Land Law

Land Law

Emma Warner-Reed

Leeds Metropolitan University

PEARSON

Harlow, England • London • New York • Boston • San Francisco • Toronto • Sydney
Auckland • Singapore • Hong Kong • Tokyo • Seoul • Taipei • New Delhi
Cape Town • São Paulo • Mexico City • Madrid • Amsterdam • Munich • Paris • Milan

LIVINGLAW

Pearson Education Limited
Edinburgh Gate
Harlow CM20 2JE
United Kingdom
Tel: +44 (0)1279 623623
Web: www.pearson.com/uk

First published 2013 (print and electronic)

ISBN: 978-1-4082-1912-6 (print)
978-1-4082-1914-0 (PDF)
978-1-2920-0348-1 (eText)

British Library Cataloguing-in-Publication Data
A catalogue record for the print edition is available from the British Library

Library of Congress Cataloging-in-Publication Data
Warner-Reed, Emma.
Land law / Emma Warner-Reed.
pages cm
Includes index.
ISBN 978-1-4082-1912-6
1. Real property – Great Britain – Outlines, syllabi, etc. I. Title.
KD829.6.W37 2013
346.4104'3–dc23
2013006778

10 9 8 7 6 5 4 3 2 1
16 15 14 13

Print edition typeset in 10.5/13pt Minion by 35
Print edition printed and bound in Great Britain by Ashford Colour Press Ltd, Gosport, Hampshire

NOTE THAT ANY PAGE CROSS REFERENCES REFER TO THE PRINT EDITION

Brief contents

Contents

Lecturers ***Teach your course, your way.***

MyLawChamber is a powerful teaching tool which you can use to assess your students, and improve their understanding.

Make the interactive Pearson eText a 'live' teaching resource by annotating with your own commentary, links to external sources, critique, or updates to the law and share with your students.

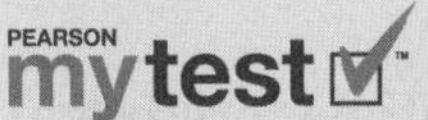

Set quizzes and mini-assessments using the bank of over 500 multiple-choice questions to gauge your students' understanding.

Use Case Navigator, a case reading resource we offer in conjunction with LexisNexis, to assign student seminar work.

For information about teaching support materials, please contact your local Pearson sales consultant or visit **www.mylawchamber.co.uk.**

The regularly maintained mylawchamber site provides the following features:

- Search tool to help locate specific items of content.
- Online help and support to assist with website usage and troubleshooting.

Case Navigator access is included with your mylawchamber registration. The LexisNexis element of Case Navigator is only available to those who currently subscribe to LexisNexis Butterworths online.

Guided tour

Key points
Identify the essential elements of each chapter, aiding your core understanding of the chapter.

Key points In this chapter we will be looking at:

- The nature of land ownership and land as a bundle of rights
- The difference between real and personal property and the importance of the distinction
- How we define land ownership and where it begins and ends
- The division of lower and upper airspace in relation to land
- The definition of fixtures and chattels
- The degree and purpose of annexation tests in relation to fixtures
- Whether a building can ever be a chattel
- The law of treasure trove and other items found in or on the ground
- Limitations on land ownership and state restrictions on the use of land, including town and country planning, compulsory

People in the law
Read the interviews from people working in Land law and gain insight from their first hand work experience.

People in the law

Name and title: William Hansen, formerly Deputy Adjudicator to the Land Registry and now at Cornerstone Barristers.

What is your role as an adjudicator to the Land Registry? The primary function of an adjudicator is to resolve disputed applications to the registrar which, if they cannot be settled by agreement between the parties, are referred by the registrar to the Adjudicator under s. 73(7) LRA 2002 who then determines the matter at a public hearing. The adjudicators are independent persons outside the structure of the Registry.

Do you often deal with cases involving overriding interests in land? The majority of cases that come before an adjudicator involve issues relating to **adverse possession**, boundaries, easements and beneficial interests in land. However, it is not uncommon to encounter

Source: William Hansen

the interest is in 'actual occupation' or (in the context of a registered disposition) whether the disponee had actual knowledge of the interest at the time of the disposition.

Law in action
Learn how the system works in practice through examples and problem scenarios found in the news.

Law in action Athlone House: home to Britain's wealthiest tramp?

Seventy-year-old tramp Harry Hallowes has at last realised his dream of property ownership. Mr Hallowes, who has been squatting on a piece of land forming one corner of the grounds to Athlone House, a £130-million-pound mansion adjoining London's Hampstead Heath, since 1986, has been awarded **possessory title** to the property by the Land Registry. This means that the land is now his to sell or pass on under the terms of a will, should he wish to. The lucky tramp has lived in a small shack on the land for over two decades.

The decision of the Land Registry to grant Mr Hallowes title to the land follows a three year battle with property developers Dwyer, who want to redevelop the huge mansion house into luxury flats. In March 2005, Dwyer attempted to evict Mr Hallowes from the site, but at a court hearing lawyers were able to show that the tramp had lived on the plot for an uninterrupted period of no less than 18 years. As it was not possible to quash the evidence, Mr Hallowes was able to use this as the basis for a successful application to the Land Registry to be granted title to the property on the grounds of adverse possession. It is estimated that his small plot adjoining the Heath, measuring only 20 by 40 metres, could be worth as much as £3.5 million subject to planning permission.

Sources: http://property.timesonline.co.uk/tol/life_and_style/property/article3671198.ece and http://www.metro.co.uk/news/50308-squatter-handed-deeds-to-3-5m-plot-on-the-heath#ixzz1j9rgvRaZ

Case summary
Learn the essential facts, details of the case and the decision, all in these concise summaries, integrated into the text yet pulled out in the margins for easy reference.

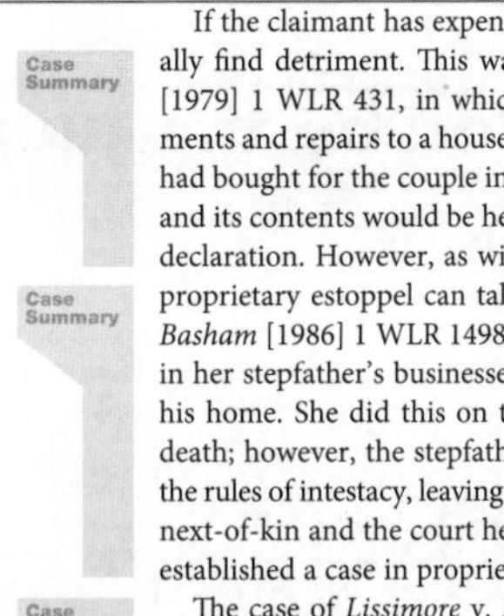

Case Summary

If the claimant has expended money in reliance on the assurance, the court will usually find detriment. This was the finding of the Court of Appeal in *Pascoe* v. *Turner* [1979] 1 WLR 431, in which a woman had spent money on redecorations, improvements and repairs to a house in which she lived with her partner for ten years. The house had bought for the couple in the man's sole name, but he had assured her that the house and its contents would be hers and she had spent money on the house in reliance on his declaration. However, as with **detrimental reliance** in constructive trusts, detriment in proprietary estoppel can take many forms, not necessarily financial. In the case of *Re Basham* [1986] 1 WLR 1498 the claimant, Joan Bird, acted to her detriment by working in her stepfather's businesses without payment for many years and caring for him and his home. She did this on the understanding that she would inherit his estate on his death; however, the stepfather died **intestate** and his estate went to his children under the rules of intestacy, leaving Joan with nothing. Joan made a claim against the stepfather's next-of-kin and the court held that she was entitled to the estate as she had successfully established a case in proprietary estoppel in the circumstances.

Case Summary

The case of *Lissimore* v. *Downing* [2003] 2 FLR 308, on the other hand, provides a good illustration of what will *not* constitute detriment. The case concerned a claim by

Case Summary

Documenting the law
See real life tort law documents reproduced within the text to give you a sense of how the law looks and feels in practice.

Documenting the law

Example of a search result from the Land Charges Department in Plymouth

LAND CHARGES ACT 1972
CERTIFICATE OF THE RESULT OF THE SEARCH

CERTIFICATE NO.	CERTIFICATE DATE	PROTECTION ENDS ON
0723135	01/11/12	22/11/12

It is hereby certified that an official search in respect of the undermentioned particulars has been made in the index to the registers which are kept pursuant to the Land Charges Act 1972. The result of the search is shown below.

PARTICULARS SEARCHED	
COUNTY OR COUNTIES	East Irkshire

Key stats
Information about what is actually happening in the real world helps you to relate to the practical side of the law.

Key stats Trends in the housing market over the past 50 years

UK house prices

- **The average UK house price has increased over the past 50 years from £2,507 in 1959 to £162,085 in 2009.** This is an increase of 273%, at an average annual rate of 2.7%: faster than the 2% per annum average rise in earnings over the period.
- **House prices recorded their biggest increase in the latest decade with a rise of 62% during the 2000s.** The worst-performing decade for house prices was the 1990s when prices fell by 22%.
- **The north/south house price divide has widened**

Source: Jules Selmes, Pearson Education Ltd

Diagrams and **Flowcharts**
These visual aids will make complex legal processes easier to follow and understand.

Figure 13.1 Assignment and subletting

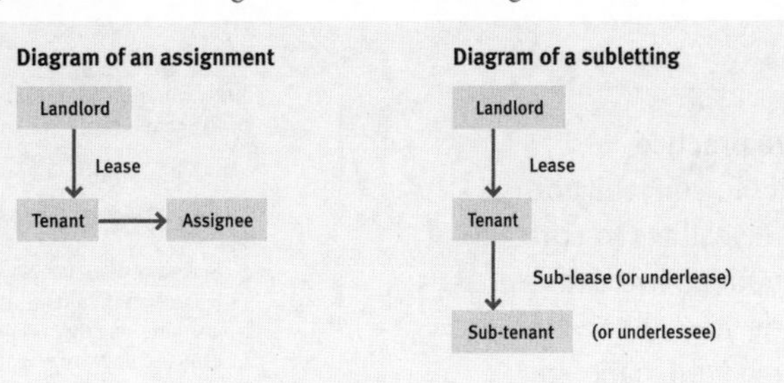

You be the Judge
Use your knowledge and apply it to as you go to real life scenarios to fully test your understanding.

You be the judge

Source: Sozaijiten

Q: Which of the following do you think constitute 'possession' for the purposes of making an adverse possession claim: (a) building and living in a house on the land; (b) cultivating the land; (c) fencing off the land; (d) putting up notices warning intruders to keep off the land; (e) parking a car on the land; (f) allowing children to play on the land; and (g) running a sewer pipe under the land?

A: In law, (a) (b) (c) and (d) are sufficient to constitute possession, whereas (e) (f) and (g) are not. Whilst (e) (f) and (g) all show a clear and consistent use of the land, they have all been considered by the courts as insufficient to constitute physical possession for the purposes of making an adverse possession claim. Further details are given in the cases below.

Writing and drafting
Put your knowledge of tort law into practice by completing the writing and drafting exercises contained throughout to enhance your practical legal skills and employability.

Writing and drafting

Imagine you are a landlord renting out your dream property. What terms would you expect to see in the lease? Which of those terms would you consider essential? Why not have a go at drafting your own lease of the property and then compare it with the sample lease below. Try to do it without looking at the example for inspiration though! Remember, it is the basic form we are interested in at this stage, not a perfect piece of legal drafting.

You should spend no more than 30 minutes on this task.

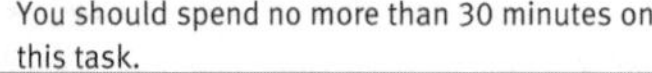
Source: Nick Pope © Dorling Kindersley

Out and about
Venture out and visit the suggested places or stay in and visit the websites to enhance your understanding of the areas covered.

Out and about

Your 'dream' property

Source: Photodisc

Go into your local estate agents or have a look at an online property search engine, such as **http://www.rightmove.co.uk** (there are, of course, others you can use), and have a look at the properties on sale. Imagine you are buying your first home. Choose a property that would be right for you and collect or print out the particulars of sale from the agent.

Take a look at the property particulars and make a note of any information provided by the particulars which you think will be relevant to the purchase of the property. Now, make a second list of additional information you think you will need to buy the property.

Reflective practice
How well did you really do? Use these sections to critically analyse your answers to exercises, deepening your understanding and raising your marks in assessments.

these leasehold rights and obligations, on which we will be focusing for the remainder of the chapter.

Reflective practice

Compare the example lease in the Documenting the Law feature with your own draft lease. You should be able to see some similarities. Consider the differences. Did you miss anything out that you now consider essential, or is there anything missing from the example that you would ordinarily expect to see in a lease?

Summaries
Identify and recall the important cases and legal principles you need to aid revision and guarantee you go into assessments with confidence.

Summary

- Resulting and constructive trusts can be created without any formality whatever, meaning that there is no need even for writing to create them (s.53(2) LPA 1925).
- In the context of the acquisition of land, a resulting trust will be created wherever property has been bought in one person's sole name but paid for, either wholly or in part, by another.
- Only contributions to the purchase of the property will be relevant in awarding a resulting trust. This may include payments towards the mortgage, but will not include any subsequent payments to the maintenance or improvement of the property, however substantial.
- The beneficial share in a property awarded in a

or where a common intention that the parties should share the beneficial interest in it can be proved.

- In the absence of an express agreement, only direct contributions to the purchase of the property will traditionally be enough to suggest a common intention to share the beneficial interest – *Lloyds Bank* v. *Rosset* (but see *Abbott* v. *Abbott* and *Hapeshi* v. *Allnatt*, which suggest a more holistic approach).
- Where there has been an express agreement, the detriment need not be financial at all, however (see *Ungurian* v. *Lesnoff*).
- In calculating the share of the property to be awarded in constructive trust cases, the court will 'undertake a survey of the whole course

Question and answer
Test and apply your knowledge of tort law by answering the questions provided using the guidance to help and structure your answers.

Question and answer*

Problem: Sanjay owned two pieces of land, a barn and paddock, depicted below.

Further reading
Annotated references to journals and websites point you to that extra reading necessary to ensure you hit the higher marks.

Further reading

McMurtry, L., 'The Section 36 discretion: policy and practicality', Conv 2002, Nov/Dec, 594–601.
This article gives a clear and useful discussion of the law relating to section 36 of the Administration of Justice Act 1970, as amended, through discussion of the case of *Barclays Bank Plc* v. *Alcorn* [2002] EWHC 498 (Ch).

***Royal Bank of Scotland plc* v. *Etridge (No.2)* [2001] 3 WLR 1021.**

McAuslan, P. 'Whose mortgage is it anyway? Producers, consumers and the law in the UK mortgage market', available online at: http://www.gla.ac.uk/media/media_129711_en.pdf.
This University of Glasgow conference paper makes a clear and thorough survey of the law of mortgages as it stands and makes suggestions for change, taking into account economic and financial factors as well as legal ones. For a really good overview of the law on this subject this is a must-read

Visit **www.mylawchamber.co.uk** to access a wealth of tools to help you develop and test your knowledge of land law, strengthening your understanding so you can excel.

The Pearson eText is a fully searchable, interactive version of *Land Law*. You can make notes in it, highlight it, bookmark it, even link to online sources – helping you get more out of studying and revision.

Case Navigator provides in-depth analysis of the leading cases in land law, improving your case-reading skills and understanding of how the law is applied.

Explore the world of **Virtual Lawyer** and develop your skills in answering legal problem questions as you apply your knowledge of the law to a range of interactive scenarios.

Use the access card at the back of the book to activate mylawchamber. Online purchase is also available at **www.mylawchamber.co.uk**.

Preface

This is the second title I have written for the Living Law series, the first having been on the subject of equity and trusts. The aim of the series is to breathe a little bit of life into the core areas of undergraduate legal study by illustrating them in a rather more practical context than other textbooks currently available on the market. The topic of land law is one of the subjects with which, traditionally, students have some difficulty. In this book I have sought to show the reader, by giving practical illustrations and examples of the law in action in a contemporary setting, that land law is not only highly relevant in both personal and business formats, but also that the subject can actually be quite interesting and, at times, even controversial (just take a look at the chapter on adverse possession!).

As both an experienced practitioner of land law and as an academic, I have always been keen to teach my students the law in a practical context. I strongly believe that students learn more effectively and their understanding of legal concepts is both deeper and more permanent if given a practical grounding on which to base those concepts. It is so easy for students to dismiss a topic as dry, dull or irrelevant if they do not appreciate it as a current, living and wholly applicable area of the law, and with land law in particular students often fail to make the connection between the academic study of land law and the practical application of land law principles in the context of conveyancing and property law and practice. As a former head of the Legal Practice course at Leeds Metropolitan University and as a Module Leader for the Property Law and Practice module which is a compulsory element of the course, it has proved a constant source of frustration for me that students come to the course with little or no knowledge or recollection of the basic building blocks upon which these topics rest, such as a working understanding of the protection of interests in land, the creation of easements and the passing of restrictive covenants to third parties. It is my hope that, by making these subjects current and accessible to students, this text will go some way toward breaking the cycle in this respect.

This text is an introductory one and thus assumes no prior knowledge of land law. In order to achieve the practical focus required for such a book, in covering the black letter law I have sought to draw out the more topical and socially relevant topics and minimise the discussion of drier and more archaic areas of the law (although I could happily talk about *profits à prendre* for hours!). Nevertheless, I have sought to include all of the topics that are covered on a typical undergraduate course.

The book also contains more practical exercises than those typically found in an undergraduate law textbook. These exercises, whilst being carefully tied to the textbook content, seek to highlight not only an application of the legal principles set out in each chapter, but also to hone the variety of skills that a law student needs to have in practice and in employment more generally, from legal research to organisational skills.

An outline of the book

The book is set out over 14 chapters. After giving a brief history of land law and introducing the concepts of tenure and estates in Chapter 1, Chapter 2 goes on to define land in a legal context. Chapters 3, 6, 7 and 8 deal with how land may be acquired, both formally (Chapter 3) and informally (Chapters 6, 7 and 8). Chapter 4 sets out the various interests in land and how these may be protected, and Chapters 10, 11 and 12 consider in detail the three most commonly used interests: easements (Chapter 10), freehold covenants (Chapter 11) and mortgages (Chapter 12). Chapters 5 and 13 consider leases and the transmission of leasehold covenants, and Chapter 9 deals with co-ownership. The final chapter, Chapter 14, is named the 'Lawyer's brief'. This comprises a series of exercises designed to consolidate your knowledge and understanding of land law by applying it in a number of ways, both academic and practical. It can be used as a revision tool at the end of the text, or as a workbook, from which you can pick and choose appropriate exercises to complete during the course of your learning.

As you will have seen from the guided tour of the text, each chapter includes a number of key features, such as People in the Law, Key Stats, Law in Action, and so on. I have tried to make all of these as interesting and relevant as possible. I would like to think that, by reading the features and undertaking some of the tasks in the linked You be the Judge, Writing and Drafting and Out and About boxes, students will gain a broader understanding of how the legal principles are applied in practice and how they affect the everyday world, the result being a deeper understanding of the principles themselves. Where possible I have provided feedback or hints to the tasks in the book and there is also more guidance available on the accompanying **mylawchamber** site.

I hope you find the book both useful and enjoyable to read. If you would like to comment on anything contained within the book or with the approach of the series in general, I would encourage you to contact me via the **mylawchamber** site, or at: **e.warner-reed@leedsmet.ac.uk**. The law is as stated on 18 October 2011. Whilst I am grateful to reviewers and colleagues for the valuable advice provided to me in earlier drafts, any oversights or errors do, of, course remain my responsibility.

Wishing you all the very best of luck with your study of land law.

Emma Warner-Reed
Senior Lecturer in Law
Leeds Metropolitan University
23 January 2012

Acknowledgements

Author's acknowledgements

This, my second attempt at textbook writing, has spanned not one but two maternity leaves, having started with the birth of Rafe Isaac in 2010 and being completed shortly before the birth of Eliza Scarlett in 2012. Consequently, its production has not been without difficulty, trying to fit in a little bit of legal writing here and there in between nappy changes and nursing breaks. However, with a lot of patience and a few delays, we finally reached the finishing post.

As ever, there are a number of people to whom I owe my particular thanks on this project:

To the editorial team at Pearson and especially my editor, Cheryl Cheasley, for her continued patience and understanding as deadlines were extended on more than one occasion!

To my students, who have acted alternately as a great sounding-board, test panel and unofficial collective reviewer for my emerging text.

To my reviewers themselves, for their useful insight and comments.

To my 'People in the Law', who allowed me to interview them, and to all those who gave me their permission to use documents and statistics to illustrate the text and bring it to life.

To my husband Jonathan, who is unwaivering in his support of all my academic pursuits and from whom I derive my strength – I thank you.

And finally to our children: Harry and baby Eliza, for their uncomplaining acceptance of my writing habit, and middle son Rafe – to whom this book is dedicated.

Publisher's acknowledgements

We are grateful to the following for permission to reproduce copyright material:

Figure

Figure on page 170 from **http://www.dailymail.co.uk/news/article-1230470/Meet-Nigella-Lawsons-new-neighbours--squatters.html**, © Nigel Howard/Evening Standard. Reproduced with permission of Solo Syndication.

Text

Crown Copyright material is reproduced with the permission of the Controller of HMSO and the Queen's Printer for Scotland.

Key stats box on p. 47 adapted from **http://www.culture.gov.uk/publications/8459.aspx**, contains public sector information licensed under the Open Government Licence

(OGL) v1.0. **http://www.nationalarchives.gov.uk/doc/open-government-licence/open-government**; Documenting the law box on pp. 38–9 from **http://www.lawsociety.org.uk/documents/downloads/dynamic/ta10_formspecimen.pdf**, © The Law Society, reproduced with permission; Documenting the law box on pp. 72–4 from Land Registry, contains public sector information licensed under the Open Government Licence (OGL) v1.0. **http://www.nationalarchives.gov.uk/doc/open-government-licence/open-government**; Key stats box on p. 118 adapted from **http://www.communities.gov.uk/publications/corporate/statistics/privatelandlordssurvey2010**, contains public sector information licensed under the Open Government Licence (OGL) v1.0. **http://www.nationalarchives.gov.uk/doc/open-government-licence/open-government**; Quote on p. 156 from Hansard source: HC Deb, 12 September 2011, c1032W, contains public sector information licensed under the Open Government Licence (OGL) v1.0. **http://www.nationalarchives.gov.uk/doc/open-government-licence/open-government**; Key stats box on p. 210 from Families and Households 2011, Office for National Statistics, Source: Office for National Statistics licensed under the Open Government Licence v.1.0; Key stats box on p. 247 from **http://www.ons.gov.uk/ons/rel/family-demography/families-and-households/2011/stb-families-households.html**, source: Office for National Statistics licensed under the Open Government Licence v.1.0; Key stats box on p. 276 from **http://lawcommission.justice.gov.uk/docs/cp186_Easements_Covenants_and_Profits_a_Prendre_Consultation.pdf**, contains public sector information licensed under the Open Government Licence (OGL) v1.0. **http://www.nationalarchives.gov.uk/doc/open-government-licence/open-government**; Key stats box on p. 336 from **http://www.official-documents.gov.uk/document/hc1012/hc10/1067/1067.pdf**, contains public sector information licensed under the Open Government Licence (OGL) v1.0. **http://www.nationalarchives.gov.uk/doc/open-government-licence/open-government**; Law in action box on pp. 345–6 from **http://www.ft.com**, © The Financial Times Limited, all rights reserved; The following law report extracts have been reproduced with the permission of the ICLR (Incorporated Council of Law Reporting): Quote on p. 125 from Street v. Mountford (1985) AC 809; Quote on p. 128 from Somma v. Hazelhurst (1978) 1 WLR 1014; Quote on p. 157 from Rains v. Buxton (1880) 14 Ch D 537; Quotes on p. 193, pp. 193–4, page 199 from Burns v. Burns (1984) Ch.317; Quote on page 196 from Banner Homes Group v. Luff Developments Ltd (2000) 2 WLR 772; Quotes on pp. 197 and 198 from Gissing v. Gissing (1971) AC 886; Quote on p. 199 from Grant v. Edwards (1986) Ch 638 (CA); Quote on p. 202 from Grant v. Edwards (1986) Ch.638 (CA); Quote on pp. 200–1 from Lloyds Bank plc v. Rosset (1991) 1 AC 107; Extract on p. 224 from Cobbe v. Yeoman's Row Management Ltd (2008) 1 WLR 1752; Quote on p. 228 from Gillett v. Holt (2001) Ch 210; Quote on p. 232 from Cobbe v. Yeomans' Row Management Ltd (2008) 1 WLR 1752; Quote on p. 233 from Pascoe v. Turner (1979) 1 WLR 431; Quote on p. 239 from Van Laethem v. Brooker, Family Law Reports [2006] 2 FLR 495; Quote on pp. 264–5 from Re K, Dec'd (1985) 2 WLR 262, 92–4; Quote on p. 277 from Phipps v. Pears (1964) 2 WLR 996; Quote on p. 289 from Pwllbach Colliery Co. Ltd v. Woodman (1915) AC 634; Quote on p. 299 from Colls v. Home and Colonial Stores Ltd (1904) AC 179; Quote on pp. 297–8 from Hulbert v. Dale (1909) 2 Ch 570; Quote on p. 366 from Re White Rose Cottage (1965) Ch 940; Quote on p. 393 from Bickel v. Duke of Westminster (1977) QB 517; Quote on p. 397 from Lurcott v. Wakely (1911) 1 KB 905.

Interviews

Interview and photograph on pp. 4–5 from Nick Talbot; Interview and photograph on p. 33 from Simon Nabarro; Interview and photograph on pp. 103–4 from William Hansen; Interview and photograph on pp. 179–80 from Andrew Vinson; Interview and photograph on p. 300 from Elizabeth de Burgh Sidley; Interview and photograph on pp. 286–7 from Hayden Glynn; Interview and photograph on pp. 403–4 from Steve Wood.

Picture credits

We are grateful to the following for permission to reproduce photographs:

Brofsky Studio Inc., Photodisc: 345; BuildPix, **constructionphotography.com**: 277; Janis Christie, Photodisc: 207; Trevor Clifford, Pearson Education Ltd: 23; Andy Crawford © Dorling Kindersley: 118; Imagemore Co. Ltd: 346; Ingram Publishing, Alamy: 251; Naki Kouyioumtzis, Pearson Education Ltd: 326; Photodisc: 19; Nick Pope © Dorling Kindersley: 379; Jules Selmes, Pearson Education Ltd: 3; Steve Shott © Dorling Kindersley: 98; Richard Smith: 276; Sozaijiten: 30, 162, 223.

In some instances we have been unable to trace the owners of copyright material, and we would appreciate any information that would enable us to do so.

Table of cases

Case Navigator provides in-depth analysis of the leading cases in land law, improving your case-reading skills and understanding of how the law is applied.

Visit **www.mylawchamber.co.uk** to access unique online support:

- **Direct deep links** to the core cases in land law
- **Short introductions** provide guidance on what you should look out for while reading the case
- **Questions** help you to test your understanding of the case, and provide feedback on what you should have grasped
- **Summaries** contextualise the case and point you to further reading so that you are fully prepared for seminars and discussions

Case Navigator cases are highlighted **in bold** below.

Please note that access to Case Navigator is free with the purchase of this book, but you must register with us for access. Full registration instructions are available online. The LexisNexis element of Case Navigator is only available to those who currently subscribe to LexisNexis Butterworths online.

Table of statutes

Table of statutory instruments

Table of European legislation

Chapter 1 Introduction to land law

Key points In this chapter we will be looking at:

- ✦ Reasons for learning land law
- ✦ The structure of land ownership in England and Wales: tenures and estates
- ✦ How the 1925 reforms simplified landholding
- ✦ The two legal estates in land: freehold and leasehold
- ✦ The new legal estate: commonhold
- ✦ Unregistered landholding and the introduction of land registration

Introduction

As a new student of the subject, you may be asking yourselves 'why learn land law?' However, a more pertinent question might be: why not? Land and property forms what can unquestionably be called the national obsession. In England and Wales, home ownership is of paramount importance to individuals and families alike. From the moment a young adult goes out and starts to work they dream of owning their own home and strive to achieve this. We live, breathe and dream property. We do DIY on our homes in our spare time to make our properties more beautiful and we watch property programmes on television to relax. Not a week goes by when the news does not mention the rise or fall in house prices. Indeed, we not only make property our homes: more and more of us buy property for investment purposes, either developing or renting it for income or profit.

The national obsession

The statistics speak for themselves. Well-known high-street bank, Halifax plc, has looked at the key trends and developments in the UK housing market over the past 50 years, using data from the Halifax's own extensive housing statistics database, the Office for National Statistics and the Communities and Local Government department. Take a look at the results of their key findings, below.

Key stats Trends in the housing market over the past 50 years

UK house prices

Source: Jules Selmes, Pearson Education Ltd

- **The average UK house price has increased over the past 50 years from £2,507 in 1959 to £162,085 in 2009.** This is an increase of 273%, at an average annual rate of 2.7%: faster than the 2% per annum average rise in earnings over the period.
- **House prices recorded their biggest increase in the latest decade with a rise of 62% during the 2000s.** The worst-performing decade for house prices was the 1990s when prices fell by 22%.
- **The north/south house price divide has widened since 1969 as prices have generally increased more quickly in the south.** However, there has been remarkably little change in the ranking of the different regions of the UK over the last 40 years, with London and the South East remaining the most expensive part of the country and Yorkshire and Humberside continuing to have the lowest average prices.

Housing ownership

- **Owner-occupation (that is, people who buy their own homes rather than renting) in the UK has increased by 25%, from 43% in 1961 to 68% in 2008.** The biggest rise in owner-occupation occurred in the 1980s following the introduction of the Right to Buy scheme* in Great Britain, helping to lift owner-occupation from 56% to 67%.
- **The proportion of homes that are privately rented has fallen significantly from 33% in 1961 to 14% in 2008.** The private rental sector was bigger than both the owner-occupied and social rented sectors until the mid-1950s.

Households

- **The number of individual households, or family units, has risen by nearly 10 million since the early 1960s,** increasing from 16.7 million in 1961 to 26.6 million in 2009, according to Halifax estimates. Over the same period, the UK population has grown by nine million from 52.8 million to an estimated 61.8 million in 2009.
- **There has been a decline in the size of the average household,** the proportion of single person households in England having increased from less than one in five households (19%) in 1971 to one in three (33%) in 2009.

Housebuilding

- **The number of houses built in the UK was an estimated 156,816 in 2009; 44% less than the 281,570 built in 1959.** The decline in house building has been driven by a fall in the creation of public sector housing, which dropped by 69% between 1959 and 2009. Consequently the proportion of house purchases completed in the private sector increased from 54% in 1959 to an estimated 75% in 2009.

Statistics are as at 20 January 2010.

*The Right to Buy scheme is a government policy which enables those living in council housing to buy their council house at a discounted rate.

Source: **http://www.lloydsbankinggroup.com/media/pdfs/research/2010/50_Years_of_Housing_UK.pdf**

The survey shows that the typical UK household today is very different from that of 50 years ago. There has been a significant shift towards owner-occupation with the majority of households now living in their own homes rather than renting. There have also been substantial changes in both the number of households and their composition. The old adage that 'an Englishman's home is his castle' has not become outmoded or outdated by a long way yet. In the People in the Law box, Nick Talbot of the Carter Jonas estate agency practice comments on the meaning of property ownership to UK householders.

People in the law

Name and title: Nick Talbot, Partner at Carter Jonas LLP, estate agents.

Source: Nick Talbot

What is your role within the practice? I am responsible for residential agency in North and West Yorkshire and advising clients on general agency matters with particular experience in the sale of period and unusual properties including substantial country houses, town houses and new developments.

How long have you been working in the estate agency business? Since 1987.

Is this a dangerous profession to be in, given the current downturn in the property market? The current weakness in the property market has meant that all costs and resources have had to be reviewed which has put pressure on everyone. However, I do believe we are well poised to take advantage now for when the market improves.

Do you think that the recent trend in buying property over shares as an investment will wane as a result of the recent price crash? Purchasers remain nervous about property at the moment and will continue to do so until they feel some reassurance that prices are not going to fall back any more and more importantly when the banks start to lend finance again. Once this changes then I do believe we will start to see buyers returning but perhaps not to quite the same level as we have seen over the last decade.

Speaking as a property professional, what are your views on the system of land ownership and transfer in this country? The current system for transferring ownership of land is slow and drawn-out and I am sure could be improved if everyone involved in it were of a like mind. However, as proved with the implementation of Home Information Packs,* it needs to be carefully thought out rather than the fiasco that they caused.

What are the cheapest and most expensive houses you've ever sold, respectively? The cheapest house I sold was a two-bedroom back-to-back terraced house that was being sold by the mortgagees in possession at auction and was bought by a residential investor for just over £4000 without seeing the property. I questioned his motivation after the auction and he quoted 'Because I liked the colour of the front door'. The most expensive property I sold was a landed estate in North Yorkshire for £10,000,000.

What is the most unusual property you have ever sold? A very small piece of woodland with a lake in the middle that had limited access and was sold as 'for the man who has everything' and sure enough a chap bought it as somewhere to go and spend some quiet time by himself.

*__Home Information Packs__ (or **HIPs**) was a government initiative aimed to simplify the conveyancing process in England and Wales, by providing the majority of information required by the buyer 'up front' in a standard format. However, the initiative was unpopular and has now been suspended indefinitely by the current government.

In the light of the above it follows that, of all the core subjects of undergraduate legal study, land law is probably the most relevant to our everyday lives in that it affects us the most directly, constantly and personally. How better to enhance an interest in property than to find out exactly how the law of property works: how the land itself is acquired and disposed of, and how rights over property can be established or defeated. This text is going to take you on a journey of exploration, through the fascinating world that is property ownership. But, before we start, let us set the scene with a little bit of history.

The structure of land ownership in England and Wales

The first important point that needs to be made about property ownership in England and Wales is that, in actual fact, no one in this country 'owns' their own property at all, all property in England and Wales, technically speaking, being owned by the Crown. What we have instead of outright ownership of the land, and what we are therefore trading in when we buy and sell property, is the right to *use* the land in varying ways and for varying periods of time.

no one in this country 'owns' their own property

As with many other concepts in English land law, the reason for this slightly unusual state of affairs lies in history, around the time of the Norman Conquest. When William the Conqueror first invaded our shores in 1066 he seized all land owned by the native Britons and claimed it for himself as king. In order to manage the land more efficiently, he then carved the country up into large sections and handed them to his most loyal and trusted nobles, allowing them the use of the land in return for services to the Crown. These rights to hold, or use, the land were known as **tenures**, deriving from the Latin verb *tenere*, which means 'to hold'.

The system of land tenures did not end at the granting of large estates to the nobility, however. The successful land management of such large parcels of property could not be achieved by the nobles alone, so they in turn granted their own lesser tenures to lesser nobles, servants and counterparts, these lesser nobles managing the land in return for services to the granting noble. A tiered system of tenures thus evolved, the land being divided into smaller and smaller pieces as each strata within the hierarchy granted tenures to its underlings. Whilst those at the bottom actually worked the land, those at the top simply managed it.

The varying types of tenure required different types of service. The highest tenures, **'free' tenures**, which were held by the nobles, did not necessarily require the **tenant** (that is, the party holding the land) to actually farm the land. Rather these higher forms of 'freeholding' required services of a more somewhat chivalrous nature, ranging from an obligation to provide the king with a certain number of horsemen equipped with arms, for a certain number of days in the year ('**knight service**'), to acting as the king's chamberlain, or carrying his banner ('**grand sergeanty**'), to providing hay for the king's horses or feeding the king's dogs ('**petty sergeanty**'). The most common form of freeholding, which was called '**common socage**', did require services of an agricultural nature, however, the tenant being required to plough the fields or graze the land for a certain portion of the year.

Below free tenures came '**unfree**' or **copyhold tenures**, which required a more onerous level of servitude to the person granting the tenure. These copyhold tenures effectively amounted to nothing more than a right to occupy the land, in exchange for various menial services of the grantor's choosing. A pictorial illustration of how the system of tenures worked at this time can be seen in Figure 1.1, below.

One might ask the question: why did William go to the trouble of creating this complicated system of landholding, rather than simply making outright gifts of the pieces of land he did not want to those who had served him well during the conquest? The answer is that he wanted to maintain control: whilst William could not possibly hope (nor wish) to occupy and manage all the land in the kingdom himself, if he gave the land away entirely he would lose control over its subsequent maintenance or use. This is a compelling reason for the preservation of this system to the present day, and something which can perhaps be better explained in the light of modern examples. The ability of the State to maintain control over the erection and use of buildings on the land in the form of **town and country planning** and **building control**, control over the maintenance of land and property by **demolition/preservation orders** and environmental protection measures and even the ability to claim the land back under certain circumstances by way

Figure 1.1 Land tenure after the Norman conquest

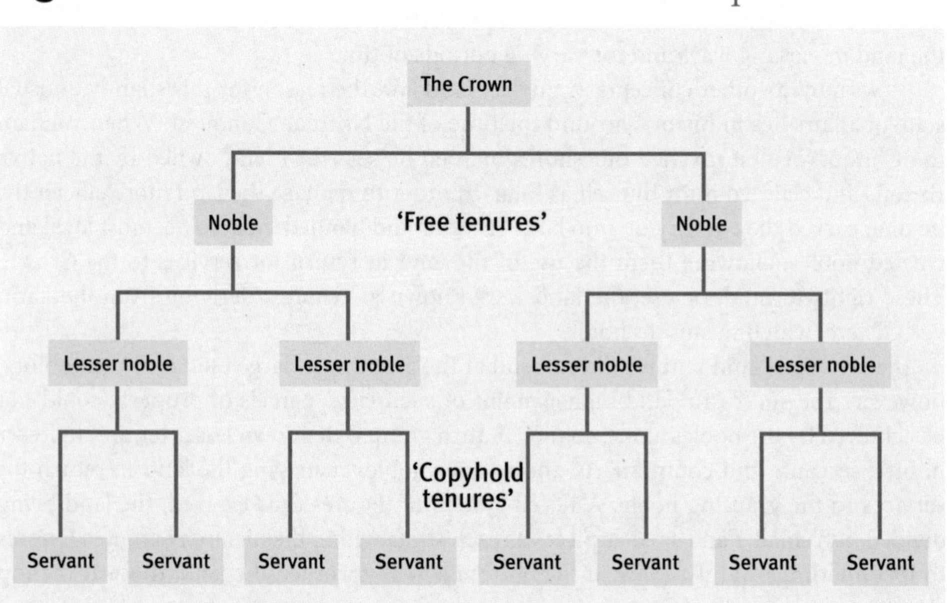

of **compulsory purchase** and the doctrine of ***bona vacantia***, which is the right of the State to reclaim 'ownerless' land, are all made possible through the system of land tenure. The issue of state control of property and the human rights issues brought about by this are discussed in further detail in Chapter 2 of this text.

Having said this, it is not to say that the system of land tenures has not been amended significantly in the last thousand years, however. Tenure as a method of landholding was bound to evolve and, as Figure 1.1 might suggest, over several centuries had become quite an unwieldy beast, with many different levels of tenure existing, all in return for different services granted in favour of different people at different times. Several attempts were therefore made to streamline the system. Initially this was done by virtue of a statute known as the *Quia Emptores* in 1290, which banned the creation of any further tenures, except by the king. This ban to all intents and purposes effected the birth of modern **conveyancing**, the process of buying and selling land, as with no new tenures being created, the only way in which a person could now acquire land was by way of substitution of the new landholder in place of the old, whether it be by inheritance, sale or gift.

The period following the abolition of new tenures also saw a change in the way in which the continuing tenures were managed on a practical level. At first, there was a shift towards incoming tenants making small payments of money to their lords instead of providing services for the land. However, eventually these payments fell away, and what could be viewed as the landlord and tenant-type relationship that existed between the **grantor** and **grantee** of the various tenures was lost altogether. Finally, in 1660 the Tenures Abolition Act converted all existing freehold tenures of any type that remained into one single tenure: that of '**free and common socage**'. The real meaning of common socage itself as a form of agricultural tenure had by this time been lost, there no longer being any requirement to farm the land. And so, in doing this, the law was massively simplified: rather than a complicated system of multi-layered property ownership, all of the in-between layers were effectively stripped away, leaving just the actual holder of the land and the Crown as absolute owner.

Finally, in the first quarter of the twentieth century one last sweeping set of changes to the law served to render the doctrine of tenures to all intents and purposes redundant: the coming into force of the Law of Property Act 1925. Under the terms of the Act all lower forms of tenure, including unfree, or copyhold tenure, were abolished. This left only one surviving form of tenure, that of the free tenure in common socage, more commonly known as the '**freehold**', which still exists today (Figure 1.2).

Figure 1.2 Land tenure after the 1925 reforms

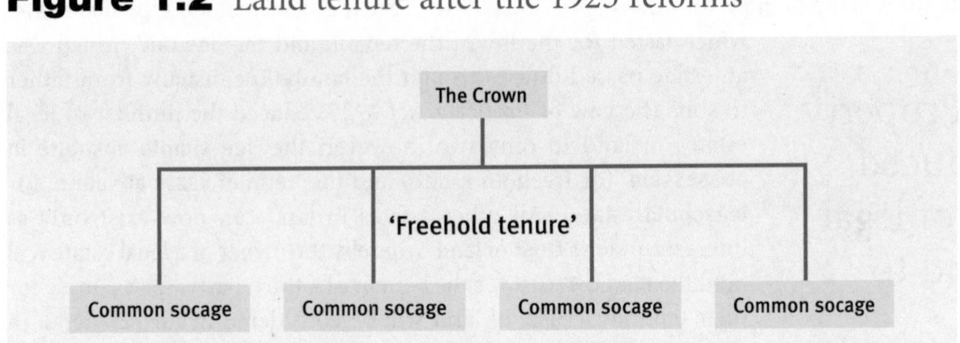

The effect is that, with only one single tenure, excepting the wider state control of property in the form of town and country planning, building control and so on alluded to above, freehold landholding is to all intents and purposes as good as absolute ownership from a practical point of view, with the freeholder being able to use the land without reference or payment to another, and being able to transfer their property freely at will.

The 1925 reforms and the doctrine of estates

The 1925 reforms took the shape of six separate statutes, which were:

- ✦ The Law of Property Act 1925
- ✦ The Trustee Act 1925
- ✦ The Land Registration Act 1925
- ✦ The Settled Land Act 1925
- ✦ The Administration of Estates Act 1925
- ✦ The Land Charges Act 1925

Together, the aim of the statutes was to consolidate and modernise the law as it stood, and to bring about a series of much-needed changes. Many of the provisions of these statutes are still in force today and underpin our modern system of land law, and you will come across them again and again as you read this text. However, most significant to our discussion of the reforms to methods of landholding in England and Wales is the Law of Property Act 1925.

We have already seen that the Law of Property Act 1925 abolished all forms of tenure of land, save for the free tenure in common socage, or freehold. The other principal change made by the Act was the reduction in the number of legal **estates** in land. It should be noted that the terms 'tenure' and 'estate' are often used interchangeably, but actually they have very distinct and different meanings. Whilst the term 'tenure' denotes how, or on what terms, property is held, the word 'estate' describes the length of time for which that right to hold the property exists. An estate in land is therefore a right to use the land for a certain period of time.

Prior to the 1925 legislation, there were many different forms of estate in land, tenures being granted for differing periods of time. Such estates included the **life estate**, which lasted for the life of the tenant, and the '**fee tail**', which was an estate passed down through the family line, usually from father to son. The Law of Property Act 1925 reduced the number of legal estates in land to only two, however: the '**fee simple absolute in possession**' (or freehold estate) and the '**term of years absolute**' (or **leasehold** estate). All other estates in land can now exist only as interests under a **trust of land**, whereby the owner of a legal estate will hold the land on trust for the benefit of a third party, for example for their lifetime. Trusts of land will be considered in further detail in Chapter 4.

The Law of Property Act 1925 reduced the number of legal estates in land to two

The two legal estates: freehold and leasehold

So what are these two estates, the term of years absolute and the fee simple absolute in possession? Exactly what kind of landholding do they describe and how do they differ? To use more modern legal terminology and to give them their less formal titles, the fee simple absolute in possession is more commonly described as the 'freehold' estate in land, and the term of years absolute as the 'leasehold' estate in land. The reason for their rather ungainly formal titles is again historic. In reducing the number of legal estates to two (remember, there is now only one legal tenure – the free tenure in common socage), it was important to describe in detail the precise attributes of each estate. Thus, each part of the term brings with it certain qualities. In the case of the freehold estate, the term 'fee simple absolute in possession' can be broken down into parts, as shown in Table 1.1.

Table 1.1 Defining 'fee simple absolute in possession'.

Fee	Simple	Absolute	In possession
The estate is inheritable.	Inheritable by anyone – even women! (This is of course no longer significant in modern society).	The right is not ended upon the happening of any certain event, i.e. it is not conditional.	The right is immediate, and does not take place in the future.

In short, then, the freehold estate is simply a current estate in land which can be sold, gifted or handed down by will, and which will continue for an unlimited period of time. The only circumstances, in fact, under which the estate will be terminated is where the freehold owner dies without leaving any relatives and leaves no valid will, in which case the property will return to the Crown under the **doctrine** of *bona vacantia*.

It should be noted that the term '**in possession**' does not require actual physical possession of the property; under section 205(1)(xix) of the Act if the freeholder is in receipt of rents or profits made from the land, this will be sufficient to denote 'possession' for legal purposes. To test your understanding of the terminology, take a look at the You Be the Judge feature below.

You be the judge

Q: **Which of the following could be a freehold estate in land: (a) a right to possess the land for the life of the tenant; (b) a right to possess the land until the tenant marries; (c) a right to possess the land for 100 years; (d) a right to possess the land on the death of the tenant's sister and (e) a right to possess the land indefinitely?**

A: Only (e) could be a legal estate in land. Answer (a) is limited to the life of the tenant, and cannot therefore be classed as a freehold, which is for an unlimited duration; answer (b) is conditional, the right determining on the marriage of the tenant; and answer (d) is a future right, coming into being only on the death of the tenant's sister. Answer (c) could be a leasehold estate, but not freehold as again it is for a limited duration.

The leasehold, or 'term of years absolute', on the other hand, is a form of landholding with a rather more limited scope and subordinate to the freehold. Unlike the freehold, a leasehold estate only exists for a finite period, a 'term of years', the estate expiring when that period comes to an end and the land returning to the freeholder. This does not mean that the leasehold is any less important than the freehold, however. In fact, residential flats aside (which are typically leasehold), around 70 per cent of commercial property in the UK is leasehold. It is therefore in real terms as important a form of landholding as the freehold.

a leasehold estate only exists for a finite period

Commonhold land

In 2002 the Commonhold and Leasehold Reform Act brought in a new form of landholding, called **commonhold**. Commonhold should not be mistaken for a new estate in land, however. In fact, it is simply an alternative method of holding freehold land. Anyone buying commonhold land is therefore buying the freehold in the property, but subject to the rules and regulations of the commonhold.

So why the need for a new system? The concept of commonhold land was devised primarily to overcome difficulties faced by owners of leasehold property in enforcing **covenants** (that is promises to do, or not to do, something) contained in the **lease** as against neighbouring property. This may be better explained by way of an example. Imagine you buy a flat in a converted four-storey Victorian terraced house. There are four flats in total, one on each floor. Your flat is on the second floor. Shortly after you move in, you start experiencing problems with the person who lives in the first-floor flat. She keeps playing loud dance music, often through the night, which is preventing you from sleeping. She also keeps leaving her bicycle lying across the landing and you keep tripping over it when you use the stairs to get to your flat. There is a covenant in your lease (you understand all the flat leases are the same) which states that tenants will not do anything which will cause a nuisance or annoyance to neighbouring properties. You contact your **landlord**, thinking that, as the owner of the freehold and the person who has let the property to you he will want to intervene, but he is not interested in the problems you are having. What can you do about it?

Well, the answer is, under the terms of the lease, absolutely nothing. It is the landlord to whom the tenant has made the promise and to whom she is contractually bound. There is no relationship between you and the tenant of the first-floor flat other than that of neighbours, so if the landlord chooses not to enforce the covenants in the lease that it entirely up to him. You have no say in the matter. Obviously this is not an ideal situation for a person buying a leasehold property. The purchaser may have paid a significant sum for the property and they will want to ensure, as a result, that the **common areas** (in this case the stairs and landing) are well maintained and that the tenants in neighbouring properties act in the appropriate manner. By registering the building as a commonhold, however, these problems would be averted because under the rules of commonhold, any member of the commonhold is able to enforce the rights or restrictions of the commonhold against any other member. For a more in-depth discussion on the enforcement of covenants in leasehold land see Chapter 13.

Commonhold landholding works as follows: Each separate property within the commonhold development is called a **commonhold 'unit'**. The common parts of the development, that is the parts of the development which are shared such as access ways to and from the property, are owned by a **commonhold association**, who are in charge of their management and maintenance. The commonhold association is a private company limited by guarantee, which is a special kind of company often used for non-profit-making organisations such as clubs, associations or charities, with every unit holder being a member of the company. Thus, all the unit holders share in the running of the common parts. The company acts upon and abides by a **commonhold community statement**, which is registered at the **Land Registry**. The statement contains the rules and regulations which apply to the commonhold. Section 26 of the Act contains details of what a commonhold community statement should contain. Unit holders are required to pay a management or **service charge** to the commonhold association for the upkeep of the common parts, rather than making such payments to the landlord, as would usually be the case.

By removing the landlord and putting the running of the development as a whole into the hands of those who live there and who therefore have a genuine interest in the welfare of the estate, commonholds avoid the problems of disconnected and uninterested landlords who are unwilling to deal with nuisance tenants. Does commonhold seem like a good idea to you? Have a look at the Writing and Drafting feature below to gain some idea of what it would be like to have your own commonhold estate.

Writing and drafting

You are a developer building an exclusive development of six houses around a central courtyard area, from which all six houses are accessed by vehicles and on foot. Because of the exclusivity of the development you would like to impose restrictions on how the courtyard is to be used and ensure the up-market tone of the development is maintained.

With this in mind, think about what you would include in your own commonhold community statement. What matters would be important to you? If you are looking for inspiration, section 31(5) of the Commonhold and Leasehold Reform Act 2002 contains examples of the types of duties which might be expected of unit holders and which may be set out in the statement.

You should spend no more than 30 minutes on this task.

Handy tip: The following web link gives guidance on the drafting of a commonhold community statement and includes a very comprehensive sample statement that you can have a look at: **http://webarchive.nationalarchives.gov.uk/+/http://www.dca.gov.uk/legist/commonhold/ccsguide.pdf.**

In addition to the control commonhold ownership gives to the unit holders, the fact that individual commonhold units are freehold and not leasehold in nature also means that they are worth more in real terms. This is because, unlike a lease which is a wasting asset – reducing in value as the length of term of the lease which remains decreases, commonhold units have all the benefits of freehold ownership, including an unlimited period of ownership of the land. Despite these perceived benefits, the uptake of commonhold as a method of landholding has been slow, however, with only 17 commonhold developments being registered at the Land Registry by 1 March 2011.

the uptake of commonhold as a method of landholding has been slow

Registered and unregistered land

The other major change brought about by the 1925 legislation was the introduction of a centralised system of land registration in England and Wales. Prior to 1925, ownership of land was proved through the production of a series of linked documents showing how the property had passed down from owner to owner over a period of time. This series of documents was collectively referred to as the '**title deeds**' to the property. An example of one such document is the deed of **conveyance** contained in the Documenting the Law feature, below.

Documenting the law

Conveyance of 5 Hall Yard, Ripon

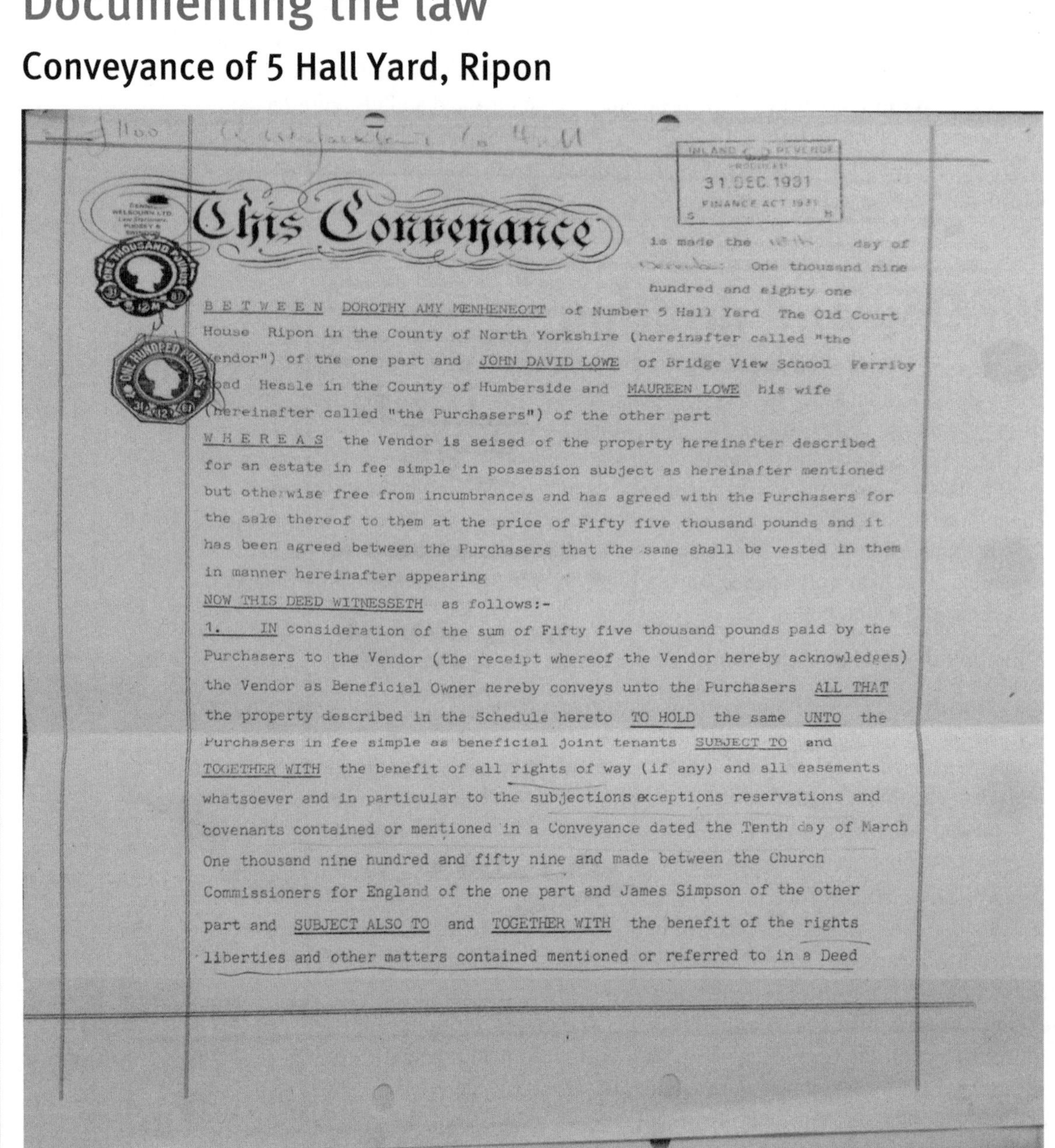

This Conveyance is made the day of One thousand nine hundred and eighty one

BETWEEN DOROTHY AMY MENHENEOTT of Number 5 Hall Yard The Old Court House Ripon in the County of North Yorkshire (hereinafter called "the Vendor") of the one part and JOHN DAVID LOWE of Bridge View School Ferriby Road Hessle in the County of Humberside and MAUREEN LOWE his wife (hereinafter called "the Purchasers") of the other part

WHEREAS the Vendor is seised of the property hereinafter described for an estate in fee simple in possession subject as hereinafter mentioned but otherwise free from incumbrances and has agreed with the Purchasers for the sale thereof to them at the price of Fifty five thousand pounds and it has been agreed between the Purchasers that the same shall be vested in them in manner hereinafter appearing

NOW THIS DEED WITNESSETH as follows:-

1. IN consideration of the sum of Fifty five thousand pounds paid by the Purchasers to the Vendor (the receipt whereof the Vendor hereby acknowledges) the Vendor as Beneficial Owner hereby conveys unto the Purchasers ALL THAT the property described in the Schedule hereto TO HOLD the same UNTO the Purchasers in fee simple as beneficial joint tenants SUBJECT TO and TOGETHER WITH the benefit of all rights of way (if any) and all easements whatsoever and in particular to the subjections exceptions reservations and covenants contained or mentioned in a Conveyance dated the Tenth day of March One thousand nine hundred and fifty nine and made between the Church Commissioners for England of the one part and James Simpson of the other part and SUBJECT ALSO TO and TOGETHER WITH the benefit of the rights liberties and other matters contained mentioned or referred to in a Deed

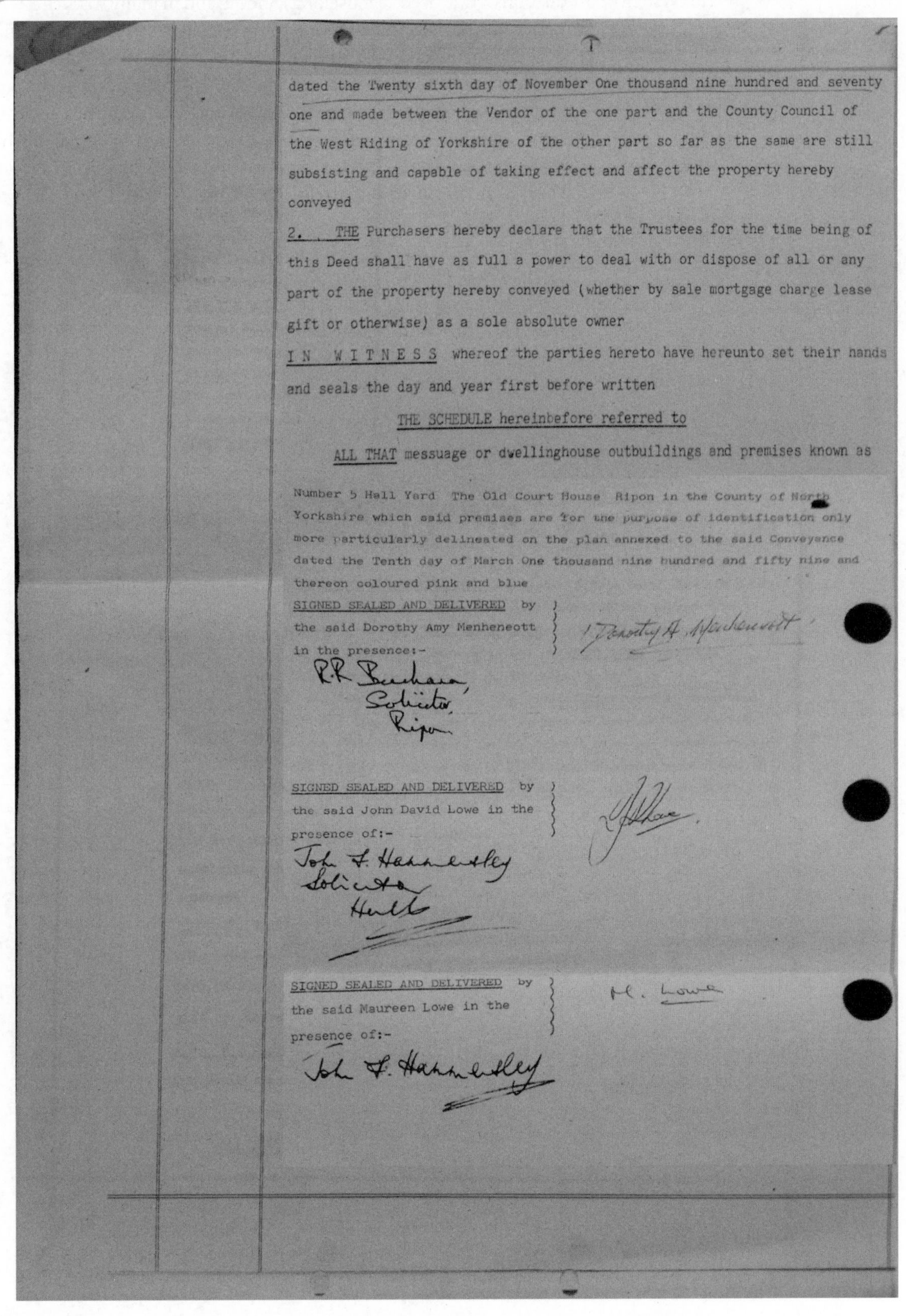
dated the Twenty sixth day of November One thousand nine hundred and seventy one and made between the Vendor of the one part and the County Council of the West Riding of Yorkshire of the other part so far as the same are still subsisting and capable of taking effect and affect the property hereby conveyed

2. THE Purchasers hereby declare that the Trustees for the time being of this Deed shall have as full a power to deal with or dispose of all or any part of the property hereby conveyed (whether by sale mortgage charge lease gift or otherwise) as a sole absolute owner

IN WITNESS whereof the parties hereto have hereunto set their hands and seals the day and year first before written

THE SCHEDULE hereinbefore referred to

ALL THAT messuage or dwellinghouse outbuildings and premises known as Number 5 Hall Yard The Old Court House Ripon in the County of North Yorkshire which said premises are for the purpose of identification only more particularly delineated on the plan annexed to the said Conveyance dated the Tenth day of March One thousand nine hundred and fifty nine and thereon coloured pink and blue

SIGNED SEALED AND DELIVERED by the said Dorothy Amy Menheneott in the presence:-

SIGNED SEALED AND DELIVERED by the said John David Lowe in the presence of:-

SIGNED SEALED AND DELIVERED by the said Maureen Lowe in the presence of:-

This system of production of title deeds, whilst longstanding and in many ways effective, was cumbersome in terms of the sale and purchase of property because it meant that every time the property changed hands the solicitor acting for the seller would have to pore over the title deeds and produce proof of an unbroken chain of ownership to the buyer's solicitor to check. As there was no prescribed form of documentation, which could span many years or even centuries, this was often a laborious and time-consuming job for both parties. The system was also problematic in that, if the title deeds were lost or stolen, proof of ownership was extremely difficult to establish. One particularly pertinent example of this happening on a massive scale was the Bradford and Bingley Building Society warehouse fire in 1998, in which literally thousands of title deeds were destroyed. Take a look at the Law in Action feature below for details.

if the title deeds were lost or stolen, proof of ownership was difficult to establish

Law in action The Bradford and Bingley warehouse fire

In November 1998 a fire swept through a warehouse in Erdington, Birmingham, destroying over 67,000 property title deeds stored there by the building society, Bradford and Bingley.

The deeds were allegedly burned when a ten-year-old boy slipped through a security fence and started a fire in the archive storage building. Of the 70,408 packets of deeds, many of which were for residential homes, 67,054 were destroyed by fire. Those which survived suffered water damage from the firemen's hoses as they fought to put out the blaze. The building society had estimated that to reissue the title deeds to the owners of the property would cost more than £17 million. Replacing registered title documents, guarantees and other documentation for each house cost up to £580. Many original historical title deeds and documents which were kept with these were lost forever.

The reissuing of title deeds in respect of registered properties would be a fairly straightforward, albeit time-consuming administrative task, completing a sworn declaration that the deeds had been destroyed by fire and requesting replacement copies of the register from the Land Registry. The loss of unregistered title documents would cause more of a problem, however. From a legal point of view, with no title deeds, the unfortunate owners of the properties had no proof of ownership of their own properties. They would therefore have to register their ownership of their properties as possessory* only, leaving them in a vulnerable position until the required ten years ownership elapsed and the title could be upgraded to absolute ownership. From a marketability angle, this would have serious consequences for anyone wishing to sell their property in the meantime.

The Bradford and Bingley issued a writ against the warehousing firm, Hays Business, for £20 million in 2000. It said that Hays Business was negligent by failing to make the building secure, for its security guards failing to prevent the boy from getting through the fence and into the building, and for failing to provide 24-hour CCTV cover. The case never came to court but a spokesman for Hays was quoted as saying that both firms were insured and their legal advisers had been in talks with the building society at the time.

*For more detail on possessory title and the law relating to adverse ownership of property, see Chapter 3.

Sources: **http://findarticles.com/p/articles/mi_qn4161/is_20000521/ai_n14505748/pg_2/?tag=content;col1** and **http://www.highbeam.com/doc/1P2-17646599.html**

An additional problem caused by the unregistered system was that the private system of document-holding prevented the State from building up any clear picture of who owned what land at any one time. This was far removed from the original vision of tenure brought over by the Normans.

It was for these reasons that the government decided to introduce a centralised system of landholding in England and Wales, whereby details of the holding of all property at any given time, together with any rights or burdens affecting that land, should be held on a central register at what was (then) to be called His Majesty's Land Registry (this title has since been shortened simply to 'the Land Registry'). The Documenting the Law feature below shows an example of what the entries in the **Land Register** for a single property might look like.

Documenting the law

Specimen copy of the register at the Land Registry

This is a copy of the register of the title number set out immediately below, showing the entries in the register on 1 March 2011.

TITLE NUMBER: YS12345

PROPERTY REGISTER

YORKSHIRE : BRADFIELD

1. (23 August 1989) The Freehold land shown edged with red on the plan of the above Title filed at the Registry and being 4 Sykes Lane, Kimmington, Bradfield (BR12 2SR).
2. (23 August 1989) The land tinted brown on the title plan has the benefit of the following rights granted by the Conveyance dated 13 June 1896 referred to in the Charges Register:-

   'TOGETHER WITH the benefit of a right of way on foot only over that part of the shared accessway belonging to 2 Sykes Lane.'
3. (23 August 1989) The land has the benefit of the rights granted by the Transfer dated 17 December 1957 referred to in the Charges Register.

END OF PROPERTY REGISTER

TITLE NUMBER: YS12345

PROPRIETORSHIP REGISTER

ABSOLUTE FREEHOLD

1. (12 September 2005): PROPRIETOR: SEAN ANDREW CONLAN and SUSAN ALICE CONLAN of 4 Sykes Lane, Kimmington, Bradfield (BR12 2SR).
2. (12 September 2005) The price stated to have been paid on 12 September 2005 was £178,000.
3. (12 September 2005) Except under an order of the registrar no disposition by the proprietor of the land is to be registered without the consent of the proprietor of the charge dated 12 September 2005 in favour of the Bradfield Building Society referred to in the Charges Register.

END OF PROPRIETORSHIP REGISTER

TITLE NUMBER: CS72510

CHARGES REGISTER

1. (23 August 1989) A Conveyance of the land tinted pink on the title plan dated 17 December 1957 made between (1) Charles Reginald MacEvoy (Vendor) and (2) James Thomas Lees (Purchaser) contains the following covenants:-

   'THE Purchaser hereby covenants with the Vendor so as to bind the land hereby conveyed into whosoever hands the same may come that the Purchaser and his successors in title will not use the premises hereby conveyed for the sale or public consumption of intoxicating liquor.'

2. (23 August 1989) The land in this title is subject to the following rights reserved by a Conveyance dated 13 June 1896 made between (1) Bradfield City Council (Vendor) and (2) Courtney Miller (Purchaser):-

   'subject to

   (i) An exception and reservation in favour of the Vendor of the right to enter upon the land hereby conveyed for the purpose of constructing a public sewer the approximate line of which is shown coloured blue on the plan annexed hereto and at all times hereafter for the purpose of inspecting cleaning repairing or renewing the said sewer.'

   NOTE:- The red line referred to is shown by a blue line on the title plan.

3. (23 August 1989) A Transfer of the land in this title dated 17 December 1957 made between (1) Henry Jordan and (2) Carlton Greenaway and Eleanor Greenaway contains restrictive covenants.

   NOTE: Copy in Certificate.

4. REGISTERED CHARGE dated 12 September 2005 to secure the moneys including the further advances therein mentioned.

   PROPRIETOR Bradfield Building Society of 1 High Street, Bradfield BR1 3FT.

END OF REGISTER

The ambitious scheme envisaged that over a period of time all property in England and Wales would become **registered**, both simplifying the conveyancing process with only one single document (the register) to look at, and creating a clear vision of property ownership nationwide. It would also mean that the loss, destruction or theft of title deeds would be less devastating in its effect, because there would always be a central record of the property and everyone who had rights over it at the Land Registry to fall back on. Furthermore, registration at the Land Registry would bring with it a state guarantee of ownership of the registered property, thereby underpinning the economy by guaranteeing the ownership of many billions of pounds worth of property.

The scheme has in many respects worked very well, albeit that it does have its difficulties. These are discussed in more detail in Chapter 4. Nevertheless, with the Land Registry now boasting the title of the world's largest property database of over 20 million titles, it would be unfair to herald the system as anything less than a resounding success. That said, the Land Registry is still a long way from providing a complete picture of landholding in England and Wales, a little over 26 per cent of land in this country remaining **unregistered** at present. The following Key Stats feature gives us some figures on the subject.

Key stats

Around £1 million of property is processed by the Land Registry every minute. However, this still leaves over 26 per cent of the land in England and Wales unregistered. Here are the statistics:

- There are in excess of 15.4 million hectares of land in England and Wales, of which around 11.35 million hectares are currently registered.
- For land registration purposes, England and Wales is divided into regions of varying sizes, the largest being Cumbria, comprising 718,000 hectares of land and the smallest being the Scilly Isles, comprising only 2,285 hectares of land.
- Wales is least registered with nine of its 22 counties having under 70% of land registered.
- Cumbria has the largest area of unregistered land, with over 200,000 hectares of land unregistered. Having said this, the amount of unregistered land in this region has almost halved since 2007, when the figure was just under 400,000 hectares.
- Lincolnshire is the next largest region, standing at over 610,000 hectares. It has 68.5% of its land registered.
- At the other end of the spectrum, four regions in England and Wales have 100% of their land registered. These are Blackpool, Middlesbrough, the Scilly Isles and Newport, Wales. The regions are four of the smallest, however, their total land mass amounting to under 34,000 hectares – only 0.2% of the land mass of England and Wales.

There is a very helpful map illustration of England and Wales at **http://www1.landregistry.gov.uk/assets/library/documents/Regdevmap.pdf**, which shows the percentage band of each region in registration terms.

Sources: **http://www.landreg.gov.uk/about_us/pressoffice/notices/default.asp?article_id=15067** and **http://www1.landregistry.gov.uk/register_dev/fholdcovertable/**

So why is there so much land that remains unregistered? Part of the reason is because of the relatively late imposition of compulsory registration on transfers of land across the country. Despite the Land Registration Act 1925 coming into force on 1 January 1926, it was not until as late as December 1990 that it became compulsory to register land throughout the whole of England and Wales. Prior to this, land registration was voluntary in many areas, compulsory registration being introduced in a piecemeal fashion to different regions at different times. Even once compulsory registration had been introduced across the board, this still only applied to a sale of property, and not to gifts of land or transfers occurring on the death of the landholder. It soon became apparent that this was not having the desired effect in attaining the Land Registry's goal of completing the registration of the entire country any time soon. So in 1998 new 'triggers' for the compulsory registration of land were introduced, including gifts of land, transfers on death and mortgaging property. This dramatically increased the rate of registration of land, so that in the last four years alone, the percentage of land registered in England and Wales has increased from only 60 per cent to over 76 per cent. That is a staggering 2.4 million hectares of additional land which has been registered during this period. The Land Registration Act 1926 was superseded by the Land Registration Act 2002, but this made very little additional change, its primary purpose being to pave the way for electronic conveyancing, something which we will look at in a little more detail in Chapter 3.

Of the areas of land across England and Wales which still remain unregistered, much is land held by the Crown. This is due to a loophole in the law brought about by the provisions of the original Land Registration Act in 1925. As the purpose of land registration is to register *estates* in land, the Crown was previously unable to register land owned by it directly. This was because, being the direct owner of the land itself and thus not holding any estate in it, there was no estate in the land which it could register. Section 79 of the Land Registration Act 2002 has solved this problem by enabling the Crown to grant an estate in land to itself and register it under the new provisions, however. Another problem area in terms of achieving 100 per cent registration was landed estates and farming land. These types of property not only often represent large areas of land, but there is a tendency for the property to be passed down through the generations and thus becoming registrable only once in a generation. The Land Registry is seeking to encourage voluntary registration of these types of properties by offering a 25 per cent discount on registration fees to anyone voluntarily registering their property for the first time. A similar problem exists for landholdings of government and other institutions, which tend to be significant landholdings that change hands rarely, if at all. As a consequence, these are unlikely to be registered under the existing statutory provisions.

So, what is the practical impact of all this? Essentially it means that, whilst the central registration of landholding across the country remains incomplete, practitioners of law will need to learn about both the unregistered and registered systems of landholding and land transfer for the foreseeable future. This text will therefore consider the rules relating to both registered and unregistered land.

Conclusion

Land law is a complex yet fascinating subject. But for those of you who are not yet convinced that land law is a subject which holds any personal interest for you, consider the professional implications it has for you as a trainee lawyer:

1. As we have already seen, land law is the basic foundation for conveyancing practice. For those students wishing to qualify as conveyancing practitioners, either residential or commercial, the subject of land law is vital to your ability to practice effectively. You will need it in the sale and purchase of houses, apartment rentals and, in a commercial context, in terms of site acquisition for commercial development. You will also need it for the sale, purchase and lease of commercial properties; take, for example, the law school you attend.
2. Those students intending to undertake the Legal Practice Course will need to draw extensively on their knowledge of land law during the property aspect of the Legal Practice Course, which is not only compulsory, but forms a major part of the course.
3. It is important to have a working knowledge of land law in the application of many other areas of practice, including:
   (a) Litigation – you will need a knowledge of land law when you have to deal with landlord and tenant disputes, both residential and commercial; boundary disputes or acting in the renewal of commercial leases
   (b) Banking law – you will be interested in the effect and application of mortgages over land, which we will be covering in Chapter 12.
   (c) Family law – a knowledge of land law will be valuable to you when examining the rights of your clients in respect of the family home and other associated issues (see Chapter 7)
   (d) Insolvency lawyers – you will be interested in land as an asset of the individual or company

This is, of course, in addition to land law's relevance to you as prospective property owners of the future.

This introductory chapter should have given you some insight into the importance of land law as a subject. Now to get you started on your own personal journey into the world of property law, take a look at the Out and About feature, below.

Out and about

Your 'dream' property

Go into your local estate agents or have a look at an online property search engine, such as **http://www.rightmove.co.uk** (there are, of course, others you can use), and have a look at the properties on sale. Imagine you are buying your first home. Choose a property that would be right for you and collect or print out the particulars of sale from the agent.

Source: Photodisc

Take a look at the property particulars and make a note of any information provided by the particulars which you think will be relevant to the purchase of the property. Now, make a second list of additional information you think you will need to buy the property.

You should take no longer than 30 minutes on this task.

Handy tip: Remember to be realistic with the house you choose – we will be using the particulars again later in the book and the most expensive house in the estate agent's window isn't likely to be the easiest to work with!

Reflective practice

Take another look at the list you have created. How many of the items on your list do you think are relevant to the legal purchase of the land and building? Have you thought about the following:

- Is the property freehold or leasehold?
- Boundaries to the property
- Shared rights of maintenance and access to the property
- Rights of others over the property
- Any rights you will need over others' property
- Relevant planning issues

On reflection, is there anything else you would add to (or remove from) your list?

Some (but not all) of the Out and About and Writing and Drafting features you will come across throughout the remaining chapters of the text will contain instructions to find and investigate your 'dream' property. You should keep all of the information you collate on the property to create your own property file. This is not designed as a complete file for conveyancing purposes; it is simply designed to gather together a number of issues which should help you when you come to revise some of the important land law issues dealt with in the text. It is hoped that you find it a useful learning tool.

Summary

- All land in England and Wales is held by the Crown. Thus there can be no absolute ownership of land by an individual in this country.
- There is only one form of tenure in modern land law: the free tenure of common socage. The doctrine of tenures is all but obsolete in its application, however, save in the case of the death of the landholder without a will or living relatives, in which case the property will return to the Crown, as *bona vacantia*.
- There are two legal estates in land: the fee simple absolute in possession (freehold) and the term of years absolute (leasehold) (section 1 Law of Property Act 1925).
- Commonhold is a method of collectively holding a freehold estate in land. It is used to get around the difficulties of enforcing covenants as between neighbouring properties in a development, residential or commercial.
- The Land Registration Act 1925 introduced a centralised system of registration for landowners. This has been superseded by the Land Registration Act 2002.
- About one quarter of the land in England and Wales is still unregistered, so it is necessary to learn about the law relating to both unregistered and registered land.

Question and answer*

Essay: English Civil War dictator Oliver Cromwell described the system of land transfer which existed in England and Wales 'an ungodly mess'. Why was this and what key changes have been implemented since this time to improve the system?

This question should be answered in 40 minutes.

* Answer guidance is provided at the end of the chapter.

Further reading

Land Registry Practice Guide 1, available online at: http://www.landregistry.gov.uk/professional/guides/practice-guide-1#guide-mark-7
This guide lists at section 3 all the circumstances under which registration of title is now compulsory in England and Wales.

Brenan, J. (2004) 'Lessee-owned blocks: moving towards commonhold', L&T Review, 8(1), 2–4.
This article provides an interesting practical discussion on the shortfalls of leasehold property ownership and why a move should be made towards the use of commonhold as an alternative form of landholding.

Useful websites

For more information on property held by the Crown, see the Crown Estate's website at: **http://www.thecrownestate.co.uk/tce_faqs.htm**.

For more information on the doctrine of *bona vacantia*, take a look at the Bona Vacantia division of the Treasury Solicitor's Department, at: **http://www.bonavacantia.gov.uk/output/**.

The Land Registry's website gives information on commonhold estates and how to go about registering one at the Land Registry. To read more go to: **http://www1.landregistry.gov.uk/education_chapter_pages_repository/commonhold/**.

Question and answer guidance

Please note that the following is not a full answer and is intended to provide guidance in outline form only as to how to answer the questions posed.

Essay: You should explain that Cromwell was referring to the practical difficulties incumbent in the transfer of land process which existed in England at that time (he ruled the country as Lord Protector between 1653 and 1658). As we have seen above, the system of unregistered land was long-winded and complicated, lawyers having to repeat the process of proving title to the property every time the land changed hands. In addition, the private ownership and holding of title deeds meant that the government was unable to keep tabs on who owned what land at any one time. There was also the problem of how to prove ownership if title deeds were lost or stolen.

There were actually a few attempts made at the introduction of a system of land registration, before it was finally successfully introduced by the Land Registration Act 1925 (for more information on the history of land registration, see the Land Registry's information leaflet, at: **http://www.landreg.gov.uk/assets/library/documents/bhist-lr.pdf**). The introduction of land registration simplified the conveyancing process, and began the task of recording the individual ownership of property across the country.

Your essay could conclude that, whilst the system is not without its flaws (for further information on this see the section on overriding interests in Chapter 4 of the text), the move towards 100% registration of land in this country is a vast improvement on the previous system.

Visit **www.mylawchamber.co.uk** to access tools to help you develop and test your knowledge of land law.

Chapter 2
What is land?

Key points In this chapter we will be looking at:

- The nature of land ownership and land as a bundle of rights
- The difference between real and personal property and the importance of the distinction
- How we define land ownership and where it begins and ends
- The division of lower and upper airspace in relation to land ownership
- The general rules as to boundaries
- The definition of fixtures and chattels
- The degree and purpose of annexation tests in relation to fixtures
- Whether a building can ever be a chattel
- The law of treasure trove and other items found in or on the ground
- Limitations on land ownership and state restrictions on the use of land, including town and country planning, compulsory purchase and the resulting human rights implications

Introduction

In Chapter 1 we considered the importance of land law and highlighted its relevance in everyday life. We also learned a little bit about the history of land law in England and Wales and we were introduced both to the concepts of **tenure** and **estates**, and **registered** and **unregistered land**. Having thus set the scene, in this second chapter we are going to start thinking about land as the basis of an academic subject of study.

What does it mean to *own* land?

We have already established that, with the exception of the Crown, no one in this country owns land outright, and that what the homeowner actually has is an estate in the land, or a right to use or enjoy the land for a certain period of time. Although we talk about 'owning' our own property therefore, in reality what we term ownership bears scant resemblance to ownership in the literal sense of the word. We cannot 'own' property in the same way as we might own an iPod or our car: ownership of land is in many ways far more limited.

Consider the following example. You are going to the Leeds Festival. You have bought a weekend ticket and are very excited. You buy a brand new tent for the occasion. You arrive at the festival and pitch your tent. You would not expect to come back from the gig and find someone else sleeping in your tent, nor would you expect other campers to take a shortcut through your tent to access another part of the site. It is your property and no one else has any rights in it. Equally, if you wanted to decorate or customise your tent to make it personal to you, no one would be able to prevent you from doing this – the tent belongs to you and you can do with it as you wish. If, when the festival comes to a close, you decide to abandon or destroy your tent rather than taking it down to use at another event, you could do this too. Just to make sure you have a clear understanding of outright property ownership, take a look at the Out and About feature, below.

Out and about

Take the further example of a pair of designer wellies you buy for the festival. Now take a few minutes to make a list of all of the different things you could do to, or with, your wellies as personal property.

Source: Trevor Clifford, Pearson Education Ltd

You should take no more than 10 minutes on this task.

Reflective practice

Take a look at the list you have created above. Would you expect to be able to do all these things with your own land?

Now that we have established what you can and cannot do with your own personal property, let us consider how the ownership of land may differ from this. Take, for example, the owners of Bramham Park, where the Leeds Festival is held. In contrast to the absolute ownership you enjoy in your tent, their ownership of the Park, whilst extensive, may also be subject to a significant number of limitations. It is quite feasible that their rights to the enjoyment of the land may be subject to a right of a third party, or even the general public, to use a right of way crossing part of it, or for their ability to build on the grazing land to be limited to agricultural buildings, or in some part no building at all. This is because land ownership is not an absolute; it is simply a right to use land in a specified way for a certain period of time. This means that, as well as being limited in time, this right to use the land may be subject to restrictions on how the land is used or what it is used for. And most importantly, because it is a right of user and not absolute ownership in the way that the term 'ownership' is commonly understood, one single piece of land can be subject to a number of different rights or users. In this regard it may therefore be more accurate to say that Bramham Park, as a property, actually amounts to no more than a mixed bundle of rights belonging to various different owners, with the Lane Foxes simply being custodians of the physical land itself for the duration of their legal estate in it.

> land ownership is not an absolute

So why is land as an entity treated so differently from all other types of property? It could be argued that there are a number of different reasons for this. One reason is perhaps because of the sheer scale of land, not just in size, but in its value as an asset too.

Land is by far the most valuable commodity most of us will ever own and its importance as such is reflected in the way in which it is viewed from a legal perspective. It is also important to recognise land's value to us as the foundation of our lives and livelihood. If you think about it, we are wholly reliant on land as a source of food, shelter, health, exercise and indeed every other aspect of our existence. For this reason above all others land is simply too important a commodity to be left entirely at the whim of the individual. One final reason for land's treatment apart from all other types of property is its longevity. The land is by its nature going to be around for a very long time – far longer than our lifetimes and even the lifetimes of our children or our grandchildren. It therefore makes sense that we should take our place simply as custodians of the land for a piece of time rather than to be so bold as to claim that we are the owners of it.

Real and personal property

The separate nature of land ownership compared with ownership of other types of property has also led to significant differences in how claims over land are dealt with from a legal perspective. The result is that, if a third party misappropriates your land, you will have the right to make a claim through the courts for the land's return. This is known as a **right 'in *rem*'** (that is, a right to recover the thing itself), or a **'real' action**. It is important to note here that the court has no discretion over whether to grant an alternative remedy, the ability to claim physical recovery of one's land being available to any landowner as of right. For this reason, all estates and interests in land are termed 'real' property or '**realty**', because of the 'real' rights which attach to them.

All other types of property, such as cars, books, clothing and so on, cannot claim the benefit of such an action. As purely personal property if someone misappropriates, for example, your netbook, you can make a claim through the courts for the return of your item. However, you have no absolute right to its return. Thus, the court may order the return of the netbook; however, they may as easily order financial compensation to the value of the item you have lost. This is known as a **personal action**, or an **action '*in personam*'**, because the action is against the person who has taken your property and not against the item or thing which has been misappropriated. For historical reasons items of personal property, or '**personalty**', are also often referred to as '**chattels**', from the old English for cattle, which were originally the most valuable and thus the most important form of personal property.

It should be noted that **leases** are a peculiar hybrid of the two types of property. Because of their contractual nature, the placing of leases historically has always been in the category of personal property, or chattels. However, due to their growing importance as a concept and ultimate recognition in the 1925 legislation as a legal estate in land, leasehold rights are now accorded the same benefit of real action as freehold property. The result is that leases are given a special category of their own in which to reside: that of **chattels real** (i.e. personal property which can be protected through a real action).

The definition of land

Having established what it means to be the owner of land, now let us turn to look at the definition of land itself: in other words, if we own a piece of land, what exactly is it that we own? Take a look at the following documents in the Documenting the Law box:

Documenting the law

Land Registry official filed plan of The Old Courthouse, Ripon (registered land)

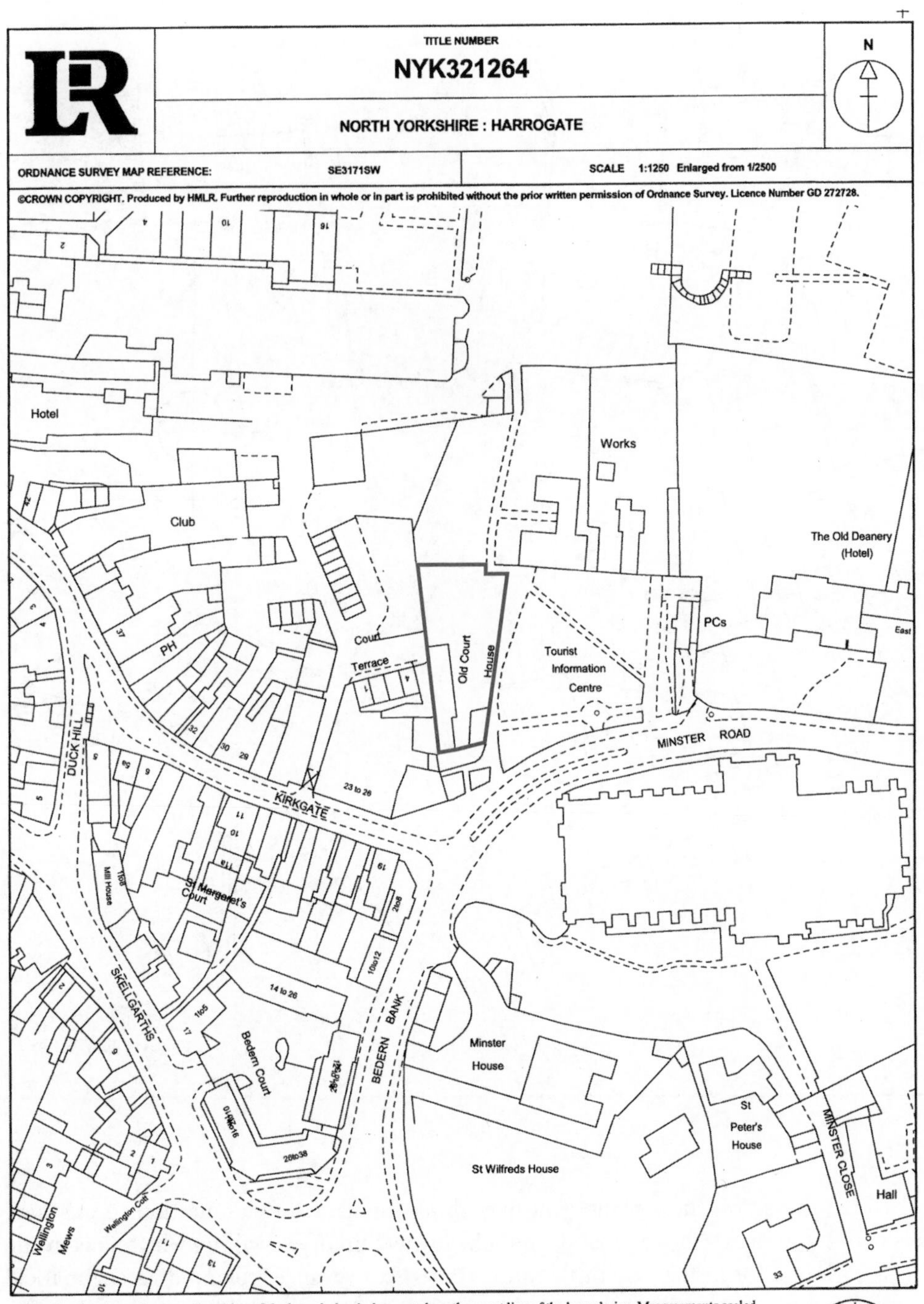

This title plan shows the general position of the boundaries: it does not show the exact line of the boundaries. Measurements scaled from this plan may not match measurements between the same points on the ground. For more information see Land Registry Public Guide 7 - *Title Plans*.
This official copy shows the state of the title plan on **6 June 2006** at **10:13:01**. It may be subject to distortions in scale.
Under s.67 of the Land Registration Act 2002, this copy is admissible in evidence to the same extent as the original.
Issued on 6 June 2006.
This title is dealt with by the **York District Land Registry.**

H.M. LAND REGISTRY
DA
06/2006

Plan from a conveyance of The Old Courthouse, Ripon dated 10 March 1959 (unregistered land)

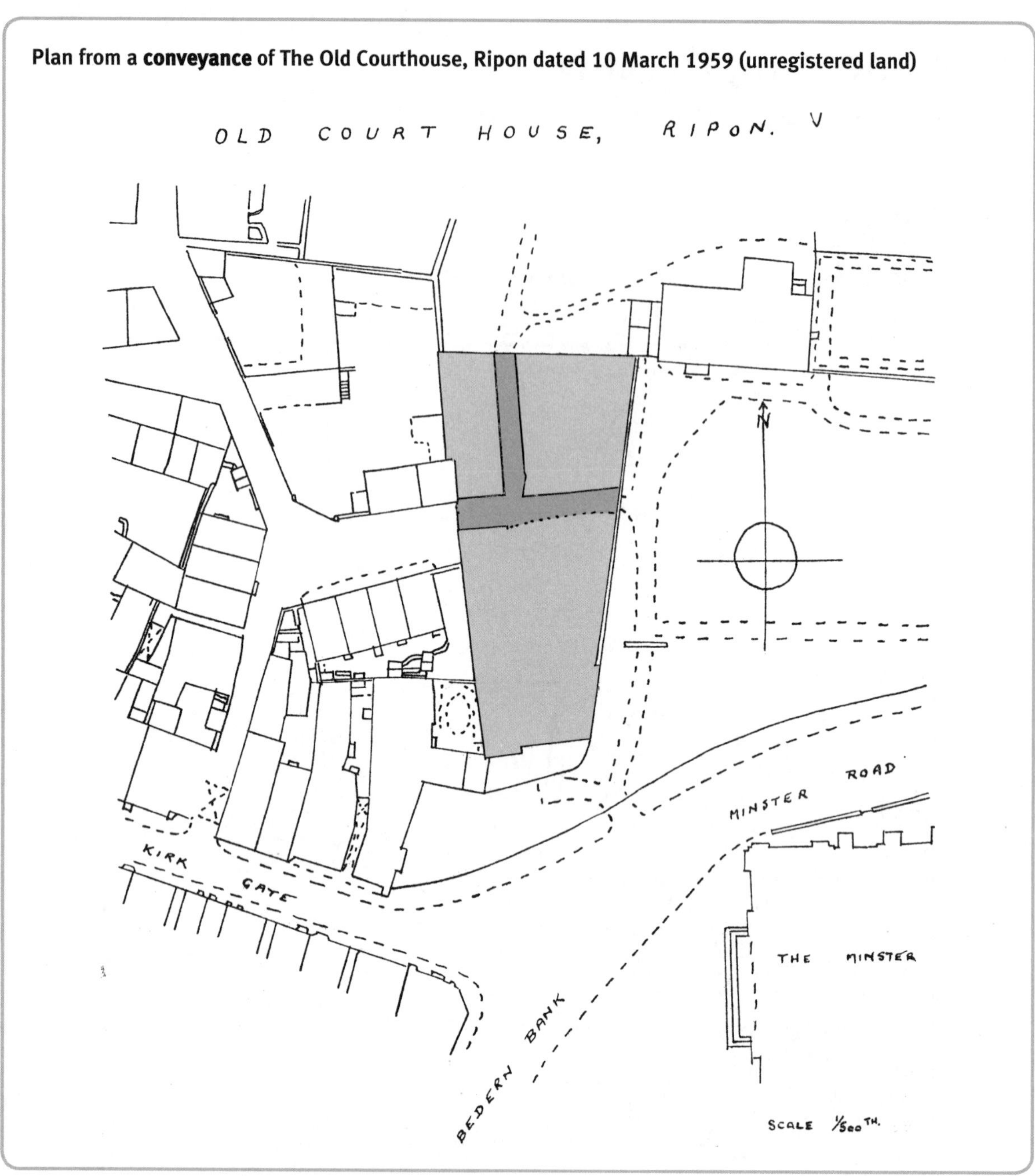

Based on these plans, you may think this is a simple question to answer: when you purchase a piece of land, you take ownership of everything which falls inside the green line (or in the case of the unregistered conveyance, coloured green) marked upon the plan. But can it really be as simple as that? To get you thinking about it, why not take a look at the Writing and Drafting feature below.

Writing and drafting

What does the term 'land' mean to you? Try drafting your own definition of land based on your understanding of the term.

You should take no more than 15 minutes on this task.

One definition of land in lay terms is: 'the part of the earth's surface that is not covered by water' (the *Oxford English Dictionary*). When trying to define it legally, however, one soon realises that the concept of 'land' is so much wider than this. To begin with, from a legal point of view the dictionary definition of land leaves unanswered a number of important questions as to the exact extent of the land. Take the following example: imagine you buy a house in the countryside with a quarter of an acre of garden. Presumably you own up to the boundaries of the property on each side (as per the plan to the conveyance of the land). But what about the earth out of which the land is made? How far down do you own? In terms of your garden, do you own just the lawn, or the earth which lies beneath it? If you wanted to plant potatoes in your vegetable patch, common sense might dictate that you owned the earth in which the potatoes were going to grow and that you could harvest them without fear of trespass onto someone else's space. But what about further down? If your neighbour decided to build a tunnel underneath your garden as a shortcut to the main road, would your neighbour be trespassing on your land or simply passing underneath it? What about the earth displaced when your neighbour created the tunnel? Would this belong to you? What if the neighbour discovered a seam of precious metal whilst they were digging? Would the metals they unearthed belong to you as landowner, or to them? Equally, what about the airspace above your land? Could you build a skyscraper on your land or does someone else own the airspace? If it is you who owns it, surely this means that if an aeroplane wished to fly over the country they would need permission from each and every landowner whose land they crossed. But surely this is not logical. And finally, would you define your land as including any buildings on it, or just the land on which those buildings stand?

Reflective practice

Go back and have a look at your definition of land. Would you change it in light of what you have read above? Is there anything you would add to your definition and if so, what?

These questions certainly provide food for thought, and we shall strive to answer each one of them throughout the rest of the chapter. In the meantime, let us have a look at what the lawyers have to say on the matter. Land is given a legal definition in Section 205(1)(ix) of the Law of Property Act 1925. The section states that:

> 'Land' includes land of any tenure, and mines and minerals, whether or not held apart from the surface, buildings or parts of buildings (whether the division is horizontal, vertical or made in any other way) and other **corporeal hereditaments** . . . **incorporeal hereditaments**, and an **easement**, right, **privilege**, or benefit in, over, or derived from land;

At first the wording seems a bit difficult, but if broken down into sections can be explained fairly simply, as follows:

'Land' includes land of any tenure . . .

We have already established in Chapter 1 that all land in this country (with the exception of Crown land) is held upon tenure; we can essentially say, therefore, that the term land includes all land in this country.

. . . and mines and minerals, whether or not held apart from the surface . . .

The definition also states that land includes any mines or minerals found either within the land or on its surface (whether physically attached to the surface or not). There are a few exceptions to this rule, as we shall see below, however.

. . . buildings or parts of buildings . . .

In addition, any buildings on the land are included within the definition.

. . . corporeal and incorporeal hereditaments . . .

The term '**hereditament**' is the one you are the least likely to be familiar with from the definition. However, it is simply an outmoded term denoting an inheritable right (think of the word 'hereditary' and you will get to 'hereditament'). 'Corporeal hereditaments' are therefore inheritable rights of a physical nature, such as the land itself, any buildings on it and anything affixed to the land (which we will discuss in further detail below); whereas 'incorporeal hereditaments' are intangible rights, such as **rights of way** over the land or perhaps a right to take something from the land, such as firewood or grass for hay. The reference to 'an easement, right, privilege, or benefit in, over, or derived from land' is just a list of some of the different types of intangible right which fall within this definition.

Essentially, then, what the statutory definition of land tells us is that land includes not only the land itself, but also anything built on it and any rights granted over it.

Land as a slice of the earth

As we have seen, the legal definition is fairly all-encompassing in terms of the surface of the earth. But what about the soil and the rock which lies below the surface and the sky which reaches above it? There is no specific mention of either of these things in the statutory definition. The only reference to the earth is by implication in the mentioning of mines and minerals contained within it. So if you own a piece of land, where does that land start and end? In order to find the answer to this question we must look to another, much older source. There is an ancient Latin **maxim** which reads: '*Cuius est solum eius est usque ad coelum et ad inferos*'.

This translates as 'he who owns the earth owns everything up to the heavens above and down to the depths below'. In other words, if you own a piece of land you own everything above it to infinity and everything below it until you reach the centre of the earth. As a general rule, this maxim still holds good today; however, certain modifications have been made over the course of time (and in particular since the advent of aeronautical engineering) to curb this to a greater or lesser extent.

'ad inferos'

In terms of the land below the surface of the earth, according to the Court of Appeal case of *Grigsby* v. *Melville* [1974] 1 WLR 80 it is indeed the case that whoever owns land owns everything below the surface of that land, to the centre of the earth. The case concerned freehold owners of adjoining properties. There was a cellar under the claimant's property which could only be accessed via a staircase leading down from the defendant's property, and which the defendant was using. The claimant wished to prevent the defendant from using the cellar, which she claimed was a trespass on her property. The court held that the cellar was owned by the claimant and therefore granted an injunction against the defendant to prevent further access to the cellar. Their judgment was based on the principle that when the claimant had purchased the land she had bought everything which lay below its surface, including the cellar. This was irrespective of the method of access.

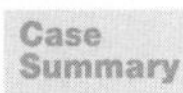

This ownership to the centre of the earth is not in reality an absolute, however, as the case would suggest. We have seen from the statutory definition of land that the landowner also owns any mines and minerals which are contained within the land; but in reality certain kinds of minerals actually belong to the State. Ownership of oil and gas within the land area of Great Britain is vested in the Crown by section 2 of the Petroleum Act 1998. Following the privatisation of the coal industry in 1994 the ownership of almost all coal now lies with the Coal Authority, which is a public body. And finally the Crown holds the rights to gold and silver as part of the **Crown Estate**. The mines of these metals are known as '**Mines Royal**'. At one time the mines royal included copper, iron, lead and tin mines as well, but the extent of the mines was curtailed by an Act of 1688. The collaborative effect of these provisions is that, in real terms, ownership of the land beneath the surface of the earth is not in fact absolute at all. The Acts have had the effect of curtailing the maxim so that it reads 'he who owns the earth owns everything down to the depths below except for any gas, oil, coal, gold or silver, which shall be owned by the State'.

Having said this, a recent case has confirmed that a landowner will still be entitled to compensation for subterranean trespass, despite the trespasser entering the land to excavate mineral deposits belonging to them, and not the landowner. In the case of *Bocardo SA* v. *Star Energy* [2010] UKSC 35, a mining company had drilled below the landowner's property in order to extract oil, without the landowner's permission. The Supreme Court ruled that a landowner owns the earth which lies beneath their property up to an undefined depth where the notion of ownership becomes absurd. Applying this principle, the court found that in this case, even mining at a depth of 2,800 feet below the earth, a trespass had occurred. However, the correct measure of **damages** would only extend to adequate compensation for the act of trespass itself (in this case the installation of pipes and not to a share in the oil mined). Damages were therefore limited to the nominal figure of £1,000.

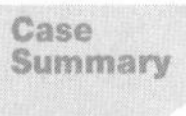

'ad coelum'

As regards the sky forming the airspace above the land, the extent of ownership is more limited still. For legal purposes the airspace above any given property is divided into two strata: the lower airspace and the upper airspace. The lower airspace is deemed to belong to the property and the upper airspace is not. Thus, any use of upper airspace above the landowner's property is not actionable by the landowner and cannot be curtailed or prevented. The case which defined this lower and upper airspace is that of

Case Summary

Bernstein of Leigh (Baron) v. *Skyviews & General Ltd* [1978] QB 479. The case concerned an aeroplane flying over land in order to take an aerial photograph. Baron Bernstein was enraged by the defendant flying over his land, which he considered a trespass and an invasion of his privacy. The court held, however, that the defendant had not committed an act of trespass. He was flying several hundred feet above the ground and this could not possibly have interfered with any use to which the Baron might have wished to put the land at that time.

Since this case was heard the enactment of the Civil Aviation Act 1982 has ensured that aircraft flying above property no longer pose issues of trespass over private property in any event. Under section 76(1) of the Act, immunity from trespass or nuisance is given to any aircraft flying 'at a height above the ground which, having regard to wind, weather and all the circumstances of the case is reasonable'. No guidance is given by the Act as to what height is generally considered to be reasonable; however, under air traffic control regulations no aircraft may fly closer to the ground than 500 feet except for on landing or take-off (see the first schedule to the Rules of the Air Regulations 1996 SI 1996/1393, section 5(1)(e)).

The lower airspace does not extend to a measured distance above the ground; rather it is limited to the amount of airspace above a person's property which is necessary for their ordinary use and enjoyment of the land and any structures built upon it. With space, particularly in built-up inner city areas, being ever more at a premium, this lower airspace can be commercially very valuable. Take a look at the Law in Action feature below which illustrates this.

Law in action Trump Tower

Did you know that American multi-millionaire property tycoon, Donald Trump, made his money leasing airspace to build skyscrapers?

Trump Towers was Donald Trump's second major construction project in New York City. Trump began work on the project in 1980, planning to build a $200 million luxury high-rise residential apartment block on Fifth Avenue with office space and retail stores below, on the site of what had previously been the Bonwitt Teller building next to the iconic Tiffany's jewellery store. The building would provide tenants with upmarket shops, high-end office space and luxurious serviced apartments with breathtaking views of the city.

Source: Sozaijiten

In order to create something worthy of such prestige, however, Trump knew that his tower needed to be taller than its neighbours. He also knew that the higher he could build the more storeys he could add and this meant more luxury apartments and inevitably more money. This presented a problem, however, because in the state of New York the planning laws require that the maximum height of a building is determined by the surface area of the land owned. The land owned by Trump was sufficient to construct a 48-storey skyscraper, but no more than this. Trump had an idea. He approached his next-door neighbour, Tiffany & Co., persuading them to sell their unused air rights above the Tiffany's store for $5 million. This allowed him to add another 20 storeys to his building, creating an apartment block some 68 storeys high. Trump Tower opened its doors in 1983. Donald Trump has since built a number of other towers, including the 90-storey Trump World Tower, also in New York City, which is recorded as being the tallest residential building in the world.

Whilst the same planning laws do not apply in England and Wales, airspace can be an equally valuable commodity for us. As we will see later in the chapter, the leasing of airspace for the oversailing of cranes in a development context, and for the placement of television and telecommunications aerials, is not only common but can be extremely lucrative for the landowners involved.

Source: **http://www.trump.com**

In England and Wales there are a number of cases relating to lower airspace, all of which follow the general principle that the lower airspace is limited to the amount of airspace necessary for the ordinary use and enjoyment of the land, and apply it fairly strictly. Thus, where a third party enters into the landholder's airspace, they will be guilty of trespass regardless of whether there is any damage caused to the property. The first two cases were set in a residential context. In *Lemmon* v. *Webb* [1895] AC 1 branches of the defendant's tree overhung the claimant's property. The court held that the claimant was entitled to lop off the overhanging branches which trespassed on the claimant's property, so long as he did not enter the defendant's land in order to do so. There was no need for the claimant to give notice to the defendant of his intended actions; however, he was not entitled to keep the branches, which belonged to the defendant. These had to be thrown back on to the neighbour's land. A slightly earlier decision that produced a similar outcome was that of *Ellis* v. *Loftus Iron Company* (1874) LR 10 CP 10. In this case the court held that the defendant had committed a trespass by allowing his horse's head to cross a dividing fence between two neighbouring properties. This shows just how strictly the offence of trespass into lower airspace is applied, given the difficulty the defendant would have had in keeping the horse's head from crossing the fence line. Luckily, in contrast to the finding in *Lemmon* v. *Webb*, the court did not grant the claimant permission to lop off the overhanging head, however!

Case Summary

Case Summary

A couple of more recent cases relate to commercial property. In the case of *Kelsen* v. *Imperial Tobacco Co.* [1957] 2 QB 334 an advertising sign put up by the Imperial Tobacco company infringed upon the airspace of Mr Kelsen's shop by only a few inches. The court nevertheless granted an **injunction** requiring the company to remove their signage immediately. In the case of *Wollerton & Wilson Ltd* v. *Richard Costain (Midlands) Ltd* [1970] 1 WLR 411 the defendant's crane overhung the claimant's premises some fifteen metres above the level of the claimant's roof. Despite the fact that this was a considerable height above the claimant's premises, an injunction was nevertheless granted to restrain the crane from trespassing over the land. It should be noted, however, that the court postponed the injunction for a year pending completion of the works because of the particular circumstances of the case. It can be seen, then, that the courts will apply a common-sense element to such claims where necessary despite the strict application of the rule. *Wollerton & Wilson* is an important case because,

Case Summary

Case Summary

in a development context, the oversailing of cranes is often an issue which arises and the use of crane oversailing licences is not only common but can be extremely lucrative for the landowners involved. In the 1989 case of *London & Manchester Assurance Co. Ltd* v. *O & H Construction Ltd* [1989] 2 EGLR 185, which turned on similar facts to *Wollerton & Wilson*, Mr Justice Harman in granting injunctions to restrain an overswinging crane said, amongst other things, that 'it is, in my view, beyond any possible question on the authorities and the law that a party is not entitled to swing his crane over neighbouring land without the consent of the neighbouring owner'. It should be noted that an injunction is not the only remedy available to the courts in such instances. The grant of an injunction is discretionary and the court could just as easily give an award of damages if they feel it more appropriate under the circumstances of the case.

Case Summary

It should be noted that leases of flats can be viewed quite differently, however. In the case of *Davies* v. *Vadegar* [1990] 1 EGLR 71, the Court of Appeal held that where a house was divided into two flats, one on the ground floor and one on the first floor, because the lease of the first floor flat was stated to include the roof, it also included the airspace above it. The more recent case of *Rosebery Ltd* v. *Rocklee Ltd*, LTL 2/2/2011 treated the matter quite differently, however. The case, which can be said to have produced a significant development in the law in terms of the strictness of its application, concerned an eight-storey apartment block. The owner of the sixth-floor apartment was granted an additional lease of the airspace above the fifth-floor flat below by the landlord of the apartment building, for the purpose of building an extension to the flat on their terrace, in the airspace above part of the roof of the fifth-floor flat. The seventh-floor flat owner subsequently sought to do the same by building on the roof of the sixth-floor flat owner's extension. The sixth-floor flat owner objected, on the grounds that it had leased all of the airspace above the extension. The court rejected the argument. In their view, the lease of airspace granted by the landlord to build the extension to the sixth-floor flat did not include the airspace above it. With a lease of part of a building there should be no presumptions about the extent of airspace included in it. Each case should be considered on its merits, the Court considering what a reasonable third party, would conclude in the individual circumstances. It can be seen here then that, in cases of leasehold apartments at least, there can no longer be any presumption made about the extent of airspace owned by any given property. This could be taken to be a logical conclusion of the courts, however, because the very nature of apartments in a block is that the land is divided horizontally as well as vertically, so that separate dwellings can be created one above the other.

Case Summary

Case Summary

Boundaries

The horizontal division of the land is not the only issue, however. Vertical division, or the definition of boundaries 'on the ground', can carry with it its own difficulties too. Take another look at the **Land Registry** plan shown in the Documenting the Law feature, above. The extent of the land at first glance would appear well-defined, including all that property which falls within the green line. But when dealing with something like land which has such a large physical presence, reducing it down to a scale so small that it can be viewed on a piece of A4 paper is bound to cause problems. Chartered Surveyor Simon Nabarro explains some of the difficulties inherent in accurately defining property boundaries.

People in the law

Source: Simon Nabarro

Name and title: Simon Nabarro, director at Nabarro McAllister & Co. Ltd, Leeds.

What is your role? I am a Chartered Surveyor.

What are the main difficulties in defining boundaries between properties? The lack of an accurate and detailed method of recording land ownership. The Land Registry system far from achieves certainty due to the **General Boundaries Rule** [see below for an explanation of this rule].

In practice, how common are boundary disputes? I deal with many boundary disputes and am only a small practice. Members of the public are very precious about their land and I find disputes on boundaries to be very common.

What are the consequences of such disputes? They cost disproportionate sums of money on legal and surveyors' fees in comparison to the issues and they tend to be very bitter.

And how can you assist in the solving of boundary disputes? I attempt to find a common-sense solution from the available evidence. Sometimes there is good evidence to point to where the boundary ought to be but sometimes it is impossible to determine. In the latter cases I attempt to get the parties to reach a compromise.

Could you give one or more examples of disputes in which you have assisted? I undertook a dispute about 15 years ago which went to Court to be resolved. It was about a boundary hedge which one neighbour claimed was his and the adjoining owner wanted to be removed. When the neighbour who believed the hedge was his went away on holiday, his neighbour removed it.

I attended Court to give evidence as did the surveyor acting on instruction from the landowner who removed the hedge. The Court ruled that indeed the hedge did belong to my client and it was unlawfully removed by the adjoining owner. Following the Court ruling the lady who removed the hedge committed suicide and the following day her sons committed GBH on my client. I tell all my clients this story to try and put them off pursuing costly and fruitless disputes but many take no notice.

Can anything be done to prevent these disputes occurring in the first place? An improved system of land registry would do this but I don't see how practically this could be achieved. If with every transaction a detailed plan with measurements was prepared the boundary detail would have to be agreed with all the neighbours. This would delay the house sale process to an unreasonable extent.

Does the Land Registry have a role to play in all of this? The Land Registry can assist with explaining their rules and systems and also being able to refer to boundary applications that have previously been determined are useful if disputing neighbours can reach agreement.

The General Boundaries Rule mentioned by Simon Nabarro in the People in the Law feature above is a rule which now has statutory authority under section 60 of the Land Registration Act 2002. The rule states that a boundary shown on the register of title of a registered property is a general boundary only and therefore does not determine the exact line of the boundary. Land Registry plans can therefore not be relied upon to determine the exact position of a boundary on the ground and only serve to give a rough guide or indication of where it should be.

Where plans and surveyors cannot help there are also some common law rules which can assist in the division of land, reducing the ambiguity inherent in such matters to a greater or lesser extent. The rules vary depending on the type of boundary, and can be summarised as follows.

Boundary fences

If the property boundary is defined with a wooden fence, the assumption is that the landowner will use their land to its fullest extent, placing the fence rails on the outermost boundary of their land, with the posts on the inside. If the fence was erected with the posts on the outside, the landowner would lose those pieces of land which stood between the posts but behind the railing. Figure 2.1 may make this easier to follow:

Figure 2.1 Boundary fences

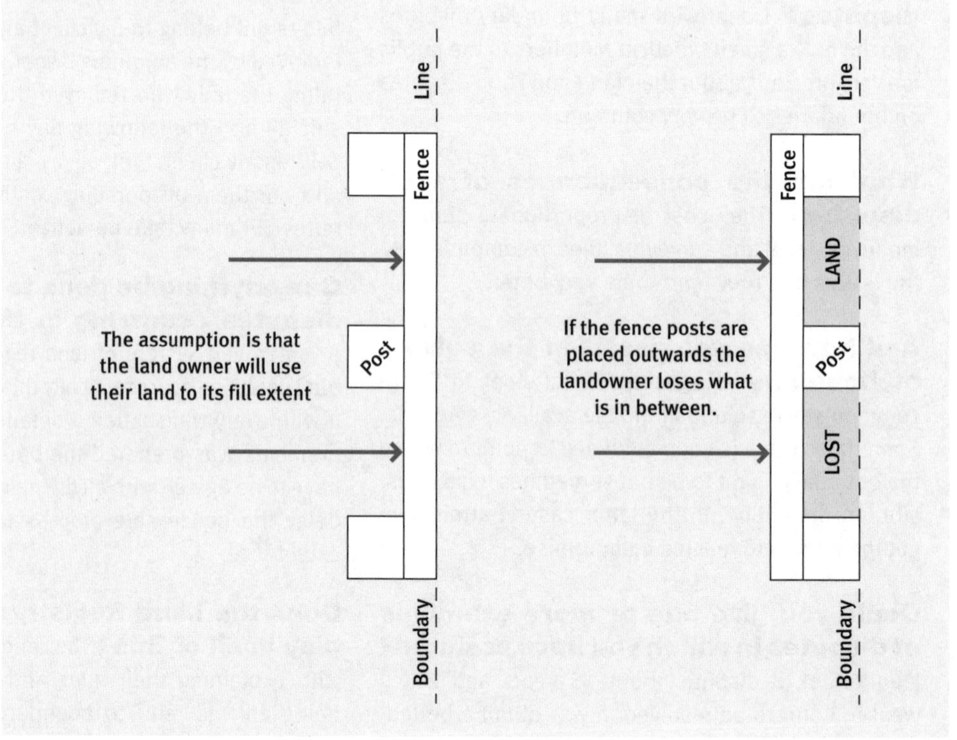

Hedges

Where two pieces of land are separated by a hedge or bank and an artificial ditch, it is presumed that the boundary runs along the side of the ditch furthest from the hedge or bank. This ancient common law rule was acknowledged by Mr Justice Bayley in the 1827 case of *Noye* v. *Reed* (1827) 1 Man & Ry KB 63, which concerned an argument between two neighbouring tenants of land owned by the same landlord. In this case it was determined that the rule would not apply as between tenants of land within the same ultimate ownership.

The general rule has been applied more recently in the Court of Appeal case of *Hall* v. *Dorling* (1996) 74 P & CR 400, CA in which Mr Hall, who was the owner of a field adjoining Mr Dorling's land, succeeded in establishing that the **Hedge and Ditch rule** should apply in the absence of evidence to the contrary. The case had concerned a dispute as to the extent of Dorling's land, which he wished to develop into a housing estate.

Roads

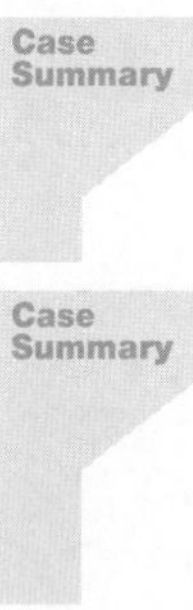

According to the case of *Goodtitle d. Chester* v. *Alker and another* [1558–1774] All ER Rep 208, if the boundary to the property is formed by a road or highway the presumed boundary line runs down the middle of the road, with the landowner owning the half of that road or highway which abuts their land, up to the middle line. It should be noted that if the local authority is responsible for the maintenance of the road, this extends only to the surface of the road itself. The earth beneath remains within the ownership of the adjacent landowner in accordance with the middle line rule, the surface reverting to the landowner should the road ever be closed (see *Holmes* v. *Bellingham* (1859) 141 ER 843).

Water

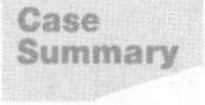

According to the case of *Wishart* v. *Wyllie* (1853) 1 Macq 389, HL the same ancient rule applies to land adjacent to non-tidal rivers (a tidal river is one where the water is subject to the ebb and flow of the tide), although the landowner does not own the water in the river: only the earth which makes up the river bed. Land which is covered with water, although not mentioned in the Law of Property Act 1925, is specifically included in the definition of 'land' given at section 132 of the Land Registration Act 2002. We will touch again briefly on the ownership of water itself later on in the chapter. This rule has been more recently tested in the 2005 case of *Herbert* v. *Pegrum* [2005] All ER (D) 307, in which the Court of Appeal found that in the absence of documentation showing sufficient evidence of agreement to the contrary, the presumption of ownership to the median line of the river would take effect. The claimant in this case had tried to rely on some wording in a 1931 conveyance as evidence of her sole ownership of the river, but this was rejected by the court.

In the case of land abutting the sea and tidal rivers, the boundary is taken to be the high tide mark; the land between the high and low tide marks, or **foreshore**, belongs to the Crown. An early authority for this rule is *Sir Henry Constable's Case* (1601) 5 Co Rep 106a, the facts of which make interesting reading. The claimant made a claim for trespass against the defendant in respect of a package of goods which the defendant had taken. The package had been washed up on the seashore following a shipwreck. The remainder of the goods from the wreck was still floating in the tide. Finding for the claimant, the court held that the package constituted shipwrecked goods and was therefore the property of the Crown; the items still floating on the foreshore were 'flotsam and jetsam' and also within the Crown's jurisdiction.

It is interesting to note that, if the river bed should change course, the landowner's boundary will change with it, provided the change is 'gradual and imperceptible'. This was the case in the Privy Council case of *Southern Centre of Theosophy Inc* v. *State of South Australia* [1982] AC 706, in which the Lords held that the tenants of land

bordered by a tidal lake which had accrued some 20 acres through the gradual deposit of soil on the shore of the lake were entitled to the additional land, such land not having been excluded from the terms of the lease.

Fixtures and chattels

So, having now established how far a landowner's property holding extends, both horizontally and vertically, let us consider the extent of that ownership in terms of those physical objects which may be placed upon the surface of the earth. In other words, if you buy a piece of land with buildings or other items on or in it, what is included in the sale? We have already established that minerals found either in or on the surface of the earth will be included (with the exclusion of fossil fuels, gold and silver), even if they are 'held apart from the surface' – in other words, even if they are just found lying on the ground. So if you were lucky enough to find a natural source of diamonds in the silt in the river at the bottom of your garden, you would be in the very fortunate position of being able to claim them as yours.

a building on the ground becomes part of the ground

We have also seen from the statutory definition that land includes any buildings on that land. The inclusion of the buildings on the land within the statutory definition is actually just the codification of a much older established common law maxim dating back to Roman times, which is encompassed by the Latin phrase '*superficies solo cedit*'. The phrase, which means that a building on the ground becomes part of the ground (or '*solum*'), creates the presumption that any house or other structure erected on the land is intended when it is built to form part of that land. This ancient maxim is confirmed not only within the wording of the statutory definition given at section 205 of the Act, it also finds expression in section 62 of the Act, which states that, in the absence of contrary intention, any transfer of land is deemed to include all buildings on it without the need to refer to them separately in the transfer documents. The wording of the section is set out below:

LAW OF PROPERTY ACT 1925
Section 62: general words implied in conveyances

(1) A conveyance of land shall be deemed to include . . . all buildings, erections, fixtures, commons, hedges, ditches, fences, ways, waters, watercourses, liberties, privileges, easements, rights, and advantages whatsoever, appertaining or reputed to appertain to the land, or any part thereof, or, at the time of conveyance . . .

(2) A conveyance of land, having houses or other buildings thereon, shall be deemed to include . . . with the land, houses, or other buildings, all outhouses, erections, fixtures, cellars, areas, courts, courtyards, cisterns, sewers, gutters, drains, ways, passages, lights, watercourses, liberties, privileges, easements, rights, and advantages whatsoever, appertaining or reputed to appertain to the land, houses, or other buildings conveyed, or any of them, or any part thereof, or, at the time of conveyance . . .

(4) This section applies only if and as far as a contrary intention is not expressed in the conveyance . . .

It would appear, then, that the issue of buildings on the land is clear-cut. However, the definition of land does not end with buildings; the matter of **fixtures** must also be considered. 'Fixtures' are not included in the section 205 definition of land, but they are specifically mentioned in section 62, as can be seen above, and will be automatically included in any conveyance of the land along with the buildings on it.

So what are fixtures, exactly? The general definition of a fixture is that it is an object with physical form, which is regarded as being part of the land and is thus transferred with it on a sale of that land. An example of such an item might be fitted wardrobe units within a house, or the kitchen sink in a fitted kitchen. A fixture by its nature is quite different from a chattel which, as we have seen earlier in the chapter, is simply a personal possession with all rights in it attaching to its owner and not the land on which it rests. But what separates a fixture from a chattel: how is it possible to differentiate between the two? The answer is twofold. An object becomes a fixture and thereby becomes a permanent part of the land on which it rests, either because of the extent of its physical attachment to the land itself or because its purpose is considered to be indivisibly connected with that of the land. The process through which fixtures merge with the land at law is known as '**annexation**', and once more comes from an ancient maxim, that of '*quidquid plantatur solo, solo cedit*' ('whatever is attached to the land becomes part of it'). This merging of the fixture with the land at law does not prevent the property owner from removing it during their ownership of the property. However, should the property be sold the presumption will be that it is automatically included in the sale of the land unless the seller specifically states otherwise.

It is for this reason that the distinction between fixtures and chattels is such an important one. If there is no mention of which items are going to be removed from the property on a sale, at law the buyer is entitled to claim any fixtures on the land at the date the parties enter into the contract to buy and sell the property, or even arguably at the time when the property is offered for sale, as was successfully argued in the case of *Taylor* v. *Hamer* [2003] 03 EG 127. In this case, the claimant had agreed to purchase a house from the defendant for the sum of £3.15 million. Thus, the seller could end up giving away with the property valuable items they would have preferred to keep. The distinction is also important for **mortgage** lenders as, where there is a mortgage over the property the fixtures will form part of the **security** for the borrowing and will be included in the sale of the property if the house is **repossessed**. In order to ensure that there is no mistake as to what is and what is not included in a sale of property, it is modern conveyancing practice for the seller to complete what is known as a 'Fixtures, Fittings and Contents' form, on which they indicate which items are to be included in the sale and which is then stapled to the contract to remove any possible ambiguity.

Case Summary

Documenting the law

Extract from the Law Society's Fixtures, Fittings and Contents form, version 2 (2009)

1 Basic fittings

Boiler / immersion heater	☐	Roof insulation	☐
Radiators / wall heaters	☐	Window fitments	☐
Night-storage heaters	☐	Window shutters / grills	☐
Free-standing heaters	☐	Internal door furniture	☐
Gas fires (with surround)	☐	External door furniture	☐
Electric fires (with surround)	☐	Doorbell / chime	☐
Light switches	☐	Electric sockets	☐
	☐		☐
	☐		☐
	☐		☐

2 Television and telephone

Telephone receivers	☐	Television aerial	☐
Radio aerial	☐	Satellite dish	☐

3 Kitchen

Hob	☐	Refrigerator / fridge-freezer	☐
Extractor hood	☐	Freezer	☐
Fitted oven and grills	☐	Free-standing oven / cooker	☐
Fitted microwave	☐	Dishwasher	☐
Tumble-dryer	☐	Washing machine	☐
	☐		☐
	☐		☐

4 Bathroom

Bath	☐	Separate shower and fittings	☐
Shower fitting for bath	☐	Towel rail	☐
Shower curtain	☐	Soap / toothbrush holders	☐
Bathroom cabinet	☐	Toilet roll holders	☐
Taps	☐	Bathroom mirror	☐
	☐		☐
	☐		☐
	☐		☐

 3 of 4 *Fittings and Contents Form* TA10

5 Carpets, curtains, light fittings and fitted units

	Carpets	Curtain rails poles/pelmets*	Curtains/ blinds*	Light fittings	Fitted units**
Hall, stairs and landing					
Living room					
Dining room					
Kitchen					
Bedroom 1					
Bedroom 2					
Bedroom 3					

If the seller wishes to further explain the answers to section 5 above, please give details:

* Delete as appropriate.
** Fitted units (for example: fitted cupboards, fitted shelves, and fitted wardrobes).

6 Outdoor area

Gerutinruf nedra		Oretaeh roodtu	
Garden ornaments		Stock of fuel	
Tsburhs,stnalp,see		Osthgil edistu	
Beucebra		Wttub reta	
Dsnibtsu		Cenil sehtol	
Gdehs nedra		Renil yrato	
Greenhouse			

Signed: .... Dated:......................................

Each seller should sign this form.

Source: http://www.lawsociety.org.uk/documents/downloads/dynamic/ta10_formspecimen.pdf

It is important nevertheless to know the default position in respect of items which may not have been mentioned on the form, however, as from a practical point of view this can have very serious financial implications for the seller or buyer if a dispute arises.

So how do we tell the difference between a fixture and a chattel? As has been already alluded to above, there are two separate tests: the '**degree of annexation**', and the '**purpose of annexation**'. These tests were set out by Mr Justice Blackburn in the case of *Holland* v. *Hodgson* (1872) LR 7 CP 328, which concerned a claim by a mortgage lender for possession of spinning looms at a woollen mill. The mortgage lender had seized the property and its contents, which included the looms, in lieu of an unpaid mortgage debt. Let us look at these two tests in turn.

Case Summary

Degree of annexation

With the degree of annexation test we are trying to establish to what extent the item in question has been physically attached to the property. So what we really want to know in the first instance is whether to remove that item would cause its destruction or significant damage to the property to which it is attached. For instance, we might be talking here about the difference between fitted wardrobe units, which could not be removed without taking them apart, and a completely freestanding wardrobe.

In applying the test, the general rule of thumb is that the more firmly an item is fixed to the land the more likely it is to be a fixture. Thus, in the case of *Aircool Installations* v. *BT* [1995] CLY 821, air-conditioning equipment which had been cut into and bolted onto the walls of a building was held to constitute a fixture; and in the case of *Melluish* v. *BMI (No. 3) Ltd* [1996] 1 AC 454 the central heating system, lifts, integrated video alarm system and swimming pool filtration systems, all of which were built into the property, were all held to be fixtures. Similarly, petrol pumps on a petrol station forecourt were held to be fixtures in *Smith* v. *City Petroleum Co. Ltd* [1940] 1 All ER 260.

Case Summary

Case Summary

Case Summary

Conversely, if the item is simply resting on the land by the force of its own weight, it will generally not be considered a fixture under the degree of annexation test. This can be illustrated by the two contrasting cases of *Holland* v. *Hodgson*, mentioned above, and *Hulme* v. *Brigham* [1943] KB 152. In the earlier case of *Holland* v. *Hodgson*, spinning looms bolted to the floor of a mill were held to be fixtures, whereas in the 1943 case of *Hulme* v. *Brigham*, heavy printing machinery which was not attached to the floor was held to be a chattel only. This does not mean that the item in question has to be big and heavy and therefore unlikely to be moved in order to be deemed a fixture, however. Each case will turn on its individual facts and small things such as extractor fans or wall cabinets in bathrooms can also be considered fixtures provided there is a degree of physical attachment between them and the property.

Case Summary

Case Summary

Purpose of annexation

If a particular item is not physically attached to the land, this will not necessarily be the end of the matter, however. It is still possible that the item may be a fixture by virtue of the purpose of annexation test. The purpose of annexation test deals not with the physical attachment of the item to the property but rather with the motivations of the owner of the item behind its installation. So the question that is being asked here is whether the object was intended to be a permanent addition to the land or whether it was intended only to create a temporary improvement or look.

The classic example of the purpose of annexation test being successfully applied is that of *D'Eyncourt* v. *Gregory* (1866) LR 3 Eq 382. Here a stone garden seat and large marble statues of lions were placed at strategic points within the landowner's garden in order to create a garden landscape design. When the question arose as to whether the rather heavy and valuable lions were fixtures or chattels the landowner argued that they were chattels and therefore belonged to him to take with him on his sale of the property. However, the court held that the placing of the statues at particular points within the garden clearly showed the landowner's intention that they would form a permanent part of the garden design and thus they acquired the status of fixtures rather than chattels despite their not being affixed to the land in any way. The case should be contrasted, however, with the 1977 case of *Berkley* v. *Poulett* [1977] 1 EGLR 86 in which a statue and sundial resting on their own weight in a garden were held to be chattels because they had been placed there by the property owner for their own individual aesthetic value and not as part of an overall garden design. The effect of the purpose of annexation test, then, is that whilst a single garden gnome in a suburban garden may constitute a mere chattel, a carefully coordinated series of such ornaments forming a permanent garden display may well establish them as a group of fixtures.

Another example of the purpose of annexation test serving to create fixtures out of a series of items particularly placed is *Kennedy* v. *Secretary of State for Wales* [1996] EGCS 17, in which three bronze chandeliers and a musical clock in a stately home were held to be fixtures because they formed part of the overall house design, although it should be noted that Lord Justice Roch in the Court of Appeal case of *Botham* v. *TSB Bank* plc (1996) 73 P&CR D1, the facts of which are outlined below, stated **obiter** that ornamental chandeliers suspended from a ceiling rose should ordinarily be treated as chattels only.

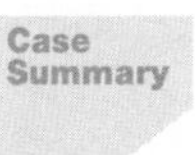

It is clear to see from the two tests that the purpose of annexation test takes precedence over the degree of annexation test and, in fact, in the case of *Hamp* v. *Bygrave* (1983) 266 EG 720 which again concerned garden ornaments, Mr Justice Botham confirmed that the purpose test should prevail over the degree test if there is any discrepancy between them. Having looked at the question of physical attachment to the land then, if this is not sufficient to warrant the item in question being termed a fixture the parties can turn to the purpose of annexation test to prove the case for their categorisation as such, should the circumstances warrant it.

Interestingly, the preferential treatment given to the purpose of annexation test over the degree of annexation test can be used to work in the opposite way as well. This means that items which are very firmly affixed to the land may still be deemed chattels if the reason for attaching them to the land is simply to facilitate their enjoyment as chattels and if the degree of annexation was no more than was necessary for the achieving of that purpose. In the case of *Leigh* v. *Taylor* [1902] AC 157 the House of Lords held that tapestries tacked to a wall were chattels, not fixtures, and thus had not become a part of the property. The tapestries had been tacked to the wall in order to be viewed and enjoyed, something which could not have been achieved in any other way. It was not the intention of the property owner in doing this to attach them permanently to the land. Equally the Canadian case of *Credit Valley Cable TV/FM Ltd* v. *Peel Condominium Corp. No. 95* (1980) 107 DLR (3d) 266 found that television cabling and antenna constituted mere chattels, the reasoning given by the court being that the equipment had been installed not for the permanent improvement of the property but simply so that the owner could better enjoy his television. This is in stark contrast to the earlier degree of

annexation cases of *Melluish* v. *BMI* and *Aircool* v. *British Telecommunications*, mentioned above, in which an alarm system and an air-conditioning system respectively were held to be fixtures.

Case Summary

In a more modern, and perhaps more mundane, context, the reasoning given in *Leigh* v. *Taylor* in respect of tapestries might apply to fitted carpets and curtains, which were discussed in some detail in the case of *Botham* v. *TSB Bank plc*, mentioned above. It was also stated in this case that integrated kitchen appliances including a freestanding cooker which, although connected electronically, remained in position by their own weight, were not fixtures. In any event, it is clear that an individual and common-sense approach should be taken in all cases. Thus, in respect of the carpets, *Botham* v. *TSB* should be contrasted with the earlier case of *La Salle Recreations Ltd* v. *Canadian Camdex Investments Ltd* (1969) 4 DLR (3d) 549, in which wall-to-wall carpeting in a hotel incorporating the hotel's design motif was held to be part of the overall hotel design and therefore constituted a fixture of the hotel.

Case Summary

Case Summary

One final case which should perhaps be mentioned is the Australian case of *Palumberi* v. *Palumberi* (1986) 4 BPR 9106, which concerned an argument between two brothers over certain fixtures in a house owned jointly by them. The brothers who lived together had fallen out and one had agreed to buy the other's half of the house from him. However, a disagreement ensued about what should be included in the sale. One particular item over which they argued was a freestanding gas stove. The court found that the stove was an essential and integral element of a kitchen and therefore a fixture. On this basis one might distinguish, therefore, a standard modern freestanding cooker from a stove, which would form a permanent fixture.

Can a building ever be a chattel?

You be the judge

Q: Consider the cases of *Holland* v. *Hodgson* and *Hulme* v. *Brigham*, above. Bearing the facts of these cases in mind, would you say that it follows that a building resting on the ground on its own weight (as opposed to being built into the ground with foundations), would be a fixture or a chattel?

A: The answer, perhaps surprisingly in spite of the cases listed above, is that it is possible for such a building to be classified as a mere chattel by the courts. See below for details.

We have seen the definition of land under section 205(1)(ix) of the Law of Property Act 1925 which states quite clearly that land includes buildings on it. However, there are nevertheless rare situations in which buildings may be deemed chattels and therefore will not form part of the land at all. The first of these can be found in *Culling* v. *Tufnal* (1694) Bull NP 34, in which a Dutch barn (a type of large, gable-roofed barn) resting on its own weight was held not to be a fixture and therefore could be removed by the landowner on sale of the property. Obviously this case significantly pre-dates the Law of Property Act; however, there are more recent examples, most notably the 1970 case

Case Summary

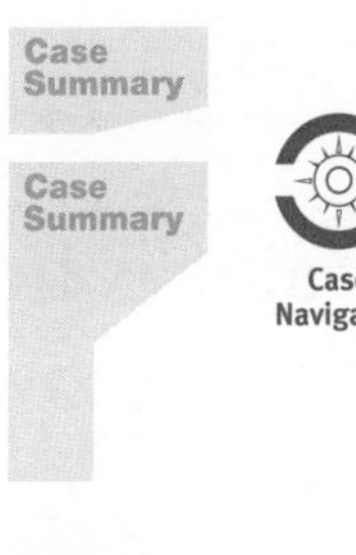

of *HE Dibble Ltd* v. *Moore* [1970] 2 QB 181, in which greenhouses which were described as 'moveable' were also considered to be chattels by the court.

The House of Lords case of ***Elitestone* v. *Morris*** [1997] 1 WLR 687 has more recently suggested that an element of common sense should be applied in such cases. Here, the Lords held that a wooden bungalow resting on concrete pillars was a fixture and not a chattel, despite the fact that it was not physically attached to the ground, because effectively it could not be moved without first demolishing it (arguably on the basis of the purpose of annexation test it might have been considered a fixture in any event). A houseboat, on the other hand, was held by the Court of Appeal to be a chattel and not a fixture in the case of *Chelsea Yacht & Boat Co. Ltd* v. *Pope* [2001] 2 All ER 409, because it could be easily removed from its moorings and did not therefore form part and parcel of the land.

Tenant's fixtures

One final point which should be made relates to items which have been affixed to the land by **tenants**. In principle, as we have already established, once a fixture is attached to the land it can only be removed by the owner of the property (that is, the freehold owner) during the course of their ownership of the property. However, the **common law** does allow by way of exception a tenant of property to remove certain kinds of fixture that they themselves have added to the property, at the end of their **letting**. This is because otherwise the **landlord** would be allowed to benefit from improvements that have been made to the property by the tenant during the duration of the lease, at the tenant's own expense. The relaxation of the general rule in relation to tenant's fixtures was recognised in the Court of Appeal case of *Spyer* v. *Phillipson* [1931] 2 Ch 183. The tenant in this case had without the landlord's consent installed valuable antique panelling and period fireplaces at the property. On the death of the tenant, his **executors** claimed the right to remove these items; however, the landlord disagreed, contending that the items in question had been installed in such a way as to become part of the fabric of the building. The Court held that in determining whether an item installed at a property was a landlord's or a tenant's fixture, the only matter to be taken into account was the purpose and object of the installation and what would happen if the item were to be removed. As long as the item could be removed without doing irreparable damage to the property, the degree of annexation was irrelevant. This common law rule extends to objects which have been attached to the property for the purpose of the tenant's trade or business, ornamental and domestic purposes and certain agricultural purposes (under section 8 of the Agricultural Tenancies Act 1995).

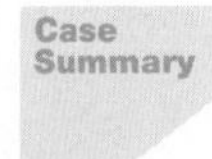

Things found on the land

Having considered the physical extent of the land in the context of ownership, and also those items built upon or affixed to it, all that remains to consider is the status in terms of ownership of an odd assortment of items which you might either find naturally occurring on the land, or which might have been lost or found there. The first of these we should look at is water.

Water

Water is not capable of being owned at law

We touched upon water in the context of boundaries earlier in the chapter, although the water itself does not actually feature in the law relating to boundaries; as you will remember the common law rules apply to the land which sits underneath the body of water, whether it is the river bed or the land comprising the foreshore. As for the water itself, this is not capable of being owned at law; thus an owner of land has no absolute right to the water flowing through their land. The common law, however, allows a landowner to take water for purposes connected with the use of the land, such as watering crops, for example, or working a mill or for use in a manufacturing process, provided the water is returned to the stream in substantially the same quantity and condition as when it was taken. Thus, in essence the water may be used, but not kept.

This use of water itself is subject to restriction, however, in that a landowner wishing to use water flowing through their land will now have to obtain a water extraction licence under section 24 of the Water Resources Act 1991. The Act requires a licence for the abstraction of all water, except for a limited amount which may be taken for domestic or agricultural purposes (excluding use in spray irrigation). It is irrelevant for the purposes of the Act whether the water is taken from a river or spring, or whether it percolates through an undefined channel.

Animals

Case Summary

Case Summary

Living animals do not form part of the land. Domestic or farm animals are chattels and belong to the landowner themselves. Wild animals, on the other hand, cannot be owned by an individual. This ancient rule was confirmed in the famous *Case of Swans* (1592) 7 Co Rep 15b, in which Henry VIII established a law against the killing of swans which still holds good today. According to the House of Lords case of *Blades* v. *Higgs* (1865) 11 HL Cas 621 though, which concerned the catching and taking of rabbits from the claimant's land, the owner of land has the exclusive right to hunt or trap wild animals found on their land (with the exception of certain protected wild animals including swans, badgers and other protected species under statute). However, if the animal being hunted flees to adjacent land though, there is no right for the hunter to stray onto their neighbour's property in order to catch it; on the contrary, the owner of the adjacent land can take up the chase. The case also stated that once a wild animal dies, its carcass becomes the personal property of the landowner, regardless of who caught or killed it.

Case Summary

In respect of fish in rivers on the land, there is an exclusive right for the landowner to fish in any non-tidal river running through their land although, as was established in the House of Lords case of *Fotheringham* v. *Passmore (or Kerr)* (1984) 48 P & CR 173 which concerned an argument over salmon fishing rights between two landowners who owned the land on opposite sides of a river, if the river forms a boundary, the landowner only has the right to wade out to the middle line of the river to cast his line, but no further.

Crops

The natural products of the soil, such as grass, wood and fruit from fruit trees, are treated as part of the land and come within the ownership of the landowner. Annual crops which require cultivation, such as potatoes or corn, however, are excluded from the land and are termed as chattels.

Treasure

What was once the ancient common law of **treasure trove** is now governed by the Treasure Act 1996. Treasure is defined in section 1 of the Act as being:

(a) objects that are at least 300 years old when found and contain at least 10 per cent gold or silver; or

(b) objects that belong to a class of object designated by the Secretary of State as being of outstanding historical, archaeological or cultural importance.

In accordance with the Treasure (Designation) Order 2002 this means that it will be treasure if any part of it is gold or silver and it is 'prehistoric', in other words if it dates from the Iron Age or any earlier period. If it does not contain any gold or silver it will still be treasure if it forms part of a find of at least two prehistoric items together.

An item found on land will also be classed as treasure if it falls within the common law definition of treasure trove which applied before the Treasure Act 1996 which, according to the Court of Appeal case of *Attorney-General of the Duchy of Lancaster* v. *G E Overton (Farms) Ltd* [1982] Ch 277, was that the object contains a substantial amount of gold or silver and is found deliberately hidden in a house, or in the earth, or other private place, with the intention of later recovery. The case concerned a find of 7,811 third century Roman coins made by the defendant on land owned and occupied by him. The coins were made of alloys of silver and base metal. Analysis showed the silver content in the coins to be minimal, averaging at around 1.6 per cent. The Duchy of Lancaster's claim to the coins on behalf of the Crown as treasure trove was rejected. The Crown's right to treasure trove was limited to objects made of gold and silver. For an article to be described as such it had to contain a substantial amount of precious metal and there were only small amounts of silver in the discovered coins. Lord Denning, Master of the Rolls, said in giving his judgment that an object should have a gold or silver content of 50 per cent or more before it could be described as gold or silver.

Case Summary

It should be noted that this case pre-dates the Treasure Act 1996. In accordance with section 8 of the Act, any object found on or in land must now be notified to the local coroner within 14 days, following which an inquest will be held to decide if the object is treasure. It is an offence not to notify the coroner of a find, punishable with up to three months' imprisonment and/or a fine of up to £5,000. If the object is found to be treasure the Crown can claim it as treasure trove. Under section 10 of the Act the Secretary of State has discretion to pay a reward to the finder, up to a value of no more than the market value of the item found. This can be quite a hefty sum, however, as the Law in Action article below shows.

Law in action The Staffordshire Hoard

On the afternoon of 5 July 2008, unemployed 55-year-old Terry Herbert made the astounding discovery of a hoard of Anglo-Saxon gold and silver in a field in Staffordshire.

Mr Herbert had been scouring the farmland with his metal detector, with the permission of the farmer. After a five-day search the hobbyist unearthed what is reputed to be the largest hoard of Anglo-Saxon gold ever found. The haul of around 1,500 items, including some 5 kg of gold and 2.5 kg of silver, was later declared to be treasure under the Treasure Act 1996 by South Staffordshire Coroner, Andrew Haigh.

Mr Herbert bought his first metal detector over 20 years ago from a car boot sale for just £2.50 and he has certainly seen a good return on his money. The find was valued at £3.3 million by the British Museum and later purchased jointly between Stoke-on-Trent and Birmingham City Councils in order to keep the find within the region. Mr Herbert and the farmer on whose land the hoard was found agreed to split the £3.3 million purchase monies equally between them.

But the historical worth of the treasure, which has since become known as the Staffordshire Hoard, is only the tip of the iceberg. The sheer scale of the find is expected to provide historians with a fascinating insight into life in Saxon England, which is a notoriously dark period in British history.

At the time of writing the Staffordshire Hoard is being exhibited at the Birmingham Museum.

Sources: **http://www.thisisstaffordshire.co.uk/news/Breathtaking-treasure-trove-come-Stoke-Trent/article-1367781-detail/article.html** and **http://www.thisisstaffordshire.co.uk/panels/s-fun-winning-lottery/article-1367790-detail/article.html**

Other objects found on the land

If an object found on the land is not classed as treasure, its ownership will depend on whether the object is found *on* or *in* the ground. If an item is buried and has to be uncovered or dug out of the ground, it belongs to the landowner. This is regardless of whether the landowner is the finder of the object and applies even if the landowner was unaware of the object's existence. The defining case in this area is *Elwes* v. *Briggs Gas Co.* (1886) 33 ChD 562, which concerned the discovery of a 2000-year-old ship found buried in mud on the bank of a river by tenants of the land when they were digging the foundations for buildings they intended to erect on the river bank. The court held in this instance that the boat was the property of the landowner, despite the boat having been excavated by the tenants.

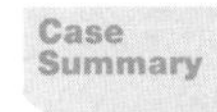

A more recent Court of Appeal case on buried objects is that of *Waverley Borough Council* v. *Fletcher* [1996] QB 334, in which the **defendant** found a medieval gold brooch in a public park, using a metal detector. The brooch was buried nine inches below the ground. The Court of Appeal held that the local authority, as owners of the park, were entitled to the ownership of the brooch.

If the object is found lying on the ground or unattached to the ground, on the other hand, the finder can keep the object (provided that the true owner cannot be traced) unless before the object is found the owner of the land has 'manifested an intention to exercise control over the land and the things which may be upon or in it'. Such an intention can be express, as with the placing of a sign signifying the owner's intention, or implied, as with a property to which access is restricted. The outcome in each case will be dictated by its individual facts.

The leading case in this area is that of *Parker* v. *British Airways Board* [1982] QB 1004. The case concerned a gold bracelet which was found by a passenger at Heathrow airport on the floor of the executive lounge. The owners of the airport argued that the bracelet should belong to them; the finder argued the same. Upon investigation the court found no evidence that the airport searched for lost property either regularly or even at all. The bracelet was therefore held to belong to the finder and not the airport owner, on the basis that the airport owner had not sufficiently manifested an intention to exercise control over lost property in the airport.

In making his judgment in the case Lord Justice Donaldson said that, in his opinion, in such cases there are two ends of a spectrum: at one end a bracelet found during a tour of a safe deposit vault, where there would be manifest intention by the landowner to exercise control, and at the other end a public park, where there would be no such intention. The unfenced front gardens of private houses, he said, would fall somewhere in between. Certainly in the case of public places, the judge's summation is well supported. In the earlier case of *Bridges* v. *Hawkesworth* (1851) 21 LJ QB 75, money found by a customer on the floor of a shop was held to belong to the customer, and not the shopkeeper, because the shop was a public place and the shopkeeper had not manifested an intention to exercise control over lost items. Lord Justice Donaldson's comment about unfenced front gardens is perhaps a little more surprising. His suggestion here would appear to be that an object found on private residential property will not automatically belong to the landowner, its ownership depending on whether the landowner has 'manifested his intention to exercise control' in spite of the private nature of the property owned. Again, an earlier case supports this, however. In the case of *Hannah* v. *Peel* [1945] KB 509, the defendant was the owner of a house that he had never occupied. The house had been requisitioned during the war and during this time the **claimant**, a soldier, had found a brooch loose in a crevice within the house. The court found in favour of the finder, although the reasoning for this judgment is not made clear. It would seem, then, that the burden placed upon landowners to show their intention to exercise control, even over their own private property, is quite onerous, the majority of case law in the area falling in favour of the finder rather than the landowner.

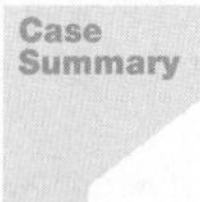

The following statistics in the Key Stats feature below give an indication of the remarkable number of possible treasure finds reported in this country every year.

Key stats Treasure finds in England, Wales and Northern Ireland

The following statistics from the Department for Culture, Media and Sport show recorded finds during 2009 and 2010:

- 778 finds of Treasure were reported.
- 67,089 finds were recorded in 2009 with the Portable Antiquities database.* In 2010 90,099 finds were recorded with the Portable Antiquities database.

Clearly, only a small proportion of finds are Treasure within the definition of the Treasure Act 1996.

Of the known methods of discovery, these were recorded as follows:

	Metal-detecting	Chance find while metal-detecting	Field-walking	Other chance find/ gardening	Controlled archaeological investigation	Building/ agricultural work
2009	82.70%	5.36%	2.31%	5.83%	2.81%	0.99%
2010	86.41%	2.02%	4.32%	3.61%	3.52%	0.12%

In 2009, 113 parties waived their right to a reward in 71 Treasure cases, allowing those treasure finds to be acquired by museums at no (or reduced) public cost.

The statistics were produced by the British Museum on behalf of the Department for Culture, Media and Sport and were released on 12 October 2011.

*The Portable Antiquities Database is a national database that coutains a comprehensive record of archaeological objects of all kinds found by the public in England and Wales.

Source: **http://www.culture.gov.uk/publications/8459.aspx**

Limitations on land ownership

We have already touched upon the idea of the State restricting the use of land in our discussion on land tenures in Chapter 1. Reference was also made to restrictions on the use of land that may be imposed by third party individuals at the beginning of this chapter, when we were considering the meaning of land ownership and the idea of landholding as a bundle of separate rights over property. We will be thinking about restrictions on the use of land by individuals in further detail later on in the text, when we take a look first at the concept of third party rights and interests in Chapter 4 and then restrictive covenants in Chapter 8. In the meantime, some brief thought should be given to the rather wider restrictions placed upon property ownership by the law and, ultimately, by the State.

As we saw earlier in the chapter, an owner of land can, generally speaking, use the land in any way they think fit, disposing of it as they wish, either in whole or in part. As a general rule of law this has traditionally even gone so far as to allow the landowner to lay **waste** or destroy their property and to protect them from liability merely on the grounds of neglect. This was illustrated in the case of *Giles* v. *Walker* (1890) 24 QBD 656, where a landowner was cleared of responsibility towards a neighbouring landowner when he allowed weeds to grow up on his land the seeds of which subsequently blew onto his neighbour's land and caused it to be overrun with thistles. It should be noted, however, that there has long been a common law liability in tort both for:

Case Summary

- injuries caused to third parties by the acts of landowners in respect of their land under the rule in ***Rylands* v. *Fletcher*** (1869) LR 3 HL 330, which concerned a reservoir which had burst its banks and caused damage to neighbouring property; and

Case Summary

- the tort of nuisance, for example as in the case of *Bland* v. *Yates* (1914) 58 SJ 612, where the landowner had allowed a large pile of manure to build up on his land attracting flies and causing an offensive smell.

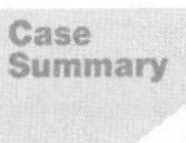

These common law restrictions aside, the State has found it necessary for a multitude of reasons, including increasing industrialisation and a rising population, to place increasingly tight controls upon the use of land over the last hundred years, both in terms of the use of the land and its preservation and maintenance. As a result, the twentieth century saw a plethora of legislation designed to protect the population, and ultimately the economy, against the individual landowner. One example of this is the Weeds Act 1959, section 1 of which states that,

> Where the Minister of Agriculture, Fisheries and Food . . . is satisfied that there are injurious weeds to which this Act applies growing upon any land he may serve upon the occupier of the land a notice in writing requiring him, within the time specified in the notice, to take such action as may be necessary to prevent the weeds from spreading.

Had this act been in force in 1890 this would have meant quite a different decision for the negligent Mr Walker and his thistles. Environmental legislation in the form of the Environment Act 1995 also has now taken its place in preventing uses of land which may have a polluting effect on the environment.

Town and country planning

> The function of the Act is to control land use and development

One major limitation which has been placed upon the individual landowner through statute is in the area of **planning control**. At common law a landowner is free to develop their land in whatever manner they see fit. However, since 1909 there has been put into force a succession of planning legislation controlling a landowner's use of the land and the buildings they place upon it, culminating in the Town and Country Planning Act 1990. The primary function of the Act is to control land use and development through the requirement of permissions given to the landowner by the relevant local authority. In this way, the local authority can both monitor and control land owned by individuals, and prevent misuse which may affect public health or safety and the economy. 'Development' in the context of the Act includes any building works carried out to property and covers not only new building and alterations but also the demolition of buildings (under section 55). In addition **building control regulations** imposed by **statutory instrument** under the Building Act 1984 ensure that building works are carried out to a specified standard from a health and safety perspective, and restrictions are placed on **listed buildings** to prevent the loss of or damage to buildings and garden schemes which are registered as being of architectural or historic importance under the Planning (Listed Buildings and Conservation Areas) Act 1990. And finally Part VIII of the Act details a number of additional 'special controls' regulating to the use and development of land, which include **tree preservation orders** to prevent the cutting down of certain protected trees on land (section 198). There is even legislation regulating the placing of advertising on the land of an individual (under section 220).

Failure to comply with these various planning controls may result in a range of actions, from the issuing of an **enforcement notice** or **stop notice** by the council requiring the rectification or cessation of the unlawful use or development of the property under section VII of the Town and Country Planning Act 1990, to summary conviction under the Planning (Listed Buildings and Conservation Areas) Act 1990 which carries a penalty of up to £20,000 by way of a fine or even imprisonment. In cases of severe neglect the local council also has the authority to force the owners to sell the property to them by way of **compulsory purchase**.

Compulsory purchase of land

It is not only by way of enforcement action that land can be compulsorily purchased under planning legislation. Under section 226 of the Town and Country Planning Act 1990 the local authority also has the right to compulsorily purchase property for development in any situation where they can show that the development in question will promote or improve the economic, environmental or social well-being of the area, or where the land is needed for public use (under section 228). Thus, a person may have their land compulsorily purchased in order to make way for a new motorway or train line being built. It should be stressed that, whilst the concept of compulsory purchase may on the face of it seem unfair, a compulsory purchase order will only be granted to a public body, such as a local authority, and never for individual gain. There is therefore no risk that a person may be forced to sell their home to a developer wishing to redevelop the land on which it stands, unless the house is in an area earmarked by the authorities for regeneration.

State control of property: the human rights implications

'every natural or legal person is entitled to the peaceful enjoyment of his possessions'

One question which has been raised on a regular basis since the imposition of these state controls is of course how this affects the human rights of the individual landowner. In particular, the incorporation of the European Convention on Human Rights into the law of England and Wales by section 3 of the Human Rights Act 1998 (which came into force on the 20 October 2000) has been significant in doing so. There are two provisions under the Convention which have a direct bearing on property ownership rights, and these are Article 1 of the First Protocol, which states that 'every natural or legal person is entitled to the peaceful enjoyment of his possessions' and Article 8, which states that 'everyone has the right to respect for his private and family life, his home and his correspondence' (although we will come across other articles which have relevance in relation to certain specific property law issues throughout the text). It should be noted that both provisions have their qualifications. Article 1 states that:

> No one shall be deprived of his possessions *except in the public interest and subject to the conditions provided for by law and by the general principles of international law. The . . . provisions shall not . . . in any way impair the right of a State to enforce such laws as it deems necessary to control the use of property in accordance with the general interest or to secure the payment of taxes or other contributions or penalties.* [emphasis added]

and Article 8 states that:

> there shall be no interference by a public authority . . . *except such as is in accordance with the law and is necessary in a democratic society in the interests of national security, public safety or the economic wellbeing of the country . . . or for the protection of the rights and freedom of others.* [emphasis added]

It could therefore be suggested that the effect of the convention on the broader scale is not as far-reaching as might at first have been anticipated. Nevertheless, the subject remains a topic for hot debate. The issue of human rights in relation to land law is discussed in more detail in Chapter 5, in the context of adverse possession claims.

Summary

- Land ownership is not an absolute; it is simply a right to use land in a specified way for a certain period of time.
- Estates and interests in land are 'real' property because they carry a right to recover the land itself. All other types of property are personal property only.
- Leases come in a special category of their own: that of chattels real, because they are personal property which can be protected through a real action.
- Land is given a legal definition in section 205(1)(ix) of the Law of Property Act 1925. Essentially, what the definition tells us is that land includes not only the land itself, but also anything built on it and any rights granted over it.
- As a general rule, if you own a piece of land you own everything below it down to the centre of the earth (*Grigsby* v. *Melville*) with the exception of coal, oil and gas, and gold and silver.
- As regards the airspace above your property, this is divided into two strata: the lower and upper airspace.
  - The upper airspace cannot be owned; the lower airspace forms part of the property of the landowner (*Bernstein* v. *Skyviews*).
  - The lower airspace extends as far as is necessary for the ordinary use and enjoyment of the property.
- The exact position of the boundary lines to a property can be difficult to establish if not clearly marked. There are various common law rules which may help if the property is bounded by a road, water, fence or hedge.
- Fixtures are items which form part of the land by virtue of their being annexed to it, either physically, or because this was the intention of the owner when they were placed there.
- There are two tests to determine whether an object is a fixture or a chattel: the degree of annexation test and the purpose of annexation test (*Holland* v. *Hodgson*).
- The degree of annexation test depends upon the level of physical attachment to the property: the better the thing is attached the more likely it is to be held a fixture (*Holland* v. *Hodgson*).

- The purpose of annexation test states that an object will be a fixture if the property owner put it there with the intention of making a permanent improvement to the property (*D'Eyncourt* v. *Gregory*).
- Treasure is defined in section 1 of the Treasure Act 1996 and belongs to the Crown. Items which are not treasure will belong either to the landowner or the finder, depending on where they are found.
- If an item is found buried in the ground, it will belong to the landowner, irrespective of who found the item and whether the landowner was aware of its existence (*Elwes* v. *Briggs*).
- If an item is found loose on the ground it will belong to the finder unless the land-owner has manifested sufficient intention to exercise control over the land (*Parker* v. *British Airways*).

Question and answer*

Problem: In 2001 Sharan bought with the aid of a mortgage an Elizabethan manor house in East Gladshire which she planned to open to the public. The house required extensive renovation, which Sharan carried out over a period of five years. She furnished the formal rooms and two bed-rooms in the house in the traditional Elizabethan style, with tapestries which she tacked to the walls and three Elizabethan wood carvings which she placed in niches in the walls of the formal rooms. She also bought a rare collection of Elizabethan taxidermy at an auction which she placed in glass display cases in the dining hall. Upstairs, Sharan furnished the walls of one of the upstairs bedrooms with some fine Elizabethan oak panelling.

The house opened to the public in 2006. Sadly the venture has not been a success, however, and following a period of spiralling debt the mortgage company has repossessed the house and contents. Sharan believes the mortgage company should not be entitled to the contents of the house, which are worth a considerable amount of money due to their age and rarity. In particular, she wishes to keep the tapestries, carvings, taxidermy and panelling. The mortgage company is arguing that these are part and parcel of the house and part of their entitlement under the terms of the repossession, however. Advise Sharan.

You should allow yourself no more than 40 minutes to complete this task.

Essay: 'No person can make his property real or personal by merely thinking it so.' Comment on the above quotation from Lord Cockburn in the case of *Dixon* v. *Fisher* (1843) 5 D 775.

This question should be answered in 40 minutes.

* Answer guidance is provided at the end of the chapter.

Further reading

***Botham* v. *TSB Bank plc* (1996) 73 P&CR D1.**
This is an excellent case to read on the subject of fixtures because Lord Justice Roch in his judgment spends some time going through in detail a number of different items and whether he considers them to be fixtures or chattels. The judgment is clearly set out and not too long – well worth a read.

Scrase, T. (2000) 'Listed building controls – shifting ground on fixtures and fittings?', JPL, Mar, 235–45.
This article gives a thorough explanation of the law relating to fixtures and fittings together with a really interesting insight into the law as it affects the removal of works of art from listed buildings.

Ross, L. and Martson, J., 'Treasure and portable antiquities in the 1990s still chained to the ghosts of the past: the Treasure Act 1996', Conv. 1997, Jul/Aug, 273–87.
This article, whilst a little dated, gives a useful and thorough overview of the law of treasure trove.

http://www.telegraph.co.uk/finance/personalfinance/4483510/Can-you-resist-compulsory-purchase.html
Easy to read article stating in layman's terms the practical implications of compulsory purchase and how it can be applied.

Howell, J., 'Land and Human Rights', Conv. 1999, Jul/Aug, 287–310.
Although this article pre-dates the coming into force of section 3 of the Human Rights Act 1988 and is therefore written in anticipation of it, this is an excellent article which sets out clearly the human rights issues and challenges likely to be faced in respect of land ownership in the future.

Question and answer guidance

Please note that the following is not a full answer and is intended to provide guidance in outline form only as to how to answer the questions posed.

Problem:

Sharan needs advice on whether the items her mortgage lender seeks to repossess are fixtures or chattels. If they are fixtures, they will be repossessed as part of the house and Sharan will lose them; if they are chattels, they are Sharan's personal possessions and she can remove them from the house at will.

There are two tests to determine whether an item is a fixture or a fitting: the degree of annexation test and the purpose of annexation test (*Holland* v. *Hodgson*). The degree of annexation test depends upon how securely affixed to the house the items are. As a general rule of thumb, the more permanently affixed the items are the more likely they are to be adjudged fixtures under this rule. The purpose of annexation test is dependent upon Sharan's intentions when she placed the objects in the house (*D'Eyncourt* v. *Gregory*). If they were merely placed there for Sharan's own enjoyment they are unlikely to be judged fixtures. If they formed part of a scheme for the house as a whole they are likely to be classed as fixtures and the mortgage company will be able to claim them.

Let us consider the degree of annexation test first.

- *The tapestries*, we are told, have been tacked to the walls but see *Leigh* v. *Taylor* in which a tapestry tacked securely to a wall was held to be a chattel only because it was only tacked there to better display the tapestry. *The carvings* have not been affixed but have been placed in niches in the formal rooms. On the degree of annexation test therefore they are likely to be chattels only.
- *The taxidermy* – has been displayed in cases in the dining hall. We are not told they are affixed in any way. In *Hill* v. *Bullock* [1897] 2 Ch 482 display cases of rare stuffed ornamental birds were held to be chattels.
- As for *the oak panelling*, we are not told how this has been displayed but presumably it has been affixed to the walls of the bedroom and thus it is likely to be a fixture. Note that *Spyer* v. *Phillipson*, which concerned wooden panelling, was a tenant's fixtures case.

On the purpose of annexation test, see *Kennedy* v. *Secretary of State for Wales*, in which bronze chandeliers and a clock in a stately home were held to be fixtures because they formed part of the overall design of the house. It could be argued that all the items form part of an overall Elizabethan design scheme, therefore, and as such are part of the house. Consider *Re Whaley* [1908] 1 Ch 615. In this case a dining room in a house had been fitted and decorated by the owner as a perfect specimen of an Elizabethan room. The room included a picture of Queen Elizabeth I painted on wood and a tapestry, both of which were nailed to the walls. It was held that both the painting and tapestries had been affixed to the walls as part of the overall scheme of decoration of the room and not simply for their better enjoyment as chattels. They were therefore fixtures not chattels.

Essay: This quotation is asking you to comment on fixtures and chattels in the context of the purpose of annexation test. Recent case law has suggested that the importance of the degree of annexation has now been overtaken by the motivation of the owner for that annexation (*D'Eyncourt* v. *Gregory*). So, whereas the physical installation points initially to its classification as a fixture or chattel, this presumption is rebuttable by evidence of some contrary purpose or scheme underlying the installation itself. The point that Lord Cockburn is making is that the use of the purpose of annexation test must be tempered with a degree of common sense, however. His inference is that the law cannot and should not be used to make an object either a fixture (in which case it forms part of the land and is realty) or a chattel (in which case it is personalty), at the whim of the claimant. You should conclude by stating either that it is possible to do this, giving examples as to why they think this, or that it is not possible to do this and that the vast array of seemingly contradicting precedent is simply evidence that each case will be examined on its own facts. You should make reference to relevant case law in this respect applying it to their argument appropriately. For example, in *Botham* v. *TSB* Roch LJ stated obiter that fitted carpets were chattels because the annexation was insubstantial and no more than necessary for the enjoyment of the items as carpets; whereas in *La Salle* v. *Camdex* wall-to-wall carpeting was held to be a fixture as it formed part of the overall design of the hotel.

Visit **www.mylawchamber.co.uk** to access tools to help you develop and test your knowledge of land law.

Use Case Navigator to read in full some of the key cases referenced in this chapter with commentary and questions:
Elitestone Ltd* v. *Morris and another [1997] 2 All ER 513

Chapter 3
The acquisition of freehold land

Key points In this chapter we will be looking at:

- An overview of how property is bought and sold in England and Wales
- How you 'prove title' to your property
- Other matters to be taken into consideration when buying land
- Different types of contract for the sale of land
- Requirements for a valid contract under s.2 Law of Property (Miscellaneous Provisions) Act 1989
- How to deal with variations in the contract for sale
- The legal effect of entering into a contract for the sale of land
- Other formalities required for the acquisition of freehold land: the process of 'completion'
- Land registration requirements under the Land Registration Act 2002
- The advent of electronic conveyancing

Introduction

In the last chapter we took some time to consider the meaning of land. Now that we know what land is, let us turn to look at how you acquire it.

We have already seen in Chapter 1 that in England and Wales land is held on **tenure** from the Crown. As it is only the Crown that can create new tenures (you will remember that this has been the case since the Quia Emptores was made law in 1290), and the grant of land from the Crown only happens in rare and exceptional circumstances, by far the most common way in which property in this country is acquired is through the transfer of an already existing tenure from one person to another. So what we are thinking about here are transfers of property by way of a sale, gift or property left by will.

The conveyancing process

Irrespective of the circumstances of the transfer of property, the correct formalities must be adhered to in order for the property to be transferred legally from one party to another. In order to be legal all transfers of property must be made by **deed** under section 52(1) of the Law of Property Act 1925 (we will return to this later in the chapter). It is rare for a transfer of land to take place simply by way of transfer, however. In order to protect the buyers and sellers of property a thorough and complete system of **conveyancing** practice has evolved over the course of time, by which the majority of property sales and purchases abide. This system aims to ensure not only that the property is transferred legally, but also that both the buyer and seller have taken all the precautions necessary before committing themselves to the purchase of the land. The reason for such caution is primarily due to a Latin **maxim** which underpins all sales and purchases of land: that of '***caveat emptor***' or 'let the buyer beware'. Essentially, as the phrase implies, the maxim dictates that it shall be the responsibility of the buyer of a piece of land to ensure that the seller is entitled to sell the property; that it is not subject to any third party rights which may affect its value or use by the buyers and that it is in good condition (or at least that it is in the condition they think it is). Unless a fraud has been committed, the seller is not liable for any matters which the buyer has failed to discover about the property they are selling; thus, the property is effectively 'sold as seen'. As has been mentioned in previous chapters, property is a valuable commodity, probably the single most expensive asset anyone buys or owns in their lifetime, so it is essential to make sure the buyer is getting what they pay for. To give you a flavour of how the system works, an outline of the conveyancing process is below.

Investigation of title

First of all, before the buyer commits to buying the land, they will want to know that the seller genuinely owns the property and is entitled to sell it. The seller will do this by proving their '**title**' to the land through the production of the relevant deeds and documents relating to the property. You will remember that you came across the two systems of proving title to land in Chapter 1: the **unregistered** system, where title is investigated by looking at the **title deeds** to the property, and the **registered** system, whereby you inspect the register of title at the **Land Registry**. Let us take another look at the Documenting the Law feature from Chapter 1 that, you will remember, shows an example of what the entries in the **Land Register** for a single property might look like.

Documenting the law

Specimen copy of the register at the Land Registry

This is a copy of the register of the title number set out immediately below, showing the entries in the register on 1 March 2011.

TITLE NUMBER : YS12345

PROPERTY REGISTER

YORKSHIRE: BRADFIELD

1. (23 August 1989) The **Freehold** land shown edged with red on the plan of the above Title filed at the Registry and being 4 Sykes Lane, Kimmington, Bradfield (BR12 2SR).
2. (23 August 1989) The land tinted brown on the **title plan** has the benefit of the following rights granted by the **Conveyance** dated 13 June 1896 referred to in the **Charges Register**:–

   'TOGETHER WITH the benefit of a right of way on foot only over that part of the shared accessway belonging to 2 Sykes Lane.'
3. (23 August 1989) The land has the benefit of the rights granted by the Transfer dated 17 December 1957 referred to in the Charges Register.

END OF PROPERTY REGISTER

TITLE NUMBER : YS12345

PROPRIETORSHIP REGISTER

ABSOLUTE FREEHOLD

1. (12 September 2005): PROPRIETOR: SEAN ANDREW CONLAN and SUSAN ALICE CONLAN of 4 Sykes Lane, Kimmington, Bradfield (BR12 2SR).
2. (12 September 2005) The price stated to have been paid on 12 September 2005 was £178,000.
3. (12 September 2005) Except under an order of the registrar no disposition by the proprietor of the land is to be registered without the consent of the proprietor of the charge dated 12 September 2005 in favour of the Bradfield Building Society referred to in the Charges Register.

END OF PROPRIETORSHIP REGISTER

TITLE NUMBER : CS72510

CHARGES REGISTER

1. (23 August 1989) A Conveyance of the land tinted pink on the title plan dated 17 December 1957 made between (1) Charles Reginald MacEvoy (Vendor) and (2) James Thomas Lees (Purchaser) contains the following **covenants**:–

   'THE **Purchaser** hereby covenants with the **Vendor** so as to bind the land hereby conveyed into whosoever hands the same may come that the Purchaser and his **successors in title** will not use the premises hereby conveyed for the sale or public consumption of intoxicating liquor.'
2. (23 August 1989) The land in this title is subject to the following rights reserved by a Conveyance dated 13 June 1896 made between (1) Bradfield City Council (Vendor) and (2) Courtney Miller (Purchaser):–

'subject to

(i) An **exception** and **reservation** in favour of the Vendor of the right to enter upon the land hereby conveyed for the purpose of constructing a public sewer the approximate line of which is shown coloured blue on the plan annexed hereto and at all times hereafter for the purpose of inspecting cleaning repairing or renewing the said sewer.'

NOTE:– The red line referred to is shown by a blue line on the title plan.

3. (23 August 1989) A Transfer of the land in this title dated 17 December 1957 made between (1) Henry Jordan and (2) Carlton Greenaway and Eleanor Greenaway contains **restrictive covenants**.

NOTE: Copy in Certificate.

4. REGISTERED CHARGE dated 12 September 2005 to secure the moneys including the further advances therein mentioned.

PROPRIETOR Bradfield Building Society of 1 High Street, Bradfield BR1 3FT.

END OF REGISTER

As you can see, the register is divided into three sections: the Property Register, the Proprietorship Register and the Charges Register.

- *Property Register*: this gives a description of the property, usually by way of its postal address, plus a reference to the registered plan for the property, an example of which you can see in the Documenting the Law feature in Chapter 2. The property register also shows rights and interests which exist over other properties. This will be discussed later in the chapter.
- *Proprietorship Register*: this records the ownership of the property, so this is where you would look for evidence that the seller is the current registered owner of the property.
- *Charges Register*: this gives details of any **mortgages** or other **incumbrances** (that is, third party rights) over the property.

As the specimen register shows, with registered land the task of proving ownership of the property is quite a simple one: the seller's solicitor simply provides an up-to-date copy of the record for the property contained on the register at the Land Registry, like the one shown above. The buyer's solicitors can then see clearly by looking at the Proprietorship Register that the owner of the property is the person selling (in this case Sean and Susan Conlan) and that is the end of the matter. As was mentioned in Chapter 1, entries on the register come with a State guarantee so the buyer's solicitor can be confident that they can rely on the information contained within the register.

entries on the register come with a State guarantee

With unregistered land the task is somewhat more convoluted, however. There is no register showing the current position of the property – so how to prove ownership? You may think it sufficient to show the buyers a copy of the deed of transfer which transferred the legal ownership of the property to the seller. However, for conveyancing purposes, this is not enough: after all, how do you know simply by looking at this one document that the seller bought the property from a legitimate source? Unregistered conveyancing practice therefore seeks to trace an unbroken '**chain of ownership**', showing how the property has passed from owner to owner over a minimum period of 15 years,

Figure 3.1 Illustration of a chain of ownership in unregistered land

Purchase deed of Mr and Mrs Doubleby in 1989
(this is the first document which is over 15 years old and so a good starting point for the chain of ownership)

Death certificate of Mr Doubleby in 2003
(evidencing his death and thus providing proof that Mrs Doubleby can sell the property on her own: if Mr Doubleby were still alive they would both have to sell the property together)

Purchase deed of Simon Cross from Mrs Doubleby in 2004

Note: this is a very basic illustration of how a chain of ownership works and in practice there are a number of other issues which will have to be considered. However, this should be sufficient to give you an understanding of the method through which title is proved in unregistered land.

ending with the present owner. An example will help to illustrate this. Imagine you are buying a property: 11 Ling Lane, from the seller, Simon Cross. Simon bought the property in 2004 from an old lady, Mrs Doubleby, after the death of her husband the previous year, with whom she jointly owned the property. Mr and Mrs Doubleby had owned the property since they bought it in 1989. The documents the seller's solicitors would need to produce in order to show an unbroken chain of ownership of the property would be as shown in Figure 3.1.

As well as reassuring themselves that the seller has the right to sell the land they are buying, the buyer will also want to find out, during this **investigation of title**, whether any third parties have rights over the land or if the use of the land is restricted in any way. For example, the next-door neighbour might have a right to use the seller's driveway in order to access their own property. There may also be restrictions on building on the property or certain uses of the land might be prohibited, and the buyer will want to find out about these so that they can make sure that they will be able to use the property they are buying for the purpose they are purchasing it. There would be no point in buying a house to run as a bed and breakfast if there is a **restriction** preventing the property being used for business purposes, for example.

Again, this information can be gleaned either from the deeds and documents of title in unregistered land, or from the Land Registry's register in registered land: if the property is unregistered, the buyer's solicitor will look at the wording of the deeds and documents provided to find evidence of such third party rights being in existence (as well as asking questions of the seller's solicitor); in registered land, a look at the Charges Register will show details of any incumbrances or restrictions on the land.

If we take a look back at our example – Charges Register in the Documenting the law feature, above – we can see that there are four incumbrances on the property:

- the first is a restriction preventing the property being used for the sale of alcohol;
- the second is a right to construct a sewer pipe through the property and for access to maintain that sewer pipe;

- ✦ the third is a restrictive covenant or covenants contained in a transfer dated 17 December 1957 (we are not told what the covenants are); and
- ✦ the fourth is a registered charge (or legal mortgage) in favour of the Bradfield Building Society.

We will be looking at third party rights over property in more detail in Chapter 4.

Investigating the condition of the property

As well as investigating the title to the property, the buyer will also want to assess the property's condition. They will inspect the land to check the position of the boundaries, and they will most likely instruct a surveyor to carry out a **building survey** on the property. As we learned in Chapter 2, they will also agree with the seller which **fixtures** and **fittings** are to be included with the property and this will be documented on the fixtures, fittings and contents form. If the buyer is buying the property with the help of a mortgage, the lender will also want reassurance that the property provides good **security** for their investment, so they will require a valuation of the property, taking into account its condition (we will be looking at mortgages in further detail in Chapter 12).

Other enquiries of the seller

In addition to enquiries of the seller as to the title and condition of the property, the buyer's solicitor will also carry out a number of other searches and enquiries. These include a search of the local land charges register via the local authority (also known simply as a **local authority search**), which will provide information about any planning restrictions affecting the property, and tell the buyer whether the property is a **listed** building or in a **conservation area** (in which case additional restrictions will apply if the buyer wishes to make changes to the property). A search of the local authority will also show the ownership of roads leading to the property and who is responsible for maintaining them. Other common searches carried out by the buyer's solicitor include:

- ✦ **coal mining searches** to check whether there are any mine shafts on or near the property which might be a danger or cause subsidence;
- ✦ **commons searches** to check the status of any open land near the property which may carry grazing or other public rights;
- ✦ **environmental reports** to make sure there is no contaminated land near the property making it dangerous to use or live there;
- ✦ **drainage searches** to check the position and maintenance of drains and sewers to the property; and
- ✦ an '**Energy Performance Certificate**' or **EPC** which rates the energy efficiency of the building and gives recommendations for improvements. An EPC is required in order to sell any domestic or commercial property in England and Wales.

The seller's solicitor will also ask questions of the seller as to other more general matters, such as whether there are any disputes with neighbours or whether there are any shared **service or management charges** attached to the property.

Formalities

Once all these investigations have been carried out and the buyer is happy to proceed with their purchase, irrespective of whether the property is registered or unregistered, the formal transfer of the property will usually take place by way of a three-part process:

- First is the contract stage, in which the buyer and seller enter into a formal binding contract for the sale of the property. This is often referred to as '**exchange**' or '**exchange of contracts**'.
- Second is the actual legal transfer of the property, which is referred to in conveyancing terms as '**completion**'.
- Third is registration of the transfer of the ownership of the property at the Land Registry.

We will consider these three stages in turn.

The contract

When buyer and seller are both happy to go ahead with the sale and purchase, they will enter into a binding contract in which the seller undertakes to legally transfer the property for an agreed price and at a future date specified in the contract. Traditionally, a deposit will be paid to the seller at this stage, which the buyer will forfeit if they do not complete the purchase. This contractual stage of the conveyancing process is not compulsory; however, it is commonplace in the majority of transactions, especially in residential conveyancing. The primary reason for entering into a contract for the purchase of property, and not for entering directly into the legal transfer of the property is a practical one. In residential property transactions the buyer and seller will need to arrange for their belongings to be removed from (and moved into) the property, for which a notice period of a couple of weeks can be helpful. The parties will also want to arrange things so that electricity and other services to the property are set up to be available at the property from the date on which they move in. In commercial property transactions, having a gap between the contract stage and completion allows the parties time to fulfil any conditions which may be contained within the contract, such as the procurement of **planning permission** for the development of the property being purchased.

traditionally, a deposit will be paid

Contracts for the sale of land are different from other contracts in that they must meet certain statutory criteria in order to be valid. These criteria are set out in section 2 of the Law of Property (Miscellaneous Provisions) Act 1989, which came into force on the 27 September of that year. Section 2 states that:

> (1) A contract for the sale or other disposition of an interest in land can only be made in writing and only by incorporating all the terms which the parties have expressly agreed in one document or, where contracts are exchanged, in each.
>
> (2) The terms may be incorporated in a document either by being set out in it or by reference to some other document.

(3) The document incorporating the terms or, where contracts are exchanged, one of the documents incorporating them (but not necessarily the same one) must be signed by or on behalf of each party to the contract.

Looking at the wording of section 2(1), we can see that it is made quite clear that a contract for the sale of land must be in writing. Thus there is no provision made for oral contracts for the sale and purchase of land.

In addition, the section states that in order to be valid the contract must incorporate 'all the terms which the parties have expressly agreed'. This means that if even one of the agreed terms is omitted from the contract then the whole of the contract will be void. Section 2(2) does make some concession to the strictness of the provision, however, by stating that the terms of the agreement may be contained in a separate document and simply incorporated by reference in the main contract. An example of how this might work in practice is in the case of fixtures, fittings and contents forms in residential property transactions, which are routinely attached to the contract for sale to show which fixtures are being left at the property by the seller.

if one of the agreed terms is omitted the whole contract will be void

The issue of secondary documentation being incorporated into the main contract is the area which has thrown up the most questions and perhaps one might say has caused the most controversy over the working of section 2. The two contrasting cases of *Record* v. *Bell* [1991] 1 WLR 853 and *Wright* v. *Robert Leonard (Developments) Ltd* [1994] NPC 49 provide a useful illustration of the different interpretations which can be given to the wording of the section by the courts.

Case Summary

The case of *Record* v. *Bell* concerned a seventeenth-century property in Smith Square in London, the title to which was registered. Two copies of the contract for sale were prepared and the buyer and seller each signed a copy, in accordance with normal conveyancing practice. Before contracts were exchanged the buyer's solicitors asked the seller's solicitor to produce an up-to-date copy of the register of title for the property, which they would have to obtain from the Land Registry. Because of the delay this would cause, however, the solicitors agreed on behalf of their clients that they would exchange contracts in any event, completion of the sale being conditional upon the production of the additional documentation. Contracts were exchanged but rather than amending the contracts to incorporate the change as they should have done, instead the solicitors simply stated in a letter and a note sent to each other together with the contracts that the agreement was to be conditional upon the presentation of the proof of title required. After exchange the seller's solicitor received the information he needed from the Land Registry and forwarded this to the buyer. The buyer, however, refused to complete the transaction, despite the request to produce the extra documentation being met (he actually wanted out of the purchase because he had lost a lot of money as a result of the Gulf War and could no longer afford to buy it). The buyer said that the contract was void because it did not incorporate all the terms of the agreement. The seller disagreed, seeking to enforce the contract under section 2. The court held in favour of the seller.

The decision, which is perhaps surprising, was based on the finding of the court that the agreement to produce the Land Registry documentation was not in fact a term of the contract for sale. Instead, the court said that it was a **collateral contract**: a secondary contract not for the sale of land, but for the production of documentation, the consideration for which was the buyer's agreement to enter into the main contract. The decision, which remains contentious, has not been followed in later cases.

Case Summary

Three years later in the case of *Wright* v. *Robert Leonard Developments* the Court of Appeal took a much stricter approach to the interpretation of section 2. The case in this instance concerned the sale of a 'show home', which was in this case a flat, and its contents. A show home is a finished property within a new development which the building company has fully decorated and furnished to give buyers an idea of what the final product will look like when they are seeking to sell properties which have not yet been built or completed. The show home is usually the last in the development to be sold, and will command a premium due to its having been furnished and decorated to a high standard, usually with the assistance of an interior designer. A dispute arose as to what was included in the sale of the show flat. Mr Wright believed that he was buying the entire contents of the flat as part of his purchase. However, the contract for the sale of the flat did not include any terms as to its contents at all. The court held that the contract did not comply with section 2 and was therefore void (it should be noted that Mr Wright did get his fixtures and fittings in the end, though, as the court ordered that the contract be **rectified** to show the inclusion of the flat contents in the sale).

Subsection (1) states that the terms of the agreement may either be contained in one document or if the contracts are to be 'exchanged', in both identical copy documents. Exchange of contracts is the term used for the situation in which, perhaps because it is impractical for both parties to sign the contract because they are in different parts of the country, two copies of the contract are drawn up, with the parties to the agreement each signing their own copy. The contracts are then physically swapped so that each party has the part of the contract that the other has signed. Exchange of contracts is commonplace in residential conveyancing transactions and it is rare for both parties to a transaction to sign the same contract in modern sales and purchases.

Case Summary

It is worth stating that the concept of an exchange of two identical documents, each signed by one party to the agreement, is quite different from an agreement reached through an exchange of correspondence. In the case of *Commission for the New Towns* v. *Cooper (Great Britain) Ltd* [1995] Ch 259 it was held that letters passed between the parties did not constitute an exchange of contracts for the purpose of section 2. It is therefore not possible to create a contract under section 2 by correspondence: there must either be one document signed by both parties to the agreement, or two identical documents with a signature on each.

Case Summary

One final point to be made about the provisions of section 2 is that both parties must have signed the contract in order for it to be valid. With reference to the requirement for a signature the typing or printing of a name does not constitute a signature. This was held to be the case in *Firstpost Homes Ltd* v. *Johnson* [1995] 1 WLR 1567. The case concerned an agreement to purchase fifteen-and-a-half acres of land. The buyer prepared a letter for the seller to sign, at the top of which the buyer's name was typed as the addressee of the letter. The letter set out the seller's agreement to sell the land 'shown on the enclosed plan'. The buyer signed the plan, but not the letter. The seller signed and dated both the letter and the plan. The court held that section 2 was not satisfied in this case. It was the letter and not the plan, which was merely a document incorporated into the agreement, which was the contract for sale and it was therefore the letter that needed to have both signatures on it. The buyer had not signed the letter and his name typed at the top of the letter was not sufficient to satisfy the provisions of the Act: a real signature was required. It should be noted that it is theoretically possible under section 7 of the Electronic Communications Act 2000 to sign contracts using an electronic signature, but it is not current practice to do so in domestic conveyancing transactions.

As regards the need for two signatures, this was explored soon after section 2 came into force, in the case of *Spiro* v. *Glencrown Properties Ltd* [1991] Ch 537. The case concerned an **option to purchase** land. An option to purchase is a special kind of contract under which a seller is paid a monetary deposit in return for their agreement to sell their property to the buyer within a specified time period, on the service of notice to them by the buyer. During the specified period the seller is not allowed to sell the property to anyone else. But if the buyer does not serve notice to exercise the option by the end of the period, the seller is then free to sell the property to a third party and also gets to keep their deposit. Options to purchase are often used in a commercial context, where a developer wishes to buy a number of adjoining parcels of land to form a development site on which to build. The developer will only want to buy the land if they can acquire all the parcels of land together (fewer would form too small a site), and so they will enter into separate options to purchase the various pieces of the planned area for purchase from the various landowners of the adjoining land to give them time to acquire all of the pieces of land that they want to form the whole.

Case Summary

The option to purchase in the case of *Spiro* v. *Glencrown* was signed by both parties to the agreement and the buyer exercised the option within the stipulated time by serving on the seller a written notice, signed only by the buyer. The seller then refused to complete, claiming that the option was invalid. He argued that, since the written notice exercising the option was only signed by the buyer, it did not comply with section 2 which requires both parties' signatures in order to be valid. However, the judge held that, whilst the option agreement itself did have to comply with section 2, the notice exercising the option did not. The seller was therefore legally bound by the option agreement and was required to sell the property to the buyer. In explaining his reasoning for the judgment, Mr Justice Hoffman said that the purpose of section 2 is to set out the formalities required for the recording of a mutual agreement for the sale of land between two parties. Whilst the grant of the option depends upon agreement between the parties, the exercise of the option through the service of notice on the seller is a unilateral act by the buyer (the seller has already agreed under the terms of the option agreement to be bound by the terms of the notice, once served). Therefore only the signature of the buyer, as the person serving the option notice, is required.

Similar arguments have been raised in relation to rights of **pre-emption**. Pre-emption rights are similar to options to purchase in that they bind the seller to sell to the buyer under certain circumstances; however, the emphasis of the agreement in a right of pre-emption is quite different. Whereas with an option to purchase the seller is bound to sell to the buyer if the buyer complies with certain conditions (to serve notice on the seller within a certain period of time), with a pre-emption right there is no obligation on the seller to sell. The agreement merely stipulates that if the seller does decide to sell, they will offer the property to the buyer first, before opening the sale up to other prospective purchasers. So, in other words, a right of pre-emption is a right of first refusal to purchase property. The status of pre-emption rights differs dependent on whether the property is registered or not. At **common law**, the rule has always been that pre-emption rights *per se* are not **interests** in land. In the case of *Pritchard* v. *Briggs* [1980] Ch 338, which concerned pre-emption rights given over land retained by the sellers on the sale of a hotel, the Court of Appeal held that a right of pre-emption did not create an interest in land until the seller decided to sell the property as, before this time, there is no requirement on the seller to sell. This was followed in the case of *Bircham & Co. (No. 2) Ltd* v. *Worrell Holdings Ltd* (2001) 82 P&CR 34, in which the Court of Appeal confirmed that a right of pre-emption would create an interest in land from the moment the seller offered the land for sale to the buyer (and thus committing the seller to the sale).

Case Summary

Case Summary

With regard to registered land, since the coming into force of the Land Registration Act 2002 pre-emption rights granted over registered land are construed as creating an interest in the land under section 115(1). This applies to any right of pre-emption granted after 13 October 2003. Prior to this date the common law rules apply. Irrespective of the date of the right being granted, or the nature of the land over which the grant is made, as an agreement relating to land, pre-emption rights must comply with section 2. This was confirmed in *Bircham* v. *Worrell Holdings*.

Now test your knowledge of the rules relating to contracts in the You Be the Judge feature below.

You be the judge

Q: **Which of the following will amount to a contract under section 2?**

(a) A typed letter containing all the terms of the agreement, signed by both parties and dated.

(b) A typed letter referring to terms contained in a memorandum attached to the letter, signed by both parties and dated.

(c) Two identical typed letters containing all the terms, one signed by each party.

A: They all will because they are all in writing, incorporate all the terms of the agreement (in the case of (b) by reference to another document), and are signed by both parties (in the case of (c) two identical documents are each signed by one of the parties).

Variations of contract

One final point which should be mentioned is where there is a variation made to the terms of the contract, such as a change in the purchase price, the amount of land to be purchased, or a change in the proposed date of completion for the sale. According to the Court of Appeal in *McCausland* v. *Duncan Lawrie Ltd* [1997] 1 WLR 38, where a contract for the sale of land is varied, the variation must comply with section 2. In the case in question the solicitors for the buyer and seller had agreed by letter to vary the date of completion for the sale and purchase to an earlier date because they realised after the contract had been entered into that the date they had agreed to in the contract was actually a Sunday. When the buyer did not provide the completion monies on the agreed earlier date, the seller sought to rescind the contract for a breach of its terms. However, the court held that as the contract did not then incorporate all the terms of the contract and was not signed by both parties, it could not comply with section 2 and the variation of the contract was found to be invalid.

So, just to recap, there are three things to remember about contracts for the sale of land under section 2 of the 1989 Act. These are that the contract:

- must be in writing
- must contain all the terms of agreement between the parties
- must be signed by both parties to the agreement

The other important points to note are that:

- the parties' signatures can be contained within two separate but identical documents which are subsequently exchanged; and
- the terms of agreement may be contained within a document separate to the contract, so long as the wording of the contract incorporates them.

You should now have a clear idea of what constitutes a valid contract for the sale of land. The Writing and Drafting exercise below gives you the opportunity to create one.

Writing and drafting

Remember the 'dream property' that you found in the Out and About feature in Chapter 1 of the text? Take a look at the information you have already gleaned on the property and, using this information, have a go at drafting the contract for the purchase of your dream property.

You should take no more than 30 minutes on this task.

Handy tip: The focus of this exercise is not to produce a perfect legal document; it is simply to get you thinking about the requirements for a valid contract. Think about what information you would need to include in the contract. How much are you paying for the property? What is the address? Who are the parties? And so on.

In order to promote efficiency in the transaction conveyancers actually tend to use a standard form of contract, although the use of such a form is not compulsory. An example of a standard contract for the sale of residential property is shown in the Documenting the Law feature, below.

Documenting the law

Contract for the sale of a residential property in standard form

CONTRACT
Incorporating the Standard Conditions of Sale (Fifth Edition)

Date:

Seller:

Buyer:

Property:

(Freehold/Leasehold):

Root of Title/Title Number:

Specified incumbrances:

Title Guarantee:
(full/limited)

Completion date:

Contract rate:

Purchase price:

Deposit:

Chattels price:
(if separate)

Balance:

The seller will sell and the buyer will buy the property for the purchase price.

This agreement continues on the back page

WARNING
This is a formal document, designed to create legal rights and legal obligations. Take advice before using it.

Signed

Seller/Buyer

SPECIAL CONDITIONS

1. (a) This contract incorporates the Standard Conditions of Sale (Fifth Edition).

(b) The terms used in this contract have the same meaning when used in the Conditions.

2. Subject to the terms of this contract and to the Standard Conditions of Sale, the seller is to transfer the property with either full title guarantee or limited title guarantee, as specified on the front page.

3. (a) The sale includes those contents which are indicated on the attached list as included in the sale and the buyer is to pay the contents price for them.

(b) The sale excludes those fixtures which are at the property and are indicated on the attached list as excluded from the sale.

4. The Property is sold with vacant possession on completion.

(or)4. The Property is sold subject to the following leases or tenancies:

Seller's conveyancers*

Buyer's conveyancers*

*** Adding an e-mail address authorises service by e-mail: see condition 1.3.3(b)**

It should be noted that the form incorporates by reference the **Standard Conditions of Sale**, fifth edition. These are a set of terms and conditions in agreed form covering a number of matters such as who should be liable for insuring the property between exchange and completion, what will happen in the event of default, and so on. It is beyond the scope of this text to look at these conditions in detail.

Reflective practice

Look at the sample standard form of contract contained in the Documenting the Law feature above and compare it with your dream property contract. Did you miss anything and, if so, what? (It is not necessary to consider the Standard Conditions of Sale for the purposes of this exercise.)

Exceptions to the requirement for writing

As with the majority of legal rules there are exceptions. Under section 2(5) of 1989 Act there are a number of types of contract which are exempt from the requirements of section 2. These are:

- a contract to grant a lease for a term not exceeding three years
- contracts made at public auction
- any contract regulated by the Financial Services & Markets Act 2000, other than a regulated mortgage contract
- resulting or constructive trusts.

A contract to grant a lease for a term not exceeding three years

This is because under section 54(2) of the Law of Property Act 1925 short leases do not require the formality of writing in order to be created and it would make no sense to require writing for a contract to create an interest in land which itself requires no formalities. The formalities required for the creation of leases will be discussed in further detail in Chapter 5.

Contracts made at public auction

At a public auction the contract is made on the fall of the hammer. Therefore the requirement for writing under section 2 cannot apply.

Any contract regulated by the Financial Services & Markets Act 2000, other than a regulated mortgage contract

Contracts made within the financial services sector are outside the scope of this text.

The creation of resulting or constructive trusts

Case Summary

Resulting and constructive trusts are, by their nature, implied and therefore do not require writing. This was confirmed by the Court of Appeal in the case of *Yaxley* v. *Gotts* [1999] 3 WLR 1217, in which the claimant, Mr Yaxley, was held to be entitled to an interest in land under a constructive trust. Mr Yaxley had acted to his detriment in reliance on an oral promise from Mr Gotts that he would be given the ground-floor flat in a development of three flats on Mr Yaxley's completion of the conversion works to all three properties. However, Mr Yaxley was never given the flat. Resulting and constructive trusts will be discussed in more detail in Chapter 7.

The legal effect of the contract

Once the contract for the sale of land has been entered into or, more colloquially, one might say once 'contracts have been exchanged', the parties are bound by the ordinary rules of contract in respect of their agreement. Thus, if either of the parties to the contract breaches any of its terms they will be entitled to contractual **damages** for breach of contract at common law.

Perhaps more importantly, however, is the effect of entering into a contract for the sale of land in **equity**, which is that, at the point of exchange, the buyer becomes the equitable owner of the property. This is because of the **equitable maxim** that 'equity regards as done that which ought to be done'. In the context of the sale of land this means that, once the contract has come into existence, 'that which ought to be done' is the completion of the transfer of the ownership of the property to the buyer. From the point of exchange, therefore, whilst the seller remains the legal owner in name, the buyer holds the **beneficial rights** to the property in equity. The equitable nature of the rights given to the buyer also means that equitable remedies are also available for breach of a contract for the sale of land. Such remedies include the equitable remedies of **specific performance** and **injunction**. Both specific performance, which forces the defaulting party to complete their sale or purchase of the property, and injunctions, which can be used to restrain a threatened breach of contract, are equitable remedies and therefore entirely at the discretion of the court.

at the point of exchange, the buyer becomes the equitable owner of the property

Completion

Once contracts have been exchanged, the next step is to complete the sale and purchase by transferring the legal estate to the buyer. As we saw at the beginning of the chapter, section 52(1) of the Law of Property Act 1925 requires that, in order to be legal, any transfer of property must be made by deed. The requirements for a valid deed are set out in section 1 of the Law of Property (Miscellaneous Provisions) Act 1989, which states that for a document to amount to a deed it must be:

- clear on the face of it that it is intended to be a deed (usually by stating somewhere in the document the words 'this deed', or 'signed as a deed');
- signed in the presence of an independent witness (that is, someone who is not connected with the signatory and has no personal interest in the transaction. Spouses and other relatives therefore cannot act as witnesses); and
- delivered.

any legal transfer of property must be made by deed

Delivery in this case does not mean actual physical delivery of the deed itself. The delivery is symbolic. All that is required from a legal perspective is that the signatories to the deed show that their intention is to commit themselves irrevocably to the terms of the deed. In most cases the dating of the deed, following signature is sufficient evidence of such an intention.

In unregistered land, there is no requirement for the deed to take any particular form. However, if the land is registered, it must be in prescribed form as set out by rule 58 of the Land Registration Rules 2003. The current prescribed form of transfer is on Land Registry form TR1, a specimen of which can be seen in the Documenting the Law feature, below.

Documenting the law

Specimen deed of transfer on form TR1

Land Registry
Transfer of whole of registered title(s)

TR1

If you need more room than is provided for in a panel, and your software allows, you can expand any panel in the form. Alternatively use continuation sheet CS and attach it to this form.

Leave blank if not yet registered.	1 Title number(s) of the property:
Insert address including postcode (if any) or other description of the property, for example 'land adjoining 2 Acacia Avenue'.	2 Property:
	3 Date:
Give full name(s). Complete as appropriate where the transferor is a company.	4 Transferor: For UK incorporated companies/LLPs Registered number of company or limited liability partnership including any prefix: For overseas companies (a) Territory of incorporation: (b) Registered number in the United Kingdom including any prefix:
Give full name(s). Complete as appropriate where the transferee is a company. Also, for an overseas company, unless an arrangement with Land Registry exists, lodge either a certificate in Form 7 in Schedule 3 to the Land Registration Rules 2003 or a certified copy of the constitution in English or Welsh, or other evidence permitted by rule 183 of the Land Registration Rules 2003.	5 Transferee for entry in the register: For UK incorporated companies/LLPs Registered number of company or limited liability partnership including any prefix: For overseas companies (a) Territory of incorporation: (b) Registered number in the United Kingdom including any prefix:
Each transferee may give up to three addresses for service, one of which must be a postal address whether or not in the UK (including the postcode, if any). The others can be any combination of a postal address, a UK DX box number or an electronic address.	6 Transferee's intended address(es) for service for entry in the register:
	7 The transferor transfers the property to the transferee

Place 'X' in the appropriate box. State the currency unit if other than sterling. If none of the boxes apply, insert an appropriate memorandum in panel 11.	8 Consideration ☐ The transferor has received from the transferee for the property the following sum (in words and figures): ☐ The transfer is not for money or anything that has a monetary value ☐ Insert other receipt as appropriate:
Place 'X' in any box that applies. Add any modifications.	9 The transferor transfers with ☐ full title guarantee ☐ limited title guarantee
Where the transferee is more than one person, place 'X' in the appropriate box. Complete as necessary.	10 Declaration of trust. The transferee is more than one person and ☐ they are to hold the property on trust for themselves as joint tenants ☐ they are to hold the property on trust for themselves as tenants in common in equal shares ☐ they are to hold the property on trust:
Insert here any required or permitted statement, certificate or application and any agreed covenants, declarations and so on.	11 Additional provisions

The transferor must execute this transfer as a deed using the space opposite. If there is more than one transferor, all must execute. Forms of execution are given in Schedule 9 to the Land Registration Rules 2003. If the transfer contains transferee's covenants or declarations or contains an application by the transferee (such as for a restriction), it must also be executed by the transferee.

12 Execution

WARNING

If you dishonestly enter information or make a statement that you know is, or might be, untrue or misleading, and intend by doing so to make a gain for yourself or another person, or to cause loss or the risk of loss to another person, you may commit the offence of fraud under section 1 of the Fraud Act 2006, the maximum penalty for which is 10 years' imprisonment or an unlimited fine, or both.

Failure to complete this form with proper care may result in a loss of protection under the Land Registration Act 2002 if, as a result, a mistake is made in the register.

Under section 66 of the Land Registration Act 2002 most documents (including this form) kept by the registrar relating to an application to the registrar or referred to in the register are open to public inspection and copying. If you believe a docume contains prejudicial information, you may apply for that part of the document to be made exempt using Form EX1, under rule 136 of the Land Registration Rules 2003.

The legal effect of the completion of the transfer deed differs dependent upon whether the land is registered or unregistered. In unregistered land, the change of ownership of the property takes legal effect at the point of completion, subject to the requirements of registration at the Land Registry, which are discussed below. In registered land, section 27 of the Land Registration Act 2002 states that the change of ownership will not operate at law until the transfer has been registered at the Land Registry.

It should be noted that under section 1(6) of the Law of Property Act 1925 in order to be the legal owner of land a person must be over the age of 18. Children therefore cannot own land except as **beneficiaries** under the terms of a trust. This concept is explained in more detail in Chapter 4.

Registration

Under sections 4 (unregistered land) and 27 (registered land) of the Land Registration Act 2002 it is now compulsory following completion of the legal transfer of any property to register the change of ownership at the Land Registry. If the property is unregistered, the change of ownership must be registered within 2 months of completion (section 6(4)); otherwise the property will revert to the seller on **trust** until another transfer has been completed. In the case of registered land, registration must take place within a '**priority period**' of 30 working days given to the seller's solicitor by the Land Registry prior to completion. The sheer volume of work this creates for the Land Registry is huge. Take a look at the Key Stats below to give you a flavour of the scale of work carried out at the Land Registry.

Key stats Volume of Land Registry applications

The volume of transactions dealt with per month by the Land Registry is phenomenal. Between the months of March and June 2010 alone, sales of property in England and Wales averaged 53,089 per month. And this does not include other types of transaction like renewals of mortgages on property, for example. The Bank of England figures show an average of 34,438 remortgages per month during the first quarter of 2011, which would also have required registration (under section 4 of the Land Registration Act 2002 remortgages of property are subject to registration at the Land Registry in addition to new mortgages taken out on a purchase of property).

Sources: **http://www1.landregistry.gov.uk/upload/documents/Annual_Report_0910.pdf** and **http://www.bankofengland.co.uk/mfsd/iadb/FromShowColumns.asp?Travel=NIxAZxI3x&FromCategoryList=Yes&NewMeaningId=ALSNAR&CategId=6&HighlightCatValueDisplay=Approvals%20-%20No.%20for%20remortgaging**

As stated above, the legal title to the property does not transfer at all until registration has been completed.

Electronic conveyancing

Provisions have been made under Part 8 of the Land Registration Act for all conveyancing transactions to become electronic in the future. The provisions for the introduction of electronic conveyancing are not yet in force and there is no set timescale for their implementation, but it is worth taking note of the proposals in any event as this is likely to happen in the intermediate future. The idea behind electronic conveyancing is that,

Figure 3.2 Five steps in a simple residential conveyancing transaction

1. **Buyer's solicitor investigates the title to the property and carries out pre-contract searches**

⇩

2. **Buyer inspects the physical aspects of the property and instructs a building survey to be carried out**

⇩

3. **Contracts are exchanged for the sale and purchase of the property**

⇩

4. **The transfer deed is prepared and completed (legal completion)**

⇩

5. **The change of ownership of title is registered at the Land Registry**

instead of having a transfer deed which is then sent to the Land Registry for registration, the seller and buyer will log on to the Land Registry's secure electronic network and complete the legal transfer of the property online. Registration will then take effect simultaneously with the transfer; the result being a much more efficient system of land transfer. Applications for the transfer of first registration of unregistered property will also take place online, subject to the paper deeds and documents of title being checked by Land Registry staff after the completion of the transaction.

This brings an end to our outline of the formal requirements for a transfer of ownership of an estate in land. There is a lot to take in, but to help to reinforce your mental picture of how this all fits together as a whole, Figure 3.2 shows in sequence the basic steps in a residential conveyancing transaction.

We will be looking at the acquisition of land through informal methods in Chapters 6, 7 and 8 of the text.

Summary

- In order to be legal a transfer of property must be made by deed (s.52(1) Law of Property Act 1925).
- All sales and purchases of land are underpinned by the Latin maxim '*caveat emptor*' or 'let the buyer beware'. Because of this, a thorough system of conveyancing practice has evolved to protect buyers before committing to purchase.
- Before the buyer commits to buying the land, they will want to know that the seller genuinely owns the property and is entitled to sell it. The seller will do this by proving their 'title' to the land through the production of the relevant deeds and documents relating to the property.
- If the land is unregistered, title is investigated by looking at the title deeds to the property; if the title is registered, title is investigated by looking at the register of title at the Land Registry.
- The buyer's solicitor will also carry out a number of other searches and enquiries, which include the local authority search and other searches relevant to the property.

- Contracts for the sale of land must be in writing, contain all the terms of agreement between the parties and must be signed by both parties to the agreement (s.2 LP(MP)A 1989).
- The parties' signatures can be contained within two separate but identical documents which are subsequently exchanged.
- The terms of agreement may be contained within a document separate to the contract, so long as the wording of the contract incorporates them.
- The typing or printing of a name does not constitute a signature (*Firstpost Homes Ltd* v. *Johnson* [1995] 1 WLR 1567).
- Where a contract for the sale of land is varied, the variation must comply with section 2 (*McCausland* v. *Duncan Lawrie Ltd* [1997] 1 WLR 38).
- At the point of exchange, the buyer becomes the equitable owner of the property.
- The formalities for the legal purchase of the property must then be completed by way of a deed of transfer of the land.
- It is now compulsory following completion of the legal transfer of any property to register the change of ownership at the Land Registry (ss.4 and 27 LRA 2002).

Question and answer*

Problem:

Shiri Mistri owns two-and-a-half acres of unregistered land at Forder Heights in Cornshire. On 21 March 2006 she sends the following letter to businessman, Jonal Hayes:

> Dear Jonal,
>
> Please take this letter as confirmation of my promise to offer my land at Forder Heights to you first, should I ever decide to sell it. The price to be paid for the land will be the market value of the property at the time of sale, to be determined by an independent valuer of my choosing.
>
> Signed,
> Shiri

In September of the following year, Ms Mistri decides to sell the land at Forder Heights. She writes to Mr Hayes as follows:

> Dear Jonal,
>
> I have now decided to sell my land at Forder Heights. In accordance with my previous letter, I am giving you the first opportunity to purchase the land at a price of £75,000.
>
> Please sign this letter on receipt.
>
> Signed,
> Shiri

Jonal signed this letter when he received it.

Two weeks later, Jonal Hayes sent the following letter to Shiri Mistri:

Dear Shiri,

As we discussed over the 'phone last week, I confirm that you will include in your sale of the land included in the sale of Forder Heights an additional half-an-acre strip adjoining the left boundary, shown on the plan attached.

Signed,
Jonal Hayes

A further three months have passed and Shiri is now refusing to sell her land to Jonal, having received a better offer from Jonal's business rival, a local man nicknamed 'Sharp Steve'. Jonal is claiming specific performance of the agreement, but Shiri is claiming that there is no contract in accordance with section 2 of the Law of Property (Miscellaneous Provisions) Act 1989. Advise Jonal.

You should allow yourself no more than 40 minutes to complete this task.

Essay: In the wake of *Record* v. *Bell* it would appear that the provisions of section 2 have not provided clarity but have served rather to muddy the waters still further. Discuss.

This question should be answered in 40 minutes.

✱ Answer guidance is provided at the end of the chapter.

Further reading

(1985) Working Paper No. 92; and Law Com. No. 164 (Formalities for Contracts for Sale, etc. of Land).
This is the Law Commission report which gives reasons for the desire to replace the then current section 40 of the Law of Property Act 1925 with what was to become section 2 of the LP(MP)A 1989. Makes very useful background reading for a wider understanding of this area.

***Spiro* v. *Glencrown Properties Ltd* [1991], Ch 537.**
This is a very helpful case because it came not long after the new provisions for contracts for the sale of land came into force and Mr Justice Hoffman, who presided in the case, sets out in detail the working of section 2 in his judgment.

Smith, R.J., 'Contracts for the sale of land: collateral contracts', LQR 1992, 108 (Apr), 217–21.
Another useful article detailing the decision in *Record* v. *Bell* and the use of collateral contracts as a tool by the courts to prevent contracts for being void for non-incorporation of their terms.

'New loophole for oral contracts', PLB 1999, 20(3), 17, 23.
Short and sweet. This case comment on the case of *Yaxley* v. *Gotts* explains how the imposition of an implied trust can be used as an alternative to the doctrine of part performance where the conscience of the court requires a remedy.

A specimen contract incorporating a copy of the Standard Conditions of Sale can be seen at: **http://www.lawsociety.org.uk/new/documents/standardconditions-specimen.pdf**

Brown, D., 'E-conveyancing – nothing to fear', NLJ 2005 155(7193) 1389–90.
This article explains how electronic conveyancing will work, outlining the present system and the key elements of the new service, including the use of electronic signatures.

Pollock, L., 'E-conveyancing: is it going to work?', EBL 2002 4(2), 16.
This practical article highlights a number of problems which may arise from the introduction of electronic conveyancing, including the risk of fraud, the need for a 24-hour Land Registry and what happens when systems break down.

Question and answer guidance

Please note that the following is not a full answer and is intended to provide guidance in outline form only as to how to answer the questions posed.

Problem: This is a dispute as to the validity of a contract for the sale of land between Shiri and Jonal. Contracts for the sale of land are governed by section 2 LP(MP)A 1989. Section 2 requires that the contract: must be in writing, contain all the terms agreed and be signed by both parties to the agreement. If these formalities aren't met the contract will be void.

The contract in question is a special kind of contract – a right of pre-emption. This is where the seller promises that if they ever decide to sell the land they will give the buyer the option of first refusal at an agreed price (usually the current market value of the property) before offering it to third parties.

Is the contract in writing? Yes, clearly the agreement is in writing (see letter dated 21 March 2006).

Is the agreement signed by both parties? We can see from the information given that the letter granting the right of pre-emption is signed only by the seller, Shiri, whereas the second letter notifying the buyer of Shiri's decision to sell is signed by both of them. The third letter is signed only by Jonal. As with option agreements, the question then arises as to which part of the agreement must comply with section 2 – the grant of the right of pre-emption or the letter notifying Shiri's decision to sell?

Shiri will want to argue that the grant of the pre-emption right contained in the first letter must comply with section 2, in accordance with *Spiro* v. *Glencrown*, and that because the grant is not signed by both parties it falls foul of section 2 and is not a valid contract. However, note Hoffman's obiter dicta in his judgment in *Spiro* in which he said that for the exercise of the option to comply with section 2 it must be countersigned. On this basis it could be argued that if the exercise of the option (or in this case the right of pre-emption) complies with section 2 this will be sufficient, even though the grant did not. *Does the contract contain all the terms*? The next problem from Jonal's point of view is that not only must the contract be signed by both parties but it must also contain all the terms. The letter which has been signed by both parties, that is the letter from Shiri confirming her sale of the land and offering it to Jonal, does not contain all the terms. These are contained in the first letter of 21 March, which only Shiri has signed.

The first point to note here is that it is no longer possible for a contract to be created through an exchange of correspondence. The parties must agree terms between them and then reduce this into writing in the form of one document (*Commission for New Towns* v. *Cooper*), albeit that it is possible to refer to an additional document expressly incorporated into the main document (see here *Record* v. *Bell*), which Jonal might try to argue.

Even if this could be argued, however, the final letter clearly introduces another essential term into the contract (the addition of an extra piece of land) which has not been included in the main contract in compliance with section 2 – see *Wright* v. *Robert Leonard Developments*. It would not be possible to argue a collateral contract (as with *Record* v. *Bell*) because of its status: it is a contract for the sale of land (regardless of whether it is additional to the original agreement) and therefore must comply with section 2 in its own right in order to be valid. In any event, *McCausland* v. *Duncan Lawrie* states quite clearly that variations to the main contract must comply with section 2.

One final point to note is that in *Wright* v. *Robert Leonard Developments*, the contract was upheld by rectification. Here, however, it is clear that it was not originally intended that the additional piece of land should form part of the sale – it was only discussed afterwards.

Essay: The question is seeking discussion of the provision in section 2 LP(MP)A 1989 which states that an agreement for the sale of land must incorporate all the terms agreed between the parties in order to be valid.

The particular point made relates to the fact that the statute allows for the terms of the agreement to be contained within a separate document but then incorporated into the main agreement (as with a fixtures and fittings list attached to a contract for the sale of residential property). The issue of secondary documentation being incorporated into the main contract has caused a deal of controversy over the working of section 2.

In particular the case of *Record* v. *Bell* [1991] 1 WLR 853 which was heard shortly after the 1989 Act came into force proved a controversial decision because of the interpretation of this provision given in this case by the court.

You should give details of the case in question, explaining the facts and the decision made. The facts are set out earlier in the chapter.

The outcome of the case was that the court held in favour of the seller, who was seeking the equitable remedy of specific performance from the defaulting buyer, forcing him to complete on the purchase of the property. Their reasoning was that the request for additional title information on the property, which was not incorporated into the contract formally, was a collateral contract for the production of information only and not a contract for the sale of land. This meant that it did not have to comply with section 2 and got around the problem of the main contract not incorporating all the terms of the agreement (which would have rendered it void).

Record v. *Bell* can be criticised because if followed the suggestion is that almost any contract could be interpreted as valid, even if terms have been omitted, thus placing us in no better position than we were with the previous statutory provision.

You should state whether or not you agree with this criticism and why, perhaps concluding by saying that the decision has been criticised and not followed in other cases (see *Wright* v. *Robert Leonard Developments*).

You can read a clear and succinct discussion of the issue raised in this question in Smith, R.J., 'Contracts for the sale of land: collateral contracts', LQR 1992, 108(Apr), 217–21.

Visit **www.mylawchamber.co.uk** to access tools to help you develop and test your knowledge of land law.

Chapter 4
Interests in land

Key points In this chapter we will be looking at:

- What constitutes an interest in land
- The proprietary nature of interests in land
- The five types of legal interest in land listed under s.1(2) the Law of Property Act 1925
- How legal interests are created
- The concept of equity and equitable interests
- The three most common types of equitable interest: restrictive covenants, beneficial interests behind a trust and estate contracts
- How equitable interests are created and transferred
- The importance of the distinction between legal and equitable interests
- The enforcement of legal and equitable interests pre-1926 and the doctrine of notice
- The enforcement of legal and equitable interests in registered land and overriding interests
- The protection of legal and equitable interests in unregistered land and the Land Charges Register in Plymouth
- The principle of 'overreaching'

Introduction

As we saw in Chapter 1, according to section 1 of the Law of Property Act 1925 there are now only two legal **estates** in land: the **fee simple absolute in possession**, or **freehold** estate, and the **term of years absolute**, or **leasehold** estate. And in the last chapter we looked at the formal steps you need to take to acquire such an estate in land. In addition to the two legal estates, however, there are also a number of ***interests*** in land which we need to consider.

You have already come across interests in land: firstly, in the guise of a **right of way** over someone else's property, as we saw in respect of the Leeds Festival site, Bramham Park, in Chapter 2; and then as a restriction on the use of property, as we saw in the Register of Title to 4 Sykes Lane in Chapter 3 (you will remember there was a restriction in the **Charges Register** preventing the use of the property for the sale of alcohol). To give you an actual definition of what an interest in land is, though, we might say that it is a lesser right in land, enjoyed by one individual over the land of another.

A person does not have to be the owner of an estate in land themselves in order to have an interest in land. Thus, whilst it is often the case that the holder of an interest in land will have a legal estate in neighbouring property, as in the case of **easements**, which we will consider in Chapter 10, this is by no means a prerequisite. For example, you could have an interest in land in the form of a right to take something from the land, such as crops or firewood, without owning any land yourself. Interests in land are nevertheless **proprietary rights**. This means that they can be transferred or sold by the owner of the interest, in the same way as an estate in land can. It also means that the holder of an interest in land can protect that interest, enforcing their right, for example as against a third party who buys the estate in which they have an interest (provided their interest is properly protected – of which more later). Because of the power of the owner of the interest to enforce against the landowner, interests in land are often also referred to as **encumbrances** on an estate. To give you an idea of just how valuable such interests over land can be, take a look at the following article in the Law in Action feature, below.

Law in action Interests in land purchased through manorial titles

In 1999 a company owned by Welsh businessman Mark Roberts bought the title of Lord of the Manor of Alstonefield, a village in the Peak District, for £10,000.

Mr Roberts claims that with the title came the ownership of all the grass verges and commons in the village, although the parish council has disputed this claim, saying it has an old legal document to prove a previous lord of the manor gave up rights to this land in the 1800s. In the meantime, Mr Roberts has been charging some villagers for access to their own properties on the basis that they have to cross land owned by him in order to get to them. In one case, a resident is reported to have paid £15,000 to Mr Roberts for some land adjoining his house.

This is not the first time Mr Roberts's purchase of a manorial title has caused controversy. Mr Roberts is also lord of the manor of the village of Peterston Wentloog, near Newport in South Wales, and residents of the Welsh village found themselves paying for access across the grass verges too.

There was a change in the law in 2005 which means that no one can charge a person for accessing their property via common land any more, as long as they can show they have been doing so for 20 years or more. This has effectively put an end to Mr Roberts's previous practice. However, titles such as these can still be valuable. As well as rights to common land, titles can also carry with them other rights over land such as rights to minerals, hunting and fishing rights, the right to hold a market and even the right to claim a beached whale, should one wash up in your manor.

Some people buy titles just for fun, like ex-boxer Chris Eubank, who is Lord of the Manor of Brighton; but for others this is a real business opportunity. Mr Roberts's company owns a total of 60 titles in all.

Source: **http://news.bbc.co.uk/1/hi/magazine/6923705.stm**

There are two types of interest in land: legal interests and **equitable interests**. We will consider these in turn.

Legal interests

As with legal estates in land, the basis of legal interests in land is statutory. According to section 1(2) of the Law of Property Act 1925, there are five legal interests which can exist over land. These are:

(a) an easement, right or **privilege** in or over land for an interest equivalent to an estate in fee simple absolute in possession or a term of years absolute;

(b) a **rentcharge** in possession issuing out of or charged on land being either perpetual or for a term of years absolute;

(c) a **charge** by way of legal **mortgage**;

(d) [**land tax**, **tithe rentcharge**] and any other similar charge on land which is not created by an **instrument** (this category of legal interest is currently obsolete);

(e) **rights of re-entry** exercisable over or in respect of a legal term of years absolute, or annexed, for any purpose, to a legal mortgage.

In order to build up a picture of what these interests are, it is helpful to look at each category of interest in a little more detail.

(a) Easements and privileges

An easement is a right attached to the land of one person to use, or in rare cases to restrict the use of, neighbouring property. The most common instance of an easement is a right of way which allows the owner of the right to cross one property in order to access another. So, you might have to use a shared driveway crossing land owned by your neighbour in order to get to your own house, for example. Other examples of easements are the right to drainage from your property over another's land, a right of light, a right to park a car or even a right to use a toilet on someone else's property!

a 'profit' is a right to take something from the land

Whereas an easement is a right of usage over another's land, a privilege is an old-fashioned legal term for a right more commonly known as a profit or '**profit à prendre**' which, as the French suggests, is a right to actually remove or take something from the land (if you took French at school you may remember that the verb 'prendre' in French means 'to take'). Profits à prendre are a very ancient class of right and examples of them are the right to fish or hunt on the land, the right to collect wood or the right to graze cattle. These rights are relatively rare in a modern context. We will be looking at easements and profits in more detail in Chapter 10.

(b) Rentcharges

A rentcharge is the right to receive a periodic payment from the owner of freehold land and so is for the property with the burden of the rentcharge, in effect, a sort of rent paid for the use of freehold land. It is the person who has the right to receive the rent who is the owner of the interest in the land. Rentcharges are a very ancient form of right, which have been in existence since the Statute of Quia Emptores in 1290. The original purpose of a rentcharge was to give a landowner willing to release land for development a regular income, quite often because, when the land was originally released in this way, there was no payment made for the land itself, and only the rentcharge was paid to the landowner. The concept of the rentcharge is now largely outdated and the creation of new rentcharges has been to all intents and purposes prohibited under the Rentcharges Act 1977. Under the Act, existing rentcharges are being phased out: all rentcharges are to cease on the expiry of 60 years from the date of the Act (that is, by 2037). The one exception to this is the **estate rentcharge**, which can still be created under the provisions of section 2(3) of the Act. An estate rentcharge is a rentcharge created to secure the performance of **covenants** for the provision of services and maintenance on an estate. Estate rentcharges can be useful when a new development of properties with shared space such as a central courtyard is being built. As we have seen in Chapter 1, the creation of a **commonhold** provides a modern alternative to this, however.

(c) Charge by way of legal mortgage

A 'charge by way of legal mortgage' is the correct legal terminology for a mortgage entered into under the Law of Property Act 1925. To explain the concept of a mortgage in brief, when a person borrows money in order to buy their house (or perhaps the money is borrowed for some other reason), the bank or building society lending them the money will take a charge or mortgage over the property, holding that property as security for the loan. The lender then has a legal interest over the property, which they will register at the Land Registry (you will remember that on the Register of Title in the Documenting the Law feature in Chapter 2 there was a mortgage over 4 Sykes Lane, in favour of the Bradfield Building Society). As the holder of a legal interest in the property, if the borrower then defaults on the loan, the lender can take the house and sell it to repay the outstanding debt. We will be looking at mortgages in more detail in Chapter 12.

(d) 'Any other similar charge not created by an instrument'

Subsection (d) refers to statutory charges: that is, charges imposed by statute, as opposed to by the usual method of formal creation by **deed** ('not created by an instrument' meaning not created by deed). We will be considering the creation of legal interests later in the chapter. The interests denoted in square brackets in our list, the land tax and the tithe rentcharge, were repealed by the Finance Act 1963, Schedule 14 Part VI and the Tithe Act 1936, Schedule 9 respectively. The words have been included here, however, to give you an idea of the type of interest to which the subsection refers. Essentially the category covers a number of periodic payments attaching to land by virtue of statute. Land tax was a longstanding annual tax on land first introduced in 1692 but abolished in 1963; the tithe rentcharge was a type of statutory rentcharge imposed in lieu of the ancient right of certain members of the clergy to receive one tenth of the produce of the land. When tithe rentcharges were abolished the owners of the rights were compensated by the government, and an annual payment to the Crown, named a 'tithe redemption annuity', was attached to the burdened land instead. These types of charge on land, however, were abolished by section 56 of the Finance Act 1977. As stated above, there is therefore no current use for this category of legal interest.

(e) Right of re-entry

A right of re-entry is the right for a **landlord** to enter tenanted property in order to repossess it, where the **tenant** has breached one or more of the terms of the letting. This is not an automatic right of a landlord, but must be reserved in writing under the terms of the **lease**. It is standard practice for the landlord to reserve such a right when letting their property, however. We will be looking at rights of re-entry in more detail in Chapter 13.

Creation of legal interests

As lesser rights over land there is no restriction on the creation of new legal interests in land, as there is with estates. This means that anyone with an estate in land can grant an interest over it, or reserve interests over land they are selling. Such interests must nevertheless accord with certain formalities in order to be created legally. Thus, according to the Law of Property Act 1925, in order for any interest in land to be legal it must satisfy two requirements. These are:

(a) it must fall within the one of the categories of interests listed under section 1(2) of the Act (in other words it must be one of the five kinds of interest detailed above); and

(b) it must be made by deed (s.52(1) LPA 1925).

As we saw in Chapter 3, a deed is a formal legal document defined under section 1 of the Law of Property (Miscellaneous Provisions) Act 1989 which, in order to be valid, must be signed by the person creating the interest; witnessed by an independent person; clear on the face of it that it is intended to be a deed; and delivered.

As well as these two prerequisites for the creation of a valid legal interest, easements and profits also share an additional requirement, and this is that they must be created for a period equivalent to a legal estate: in other words they have to be granted to the beneficiary of the interest either forever (in fee simple absolute), or for a fixed and certain period of time (term of years absolute). This means that an easement granted for a ten-year period could be a valid legal interest, but an easement granted for the lifetime of the grantee cannot. Any attempt to create such an interest would take place in **equity** only. We will be looking at this in more detail in the next section of this chapter.

In the case of registered land, easements granted by deed must also be registered at the Land Registry in order to become a valid legal interest. This is under the compulsory registration requirements under section 27(2)(d) of the Land Registration Act 2002. Again, failure to register an easement under the statutory requirements will result in the easement taking place in equity only.

Equitable interests

Under section 1(3) of the Law of Property Act 1925, any interest in land which does not fall within the categories listed at section 1(2) of the Act, such as a **restrictive covenant** or an **estate contract**, for example, or which is not created in the correct manner in order to make it legal (that is, if the interest has not been made by deed, or if an easement or profit is not for a period equivalent to a legal estate in land as stated above), cannot be a legal interest and will therefore exist only in equity.

As a law student you may already be aware of the existence of equity through your study of the English Legal System; in any event, you will certainly become aware of it when you come to study the concepts of equity and trusts. The law of equity is a system of law unique to England and Wales that runs alongside the traditional precedent-based system of common law which we use in this country. The law sprang up in order to complement the existing law, providing 'equitable' remedies where the existing law was unnecessarily harsh or unbending. Equitable principles, in the first instance, are not based on **precedent**, but rather are based on a set of **equitable maxims**, or guidelines, used by the court as a sort of 'moral compass' against which to measure whether or not an equitable remedy should be given under the circumstances. One of the most famous of these maxims is that 'he who comes to equity must come with clean hands'; in other words a person should not seek a remedy from the court of equity if they have done something morally or legally wrong which has put them in the position against which they are seeking a remedy. Another of these maxims is that 'equity will follow the law', meaning that as a general rule the court of equity will look to the law for a remedy before it will consider applying one of its own.

Although equitable rules feature heavily in land law, it is not the place of this text to spend a great deal of time examining the law of equity as a whole: this is a subject of study in its own right and worthy of separate study. For those of you who are interested in gaining further insight into the law of equity and trusts you should read the *Equity and Trusts* title in the Living Law series of texts.

Equitable interests in land are many and varied, but the most common of these interests and the ones which we are going to consider in this text are restrictive covenants, beneficial interests under a **trust** and estate contracts.

Restrictive covenants

Restrictive covenants do not appear as one of the five categories of legal interest listed under section 1(2) of the Law of Property Act 1925 and therefore can take place only in equity. A covenant is a promise made by deed. A restrictive covenant therefore is a promise not to do something, made by deed. Restrictive covenants by their nature restrict the use of the land in some way, perhaps by preventing the owner of the land from building on the land, or from using it in a certain way, attaching to the land itself, rather than just being attached to the people who made them. Thus, if Angie, a buyer, covenants with the seller of a property, Den, not to use the premises for business purposes, that covenant will attach to the premises themselves, preventing any future owners (and not just Angie) from using the property for this purpose. Another example of a restrictive covenant is the promise contained in the Charges Register of 4 Sykes Lane in the Register of Title contained in Chapter 3. We will be looking at restrictive covenants in more detail in Chapter 11.

Beneficial interests under a trust

A person who receives the benefit under the terms of a trust of land has an equitable interest in that land under section 1(3). Trusts are what have often been called the most important invention of equity. To explain a little further what a trust is, we can say that a trust will exist wherever one person holds the legal title to property on behalf of, or for the benefit of another. At **common law** only the legal ownership of the property is recognised; but equity recognises the rights of the person on whose behalf the property is held, or **beneficiary**. This is because the court of equity sees that it would be unfair to uphold strictly the rights of the legal owner to the detriment of the beneficiary under such circumstances.

The need to recognise this division between legal and equitable ownership of property arises in a number of situations in the study of land law. One example might be where property is bought for a minor (that is, someone under the age of 18). As you will remember from Chapter 3, under section 1(6) of the Law of Property Act 1925 it is not possible for anyone under the age of 18 to legally own property. This means that for a child to have the benefit of the property that property will have to be held on trust for the child until they reach the age of majority. Thus, the trustees will hold the legal title to the property, with the child holding the equitable, or beneficial interest in it.

Another common example of where trusts of property arise is in the context of shared property. Where land is jointly owned by two or more persons, a trust of land is automatically imposed by virtue of statute. We will consider this concept in further detail in Chapter 9 on co-ownership. In addition, it is also possible for a trust to arise in favour of a person living in a property even if they are not legal owners of it, but they have nevertheless contributed to the purchase of the property. This is particularly common in a husband and wife scenario, and will be discussed in further detail in Chapter 7. In any event, you should begin to see just from the brief examples given that beneficial interests under a trust are an important type of equitable interest and one which you will come across in a variety of circumstances.

Estate contracts

an estate contract is a contract for the sale and purchase of land

The third equitable interest in land which you are certain to come across is the estate contract. Put simply, an estate contract is a contract for the sale and purchase of land. The contract for the purchase of residential property described in detail in the previous chapter is the most common form of estate contract but, as we have seen, there are also other forms of estate contract, including **options to purchase** and **pre-emption rights**.

At common law, a contract for the sale of land gives the parties to the contract the contractual right to **damages** if the contract is not performed. However, as we saw in Chapter 3, estate contracts also give rise to equitable rights and obligations. In particular, this means that one party to an estate contract can rely on equitable remedies if the other party does not comply with their obligations under the contract. Such equitable remedies include the remedy of **specific performance** and **injunction**.

The creation and transfer of equitable interests

In order for an equitable interest to be created a deed is not required. Instead, with the exception of certain types of **implied trust** which, due to their nature are often created without writing (these will be discussed in further detail in Chapter 7), equitable interests must be created in writing, in accordance with section 53(1)(a) of the Law of Property Act 1925.

There are four basic situations in which an equitable interest will be created:

- Firstly, where the interest created is one which is recognised in equity only and not in law (so this is any interest created which does not come within the categories listed in section 1(2)). This would apply to the creation of any new restrictive covenant, for example.
- Secondly, where the parties have tried to create a legal interest in land, but their attempt has failed for whatever reason. This might be because the interest has not been created properly by deed, for example.
- Thirdly, where an easement or profit has not been created for a period equivalent to an estate in land (either freehold or leasehold), even if it is created by deed the result will be an equitable interest. You will remember that this would be the case if an easement for the period of someone's lifetime were created.
- Fourthly, where the person creating the interest themselves only has an equitable estate in the land, they cannot create a legal interest out of it and therefore the best interest they can create will be equitable. This is formed upon the basis of the Latin **maxim** '*nemo dat quod non habet*': you can't give what you don't have. In other words, you can't give something greater than you own and so you cannot create a legal interest out of an equitable one.

Some additional explanation of the second situation is required. The ability of equity to interpret a failed attempt to create a legal interest in land as an equitable one relies on a legal fiction established in the case of ***Walsh* v. *Lonsdale*** (1882) 21 Ch D 9. What the case says is that, where an attempt to create a legal interest has failed, as no deed has been used, a legal fiction will be created whereby equity will regard the failed attempt as a contract to create that interest. Provided the contract is valid therefore, in other words: provided it complies with section 2 of the Law of Property (Miscellaneous Provisions) Act 1989 (which states that a contract for the sale of land must be in writing, contain all the terms agreed between the parties and be signed by both parties to the agreement) *and* that specific performance is available on the facts of the case, an equitable interest is created on the basis of the equitable maxim that 'equity sees as done that which ought to be done'. The case of *Walsh* v. *Lonsdale* itself concerned an argument over the lease of a mill. The **formalities** for the creation of a legal lease were never completed (in other words, there was no deed for the grant of the lease). When the tenant failed to pay his rent, the landlord tried to claim equipment kept upon the premises in lieu of payment, which he was entitled to do under the terms of the lease. The tenant argued he could not do this because no legal lease had been created. The Court of Appeal found that there was an equitable lease and the landlord was allowed to take the equipment from the property. It should be noted that the failure of the fictional contract to comply with the provisions of section 2 would also fail to create an equitable interest in the land.

A further fictional example will help to illustrate the point. Imagine Jed, a landowner, sells part of his front garden to Astrid on which to build a house. Following the sale of the garden to Astrid, Jed's own property will no longer adjoin the road (although there is a path from which he can access his property by foot to the rear of the house), so Jed reserves for himself a right of way with vehicles over the land he is selling to Astrid via which he can access his property by car. The deed is drawn up and both parties sign the document; however, Jed does not realise that his signature must be witnessed in order for the deed to be valid. Following the sale of the land to Astrid, she refuses to allow him access across her land, saying that there is no valid right of way over the property as the deed is invalid. In this case, equity would step in and say that as long as the deed of grant of the right of way was in writing, contained all the terms of their agreement (or incorporated them by reference to another document), and was signed by both the parties to the agreement (thus complying with section 2), and provided the agreement was one capable of specific performance (in this case it would be, as Astrid could be forced to allow Jed to cross her land), this would be sufficient to create an agreement to enter into a grant of a formal right of way across the property, and an equitable interest over Astrid's land in favour of Jed would be created.

Importance of the distinction between legal and equitable interests

Having gone to all the trouble of setting out the different legal and equitable interests separately you may be wondering exactly what the importance of the distinction between legal and equitable interests is. Obviously they are treated differently in terms of their creation. As we have seen above, the rules for the creation of equitable interests are less stringent than for the creation of legal ones. But there is more to it than this. For a number of reasons, a legal interest is superior to an equitable one and it is this that makes the distinction so important. These reasons can be summarised as follows:

- Remedies are available as of right with a legal interest. Equitable remedies are only available at the discretion of the court.
- It is easier to enforce legal rights than equitable ones (in theory).

Let us now look at these issues in a little more detail.

Legal remedies are as of right; equitable remedies are discretionary

If a person has a legal interest in land, and someone interferes with that interest in some way, the holder of the legal interest will have an automatic right to claim damages from the defaulting party at common law. It is important to note that this right is automatic as it means that, if the matter were to go to court, the judge has no discretion in making their decision to take into consideration the merits of the case. The fact that the claimant's legal interests have been infringed is all that is required to be proven and the judge is bound to apply the law and give damages, regardless of how fair an outcome this would be in the circumstances. To give an example, imagine Keiko has a right of way over a strip of land owned by Hera, to the side of Hera's house. Should Hera block up the right of way to stop Keiko from using it, Keiko will be entitled to go to court and claim damages for the breach of her legal interest. This will be the case even if Keiko is driving across the land with a heavy vehicle and damaging Hera's flower beds every time she uses the right of way. In short then, the right to damages is not affected by the perceived fairness (or otherwise) of the claim.

The remedies available in equity are more varied than the simple right to common law damages, and can include an order for specific performance, an injunction, **rescission** (this would have the effect of restoring the parties to the position they would have been in before the infringement of the interest occurred) or **rectification**, which is an order correcting a document which has, because of a mistake by the person drafting the agreement, recorded the agreement made between the parties incorrectly.

The remedies provided by equity, whilst they provide the claimant with a greater choice of solutions, work quite differently from the award of damages at common law, however. Going back to our example of Keiko and Hera, if Keiko's interest was equitable the court would not be bound by the strict rules of the common law. Instead, they would have a complete discretion as to whether to grant an equitable remedy in her favour, taking into account in making their decision equitable maxims, such as 'he who comes to equity must come with **clean hands**'. On this basis if, looking at the facts of the case, they decided that Keiko had been deliberately damaging the flower beds in the exercise of her right they would have the freedom to decide to deny her a remedy for Hera's infringement of that right (by blocking her path over the land).

Case Summary

A further example of how this can work in practice can be seen in the case of *Coatsworth* v. *Johnson* (1886) 55 LJ QB 220. The **claimant** in this case was the tenant of a 130-acre farm in Kent called 'Stocks Green Farm'. The farm was owned by the **defendant** farmer and the claimant had entered into possession under the terms of an agreement for lease (which thus formed an equitable lease under the rule in *Walsh* v. *Lonsdale*, considered above). The agreement required the tenant, amongst other things, to cultivate the land 'in a good and husbandlike manner'. The tenant did not cultivate the land and, fearing irreparable damage to the land through neglect, the farmer gave notice to the tenant to quit the premises. The tenant applied to the court for the equitable remedy of specific performance of the agreement for lease, but the Court of Appeal found that, because the tenant was in breach of the terms of his agreement, he had not come to equity with clean hands, and his application was refused.

It is perhaps worth noting here that a person with a legal interest in land is not limited to the common law remedy of damages alone. One of the primary functions of the court of equity is to step in with a remedy wherever the common law is found wanting. Thus, in any particular case if the common law remedy of damages is inadequate, the court may order in addition any of the remedies available to equity. The point to be remembered here, though, is that equitable remedies are discretionary, regardless of whether the right being enforced is a legal or an equitable one. Thus, once it comes to equitable remedies, both legal and equitable interests are treated the same.

Enforcement of legal and equitable remedies

The automatic right to damages for breach of a legal interest is obviously important. But the main reason for the need to differentiate between those interests which are legal and those which are equitable is not because of the differing range of remedies available to them. Rather it is because of the basic ability of the holders of those interests to enforce their rights against a third party in the first place. To help you get a feel for this, let us expand upon our example of Keiko and Hera once more. We have already said that Keiko has a right of way over Hera's land. Let us assume this right of way was granted for an unlimited period by deed. In the same deed, Hera has also entered into an agreement with Keiko which states that Hera will not erect any buildings on her land.

You be the judge

Q: Looking at our example above, what kinds of interest in the land have been created in favour of Hera?

A: The right of way is a type of easement. It has been created by deed and for a period equivalent to an estate in land and is therefore a valid legal interest. The agreement not to build is a restrictive covenant and is therefore an equitable interest, despite having been created by deed because it falls outside the categories listed in s.1(2) LPA 1925.

If Hera then sells her land to Josh, and Josh blocks Keiko's right of way by building a conservatory over the top of it, the question we need to answer is: can Keiko enforce her rights against Josh? In order to answer this question we need to understand the law relating to the enforcement of interests over land in the case of land which is both registered and unregistered. But first we need to turn back the clock and look at the position prior to 1 January 1926, when the Law of Property Act 1925 came into force.

Enforcing interests in land pre-1926

First of all we should deal with legal interests in land. The position pre-1926 was simple. Under the terms of the historical legal maxim: 'legal rights bind the whole world' (unusually this is not translated from the Latin), any person holding a legal interest in land could enforce that interest against anyone taking possession of the land, for example by buying the freehold in the land, regardless of whether or not the buyer was aware of the existence of the legal interest when they bought it. This meant that, using our example, Keiko would be able to enforce her legal right of way against Josh, obtaining either damages or a more appropriate equitable remedy, regardless of whether Josh knew about that right when he bought the property.

The position with equitable interests, pre-1926, was quite different, however. The maxim 'legal rights bind the whole world' did not apply to equitable rights, and so could not afford any protection to the holder of an equitable interest. Instead, the court of equity applied its own equitable **doctrine**, which said that a purchaser of land would have to take that land subject to any equitable interests which existed over it *unless* they could show that they were a '***bone fide*** **purchaser for value of the legal estate without notice**' in the land. This doctrine was called the **doctrine of notice** and still applies to unregistered land under certain circumstances today. We will be considering these circumstances later in the chapter.

The idea behind the doctrine of notice was that, contrary to the position with legal interests (which were automatically binding on purchasers of the property burdened by the interest), equity would only intervene and enforce an interest against a third party where that person's conscience had been pricked in some way, making it equitable for the third party to take the land subject to it. This 'pricking of the conscience' would occur principally when the third party knew about the equitable interest when they bought the property: the idea being that the buyer's conscience simply could not allow them to take the land free from the interest when they had notice of it. Conversely, however, where a purchaser was a bona fide purchaser for value of a legal estate in the land who had no notice of the prior interest, they would acquire the land free of that interest because there was no reason for equity to interfere with their legal ownership of the land. So essentially, in order to be able to enforce the benefit of the restrictive covenant against Josh, Keiko from our example would have to show that Josh was not a bone fide purchaser for value without notice of the land. But how would she do this?

In order to gain protection from the doctrine of notice, any buyer would have to show that they had complied with all of the elements of the doctrine. Failure to comply with any part of it would mean that they would have to take subject to the equitable interests over the land. The easiest way to understand the implications of this is to look at each elements of the doctrine individually:

Bona fide

Translated '**bona fide**' quite literally means in good faith. The requirement then is that the buyer is an innocent party in the transaction whose motives in the purchase of the property are genuine. There must be no fraud or dishonesty involved in the transaction (which there would be if, for example, the buyer pretended not to know about the equitable interest when in reality they were aware of it).

Purchaser for value

The use of the word 'purchaser' is significant because it means that only a person who buys the land can benefit from the doctrine of notice. Someone who inherits the land will therefore take subject to any rights over it, regardless of whether they are legal or equitable. Equally someone to whom the property is gifted (and therefore no money changes hands) would take subject to any equitable interests in the land. The term '**for value**' refers to money or money's worth, so an exchange of property for goods or services instead of money would be included in the definition.

only a person who buys the land can benefit from the doctrine of notice

Of the legal estate

The significance of this is that only the purchaser of a legal estate in the land can take free from equitable interests: in other words someone who has bought the freehold or leasehold of the property. A person acquiring an equitable interest in the property (such as the beneficiary under a trust) would not benefit from the doctrine.

Without notice

there are three kinds of notice: actual, constructive and imputed

The notice requirement is the element of the doctrine which can be attributed the widest range of interpretation and which is therefore the point which requires the greatest consideration. For the purposes of the doctrine, there are three kinds of notice: **actual notice, constructive notice** and **imputed notice**. A finding of any one of the three types of notice will result in the buyer taking the land subject to the equitable interest in question.

Actual notice

Case Summary

This is the most straightforward type of notice. As its name suggests, actual notice is when the buyer actually knew about the equitable interest when they bought the land. There is no requirement on the buyer to have learned of the interest from any particular source; it is simply sufficient that they knew about it before they bought the land. The facts of *Lloyd* v. *Banks* (1868) LR 3 Ch App 488 did not centre on a buyer's knowledge of an interest in land, but rather to knowledge of an insolvent beneficiary under a trust. The principle, however, is the same. In this case, the defendant had learned about the bankruptcy through a newspaper article. The rule now has statutory force under section 199(1)(ii)(a) of the Law of Property Act 1925, which states that 'a purchaser shall not be prejudicially affected by notice of . . . any . . . instrument or notice or any fact or thing unless it is within his own knowledge . . .'.

Constructive notice

Case Summary

The requirement for actual notice historically had led to buyers choosing not to make any enquiries about property they were purchasing in the belief that, if they did not know about any equitable interests over the land, they would not have to be bound by them. However, the court soon put a stop to this practice. In the case of *Jones* v. *Smith* (1841) 66 ER 943, which concerned a wife's undeclared interest in lands which formed part of an estate on which a lender proposed to offer a mortgage, the court found that not to make the searches ordinarily carried out in the purchase of land was in itself an act of bad faith and therefore did not comply with the doctrine of notice (although it should be noted that in this particular case the lender was found to have carried out extensive enough enquiries to take free from the interest). Buyers were subsequently deemed to have constructive notice of any information which they should have learned by undertaking the 'usual' searches on the property.

Case Summary

The two types of search considered necessary, or usual, in the course of an ordinary conveyancing transaction were the examination of the **title deeds** to the property and a physical inspection of the land being purchased. The consequences of not examining the title deeds to a property fully can be seen in the case of *Worthington* v. *Morgan* (1849) 16 Sim 547. Here a lender took a mortgage over a property without examining the title deeds. It transpired that the property was already mortgaged to a third party and as a result the lender was bound to take the property subject to the earlier mortgage (thus significantly reducing his security on the loan). The court held that the lender was deemed to have constructive notice of the earlier mortgage, which he would have discovered but for his negligence in not checking the title deeds to the property. An example of an interest in land incorporated into a conveyance of unregistered land can be seen in the following extract contained in the Documenting the Law feature, below.

Documenting the law

Extract from a conveyance showing an interest in land

NOW THIS DEED WITNESSETH as follows:-

1. In consideration of the covenant hereinafter contained the Grantor as trustee in exercise of the powers conferred on him by the Settled Land Act 1925 and of every power him enabling hereby grants unto the Authority for the Authority and its successors in title owners or occupiers of Breary Banks or any part thereof

(i) Full right and liberty to drain through the said drain sewage water and soil from Breary Banks or any part thereof into the said septic tank

(ii) Full right and liberty to enter upon the premises upon giving reasonable notice in writing (except in case of emergency) so far only as may be necessary for the inspection repair and maintenance of the said drain and septic tank or any part thereof and for emptying the septic tank as may be required by law or any competent authority

The requirement that any purchaser of property should undertake a physical inspection of the property and question any occupants as to their interest in it, is enshrined in the 1902 Court of Appeal case of *Hunt* v. *Luck* [1902] 1 Ch 428. In this case a buyer was held by the court to have notice of all of the rights of a tenant who occupied the property, on the basis that they should have had an awareness that the property was not occupied by the freeholder because they were in receipt of rents on it. Following this, the buyer's solicitors should have made all necessary enquiries of the freeholder as to who was in occupation and on what basis the rent was being paid. This was a significant finding because it meant that, as a result, anyone buying property would have constructive notice of any rights belonging to anyone other than the legal owner who occupied the property. This led to a need for extensive enquiries being made of anyone living at the property.

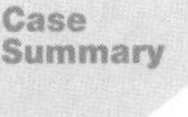

In particular, the finding in *Hunt* v. *Luck* poses problems in relation to property purchased from married couples, where one spouse is the legal owner but both occupy the

Case Summary

property together. It used to be thought that spousal interests did not raise the spectre of constructive notice: in the case of *Caunce* v. *Caunce* [1969] 1 WLR 286, the court even going so far as to state that any buyer of residential property was entitled to presume that the spouse of the seller was there only by virtue of their marriage to the legal owner, and did not have any further interest in the property. This case has been heavily criticised, however, and in the more recent case of *Kingsnorth Finance Co. Ltd* v. *Tizard* [1986] 1 WLR 783 the position of the court was reversed, meaning that now it is wise for the buyers of property in joint occupation to make enquiries of any occupier who is not a legal owner of the property and obtain written confirmation of their consent to the sale.

Case Summary

The facts of *Kingsnorth* v. *Tizard* were as follows: a husband purchased property with the help of money from the wife, but the house was put into the husband's sole name (as was common at that time). Despite the husband being the legal owner, however, the wife's financial contribution gave her an equitable interest in the property. We shall be looking at how such interests are acquired in more detail in Chapter 7. The husband and wife separated and the wife moved out, returning each day to look after the children and run the house. There were a number of her possessions still left at the property. During this time the husband remortgaged the property, arranging for the mortgage company to carry out an inspection of the property whilst the wife was away. The husband subsequently failed to make payments on the mortgage and the mortgage company sought to repossess the property. The wife claimed that the mortgage company had constructive notice of her equitable interest in the property and should take subject to it. The court agreed. Whilst they conceded that a proper inspection of the property for the purposes of constructive notice did not go so far as to 'open drawers or hunt in cupboards' (which would have revealed the wife's possession still at the property), the mortgage company were aware of the couple's recent separation and should have made further enquiries.

The judgment in this case is very helpful in detailing the type of search which would be required by a prospective purchaser of property in order to avoid constructive notice of any equitable interests of an occupier of the property under the doctrine of notice. Why not take some time to read through it and answer the questions in the Out and About feature, below.

Out and about

Read the judgment of Judge John Finlay, QC, in *Kingsnorth Finance Co. Ltd* v. *Tizard* [1986] 1 WLR 783 and answer the following questions:

1. Was Mrs Tizard held to have been in occupation of the property?
2. How was Mrs Tizard's physical presence in the property established?
3. The judge in the case said that occupation of the property in unregistered land would not be enough to constitute notice. What did he say would be sufficient?
4. What information was the lender given that the court felt should have prompted them to make further enquiries of the borrower?
5. What was the judge's difficulty with the inspection of the property that was made by the lender's agents?
6. What was the ultimate outcome for the lender in this case, and why?

As you will have seen from your reading of the judgment, above, the finding of constructive notice in the case of occupiers of a property is all the more salient because constructive notice actually now has a statutory voice under section 199(1)(ii)(a) of the Law of Property Act 1925, which states that:

> a purchaser shall not be prejudicially affected by notice of . . . any . . . instrument or matter or any fact or thing unless it . . . would have come to his knowledge if such inquiries and inspections had been made as ought reasonably to have been made by him.

Thus, there is not only a common law, but also a statutory, requirement to make reasonable enquiries and inspections of the property to be purchased, failure to do so resulting in constructive notice of the interest.

Imputed notice

This is where an agent of the purchaser has either actual or constructive notice of the interest in question. In these circumstances, the purchaser is themselves deemed to have imputed notice of the interest because their agent was acting on their behalf and should have relayed the information to them before they committed to the purchase of the property. An example of imputed notice in a conveyancing transaction might be where a solicitor failed to carry out a coal mining search in a coal mining area and the property then turned out to have a mine shaft in the back garden. The buyer would have imputed notice of the mine search because the information was a matter of public record and their solicitor should have discovered it by carrying out the relevant search on the property. This rule does not apply, however, if the agent of the purchaser finds out about an issue regarding the land but then deliberately conceals it from the purchaser. Such was the case in *Cave* v. *Cave* (1880) 15 Ch D 639, where a solicitor acting as a trustee of a trust fund fraudulently released money out of the trust fund to purchase property in his brother's name. The solicitor then took a legal mortgage out on the property, acting on behalf of both the lender and the borrower (his brother). The court held that the lender's charge over the property could take precedence over the equitable interests of the beneficiaries under the trust, because the solicitor's fraud prevented knowledge of the interests being imputed to the lenders for whom he was agent. As with the other two forms of notice, imputed notice has now found statutory form in section 199(1)(ii)(b) of the Law of Property Act 1925, which states that:

Case Summary

> A purchaser shall not be prejudicially affected by notice of any . . . instrument or matter or any fact or thing unless . . . in the same transaction with respect to which a question of notice to the purchaser arises, it has come to the knowledge of his counsel, as such, or of his solicitor or other agent, as such, or would have come to the knowledge of his solicitor or other agent, as such, if such inquiries and inspections had been made as ought reasonably to have been made by the solicitor or other agent.

Now check your understanding of the requirements with the following short exercise.

You be the judge

Source: Steve Shott © Dorling Kindersley

Q: Which of the following purchasers of 12 Silver Street would be bound by a covenant in favour of 10 Silver Street not to keep or breed any animals on the land, created before 1926: (a) John, who has a pet Labrador, and buys 12 Silver Street for £100,000 without notice of the covenant; (b) Jason, who keeps tropical fish, and buys 12 Silver Street for £110,000 with notice of the covenant; (c) Mary-Ellen, who breeds poodles, and inherits 12 Silver Street from her aunt without notice of the covenant; (d) Erin, who wishes to run a cattery from the premises, and is given 12 Silver Street by her father as a wedding present without notice of the covenant; (e) Jim-Bob, who keeps hens, and swaps 12 Silver Street for his property in the country without notice of the covenant; (f) Elizabeth, who has a pony, and buys 12 Silver Street for £125,000 without notice of the covenant? There is a note of the interest in the title deeds to the property, but Elizabeth's solicitor failed to notice it.

A: All of them except for John, in scenario (a), and Jim-Bob, in scenario (e), would be bound by the covenant. Jason has direct notice of the covenant; Mary Ellen inherits the property and is therefore not a purchaser for value of the property; the same applies to Erin who receives it as a gift; Elizabeth has imputed notice because her solicitor would have had constructive notice of the covenant, which appeared in the title deeds. Both John and Jim-Bob are bone fide purchasers for value of the covenant without notice. In Jim-Bob's case, the value is represented by the property in the country which he swaps for 12 Silver Street.

So, these are the requirements for a purchaser wishing to take free of an equitable interest of land created before 1926. But if someone does manage to fulfil all of the stringent requirements needed in order to be a bone fide purchaser for value of the legal estate without notice, what does this mean for the owner of the equitable interest? The answer quite simply is that the equitable interest is void, or invalid, as against that purchaser. The practical outcome is that the interest is effectively extinguished because, once this has happened, the interest cannot later be revived against any subsequent purchaser who had knowledge of it. The person with the equitable interest therefore loses their right in the land.

This concludes our discussion of legal and equitable interests in respect of interests in land created pre-1926. The following Writing and Drafting exercise will help to consolidate your reading.

Writing and drafting

What are your views on the ability to enforce legal and equitable interests in the land prior to 1926? Why not spend a little time creating a table to show the pros and cons of being an owner, both of a legal or equitable interest in land and the buyer of land affected by a legal or equitable interest pre-1926.

You should spend no more than 30 minutes on this task.

Handy tip: Remember that, prior to 1926, legal rights bind the whole world; equitable rights bind everyone except a bone fide purchaser for value without notice. Think about what you would need to do as a purchaser to discover what rights affected the property.

Reflective practice

Now that you have created a table of pros and cons, take some time to reflect on it. Who do you think benefited most from the old system – the owner of the interest or the purchaser of the land?

It is evident from the discussion above that the system prior to the changes made by the Law of Property Act 1925 was inadequate. From the point of view of a buyer of land, it meant that they had to carry out extensive and time-consuming enquiries on the property, with no guarantee of the discovery of the interest; from the owner of the interest's point of view, their right (if equitable) could be easily extinguished and there was little they could do to protect it. The response to this, as well as to many other aspects of the **conveyancing** process which, until then, had been quite convoluted, was the 1925 law of property legislation and, in particular, the Land Registration Act 1925, which has now been largely superseded by the Land Registration Act 2002. If you wish to refresh your memory about the 1925 property legislation you may wish to refer back to Chapter 1 of the text at this point.

Enforcement of interests in registered land

As we saw in Chapter 1, the idea behind the land registration system was that all property in England and Wales would become **registered**, with the result that any given property would appear on the Register together with a note of any rights or interests over it and any burdens attached to it. The position would be quite simple: a purchaser of the land would be bound only by those interests and burdens which appeared on the Register, regardless of whether those interests were legal or equitable in nature. Anything not recorded on the Register would be unenforceable. In addition all registered property would be backed by a State guarantee so all uncertainty and the need for extensive searches and enquiries to discover otherwise undisclosed rights over the subject property which may not have been recorded would be removed.

That was the theory: and it was a good one. Unfortunately the system of land registration which transpired did not quite cover all eventualities when it came to dealing with interests in land. The effect is that we have a system of land registration in which there are a number of interests which do not appear on the Register but which nevertheless bind a purchaser of the property. Arguably, this makes a nonsense of the registered land system altogether. Nevertheless, these unregistrable interests remain and it is necessary as students of law to know about them and to know how to guard against them. The current system of land registration separates rights and interests in land into three categories. These are:

- registrable interests or dispositions
- third party rights and interests
- unregistered or 'overriding' interests

Registrable interests

Registrable interests are listed under section 27(2) of the Land Registration Act 2002. Included in this category are the four notable legal interests in land listed under section 1(2) of the Law of Property Act 1925. These are:

- legal mortgages over property;
- rentcharges;
- rights of entry; and
- expressly granted legal easements.

Rights in this category must be registered in order to take legal effect. If they are registered, they will bind any purchaser of a legal estate in the land affected by the interest.

Third party interests

Any other kind of interest in land (in other words any equitable interest, including equitable easements and mortgages, restrictive covenants, interests behind a trust and estate contracts) is classed under the Land Registration Act 2002 as a third party interest in land. These interests do not require registration *per se*, but the owner of the right or interest is able to protect their interest by registering it against the property over which they hold the right, either by way of a '**notice**' or '**restriction**' on the Register of Title for that property. Notices appear in the **Charges Register** for the property and restrictions appear in the **Proprietorship Register**. As their names might suggest, a notice does not prevent the sale of the property, it only gives a potential purchaser notice of an interest claimed in the land. It is not proof that the interest is legal, only that it is being claimed and is protected (through registration) if it is proven to be valid. An example of a notice would be the burden of an easement or a restrictive covenant over the land. A restriction on the other hand will prevent registration of a change of ownership at the Land Registry unless the terms of the restriction are complied with. This might be obtaining the consent of the person who has entered the restriction, or giving notice to them. An example of a restriction entered on the Proprietorship Register would be a restriction entered by the bank or building society preventing the land from being sold without their loan against the property being repaid. You can see examples of both notices and restrictions in the example Register for 4 Sykes Lane, contained in the Documenting the Law feature in Chapter 3. Failure to register an interest as a notice or a restriction will allow a buyer of the property to take free from it unless that interest is **overriding** in nature (see below). This is irrespective of whether the purchaser knew about the interest or not. This is illustrated by the caser of *De Lusignan* v. *Johnson* (1973) 230 EG 499, in which a solicitor acting for a lender had express notice of a contract for the sale of the property over which the charge was being taken, but nevertheless took free from it because the contract had not been duly protected by registration.

Case Summary

Unregistered or 'overriding' interests

This third category of interests is listed in Schedule 3 of the Land Registration Act 2002. Unregistered, or 'overriding' interests, fall outside the system of land registration because they have the effect of binding a purchaser of registered land despite there being no way of entering them onto the Register of Title at the Land Registry. Whilst there are interests in land which are not capable of registration (such as legal leases for less than three years' duration under section 32(1) of the Land Registration Act 2002, for example), it is not necessarily always the case that overriding interests *cannot* be registered as a third party interest on the Register of the property affected by the interest. Rather, it is simply that they will survive any change in ownership of the subject property without the need for registration. Thus, an interest under a trust of land, if it is not entered as a restriction on the Proprietorship Register of the property it affects, may still take effect as an overriding interest if it falls within one of the categories listed below.

For this reason this really is the category of interests, therefore, that we must watch out for with registered land. So what do they include? According to Schedule 3, overriding interests include:

- *Legal leases granted for seven years or less* (Schedule 3, paragraph 1). Remember that legal leases granted for over seven years must be registered in order to take legal effect as an estate in land. Legal leases for less than seven years but more than three years can be entered as a notice on the Charges Register, but will nevertheless be overriding if they are not registered. Leases for less than three years are incapable of entry as a notice or restriction and so are truly overriding in this sense.
- *Legal easements acquired by implication or* ***prescription*** (Schedule 3, paragraph 3). These are easements which are acquired informally and therefore do not require the formality of easements which have been expressly granted. We are going to deal with how such easements are acquired in Chapter 10. It should be noted that the statute has preserved the notice element for this category of overriding interest to a small extent in that the Act requires that such easements will only be overriding if either:
  - their existence is known to the purchaser of the burdened land; or
  - it is obvious upon a reasonable inspection of the land; or
  - the easement has been exercised within one year prior to the disposition.

  There is therefore a proviso here that if the buyer of the land does not know about the easement and either couldn't have discovered it by inspecting the property or the easement hadn't been in use for the last year, they will still be able to take free of the interest when the land is bought.
- *Interests of people 'in actual occupation of the property'* (Schedule 3 paragraph 2). This class of interest includes the equitable rights of, for example, a husband or wife living in the family home, where the house is registered in the sole name of the other spouse. Another example might be where a grandparent is living with their son or daughter and their family, and might have contributed towards the purchase of a larger house to accommodate the extended family. As with easements acquired informally, there is an element of notice in this type of interest as well. Paragraph 2 says that interests of people in actual occupation of the property will *not* be overriding if either:
  - It is not disclosed on reasonable enquiry; or
  - The occupation would not have been obvious on a reasonable inspection of the land.

  Thus, if we were to revisit the facts of the case of *Kingsnorth* v. *Tizard*, we can see that in this case under the provisions of the statute the equitable interest of the wife in the property would not have been protected against the bank's repossession of the house because her belongings, and therefore her occupation of the property, were not obvious on reasonable inspection. You will remember that in this case, however, the circumstances were such that the bank should have been put on notice and made further enquiries

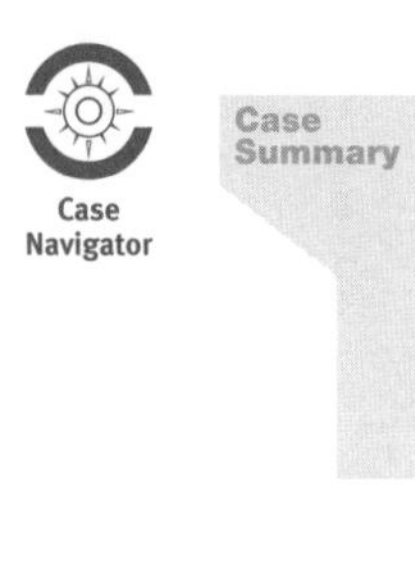

about the wife's interest in the property in any event. In contrast to this is the case of ***Williams & Glyn's Bank Ltd* v. *Boland*** [1981] AC 487. In this case Mrs Boland had an equitable interest in the property through her contribution to the purchase price. However, she was found to be in actual occupation of the property when her husband later mortgaged the property without her knowledge or consent and subsequently defaulted on the loan. The court therefore held that she did indeed have an overriding interest in the property and the bank was bound to take the house subject to it.

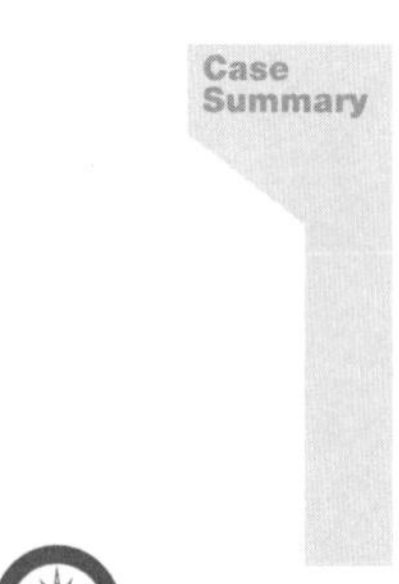

It is worth spending a moment or two thinking about what occupation actually means in this context. Apart from the occupation of the person with the interest being obvious upon a reasonable inspection of the property (in other words, is there an additional toothbrush in the bathroom? Are there coats or shoes, or belongings of that person around the house?), the occupation must have some form of continuity or permanence about it. In the case of *Strand Securities* v. *Caswell* [1965] Ch 958 the defendant, Mr Caswell, lived in the country but had a flat in London which he used as a base when he was working in the city. He also allowed his daughter to live in the apartment rent-free. When his bank sought to repossess the property the court said, however, that Mr Caswell did not live permanently at the property and could not call it his home: he therefore did not have an interest in actual occupation. Neither could he claim an interest through his daughter's occupation, as in order to benefit he had to occupy the property himself. Mr Caswell failed in his claim. This should be contrasted against the House of Lords case of ***Abbey National Building Society* v. *Cann*** [1990] 2 WLR 832, in which Lord Oliver said, **obiter**, that occupancy did not necessarily require the physical presence of the holder of the interest and that, as such, a caretaker could occupy property on behalf of his employer and an employee on behalf of his company. The case in question actually centred around an argument over whether a family who had completed the purchase of a house but had not yet moved in were in actual occupation at the time that a mortgage was created. The House of Lords followed the decision of the Court of Appeal, finding that they were not as they had not yet moved into the property at the time the mortgage was created. In any event, the difference between *Strand Securities* and the scenario set out in Lord Oliver's **dictum** is, of course, is that whereas Mr Caswell's daughter just happened to be staying in the property, albeit rent-free, but independently of her father, if Mr Caswell had been employing somebody to stay in the flat and keep house for him in his absence, they would be considered an agent occupying and keeping house on Mr Caswell's behalf.

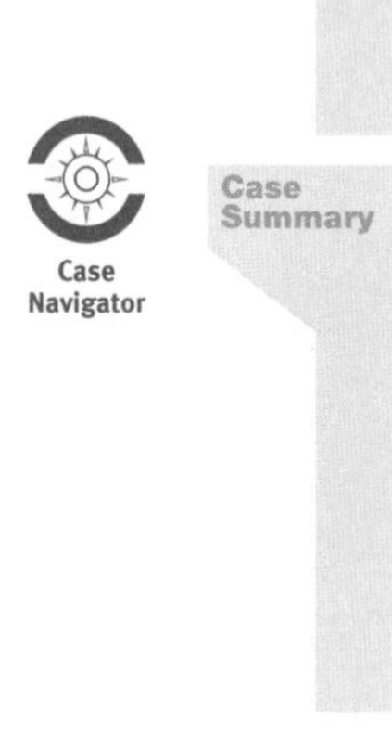

One final point to note here is that, whilst occupation in this sense must be permanent, short absences in hospital or on holiday will not affect the rights of the holder of the interest. In the case of *Chhokar* v. *Chhokar* [1984] Fam Law 269, the husband sold the family home, which was in his sole name, whilst his wife was in hospital having a baby. When she returned home from hospital she found that the locks had been changed and a stranger was living there. The court found that the wife had been in occupation of the property at the time of the sale and therefore the buyer took subject to her interest in the property.

It should be noted that, technically speaking, the use of the term 'overriding interests' is incorrect. Under the Land Registration Act 2002 these are '**unregistered interests**' in land. The reference to overriding interests refers back to the pre-2002 position under section 70(1)(g) of the Land Registration Act 1925, which the 2002 Act superseded. However, this category of interests is still commonly taught and referred to in practice as 'overriding' in order to avoid confusion with interests in unregistered land.

Electronic conveyancing

Under the proposed scheme of electronic conveyancing, authorised by Part 8 of the Land Registration Act 2002, it will be impossible to create certain interests unless they are entered electronically on the Register of Title of the relevant land (section 93). This could theoretically be an opportunity to further improve the registered system; however, the suggestion is that it will not apply to all types of interest and there is currently no indication as to which interests this will apply to. Thus, in all likelihood, electronic conveyancing will do little to curtail the use of the current system of overriding interests, albeit that it may seek to limit the circumstances in which overriding interests can arise. Barrister William Hansen, who is a Deputy Adjudicator at the Land Registry, comments on the efficacy of the registered system in the People in the Law feature, below.

People in the law

Name and title: William Hansen, formerly Deputy Adjudicator to the Land Registry and now at Cornerstone Barristers.

Source: William Hansen

What is your role as an adjudicator to the Land Registry? The primary function of an adjudicator is to resolve disputed applications to the registrar which, if they cannot be settled by agreement between the parties, are referred by the registrar to the Adjudicator under s. 73(7) LRA 2002 who then determines the matter at a public hearing. The adjudicators are independent persons outside the structure of the Registry.

Do you often deal with cases involving overriding interests in land? The majority of cases that come before an adjudicator involve issues relating to **adverse possession**, boundaries, easements and beneficial interests in land. However, it is not uncommon to encounter cases involving overriding interests, particularly legal easements.

What are the main causes of dispute in this area? Overriding interests frequently arise in the context of applications for first registration and registered dispositions, where the issue is whether there is some overriding interest (often a legal easement or the interest of a person in actual occupation) which binds the proprietor's estate. The dispute is often as to whether the person claiming the interest is in 'actual occupation' or (in the context of a registered disposition) whether the disponee had actual knowledge of the interest at the time of the disposition.

Do you consider that the system is adequate in protecting third party interests in land? On balance yes, although the LRA 2002 has deliberately reduced the number of overriding interests (e.g. by the exclusion of equitable easements: see paragraph 3 of Schedule 1) and tightened up the requirements for attracting overriding status (e.g. the obvious on inspection test in paragraph 3 of Schedule 3).

The concept of unregistered (overriding) interests is a bit of an anomaly, though, isn't it? Yes, particularly given that one of the main objectives of the LRA 2002 was to make the Register as accurate and complete a record of the title as is possible. In this context, the continued existence of rights that bind a registered estate but yet do not appear on the Register is somewhat at odds with the fundamental objective of the LRA 2002.

Does this make your work more difficult? Not really, because we are very used to the concept of overriding interests going back to the LPA 1925.

How do you think the law could be improved in this area? There is clearly a delicate balance to be struck between the desirability of a complete and accurate Register of Title on the one hand, and the protection of legitimate third-party interests on the other hand. In my view, the LRA 2002 strikes the right balance.

Do you think this will be achieved with the advent of e-conveyancing? The concept behind e-conveyancing and the aim of a conclusive Register are inconsistent with overriding interests. This has been recognised, hence the attempt at reducing the number of overriding interests. However, for the Register to be genuinely conclusive with all aspects of conveyancing being done online, overriding interests would ultimately have to be eliminated but this would presumably be too draconian and would itself result in injustice. There will therefore always be a core of overriding interests.

You can find out more about Cornerstone Barristers and the work of William Hansen at **http://cornerstonebarristers.com/barrister/william-hansen**

Enforcement of interests in unregistered land

The system of land registration brought in by the Land Registration Act 1925, whilst flawed, did to a large extent bring about an end to the uncertainty caused by the doctrine of notice in respect of the property to which it applied. Take a look at the Key Stats feature below to see how big the problem was at the time.

Key stats

If you go back 50 years to 1963, the position was considerably worse, with only 2 million titles in the country being registered; this equates to only one tenth of the current registration figures (there are around 20 million titles registered in England and Wales today). So if only 7.5 per cent of the country was registered in 1963, despite registration this left the vast majority of land in England and Wales still subject to the pre-1926 unregistered system and the doctrine of notice at that time. Clearly interim measures needed to be taken until such time as all land in the country was registered and the doctrine of notice ceased to be in use.

Source: **http://www1.landregistry.gov.uk/upload/documents/bhist-lr.pdf**

A temporary solution was provided in the guise of the Land Charges Act 1925, the provisions of which have now been superseded by the Land Charges Act 1972. The Act provided that certain interests in land, most of which are equitable, would have to be registered in a central public register, called the **Land Charges Register**, in order to be protected against purchasers of the land over which the interests were held. So in effect what was created was a system of partial registration, relating to interests in unregistered land only. It should be noted that the Land Charges Register is quite separate from the Land Registry, which itself holds details of registered land. The Register is held in a single location (currently in Plymouth, Devon) and records equitable interests against the name of the owner of the property affected by that interest, as opposed to against the property itself (under section 3(1) of the 1972 Act). The following Documenting the Law feature shows what the results of a search of the Land Charges Register looks like.

Documenting the law

Example of a search result from the Land Charges Department in Plymouth

LAND CHARGES ACT 1972

CERTIFICATE OF THE RESULT OF THE SEARCH

CERTIFICATE NO.	CERTIFICATE DATE	PROTECTION ENDS ON
0723135	01/11/12	22/11/12

It is hereby certified that an official search in respect of the undermentioned particulars has been made in the index to the registers which are kept pursuant to the Land Charges Act 1972. The result of the search is shown below.

PARTICULARS SEARCHED			
COUNTY OR COUNTIES	East Irkshire		
NAME(S)	Particulars of Charge	PERIOD	FEES
(1) JOHN ABEL TUNNARD (2) 23.05.1999 (3) C(iv) (4) HAZLEMIRE (5) EAST IRKSHIRE *************** (1) JOHN ABEL TUNNARD (2) 23.05.1999 (3) D(ii) (4) HAZLEMIRE (5) EAST IRKSHIRE ************** ---------------------------END OF SEARCH ----------------------		1999 - 2012 1999 - 2012	

APPLICANT'S REFERENCE	JR/TUN759	APPLICANT'S KEY NUMBER	83647-9	AMOUNT DEBITED £	

SNIPES HALL SOLICITORS CRANBER COURT HAZLEMIRE EAST IRKSHIRE	Any enquiries concerning this certificate to be addressed to:- The Superintendent Land Charges Department Burrington Way Plymouth PL5 3LP
	IMPORTANT PLEASE READ THE NOTES OVERLEAF (NOTE: not provided for the purposes of this assessment)

There are six classes of interest which can be registered against unregistered land in this way, all of which are listed A to F in section 2 of the 1972 Act. The classes are then subdivided further into more specific types of interest. Not all of the interests listed in the Act are of practical significance today, and we shall only be looking at the most common types of interest that you are likely to come across in practice. These are as follows.

Class C(i) – Puisne mortgages

Puisne mortgages (pronounced 'puny') are legal mortgages which are not protected by the deposit of the title deeds with the lender. This would be the case where the mortgage is a second or third mortgage on the property, and the original lender has the deeds already so there are none to hand over. The practice of giving the title deeds to property to the lender in unregistered land is to prevent the property owner from dealing with the property in any way during the continuation of the loan; it thus secures the property in favour of the lender. This was common practice with unregistered land, but is no longer necessary today because taking out a mortgage requires the property to be registered and so title deeds are no longer necessary.

Puisne mortgages are the only legal interest capable of registration under the Land Charges Act. The others are all equitable interests. Whilst, technically speaking, outside the Land Registration Acts legal interests bind the whole world and therefore a puisne mortgage should be protected regardless of registration, from a practical point of view it would be very difficult to discover a second or third mortgage against a property without registration of the interest. It is for this reason that this one legal interest is required to be registered under the Act.

Class C(iv) – Estate contracts

You can see a Class C(iv) search result in the Documenting the Law feature, above. As you will remember from earlier in the chapter, an estate contract is the legal term for a contract for the sale of land and includes ordinary contracts for the sale of land as well as options to purchase and rights of pre-emption. Remember that when the parties enter into a contract for the sale of land this creates an equitable interest in the land in favour of the buyer. It is this interest that is protected by registration at the Land Charges Registry.

Class D(ii) – Restrictive covenants

You can see a Class D(ii) search result in the Documenting the Law feature, above. You will be familiar with the concept of restrictive covenants from your earlier reading. Class D(ii) applies only to restrictive covenants created after 1926. Any created before this are still subject to the doctrine of notice.

Class D(iii) – Equitable easements

Again, equitable easements were considered earlier in the chapter. An equitable easement will usually be created in situations where either an attempt to create a legal easement has failed, because the correct formalities have not been adhered to, or where the easement has not been created for a duration equivalent to a legal estate in land. This category would therefore include an easement created for life, for example. Class D(iii) applies only to equitable easements created after 1926. All equitable easements created before this date are still governed by the old doctrine of notice.

Class F – Charges under the Family Law Act 1996

The Family Law Act 1996 gives a spouse a right of occupation in the matrimonial home where that spouse is not a legal owner of the property. It is important to note that this is a right of occupation only and does not give the spouse any equitable interest in the property or a right to a share in the house on its subsequent sale. If a spouse registers such a charge the legal owner of the property will be unable to sell the property until the charge is cancelled (because they will be unable to force the non-owning spouse out of the property).

Non-registration of interests under the Land Charges Act 1972

If a person with an interest in unregistered land fails to register their interest under the Land Charges Act 1972 the effect will depend on the type of interest they have failed to register. Under section 4 of the Act:

- Unregistered puisne mortgages under class C(i) and Class F charges under the Family Law Act 1996 will be **void** (invalid) against a purchaser of any interest in the land (including an equitable one). They would therefore remain binding against a person who was given the land as a gift, for example.
- Unregistered equitable interests, including estate contracts (class C(iv)), restrictive covenants (class D(ii)) and equitable easements (class D(iii)), will be void against a purchaser *for money or money's worth* of a legal estate in the land. They would therefore remain binding against the purchaser of an equitable interest in the land or a person receiving the legal estate as a gift.

The different wording contained in the statutory provisions initially caused some uncertainty over whether or not the use of the words 'money or money's worth' as regards equitable interests in the land required a different interpretation to the simple requirement of a purchaser in respect of the other interests listed. Any controversy was ironed out in the House of Lords case of *Midland Bank Trust Co. Ltd* v. *Green* [1981] AC 513, however. The case concerned a falling-out between father and son. The father owned an unregistered farm and gave his son an option to purchase the farm at any time over the next ten years. The son should have registered the option as a Class C(iv) **land charge** (an estate contract), but he did not do so. The father and son subsequently argued and out of spite the father instead sold the farm to his wife for £500 (the farm was then worth around £40,000). The wife knew about the option which had been given to her son and the question arose as to whether she should take the farm subject to the option. The

Court of Appeal found that the wife was bound by the option. They said that 'money or money's worth' meant a fair price and that as the property had been sold for considerably less than this was worth this did not constitute a sale of the legal estate for 'money or money's worth'. The House of Lords overturned the decision, however. They held that the wife was not bound by the option. In their view, the term 'money or money's worth' meant the same as 'value'. The £500 paid for the farm was a genuine payment of money and the amount was irrelevant. In addition, the wife's knowledge of the option was irrelevant: the option had not been registered and so it was void against her as a purchaser of the land.

We can see, then, that although the wording differs slightly dependent on the type of interest in question, the overall effect of registration under the Land Charges Act 1972 is that failure to register an interest under the terms of the Act will result in it being void against a purchaser of the property burdened by that interest. For these interests, the doctrine of notice no longer applies and knowledge of the interest is irrelevant to enforcement. One further case which illustrates this is the case of *Hollington Bros* v. *Rhodes* [1951] 2 All ER 578. In this case a property was sold to the buyer who had knowledge of a tenant in possession of the property under an unregistered equitable lease. After the sale of the property had been completed, the new owners served notice on the tenant to quit the property. The tenant argued that the property had been purchased subject to their interest and therefore that it should be upheld against the buyer, but the court disagreed. The equitable lease should have been registered as an estate contract under Class C(iv) of the (then) Land Charges Act 1925. The buyer was a purchaser of the legal estate for money and therefore took free of the rights of the tenant regardless of notice. The status of equitable leases will be considered in further detail in Chapter 5.

Case Summary

Legal interests in unregistered land

As regards legal interests in unregistered land, with the exception of puisne mortgages, dealt with above, all legal interests in unregistered land still abide by the common law rule that 'legal rights bind the whole world'. A purchaser of unregistered land will therefore buy the land subject to any legal rights over it, regardless of whether they were aware of that right when they purchased the property.

Any other interests in the land not covered by the provisions of the Land Charges Act 1972 will also still be governed by the pre-1926 rules and the doctrine of notice. Thus, restrictive covenants and equitable easements created before 1926, which are expressly excluded from the 1972 Act, beneficial interests under a trust and other interests which may arise informally over the land (such as resulting or constructive trusts, or interests arising by **estoppel** – all of which we will consider in further detail in Chapters 7 and 8), all of which do not feature in the legislation, will bind a purchaser of the legal estate affected by that interest unless they are a bona fide purchaser for value without notice.

So what does this leave us with, altogether? We have a system of unregistered land which requires registration of certain interests in order to protect them, and a system of registered land which includes a number of interests which are incapable of registration. The system is convoluted, at best. Table 4.1 should help to clarify the position as it stands at present.

Table 4.1 Protection of interests in registered and unregistered land

Registered land	
Legal interests	**Equitable interests**
Registrable dispositions (i.e. legal mortgages over property; rentcharges; rights of entry; and expressly granted legal easements) must be registered in order to be protected against a third party purchaser of the land.	Third party interests (i.e. equitable easements and mortgages, restrictive covenants, interests behind a trust and estate contracts) must be registered as a Notice or Restriction on the register of title in order for them to be protected against a third party purchaser.
Overriding interests under Sched.3, para.2 LRA 2002 (including legal leases of 7 years or less and implied legal easements) will bind a third party purchaser despite not being registered	Interests of people in actual occupation (including those with an equitable interest in the property) will have an overriding interest under Sched.3, para.2 LRA 2002, although any interest under a trust can be overreached if the purchase monies are paid to two trustees.
Unregistered land	
Legal interests	**Equitable interests**
Legal interests 'bind the whole world'	Equitable interests created pre-1926 are bound by the doctrine of notice, meaning any purchaser will be bound unless they are a bone fide purchaser for value of the legal estate without notice
Puisne mortgages must be registered as Land Charges in order to bind any purchaser of the land.	Equitable interests created after 1926 (including estate contracts, restrictive covenants and equitable easements) must be registered as Land Charges in order to bind a purchaser for money or money's worth, of the land.

Overreaching – a little help at hand

Clearly the biggest area of concern here is interests under a trust of land and in particular interests in the land which may arise informally, as these are neither capable of registration as a land charge in unregistered land nor as a Notice or Restriction in registered land. Luckily, the statutory concept of **overreaching** provides assistance to purchasers of the legal estate in respect of all interests under a trust of land, including those registered as a Restriction on the Proprietorship Register in registered land. Under section 2 of the Law of Property Act 1925, any interest under a trust of land can be 'overreached' by a purchaser of the legal estate of the land affected by the interest, provided that the buyer pays the purchase money to two **trustees** of the trust or a **trust corporation** (that is a company paid to act professionally in the place of trustees to a trust). But what does this

overreaching is where the equitable interest attaches to the proceeds of sale

mean? The concept of overreaching sounds complicated but in reality is simple: overreaching is where the equitable interest detaches itself from the land and instead attaches to the proceeds of sale of the property, leaving the purchaser free of the equitable interest without the interest being extinguished. An example will make this clearer. Imagine Bert and Lesley buy a flat on trust for the benefit of their son, Ernest, who is only 17 and therefore unable to hold the legal title to the flat. When they later decide to sell the flat, what happens to Ernest's interest in the property? As long as the purchase money is paid to two trustees, in this instance Bert and Lesley, the property can be sold free of Ernest's interest and the buyer can take possession of the property safe in the knowledge that it is not encumbered in any way. Ernest's interest has not been extinguished, though. Instead, his parents now hold the proceeds of sale of the property on trust for Ernest. Thus, his equitable interest is now in the money instead of the land. Consequently Ernest's parents, as trustees of the trust, will not be able to spend that money except on behalf of Ernest for the benefit of the trust.

To give another example, imagine a couple living in a property, 6 Gretel Street, with the husband's mother. The mother sold her own property and used £100,000 from the proceeds towards purchasing 6 Gretel Street together with her son and daughter-in-law so that they could all live in it together. Unfortunately the arrangement doesn't go well and the two generations decide to part ways. The couple sells the property for £300,000 and the purchase money is paid into their joint bank account. However, whilst the mother's interest has been overreached by the sale, of the purchase money they receive, £100,000 of that money will be held on trust by them for the husband's mother, in lieu of her equitable interest in the property. They cannot therefore spend this money as their own, as it is held on trust for her benefit.

Is it important to realise that the need for the money to be paid to two trustees is crucial for the concept of overreaching to work. Two contrasting cases illustrate the importance of this. In *Williams & Glyn's Bank Ltd* v. *Boland* [1981] AC 487, the matrimonial home was registered in the husband's sole name on trust for himself and his wife. The husband took out a mortgage against the property without the knowledge of the wife. However, it was held that the bank took subject to the wife's interest in the property because there had been no overreaching, the money having been paid to only one trustee (the husband). The wife's interest in the property was not registered at the Land Registry, but took effect as an overriding interest because she was in actual occupation of the property.

Case Summary

Case Navigator

Case Summary

In the later case of ***City of London Building Society* v. *Flegg*** [1988] AC 54, a husband and wife were trustees of a trust in favour of the wife's mother and father, who lived with them and had contributed towards the purchase of the property. The husband and wife took out a mortgage over the property without the knowledge of the wife's parents. When the husband and wife then failed to make payments on the mortgage, the building society sought possession of the property as security for the loan. The parents tried to argue that the building society should take subject to their equitable interest in the property. However, it was held that the interests of the parents had been overreached because the loan monies had been paid out to two trustees (the husband and wife). This was even though the parents were in actual occupation of the property.

It can be seen from this case, then, that overreaching will defeat even an overriding interest in the land, if the money is paid to two trustees. In the case of the mother and father, the outcome may seem a little unfair. However, the law of overreaching is designed to protect the innocent purchasers of a property, and not those with an interest in the land. The interests of the parents in theory are protected by the law of trusts, in which their daughter and son-in-law will be responsible to them as trustees of the monies received by them from the mortgage company, which they will have had a duty to hold in trust on behalf of the parents in proportion to their share in the property. The reality, of course, is that the daughter and son-in-law have no money (hence the house being repossessed) so the likelihood of the parents ever seeing their money (or their home) again is slim. For a more detailed look at trustee responsibility read Chapter 10 on duties of trustees in Warner-Reed on *Equity and Trusts*, in the Living Law series of books.

Summary

- There are five legal interests which can exist in land: easements, rentcharges, mortgages, similar charges not created by instrument, and rights of entry (s.1(2) LPA 1925).
- In order for an interest to be legal it must fall within one of the categories listed in the LPA 1925 and be created by deed (s.52 LPA 1925).
- All other interests in land take place in equity only (s.1(3) LPA 1925). These include restrictive covenants, interests under a trust and estate contracts.
- With the exception of certain types of trust, equitable interests require writing under section 53(1) of the LPA 1925.
- The ability to enforce interests in land depends on whether they are legal or equitable, and whether the land over which the interest is held is registered or unregistered.
- In unregistered land, with the exception of puisne mortgages, legal interests bind the whole world.
- Puisne mortgage, equitable interests (notably restrictive covenants, estate contracts and equitable easements created after 1926) and the right to occupy under the Family Law Act 1996 require registration at the Land Charges Registry in Plymouth in order to bind a purchaser of the land.
- All other interests in land are bound by the old doctrine of notice, which says that any purchaser of the land will be bound by interests over it unless they are a bone fide purchaser for value of the legal estate without notice.
- In registered land, whether an interest will bind a purchaser of the land affected by it will depend for the most part on registration either as a registrable disposition or as a notice or restriction on the Register of Title.
- Certain interests that do not appear on the Register are overriding, however, meaning a purchaser of the land will take subject to those interests despite them not appearing on the Register. These are legal leases of seven years or less, implied legal easements, and interests of people in actual occupation of the property (Sched.3, para.2 LRA 2002).
- Beneficial interests under a trust can be overreached in both registered and unregistered land by the payment of the purchase monies to two trustees or a trust corporation (s.2 LPA 1925). Overreaching takes precedence both over the registration of an interest as a restriction in registered land and over any overriding interest which may exist in the property.

Question and answer*

Problem: Your client, Jessica, has just bought 18 Travis Court, which has registered title. Say which, if any, of the following rights or interests will bind your client:

(a) 16 Travis Court's right of way across the garden of the property; (b) a covenant made with 16 Travis Court not to use the property for business purposes; (c) Trish's option to purchase the property at any time within the next five years; (d) Serena's right to live in 18 Travis Court together with her husband, who was the sole legal owner of the property; (e) Hardeep's legal five-year lease over the premises; (f) Jayden and Karmel's equitable right in the property, in which they live with their son and daughter-in-law, Serena. They are not legal owners of the property but paid a quarter of the purchase price

You should allow yourself no more than 45 minutes to complete this task.

Problem: What would be your answers if the property had unregistered title?

You should allow yourself no more than 30 minutes to complete this task.

* Answer guidance is provided at the end of the chapter.

Further reading

Warner-Reed, E. (2011), *Equity and Trusts*, 1st edn, Living Law series, Harlow: Pearson.
Chapter 1 gives an explanation of the birth of equity which provides useful background to this chapter and to the concepts of equity which you will come across throughout the text. Worth taking a look at for some background reading and to gain a fuller understanding of the theory behind some of the concepts (such as co-ownership) you will come across in this text.

***Kingsnorth Finance Co. Ltd* v. *Tizard* [1986] 1 WLR 783.**
The judgment in this case is very helpful in detailing the type of search which would be required by a prospective purchaser of property in order to avoid constructive notice of any equitable interests of an occupier of the property under the doctrine of notice, and is therefore worth a read.

Howell, J., 'The doctrine of notice: an historical perspective', Conv. 1997, Nov/Dec, 431–41.
A useful article detailing the doctrine of notice and the reasons for change in the law, together with a summary of the law as it stands regarding the doctrine of notice today.

Jackson, N., 'Title by registration and concealed overriding interests: the cause and effect of antipathy to documentary proof', LQR 2003 119 (Oct), 660–91.
This article gives a thorough critique of overriding interests and makes a case for reform in this area of the law.

Question and answer guidance

Please note that the following is not a full answer and is intended to provide guidance in outline form only as to how to answer the questions posed.

Problem:

(a) A right of way could be a type of easement over the property, although we are not told whether the easement in question is legal or equitable. If legal, either the right of way will have been expressly granted or granted by implication or prescription. If expressly granted it will be a registrable disposition under s.27(2)(d) LRA 2002 and will require registration in order to bind a purchaser. Thus Jessica will only be bound if it appears as a notice on the Charges Register of her registered title as a burden over her property.

If the right of way has been acquired informally, on the other hand, either by implied grant or reservation, or by prescription, it will be overriding under Sched.3 para.3 LRA 2002 and so will bind Jessica regardless of whether it appears on the Register, provided that it is either within Jessica's actual knowledge when she bought the property, or obvious on a reasonably careful inspection of the land she is buying and has been exercised within a year before the date of the purchase.

If the easement is equitable it should have been protected by way of a notice in the Charges Register of Jessica's land. If it has not been it will not bind Jessica.

(b) A covenant restricting Jessica's use of the property is a restrictive covenant and therefore equitable in nature. It must therefore be entered as a notice in the Charges Register of Jessica's land in order to bind her.

(c) An option to purchase is a type of estate contract and therefore equitable in nature. It must therefore be entered as a notice in the Charges Register of Jessica's land in order to bind her.

(d) This is suggestive of a right under the Family Law Act 1996, acquired by Serena by virtue of her marriage to the owner of the property. This right is created by statute and is protected by entry of a notice in the Charges Register. This is called a 'matrimonial rights notice' and gives a right of occupation in the matrimonial home. If such a notice is registered, Serena will have the right not to be evicted or excluded from the house except in pursuance of a court order, and Jessica will be bound by this. If no notice is present, Jessica will not be bound. Serena's occupation of the property cannot be overriding because matrimonial homes rights do not amount to an interest in land.

(e) A legal lease of seven years or less is overriding under Sched.3 para. 1 LRA 2002 and will therefore bind Jessica regardless of whether it appears on the register of title or not. As a lease of over three years it can be entered as a notice in the Charges Register against Jessica's title, however, so she may have been aware of it. If the lease is equitable again it should have been registered as a notice in the Charges Register of Jessica's title. If it was not, Hardeep's lease could nevertheless be overriding if he is in actual occupation of the premises under Sched.3. para 2, LRA 2002.

(f) Jayden and Karmel have an equitable interest by virtue of a resulting trust, on account of their contribution to the purchase price of the property. They could have entered a restriction in the Proprietorship Register for 18 Travis Court preventing the property from being sold to Jessica without their permission. If they have not done this, they will still have an overriding interest in actual occupation under Sched.3 para.2 LRA 2002, provided their occupation is obvious upon reasonable inspection and was disclosed upon reasonable inquiry by the purchasers. Their interest could not have been overreached by Jessica as she is a sole purchaser of the property. Her purchase is therefore bound by their interest.

Problem: If the property had unregistered title, the answers would differ as follows: (a) legal rights bind the whole world; an equitable easement must be registered as a Class D(iii) Land Charge. Otherwise it would not bind Jessica provided she was a purchaser of the legal estate for money or money's worth; (b) a restrictive covenant is equitable in nature and should be registered as a Class D(ii) Land Charge, as above; (c) an option to purchase is equitable and should be registered as a Class C(iv) Land Charge, as above; (d) a right to occupy under the LFA 1996 must be registered as a Class F Land Charge. If it is not, it will not bind a purchaser of the land, whether legal or equitable; (e) if the lease was legal it will bind Jessica as legal rights bind the whole world; if it was equitable then technically speaking it is a type of estate contract (a contract to create a lease under the doctrine in *Walsh* v. *Lonsdale*) and therefore should have been registered as a Class C(iv) Land Charge, as above; (f) Jayden and Karmel's interest is not capable of registration under the Land Charges Act 1972 and cannot be overreached as the purchase monies were paid to a sole trustee i.e. Jessica. Therefore whether Jessica is bound by the interest will depend upon the doctrine of notice, i.e. is Jessica a bona fide purchaser of the legal estate for value without notice. If she is, she will not be bound by their interest.

Visit **www.mylawchamber.co.uk** to access tools to help you develop and test your knowledge of land law.

Use Case Navigator to read in full some of the key cases referenced in this chapter with commentary and questions:

Walsh* v. *Lonsdale [1881–5] All ER Rep Ext 1690
Williams & Glyn's Bank Ltd* v. *Boland [1980] 2 All ER 141
Abbey National Building Society* v. *Cann [1990] 1 All ER 1085
City of London Building Society* v. *Flegg [1988] 2 AC 54

Introduction

Chapter 5
The leasehold estate

Key points In this chapter we will be looking at:

- Why we need leases, from a legal and a practical point of view
- The terminology of leases
- The definition of a lease and different types of leases, including fixed term and periodic tenancies
- Leases and licences and why it is important to distinguish between them
- The essential characteristics of a lease as set out in *Street* v. *Mountford*
- What equates to 'exclusive possession'
- The need for a determinate term in the lease
- Exceptional circumstances in which a lease will not be created: the '*Facchini* categories'
- Formalities for the creation and transfer of leasehold interests, including registration
- Equitable leases: their nature and inherent flaws
- How leases are brought to an end: different methods of termination

Introduction

Having discussed, in Chapter 3, the requirements for the acquisition of a **freehold** estate in land and then, in Chapter 4, the requirements for the creation or transfer of both legal and **equitable interests** in land, it would be prudent to spend a little time thinking about the concept of the **leasehold** estate and its creation and transfer. This chapter, therefore, will do exactly that.

In Chapter 1 we learned that the Law of Property Act 1925 reduced the number of legal estates in land to only two: the **'fee simple absolute in possession'**, or freehold estate, and the **'term of years absolute'**, or leasehold estate. We also learned that the leasehold, or 'term of years absolute', is a form of landholding with a rather more limited scope and subordinate to the freehold, and we discovered that, unlike the freehold, a leasehold estate only exists for a finite period, a **'term of years'**, the estate expiring when that period comes to an end and the land returning to the freeholder. But what is the point of the leasehold estate? If it is inferior to the freehold, why bother having it at all? Let us start by considering this point.

Why do we need leases?

So why are leases necessary? We need them from both a business and residential perspective. The Law in Action feature below gives us some insight.

Law in action More people could be renting than buying within a generation

According to independent research carried out for the UK's largest listed landlord, Grainger, by Brunswick, there may be more renters in the UK than homeowners within the next 15 years.

The Brunswick Research project questioned 2,220 members of the general public and found that 54% expect that in 15 years' time there will be more people in the UK renting than owning their homes. Findings also suggest that the stigma associated with renting is disappearing, with only 31% of those questioned believing that opportunities for first-time buyers will improve over the next few years.

When questioned by Brunswick, Nick Jopling, executive property director of Grainger, said: 'There is a new housing reality dawning on Britain. The financial crisis has tightened mortgage lending; house prices continue to be uncertain; and there are simply too few homes for demand.'

And the answer to all this? Some say the Government should do more to back the private rented sector. Or perhaps it is just time to accept a reality that has been the norm on the continent for decades: the majority of households simply rent. The solution remains to be found.

Source: **http://www.lettingagenttoday.co.uk/news_features/More-people-could-be-renting-than-buying-in-15-years-say-public**

As we can see from the feature above, in a residential context one reason is simple financial need: a **tenant** of residential property may be renting because they cannot afford to buy at that time in their lives. Another equally practical reason, however, might be simply because they are living in a locality on a temporary basis (such as a student studying at university). From a **landlord**'s point of view they might own surplus property that they have no current use for, so rather than that property standing empty they may wish to rent it out for a period of time. Alternatively, they may buy property specifically with the idea of renting it out as an investment, to receive income from it.

From the point of view of a business tenant, they may wish to test the water by renting a property for a few years, with a view to making a more permanent commitment at a later date. Alternatively they may wish to test the market in a particular location, and therefore may wish to rent before taking the step of buying in a particular area. They may also not have the money required to buy commercial premises. As we saw in Chapter 1, over 70 per cent of business premises are rented, so this is no small market. The following Key Stats feature below gives us some statistics on the rental market in England and Wales.

Key stats The Private Landlords Survey

The Private Landlords Survey is a national survey commissioned by the Department for Communities and Local Government of landlords and managing agents who own and/or manage privately-rented properties in England. Some key findings of the latest survey published in October 2011 are shown below:

- 89% of landlords were private individual landlords responsible for 71% of all private rented dwellings, with a further 5% of landlords being company landlords responsible for 15% of dwellings.
- More than three quarters (78%) of all landlords only owned a single dwelling for rent, with only 8% of landlords stating they were full-time landlords.
- The majority (54%) of dwellings met the Decent Homes Standard though this rose to nearly three-quarters (74%) for those let by new landlords.
- 51% of all dwellings were acquired since 2000, 25% in the ten years between 1990 and 1999.
- In terms of formal **letting** and management practices, nearly all landlords and agents (97%) made use of a written tenancy agreement.

Source: **http://www.communities.gov.uk/publications/corporate/statistics/privatelandlordssurvey2010**

The reasons given above for creating leases over property are mostly financial in nature; however, there are also sound practical reasons why the existence of leasehold tenure is necessary. In a scenario where there are a number of flats in one building, for example, the vehicle of leasehold ownership provides a very practical solution where freehold tenure would be an entirely unsatisfactory form of landholding.

Imagine a house over four storeys that has been converted into flats, one on each floor: there is a basement, or 'garden' flat, and flats at ground, first and second floors. From a theoretical point of view, there is no reason why each flat cannot be owned as a freehold. After all, according to the statutory definition of land under section 205 of the Law of Property Act 1925 it includes '. . . buildings or parts of buildings . . . whether the division is horizontal, vertical or made in any other way . . .'. However, to do this would have massive practical implications. Take a look at the Writing and Drafting feature below and see if you can figure out what these might be.

Writing and drafting

In the paragraph above, the text comments that to divide property horizontally (thus creating a freehold flat), whilst possible from a legal point of view, would have massive practical implications for the landowner. Can you think of what any of these are? Spend ten minutes writing a list of the problems you can see with owning a freehold flat.

Handy tip: Consider the following – who owns the roof and the foundations of the property? Who owns the stairs and landing? What practical difficulties might this pose for owners of each of the separate flats, if their ownership was freehold?

Source: Andy Crawford © Dorling Kindersley

As you have considered above, owning a freehold flat has a number of serious implications on a practical level. To begin with, there is the issue of the structure of the property. Who is responsible for this? Is the owner of the top-floor flat also responsible for repairs to the roof, and the owner of the basement flat responsible for the foundations of the building? If the basement flat owner does nothing to deal with an inherent rising damp problem and the whole house is condemned, as freeholders the other flat owners can do nothing to protect their interests because they have no say over what the basement flat owner does with their own property. Equally, is it fair to expect the basement flat owner to organise and pay for structural repairs to the building without any financial input from the other flat owners who will benefit from those repairs.

There is also the issue of maintenance of and access through the **common parts** of the building. Does the owner of each floor own their respective part of the staircase and landing to the other flats? What if there is a lift – who owns that? Individual freehold ownership would presumably require **easements** being granted to the owner of the first-floor flat to access their flat via the ground floor entrance, and the owner of the second-floor flat through the ground and first floors, and so on. This is complicated at best. In addition there is the question of who is responsible for repair of the common parts. What if the owner of the ground floor flat did not look after the entrance hall, or left it full of rubbish, and yet you had to walk through it every day to access your own property? For a further discussion of easements and how they work see Chapter 10.

Reflective practice

Take a look at your answers to the Writing and Drafting feature above. Had you considered all of the difficulties listed above? Can you think of any others?

As you can see, the ownership of individual freehold flats would be fraught with complication, so much so that mortgage lenders are loath to lend money against freehold flats. Traditionally these problems have been circumvented with the use of leases of each flat, the building remaining in the ownership of a landlord who has responsibility for the structure and common parts of the building. More recently, the advent of **commonhold** as a method of ownership provides a suitable alternative; however, the uptake on commonhold is slow and leases are still very much the preferred method of landholding where single buildings are in shared occupation. Responsibility for repairs and the issue of leasehold **covenants** will be dealt with in more detail in Chapter 13.

The terminology of leases

Before we begin to think about leases as a concept, it may be a good idea to familiarise ourselves with a few terms you are going to come across in the context of leasehold property.

First of all we have the landlord and tenant, who are also known as the **lessor** and **lessee**. These terms can be used interchangeably and refer to the person who owns the freehold (or longer lease as you can create a lease out of a larger leasehold estate. We will look at this in more detail shortly) of the property (the landlord or lessor) and the person who rents or leases it (the tenant or lessee).

The agreement between landlord and tenant is referred to as either a **lease** or a **tenancy**. Again, the terms are interchangeable, except that it tends to be the case that longer leaseholds tend to be referred to as leases and shorter ones as tenancies.

The freehold (or leasehold) estate that is subject to the lease is referred to as the **reversionary estate** or simply the **reversion**. This is because the property will return, or 'revert' back to them at the end of the term of the lease, as shown in Figure 5.1, below.

Figure 5.1 Simple illustration of a lease or tenancy

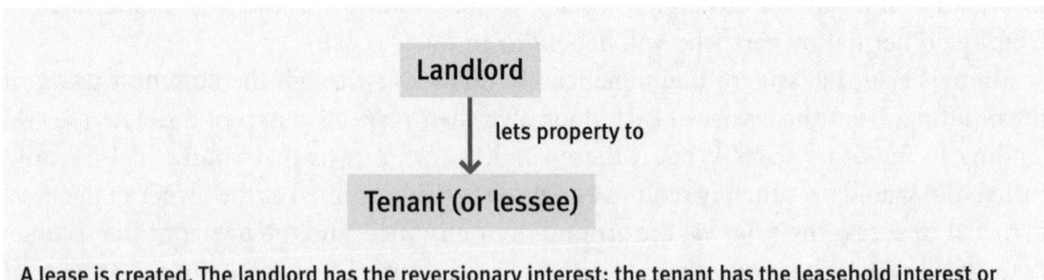

A lease is created. The landlord has the reversionary interest; the tenant has the leasehold interest or tenancy.

A lease which is granted out of leasehold property is termed a **sub-lease** or **underlease**, and the tenant of the sub- or underlease is referred to as the **sub-tenant** or **underlessee**. As shown in Figure 5.2, the owner of the freehold then becomes the **head landlord** (being the landlord of the underlessee).

Figure 5.2 Illustration of an underlease

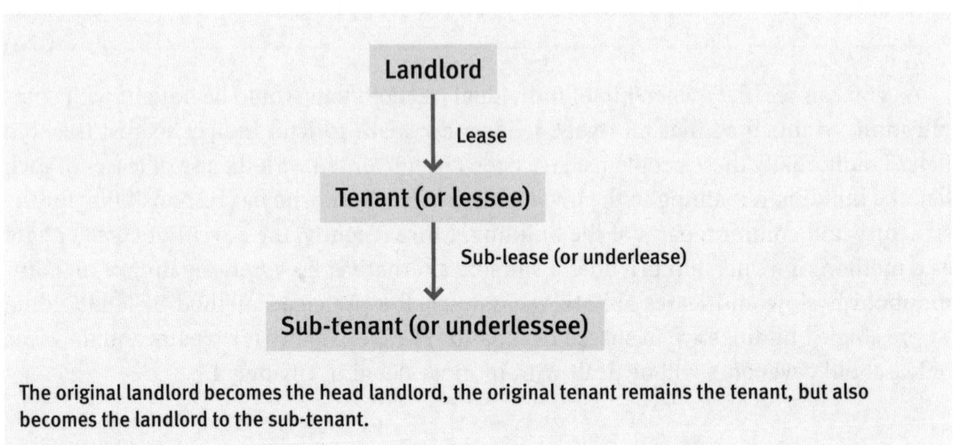

The original landlord becomes the head landlord, the original tenant remains the tenant, but also becomes the landlord to the sub-tenant.

One final piece of terminology you need to know is where a leasehold estate is sold or otherwise transferred to a third party, and this is known as an **assignment**. The original, or outgoing, tenant is termed the **assignor** and the new, or incoming, tenant is termed the **assignee**. Once the assignment, or transfer of the lease, is completed, the landlord becomes landlord to the new tenant (also known as the assignee or incoming tenant), and the original, or outgoing, tenant is no longer a party to the lease. This is illustrated in Figure 5.3.

As you can see, there is a significant amount of terminology peculiar to leases, much of which is interchangeable, and you may wish to keep referring back to this section until you a comfortable with it. Alternatively, all the terms are detailed in the glossary at the back of the text.

Figure 5.3 Illustration of an assignment

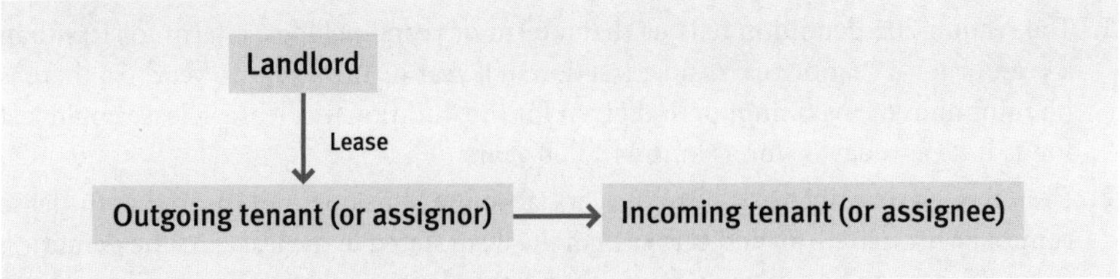

What is a lease?

Now that we are comfortable with why we need leases and the terminology of leases, let us take some time to think about what exactly constitutes a lease. From the point of view of a lay person the concept of a lease may be perfectly straightforward: a landlord rents or lets their property to a tenant in return for the payment of rent, thereby letting them reside in that property for residential or business purposes for an agreed amount of time. In broad terms this is absolutely correct. However, as students of law we have to be much more specific.

A good place to start from a legal perspective is the statutory definition of the lease, the 'term of years absolute', contained in section 205(1)(xxvii) of the Law of Property Act 1925. Here we can see that the definition states:

> (xxvii) 'Term of years absolute' means a term of years (taking effect either in possession or in reversion whether or not at a rent) with or without impeachment for waste, subject or not to another legal estate, and either certain or liable to determination by notice, re-entry, operation of law, or by a provision for cesser on redemption, or in any other event (other than the dropping of a life, or the determination of a determinable life interest); but does not include any term of years determinable with life or lives or with the cesser of a determinable life interest, nor, if created after the commencement of this Act, a term of years which is not expressed to take effect in possession within twenty-one years after the creation thereof where required by this Act to take effect within that period; and in this definition the expression 'term of years' includes a term for less than a year, or for a year or years and a fraction of a year or from year to year;

As with much of the Law of Property Act 1925, the description is nothing if not thorough. However, if we compare the definition with its counterpart definition of the freehold, it is what is missing from the definition that is immediately significant. If we look at the 'term of years absolute' we notice that, unlike the freehold (the fee simple absolute in possession) its description does not include the words '**in possession**'. A first and fundamental difference therefore between freehold and leasehold estates is that a lease can take effect in the future: it does not have to commence immediately. Thus, it is possible to grant a lease on 1 January the term of which does not start until 1 December. And, in fact, we can see from the statutory definition of the term of years that a lease can take effect in possession (that is, that it can start) at any time within 21 years from the date of its creation. To term the two types of leases correctly, we call leases which start immediately leases 'in possession', and leases which take effect at some time in the future leases '**in reversion**'.

As for what is included in the definition, in terms of the duration of a legal lease, you should note the following:

1. The section 205 definition tells us that a term of years includes 'a term for less than a year, or for a year or years and a fraction of a year or from year to year'. So there is no minimum or maximum period given for the duration of a lease: a lease could last for as little as a day or for as long as 1,000 years.
2. Even though described as a term of years 'absolute', this does not mean that the lease cannot be brought to an end earlier than the term stated in the lease. As the definition states, a lease can be subject to premature determination (that is, it can be brought to an end early) by notice, for example if there is a provision in the lease for either party to bring an end to the lease early by giving notice of this (otherwise known as a 'break clause'); by the presence of a **re-entry** or **forfeiture** clause in the lease, which allows the landlord to repossess the premises in the event of a breach (forfeiture will be discussed in more detail in Chapter 13); or for a number of other reasons, including where the tenant buys the freehold, thereby causing the leasehold and freehold titles to merge ('**merger**') and **surrender** – where the tenant enters into a formal agreement to bring the lease to an end.
3. A term of years is described as 'whether or not at a rent'. We can see, therefore, that whilst it is usual for rent to be payable to the landlord in exchange for the right to occupy the property, from a legal point of view this is not an essential component of a leasehold interest in land. We will be considering this point in a little more detail later on in the chapter.

And finally, we should look at what is specifically excluded from the definition, and this is leases determinable with a life or lives: in other words, you cannot grant a lease for the duration of somebody's lifetime. The reason for this is simple: a lifetime is not a period calculable from the date of commencement of the lease – it is not an absolute term. No one can say with certainty how long a person is going to live for. A lease for life can therefore only take effect in **equity**.

Different types of lease

There are two main types of lease or tenancy: these are commonly known as the **fixed term tenancy** and the **periodic tenancy**.

Fixed term tenancies

As its title suggests, the fixed term tenancy is a lease granted for a fixed period of time, say five years, ceasing at the end of the term granted. With a fixed term tenancy, both the landlord and the tenant know exactly when the lease is going to start and end from the outset and, once fixed, neither party has the right to bring the lease to an end earlier than the date of the fixed term, unless there is provision to do so in the lease. If such a provision does exist, it will usually be in the form either of a '**break clause**', which is a clause enabling either or both parties to end the lease either after a specified period or by giving a fixed period of notice, or by virtue of re-entry, or forfeiture, provisions on the part of the landlord. These are provisions which allow the landlord to reclaim the premises and end the lease if the tenant breaches their obligations under the terms of the lease agreement. Rights of re-entry will be discussed in more detail in Chapter 13 on leasehold covenants.

Periodic tenancies

A periodic tenancy, on the other hand, is measured not by reference to a single fixed time period, but by reference to a shorter term: usually dictated by the mode of rental payment, which is simply renewed automatically at the end of each term and which continues to run until notice to end the lease is served by either party to the agreement. Thus, a periodic tenancy might commonly be weekly, monthly, quarterly, or annually. If the rent is payable quarterly (that is, four times yearly) the rent will usually be paid on the 'usual **quarter days**'. These are traditionally stated to be Lady Day (25 March), Midsummer Day (24 June), Michaelmas Day (29 September) and Christmas Day (25 December).

Periodic tenancies can be express or implied. When implied they generally come into being by virtue of the tenant being in occupation of the premises and paying rent at regular fixed intervals. If there is an agreement but nothing in writing specifying the length of the periodic term, this will be calculated by reference to the period by which the rent is stated to be payable in the agreement. Therefore if the rent is stated to be £500 per month in the agreement, the tenancy will be a monthly periodic tenancy. However, an agreement to pay rent of £6,000 per annum (year) payable by monthly instalments, the tenancy will be an annual (yearly) periodic tenancy, and not a monthly one. This is because the rent is stated to be a yearly lump sum; how this amount is broken down and paid for practical or administrative purposes is irrelevant. Bearing this in mind, take a look at the You Be the Judge feature, below, and see if you can tell whether the tenancies detailed are periodic or fixed.

You be the judge

Q: **Say what type of tenancies are the following: (a) a landlord lets premises to a tenant for a period of three years commencing on 1 June 2013; (b) a landlord lets premises to a tenant on a six-monthly tenancy, renewable indefinitely until such time as either the landlord or tenant serves six months' notice to quit on the other; (c) a landlord lets premises to a tenant. An agreement is made to pay an annual rent of £12,000, payable on the usual quarter days; (d) a landlord allows a tenant into their premises on an informal basis. The tenant pays £200 per month to the landlord for the letting.**

A: (a) is a fixed term tenancy; (b) is an express six-month periodic tenancy; (c) is an express annual periodic tenancy; (d) is an implied monthly periodic tenancy.

Tenancies at will

You may also see reference to the term, '**tenancy at will**'. The term is a misleading one because, in fact, this is a situation in which there is actually no legal interest created in the land at all (and therefore there is no tenancy). A tenancy at will is created where the landlord allows the tenant to occupy the premises on a purely informal basis, on the understanding that either party may end the agreement at any time. A tenancy at will, therefore, is not a real tenancy; rather it is a personal agreement between the parties that creates no estate or interest in the land. A classic example of a tenancy at will arising is where a proposed tenant is allowed into possession of premises whilst the terms of the lease are still being negotiated. This was the case in *Javad* v. *Mohammed Aqil* [1991] 1 WLR 1007. Once the lease is signed, the tenancy at will falls away and the parties are left with a formal legal lease of the land.

Licences and the lease/licence distinction

Like a tenancy at will, a **licence** is a purely personal agreement between two parties to occupy land which does not create any interest in the land itself.

Whereas a lease creates an estate in the land which gives the tenant exclusive control over and possession of the property for the duration of the tenancy, a licence is simply a personal permission for the license holder, or **licensee**, to occupy the property, effectively making legal what would otherwise constitute a trespass. A licence therefore confers no **proprietary right** in the land; it is simply a personal arrangement between two parties. As such, a licence cannot be transferred to a third party (you cannot assign a licence or create a sub-licence) and a licence will not survive a sale of the freehold estate. If the landlord, or **licensor**, sells their property the licence will automatically be brought to an end. The only way the licensee could remain in the property under these circumstances is if they were to agree a new licence with the new owner of the freehold.

For these reasons alone it will always be preferable for a tenant of property to hold that property under a lease and not a licence. However, there are also significant historic reasons for landlords wanting to avoid entering into leases of property. Prior to the Housing Act 1988, which significantly reduced the rights of tenants by creating the **assured shorthold tenancy** (a short form of tenancy which confers on the tenant no rights of renewal or rent-capping), landlords were keen for tenants to enter property on the basis of a licence only and not a lease in order to prevent them from acquiring both **security of tenure** in the form of the right to renew their leases under the Rent Act 1977, and the right to cap rent at a level which could amount to a figure significantly lower than current market rental values. Landlords would often therefore allow would-be tenants into their properties under purported licence agreements, even though in reality the licensee's occupation of the property was clearly that of a tenant. For landlords of business premises the desire to create licences instead of leases still carries with it a similar benefit, in that a lease will afford a business tenant the right to renew their lease under the provisions of the Landlord and Tenant Act 1954, whereas a licensee will not benefit from the statute. These statutory provisions in respect of business premises are still current today. As a consequence there exists a whole wealth of case law discussing what constitutes a licence and when a so-called licence agreement will in actual fact amount to a lease. In order to distinguish between the two it is necessary to consider what are the essential characteristics, or ingredients, of a lease.

Essential characteristics of a lease

So, we know already that a legal lease is the right to possess land for a limited period of time, but can we define this more precisely? How do we define possession and what period of time are we talking about? The requirements for a lease of land were famously and definitively set out in 1985 in the House of Lords case of *Street* v. *Mountford* [1985] AC 809. Before we discuss the case further in the text, why not have a look at the Out and About feature, below.

Out and about

***Street* v. *Mountford* [1985] AC 809, Lord Templeman's judgment**

Find a copy of *Street* v. *Mountford* either online or in paper form at your law library and read Lord Templeman's judgment. Whilst the text below gives an outline and commentary on some of the essential features of the case, there is no substitute for reading the original and it would be well worth your time to make a point of reading the full judgment to give you a full understanding of the reasoning behind the decision made in this seminal decision.

The facts of *Street* v. *Mountford* were as follows: Roger Street let two rooms at 5 St Clements Gardens, Bournemouth to a Mrs Wendy Mountford, for a rent of £37 per week and subject to termination by either party on 14 days' written notice. The argument arose as to whether the letting amounted to a lease, in which case it would be afforded the protection of the Rent Acts, or whether it was merely a licence.

Case Summary

Despite Mrs Mountford having signed a declaration in the agreement stating that the agreement amounted to no more than a licence and not a tenancy agreement, Lord Templeman found in her favour, confirming that the letting was in fact a tenancy. In explaining his decision, Lord Templeman helpfully described a lease of land as being capable of reduction into three constituent parts: 'exclusive possession, for a term, at a rent'. As far as the agreement itself was concerned, its label as a licence was irrelevant. It was the substance of the agreement, and not the form, that mattered. In perhaps what is one of land law's most famous quotes, he said:

> If the agreement satisfied all the requirements of a tenancy, then the agreement produced a tenancy and the parties cannot alter the effect of the agreement by insisting that they only created a licence. The manufacture of a five-pronged implement for manual digging results in a fork even if the manufacturer, unfamiliar with the English language, insists that he intended to make and has made a spade.

The exact wording of the agreement is replicated in the Documenting the Law feature below.

Documenting the law

The following reproduces the wording of the agreement made between Mr Street and Mrs Mountford for the letting of 5 St Clements Gardens:

I Mrs. Wendy Mountford agree to take from the owner Roger Street the single furnished room number 5 and 6 at 5 St. Clements Gardens, Boscombe, Bournemouth, commencing 7 March 1983 at a licence fee of £37 per week.

I understand that the right to occupy the above room is conditional on the strict observance of the following rules:

1. No paraffin stoves, or other than the supplied form of heating, is allowed in the room.
2. No one but the above-named person may occupy or sleep in the room without prior permission, and this personal licence is not assignable.

3. The owner (or his agent) has the right at all times to enter the room to inspect its condition, read and collect money from meters, carry out maintenance works, install or replace furniture or for any other reasonable purpose.
4. All rooms must be kept in a clean and tidy condition.
5. All damage and breakages must be paid for or replaced at once. An initial deposit equivalent to 2 weeks' licence fee will be refunded on termination of the licence subject to deduction for all damage or other breakages or arrears of licence fee, or retention towards the cost of any necessary possession proceedings.
6. No nuisance or annoyance to be caused to the other occupiers. In particular, all music played after midnight to be kept low so as not to disturb occupiers of other rooms.
7. No children or pets allowed under any circumstances whatsoever.
8. Prompt payment of the licence fee must be made every Monday in advance without fail.
9. If the licence fee or any part of it shall be seven days in arrear or if the occupier shall be in breach of any of the other terms of this agreement or if (except by arrangement) the room is left vacant or unoccupied, the owner may re-enter the room and this licence shall then immediately be terminated (without prejudice to all other rights and remedies of the owner).
10. This licence may be terminated by 14 days' written notice given to the occupier at any time by the owner or his agent, or by the same notice by the occupier to the owner or his agent.

Occupier's signature
Owner/agent's signature
Date 7 March 1983

I understand and accept that a licence in the above form does not and is not intended to give me a tenancy protected under the Rent Acts.

Occupier's signature

Reflective practice

Take a look at the agreement in the Documenting the Law feature, above. Are there any clauses in the agreement that you think are unusual? Which elements of the agreement, if any, do you think might suggest that this could be a licence and not a lease?

Let us now turn to look at Lord Templeman's three essential elements of a lease in a little more detail.

it would be illogical to say a person could be the possessor of land without having territorial control over it

Exclusive possession

Exclusive possession can be described as the right to exclude all others from the property, and this includes the landlord. This is completely logical, of course. If you cast your mind back to Chapter 1, when we considered the meaning of estates in land, you will remember that the definition of an estate in land was that it is the right to possess property for a certain period of time. It would be illogical, nonsensical even, to say that a person could be the possessor of land without having territorial control over it; and territorial control means the ability to protect the property in your possession from others – any others – and that includes the landlord themselves. It follows then that if the landlord, or anyone else for that matter, had free rein to come onto your property at any time and without your express permission you could not be said to have exclusive possession, or the sole right to occupy it.

Imagine the following scenario, which just happens to be a true story (luckily, the case never reached the courts!). A husband and wife, let us call them Jared and Vanessa, own a shop business, which they run from premises owned by Jared's parents. Jared's parents have lived in the flat above the shop for the last thirty years, but are now moving out as they have bought another property to renovate as a retirement project. They let the flat to Jared and Vanessa. However, things soon start to go awry when it becomes apparent that her in-laws are having some difficulty in 'letting go' of the flat. Whenever they have a tea-break (they also work in the shop), they let themselves into the flat and use Vanessa's kettle to make themselves a cup of tea. They help themselves to Vanessa's teabags and milk from Vanessa's fridge. They make themselves comfortable in her sitting room whilst they drink the tea and read the newspaper. Jared's father has even been known to help himself to Vanessa's chocolate HobNobs! And the problems don't end at the close of business. The other night, Vanessa was awoken by a noise in the flat. She went to investigate and, to her great surprise, found her father-in-law using the toilet on his way home from the pub! When she challenged him about why he was doing this, he simply said 'because it was convenient'. Needless to say, Jared feels awkward about challenging his parents over the intrusions and it is causing a great deal of strain in his and Vanessa's relationship.

This is obviously quite distressing for the couple on an emotional level, but from a legal point of view, the question that needs to be asked in this situation is: do Vanessa and Jared have a lease or a licence of the flat? They certainly aren't being given exclusive possession of the property, but does their agreement with Jared's parents entitle them to this? If it does, Jared's parents are clearly in breach of their agreement as landlords and the couple have the legal right to eject them from the property, at least while the lease continues. This does not make the situation any easier for them from a personal viewpoint, of course, but this is something for Vanessa and Jared to work out. At least they know they have the force of the law behind them.

As the illustration above shows, the idea of the tenant having exclusive possession of the property for the duration of their agreement with the landlord goes to the heart of what constitutes a lease, as opposed to a mere licence of land, and is fundamental when making the distinction between the two. As a consequence there is much case law discussing the nature of exclusive possession and what will or will not be sufficient to constitute a leasehold interest.

exclusive possession goes to the heart of what constitutes a lease

Prior to *Street* v. *Mountford* there had been a tendency by the courts to look at the form of any written agreement and to accept it as written. Thus, the Court of Appeal in the case of *Somma* v. *Hazelhurst* [1978] 1 WLR 1014 was happy to accept as evidence of a licence two identical but separate agreements allowing a young unmarried couple exclusive possession of a bedsit for a weekly rent, despite the fact that they were clearly sharing the bedsit on the basis of a joint tenancy. The two agreements said that each could be terminated separately, and that in this event either of them should be prepared to share the room with any other person that the landlord should nominate; however, this was clearly a fiction, as Lord Templeman was keen to point out in his judgment in *Street* v. *Mountford*.

Case Summary

Taking a highly critical view of the decision, Lord Templeman said that the outcome in *Somma* v. *Hazelhurst* should be disapproved, together with several other cases in the same vein. In his own words:

> The sham nature of this obligation would have been only slightly more obvious if H. and S. had been married or if the room had been furnished with a double bed instead of two single beds. If the landlord had served notice on H. to leave and had required S. to share the room with a strange man, the notice would only have been a disguised notice to quit on both H. and S. The room was let and taken as residential accommodation with exclusive possession in order that H. and S. might live together in undisturbed quasi-connubial bliss making weekly payments. The agreements signed by H. and S. constituted the grant to H. and S. jointly of exclusive possession at a rent for a term for the purposes for which the room was taken and the agreement therefore created a tenancy . . . the court should, in my opinion, be astute to detect and frustrate sham devices and artificial transactions whose only object is to disguise the grant of a tenancy and to evade the Rent Acts. I would disapprove of the decision in this case that H. and S. were only licensees . . .

It is clear to see, then, that following Lord Templeman's judgment in *Street* v. *Mountford* it is the true intention of the parties that will now be sought in lease/licence distinction cases, rather than any label which is put on the parties' agreement. If there is exclusive possession, for a term, at a rent, there will be a lease, regardless of what the parties choose to call it.

Case Summary

Accordingly five years later in the case of ***Antoniades* v. *Villiers*** [1990] 1 AC 417, the House of Lords on appeal held that two purported licence agreements signed by an unmarried couple to occupy a flat had created a tenancy, despite the description of the agreements as individual licences. The facts of the case were almost identical to those of *Somma* v. *Hazelhurst*, in that the case concerned a couple, Mr Villiers and Miss Bridger, renting an attic flat in London together under separate but identical 'licence' agreements. When the couple was shown around the flat, which consisted of a single room with adjoining kitchen and bathroom, they asked if the landlord, Mr Antoniades would provide a double bed, which he agreed to do. However, as in *Somma* v. *Hazelhurst*, when it came to signing the agreements the documentation stated that the couple did not have exclusive possession of the premises and that the licensor (or landlord, as he turned out to be), or indeed anyone else of the landlord's choosing, could use the rooms along with the couple. It would have been interesting if the landlord had decided to carry out this provision, the flat only containing one double bed on which to sleep! Whilst the Court of Appeal held that the agreements created two separate licences, the House of Lords reversed this decision, Lord Oliver stating that there was 'an air of total unreality' about the documentation when read as separate and individual licences, particularly in the light of the fact that the couple were seeking a flat to live in together as a quasi-matrimonial home. Lord Oliver went on to say that the unreality of the documentation was only enhanced by the reservation of the right of eviction without court order, and by the accompanying agreement not to get married which, he said, 'can have been only designed to prevent a situation arising in which it would be quite impossible to argue that the "licensees" were enjoying separate rights of occupation'.

This does not mean that there will not be situations in which a licence will have been created genuinely, however, and there is also plenty of case law to support such situations

Case Summary

occurring. In the case of *Hadjiloucas* v. *Crean* [1988] 1 WLR 1006 two friends, Miss Crean and Miss Broderick, rented a two-bedroom ground-floor flat in North London. The two girls entered into separate licence agreements to rent the flat for a period of six months, each agreeing to pay a total rent for the flat of £260 per month, which they actually split between them. The licence agreements specifically stated that the agreements constituted a licence to share the flat with one other person and that neither one of them would have exclusive possession of the premises. The two girls lived in the flat together for around two months, when Miss Broderick left. Miss Crean asked the landlord what would happen to the room, and he said he was going to advertise it. Miss Crean said that she had a friend, Miss Rollins, who might be interested. The landlord approved of her and Miss Rollins moved in, entering into a separate licence agreement for four months' duration, ending on the same date as Miss Crean's agreement. When the licence agreements were due to end, Miss Crean asked the landlord if he would be willing to grant new licences to her and a different friend, Miss Richards. The landlord agreed, but said the rent would be increased by £10 per week. Miss Crean did not agree with this and sought that the rent be fixed in accordance with the Rent Acts. The landlord sought confirmation from the court that the licences were indeed licences and did not amount to leases. The Court of Appeal ruled that the girls held the property under licences only. In this instance the agreement was not a sham: the facts of the case clearly showed that the sharers were genuinely occupying the property as individual licensees each without exclusive possession of the whole and not as joint tenants occupying the property together.

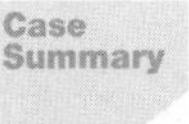

A similar decision was reached in the Court of Appeal case of *Stribling* v. *Wickham* (1989) 21 HLR 381, which concerned three flat sharers renting a three-bedroom flat under separate licence agreements, terminable on 28 days' notice. As with *Hadjiloucas* v. *Crean*, two of the three flat sharers were subsequently replaced and their licence agreements renewed several times on a six-monthly basis. When the landlord sought possession of the flat, the original tenant refused, claiming a protected tenancy under the Rent Acts. However, the court found against him. The 28-day notice period and regular replacement of tenants clearly showed that the flat was shared on the basis of three genuine and separate licence agreements and not a jointly-held lease. The agreements were not a sham and the court consequently made an order in favour of the landlord for possession of the flat.

Having been considered and followed by the Court of Appeal on two consecutive occasions, the House of Lords was finally given the opportunity to reflect on the issue in the 1990 case of ***AG Securities* v. *Vaughan*** [1988] 3 WLR 1205. The case was actually heard in conjunction with *Antoniades* v. *Villiers*, which as we have seen above had a different outcome and provides a good contrast to this matter. In *AG Securities* v. *Vaughan* there were four flat sharers, each being granted at different times and on different terms a six-month licence to occupy the flat in conjunction with three others at the landlord's discretion, and each paying different amounts for the use of their room within the flat. The House of Lords held that, again, these were four genuine and separate licences and did not together constitute a jointly shared lease of the property.

In handing down their ruling the Lords made a very helpful and valid point about the nature of **joint tenancy**. As you will see when we come to look in detail at joint ownership of property in Chapter 9, it is a well-established rule of **common law** that, for a joint tenancy to exist, the '**four unities**' must be present: these are the unities of possession, interest, title and time. The rule states that, in order to have joint ownership of property all four unities must coexist between the parties; in other words, the tenants must all be in possession of the property at the same time; the tenants must have the same rights under their agreements, paying the same rent, and so on; the tenancies must last for the same amount of time and be of the same property; and they must start and end at the same time. All these matters are essential to the nature of joint ownership. In the case of *AG Securities* v. *Vaughan* the four unities were not present. The occupation of the flat consisted of a shifting population of sharers and, as such, the Lords considered that it would be artificial to force the flat sharers' contracts into the mould of a joint tenancy.

Case Summary

One further distinguishing case on the subject of exclusive possession is that of *Aslan* v. *Murphy* [1990] 1 WLR 766. In this case the Court of Appeal considered three separate appeals which they decided in one single judgment. None of the cases dealt with the issue of shared occupancy, but each purported licence agreement contained terms which the court considered to be a pretence and therefore in each case the occupier was found to have a tenancy. The most remarkable of these was the first case, in which the occupier of a basement room was supposed to vacate the room entirely between 10.30am and 12pm each day, and have non-exclusive occupation for the rest of the time. In another case, the landlord also retained a key to the premises, purportedly in order to provide services to the tenant. However, the Court of Appeal found that, although keys had been retained, no services were actually provided, so the occupier did in fact have exclusive possession of the premises, allowing a tenancy to be established. The Court of Appeal was keen to state in giving their judgment on the three cases that it was the true bargain that was made between the parties which was relevant in determining exclusive possession; not any pretence which might appear on the face of the agreement. In other words, following in the footsteps of *Street* v. *Mountford*, it is all about substance and not form.

Case Summary

The final case in point is that of *Westminster City Council* v. *Clarke* [1992] 2 AC 288. Here the council ran a hostel for single homeless men with personality disorders or learning disabilities. The premises contained 31 rooms, each with a bed and limited cooking facilities. The premises were overseen by a warden and a team of social workers. The hostel was intended as a temporary place for the men to stay, in the hope that in time they would move on to live in permanent accommodation. Each room was occupied under a licence agreement which specified that the occupant could be required to change rooms at any time or to share it with another person. The House of Lords held that these agreements were indeed mere licences and did not grant exclusive possession nor amount to a tenancy. It is important to note here that the social workers were entitled to access the rooms at any time without notice in order to facilitate the occupants, the suggestion being that the social workers were on hand to provide psychological support, rather than simple attendant services.

The term of the lease

Going back to Lord Templeman's essential characteristics of a lease, then, you will remember that he said there must be exclusive possession, for a term, at a rent. Let us now consider the issue of the term or duration of the lease. The law here states that there must be a '**determinate term**': in other words, the term must start on a specified date and the end date must either be known at the commencement of the term or calculable at that time (in other words you can work out when it is going to end). It is for this reason that we can see in the section 205 definition of the term of years absolute that a lease for life cannot be legal, because no one can say when a person's life is going to end.

the end date must either be known or calculable

There are, of course, other examples of indeterminate terms causing a claim for a lease to fail. In the Court of Appeal case of *Lace* v. *Chantler* [1944] KB 368 a lease 'for the duration of the war' was held unable to form the basis of a legal lease because no one could say for how long the war (the Second World War, in this case) was going to continue. The lease was therefore for an indeterminate term. It should be noted that the provisions of the Validation of Wartime Leases Act 1944 actually later served to circumvent the problem arising in this particular set of circumstances, as it converted all wartime leases to a term of 10 years with a proviso that either landlord or tenant could terminate the lease once the war ended by giving a month's notice. The Act was repealed in 1976.

Another case which dealt with the issue of term is ***Prudential Assurance Co. Ltd* v. *London Residuary Body*** [1992] 3 WLR 279. The facts were that a piece of land was bought by the council and leased back to the seller on a tenancy which was stated to continue until the land was required by the council for road-widening purposes. The House of Lords held that the lease was for an uncertain period and therefore **void**. However, this case turned out to have a happy ending as the tenant was nevertheless held to have an implied yearly periodic tenancy by virtue of their possession of the land and the fact that they were paying an annual rent. Now take a look at the You Be the Judge feature, below. Which of the agreements listed do you think have a determinate term?

You be the judge

Q: Which of the following are capable of forming a valid legal lease: (a) a lease until the new moon; (b) a lease until the birth of the Duke and Duchess of Cambridge's second child; (c) a lease for the duration of the Coalition?

A: the answer is that only (a) is capable of forming a valid legal lease. We can calculate when the new moon will be, and thus when the lease will end, by looking at lunar charts. The other two, however, are not determinate terms because we cannot say definitively when, or even if, these events will ever occur.

One final recent case the outcome of which is somewhat controversial is the **Supreme Court** decision in *Berrisford* v. *Mexfield* [2011] 3 WLR 1091. The case concerned a property in Barnet, London, let in 1993 to a Mrs Berrisford by a local housing association (the Mexfield Housing Co-operative). Mrs Berrisford entered the property on the basis of an occupancy agreement which was stated to be on a monthly tenancy 'until determined as provided'. The provisions of the agreement then went on to allow Mrs Berrisford to end the agreement by one month's notice in writing; the housing association, on the other hand, were only given the right to bring the agreement to an end either if:

1. the rent was in arrears; or
2. Mrs Berrisford had breached one of the terms of the agreement; or
3. the housing association ceased to exist.

Despite this, in 2008 the housing association sought to remove Mrs Berrisford from the property by serving notice to quit on her, followed by possession proceedings. The question arose as to whether or not the agreement had created a tenancy and consequently whether the housing association had the right to do this, the suggestion being

that if the agreement was held to be a licence only the landlords would be within their rights to remove her by service of a simple notice to quit.

Effectively, looking at the terms of the agreement, the inability of the housing association to bring the tenancy to an end except in the event of tenant default meant that the agreement was for an uncertain term because, in effect, there was no provision for the agreement to be brought to an end at any particular or specifiable time. Whilst the judge at first instance and the Court of Appeal, albeit with dissent, therefore made the finding that the agreement had given rise to a licence only and granted the housing association a possession order, the Supreme Court did not agree. With Lord Neuberger leading the judgment of the Court, the Court held that the agreement, whilst void for uncertainty in law, nevertheless gave rise to a tenancy for life. The terms of the agreement did not state that the housing association had the right to bring it to an end on one month's notice; to the contrary, it stated that the association could only re-enter the premises where the occupant was in default. It would therefore be inequitable to imply into the agreement terms which were clearly never the original intention of the parties to it.

Seemingly, the implication here is that the outcome of the case enables Lord Templeman's requirement that a lease be 'for a term' certain to be overruled, or at least circumvented, wherever equity sees fit to do so. However, academic commentary would point firmly to the fact that the application of the decision was intended only to apply to the provision of social housing and not in wider circumstances (see Pawlowski, M., 'Uncertainty of term – orthodoxy side-stepped in favour of a just result' and Hunter, C. and Cowan, D., 'The future of housing co-operatives: Mexfield and beyond', the full citations for which are given at the end of the chapter). Nevertheless, the outcome contradicts the general view of the law in this area, particularly in the light of the recent call for a reform of the law limiting the security of tenure in respect of housing provided by housing associations and co-operatives (as seen in MP Jonathan Reynolds's Co-operative Housing (Tenure) Bill, published in October 2011). A more detailed discussion of the law as it relates to social housing is beyond the scope of this text. Whether there will be further ruling on this topic and how it might impact on the more general law remains to be seen.

The requirement for rent

As we have seen in the Law of Property Act 1925 definition above, technically rent is not a formal requirement of a valid legal lease (you will remember that section 205 states that a lease is a term of years 'whether or not at a rent'); however, it does help from an evidential viewpoint to prove the existence of a formal interest in land where this is present. As we shall see later on in the chapter, the payment of rent at the current market value on the property is a even made a prerequisite for the creation of a short legal lease of three years or less, if that lease is to be created in some way other than by deed (under section 54(2) LPA 1925). This point will be dealt with in more detail in the section on formalities in leases.

Case Summary

It is worth noting here the Court of Appeal case of *Ashburn Anstalt* v. *Arnold* [1988] 23 EG 128, which confirmed that although Lord Templeman had described the essential characteristics of a lease as being 'exclusive possession, for a term, at a rent', this did not preclude a lease under the terms of which no rent was payable from being valid. The case itself concerned an agreement following the sale of shop premises in which the seller was allowed to remain in the premises for a further six months rent-free under a licence agreement. The Court of Appeal held that the seller had a lease and was therefore entitled to remain in the premises.

Street v. *Mountford* and business tenancies

One additional point to remember about the requirements of *Street* v. *Mountford* is that, although the majority of cases considered above relate to occupiers of residential flats, *Street* v. *Mountford* has also been held by the courts to apply to business tenancies. A case in point is that of *Dresden Estates* v. *Collinson* [1987] 1 EGLR 45, although in this particular case the court made the finding that the agreement in question was in fact a licence, and not a lease. The case concerned a licence to occupy a workshop and store on an industrial park in Stoke-on-Trent. The agreement allowed for the owner of the workshop to require the occupier to move to a different unit within the park at the owner's request; it also allowed for the licence fee to be increased by the owner, subject to notice being given of the increase. The Court of Appeal held that the terms were inconsistent with giving exclusive possession and that therefore the agreement was effective only to create a licence.

Case Summary

Situations in which there can only be a licence

We have already established that if the tenant does not have exclusive possession of the premises, or that if the term of the lease is indeterminate, there can be only a licence over the land in question. However, there are also a number of situations in which no tenancy will be created, despite the preconditions of exclusive possession and a determinate term being met.

The landlord must have authority to grant the lease

The first of these, which is given only brief mention in *Street* v. *Mountford* but which is a vital prerequisite of any lease, is that the landlord must have been in a position to let the property in the first place. In other words, they must have had the legal authority to rent the premises out and also that they must have sufficient interest in the premises in the first place to let them. A couple of examples will make this clear. Take the owner of a freehold first of all. Their landholding is unrestricted and for an indefinite period of time, thus enabling them to let the property for any term they wish, and without restriction. But what if the prospective landlord was the owner of leasehold land? The lease would be limited to a certain duration, meaning that the landlord could not grant a lease out of their landholding longer than they had themselves. So the owner of a 10-year lease could not grant out of their landholding an 11-year tenancy. Equally, there may be covenants (or promises) in the lease not to sublet the premises, or not to sublet without the consent of the landlord. In these circumstances to create a tenancy either without their landlord's consent, or even at all, would preclude a lease from being created.

the owner of a 10-year lease could not grant an 11-year tenancy

Case Summary

An example of this in practice is the Court of Appeal case of *Gray* v. *Taylor* [1998] 1 WLR 1093, in which it was held that a charitable trust which owned almshouses in Peterborough were unable to grant tenancies of them on the basis that this could run contrary to the purpose of the **trust**. A pensioner, Dorothy Taylor, was permitted to occupy a flat in one of the almshouses owned by a charitable trust, paying a weekly sum towards the upkeep of the properties. However, the trustees later sought to terminate Dorothy's occupation on the basis of her vexatious conduct towards other occupants of the almshouses. Mrs Taylor claimed that she had been granted exclusive possession of the flat for a term at a rent, and therefore she was a tenant whose occupation could only be terminated by court order. However, the Court of Appeal held that she occupied the almshouse as a personal privilege in her capacity as a **beneficiary** under the trust and therefore the legal relationship between the parties could be seen as no more than a licence. The **trustees**' power to grant Mrs Taylor a right to occupy the flat did not extend to allowing them to grant a tenancy which could run contrary to the purpose of the trust by allowing her to continue to occupy the flat after she no longer qualified as a beneficiary under the terms of the trust.

Case Navigator

Case Summary

One rather odd case which seems on the face of it to contradict the premise that a landlord cannot create a tenancy out of a lesser right to the land is the much-criticised House of Lords ruling in ***Bruton* v. *London & Quadrant Housing Trust*** [2000] 1 AC 406. In this case, the Trust did not have the authority to lease the property to its tenants, as it held the property on licences from the local authority in the first place. However, the House of Lords nevertheless ruled that there was a tenancy and therefore that the Trust had a statutory responsibility to carry out repairs to the residential premises. The House of Lords explained this by stating that what had been created was a non-proprietary tenancy, or a purely contractual lease, if you will, that existed as a tenancy because of its conformity with the requirements of *Street* v. *Mountford*, but which was limited to the occupation of the current owner and which lacked all other proprietary rights due to the limited rights of the Trust that granted it. It is suggested that the non-proprietary lease is an anomaly brought about by the House of Lords' desire to fit the law to a unique situation under which the Trust would have been, in any other circumstance, forced to comply with a statutory obligation to repair the accommodation. There is a lot of commentary on this ruling but, for a relatively recent and comprehensive explanation of the decision and its implications, see Michael Lower's 'The Bruton Tenancy', at Conv 2010, 1, 38–56.

The Facchini categories

Case Summary

The other situation or set of situations in which exclusive possession, for a term, at a rent, will fail to create a tenancy, are what is known as the 'Facchini categories', taking their name from the case of *Facchini* v. *Bryson* [1952] 1 TLR 1386, in which the categories were established. According to the case, which was cited and approved by Lord Templeman in his judgment in *Street* v. *Mountford*, and which concerned the occupation of a house by a former employee, there are three categories of occupation in which no tenancy can be created, regardless of the overall nature of the letting. These are:

1. where there is no intention to create legal relations
2. service occupancies
3. lodgers

No intention to create legal relations

Where there is no intention to create a legal relationship between the parties, there will be no tenancy created, regardless of whether the *Street* v. *Mountford* criteria for the existence of a lease are met. Such situations include where there is a family relationship between the parties, the landlord allowing a person into occupation of premises as an act of friendship or generosity, and other personal relationships (thus excluding business relationships) where the circumstances of the case are such that there is clearly no intention to create a tenancy. A good example of such a situation occurring is the wartime case of *Booker* v. *Palmer* [1942] 2 All ER 674, in which the owner of a cottage allowed his friend to install an evacuee there during the Second World War. The evacuee subsequently tried to claim the benefit of a tenancy, but the court held that they were occupying the cottage under a licence and not a tenancy, because there had been no intention to create legal relations. The occupation of the property was simply down to an act of generosity or charity on the part of the landowner.

Case Summary

Another case involving an act of generosity is the Court of Appeal case of *Heslop* v. *Burns* [1974] 1 WLR 1241. Here a man and wife were given a house to live in free of rent. The owner of the house had employed the wife for a short time and felt sorry for her and her husband's circumstances. The man visited the couple at the house every day and frequently took meals with them. When the man died the couple sought to claim the benefit of a tenancy of the house. The Court held that under the circumstances it was impossible to infer any intention to create a tenancy. The owner of the cottage had clearly intended to be the couple's benefactor and they therefore held it under licence only.

In the above situations it is not difficult to see why the court ruled against the creation of a tenancy. In cases where there is a family relationship the intention of the parties can be more difficult to ascertain, however, and care should be taken to look at the nature of the agreement made between them. Remember that it is the facts of the case that will determine whether an intention to create legal relations existed between family members; the fact of their being family alone will not be sufficient to prevent a relationship of landlord and tenant being created. A case in point is that of *Nunn* v. *Dalrymple* (1989) 21 HLR 569. Here a couple, Mr and Mrs Dalrymple, took up occupation of a farm building belonging to their son-in-law's father, which they intended to renovate. The couple gave up their council house in order to do this. Once the renovations were complete, the Dalrymples moved into the building and began paying a weekly rent of £10. Over a period of years the rent gradually increased until in 1987 it had reached the sum of £100 per month. In the same year the owner of the building sold it to a third party, who began possession proceedings against the Dalrymples. The court at first instance ordered possession, but the Court of Appeal overturned the decision, stating that the couple had exclusive possession of the premises and paid rent on a regular basis, thus creating an implied periodic tenancy. The finding of a family relationship between the parties was not conclusive as to their intention to create legal relations.

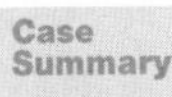

Service occupancies

Where a person occupying property is required to do so in order to perform their duties as an employee, this will be classed as a **service occupancy** and no tenancy will be created. This is the case even where the employee pays rent in accordance with the terms of their employment. An example of what might be categorised as a service occupancy includes a live-in nanny or nurse, a caretaker, gardener and so on. One such example of a service occupancy is the Court of Appeal case of *Norris* v. *Checksfield* [1991] 1 WLR 1241. In this case, a coach driver was granted a licence by his employer to live in a bungalow near to where he worked 'for the better performance of his duties'. The sum of £5 per week was deducted from his wages for his occupation of the bungalow. However, he was later dismissed when his employer found out he was a disqualified driver. The employer then sought possession of the bungalow. The court held that the licence was determinable without notice when the employee ceased to work for his employer. A court order was not necessary to evict him.

What is important to remember here is that in order for the occupation to constitute a licence only, the occupation must be necessary in order for the employee to better perform their duties for their employer. Therefore, if the occupation is merely incidental to their employment, or a reward, or for the employee's own personal convenience, it can still be viewed as a tenancy. This is illustrated in the case of *Royal Philanthropic Society* v. *County* (1985) 18 HLR 83. Mr County was employed as a house master at a school in the London borough of Wandsworth. Whilst he remained single he lodged at the school in a room adjoining a dormitory in the boarding house. However, when he decided to get married he asked the society about the possibility of a school house being provided, whereupon the school agreed to let him a house two miles from the school on a yearly tenancy. When Mr County ceased to work for the school he was asked to vacate the house, but he refused to do so, claiming the benefit of a tenancy over the property. The court at first instance dismissed his claim, but this ruling was overturned by the Court of Appeal, who said that there was no reason to construe Mr County's occupation of the house as a service tenancy The difference between the former accommodation occupied by Mr County and the latter was marked: the room in which he had lodged as a single man had been provided with furniture, linen, light, heat, laundry and cooking facilities. However, the house which he subsequently let on a yearly tenancy was granted with exclusive possession in exchange for rent with no attendant services. Therefore, as Mr County's occupation complied with the requirements of Lord Templeman in *Street* v. *Mountford*, he clearly held a lease and not a licence.

Lodgers

The third type of agreement that will not amount to a tenancy is where a property owner takes in a lodger. A lodger can generally be described as a person who resides in the home of the landlord as a paying guest. The lodger will have a room of their own, but the landlord will retain unrestricted access to that room in order to provide attendant services such as cleaning the room and making or changing the bed linen, and to provide the lodger with meals at mealtimes. In such circumstances the landlord obviously does not grant exclusive possession of the premises and thus the lodger remains a licensee, not a tenant. An example of one such case is that of *Marchant* v. *Charters* [1977] 1 WLR 1181, in which a bedsit was occupied on terms that the landlord cleaned the room daily and provided clean linen once a week. The Court of Appeal held that this was a licence, and not a tenancy. A second case in point is the Court of Appeal case of *Markou* v. *Da Silvasesa* (1986) 18 HLR 265, in which an agreement provided for services to be provided including a housekeeper, the provision of a telephone, the collection of rubbish and the provision and laundering of bed linen. Again the Court held that this was a licence only and that the occupier was a lodger. In making his

judgment in the case, Lord Justice Gibson commented on the meaning of unrestricted access, saying:

> I take the meaning of the word 'unrestricted' in this context to be primarily concerned with the landlord's need to go into and out of the lodger's rooms at the convenience of the landlord and without the lodger being there to let the landlord in.

It should be noted, however, that if the landlord is contracted to provide services on the tenant, but these can be fulfilled without the landlord having to enter onto the premises, or if they can be carried out subject to the landlord entering the premises on a restricted basis only, there may still be a tenancy. Equally, as we have seen in *Aslan* v. *Murphy* above, if the attendant services are actually never provided and the provision is simply a 'sham' in the agreement, then subject to the *Street* v. *Mountford* criteria being met the agreement will be held to be a lease. It is important to remember that the provision of services was a ploy often used by landlords wanting to construe an agreement as a licence and not a lease in order to avoid the Rent Acts. However as we have seen above, following *Street* v. *Mountford*, it was made clear that it is the nature of the actual relationship that exists between the parties, and not the labelling of that agreement, that will determine whether it is a licence or a tenancy.

Formalities for the creation or transfer of a lease

You should now have a good idea of what are the essential characteristics of a lease. However, this is not the end of the matter: having established whether or not a particular agreement is capable of forming the subject matter of a lease, we then need to look at whether the relevant **formalities** have been followed in order to create it. This is particularly important as complying with the correct formalities will determine whether the lease created is legal, or equitable, or even whether a lease has been successfully created at all.

Legal leases

As we know from our study of formalities in Chapter 2, in order to create or transfer a legal estate or interest in land we need a **deed**. And this is according to section 52 of the Law of Property Act 1925. So, in order to create a legal lease, which is a legal estate in land, we need a valid deed. The requirements for a valid deed, as we have also seen in Chapter 2, are that we have a written document that is:

- ✦ clear on the face of it that it is intended to be a deed;
- ✦ signed;
- ✦ witnessed; and
- ✦ delivered.

And you will remember that these requirements are set out in section 1 of the Law of Property (Miscellaneous Provisions) Act 1989. For a more detailed reminder of the provisions you should refer back to the earlier chapter.

So the general rule is that, in order to create a legal lease, we have to have a deed. As with most legal rules there is an exception, of course, and this is detailed at section 54(2) of the 1925 Act. Section 54(2) states that leases of three years or under do not require writing in order to be valid. Thus, a lease of three years or less can be created with no formality at all – even orally. There are a couple of provisos to this rule, which we should deal with here:

- The first is that the lease must take place 'in possession'; in other words it must start straightaway. Therefore a lease entered into on 1 January, the term of which does not commence until 1 December, must be created by deed in order to be a valid legal lease, regardless of the length of its term.
- The second proviso is that the lease must be 'at the best rent which can reasonably be obtained without taking a **fine**'. This means essentially that the lease must be at a market rent, and that no **premium** or fine is charged for it. A premium or fine in this context refers to the payment to the landlord of a one-off fee, or purchase price, for taking the lease. Such payments are commonly seen in commercial property transactions, where the tenant might pay a premium for taking a lease in a prime retail location (in a prime location on the high street, for example), or in residential leases where the lease is very long, say 99 years, and the rent is minimal. In such cases a person buying the lease from an existing tenant is likely to pay a premium for the lease, in the same way as a purchase price is offered for freehold property.

This seems straightforward; but what about periodic tenancies? Where do they fit in? Whilst the periodic term is likely to be for a period of less than three years it can, in theory, extend indefinitely by virtue of the periodic term being renewed at the end of each period. Take a look at the You Be the Judge feature below and judge for yourself.

You be the judge

Q: **Does a legal periodic tenancy require a deed for its creation?**

A: No. Under section 54(2) of the LPA 1925, a periodic tenancy is considered to be a term of three years or under, regardless of how long it has continued to be renewed for. Thus a periodic tenancy can be created without the need for writing.

The authority for the answer in the You Be the Judge feature, above is the case of *Hammond* v. *Farrow* [1904] 2 KB 332, which concerned a dispute as to whether the tenant was liable for the payment of rates. In giving his judgment in the case, Mr Justice Wills affirmed the position that, 'it has always been considered, so far as I know, that a lease from year to year is a lease for a term not exceeding three years, and can, therefore, be created by parol' (parol meaning orally).

Failure to create a legal lease

If a landlord fails to create a lease by deed and it does not fall within the section 54(2) exception, the position is different at law and in equity. In the eyes of the common law, if the landlord fails to comply with section 52 and there is no deed, but the tenant enters into possession of the premises and pays rent on a regular basis, thereby creating a renewable rental period, an implied legal periodic tenancy will be created (for a reminder on periodic tenancies see the section on types of leases, above).

In the eyes of equity, however, failure to grant a valid legal lease will be seen as a contract to create one, on the basis of the **equitable maxim** (that is a rule or guideline followed by the courts of equity) that, 'equity looks upon that as done which ought to be done'. Thus, failure to grant a valid legal lease may result in the creation of an equitable one.

Equitable leases

The application of the equitable maxim to the issue of imperfectly created leases was confirmed in the case of ***Walsh* v. *Lonsdale*** (1882) 21 Ch D 9, in which it was stated that 'an agreement for a lease is as good as a lease'. In other words, in the eyes of equity in this situation a lease has already been granted. The facts of the case were as follows: a landlord attempted to create a 7-year lease of a spinning mill. An agreement was made between the parties that the tenant would pay the rent on the mill yearly in advance; however, the lease was never formalised and the tenant was let into possession of the premises and paid six-monthly in arrears for a period of 18 months. The landlord then tried to claim a year's rent in advance and, when it was not forthcoming, took steps to levy **distress** on the property (this means that the landlord seized goods belonging to the tenant to the value of the amount outstanding on the rent). The tenant tried to claim that the landlord could not levy distress because this was a legal remedy and there was no valid legal lease. However, the court held that, as the remedy of distress would have been legal had the lease been effectively granted, and because equity 'looked upon as done that which ought to be done', the landlord's actions were lawful in equity.

The rule is not without its limitations, however. It is not the case that any failure to create a valid legal lease will automatically create an equitable one. The court is still quite strict about compliance with legal formality, the outcome being that if a failure to grant a valid lease is seen as a contract to create one, that contract must have been created in accordance with the requirements for a valid lease for the disposition of land under section 2 of the Law of Property (Miscellaneous Provisions) Act 1989. You may remember from your consideration of the formation of contracts for the sale of land in Chapter 3 that this means there must be created a document that is:

- ✦ in writing;
- ✦ contains all the terms as agreed between the parties; and
- ✦ is signed by both parties to the agreement.

Thus, if a deed is not properly witnessed, but has been signed by both parties, it will form a valid equitable lease. However, if the deed has only been signed by the landlord or tenant individually, it will not be capable of forming either a valid legal or equitable lease. In this situation, then, the only option left to the tenant is to claim the benefit of an implied periodic tenancy at common law.

Legal tenancy or equitable lease?

If a failure to create a valid legal lease can create either an implied periodic tenancy or an equitable lease, which takes precedence over the other, or is it for the parties to choose? In *Walsh* v. *Lonsdale* the court confirmed that, following another equitable maxim which states that, 'in the event of conflict between law and equity, equity shall prevail', the equitable lease should take precedence over the common law periodic tenancy. Thus, the tenant gained the benefit of an equitable 7-year lease, as opposed to a six-monthly periodic tenancy. The practical advantages of this are immediately obvious: the tenant is in a far more secure position knowing that they can remain in the premises for the full 7 years, on terms mirroring that of the original legal lease they intended to enter into, as opposed to an implied legal tenancy renewable on a six-monthly basis, which the landlord could end at any time on giving six months' notice for the tenant to quit the premises.

However, despite the claim in *Walsh* v. *Lonsdale* that 'a contract for a lease is as good as a lease' there are a number of less obvious disadvantages to claiming the benefit of an equitable lease, rather than a legal one. These are as follows:

- *Specific performance*: The doctrine in *Walsh* v. *Lonsdale* relies on the lease being capable of **specific performance**. This is the equitable remedy whereby the court can require the parties, in this instance, to comply with the terms of the lease. However, the remedy of specific performance is equitable and at the discretion of the court. This means that if the tenant is in breach of one of the terms of the lease, for example not paying the rent, this remedy may be unavailable to them. If the lease was legal, the courts would be bound to enforce the terms of the lease, regardless of any fault on the part of the tenant.
- *Third party enforceability*: Depending on whether the **title** to the freehold is registered at the **Land Registry** or remains **unregistered**, an equitable lease may not be as easily enforceable against a new landlord, should the freehold of the property be sold, as a legal lease would be. You should refer back to the relevant sections of the previous chapter for a reminder of the relevant provisions; however, in short: in unregistered land the **doctrine of notice** applies to legal leases only and not equitable ones; and in **registered land** if the tenant is not in occupation of the premises (and thereby able to benefit from an **overriding interest** in actual occupation under Schedule 3, paragraph 2 LRA 2002), the equitable lease will take effect only as a **minor interest** and will require registration on the **Charges Register** in order to be protected.
- *The creation of an equitable lease is not a 'conveyance'*: A contract for a lease is not a '**conveyance**' under the wording of section 62 of the Law of Property Act 1925 and will therefore not carry with it the benefit of rights listed in that section, including the benefit of easements acquired under section 62 (for further discussion of the mechanism of section 62 see Chapter 10 on easements).
- *Enforceability of leasehold covenants*: In leases granted prior to 1 January 1996, the benefit of covenants (that is, promises) made by either the landlord or the tenant in an equitable lease will not pass on to third parties. This means effectively that the landlord will not be able to sue an incoming tenant on assignment for breaches of their covenants in the lease. We will be considering the transmission of leasehold covenants in more detail in Chapter 13.

Registration requirements

Once the lease has been successfully created, in order to protect the lease against a third party purchaser of the landlord's estate, it may be necessary to register it at the Land Registry. The position differs depending on whether or not the landlord's title to the property is registered, and we shall look at each scenario in turn.

Registered land

You may remember from your reading of Chapter 4 on interests in land that the grant of a new lease of more than seven years' duration or the assignment of a lease with still more than seven years left to run on it are **registrable interests or dispositions** under section 27 of the Land Registration Act 2002. This means it is compulsory to register your interest as a tenant against the landlord's title to the property. If you do not do this, your interest will not be protected against a third-party purchaser of the landlord's estate in the land.

Leases of seven years or less, on the other hand, are overriding interests by virtue of Schedule 3, Paragraph 1 of the LRA 2002, meaning that they will be enforceable as against a purchaser of the landlord's title to the property, even though they do not appear on the register of title.

In the case of leases of three years or less which fall within the section 54(2) LPA 1925 exclusion, in fact it is not possible to register such interests at the Land Registry even if you wanted to (and this does not matter because they are overriding). As for everything in between, that is leases of over three years' duration and no more than seven years' duration, or leases which otherwise do not fall within the section 54(2) exclusion, these are classed as minor interests and should be registered in the Charges Register of the landlord as such. If leases which fall into this category are not registered as minor interests, it does not matter, however, because they are overriding under Schedule 3, Paragraph 1 in any event.

And finally, as for equitable leases, they should be protected as a minor interest by the entry of a **notice** in the Charges Register of the landlord's title under section 32 of the Land Registration Act 2002. If a tenant of an equitable lease fails to do this, then according to section 29 of the 2002 Act their interest will not be protected against a purchaser of the landlord's estate, unless the tenant is in occupation of the property and can establish the existence of an overriding interest in actual occupation under Schedule 3, Paragraph 2 of the Land Registration Act 2002. Table 5.1 summarises the position in registered land.

Table 5.1 Protection of leases in registered land

New leases of over 7 years' duration	Registrable dispositions and so must be registered (s.27 LRA 2002).
Assignments of leases with over 7 years left to run	Registrable dispositions and so must be registered (s.27 LRA 2002).
Leases of between 3 and 7 years' duration	Minor interests (capable of registration on Charges Register), but also overriding, so no registration actually required (sched.3 para.1 LRA 2002).
Leases of 3 years or less	Cannot be registered (s.33 LRA 2002), but overriding.
Equitable leases	Minor interests (capable of registration on Charges Register), capable of being overriding interests if the tenant is in actual occupation of the premises (sched.3 para.2 LRA 2002).

Unregistered land

You will remember that in unregistered land the default position is that 'legal rights bind the whole world'. Any purchaser of the landlord's estate will therefore be subject to any legal leases existing over the property, regardless of how long the lease is for. However, it should be noted that:

1. The grant of a new lease of over seven years or the assignment of a legal lease with over seven years left to run is a registrable disposition and as such will require compulsory first registration of the landlord's title under the Land Registration Act 2002. Therefore any leases of longer duration will become registered in any event.
2. Legal leases with a duration of seven years or less are overriding and, as such, will bind a purchaser of unregistered land even though they do not appear on any register, and this will remain the case even if the landlord subsequently sells their title to the property (thereby triggering compulsory registration).

For a reminder of how compulsory registration works take another look at the relevant section in Chapter 3.

Termination of leases

Having dealt with the creation of leases, the last thing to deal with in this chapter is how to bring a lease to an end. There are various methods of doing this, which can be summarised as follows:

Effluxion of time

At common law this is the usual way for fixed term leases to come to an end. The lease runs for the length of its fixed duration and then ends automatically at the end of this time. On the expiry of the lease, the tenant moves out of the premises and the landlord gets their property back. There are certain circumstances where statute may intervene to allow the tenant to remain in the premises at the end of the fixed term, however. These are under the Rent Act 1977 and Housing Acts 1985 and 1988, which may under certain limited circumstances give the tenant 'security of tenure', meaning that they have the right to stay on in the property after the end of the original term; and under the Landlord and Tenant Act 1954, Part II, which states that business tenants may have the right to renew their leases at the end of the term. Further discussion of the law relating to security of tenure is outside the scope of this book.

Notice to quit

This is the way in which a periodic tenancy is brought to an end – by the service of a notice by either party stating that they wish to bring an end to the tenancy within a specified time period. Usually the period of notice will equate to the period by which the periodic tenancy is measured, so a weekly tenancy would require a week's notice; a monthly periodic tenancy would require a month's notice, and so on. For an annual tenancy, a concession is given, however, so that either party only has to give six months' **notice to quit**, the notice ending on the anniversary of the commencement of the tenancy.

One further provision which needs to be mentioned in respect of notices to quit is that of the Protection from Eviction Act 1977, which states that a notice to quit in relation to a dwelling house must be for a minimum of four weeks, and that it must be in writing and contain prescribed information informing the tenant of their rights, for example to security of tenure under the terms of the Act. An example of a notice to quit is contained in the Documenting the Law feature, below.

Documenting the law

NOTICE TO QUIT A DWELLING

To:

Of:

I/We [as] [on behalf of] your [landlord(s)] [licensor(s)] named in the Schedule below HEREBY GIVE YOU NOTICE TO QUIT AND DELIVER UP POSSESSION to [me/us] [your] [landlord(s)] [licensor(s)] of the premises described in the Schedule below and which you hold of [me/us] [your] [landlord(s)] [licensor(s)] as [tenant(s)] [licensee(s)] on ....20.... or at the end of the period of your [tenancy] [licence] which will end next after the expiration of four weeks from the service upon you of this notice.

Your attention is drawn to the information set out in the Schedule below and headed 'Prescribed Information'.

Dated ....

Signed* ....

*If notice is given by an agent for the landlord, the agent's name and address and capacity (e.g. 'landlord's solicitor') should also be given.

SCHEDULE

The Premises:

Name and address of your [landlord(s)] [licensor(s)]:

Prescribed Information

1. If the tenant or licensee does not leave the dwelling, the landlord or licensor must get an order for possession from the court before the tenant or licensee can lawfully be evicted. The landlord or licensor cannot apply for such an order before the notice to quit or notice to determine has run out.
2. A tenant or licensee who does not know if he has any right to remain in possession after a notice to quit or a notice to determine runs out can obtain advice from a solicitor. Help with all or part of the cost of legal advice and assistance may be available under the Legal Aid Scheme. He should also be able to obtain information from a Citizens' Advice Bureau, a Housing Aid Centre or a rent officer.

Surrender

Surrender is where the tenant gives up their lease of the property, returning possession to the landlord with the landlord's consent. So it is, in effect, a method of bringing the lease to an end before its official expiry date, by mutual agreement.

Merger

This is where the tenant buys the landlord's interest in the property, thus becoming their own landlord. Obviously you cannot be your own landlord and so the lease will cease to exist.

Break clauses

As we have seen previously, a break clause is a provision in a lease allowing either party to the lease to serve notice on the other at specified points during the lease and thereby bring the lease to an end before the end of the term. For example, a ten-year lease might have a break clause in it allowing either party to bring the lease to an end at the midway point, after five years of the term has elapsed.

Forfeiture

As you may remember from the previous chapter, forfeiture is the right of the landlord to re-enter and thereby reclaim possession of the premises when the tenant has breached one or more of their covenants within the lease. Also known as the **right of re-entry**, forfeiture is one of the five legal interests in land specified under section 1(2) of the Law of Property Act 1925. The right to forfeit is not automatic, but depends on a specific provision being placed in the lease giving the landlord the right to forfeit under specified circumstances. The rules of forfeiture are quite precise, differing dependent on the type of breach committed by the tenant. We will be considering the rules of forfeiture in more detail in Chapter 13, when we look at the remedies available to the landlord in the event of a breach of a tenant covenant.

Summary

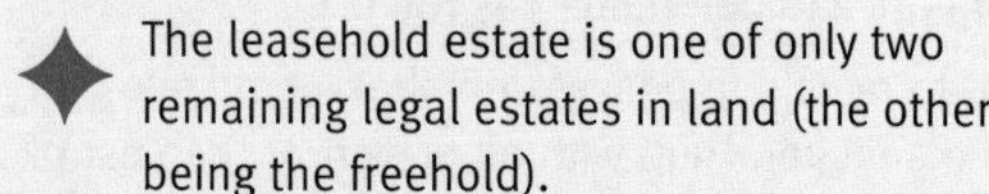

- The leasehold estate is one of only two remaining legal estates in land (the other being the freehold).
- Leases are subordinate to freeholds but equally important: leases are necessary for a number of important economic and practical reasons.

- Unlike freehold property, leases can take effect in possession or in reversion (s.205 LPA 1925).

- There is no minimum or maximum duration of a lease, save that the term should be less than that owned by the landlord.
- Leases can either exist as a fixed term or periodic tenancy. Periodic tenancies can be express or implied.
- Whereas a lease creates a proprietary interest in land, a licence is simply a personal agreement between two parties, which is incapable of transfer to third parties.
- According to the case of *Street* v. *Mountford*, in order to have a lease, you must have exclusive possession, for a term, at a rent.
- Exclusive possession means territorial control over the property. If the tenant is unable to exclude anyone from the property, including the landlord, they cannot therefore have a valid lease.
- When considering whether exclusive possession has been granted by the landlord, the courts will look to the substance, not the form of the agreement (i.e. what is the genuine position of the parties as opposed to what it says on the paperwork). The court will not give credence to 'sham' agreements (*Somma* v. *Hazlehurst*; *Antoniades* v. *Villiers*).
- Equally, a shifting population of flat sharers will not constitute a joint tenancy and can only amount to a series of separate licences (*AG Securities* v. *Vaughan*).
- If the landlord retains keys to provide services, there can be no exclusive possession, assuming those services are genuinely provided (contrast *Aslan* v. *Murphy*; *Westminster City Council* v. *Clarke*).
- The term of the tenancy must be determinate: in other words it must have a definite start and end date. The end date can be specified in the lease, or calculable from the date of its commencement (*Lace* v. *Chantler*).
- Rent is not actually a legal statutory requirement of the term of years absolute (see s.205 LPA 1925), but is helpful in the establishing of a lease from an evidential viewpoint (*Ashburn Anstalt* v. *Arnold*). It is also a necessary requirement for short leases created informally under section 54(2) LPA 1925.
- In order for a lease to be created, the landlord must have the authority to create one in the first place (see *Gray* v. *Taylor*; but note the anomalous decision of *Bruton* v. *London Quadrant Housing Trust*).
- If any of the Facchini categories apply, no tenancy will be created, even if *Street* v. *Mountford* is complied with. The Facchini categories are: no intention to create legal relations (including acts of generosity or charity), service occupancies and lodgers.
- Legal leases must be created by deed (s.52 LPA 1925), unless they are for three years or less, start immediately, and are charged at market rent without a premium or fine (s.54(2) LPA 1925).
- If a lease fails to be created by deed, it can either take effect as an implied periodic tenancy, or as an equitable lease under the rule in *Walsh* v. *Lonsdale*. In order to take effect as an equitable lease, it must comply with the requirements for a valid contract for a disposition of land under s.2 LP(MP)A 1989.
- Leases of over seven years' duration must be registered at the Land Registry in order to be protected against a third party purchaser of the landlord's estate. Leases of seven years or less are overriding, and therefore do not require registration.
- Equitable leases should be protected by entry of a notice on the Charges Register. Failing this, they can take effect as overriding interests in actual occupation, provided that the requirements of Sched.3 para.2 LRA 2002 are met.

Question and answer*

Problem: Last year, Kayla inherited a large country house and grounds, 'Pinewood', from an elderly relative. She could not afford to run the house by herself and, in fact, it was far too large for her to live in alone, so she decided to convert it into flats. She created three flats, one in the basement and two further flats on the ground and first floors.

The flat on the first floor of the building, Kayla has kept for her own use. Kayla has advertised the ground floor flat for sale in the local paper as 'a one-bedroom flat for two to share'. A young couple, Josh and Levi, responded to the advert and Kayla agreed to rent the flat to them. They required the flat to be furnished and specifically requested a double bed to be provided, as opposed to two singles.

Josh and Levi signed two separate but identical six-monthly 'occupancy agreements' which stated, amongst other things, that Kalya or anyone working for her could enter the flat at any time and that, if one of the occupants moved out, Kayla could find a substitute sharer to replace them. The couple each assumed individual responsibility to pay half of the rent.

Unfortunately the relationship between Josh and Levi has soured. It transpires that Levi has fallen in love with an Art and Design student called Adrian, and last week they eloped to the South of France together. Josh has offered to make up Levi's half of the rent to prevent Kayla from taking on another tenant in Levi's place. Advise Kayla as to the nature of the arrangement.

You should take no more than 40 minutes on this question.

Problem: Kayla has also allowed her long-time friend and gardener, Boris, who is landscaping the gardens at Pinewood, to live in the basement flat 'as a perk of the job'. This was following his recent marriage break-up, which Kayla felt had left him rather vulnerable and she wanted to keep an eye on him. The flat is quite small and dark, and Boris pays a much lower rent for it than the occupants of the other flat. Sadly, Kayla has recently had to sack Boris for being drunk in charge of the lawnmower. Now he refuses to move out. Advise Kayla whether and on what basis she can remove Boris from the flat.

You should take no more than 30 minutes on this question.

* Answer guidance is provided at the end of the chapter.

Further reading

Consultation document: 'Investment in the UK Private Rented Sector', available online at: http://www.hm-treasury.gov.uk/d/consult_investment_ukprivaterentedsector.pdf.
This consultation document gives an interesting overview of the social perspectives behind the changing role of renting in the private sector and provides useful background.

***Street* v. *Mountford* [1985] AC 809, Lord Templeman's judgment.**
As the definitive case on the lease/licence distinction it is essential reading. The law is set out clearly and concisely and is well worth taking a look at for a clear understanding of the requirements of the law in this area.

Pawlowski, M., 'Uncertainty of term – orthodoxy side-stepped in favour of a just result', L&T Review 2012, 16(1), 16–22
This article gives a really clear overview of the recent Supreme Court case of *Berrisford* v. *Mexfield* and comments on the ability of the court to circumvent the need for certainty of term on equitable grounds.

Hunter, C. and Cowan, D., 'The future of housing co-operatives: Mexfield and beyond', JHL 2012, 15(2), 26–32.
This further article on the recent decision in *Berrisford* v. *Mexfield* further highlights the difficulties inherent in the decision and comments on the need for change in the law in this area. The article comments from a housing law perspective on the proposed reform bill which calls for a separate system to be put into place for housing association property.

Co-operative Housing (Tenure) Bill, available online at: http://www.publications.parliament.uk/pa/bills/cbill/2010-2012/0231/2012231.pdf.
This is the link to a full copy of the bill which calls for a reform of the law limiting the security of tenure in respect of housing provided by housing associations and co-operatives.

Lower, M., 'The Bruton Tenancy', Conv. 2010, 1, 38–56.
As stated earlier in the chapter, this article gives a no-nonsense explanation of the unpopular decision in *Bruton* v. *London & Quadrant Housing Trust.*

Question and answer guidance

Please note that the following is not a full answer and is intended to provide guidance in outline form only as to how to answer the questions posed.

Problem: The flat on the ground floor is shared by Josh and Levi, who have signed separate but identical occupancy agreements. The agreements state that if one of the occupants moves out, Kayla can find a substitute sharer to replace them. We are also told that both Josh and Levi assume individual responsibility for their share of the rent; however, when the couple split up and Levi moves out, Josh has offered to pay Levi's share of the rent so he can continue to live there by himself – although it is not surprising he doesn't want to share his double bed with anyone else.

The facts of this case are very similar to that of *Antoniades* v. *Villiers*, which concerned a one-bedroom flat let to a cohabiting couple. In the case, they signed separate but identical 'licence agreements', which were signed at the same time, and the agreement provided that the licensor would be entitled to use the room together with the licensee. The Court of Appeal in the case said that the agreement was only a licence, but at the House of Lords it was held that the agreement was in fact a lease. The reasons they gave for this were: 1. the agreements were interdependent, that is, that they were identical agreements signed at the same time; 2. there was only one bedroom in the flat and couple had opted for a double bed; 3. the four unities were present: possession, interests, title and time, which indicated the presence of a tenancy and not a licence.

If you apply these circumstances to the facts of the problem question, you can see that they are very similar: here we have a couple, Josh and Levi, living in a one-bedroomed flat; they've opted for a double bed, and when Levi left Josh offered to pay Levi's share of the rent to avoid having anyone else in the flat. The fact that Kayla called the agreement an 'occupancy agreement' and that she provided that she could enter the flat at any time was really just a smokescreen; provided she never actually entered the flat unannounced, the likelihood is that this agreement is a tenancy.

On the other hand, the facts are also similar to another case, that of *Mikeover* v. *Brady* (1989) 21 HLR 513. That case also concerned a couple that signed separate but identical licence agreements, and the flat had been advertised in the paper as a 'flat for two people to share', similar to our scenario. Where the facts differ is that when one of the couple, Ms Guile, moved out of the flat, the property owner allowed Mr Brady to pay just his half of the rent. In court Mr Brady argued that there was nothing in the agreement purporting to discount exclusive possession of the premises and that therefore the agreement must be a lease. However, the court held that, as there was no joint responsibility to pay rent and the agreements were not interdependent, there could only be a licence.

We can perhaps distinguish the facts of *Mikeover* v. *Brady* from our case, where Josh paid the full rent and not just his share when Levi left. Decide which conclusion you would reach on the facts and give your answer. Some other cases you may wish to rely on in coming to your finding are: *Stribling* v. *Wickham*; *Hadjiloucas* v. *Crean*; and *Aslan* v. *Murphy*.

Problem:

Boris is Kayla's gardener and also an old friend. She has allowed him to live in the basement flat as a 'perk of the job', which is that he is landscaping the gardens at Pinewood. We are told that he pays much less rent than the occupants of the ground floor flat (although we are told that this flat is much smaller, darker etc.). We are not told that there is any question as to his exclusive occupation of the flat.

Under the requirements of *Street* v. *Mountford*, if he has exclusive possession and is paying rent, he is likely to have a tenancy. He must also be in the flat for a determinate term. We are not told how long it is intended Boris is to stay at the flat, but if he is paying the rent on a regular basis, this will imply a periodic tenancy in any event. We are not told that the tenancy is intended to end when Boris finishes landscaping the garden; only that the flat is a 'perk of the job'.

On the face of it, it would appear that Boris has a tenancy. In order to claim that Boris has only a licence, and therefore to assist Kayla in removing him from the premises quickly, what we need to consider in this situation is whether any of the categories set out in *Facchini* v. *Bryson*, cited by Lord Templeman in *Street* v. *Mountford* apply. These are the exceptional circumstances in which an occupier will not be granted a tenancy, despite the fact that they may have exclusive possession, for a term, at a rent.

There are three types of exceptional circumstance: no intention to create legal relations, service occupancies and lodgers. There is no suggestion that Boris is a lodger, as Kayla doesn't provide him with any attendant services – he simply occupies the flat. It could be argued that there is no intention to create legal relations, because he is a friend in need and she has helped him out in a difficult situation; however, it seems unlikely that this act of helping out a friend would be considered sufficiently 'exceptional' to apply here (although see *Heslop* v. *Burns*, above).

The most likely Facchini category to put this into would be that of a service occupancy. However, the requirement here is that the occupier needs to live at the property in order to better carry out the job they are doing. So if Boris needs to live in the flat in order to carry out the landscaping, then this is okay; but otherwise it will not be accepted within this category. It is unlikely here that Boris needs to be in the flat to better carry out his work, since the flat is referred to as being a 'perk' which denotes an advantage rather than a necessity of the landscaping work.

Again, you should draw your own conclusions from the case law. Possible cases you may wish to discuss here are *Norris* v. *Checksfield* and *Royal Philanthropic Society* v. *County*.

Visit **www.mylawchamber.co.uk** to access tools to help you develop and test your knowledge of land law.

Use Case Navigator to read in full some of the key cases referenced in this chapter with commentary and questions:

Antoniades **v.** ***Villiers and another*** [1990] 1 AC 417
AG Securities **v.** ***Vaughan and others*** [1990] 1 AC 417
Bruton **v.** ***London and Quadrant Housing Trust*** [1999] 3 All ER 481
Prudential Assurance Co. Ltd **v.** ***London Residuary Body and others*** [1992] 2 AC 386
Walsh **v.** ***Lonsdale*** [1881–5] All ER Rep Ext 1690

Chapter 6 Informal methods of acquisition: adverse possession

Key points In this chapter we will be looking at:

- The concept of adverse possession as an informal method of land acquisition
- Why adverse possession is such a controversial topic and changes that have been made to the law to redress the balance between possessor and landowner
- What actually constitutes adverse possession
- The mechanics of claiming adverse possession in both registered and unregistered land
- Ways in which a landowner can prevent an adverse possession claim
- Adverse possession of leasehold property
- Human rights and the law of adverse possession
- Changes to the law relating to squatting in residential buildings

Introduction

In Chapter 3 we learned about the formal acquisition of land, looking in brief at the **conveyancing** process and considering the **formalities** for the creation of contracts for the sale of land. We found that in order to transfer an **estate** in land legally from one party to another (remember that absolute ownership of the land is reserved to the Crown), we require a **deed** of transfer. We also saw that, in order to comply with the provisions of the Land Registration Act 2002, any transfer of land must in addition be **registered** at the **Land Registry** within certain timescales. But is there any situation in which the transfer of land from one party to another does not require such formality? The answer to this question is 'yes'. As with all rules, there are exceptions and we are going to look at the first of these, the informal acquisition of land through **adverse possession**, in detail in this chapter.

What is adverse possession?

So what is 'adverse possession'? What does it mean? Put simply, adverse possession is a means of acquiring land belonging to another person by occupying, or 'possessing' that land for an extended period of time. Thus with adverse possession there is no purchase of the land; nor is there any other form of acquisition made with the permission of the previous landowner (like, for example, a gift or inheritance). Instead, a person acquiring land through the medium of adverse possession acquires title to that land simply through their possession of it; one might say by '**squatting**' on it. So how does it work? Essentially, it is an ancient **common law** rule that, if a person (or persons) enters and occupies land owned by another person for an uninterrupted period of at least twelve years, they can after that period claim **title** to the land for themselves. Let us look at an example:

Imagine Simon, a property developer, buys an acre of land in Todmorland in 1996, on which he hopes to build a number of houses. Unfortunately, the planning authorities do not agree with his plans and refuse to give planning permission for the development. After several years of wrangling with the authority and a number of appeals, Simon runs out of money and patience with the project and moves on to another development, leaving the land at Todmorland vacant. In the meantime, Lila notices that the land is not being used and in 1998 decides to fence off a corner of it to use to keep her Indian runner ducks. She builds a duck house for them on the land and excavates a pond, visiting the land twice daily to feed and water the ducks. After a few months Simon becomes aware of Lila's presence on the site. He asks her to leave, but when she does not, as he has no use for the site until planning permission is granted on it, he decides that there is no hurry to evict her and so he does nothing further to remove her from the site. At the end of 2010 a new Development Plan is drawn up for the Todmorland area which indicates that the planning authority may be more sympathetic to Simon's development plans. In the spring of 2011 Simon makes a renewed planning application for the development of the site, but his application is opposed by Lila, who claims ownership through adverse possession of the part of the site on which she keeps her ducks. The outcome is that, in accordance with the law of adverse possession, as Lila has had uninterrupted use of the site for twelve years her claim is good. Simon can do nothing to get his land back.

A further example of how adverse possession can work in practice is in the Law in Action feature below.

Law in action Athlone House: home to Britain's wealthiest tramp?

Seventy-year-old tramp Harry Hallowes has at last realised his dream of property ownership. Mr Hallowes, who has been squatting on a piece of land forming one corner of the grounds to Athlone House, a £130-million-pound mansion adjoining London's Hampstead Heath, since 1986, has been awarded **possessory title** to the property by the Land Registry. This means that the land is now his to sell or pass on under the terms of a will, should he wish to. The lucky tramp has lived in a small shack on the land for over two decades.

The decision of the Land Registry to grant Mr Hallowes title to the land follows a three year battle with property developers Dwyer, who want to redevelop the huge mansion house into luxury flats. In March 2005, Dwyer attempted to evict Mr Hallowes from the site, but at a court hearing lawyers were able to show that the tramp had lived on the plot for an uninterrupted period of no less than 18 years. As it was not possible to quash the evidence, Mr Hallowes was able to use this as the basis for a successful application to the Land Registry to be granted title to the property on the grounds of adverse possession. It is estimated that his small plot adjoining the Heath, measuring only 20 by 40 metres, could be worth as much as £3.5 million subject to planning permission.

Sources: **http://property.timesonline.co.uk/tol/life_and_style/property/article3671198.ece** and **http://www.metro.co.uk/news/50308-squatter-handed-deeds-to-3-5m-plot-on-the-heath#ixzz1j9rgvRaZ**

Reflective practice

Look at the Law in Action feature above. Do you find it shocking that Harry Hallowes should have acquired the land in this way? Do you think that the tramp should be entitled to become the owner of land he has not bought or paid for? If you do think Harry is entitled to the land, why is this?

Squatters are often in the news and this is perhaps the type of occupation of property which comes to mind when one thinks of adverse possession. However, there is a far greater number cases of adverse possession which arise in a more mundane context. The lines which form the boundaries between residential properties and either neighbouring residential properties or other open land (often farmland) are frequently the subject of uncertainty and dispute and there are many cases of residential property owners extending their gardens by encroaching onto neighbouring property, little by little and often over an extended period of time. When boundary fences are replaced it is not uncommon for the fence to be moved slightly forwards or backwards, which leads to the landowner losing or gaining a piece of land. Equally, where properties back onto fields property owners will often steal or 'borrow' a piece of the field to accommodate a compost heap or vegetable patch, and over a period of years if the field owner does not take steps to reclaim their land this may become part of the property owner's garden.

In the case of **unregistered land**, squatter's rights are not the only reason the law of adverse possession exists. Mention was made in Chapter 1 of the difficulty with the system of unregistered land if title deeds were lost or stolen and we looked at the Bradford and Bingley Building Society warehouse fire, in which thousands of title deeds belonging to homeowners were lost. In such a situation, because there is no central register of property ownership in unregistered land (proof of ownership resting solely with the title deeds to the property) the only option left to property owners is to wait for twelve years and re-stake their claim to the property as adverse possessors of it. Then, after a further period of time they can apply to the Land Registry to upgrade the status of their title from 'possessory' to 'good' title. We can see, then, that the law of adverse possession in respect of unregistered land exists as a method of perfecting the landowner's title to property where title deeds have been lost or destroyed.

Adverse possession: a controversial method of land acquisition?

You were asked above, in the Reflective Practice exercise, to think about whether or not you thought it was right that a person should be able to acquire land they have not bought or paid for, simply through possessing it over a period of time, and you may have formed your own conclusions, one way or another. However, here is a little more food for thought: what if a person in adverse possession of land spends a lot of money on that land, for example by building a house on it. If the landowner has neither made any objection to the adverse possessor being on the property nor taken steps to remove them, should it be right that, after twenty years of living in the property built on the land by that adverse possessor, the landowner can come along and demand the land and the house back, simply because they are the legal **'paper' owner** of it? (You will remember from Chapter 2 that, under section 205(1)(ix) of the Law of Property Act 1925, when a house is built on land it becomes a part of that land.)

On the face of it this certainly might not seem fair. The person occupying the land has made no secret of their occupation of it; nor have they defrauded the legal owner of their title to the land. On the other hand, why should the legal owner be vulnerable to a third party gaining ownership of their land if they do not keep a sufficiently close eye on it? In a number of attempts to address this issue fairly, various statutory provisions were brought into force, culminating in the Limitation Act 1980 which consolidated the previous legislation. The Act limits the period of time a landowner has to bring a claim against a squatter for adverse possession of land to twelve years. After this time, the landowner is **statute-barred** from taking action against them. The idea, therefore, is that any given landowner should have a substantial window of opportunity within which to evict an unwanted occupier from their land, after which if they have done nothing to protect what is theirs their right to do so should be extinguished. This seems logical, but the legislation was seen as flawed. Legal critics considered that the statutory provisions favoured the squatter over the landowner by putting restrictions on a landowner wishing to recover their own land. As we have seen above in the case of Harry Hallowes (Law in Action), the limitation period on legal actions to recover land, albeit lengthy, has nevertheless enabled property worth a lot of money to be acquired by squatters, either simply because of an oversight on the part of the landowner (if the landowner was not aware of the squatter's presence) or because the landowner was too tolerant of the squatter's occupation of the site (as with the example of Simon and Lila given above).

critics considered that the statutory provisions favoured the squatter

Given that there is nothing in the law to require even a token payment of compensation to the landowner by the squatter it was felt by the Law Commission that further changes to the law should be made in order to redress the balance between squatter and landowner. In their report entitled *Land Registration for the 21st Century*, published in July 2001, the Law Commission made recommendations for wholesale changes to the law, in particular as related to the adverse possession of registered land. The result was the provisions appertaining to adverse possession which appear in the Land Registration Act 2002. The provisions do not bring about any change to the meaning of 'adverse possession' which the Act specifically states, at Schedule 6, paragraph 11(1), shall remain the same as under the previous law. However, they do mark a significant shift in emphasis on the twelve-year limitation period provided for in the Limitation Act 1980. Whereas, with the Limitation Act, after twelve years of continuous adverse occupation of a site the legal owner is statute-barred from taking action to recover their property, the Land Registration Act 2002 provides no such limitation period. Rather, the Act stipulates in Schedule 6, section 1 that, after a period of no less than ten years, a squatter can apply to register their possessory title against the landowner. This triggers a notice or 'warning off' period of two years, at the beginning of which the legal owner is notified of the squatter's intentions to dispossess the owner of their land and during which time the legal owner of the property is given the opportunity to take steps to evict the squatter. Subject to certain provisos, if the legal owner has not commenced eviction proceedings within two years of the notice being served, their rights will be lost and the squatter will be entitled to register a possessory title to the property at the Land Registry. A detailed account of the provisions of the Land Registration Act 2002 as they relate to applications by adverse possessors of property is given later in the chapter. The important point to make here, however, is that the new provisions mean that, whilst theoretically a squatter could still make a claim for adverse possession of property within a twelve-year period, they accrue no legal rights in the land until the time the notice is served on the landowner. Before this, it does not matter whether the squatter has been in possession of the property for ten, twenty or even more years, until notice is served they have no rights and the passing of time alone will not prevent the legal owner from asserting their rights over the property and dispossessing a squatter. This could be said to go a long way towards redressing the balance back in favour of the landowner.

As well as removing the limitation period for adverse possession and thereby taking time pressure off the landowner, the notice system has the additional benefit of alerting a property owner who might not be aware of an adverse possessor on their property to an unwanted presence which needs to be dealt with. You may ask 'how can a landowner not be aware that there are squatters on their land?' However, the problem is more common than one might think. The following Law in Action feature explains one of the ways in which this can happen:

Law in action Nigella's unwelcome neighbours: 'serial squatters' move into £33m Belgravia mansion house

In 2009 celebrity chef Nigella Lawson was the unhappy recipient of new neighbours – a gang of 'serial squatters' who have taken over the house next door to Nigella's exclusive London home in Eaton Square, west London. The aptly-named Belgravia Squatters moved in to the 34-room mansion house after being evicted from another similar house in Belgravia. It is reported that they gained access to the empty house through an open first-floor window. The squatters then attached a notice to the front door of the house, asserting squatters' rights and warning against interference with their occupation of it.

A spokesman for the Belgravia Squatters was reported to have said that when the police evict them from their Eaton Square abode, they have nothing to worry about because there is another empty house waiting for them around the corner. And his comments would appear to be true: the figures show that these and other squatters have plenty of homes to choose from. The Empty Homes Agency reports that there are more than 80,000 empty properties in London – which number forms a staggering two-and-a-half per cent of all homes in the capital. Of course, not all of these homes are in Eaton Square, which is considered by many to be one of the most prestigious addresses in London. However, there is no shortage of empty houses in exclusive neighbourhoods such as Belgravia and Mayfair which are often owned by foreign investors who buy property in these locations purely as a financial asset but continue to live elsewhere.

Source: **http://www.dailymail.co.uk/news/article-1230470/Meet-Nigella-Lawsons-new-neighbours--squatters.html**

Whilst the Law in Action feature cites property investors and foreign ownership as one reason for unoccupied property being vulnerable to squatters, in the case of farmland, it may well be that a farmer who owns a lot of land may not have the wherewithal to police their own perimeters regularly. Other reasons for properties standing empty are the financial inability of the landowner to maintain them, and divorce or inheritance issues preventing the property from being occupied. Whatever the reason for the property being abandoned, the law of adverse possession is a touchy subject which is open to criticism and changes in the law must be drafted carefully so as not to penalise landowners just by virtue of their ownership of a significant or excess amount of property.

But how many people does this controversial law affect? The Key Stats feature below gives us an indication.

Key stats

When asked in September 2011 how many applications for adverse possession of plots of land were made to the Land Registry in each of the last ten years, and how many such applications were successful, Edward Davey, Parliamentary Under-Secretary of State (Employment Relations, Consumer and Postal Affairs), Business, Innovation and Skills was able to give the following answer:

Applications for registration as the owner of land on the basis of adverse possession can be divided into two types. First, there are those where the land concerned is unregistered and the application is to register the squatter as the first 'registered proprietor' (in other words, the first registered owner). Secondly, those where the land has already been registered and the application is to register the squatter as the new registered proprietor.

Land Registry does not have reliable statistics for the first type of application. One of the main reasons for this is that it is not unusual for these 'first registration applications' to be made on more than one basis. For example, the title deeds may not be entirely clear, and so, while Land Registry is satisfied that the applicant can properly be registered as proprietor and completes the application, it might not be clear whether he or she has a 'documentary title' (the land involved falling within the extent covered by the title deeds) or a 'possessory title' (the land falling outside the title deeds but the applicant having acquired title by virtue of adverse possession). Such an application may well not be recorded as being an adverse possession application.

Land Registry does have statistics for the second type of application for the financial years 2008–9, 2009–10 and 2010–11: these show that the number of successful applications of this type in these years were 1,111, 1,059 and 868 respectively.

Source: Hansard source (HC Deb, 12 September 2011, c1032W) **http://www.theyworkforyou.com/wrans/?id=2011-09-12b.70891.h**

Acquiring land through adverse possession

So is it really as simple as that? If someone wants to acquire other property or even to extend their own property, can they simply move onto someone else's land and subsequently stake their claim?

In theory the answer is yes, you could just move onto someone else's land and wait for the relevant time period to expire. But in reality, of course, apart from the practical difficulties, there are a number of legal hoops the squatter needs to jump through in order to obtain property in this way. Let us now take a look at the rules which apply to the acquisition of land through adverse possession.

'Dispossession' or 'discontinuance'

The first question we need to answer is 'what does the squatter need to do to take possession of a property in the first place?' From a legal perspective, at what point will the clock start to run on their adverse possession of property?

Schedule 1, paragraph 1 of the Limitation Act 1980 states that:

> Where the person bringing an action to recover land, or some person through whom he claims, has been in possession of the land, and has while entitled to the land been dispossessed or discontinued his possession, the right of action *shall be treated as having accrued on the date of the dispossession or discontinuance* (emphasis added).

The same rules apply to the running of time in an adverse possession claim under the Land Registration Act 2002 (Schedule 6, para. 1).

So we can see that a claim for adverse possession starts from the time at which the legal owner of the land is either dispossessed of the land, or discontinues their possession of it. The difference between the two terms was explained by Mr Justice Fry in the case of *Rains* v. *Buxton* (1880) 14 Ch D 537 as follows:

> In my view, the difference between dispossession and the discontinuance of possession might be expressed in this way – the one is where a person comes in and drives out the others from possession [dispossession], the other case is where the person in possession goes out and is followed into possession by other persons [discontinuance].

The case of *Rains* v. *Buxton* itself concerned an application for an **injunction** against landowners who intended to carry out works which would disturb the squatters' use of a cellar under the **defendant** landowners' property which the **claimants** had occupied for the last sixty years. The claimants maintained that the defendants had discontinued their possession of the cellar, but the defendants said that this could not have been the case, as they were not even aware of the existence of the cellar until shortly before the court proceedings commenced. In order to discontinue their possession, thereby making the conscious decision to abandon the property (in this case the cellar) they had to be aware that they were owners of it in the first place. In any event, Mr Justice Fry came to the conclusion that the claimants' uninterrupted use of the property for sixty years meant that the landowners must necessarily have been dispossessed of the cellar, and the injunction was granted.

In truth, then, it can be seen that the line between discontinuance and dispossession is a fine one. As we have seen from the previous chapter on leasehold property, legal 'possession' of property does not have to be measured by the landowner's constant physical occupation of it. Thus, in the case of Simon and Lila above, although Simon is not physically occupying the development land when Lila fences off a corner of it in which to keep her ducks, the fact that Simon is discussing plans for the property with the council and making site visits is enough to suggest that he is still in possession of the property and has not abandoned it. Lila has therefore dispossessed Simon of that corner of the property, not followed him onto it following a discontinuance of possession. Proving discontinuance by the landowner is fraught with difficulty and in most cases the squatter will be viewed as having dispossessed the landowner by their occupation of the property. A good illustration of this is the case of *Powell* v. *McFarlane* (1979) 38 P&CR 452 in which the disputed land, a three-acre Christmas tree plantation just outside Reigate in Surrey, had been fenced off by the claimant and used to graze the family cow and later to cut hay from and to park vehicles. The landowners visited the land infrequently and their inspections of it were of a cursory nature, often consisting of the landowner viewing the property from the road whilst remaining seated in their car. Nevertheless, the court held that this was sufficient to indicate that the land had not been abandoned and therefore that the squatter had dispossessed them.

It would appear that the only situation in which the landowner can be said to have effectively discontinued their possession of land is in disputed boundary cases where the landowner has cut themselves off from their own property by moving the boundary fence inwards. This is explained by Lord Justice Farwell in the case of *Hounslow LBC* v. *Minchinton* (1997) 74 P&CR 221, which concerned a dispute over a strip of land owned by the council which bordered the claimant's garden and upon which the claimant had built a summer house. The judge said that 'in my judgment the fact that the council's

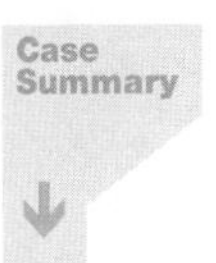

predecessor in title erected the fence and thereby denied itself access to the land lying beyond it was capable of constituting a discontinuance of possession.'

Having established the difference between dispossession and discontinuance, let us now move on to the *nature* of the occupation the squatter must have in order to be an adverse possessor of property.

'Adverse' possession

It is a fundamental tenet of the law of adverse possession that the squatter's possession of the property must be 'adverse': in other words that it must be without the permission of the property owner. It follows, then, that if a person occupies property under the terms of a **lease** or **licence** of any kind (even an implied one), their possession cannot be adverse because it is implicit in the granting of a lease or licence that the landowner has given their permission for the occupier to be there. Put simply, permission is a bar to adverse possession. This can be illustrated by the case of *Trustees of Grantham Christian Fellowship* v. *Scouts Association* [2005] EWHC 209 (Ch). The Fellowship had granted the scouts a licence to occupy some land, provided they kept it tidy. The scouts used the land for scouting activities between 1959 and 2002, building a rockery and a shed on it. In 2002, the scout group decided to claim ownership of the land by adverse possession. The court rejected their claim, however, on the ground that the licence had never been revoked or expired. The scouts had always been on the land with the permission of the owner and therefore had at no time been in adverse possession of it.

Case Summary

The case of *BP Properties* v. *Buckler* (1987) 55 P&CR 337 is also a case centring on a licence to occupy property. However, the facts of this case are quite different. Despite the landowners, BP Properties, having legally obtained an eviction order against Mrs Buckler, who lived in the property with her son, she had refused to leave the property. However, Mrs Buckler was disabled and the case had attracted a lot of unwelcome publicity against BP. The company therefore decided to offer Mrs Buckler a licence to occupy the property rent-free in order to stem the public outcry at their attempts to evict the disabled woman. Mrs Buckler had never formally accepted the offer of a licence but had continued to live in the property until her death. When her son then claimed possessory title to the property on the grounds of adverse possession, however, the court found that there had been a licence granted to Mrs Buckler to occupy the property and that there was therefore no adverse possession claim to be made. The case has been criticised, however, because the licence was never formally entered into and it begs the question whether a landowner can simply unilaterally grant licences to unwanted occupants of their property in order to defeat adverse possession claims. This is not a question that has been answered by the courts, other than the justification given by Lord Justice Dillon in the case itself that, in order to prevent the licence from coming into being, Mrs Buckler should have rejected the offer in writing. However, a series of cases dealing with the issue of implied licences, discussed below, suggests that this was a singular case distinguished by its facts and that the courts may in the future reject any such line of attack put forward by dispossessed landowners. For a more in-depth critique of this case and its implications see Herbert Wallace, 'Limitation, prescription and unsolicited permission', Conv. 1994, May/Jun, 196–210.

Case Summary

A note should be made of the situation in which a former **tenant** remains in possession of property. This can go one of two ways: if the landowner grants a lease of land which then expires and the tenant remains on the land without the landowner's consent, there may be a case for adverse possession. An example of this is the case of *Long* v. *Tower Hamlets London BC* [1996] 3 WLR 317, a case which concerned Mr Long's claim for adverse possession of a shop and flat above in Tower Hamlets, London which, on appeal, was allowed. Mr Long had initially taken a lease of the property but had subsequently occupied the property without paying rent for 18 years. The controversy in the case came over an argument between the parties as to when adverse possession of the property had actually commenced: the landlord's **notice to quit** the property having only expired 11 years before the commencement of proceedings. There was never any dispute that Mr Long, as a former tenant of the property remaining in occupation, could not become a squatter, however. An earlier case in point is the Court of Appeal case of *Hayward* v. *Chaloner* [1967] 3 WLR 1068. In this case, there was a dispute between farming landowners and a rector who had previously let the land for use as amenity land behind the gardens of cottages owned by the Church. Whilst Lord Denning was dissenting in this case, his disagreement was on the ground that there had not been continuous possession of the land by the rector for the duration of the limitation period. As with the *Tower Hamlets* case, there was no question that a former tenant of property could become an adverse possessor of land and this was clearly stated by Lord Justice Russell in *Hayward* v. *Chaloner*. The position has now been clarified by Schedule 1, paras. 5(1) (**periodic tenancies**) and 6(1) (leases in writing) of the Limitation Act 1980 which provide that, in an adverse possession claim, time will start to run from the date of the last receipt of rent on the property.

The opposite is of course true if a tenant remains in possession of the land after the expiry of their lease with the landowner's consent. In this situation, they become a **tenant at will** of the property and, since they are in occupation of the land with the landowner's consent, their possession cannot be seen to be adverse.

An interesting line of cases dealing with the issue of implied tenancies can be seen developing from the Court of Appeal case of *Wallis's Cayton Bay Holiday Camp Ltd* v. *Shell-Mex and BP Ltd* [1974] 3 WLR 387. In this case Lord Denning argued that a squatter's occupancy of the property in dispute was by virtue of an implied licence by the owner, and as such there could be no adverse possession of it. The case concerned a dispute over a piece of land in North Yorkshire on the Scarborough road which adjoined a petrol station abutting farmland. The land was not fenced off from the remainder of the farm, having been sold to the petrol company by a former owner of the farm some years previously. Although the land was clearly omitted from the plan of the farm when it was sold, the new owners of the farm proceeded to use the petrol company's land for grazing their cattle, incorporating it into their own field. The petrol company had initially planned to use the land for development in anticipation of a new road scheme which never came into being. After eleven years had passed, however, the petrol company wrote to the farmer offering to sell the piece of land to him, but the farmer did not respond to their letters. When the petrol company subsequently took steps to fence off the land, the farmer claimed ownership of it by adverse possession. Initially, the farmer's claim was upheld, but the Court of Appeal subsequently found in favour of the paper owners of the site, BP Ltd, Lord Justice Stamp dissenting from the majority.

Following the finding of the much earlier cases of *Leigh* v. *Jack* (1879) 5 Ex D 264, which concerned a failed attempt to claim a strip of land set aside by the landowner to be dedicated to the public as a highway at some point in the future which the claimant had been using to dump scrap from his metalworking business, and *Williams Brothers Direct Supply Ltd* v. *Raftery* [1958] 1 QB 159, where a strip of land intended by the

owner to be used in the future for development was used during and after the Second World War for the growing vegetables and keeping greyhounds, Lord Denning said that where an owner of land intends to use it for a particular purpose in the future but meanwhile has no immediate use for it and so leaves it unoccupied, the owner should not lose their rights to that land because a third party comes on it and uses it for 'some temporary or seasonal purpose', such as stacking materials or growing vegetables. In such a case, Lord Denning asserted that the third party's use of the land could be ascribed to an implied licence or permission granted by the landowner. In this particular case, Lord Denning went on to say that the failure of the adverse possessors to respond to the landowner's correspondence amounted to wrong-doing sufficient to estop them from claiming possessory title to the property. His suggestion in this case, then, was that:

(a) land used by a third party in a way which does not contradict the landowner's future plans for the property is occupied under an implied licence and not eligible to become the subject of an adverse possession claim; and

(b) a failure to respond by the occupier of land rendered them unfit in **equity** to make a claim under the law of adverse possession because of their dishonesty in hiding their true intentions about the land.

Lord Justice Stamp disagreed with Lord Denning on both counts, however, stating that the only issue which should be relevant to the case was the fact of the farmer's possession of the land over the requisite twelve-year period. The facts of the case were distinguished in the subsequent case of *Treloar* v. *Nute* [1976] 1 WLR 1295, which concerned a dispute of a small piece of land in Cornwall amounting to about one-seventh of an acre, owned by an elderly lady, Mrs Treloar. Unlike the land in *Wallis's Cayton Bay Holiday Camp*, the landowner had no intended future use for the property. The land, which had previously been used by Mrs Treloar as part of her farming business, was now redundant and had stood empty for a number of years. Mr Nute had purchased a house adjacent to the disputed land and believed it to be included in the purchase. In accordance with his beliefs he used the land as if it were his own for both storage and amenity. In 1963 Mr Nute had sought to fence off the land. Mrs Treloar objected and pulled the fence down but Mr Nute re-erected it. The fence remained in situ until the hearing of the initial court case in 1975. At first instance the court found that, although Mrs Treloar had no specific use in mind for the land in question, Mr Nute's actions had not in any way inconvenienced the landowner and therefore were not adverse to her possession of it. The rule set out in *Wallis's Cayton Bay Holiday Camp* was applied. However, on appeal the court reversed the decision, stating that there was nothing in the Limitation Act 1939 (then in force) to require that acts of adverse possession should be in direct opposition to the landowner's actual or intended use of the property. Thus, as Mr Nute had occupied the land for the requisite amount of time his claim to possessory title of the land was upheld.

Case Summary

Following the outcome of *Treloar* v. *Nute*, in 1977 the Law Reform Committee, in their Final Report on Limitation of Actions (1977) Cmnd 6823, condemned the findings of the Court of Appeal in *Wallis's Cayton Bay Holiday Camp*, expressing the view that if the principle set out in the case continued to be followed it would amount, in effect, 'to a judicial repeal of the statute' (see page 45, para 3.50 of the report). The issue was later specifically addressed in the wording of section 4 of the 1980 Limitation Amendment Act, which ruled out the making of an assumption of an implied licence being granted to the squatter by the landowner, stating:

For the purpose of determining whether a person occupying any land is in adverse possession of the land it shall not be assumed by implication of law that his occupation is by permission of the person entitled to the land merely by virtue of the fact that his occupation is not inconsistent with the latter's present or future enjoyment of the land.

Case Summary

In *Buckinghamshire County Council* v. *Moran* [1989] 3 WLR 152 the doctrine was conclusively held by the Court of Appeal to have been negated by the new legislation. The case concerned a plot of land purchased by the Council in 1955 with a view to using the land at some point in the future for a road diversion. In 1967 the defendant's predecessors began to use the plot which adjoined their garden by mowing the grass and trimming the hedges, and using it for their own purposes. On their subsequent sale of their house in 1971 to the defendant, Mr Moran, they swore a statutory declaration that they had occupied the property unchallenged since 1967. Mr Moran secured the property with a new lock and chain to the gate on the eastern side of the property and continued to use it for his own purposes. In 1975 the tennis club applied to the Council for permission to lay a drain across the property and the Council became aware of Mr Moran's use of the plot. There was some correspondence between the parties, culminating in Mr Moran's solicitors writing to the Council in March 1976 claiming ownership of the land by adverse possession. The Council did not take any action against Mr Moran, however, until October 1985, when they started proceedings to recover the land. On appeal it was held that Mr Moran's acts 'amounted to an unequivocal demonstration of his intention to possess the plot' and he was granted title to the land. The Court of Appeal was categorical in stating that it did not matter that the Council had plans for the future use of the land in question. Referring to the provisions of the Limitation Act 1980, the Court said that if any other interpretation of the Act was given it would mean an end to the concept of adverse possession altogether on the ground that implied licences were granted by the landowner to each and every would-be adverse possessor of property.

It should be noted, however, that the Limitation Act 1980 is nevertheless clear in stating that this will *not* prevent a licence from being implied where the facts of the case support this. Section 4 provides that:

This provision shall not be taken as prejudicing a finding to the effect that a person's occupation of any land is by implied permission of the person entitled to the land in any case where such a finding is justified on the actual facts of the case.

Case Summary

This is evidenced in the case of *Pulleyn* v. *Hall Aggregates (Thames Valley) Ltd* (1992) 65 P&CR 276. The case concerned a claim for adverse possession of land adjacent to a sailing club. The land was owned by a farmer, who was also the **landlord** of the sailing club itself. Mr Pulleyn owned a house and other adjoining land, but believed he had also purchased the land in question at the time he purchased his house. Over a period of years Mr Pulleyn gave the sailing club permission to use the land as an overflow car park and for general storage. When it transpired that Mr Pulleyn did not in fact own the land in question, he made a claim for adverse possession of it. However, the Court of Appeal found that because the landowner had been happy for the sailing club to use the land as an extension of the land they already leased from him, Mr Pulleyn could not claim this use of the land as proof of his own adverse possession of it.

The provisions of the Limitation Amendment Act 1980 cited above have now been consolidated under Schedule 1, paragraph 8(4) of the Limitation Act 1980.

the squatter needs to assert 'an appropriate degree of physical control'

Possession

In order for there to be adverse possession the squatter must be in actual possession of the land. What constitutes possession is something which is difficult to quantify. According to Mr Justice Slade in *Powell* v. *MacFarlane* (the Christmas tree plantation case), in order to sufficiently possess the property for adverse possession to run the squatter needs to assert 'an appropriate degree of physical control'. But what exactly does 'an appropriate degree of physical control' include?

You be the judge

Q: Which of the following do you think constitute 'possession' for the purposes of making an adverse possession claim: (a) building and living in a house on the land; (b) cultivating the land; (c) fencing off the land; (d) putting up notices warning intruders to keep off the land; (e) parking a car on the land; (f) allowing children to play on the land; and (g) running a sewer pipe under the land?

Source: Sozaijiten

A: In law, (a) (b) (c) and (d) are sufficient to constitute possession, whereas (e) (f) and (g) are not. Whilst (e) (f) and (g) all show a clear and consistent use of the land, they have all been considered by the courts as insufficient to constitute physical possession for the purposes of making an adverse possession claim. Further details are given in the cases below.

Case Summary

In the case of *Seddon* v. *Smith* (1877) 36 LT 168, an adverse possessor, Mr Smith, had fenced off land forming about three-quarters of a field belonging to the claimant, Mr Seddon. Mr Smith then incorporated the fenced-off land as part of his farm, ploughing the land and using it continuously in this way for a period of over twenty years. Chief Justice Cockburn said in this case that his fencing-off of the land was 'the strongest possible evidence of adverse possession'. This is as one might imagine and has been followed as a matter of course in adverse possession claims. In the more recent case of

Case Summary

Williams v. *Usherwood* (1983) 45 P&CR 235, the land in dispute formed a driveway between a pair of semi-detached houses which had originally been used as a shared access for both properties. However, at some point a fence had been put up on one side of the driveway so as to reserve the whole of it for only one of the houses. On the later sale of the house that had been deprived of its use of the shared driveway, the new owners sought to claim part ownership of the driveway and reinstate its former shared user. However, the claim failed, the defendants successfully proving ownership of the whole on grounds of adverse possession over a period of some forty years.

Case Summary

The fencing-off must be effective and permanent, however. The 1992 case of *Marsden* v. *Miller* (1992) 64 P&CR 239 is an interesting one because it does not actually feature the landowner of the property at all. Rather, it is an argument between two alleged adverse possessors of property. The case concerned two neighbours whose families had both made use of unregistered land of unknown ownership over a number of years – one

family since the 1940s and the other since the 1960s. In 1981, one party put up a fence around the property, complete with a notice board claiming ownership of the land. However, the neighbours pulled the fence down within 24 hours of its erection, and both parties subsequently continued to use the land as they had before. Three years later in 1984 the party that had erected the fence sought a declaration of their ownership of the land and an injunction to prevent the neighbours from entering it. Their grounds for doing so were that they had acquired the property through their adverse possession of it. However, the court (and subsequently the Court of Appeal) dismissed their claim. The claimants had not successfully taken control of the property, the fence enclosing the land having been in position for only 24 hours.

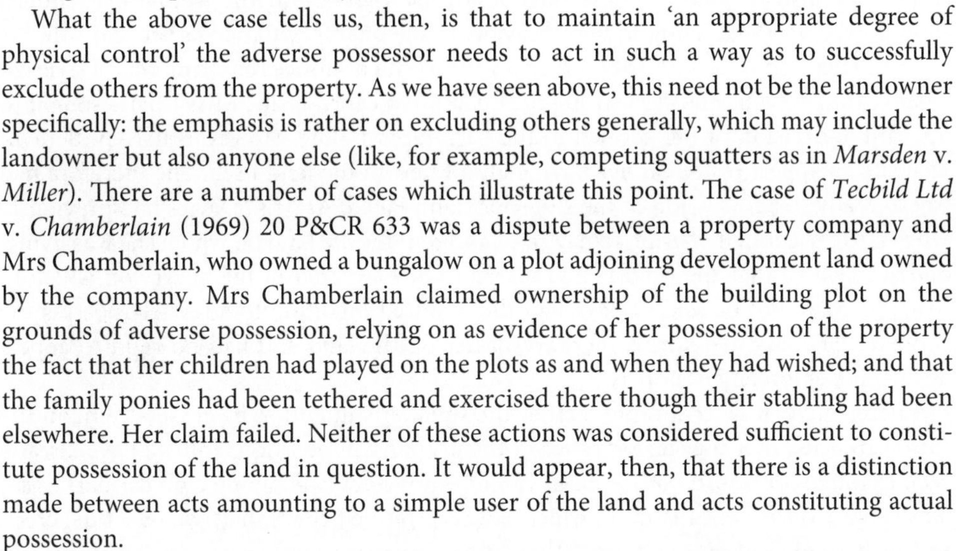

What the above case tells us, then, is that to maintain 'an appropriate degree of physical control' the adverse possessor needs to act in such a way as to successfully exclude others from the property. As we have seen above, this need not be the landowner specifically: the emphasis is rather on excluding others generally, which may include the landowner but also anyone else (like, for example, competing squatters as in *Marsden* v. *Miller*). There are a number of cases which illustrate this point. The case of *Tecbild Ltd* v. *Chamberlain* (1969) 20 P&CR 633 was a dispute between a property company and Mrs Chamberlain, who owned a bungalow on a plot adjoining development land owned by the company. Mrs Chamberlain claimed ownership of the building plot on the grounds of adverse possession, relying on as evidence of her possession of the property the fact that her children had played on the plots as and when they had wished; and that the family ponies had been tethered and exercised there though their stabling had been elsewhere. Her claim failed. Neither of these actions was considered sufficient to constitute possession of the land in question. It would appear, then, that there is a distinction made between acts amounting to a simple user of the land and acts constituting actual possession.

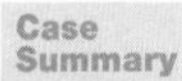

The case of *William Sindall plc* v. *Cambridgeshire County Council* [1994] 1 WLR 1016 failed on similar grounds although the facts were very different. Here, a company claimed adverse possession of land which occupied the space through which a sewer pipe ran. The sewer had been installed by the claimant on the council's land without their permission some years before. The company's claim failed as amounting to user only and not possession. The court held that any right to use the pipe, if such a right existed, amounted to an **easement** (that is, a right of user) over the land, and not adverse possession of it.

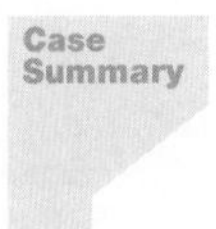

Clearly what constitutes sufficient in terms of exclusion is a matter of fact and degree. The case of *Fowley Marine (Emsworth) Ltd* v. *Gafford* [1968] 2 WLR 842 concerned a tidal creek in Chichester Harbour called Fowley Rythe. The claimants, Fowley Marine, believed themselves to be the legal owners of the creek, having purchased it from another company two years earlier. (It transpired that there was some question as to the strength of the title to the property, however – hence the adverse possession claim.) Nevertheless, the property had been occupied by Fowley Marine and their successors in title since as early as 1878, the owners managing the creek and charging a mooring fee for boats wishing to use it. The defendant, Mr Gafford, refused to acknowledge the company's ownership of the creek, claiming the land belonged to the Crown and that, as such, he had a customary right to moor there free of charge. Fowley Marine sought to remove him. The company won their claim. Their management of the land, coupled with their policing of it and the charging of a mooring fee were, according to Lord Justice Wilmer, 'as sufficient as the location in question would permit' in terms of evidencing their possession of it.

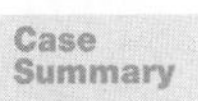

The intention to possess

We have seen above that there must be physical possession of the land in order to mount a successful claim in adverse possession. However, the law also requires that the squatter intended to occupy, or possess, the property. Thus, 'possession' in adverse possession also has a mental as well as a physical aspect. The intention to possess is known as '*animus possidendi*'. Anything short of an intention to *possess* the property will not be sufficient to found a claim in adverse possession. In the case of *R* v. *Secretary of State for the Environment, ex p. Davies* (1990) 61 P&CR 487 a woman sought to claim the right to live in a disused quarry on grounds of adverse possession. The woman had moved onto the site in 1987, living in two caravans in the quarry with her father and son. Six months later, the local authority served an enforcement notice requiring Miss Davies to remove the caravans and cease using the quarry as a caravan site. Miss Davies sought to appeal the decision of the council to the Secretary of State. However, her entitlement to make an appeal rested on her having an interest in the land itself. She therefore had to claim adverse possession of the site. Her claim failed. As Miss Davies had previously written to the council offering to pay rates and rent for the land on which she was living, and even stated that she would be prepared to buy a corner of the quarry on which to live, she could not be said to have had the required intention to adversely possess the property. She was therefore a mere trespasser on the land and had no right to appeal against the enforcement notice.

Case Summary

Interestingly, it is irrelevant whether the squatter's intention to possess came in the mistaken belief that they already owned the property in question, and we have already seen examples of this in both *Pulleyn* v. *Hall Aggregates* (the sailing club car park case) and *Fowley Marine* v. *Gafford*, in which Fowley Marine believe they owned a tidal creek in Chichester called Fowley Rythe. There are numerous examples of adverse possession claims coming out of a longstanding misunderstanding as to the true ownership of the property. Another such example is the Court of Appeal case of *Hughes* v. *Cork* [1994] EGCS 25. In this case, Mr Hughes had mistakenly believed that a triangular plot of land measuring some 50 metres by 12 at its widest point, formed part of a plot of undeveloped land at Cellar Hill in Sittingbourne, Kent, bought by him and on which he intended to build a house. It was held that his removal of fencing put up by the true owners and regular maintenance of the site during the period of his ownership of the adjoining land was sufficient to evidence his intention to possess it, despite the fact that he had done this in the belief that he already owned the land. Thus it can be seen that the intention of the squatter must be simply to possess, and not to adversely possess (although as we have seen to possess adversely is itself a fundamental part of adverse possession).

Case Summary

Although both physical possession and the intention to possess must be proved in order to mount a successful claim for adverse possession, often the physical possession of the property is in itself enough to evidence an intention to possess it. As with factual possession, it is not necessary that the squatter intended specifically to exclude the landowner, provided that they intended to exclude everyone, including the landowner. This was the case in *Buckinghamshire CC* v. *Moran*, in which the adverse possessor of the property had gated and padlocked the land in question, against intrusion by all others, including the council themselves.

The mechanics of claiming adverse possession

We now know the nature of possession the squatter has to prove in order to establish a claim for possession. But what are the mechanics of making an actual claim? Apart from the entering into possession of the land itself, what else does a squatter have to do to successfully acquire the land? Earlier in the chapter brief description was made of the requirements for making a claim of adverse possession over land. However, let us now take some time to set out the mechanics of making an adverse possession claim in full.

The first thing you need to know is that there are two applicable sets of rules in cases of adverse possession: one relating primarily to unregistered land, but also to registered land the period of adverse possession for which has run out prior to a certain date, and the other relating purely to registered land. These are as follows:

Limitation Act 1980

The provisions of the Limitation Act 1980 apply both to unregistered land, and to registered land where the rights of the squatter have been acquired prior to the coming into force of the Land Registration Act 2002 (on 13th October 2003). Section 15 of the Act provides that:

> (1) No action shall be brought by any person to recover any land after the expiration of twelve years from the date on which the right of action accrued to him or, if it first accrued to some person through whom he claims, to that person.

As we saw earlier in the chapter, Part I of Schedule 1 of the Act provides that a right of action starts to accrue from the date of the landowner's dispossession or discontinuance from the land.

The law is therefore completely straightforward prior to the Land Registration Act 2002. All a squatter need do is to dispossess the landowner or follow them onto the property following the owner's abandonment of it and adversely occupy that property for a continuous period of twelve years or more, in the case of registered land, that period being completed before 13 October 2003. As long as the required twelve-year period has elapsed (under section 15(7) this period is thirty years for Crown land and sixty years for **foreshore**, which is the part of the seashore that lies between the low and high tide marks) the original landowner is powerless under the terms of the act to bring any action to recover the land. As far as the landowner's title to the property is concerned, under section 17 of the Act the former landowner's rights to the property are automatically extinguished at the end of the limitation period and therefore cease to exist. If the land in question is registered, there is a small complication in that, whilst the landowner's rights will still lapse after completion of the limitation period, they will nevertheless remain on the Register at the Land Registry until they are removed. Section 75 of the Land Registration Act 1925 therefore provides that after the expiration of the limitation period the landowner will be deemed to hold the land on trust for the squatter until such time as the squatter registers their own possessory title to the land at the Land Registry.

Land Registration Act 2002

All claims for adverse possession in registered land, the rights to which have been acquired after 13 October 2003, are governed by the Land Registration Act 2002. A squatter of registered land could therefore acquire land by one of two means. Table 6.1 shows which provisions apply:

Table 6.1 Which rules apply to adverse possessors of land

Type of land	Applicable statute	When to apply
Unregistered land	Limitation Act 1980	After 12 years' adverse possession
Registered Land	Limitation Act 1980	Where the squatter has been in possession for a period of 12 years ending prior to 13 October 2003.
Registered Land	Land Registration Act 2002, Sched. 6	Where the squatter has been in possession for a period of 10 years or more, ending after 13 October 2003.

As we saw earlier in the chapter, there is no limitation period governing adverse possession under the 2002 Act, although the minimum period within which a squatter can acquire property by adverse possession is still twelve years. The relevant provisions are contained in Schedule 6 of the Act. The Schedule stipulates, at paragraph 1(1), that after a period of no less than ten years' adverse possession, a squatter can apply to be registered as the proprietor of the land (under Schedule 6 paragraph 13 the minimum period is 60 years for any land belonging to the Crown). On receipt of the squatter's application for registration, the land registrar is required to notify the landowner of the application. On this first application by the squatter, their application will be rejected unless one of three conditions set out at paragraph 5 of Schedule 6 are met. These are:

5(1) If an application under paragraph 1 is required to be dealt with under this paragraph, the applicant is only entitled to be registered as the new proprietor of the estate if any of the following conditions is met.

(2) The first condition is that—

(a) it would be unconscionable because of an equity by estoppel for the registered proprietor to seek to dispossess the applicant, and

(b) the circumstances are such that the applicant ought to be registered as the proprietor.

(3) The second condition is that the applicant is for some other reason entitled to be registered as the proprietor of the estate.

(4) The third condition is that—

(a) the land to which the application relates is adjacent to land belonging to the applicant,

(b) the exact line of the boundary between the two has not been determined under rules under section 60,

(c) for at least ten years of the period of adverse possession ending on the date of the application, the applicant (or any predecessor in title) reasonably believed that the land to which the application relates belonged to him, and

(d) the estate to which the application relates was registered more than one year prior to the date of the application.

Put in layman's terms, these three conditions can be explained as follows:

1. Circumstances are such that it would be **unconscionable** (unjust or unfair) for the landowner to enforce their 'paper' title against the squatter. Such a situation might occur where the squatter has built a house on land belonging to the landowner for them and their family to live in, in the mistaken belief that the land belongs to them, and the landowner encourages the squatter to do so, knowing that in actual fact the land belongs to the landowner. In this situation it would be unconscionable for the landowner to claim the land back, together with the house on it – bought and paid for by the squatter. We will be looking at the law of equity by **estoppel**, or **proprietary estoppel** as it is more commonly known, in the next chapter.
2. Where the squatter has purchased the land but for whatever reason the formal transfer has never been completed and so legal ownership remains with the previous landowner.
3. Where there is a boundary dispute and the squatter genuinely believed that the land belonged to them.

If none of the three conditions apply, the squatter's application to be registered as the proprietor of the land will be rejected by the Land Registry. From this point onwards, the landowner has two years in which to take enforcement action against the squatter and evict them from the land. If, at the end of this two-year period, under Schedule 6 paragraph 6 of the Act, the landowner has neither commenced proceedings against the squatter, nor secured their eviction from the site, the squatter may make a renewed application to the Land Registry to be registered as proprietor of the land and the land registry is required to accept their application for registration. The squatter will thereby acquire possessory title to the land in question and the former landowner's title to the land will be extinguished.

As we saw earlier in the chapter, it is important to note that until the squatter makes their first application to be registered as proprietor of the land, they have no formal rights in the land. This is regardless of how long they have occupied it. It is the first application that triggers the squatter's rights, therefore, and not the simple lapse of time, as with the Limitation Act 1980. Figure 6.1 summarises the procedure for applying to become the registered proprietor of land under the Land Registration Act 2002.

Figure 6.1 Procedure for claiming adverse possession under the LRA 2002

After 10 years' adverse possession:

- apply to register possessory title at the Land Registry
- if one of the three circumstances under schedule 6, para.5 applies (estoppel, boundary dispute or other reason), title will be registered
- if not, application will be rejected

After a further two years from the date of rejection of the original application:

- reapply to register possessory title
- title must be awarded to the squatter provided proceedings have not been commenced against them by the paper owner or an eviction order awarded

After a further 12 years from the date of registration of possessory title:

- apply for title to be upgraded to absolute freehold or good leasehold title (see below)

Successive periods of adverse possession

So far we have talked about the situation where there is only one squatter occupying property for a given period of time. But what if there are a number of squatters, occupying one after another? The issue of successive squatters raises two issues:

1. Firstly, what rights does each subsequent squatter have against the other squatters? and
2. Secondly, can the squatter in possession of the property at any given time use the periods of possession of previous squatters to add up to the required time period for the purposes of making a claim?

The answer to the first question is that if there is a succession of squatters adversely possessing a property, each successive squatter retains the right to reclaim the property as against subsequent squatters on the grounds of their prior claim until twelve years have passed from the date of their being ousted from the property. So, to give an example: imagine Lydia has been a squatter in High Hails, Mayfair for three years. After leaving the property for a long weekend at her friend's beachside squat, she returns to find that she has been ousted by Jaime, who has entered the property through an open first-floor window and changed the locks. Lydia will then have twelve years from the date on which she is dispossessed in order to stake her claim against Jaime before her right to do so expires. If, after two years' occupation of High Hails, Jaime is then herself dispossessed by Rita, Lydia will nevertheless have the right to stake her claim against Rita, as the current occupier of the property, for a further ten years (until the full twelve-year time period has elapsed). Jaime will also have a twelve-year period starting with the date of her own dispossession within which she can make a claim against Rita.

The answer to the second question is yes, it is possible for a squatter to pass on their accrued rights of possession to a subsequent adverse possessor of property. Therefore we can have a scenario where Brendan sells the freehold to his house in Robin Hood's Bay to Gino, together with such rights as he has acquired over a strip of land adjoining his back garden which he has been using as a vegetable patch for the last nine years. Gino will then be able to claim adverse possession rights over the land either after a further year in the case of unregistered property or after a further three years in the case of registered property. It should be noted that the sale of land now triggers compulsory registration under the Land Registration Act 2002 and so if this happened today, the registered system would automatically apply. It should also be noted that the Acts require a continuous period of possession so there must not be a gap between successive periods of occupation in order for the transfer of occupation rights from one squatter to another, to work.

Upgrading the squatter's title

Brief mention should be made here about possessory title. For conveyancing purposes, the Land Registry gives different grades of title to landowners. The most common (and best) grade of ownership of either freehold or leasehold land is **'absolute' title**. The greatest significance of acquiring this grade of title is from the point of view of obtaining a **mortgage** on, and therefore the ability of the owner to sell, the land. Few mortgage companies will lend on the strength of a possessory title and therefore if the squatter wishes to sell their land (purchased by their buyers with the aid of a mortgage) or obtain finance secured on their property, they are likely to be unable to do so. There is also the issue of relativity of title, which we will be considering below. A person with possessory title is always at risk of someone with a better title coming along and dispossessing them of their property. Someone with absolute title to the property, on the other hand, is at the top of the chain, so to speak, and therefore has the greatest security over their property (subject to another squatter coming along, that is!). Despite having achieved possessory title of the land, therefore, and having registered that title, from a practical point of view a squatter with possessory title would be wise to seek to upgrade their title at the earliest opportunity to realise the full potential and marketability of their property. Under sections 62(4) and (5) of the Land Registration Act 2002, a squatter can apply to upgrade their possessory title either to an absolute freehold or good leasehold title once the possessory title has been registered for 12 years. (It should be noted that absolute leasehold title can only be granted where the landlord's freehold title to the property has been provided. Good leasehold title is sufficient for most purposes, however. Further discussion of the conveyancing principles involved are outside the scope of this book.)

Few mortgage companies will lend on the strength of a possessory title

Getting the squatter out

Having considered what the squatter needs to do to obtain legal title to the property, let us now spend some time thinking about the landowner's position and what they are able to do to get a squatter off their land before the squatter is able to take possession of it permanently.

Relativity of title to land

Mention was made of the concept of relativity of title in the previous section and it is vital that we understand this concept when we start to think about evicting a squatter from any given property. You may have heard of the expression that 'possession is nine-tenths of the law'. With land law, this is certainly the case. The case of the Belgravia Squatters in the Law in Action feature, above, is the perfect example of this. The squatters have entered into the house and are living there, amid serious consternation from neighbouring house owners. However, it is important to note that the unhappy neighbours can do nothing about the squatters: they have no right to interfere with the squatters' occupation of the property at all. As occupiers of the land, the only person who can evict the squatters is someone with a superior right to the property than the squatters themselves have. This would be the legal owner of the property themselves, or perhaps a tenant of the property, or someone who inherited or was given the property as a gift. The neighbours, having no legal rights in the property, are powerless to act. The following notice shown in the Documenting the Law feature below shows just how serious unlawful interference from the neighbours (or anyone else without a superior title to the property) can be.

Documenting the law

The following is a copy of the notice attached to the door of the mansion house next door to Nigella Lawson and Charles Saatchi that was entered by the Belgravia Squatters.

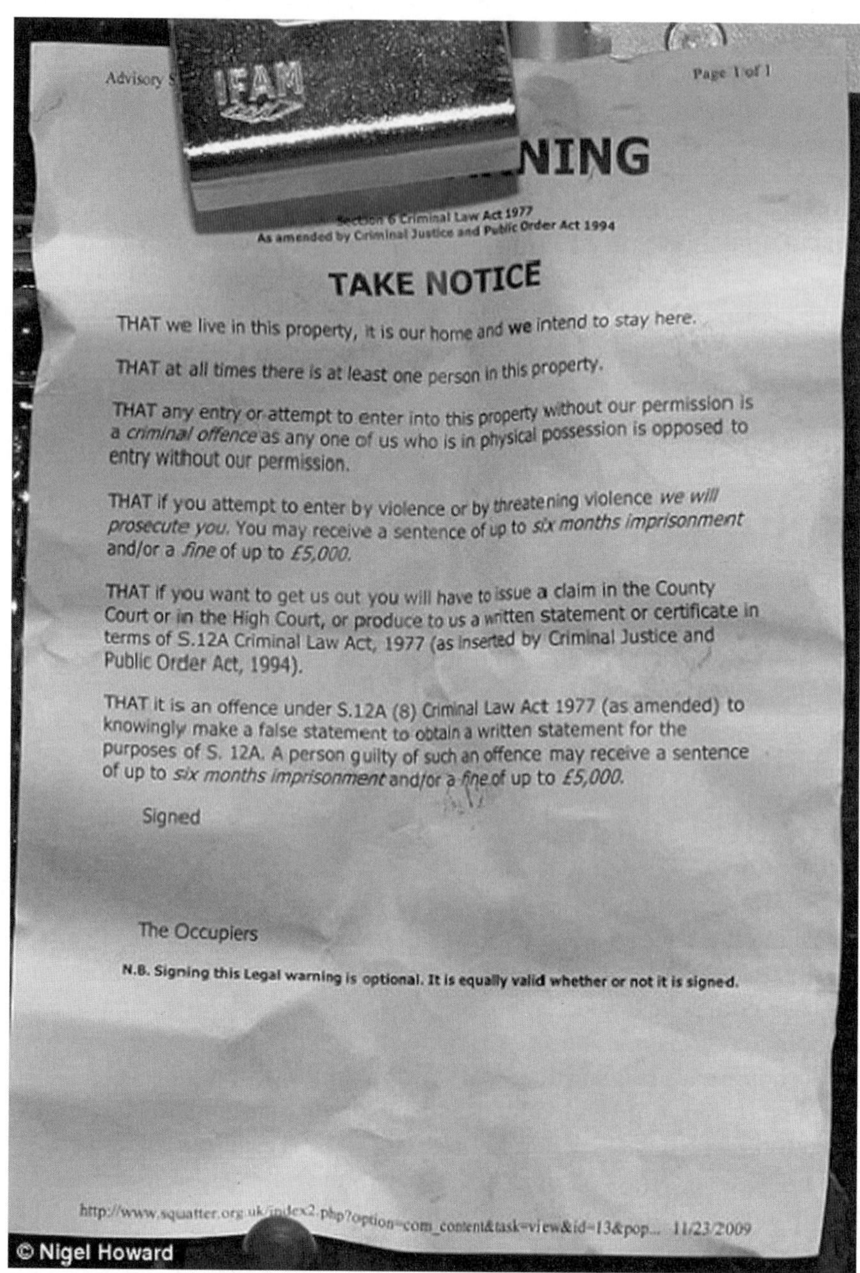

Advisory S Page 1 of 1

NING

Section 6 Criminal Law Act 1977
As amended by Criminal Justice and Public Order Act 1994

TAKE NOTICE

THAT we live in this property, it is our home and we intend to stay here.

THAT at all times there is at least one person in this property.

THAT any entry or attempt to enter into this property without our permission is a *criminal offence* as any one of us who is in physical possession is opposed to entry without our permission.

THAT if you attempt to enter by violence or by threatening violence *we will prosecute you.* You may receive a sentence of up to *six months imprisonment* and/or a *fine* of up to *£5,000.*

THAT if you want to get us out you will have to issue a claim in the County Court or in the High Court, or produce to us a written statement or certificate in terms of S.12A Criminal Law Act, 1977 (as inserted by Criminal Justice and Public Order Act, 1994).

THAT it is an offence under S.12A (8) Criminal Law Act 1977 (as amended) to knowingly make a false statement to obtain a written statement for the purposes of S. 12A. A person guilty of such an offence may receive a sentence of up to *six months imprisonment* and/or a *fine* of up to *£5,000.*

Signed

The Occupiers

N.B. Signing this Legal warning is optional. It is equally valid whether or not it is signed.

http://www.squatter.org.uk/index2.php?option=com_content&task=view&id=13&pop... 11/23/2009

Source: http://www.dailymail.co.uk/news/article-1230470/Meet-Nigella-Lawsons-new-neighbours--squatters.html

The point being made here is that the Belgravia Squatters cannot be evicted from the home they are adversely possessing by virtue of the fact that they do not have good title to the property: they cannot be attacked because of the weakness of their own claim to the land; they can only be ousted because someone else's claim is stronger. If Nigella Lawson wishes the squatters to leave their Belgravia home, therefore, her best bet is to contact the legal owners of the property and ask them to take action.

This idea, that the only person who can turn out, or 'dispossess', a person from the property they occupy is someone with a better claim to the land than they themselves have, is called 'relativity of title'. To make sure you have a clear grasp of this, take a quick look at the You Be the Judge feature, below.

You be the judge

Q: **Julia puts her caravan and sets up home on an apparently vacant piece of land adjoining the Canderberry Bypass. Who can oust her from the land:**
(a) the freehold owner of the land; (b) Farmer Giles, who took a five-year lease of the land from the freeholder in 2010; (c) Mischa, who has been grazing her horses on the land with Farmer Giles's knowledge and permission for the last twelve months; (d) Farmer Brown, who owns a field adjoining the land and doesn't like Julia's presence on the site?

A: All the parties have a right to oust Julia, with the exception of Farmer Brown. He has no rights to possess the land and therefore cannot do anything to remove her as he does not have a superior right to hers.

To conclude, then, we can see that under the theory of relativity of title, the only person who can evict a squatter is someone with a better right to the property than they have.

Preventing time from running

Once a squatter is in adverse possession of land, there are three things that will prevent time from running in the squatter's favour and thus building up a continuous 12-year period of occupancy with which the squatter can claim ownership of the land. These three things are:

1. The commencement of legal proceedings by the landowner to recover their land;
2. The acknowledgement by the squatter in writing of the landowner's title to the property; and
3. Under section 32 of the Limitation Act 1980, fraud, concealment or mistake (these also apply to registered applications under the Land Registration Act 2002).

Commencement of legal proceedings

We have seen above that under Schedule 6, paragraph 6 of the Land Registration Act 2002 the commencement of legal proceedings during the two-year period following the squatter's application for registration of a possessory title will prevent the squatter's title being registered. We also know that under the terms of the Limitation Act 1980 legal proceedings are barred after the twelve-year period has elapsed. It should be noted, however, that the commencement of legal proceedings should not be an idle threat. In the House of Lords case of *Ofulue* v. *Bossert* [2008] 3 WLR 1253 possession proceedings were commenced by the landowner. However, they failed to follow up on the proceedings and they were subsequently stayed by the court and then struck out for lack of progress. The proceedings were held by the court to be insufficient to break the continuity of possession of the squatter.

Case Summary

Acknowledgement of the landowner's title

If a squatter who is in adverse possession of the landowner's land acknowledges in writing and signs a communication from the landowner giving the squatter permission to be on the land, then the acknowledgement will bring to an end the 12-year period that has been running in the squatter's favour (sections 29 and 30 Limitation Act 1980), or in the case of applications under the Land Registration Act 2002 the minimum ten-year period preceding the squatter's application for registration of title. This is illustrated by the Court of Appeal case of *Archangel* v. *Lambeth Borough Council* (2001) 33 HLR 44. In the case, the subject of which was an appeal against a possession order granted against the tenant of a house owned by the council, the defendant had referred to the house in correspondence between him and the council as 'Lambeth's property'. The court held both at first instance and on appeal that this was clear acceptance of the council's ownership of the property. Accordingly the squatter's adverse possession claim was dismissed.

Case Summary

Acknowledgement of the landowner's title can take place both expressly and impliedly. Offering to buy the land or to pay rent, as in the case of *R* v. *Secretary of State for the Environment, ex p. Davies* (the caravan in the quarry case) have both been viewed as sufficient to end the squatter's period of adverse possession. In the case of *Lambeth London Borough Council* v. *Bigden* (2001) 33 HLR 43 signatures on a petition were even deemed sufficient to constitute an acknowledgement of the landowner's title to the property. In the case, a squatter's adverse possession claim of a flat within a block owned by the council failed because a petition delivered to landowner in 1989 which formed part of a campaign by the occupiers to prevent the sale of the block to a housing association was held sufficient acknowledgement of the landowner's title for the purposes of the Limitation Act 1980. The court held that the petition, by its very nature, acknowledged implicitly that the landowner had the power to sell.

Case Summary

If after the squatter's acknowledgement of the landowner's title the squatter then remains in possession of the property, under the provisions of the Limitation Act 1980 the landowner's title will become statute-barred at the expiry of 12 years from the date of the acknowledgement. In the case of the Land Registration Act 2002, the 10-year period will start to run again from that same date. Under the Limitation Act, once the landowner's right to recover the land becomes statute-barred, an acknowledgement by the squatter of the landowner's title will not revive the landowner's title. In the case of *Sanders* v. *Sanders* (1881) 19 Ch D 373 the Court of Appeal held that once the limitation period had expired and the landowner's title to property had been extinguished, no subsequent payment of rent or acknowledgement of title by the occupier could restore the former landowner's title. As we have already seen, the provisions of the 2002 Act

Case Summary

remove the limitation period and therefore the squatter has no rights until their post-ten-year application for registration has been made. After the initial application has been made, it is only the commencement of court proceedings or the securing of an eviction order by the landowner that will suffice in preventing the squatter's further application for registration.

There is a view that if a squatter ignores communication from the landowner in which the landowner expressly or impliedly asserts their rights over the property, the squatter's adverse possession will not be affected and the period of occupation will remain interrupted. This is a somewhat controversial viewpoint, however. In *Wallis's Cayton Bay Holiday Camp* Lord Denning toyed with the idea (amid dissent from his fellow judges) that the squatter's lack of response to the landowner's letters had amounted to an unconscionable act sufficient under equitable rules to prevent the squatter from making a claim in adverse possession at all. As we have seen above, however, the decision in this case has now been discredited by the courts. As we also saw earlier the Court of Appeal in the case of *BP Properties Ltd* v. *Buckler* (1987) 55 P&CR 337 also held that an unacknowledged unilateral communication to a squatter stating that they were permitted to remain on the land as a **licensee** was sufficient to create a licence in the squatter's favour and stop time running under the Act. The case has been heavily criticised, however, and is unlikely to be followed.

Fraud, concealment or mistake

Section 32 of the Limitation Act 1980 states that the squatter's adverse possession of the property will cease if the squatter's action is in any way fraudulent, or is based upon a mistake, or if any fact relating to the squatter's occupation of the property has been deliberately concealed. Furthermore, the occupation period will not begin to run again until the relevant action has either been discovered or 'could with reasonable diligence have discovered it'. In the case of *Beaulane Properties Ltd* v. *Palmer* [2005] 3 WLR 554, which concerned a dispute over a two-and-a-half-acre field, the court held that the commencement of the limitation period should be postponed because the squatter, Mr Palmer, had misrepresented his occupation of the land as a squatter to the landowner's agents. He had done so by stating that he had a previous arrangement with the former owner of the land when in fact he did not and was in adverse possession of the land. In the event, the postponement did not affect the overall outcome of the case, however, as Mr Palmer remained in adverse possession of the property for in excess of twelve years after the discovery of the lie.

Leaseholds and adverse possession

The scenarios we have been considering throughout the course of this chapter have all related to adverse possession of freehold land. However, it is also possible to claim a leasehold title to property through adverse possession.

Adverse possession against a tenant

If a squatter enters onto a tenant's land and remains there for twelve years without the tenant taking steps to evict them, the squatter will acquire a possessory leasehold title to the land in exactly the same way as they would in the case of freehold land. The point to remember here, however, is that the squatter does not and cannot stake their claim to possessory title as against the freeholder. So when the lease on the land expires, all the squatter's rights as the possessory tenant are lost too. The freeholder then has just as much right to evict the squatter as they would to remove the original tenant if the tenant remained in occupation of the property after the expiration of their lease. If the squatter wants to get their hands on the freehold, therefore, they will have to start the adverse possession process all over again by commencing a new period of adverse occupation as against the freehold landowner.

For the duration of the squatter's occupation of leasehold property, the relationship between the landlord and the squatter is complex. The fact that the squatter is occupying the property does not automatically make them the landlord's tenant and, as such, the **covenants** (for example to pay rent) contained within the lease are not enforceable by the landlord against the squatter. Having said this, the landlord has a certain amount of persuasive power if there is a **right of re-entry** contained within the lease (that is, a right for the landlord to enter the property and remove the tenant if they do not comply with any of the covenants in the lease). In this situation, the landlord can threaten to re-enter the property if the rent is not paid, or indeed if any of the other covenants contained within the lease are not complied with. The fact that the covenants are the responsibility of the ousted tenant and not the squatter is irrelevant here – the practical outcome for the squatter is that the landlord re-enters their building and the squatter loses their property, so this is a real threat. If the squatter then pays the rent and that rent is payable periodically (for example weekly, monthly, quarterly or annually), at common law the squatter will become a periodic tenant of the property and is therefore no longer an adverse possessor of it. For further discussion of periodic tenancies you should see the chapter on leases.

Paying rent is not the only way in which a squatter can fall into the landlord-tenant trap. If the squatter takes advantage of any of the benefits provided by the landlord under the terms of the lease, they will automatically become bound by all the terms contained within the lease and be estopped (that is that they will be prevented in equity) from claiming that they do not occupy the property under the lease. This is illustrated in the case of *Ashe* v. *Hogan* [1920] 1 IR 159, an Irish Law Reports case in which the tenant was estopped from claiming that they were not bound by the lease because they had accepted reduced rent offered under the terms of the lease by the landlord. The landlord had offered a reduced rent under lease provisions as an incentive for complying with the lease covenants, in particular a covenant not to use the property for the sale of wine, liquor and spirits. The occupier of the premises had been using them as licensed premises for the sale of alcohol.

Case Summary

One final fly in the ointment for a would-be adverse possessor of leasehold property is if the tenant decides to surrender their lease of the property to the landlord. If the land is unregistered, even though after twelve years the tenant is time-barred from taking steps to remove the squatter from the property, they can instead choose to surrender their lease to the landlord who will then as freeholder have the right to evict the squatter from the property themselves. This was the outcome in the House of Lords case of

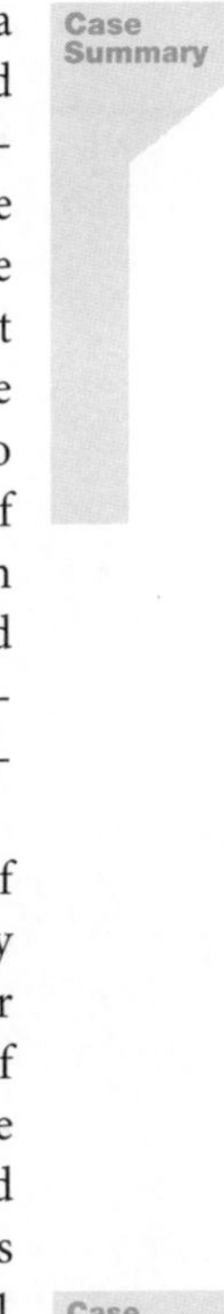

Fairweather v. *St Marylebone Property Co. Ltd* [1962] 2 WLR 1020, which concerned a 99-year lease of residential property. In the case the squatter had successfully acquired the lease of the property through their adverse possession of it and the tenant was time-barred from taking steps to evict them. The tenant then proceeded to surrender the remainder of the term of the lease to the landlord who immediately sought to evict the squatter. The landlord's application was successful. The court held that the tenant's right in title was extinguished as against the squatter but not the landlord. It was therefore possible for the tenant to surrender their rights to the landlord to enable the landlord to take direct action against the squatter. This decision effectively means that the rights of an adverse possessor to unregistered leasehold property are considerably weaker than those of a squatter on unregistered freehold land. Whereas a squatter in unregistered freehold premises knows they are safe after the twelve-year period has elapsed, a possessor of leasehold property will always live in fear of their possessory title being extinguished on the surrender of the tenant's lease to the landlord.

The position with registered land is different. If a squatter has under section 75 of the Land Registration Act 1925 succeeded in registering themselves with possessory title to the leasehold at the Land Registry, an attempt by the original tenant to surrender of the lease will have no effect. This is because the term of the lease is from the time of registration formally vested in the squatter and the tenant has no power to dispose of it. The effect is that, once the squatter's possessory title is registered, the landlord will have no right to claim possession from them until the expiry of the lease. This point is illustrated in the case of *Spectrum Investment Co.* v. *Holmes* [1981] 1 WLR 221 which, again, concerned a 99-year lease of residential property. Here it was held that because the squatter had registered possessory title to the lease at the Land Registry the tenant no longer had any rights in the property to surrender and consequently the landlord had no authority to enforce his rights as freeholder until the lease had come to an end.

Adverse possession by tenants

The other situation in which tenants play a part in adverse possession claims is where a tenant encroaches from their leased land onto neighbouring property in the ownership of a third party (not the landlord), thereby becoming an adverse possessor of it. In such a situation there is a rebuttable presumption that the tenant is claiming that property as the agent of the landlord. This means that if a tenant succeeds in claiming occupied property through adverse possession, unless there is evidence to show that the tenant did so for his own purposes and not simply to form an extension of the land leased, it is the landlord who will receive the benefit of that claim and in whose name the land will be placed. The tenant will benefit in so far as they can remain in possession of the additional property until the expiry of the lease, but once the lease has ended the landlord can enter into occupation of it as possessory owner. This point may be better understood in the light of an example. The case of *Kingsmill* v. *Millard* (1855) 11 Exch 313, concerned a tenant who had enclosed a strip of wasteland adjoining his rented property (a cottage and gardens in Chewton Mendip, Somerset). The tenant subsequently purported to sell the wasteland to a third party who built two cottages on it. The court was asked to determine whether the tenant had acquired this land for his own purposes and therefore for his own personal benefit, or whether he had acquired the land for the benefit of his landlord. The key question in the case, therefore, was whether the presumption of

acquisition on the landlord's behalf had been rebutted. In the event, the court found that the land had been acquired by the tenant independently of his lease and therefore it was his by virtue of his adverse possession of it to deal with as his own. In making their judgments the court said that, if there had been proof that the tenant had used it as an extension of the garden let to the tenant under the terms of the lease, the outcome would have been reversed.

The presumption of acquisition by a tenant on behalf of their landlord has recently been extended to provide that, in a subsequent purchase by the tenant of the leased property, any land acquired by virtue of the tenant's adverse possession of it will automatically be included in the sale. This was the decision in the case of *Tower Hamlets London Borough Council* v. *Barrett* [2006] 1 P&CR 132, in which the tenants of a public house acquired land adjacent to the pub by means of adverse possession. On the tenants' subsequent purchase of the freehold of the pub from their landlord, the land they had acquired next door was deemed to be included in the sale.

Case Summary

If the land onto which the tenant encroaches belongs to the landlord then the presumption is slightly different. If the tenant's occupation of the additional land can be viewed as a 'mere extension of the locus of his tenancy' (as stated by Lord Russell JC in the case of *Hastings* v. *Saddler* (1898) 79 LT 355, the facts of which are given below), as would have been the case in *Kingsmill* v. *Millard*, above, had the tenant simply occupied the additional land as part of the garden of the property rented by him, then the landlord's title to the land will be unaffected and will revert to the landlord at the end of the tenancy. The tenant will, however, be entitled to occupy the land possessed until the end of his tenancy. This is illustrated by the aptly named Court of Appeal case of *Smirk* v. *Lyndale Developments Ltd* [1975] Ch 317. In this case Mr Smirk was granted a weekly tenancy of a house and garden by his employers, British Railways Board. Soon after taking possession of the property Mr Smirk began to cultivate a strip of land forming part of wasteland to the rear of the house which also belonged to the Board. Thirteen years later Lyndale Developments bought the freehold of Mr Smirk's as well as the wasteland from the Board. Mr Smirk continued to cultivate the strip of wasteland for a further three years until Lyndale Developments began to make preparations to develop it. At this point Mr Smirk sought a declaration that he had a good possessory title to the strip of wasteland and that he held it as an extension of the locus of his tenancy. The Court of Appeal held that Mr Smirk had extended the locus of his tenancy to include the strip. He was therefore entitled to remain in possession of the strip until his tenancy expired.

Case Summary

If, on the other hand, the tenant is seen upon the facts to have been occupying the land 'adversely' to the landlord, then after the requisite period the tenant will be given good possessory title to the property and the landlord will lose that land, in accordance with the ordinary law of adverse possession. This was the outcome in the case of *Lord Hastings* v. *Saddler*. In this case Lord Hastings had leased an island to his tenant. However, during the term of his tenancy the tenant also took adverse possession of two other plots of land owned by Lord Hastings which were situated on the mainland, somewhere between half-a-mile and a mile away from the island leased by the tenant. After more than twelve years had elapsed and when the tenant's tenancy of the island had ended, Lord Hastings brought an action against the tenant's successor in title to obtain possession of the two plots of land. His claim failed. The court found that there was nothing to show that the tenant had occupied the plots as an extension of the island. The presumption that the tenant had occupied the plots of land as part of his lease was rebutted on the evidence. Lord Hastings was therefore not entitled to recover possession of the plots.

Case Summary

The political aspect

adverse possession diminishes the absolute nature of a landowner's rights over land

As one might imagine, the acquisition of land through adverse possession has caused a great deal of controversy over the years. We have already seen that the rights of adverse possessors and landowners are finely balanced and we have looked at what the Land Registration Act 2002 did to address the issue in respect of registered land. Whichever way you look at it, though, it does not change the fact that the law of adverse possession effectively diminishes the absolute nature of a landowner's rights over their land. So why allow it? What are the policy reasons for continuing to allow a law of adverse possession?

We looked earlier at the problems caused by unregistered land if title deeds are lost or stolen and we have seen that adverse possession is a tool through which such unregistered titles can be corrected. This is a good practical reason for maintaining adverse possession laws as they apply to this specific problem. But with over 75 per cent of estates in land in England and Wales now registered it is an argument that is ever-diminishing and we could even go as far as to say that in this respect the law of adverse possession is fast becoming an irrelevance. Another argument for maintaining a law of adverse possession is that it is in the public interest to do so. Land in England and Wales is naturally limited and if a landowner is not making use of their land why should it not be given over to someone who has a better use for it? In this context, it makes perfect logical sense that a limit should be put on the time a landowner can ignore either their property or another's possession of it. The time frames are generous, so why should a landowner who cannot be bothered to keep an eye on their property and police it be protected by the law against another person who will make better economic use of it?

Considered objectively, though, is this really fair? Is it right that a person should be able to take property from another without compensating the landowner for their loss? With unregistered land, one might have argued that there are cases where an occupier of land wishes to purchase or rent vacant land but is unable to ascertain the identity of the landowner. Registration of title puts an end to all this, however. Now, all a would-be possessor need do is to look at the register of title for the property on the centralised Land Register and the landowner will be revealed to them. If the occupier really wants the land, why should they not simply approach the landowner with an offer to buy or lease the property from them?

Of course, the most fundamental question this raises is one of human rights: how does the law of adverse possession affect the human rights of the landowner? The question was first given consideration in the case of *Family Housing Association* v. *Donellan* [2002] 1 P&CR 34. The case concerned a claim by the Family Housing Association that the grant of a possessory title to Mr Donellan in accordance with the provisions of the Limitation Act 1980 was in breach of the Housing Association's human rights under Protocol 1, Article 1 of the European Convention on Human Rights. You will remember from Chapter 2 that the Article provides:

> Every natural or legal person is entitled to the peaceful enjoyment of his possessions except in the public interest and subject to the condition provided for by law and by the general principles or international law.
>
> The preceding provisions shall not, however, in any way impair the right of a State to enforce such laws as it deems necessary to control the use of property in accordance with the general interest or to secure the payment of taxes or other contributions or penalties.

The decision, which was a High Court decision on appeal from the county court, was that the Article was not directed at matters of private law, but rather was concerned with the removal of property by or on behalf of the state for public purposes. The provisions of the Limitation Act 1980 did not breach Article 1 of the Convention. The finding was never appealed to a higher court.

Case Summary

The matter was again raised in the 2005 case of *Beaulane Properties* v. *Palmer*, but this time the courts reached a radically different conclusion. You may remember from earlier in the chapter that *Beaulane Properties* concerned a dispute over a two-and-a-half acre field used for agricultural purposes. The landowner, Beaulane Properties, intended to develop the land at a future date. The defendant, Mr Palmer, had in the meantime been using the field to graze horses. Beaulane Properties sought to have Mr Palmer evicted from the land. Whilst the court found that Mr Palmer had occupied the land for the required period of time to effect a successful claim under the Limitation Act 1980, it was held that Mr Palmer's claim to the land went against Article 1 of the Convention. It should be noted that by this time the provisions of section 3 of the Human Rights Act 1998 had come into force (they were not yet in force at the time of *Donellan*). The Act serves to incorporate the provisions of the Convention into domestic law and provides that, where domestic laws are found to be incompatible with the Convention, they should wherever possible be interpreted so as to accord with it. Focusing on the second part of Article 1, the court were unable to find any reason in the general interest why the landowner should be deprived of their land without compensation. However, unable to find a suitable interpretation of the provisions of the Limitation Act 1980 that would allow them to make a compensation payment to the landowner for the land, the court sought instead to revisit Lord Denning's invention of the implied licence (from his judgment in *Wallis's Cayton Bay Holiday Camp*) over adversely possessed land and duly held that, because the actions of Mr Palmer were not inconsistent with Beaulane's intended use of the land in the future, the claim of adverse possession could not be made. The decision to resurrect the fiction of the implied licence was immediately criticised and this interpretation of the law has now been superseded by the decisions in the ***Pye* v. *Graham*** cases.

Case Navigator

Case Summary

The first hearing of *JA Pye (Oxford) Ltd* v. *Graham* [2000] 3 WLR 242 actually took place before *Beaulane Properties*, in 2000. At this time the Human Rights Act 1998 had not yet been brought into force and so the issue of human rights was not considered. However, the case was later brought to the European Court of Human Rights by the UK government where, by a slim majority of four to three, it was held that the provisions of the Limitation Act 1980 imposed on landowners 'an individual and excessive burden' and 'upset the fair balance between the demands of the public interest on the one hand and the applicants' right to the peaceful enjoyment of their possessions on the other'. The country's adverse possession laws were therefore in breach of Article 1 of the Convention. It should be pointed out here that this was a very closely held majority, the minority stating that the law of adverse possession is well known and that the claimant should have been aware of it. They furthermore expressed the view that anyone leaving their property unattended for so long should realise it is at risk from squatters. Unhappy with the verdict, the UK government then referred the case one final time to the highest court in Europe, the Grand Chamber of the European Court of Human Rights, from which there is no appeal. The Grand Chamber found, this time by a majority of ten judges to seven, that the provisions of the Limitation Act 1980 were not in breach of Article 1. These were

anyone leaving their property unattended for so long should realise it is at risk

not statutory measures put into place to allow the State to take property from its paper owner; rather, the provisions were part of the general law intended to regulate limitation periods, which was a legitimate aim in the general interest. The Grand Chamber felt that the length of the limitation period on actions to recover land, coupled with the relative ease with which an adverse possession claim could be prevented (for example, by the landowner commencing possession proceedings against the squatter) meant that, even though no compensation was payable to the landowner following a successful adverse possession claim by a squatter, there was nevertheless no breach of Article 1.

Following the Grand Chamber decision in *Pye*, the House of Lords have now had the opportunity to give their thoughts on the issue of human rights in the adverse possession arena. In the Court of Appeal decision in *Ofulue* v. *Bossert* [2008] 3 WLR 1253, a case which concerned a claim to adverse possession of residential property made by the Bosserts, the Court held that in their opinion there was no reason to depart from the finding of the European Court of Human Rights that the legislative provisions of the Limitation Act 1980 were not Convention compliant. Accordingly, Mr Bossert was allowed to retain the property that he had acquired through adverse possession. This decision has effectively brought an end to any further claims being made that the law of adverse possession is in breach of human rights law.

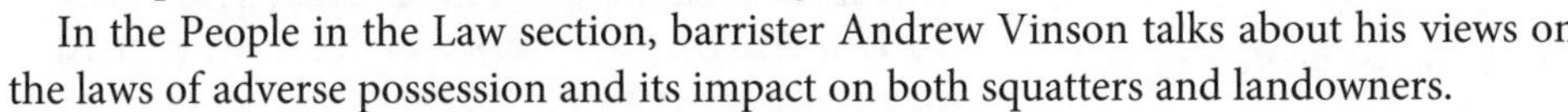

In the People in the Law section, barrister Andrew Vinson talks about his views on the laws of adverse possession and its impact on both squatters and landowners.

People in the law

Name and job description/area of expertise: Andrew Vinson, Chancery and Commercial Barrister

Source: Andrew Vinson

What made you choose this area of the law? I started out with a history degree and this area seemed to fit neatly with the sort of analysis that I had undertaken and topics that I had studied in that regard. Once at the Bar, it was amazing how a subject often accused of being dry revealed human interest. Very early on I was presented with a set of papers where one neighbour had cut the other's garage in half in the middle of the night on the basis of his interpretation of their paper titles!

Now that 75% of land in England and Wales is registered, do you think there is still a case for a law of adverse possession in modern conveyancing practice? Bluntly, yes. Even where land is registered, most boundaries shown are general. Adverse possession can cover a wide range of situations, but take for the moment the common example of a dispute over where a garden boundary lies. There needs to be some means of reflecting the longstanding reality on the ground where there has been no boundary agreement and the conveyance is unclear. Whilst it may not prevent the types of neighbour dispute that make the blood of many judges run cold, it at least provides a means for their solution.

Is not the acquisition of land through adverse possession, in effect, legalised stealing? Adverse possession has such a wide-ranging potential application that I don't think it's possible to generalise in that way. Where someone has simply tended an area which is ostensibly part of their land in the belief that it was, I don't see that you can equate that with theft. The boundaries become more blurred when you move into the realm of residential squatters.

Do you feel the provisions of the Land Registration Act 2002 have gone far enough to redress the balance between squatters and dispossessed land-owners? Yes – you will have to be pretty idle in relation to your registered land to lose it from this point on.

Where does our moral obligation lie, and should this play any part in our interpretation of the law in this field? Such an easy question! I would say that all laws must derive from some form of societal moral code. They are to distinguish between what is felt broadly to be allowable and not. To that extent, morals will inform the law. I don't see any easy moral decisions in this area though. In the example of the gardens I mentioned earlier, it is possible to have two people who are both acting in accordance with broadly accepted morals and have no idea as to the paper title situation. What moral guideline does one use to help choose between them? In other examples, such as residential squatting, how do you vary the test? What is the factor which would morally limit the application of the doctrine? The area in question, its value, the nature of the property?

We looked earlier in the chapter at the case of the Belgravia Squatters, who have entered and occupied a string of multi-million pound mansion houses in and around the Eaton Square area of London. Do you believe the law should afford these 'serial squatters' the opportunity to acquire unoccupied property in this way? Do you think the new s.144 of the Legal Aid, Sentencing and Punishment of Offenders Act 2012 will put an end to this kind of squatting? As I've set out above, once the doctrine of adverse possession is accepted, it is difficult to see how to mould it so as to exclude such situations. Where is the line to be drawn (if at all) between a strip of garden and 100 acres or a house? Personally, I have issues with such actions, but I don't see an easy cure. Under the 2002 Act, of course, it should be increasingly difficult for such claims to succeed. Section 144 might go some way towards putting an end to it, but I'm not entirely sure that respect for the law (whether civil or criminal) plays too much upon the minds of many of the occupiers.

What are your views on the most recent decision made by the Grand Chamber of the European Court of Human rights in the case of *Pye* v. *UK*? The minority expressed some powerful views. If the title is registered, and the point of registration is to provide a state guarantee of title, why should possession matter? That said, I tend to agree with the majority. It's a question of meshing the ideal with the practical reality. There needs to be some means of regulating situations on the ground which can frequently be very different from that on the registered title. I don't see that the State should pay the price for having a fallback provision concerning this.

Do you think there will be any call to revisit this issue in the future? Absolutely. This is a controversial area in which extreme examples are always likely to crop up and lead to the need for reconsideration of the principles involved.

Is there anything else you would like to add? Just to repeat what I mentioned earlier about not dismissing this area as dry or overly technical. In cases for private individuals you are often dealing with the most valuable asset that they have, and they will do some very strange things to protect it! In others, the stakes involved can be as proportionately high. There is human interest and enjoyment to be found within it.

Changes in the law affecting adverse possession claims

It should be noted that, as mentioned in the People in the Law interview above, in November 2011 Parliament added a new section to the Legal Aid, Sentencing and Punishment of Offenders Bill (HL Bill 109), making squatting in residential buildings an offence. The Bill received Royal Assent on 1 May 2012. The wording of the new Leqal Aid, Sentencing and Punishment of Offenders Act states, at Chapter 9 (Offences), that:

144

(1) A person commits an offence if–

(a) the person is in a residential building as a trespasser having entered it as a trespasser,

(b) the person knows or ought to know that he or she is a trespasser, and

(c) the person is living in the building or intends to live there for any period.

The section further states that:

(5) A person convicted of an offence under this section is liable on summary conviction to imprisonment for a term not exceeding 51 weeks or a fine not exceeding level 5 on the standard scale (or both).

Building a claim of adverse possession through squatting in residential buildings is therefore set to become increasingly difficult for those who would wish to acquire property in this way.

Writing and drafting

Having now read all about the rationale behind the laws of adverse possession and having digested the views of a barrister on the subject, why not take some time to write a list of pros and cons for the law of adverse possession.

You should take no more than twenty minutes on this task.

Handy tip: This is a straightforward but very useful writing task. Forming a list like this will not only help you to revise the theory behind the law but will also be a helpful preparation if you are asked to write an essay on the topic in an assessment scenario.

Reflective practice

Following the writing and drafting exercise above you should now have a more informed view of the law of adverse possession and the reasons behind it. Looking at your list of pros and cons, what are your personal views now on the law of adverse possession? Has your initial view, reached in the earlier Reflective Practice exercise changed at all? If so, why do you think this is?

Summary

- A squatter can acquire a possessory title to land through their uninterrupted occupation of it over a specified period of time.
- There are two sets of rules applicable to the law of adverse possession, the Limitation Act 1980, which applies to unregistered land and registered land acquired through adverse possession before 13 October 2003; and the Land Registration Act 2002, which applies to all registered land acquired through adverse possession since 2003.
- Adverse possession takes place through the dispossession or discontinuance of the owner's occupation of the land. In most cases there will be a dispossession, as discontinuance (or abandonment) of the land is so difficult to prove.
- Possession of the property must be adverse: that is, it must be without the consent of the landowner. Any form of consent, whether express or implied, by the landowner will negate the squatter's claim.
- The squatter must have both physical possession of the property and the intention to possess, or '*animus possidendi*'. What amounts to physical possession will depend upon the facts of the case, but in most cases enclosure will be adequate proof of possession. Mere user will not.
- The intention to possess will not be negated if the squatter believed they were the true owner of the land they were possessing.
- Under the Limitation Act 1980, after 12 years' adverse possession of property, the landowner will be statute-barred from taking action to recover the land, and their title to the property will be extinguished.
- Under the Land Registration Act 2002, after 10 years' adverse possession of property, the squatter may apply to be registered with possessory title to the property. If one of three specific conditions are met, they will be registered; otherwise their application will be rejected.
- Following the rejection of the squatter's application, the landowner has two years in which to commence possession proceedings against the squatter and/or procure an eviction order against them. If the landowner does not do this, the squatter may reapply for registration of their possessory title at the end of this period and the Land Registry must comply with their request.
- After a further twelve years have passed, the possessory title holder can apply for their title to be upgraded to good or absolute title.
- Leasehold property can be acquired by adverse possession as well as freehold property; however, at the end of the lease the freehold will revert to the landowner and the squatter will be required to vacate the premises.
- If a tenant acquires property by adverse possession, there is a general presumption that the tenant is acquiring land on behalf of their landlord, unless there is evidence to the contrary. If the land acquired belongs to the landlord, it will be assumed that the tenant is simply extending the area leased, unless it can be proven that the tenant's acquisition of the land was completely unrelated to their adjoining lease.
- Following protracted consideration, it would now appear settled law that the acquisition of land through the law of adverse possession is not in contravention of Article 1 of the European Convention on Human Rights (*Pye* v. *UK; Ofulue* v. *Bossert*).
- Section 144 of the Legal Aid, Sentencing and Punishment of Offenders Act now makes squatting in residential buildings an offence, which should help to reduce the number of claims by residential squatters.

Question and answer*

Problem: In 1976 Boris buys the freehold to two adjacent plots of unregistered land which he names Nineacre and Tenacre. In 1998 he leases Tenacre to Yolanda on a 25-year lease, which she intends to use for her market gardening business. Boris leaves Nineacre empty, planning to build a small warehousing and distribution site on it in the future. Initially Yolanda's business booms: so much so that in 1999 she asks Boris if she can rent from him a further strip of land, which forms part of Nineacre. Boris says no as he wishes to keep the sites separate for the purposes of his planning application. However, when Yolanda ignores his wishes and proceeds to plant cabbages and alfalfa beans on the Nineacre site, in several rows running parallel to the border between the two properties, Boris does nothing, figuring that he has plenty of time before his planning permission is granted and that it is not doing any harm. After some wranglings with the planning authorities, Boris realises the grant of planning permission is going to take considerably longer than he thought. In 2001, to bring some revenue in from Nineacre, Boris lets the field on an informal basis to Trinny as grazing for her horses. Trinny is rather unreliable and after mid-2002 stops paying rent. Boris asks Trinny to remove her horses from the field but she does not do so. In the meantime Yolanda has fenced off the part of Nineacre she has been using to protect her vegetables from the horses. In 2004 Boris dies suddenly, leaving both Nineacre and Tenacre to his only living relative – a nephew in Canada called Dexter. Initially Dexter is uninterested in the two fields he has inherited. However, after a few more years pass, he realises there may be some value in the land if it can be developed. After some renewed discussion with the local council in 2010 Dexter learns that he can obtain planning permission to build thirty houses on the combined site and it is worth a fortune. He contacts an estate agent to put the land up for sale. However, the agents soon inform him that both Yolanda and Trinny are claiming adverse possession of their respective portions of Nineacre. It is now 2012.

(a) Advise Dexter whether either Yolanda or Trinny have a right to claim Nineacre and on what grounds, and (b) explain how your advice would differ if the land was registered.

You should allow yourself no more than 40 minutes to complete this task.

Essay: Should a freeholder who makes no use of his land lose it? Is there a public interest in land being put to use? (Answer in the light of the recent case of *Pye* v. *Graham/Pye* v. *UK*)

This question should be answered in 40 minutes.

* Answer guidance is provided at the end of the chapter.

Further reading

Law Reform Committee, Final Report on Limitation of Actions (1977) Cmnd 6823.
This report is now dated but is worth taking a look at to gain a better understanding of the legislative provisions put into place in the Limitation Act 1980 and the reasoning behind them.

Law Commission, *Land Registration for the 21st Century: A Conveyancing Revolution*, Report No. 271 (2001), Paragraphs 2.69 et seq.
Again, this report is useful in that it provides an explanation of the rationale behind the reform of land registration, resulting in the Land Registration Act 2002. See http://lawcommission.justice.gov.uk/docs/lc271_land_registration_for_the_twenty-first-century.pdf

Wallace, H., 'Limitation, prescription and unsolicited permission', Conv. 1994, May/Jun, 196–210.
This article discusses the issue of permission in adverse possession cases and whether it is possible for a landowner to unilaterally grant a licence over adversely occupied land.

McCormack, G., 'Adverse possession – the future enjoyment fallacy', Conv. 1989, May–Jun, 211–16.
This is a superb article discussing the decision in the *Wallis's Cayton Bay Holiday Camp* case and the cases which followed it and whether the future plans of the landowner for the property should be relevant in determining an adverse possession case.

Dockray, M., 'Why do we need adverse possession?' (1985), Conv. 272
A great article considering the policy reasons for retaining a law of adverse possession.

Katz, L. M. (2010), 'The Moral Paradox of Adverse Possession: Sovereignty and Revolution in Property Law', McGill Law Journal, vol. 55, 47.
Although a Canadian article, as a piece of wider reading this really gets you thinking about the moral questions and dilemmas produced by the issues of squatters' rights and adverse possession laws.

Dixon, M., 'Human rights and adverse possession: the final nail?' Conv. 2008, 2, 160–65.
A clear and succinct article explaining the Court of Appeal decision in *Ofulue* v. *Bossert* and exploring the significance of the Grand Chamber ruling in *Pye* v. *UK*.

Question and answer guidance

Please note that the following is not a full answer and is intended to provide guidance in outline form only as to how to answer the questions posed.

Problem:

(a) There are two sets of rules applicable to the law of adverse possession, the Limitation Act 1980, which applies to unregistered land and registered land acquired through adverse possession before 13 October 2003; and the Land Registration Act 2002, which applies to all registered land acquired through adverse possession since 2003. We are told that the land purchased is unregistered and therefore the Limitation Act applies. In order to make a claim for adverse possession, therefore, Yolanda and Trinny must show that they have been in adverse possession of the property for a continuous period of 12 years. After this period has elapsed, Dexter will lose all rights that he has in the property and his title will be extinguished. The ladies will have possessory title to the property.

In order to establish that they have been in adverse possession of the property under the Limitation Act 1980, Trinny and Yolanda must show either that they have dispossessed the landowner from the land, or that there has been a discontinuance in the landowner's possession of it, following which the ladies have taken possession of the land (*Rains* v. *Buxton* (1880)). Discontinuance is very rare and in most cases dispossession will apply. Yolanda's cultivation of part of the Nineacre site against Boris's wishes would certainly constitute a dispossession, as would Trinny's occupation of the site with her horses following Boris's request for her to leave the site.

In so far as possession itself is concerned, we are told that Yolanda has fenced off the area of land she is cultivating. This is the best proof of possession (*Seddon* v. *Smith*). In other cases, such as Trinny's, where she is simply grazing horses on the land, it will be a matter of fact and degree, but the possessor must maintain an 'appropriate degree of physical control'. Given that she was a tenant of the land before she ceased to pay rent on it, it would be safe to assume her occupation was valid, but you may wish to illustrate the point using a couple of cases such as *Tecbild* v. *Chamberlain* and *Fowley Marine* v. *Gafford*.

Possession of the property must be adverse: that is, it must be without the consent of the landowner. Any form of consent, whether express or implied, by the landowner will negate the squatter's claim. In both cases, Boris has made it clear he does not want the ladies on the land in question and so this is satisfied. In Yolanda's case she asked to rent the additional space and Boris said no, but she took possession of it anyway; in Trinny's case, she was renting the land but ceased paying rent and Boris asked her to leave, but she remained in possession (see *Long* v. *Tower Hamlets* and *Hayward* v. *Chaloner*).

Mention could be made here of the controversy surrounding the suggestion that if the landowner does not have a conflicting use of the property planned there will be an implied licence of that land to the adverse possessor, as per *Wallis's Cayton Bay Holiday Camp*, given the facts in our scenario are that Boris was simply keeping the land with a view to obtaining planning permission on it at a later date. This can be contrasted with the case of *Treloar* v. *Nute*, in which the landowner did not have any other plans for the property.

The squatter must have both physical possession of the property and the intention to possess. There is no suggestion here that either lady was occupying the property under the misapprehension that they owned it, or that their intention was otherwise than to occupy the property adversely.

Has the 12 years elapsed? We are told that Yolanda has been cultivating the additional part of Nineacre since 1996 and fenced it off in around 2002. She has therefore been in adverse possession of the piece of land for the required amount of time and Dexter's title is extinguished. It is irrelevant that Boris was the previous owner of the property and that the freehold has now been passed to Dexter. However, as Yolanda is a leaseholder her acquisition of the land will only be to the extent that she is extending the area already leased to her, unless it can be proven that her acquisition of the land was completely unrelated to her adjoining lease. As it is an extension of her market gardening business, run from the leased site, this is unlikely. Once the 25-year lease runs out, therefore, she will be obliged to return both Tenacre and the additional strip of land acquired to Boris.

As for Trinny, she was formerly a tenant of the property but has been adversely possessing it without the payment of rent since 2002. We are told that it is 2012 and so she has only been in adverse possession of the land for 10 years, however, so she needs to wait another 2 years before Dexter's title will be extinguished.

(b) If the land was registered, the provisions of the LRA 2002 apply. These provide that, after 10 years' adverse possession of property, the squatter may apply to be registered with possessory title to the property. In this case, therefore, both Trinny and Yolanda will be in a position to apply to the Land Registry for possessory title to be registered. Following their applications, Dexter will then have two years in which to commence possession proceedings against both Trinny and Yolanda and/or procure eviction orders against them. If he does not do this, the ladies may reapply for registration of their possessory title at the end of this period and the Land Registry must comply with their request. After a further twelve years have passed, they can then apply for their title to be upgraded to good or absolute title.

Essay: This essay question is really just an opportunity for you to give your opinion on adverse possession and to say whether or not you think it is a fair method of land acquisition. Whether you agree with it or not in principle does not really matter, as long as you back up your answer with case law and examples, and take into account the available commentary on the issue.

One suggested way to start would be to cover the issue of lost or stolen title deeds and the need for there to be an ability to deal with such situations. However, admittedly this is a fairly limited (and diminishing) scenario which presumably could be contained within its own rules, rather than being a very small residual part of what is now a much larger issue.

The other common reason given for maintaining a law of adverse possession is that it is in the public interest to do so because land is limited and if a landowner is not making use of their land it makes sense that it should be given to someone who will put it to use. This argument flows contrary to the right of the landowner to do what they like with their own land, however, which many may argue takes precedence ultimately over the idea of the free flow and use of land. It also begs the question, if the adverse possessor wishes to have the land should they simply not just lease or buy it from the current landowner?

The issue of adverse possession has recently been placed in the spotlight in the human rights arena, in the cases of *Pye* v. *Graham* and *Pye* v. *UK*. The finding in *Pye* v. *Graham*, whilst the court acknowledged that a person who leaves their property unattended for such a long period of time should realise it is at risk, was that the laws of adverse possession did breach the European Convention on Human Rights, Article 1, in that they imposed an excessive burden on the individual to protect their property and upset the fair balance between the demands of the public interest on the one hand and the applicants' right to the peaceful enjoyment of their possessions on the other. However, the Grand Chamber of the ECHR overturned this decision, finding that the provisions of the Limitation Act 1980 were not in breach of Article 1.

Their decision confirmed that the provisions were part of the general law intended to regulate limitation periods, which was a legitimate aim in the general interest. The length of the limitation period on actions to recover land, coupled with the relative ease with which an adverse possession claim could be prevented (for example, by the landowner commencing possession proceedings against the squatter) meant that, even though no compensation was payable to the landowner following a successful adverse possession claim by a squatter, there could nevertheless be no breach of Article 1. The Court of Appeal decision in *Ofulue* v. *Bossert* [2008] has since affirmed their finding.

You may find the opinions of barrister, Andrew Vinson, from the People in the Law feature, useful in forming your opinion on the matter. Specifically, he gives practical and clear reasoning for the continued need for a law of adverse possession and comments that, since the provisions of the LRA 2002 were brought in, 'you would have to be pretty idle' to lose your land under an adverse possession claim for registered land. The articles listed in the Further Reading by Katz, Dixon and Dockray also all make useful and informative reading for a student wishing to write an insightful and informed essay on this topic.

Visit **www.mylawchamber.co.uk** to access tools to help you develop and test your knowledge of land law.

Use Case Navigator to read in full some of the key cases referenced in this chapter with commentary and questions:

Pye* v. *Graham [2002] UKHL 30
Pye* v. *UK [2005] ECHR 44302/02

Chapter 7 Informal methods of acquisition: resulting and constructive trusts

Key points In this chapter we will be looking at:

- ✦ The nature of resulting and constructive trusts as informally created interests in land
- ✦ The concept of resulting trusts and how they arise
- ✦ What constitutes a contribution to the purchase price in resulting trusts
- ✦ Constructive trusts and how they differ from resulting trusts
- ✦ The importance of unconscionability in constructive trusts and how it is defined
- ✦ What constitutes detrimental reliance in constructive trusts
- ✦ How the share of an interest in the property is calculated in constructive trusts
- ✦ The difficulty with quantification of share in respect of unmarried couples
- ✦ Surveying the whole course of conduct of the parties and whether this can be used to award an interest in the property, as well as quantify one
- ✦ Other uses for constructive trusts

Introduction

In this chapter we continue to look at the informal creation of rights in land. However, whereas in Chapter 6 we read about the acquisition of a legal **estate** in land by means of **adverse possession**, in this chapter we are going to consider the creation of **equitable interests**, in the form of a **trust of land**. You will remember that interests in land are a lesser form of right in the land, albeit that they can nevertheless be a very powerful and valuable thing to possess, as we shall see as we progress through the chapter.

As the law currently stands informally created trusts of land fall broadly into two categories:

- ✦ **resulting trusts**; and
- ✦ **constructive trusts**.

Unlike legal interests in land, which require a **deed** for their creation or transfer (s.52 LPA 1925), and even the majority of equitable interests, which at the very least require writing (s.53(1) LPA 1925), resulting and constructive trusts are different from other interests in land in that they do not require any **formality** for their creation. Thus, a resulting or constructive trust can be created without the need for writing at all. This is as a result of a special exclusion contained in section 53(2) of the Law of Property Act 1925, which specifically excludes from the requirement for writing the creation or operation of resulting or constructive trusts.

Resulting and constructive trusts have a wide range of uses and any textbook on the law of **equity** and **trusts** will give you a long list of different circumstances in which they can be created. However, in the context of land law, the use of resulting and constructive trusts tends to be in relation to the family home, and it is in this context that we will be considering both types of trust in this chapter. So what kind of circumstance are we talking about here? Imagine the scenario of a man and woman, Tim and Anna, buying a house together to live in. For some reason the **legal title** to the property is put into Tim's sole name, although Anna lives in the property and contributes to the purchase price, upkeep or maintenance of the property. After 10 years of living together the couple split up, and Anna asks for the property to be sold, so that the proceeds can be distributed between them. Tim refuses: the property is in his name, he says, so Anna has no rights to a share in the property at all. From a strictly legal viewpoint, of course, Tim is correct: Anna has no legal rights in the property and has no claim to the house or the proceeds of sale, if it is sold. In the eyes of equity, however, the matter is quite different. Although Anna has no claim at law to the property, through equitable principles she has contributed to the purchase or upkeep of the property and thus should have a claim in equity to a share of it. This may be achieved either through the medium of a resulting or a constructive trust.

We will be looking at resulting trusts in the first part of the chapter and the more contentious area of constructive trusts in the latter part.

Resulting trusts

In the context of land law, resulting trusts are most commonly encountered where a house or land is purchased in the name of one person, but the purchase money is provided either wholly or partially by another. In these circumstances, the legal owner of the property will be viewed as holding the property on trust together for themselves and the person who contributed to the purchase price, in proportion to the shares they put into the property.

So to use our example of Tim and Anna, where Tim has bought the property in his sole name but Anna has provided some or all of the money for the purchase, then a resulting trust will be created in favour of Anna, in line with her contribution towards the purchase price. In this scenario, the resulting trust is based on the presumption that the settlor (Anna) gave the money fully intending that it should be held on trust for their benefit. So the reasoning behind the imposition of the trust is that Anna, in putting money towards the purchase price of the house, intended that by virtue of her contribution she would receive a **beneficial interest** in the property.

Resulting trusts will not solely operate in situations such as Anna's. In fact, the presumption of a resulting trust may exist in any of the following situations:

- Where Tim and Anna have both contributed to the purchase of a property, but the property is put into Tim's sole name, as above (in which case there will be a resulting trust in favour of Anna);

- ✦ Where Tim has purchased property with his own money, but has put that property in Anna's sole name (in which case there will be a resulting trust in favour of Tim);
- ✦ Where Tim has made an outright gift of property to Anna (in which case there may again be a resulting trust in favour of Tim).

It is a well-established principle of equity that, if there is no evidence of an intention to the contrary, wherever property is purchased either party or wholly by one person in the name of some other person it will be held on a resulting trust for the person who has paid for the purchase. This is illustrated in the case of *Bull* v. *Bull* [1955] 1QB 234 (CA), which concerned a disagreement arising between a mother and son following the son's marriage. Mrs Bull and her son bought a property at 101 Rishden Gardens, Ilford, Essex in 1949. Both mother and son contributed towards the purchase price for the property, but the son provided the greater part of the money and the property was conveyed into his sole name. In April 1953 the son married and it was arranged that his mother should keep two rooms in the house whilst he and his wife would have the rest. Soon afterwards, however, differences arose between the mother and her daughter-in-law and the son told his mother to leave the house. The mother contended that, despite the house being in her son's sole name, she had a right to live in the property by virtue of her contribution towards the purchase of it. The court agreed, finding that she had not intended to make a gift of the purchase money to her son and that therefore there should be a resulting trust imposed in her favour. In making his judgment Lord Justice Denning confirmed that, whilst the son was undoubtedly the legal owner of the house, the mother and son owned the house together in equity. The mother was therefore entitled to a share of the house proportionate to her contribution to the purchase price.

Case Summary

Another example is provided by the case of *Springette* v. *Defoe* [1992] 2 FLR 388 (CA). Here, the property in question was in fact purchased in the joint names of the contributing parties; the disagreement extended only to an argument over what should be the extent of the parties' entitlement to the property in equity: in other words, in what proportion should the property be divided? The facts of the case were that Mrs Springette and Mr Defoe lived together in Mrs Springette's council flat. The council subsequently offered the couple a council house which they moved into as **joint tenants** in 1982. In the same year, the council offered to sell the council house to Mrs Springette and Mr Defoe for £14,445. This included a discount of 41 per cent of the purchase price on the basis that Mrs Springette had been a council **tenant** for more than 11 years. The couple took out a **mortgage** in their joint names for £12,000, Mrs Springette paying the balance of the purchase monies from her savings. The couple agreed that they would contribute equally towards the repayment of the mortgage. On the couple's subsequent break-up, Mr Defoe claimed that he was entitled to a 50 per cent share in the house. However, the court found that the property was held on a presumed resulting trust, Mrs Springette being entitled to a 75 per cent cent share in the property by virtue of the contribution she had made out of her savings to the purchase price, and the council discount from which the couple had benefited. The court held that Mrs Springette should benefit from the full amount of the discount, which would not have been available to them had Mrs Springette not been a council tenant for 11 years and without which the couple would not have been able to afford to buy the property.

Case Summary

Case Summary

Clearly this is an instance in which the courts were prepared to construe a discount on the purchase of a property as having an equivalent cash value in determining proportionate shares under a resulting trust. But what else can be included in the purchase price for the purposes of calculating contribution?

What is included in the purchase price?

We have seen above that whoever provides the purchase money for the property will be viewed in equity as having an interest in that property, in the form of a resulting trust in their favour. The timing of the creation of the interest is crucial in the resulting trust scenario: resulting trusts are based on the presumed intention of the parties at the time the property is acquired and the courts are really quite strict in construing this. So it is only those contributions made towards the actual purchase of the property, and not any subsequent payments, which will go to form the interest of the contributing party. A number of cases illustrate this point.

As we have already seen in *Springette* v. *Defoe*, payments towards mortgage instalments will be construed as payments towards part of the purchase price of the property, albeit that they are paid over a period of time and not just at the time of purchase. So, in the most straightforward example of this, in the case of *Cowcher* v. *Cowcher* [1972] 1 WLR 425 (CA), Mr and Mrs Cowcher bought a house with the aid of a mortgage, the house being put into Mr Cowcher's sole name. The mortgage was subsequently paid off by Mr and Mrs Cowcher together, and the courts held that Mr Cowcher would hold an interest in the property on a resulting trust for the wife on account of this.

But what about such smaller items as legal fees and removal expenses? In *Curley* v. *Parkes* [2004] 1 P & CR DG 15 the court considered a claim in respect of such payments. Mr Curley and Miss Parkes had been living together in a house in Richmond, London, bought by Miss Parkes and registered in her sole name. Mr Curley's employer subsequently asked him to relocate to the company's offices in Luton, offering in return a relocation package which consisted of money to help with the moving costs and with the purchase of a new property in the locality. The company also agreed to buy Miss Parkes's property from her as part of the relocation. Miss Parkes then purchased another property in Luton, again in her sole name, and with her own money. Mr Curley paid no proportion of the purchase price of the new property. Over the course of the following six months, Mr Curley did pay Miss Parkes a total of £9,000, however, which he later said was to compensate her for the deposit paid by her on the new house and for legal and removal expenses. When the couple separated, Mr Curley claimed an 8.5 per cent share of the property on resulting trust on the basis of money contributed towards the purchase price. However, the court dismissed his claim, as there was no evidence that the payments made to Miss Parkes had been designed to contribute to the purchase price of the property.

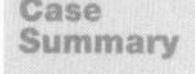

Curley v. *Parkes* shows us that contributions to the purchase price must be both specific and contemporary to the purchase. In addition, the courts must be able to attribute to such payments a genuine intention to contribute to the purchase price of the house: general contributions towards rent or household expenses will not be sufficient. In *Savage* v. *Dunningham* [1974] Ch 181 three men shared a furnished flat together, the **lease** for which was in the name of only one of them. All three parties made equal payments towards the rent and other outgoings. Mark Dunningham, who was the leaseholder, was offered the chance by the **landlord** to purchase the flat for himself. He agreed to buy the flat but did not tell his flatmates about the opportunity or give them the option to purchase the flat along with him. Shortly after buying the flat he served notice on his flatmates to vacate the property. The flatmates argued that Dunningham held the property on resulting trust for all three of them. However, it was held that there was no resulting trust. The contributions which had been made to the rent and household expenses did not equate to any payment towards the purchase price of the property.

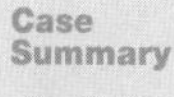

Do you think you are clear on which contributions will be sufficient to form a resulting trust? Test your knowledge and understanding by taking a look at the Writing and Drafting exercise below.

Writing and drafting

You are a trainee solicitor at Walker Smiles solicitors. Your principal has asked you to see a client, Jerome Harling. Jerome tells you that he and ex-girlfriend, Tika, purchased 10 Marlins Walk eight years ago. However, Jerome was credit blacklisted at the time, due to some outstanding student debts, and so the house and mortgage was put into Tika's sole name. Now the couple has separated. Tika is saying the house belongs to her legally and Jerome isn't entitled to a thing. However, he made a number of contributions to the property and believes he is entitled to a share in it. His contributions were as follows: (a) payment of the 10% deposit on the property; (b) payment of the estate agents and legal fees on the purchase; (c) making payments towards the mortgage; (d) payment of household bills, and (e) paying for a conservatory to the rear of property.

Write a letter to Jerome, explaining which of his contributions you think would be sufficient establish a beneficial interest in the property under a resulting trust.

You should take no more than 40 minutes on this task.

Handy tip: Remember it is the timing of the contributions that is important in a resulting trust. Which can be genuinely attributed to the property's purchase?

From the examples above we can see that the courts take quite a strict approach as to what payments will and will not be included as contributing to the purchase of a property, particularly in the case of payments made some time after the date of purchase. In the case of subsequent payments, these are unlikely to amount to a beneficial interest under a resulting trust, regardless of the amount of the payments or the period of time over which they were made. Certainly payments of a more trivial nature will not be sufficient. The case of *Gissing* v. *Gissing* [1971] AC 886 illustrates this. The case concerned a husband and wife, Violet and Raymond Gissing. Violet and Raymond lived together in a house which was registered in Raymond's sole name. He had paid for the house partly with a mortgage and partly with a loan from his employers. When Raymond left Violet for a younger woman, Violet claimed an interest in the house, claiming that she had contributed £220 from her savings to pay for a new lawn and furniture for the house. She said that she had later contributed from her earnings to the housekeeping and paid for her own and her son's clothes. However, Violet's claim was dismissed by the Court of Appeal: her limited contributions had not been enough to earn her a beneficial interest in the house.

Case Summary

A similar outcome was achieved in the House of Lords case of *Pettitt* v. *Pettitt* [1970] AC 777. The case concerned an argument over the family home of Harold and Hilda Pettitt. Hilda had inherited a house which she and her husband lived in for a number of years. Hilda then sold the house, using the proceeds to buy a plot of land on which to build a bungalow for her and Harold to live in. The bungalow was again bought in Hilda's sole name. Hilda subsequently left Harold, taking their two children with her, and made an application for divorce on grounds of cruelty. Harold claimed a share of the bungalow on the grounds that he had spent money and effort in redecorating and

Case Summary

improving it; but the House of Lords rejected Harold's claim. The improvements Harold was claiming to have made bore no relation to the purchase of the house and could therefore not amount to a beneficial interest under a resulting trust.

Both of the above cases give us an important insight into the thinking of the courts regarding the interpretation of claims for resulting trusts at that time. However, perhaps one of the most influential decisions relating to contributions in respect of the family home is the Court of Appeal case of *Burns* v. *Burns* [1984] Ch 317. The case concerned a couple, Valerie and Patrick Burns, who had lived together for almost 20 years and who had children together, although they were not actually married. The house they lived in was paid for by Patrick with part cash and part mortgage. The mortgage was paid off with Patrick's earnings while Valerie stayed at home to look after the house and children. When Valerie returned to work she used her own earnings to buy furniture, **fixtures** and **fittings** for the house and did some painting and redecoration, although her money was not needed to pay for any of the household expenses. The relationship broke down and Patrick sought a declaration as to whether Valerie had a beneficial interest in the house. The Court of Appeal held that Valerie had no interest in the house: she had made no contributions referable to the acquisition of an interest in the property. The fact that the relationship had lasted 19 years was irrelevant in claiming an interest in the property under a resulting trust.

Case Summary

This case is particularly useful in the study of resulting trusts because of Lord Justice May's really detailed summary of the position in equity, depending on whether the house is purchased in the joint names of the contributors or in the sole name of one party only. In the case of a purchase in joint names, he says:

> . . . both the man and the woman are entitled to a share in the beneficial interest. Where the house is bought outright and not on mortgage, then the extent of their respective shares will depend on a more or less arithmetical calculation of the extent of their contributions to the purchase price. Where, on the other hand, as is more usual nowadays, the house is bought with the aid of a mortgage, then the court has to assess each party's respective contributions in a broad sense; nevertheless, the court is only entitled to look at the financial contributions, or their real or substantial equivalent, to the acquisition of the house; that the husband may spend his weekends redecorating or laying a patio is neither here nor there, nor is the fact that the woman has spent so much of her time looking after the house, doing the cooking and bringing up the family.

Whereas, if the house is purchased in the sole name of one party:

> . . . then if the woman [assuming the property is bought in the man's sole name] pays or contributes to the initial deposit this points to a common intention that she should have some beneficial interest in the house. If thereafter she makes direct contributions to the instalments, then the case is [strengthened] and her rightful share is likely to be greater. If the woman, having contributed to the deposit, but although not making direct contributions to the instalments, nevertheless uses her money for other joint household expenses so as to enable the man more easily to pay the mortgage instalments out of his own money, then her position is the same. Where a woman has made no contribution to the initial deposit, but makes regular and substantial contributions to the mortgage instalments, it may still be reasonable to infer a common intention that she should share a beneficial interest from the outset . . . Finally, where the house is taken in the man's name alone, if the woman makes no 'real' or 'substantial' financial contribution towards either the purchase price, deposit or mortgage instalments by means of which the family

> home was acquired, then she is not entitled to any share in the beneficial interest in that home even though over a very substantial number of years she may have worked just as hard as the man in maintaining the family, in the sense of keeping house, giving birth to and looking after and helping to bring up the children of the union.

Lord Justice May's judgment is interesting because it suggests that the contributions made to the purchase of a house may be broadly divided into two categories: direct or indirect. Direct contributions include such payments as those which are made specifically towards the deposit or the purchase price and the payment of mortgage instalments, whereas **indirect contributions**, he suggests, may include payments towards household expenses which the legal owner of the property would otherwise be unable to meet, in addition to making the mortgage payments. There was some initial concern on the part of the judiciary following Lord Justice May's judgment that this second category of indirect contributions might cause confusion as to what exactly could be included in defining the resulting trust. The fear was that an inaccurate interpretation of the wording of the judgment might lead to an opening of the floodgates for claimants making applications for resulting trusts on the basis of contributions which bore no relation to the purchase of the property whatever. However, it is arguable that Lord Justice May was quite clear in his statement that any indirect contribution must be directly related to the acquisition of an interest in the house, which the other party could not have otherwise made (in other words, they could not have made the mortgage payments without help in paying the other household bills from their partner).

One point which does remain unaffected by the judgment in *Burns* v. *Burns* is that any beneficial share of property acquired under a resulting trust will be established at the time the property is purchased and will be unaffected by any later payments for improvements to the house or contributions to its upkeep.

Reflective practice

Consider the position of those who have either made no contribution or only paid a small amount towards the purchase of property, but who have then spent a great deal of money adding an extension to the house or maintaining the family home over a period of years. Do you think the law of resulting trusts is harsh in this respect? What do you think is the correct point at which a beneficial interest should be established in the home?

In respect of married couples, the position has been somewhat alleviated by section 37 of the Matrimonial Proceedings and Property Act 1970, which states that:

> Where a husband or wife contributes in money or money's worth to the improvement or **real** or **personal property** in which or in the proceeds of sale of which either or both of them has or have a beneficial interest, the husband or wife so contributing shall, if the contribution is of a substantial nature and subject to any agreement to the contrary express or implied, be treated as having then acquired by virtue of his or her contribution a share or an enlarged share, as the case may be, in that beneficial interest.

Section 65 of the Civil Partnership Act 2004 contains a similar provision. It should be noted that the wording of the Acts state that the work must be of a substantial nature.

So the erection of a conservatory or installing a central heating system will count, but repainting and keeping the house will not.

Section 37 is helpful to a point, but it is inherently flawed in that it does not assist unmarried couples. Thus, in *Burns* v. *Burns*, Valerie was not entitled to bring proceedings under the matrimonial legislation because they were unmarried. Given the increased trend for cohabitation, the courts tend to favour, as we shall see below, the mechanism of the constructive trust over resulting trusts when it comes to dividing the property of separating couples.

Constructive trusts

We have now established that wherever a person makes contributions to the purchase price of a property, whether they are registered as the legal owner of the property or not, they will acquire an equitable interest in the property in the form of a resulting trust, proportionate to the amount of their contribution. We have also learnt that if a person does not make a financial contribution to the purchase price, but they subsequently spend money on that property, perhaps by paying for repairs or maintenance to the property, or even by carrying out substantial works, such as an extension to the property, under the **doctrine** of resulting trusts they will nevertheless gain no entitlement to any proportion of the property, because they have not contributed towards the purchase price. Equally a person who makes no direct financial contribution to the property itself, but who stays at home and runs the household or brings up the children of the family over a number of years, will be entitled to nothing under the doctrine of resulting trusts. It may come as a relief to know that the rather harsh results meted out by the doctrine of resulting trusts in such situations do find a solution in the doctrine of constructive trusts, however; and this is what we are going to be looking at for the remainder of the chapter. This is not to say, of course, that resulting trusts do not have their place in the law; it is simply that the doctrine of constructive trusts has evolved to deal specifically with such situations as the family break-up, and is therefore more suited to the needs of persons who find themselves in this position.

What is a constructive trust?

Constructive trusts are fundamentally different from resulting trusts, not only in what they are designed to achieve (although perhaps because of this), but also in the basis on which they operate. Whereas we have seen that a resulting trust will be imposed irrespective of the legal owner's conduct – one might even say in spite of it – the assumption being that the settlor does not intend to benefit the person to whom legal title is given or transferred, a constructive trust, on the other hand, is said to arise by operation of law, specifically *on account of* the legal owner's conduct. With a constructive trust, it is all about finding the just, or equitable, outcome, based on the circumstances of the case, and the conduct of the parties plays a huge part in this.

a constructive trust said to arise *on account of* the legal owner's conduct

The concept of implied or constructive trusts is a relatively complex one which has been subject to a great deal of change over recent years. As we shall see, much of the case law relating to informally created trusts relates to the division of the family home or co-owned assets in the event of a family break-up. As a result of this, changes in the law in this area have often happened by way of reaction to changes in social norms and the increase in cohabiting couples which have rendered much of the surrounding law out of date. This makes the law in this area a constantly evolving area and, whilst there has been significant change over recent years, as we shall see throughout the remainder of the chapter, there are still plenty of areas for improvement.

changes in the law have often happened by way of reaction to changes in social norms

To give you a flavour of where a constructive trust will be imposed, let us have a look at an example. Say Nadia and Tomas set up home together. Tomas pays the deposit on the house from some savings and pays the mortgage. The property is registered in Tomas's sole name. However, Nadia subsequently buys a new central heating system for the property, pays for repairs to the roof and redecorates and furnishes the property throughout on the understanding that the house is going to be their home together and in the expectation that she will therefore have an interest in it. This is a situation we have come across in before in the context of resulting trusts and we have seen that Nadia's entitlement would be nothing in that context. However, in the context of a constructive trust, we must ask: 'would it be fair for Tomas to deny Nadia a beneficial entitlement to the property, knowing that she has spent many thousands of pounds on improving it and turning it into a comfortable home for the couple?' If, on considering this, your answer would be no, if would not be fair, then you are likely to have a constructive trust.

Case Summary

Lord Justice Chadwick in the case of *Banner Homes Group* v. *Luff Developments Ltd* [2000] 2 WLR 772 said that, with constructive trusts, it is a matter of **unconscionability**. The facts of this case were quite different from those of Nadia and Tomas, above. Here, the parties in question were companies, not individuals, and the disputed property consisted of a 4.8 acre development site, which the companies had agreed to buy and develop as a joint venture, for a purchase price of £3.4 million. Luff Developments Ltd had agreed to enter into a joint project to purchase the land, but had subsequently changed their minds, deciding to go ahead with the purchase without the **claimant**. However, they chose not to tell the claimant, Banner Homes, of their change of heart, for fear that the company would make a rival bid for the land. The court held in the event that Luff Developments had purchased the land on a constructive trust in favour of themselves and Banner Homes, in equal shares, and that all profits made from the site should be split equally between them. Quoting Lord Justice Millet from an earlier case, Lord Justice Chadwick said of constructive trusts:

> A constructive trust arises by operation of law wherever the circumstances are such that it would be unconscionable for the owner of property (usually but not necessarily the legal estate) to assert his own beneficial interest in the property and deny the beneficial interests of another.

The facts of this case may be quite different from the traditional view of constructive trusts set out in our earlier example of Nadia and Tomas; however, the principle is the same: that the legal owner of the property is deemed to have acted in an unconscionable manner in seeking to deny the claimant a beneficial interest in the property. The question to be asked here, then, with reference to Lord Justice Chadwick's judgment, is: when exactly will the circumstances be such that it would be unconscionable for the owner of the property to assert their beneficial interest over that of the claimant?

Defining unconscionability

The House of Lords was first given the opportunity to consider this question in *Gissing* v. *Gissing* [1971] AC 886, a case which we have already come across in the context of resulting trusts. You may remember that the case concerned a claim by a wife to a beneficial interest in the family home. The couple lived together in the family home which had been paid for by Mr Gissing. The house was in Mr Gissing's sole name. After 25 years of marriage, Mr Gissing left his wife for a younger woman. Mrs Gissing made an application to the court for an order in respect of her beneficial interest in the house.

The judges in the case did not consider the issue of constructive trusts in the context of 'unconscionability'; this expression was a much later description of the general equitable principles surrounding the imposition of the constructive trust and the law concerning constructive trusts was still very much in its infancy at this point. Rather, the judges' focus was that the imposition of a constructive trust should be reliant on some evidence of a **common intention** between the parties that they would share the beneficial ownership in the property in question. Whilst Lord Diplock's judgment is the most frequently quoted in respect of this case, the words of Viscount Dilhorne perhaps provide the simplest analysis of the position in equity. Viscount Dilhorne said that:

> . . . a claim to a beneficial interest in land made by a person in whom the legal estate is not **vested** and whether made by a stranger, a spouse or a former spouse must depend for its success on establishing that it is held on a trust to give effect to the beneficial interest of the claimant . . . Where there was a common intention at the time of the acquisition of the house that the beneficial interest in it should be shared, it would be a breach of faith by the spouse in whose name the legal estate was vested to fail to give effect to that intention and the other spouse will be held entitled to a share in the beneficial interest.

So, in effect, what Viscount Dilhorne is saying here is that it would be unconscionable for the legal owner of the property to deny a person an equitable interest in the property wherever there was a common intention between the parties that they should share the beneficial interest in it.

Of course, the problem with common intention, particularly in disputes between couples in the process of a relationship break-up, is proof. There will rarely have been an explicit agreement between the couple as to how the property is to be shared at the time of the purchase and any agreement, such as it was, is likely to have been oral. Viscount Dilhorne was quick to acknowledge this difficulty, stating that an absence of common intention could not be filled with inferences as to what the parties might have done if they had thought about it at the time, thus 'imputing' their intention: the common intention must have been a real one. However, in the absence of evidence of a specific agreement or discussion on the subject, Viscount Dilhorne did concede that reference could be made to the conduct of the parties and inference be made from that conduct. He said that:

an absence of common intention could not be filled with inferences as to what the parties might have done

> . . . in determining whether or not there was such a common intention, regard can of course be had to the conduct of the parties. If the wife provided part of the purchase price of the house, either initially or subsequently by paying or sharing in the mortgage payments, the inference may well arise that it was the common intention that she should have an interest in the house . . . Payment for a lawn and provision of some furniture and equipment for the house does not of itself point to the conclusion that there was such an intention.

The suggestion is, then, that common intention can be inferred from conduct under certain circumstances, in the absence of express agreement; although it would appear that where common intention is implied by conduct and not specifically expressed only direct contributions to the purchase of the house, such as contributions towards the mortgage payments, will be considered sufficient to conclude that this is what the parties intended. On the facts of *Gissing* v. *Gissing*, the decision of the judges was in fact that the contributions made by Mrs Gissing were not sufficient to conclude that there was a common intention between the parties. The appeal was therefore allowed, and Mr Gissing was thus declared to retain the sole beneficial interest in the property.

But what about situations in which the agreement is express? In the 1975 case of *Eves* v. *Eves* [1975] 1 WLR 1338 the court took a somewhat more relaxed approach to the issue of indirect contributions. The case concerned a couple, Janet and Stuart Eves. Janet and Stuart were not married (in fact, they were both married to other people), but Janet changed her surname to Eves when they had a child together. Stuart bought a house for them to live in with the aid of a mortgage, which he registered in his sole name. He told Janet this was because Janet was under the age of 21 and therefore unable to go on the **title deeds**. However, Stuart said he would rectify this when she reached the **age of majority**. As a result of this, whilst Janet did not contribute to the mortgage payments, she did a lot of renovation work on the house and maintained the house and garden. Stuart subsequently left Janet and married another woman, named Gloria, and Janet made an application to the court claiming an equitable interest in the house.

Case Summary

Unlike the case of *Gissing* v. *Gissing*, in which common intention was implied, in this case there was an express agreement between the parties regarding beneficial ownership of the property, Stuart telling Janet that the house would be transferred into her name when she reached the age of 21. As a result of this, the court held that Janet's contributions to the renovation of the property and maintenance of the house and garden were sufficient by way of indirect contribution to confer a beneficial interest on her. The Court of Appeal held that Janet should be entitled to a quarter share in the property.

The later case of *Grant* v. *Edwards* [1986] Ch 638 (CA) turned on similar facts. The claimant, Linda Grant, who was separated from her husband, set up home with a man named George Edwards. In 1969 George bought a house and moved into it with Linda, their child and the two children of Linda's previous marriage. The house was purchased in the joint names of George and his brother, Arthur, who had no beneficial interest in the property and had been named on the title deeds solely for the purpose of assisting in obtaining a mortgage. George told Linda that the reason her name was not included on the title was because it would prejudice the matrimonial proceedings which were pending against her husband. George paid the deposit and the mortgage instalments, while Linda made substantial contributions to the general household expenses. The couple lived in the house until it was damaged by fire, when they moved

Case Summary

into council accommodation. Part of the insurance money received was used to repair the house and the property was subsequently let. The leftover money was placed in the couple's joint account. In 1980 Linda and Stuart separated and Linda claimed a beneficial interest in the house.

As with *Eves* v. *Eves*, the court was happy to infer in *Grant* v. *Edwards* that there was a common intention between the parties that Linda was to have a beneficial interest in the property. The lack of formality was purely, in this case, to avoid complications in Linda's divorce proceedings. Again, indirect contributions, of a financial nature this time, were therefore held to be sufficient to confer a beneficial interest on the claimant. Lord Justice Nourse explained his reasoning:

> From the . . . facts and figures it is in my view an inevitable inference that the very substantial contribution which the **plaintiff** made out of her earnings after August 1972 to the housekeeping and to the feeding and to the bringing up of the children enabled the defendant to keep down the instalments payable under both mortgages out of his own income and, moreover, that he could not have done that if he had had to bear the whole of the other expenses as well. For example, in 1973, when he and the plaintiff were earning about £1,200 each, the defendant had to find a total of about £643 between the two mortgages. I do not see how he would have been able to do that had it not been for the plaintiff's very substantial contribution to the other expenses . . . In the circumstances, it seems that it may properly be inferred that the plaintiff did make substantial indirect contributions to the instalments payable under both mortgages.

One question to ask here is whether there are any circumstances in which indirect contributions will not be sufficient in the case of an express agreement, to confer an interest on the contributing party. The case of *Burns* v. *Burns*, which again we have already come across in the context of resulting trusts, answers this question. As you may remember, the case concerned a couple, Valerie and Patrick Burns. The house they lived in was bought and paid for by Patrick, with Valerie staying at home to look after the house and children. She also bought furniture, fixtures and fittings for the house and did some painting and redecoration. Unlike the situation in *Grant* v. *Edwards*, however, Valerie's money was not needed to pay for any of the household expenses. The Court of Appeal held that Valerie had no interest in the house because she had made no contributions referable to the acquisition of an interest in the property. Lord Justice Fox said:

> So far as housekeeping expenses are concerned, I do not doubt that (the house being bought in the man's name) if the woman goes out to work in order to provide money for the family expenses, as a result of which she spends her earnings on the housekeeping and the man is thus able to pay the mortgage instalments and other expenses out of his earnings, it can be inferred that there was a common intention that the woman should have an interest in the house – since she will have made an indirect financial contributions to the mortgage instalments. But that is not this case.

The suggestion here is therefore that, even in the case of indirect contributions, nothing short of substantial contributions enabling the legal owner to pay mortgage instalments which they could not otherwise have afforded will suffice. How this sits against the outcome in *Eves* v. *Eves*, in which Janet Eves had carried out renovation works to the property but did not contribute substantially from a financial perspective, is unclear. However, it should perhaps be noted that, on the facts of the two cases, whereas Valerie Burns had made no contribution of her own money to the property, her only contribution being out of housekeeping money given to her by her husband, Janet Eves had made a substantial contribution of her own time and effort.

The House of Lords was given the opportunity, some twenty years after *Gissing* v. *Gissing*, to consider for a second time the issue of common intention in constructive trusts.

Case Summary

In the case of *Lloyds Bank plc* v. *Rosset* [1991] 1 AC 107 a husband and wife, Mr and Mrs Rosset, planned on buying a semi-derelict property together as a home for themselves and their two children. The house was to be paid for with money from Mr Rosset's family trust in Switzerland and the **trustees** insisted on the house being registered in Mr Rosset's sole name. The purchase was to be made without the assistance of a mortgage but, unbeknown to Mrs Rosset, shortly before the purchase was completed Mr Rosset acquired a loan from Lloyds Bank plc for £15,000 to meet the cost of the renovation, which he secured against the property. Mrs Rosset made no financial contribution either to the purchase of the property or to the cost of renovation. However she project-managed the renovation and personally carried out much of the decorating work. Mr Rosset left the following year, after matrimonial difficulties, leaving Mrs Rosset and their children at the property. After a formal demand for repayment of the loan had not been met, the bank claimed possession and applied for a court order for the sale of the property. Mr Rosset did not resist the claim, but Mrs Rosset said that she had a beneficial interest in the property under a constructive trust.

Whilst the Court of Appeal had found that, on the facts of the case, the wife's activities in relation to the renovation of the property were sufficient to justify an inference of a common intention, the House of Lords disagreed, reversing their decision. In a dramatic departure from the mood of previous judgments, the Lords found against Mrs Rosset, stating that her contributions were insufficient to create a resulting trust. The Lords were keen to stress that, in their opinion, there was a fundamental distinction between cases in which there was evidence of an express discussion between the parties or representation from the legal owner regarding the beneficial interests the contributor would have in the property, and the inference of a common intention through conduct alone. They said that, where common intention was to be inferred by the parties' conduct, nothing less than direct contributions to the purchase price by the non-owning party would be sufficient evidence of such an intention, and Mrs Rosset had not provided this. Accordingly, the husband was declared to be the sole beneficiary of the property and the bank was allowed to **repossess** the house.

Using the opportunity to restate the law as applied by the House of Lords in *Gissing* v. *Gissing*, Lord Bridge said:

> The first and fundamental question which must always be resolved is whether, independently of any inference to be drawn from the conduct of the parties in the course of sharing the house as their home and managing their joint affairs, there has at any time prior to acquisition, or exceptionally at some later date, been any agreement, arrangement or understanding reached between them that the property is to be shared beneficially. The finding of an agreement or arrangement to share in this sense can only, I think, be based on evidence of express discussions between the partners, however imperfectly remembered and however imprecise their terms may have been. Once a finding to this effect is made it will only be necessary for the partner asserting a claim to a beneficial interest against the partner entitled to the legal estate to show that he or she has acted to his or her detriment or significantly altered his or her position in reliance on the agreement in order to give rise to a constructive trust . . .

> In sharp contrast with this situation is the very different one where there is no evidence to support a finding of an agreement or arrangement to share . . . and where the court must rely entirely on the conduct of the parties . . . as the basis from which to infer a common intention to share the property beneficially . . . In this situation direct contributions to the purchase price by the partner who is not the legal owner, whether initially or by payment of mortgage instalments, will readily justify the inference necessary to the creation of a constructive trust. But, as I read the authorities, it is at least extremely doubtful whether anything less will do.

In Lord Bridge's view, therefore, only direct contributions would suffice in cases of common intention based on the conduct of the parties alone.

In essence, the judgment in *Lloyds Bank* v. *Rosset* can be seen to have significantly tightened up the category of indirect contributions, restricting it to incorporate financial contributions which assisted in the payment of the mortgage instalments only (in other words, only situations such as those described in *Grant* v. *Edwards*).

Have you understood the law relating to direct and indirect contributions stated above? Test your understanding in the You Be the Judge feature below:

You be the judge

Q: **When will indirect contributions be sufficient to impose a finding of a constructive trust of property?**

A: Only where there has been an express agreement as to how the beneficial interest in the property is to be held. In all other circumstances, only direct contributions will suffice.

What is interesting to note from the wording of Lord Bridge's judgment was that, whilst it has the effect of cutting back significantly on the type of contribution which will amount to an indirect contribution for the purposes of gaining a beneficial interest in property, the Lords in *Lloyds Bank* v. *Rosset* have at the same time chosen to add not one, but two, new facets to the requirement for common intention. In Lord Bridge's view, common intention alone will now not be sufficient for a constructive trust to be imposed: there is also a need for the contributing party to have:

1. relied on the agreement between the parties; and
2. acted to their detriment or significantly altered their position as a result of that reliance.

Of course, Lord Bridge did not pull these 'new' requirements out of thin air. Although *Lloyds Bank* v. *Rosset* was the first House of Lords case to consider the issue of constructive trusts in the context of the family home since *Gissing* v. *Gissing*, as we have seen there had been a long line of Court of Appeal cases running from the judgment in *Gissing* v. *Gissing* up until the House of Lords hearing of *Lloyds Bank* v. *Rosset* and Lord Bridge was simply responding to, and consolidating, the various results of these. Nevertheless, this still leaves us with the question of how to show proof of reliance and how to define 'detriment'. Lord Bridge is quite clear that, in cases of financial contribution, whether direct or indirect, proof of the contributions will in itself be proof enough of detrimental reliance. But will any other kind of detriment suffice? If one chooses to stick slavishly to the judgment itself in *Lloyds Bank* v. *Rosset*, the answer of course would be no: absolutely not. But judgments which were being made in other contemporary cases, and certainly a number of judgments which have followed the decision in *Lloyds Bank* v. *Rosset*, would appear to suggest otherwise.

What amounts to detrimental reliance?

If we look at case law prior to *Lloyds Bank* v. *Rosset*, the interpretation of the facts in *Grant* v. *Edwards* stands out as supporting Lord Bridge's view. Here the evidence of **detrimental reliance** is clear: Linda Grant relied on George Edwards's representation to her that the only reason she didn't appear on the title deeds to the property was because of her marital situation and, as a result, acted severely to her detriment by making significant financial contributions to the running of the house, in turn allowing her partner to afford to make the mortgage instalments. Lord Justice Nourse in making his judgment in *Grant* v. *Edwards* gave the following, very logical, analysis of the facts:

> The defendant told the plaintiff that her name was not going onto the title because it would cause some prejudice in the matrimonial proceedings between her and her husband. The defendant never had any real intention of replacing his brother with the plaintiff when those proceedings were at an end. Just as in *Eves* v. *Eves*, these facts appear to me to raise a clear inference that there was an understanding between the plaintiff and the defendant of a common intention, that the plaintiff was to have some sort of **proprietary interest** in the house, otherwise no excuse for not putting her name onto the title would have been needed . . . Was the conduct of the plaintiff in making substantial indirect contributions to the instalments payable under both mortgages conduct upon which she could not reasonably have been expected to embark unless she was to have an interest in the house? I answer that question in the affirmative. I cannot see upon what other basis she could reasonably have been expected to give the defendant such substantial assistance in paying off mortgages on his house. I therefore conclude that the plaintiff did act to her detriment on the faith of the common intention between her and the defendant that she was to have some sort of proprietary interest in the house . . .

Having established a common intention a finding of detrimental reliance was easy. Linda had clearly gone over and above what she would have been expected to do as a member of the family under circumstances in which she did not expect to receive an entitlement: in short, a person quite simply would not go to such great lengths whilst expecting nothing in return. Later cases have proved less straightforward, however. The concept of 'detriment' has never been given a legal definition in the context of constructive trusts and there is therefore any number of situations to which the term might conceivably be applied. The only question this leaves is whether such examples of detriment tie in with the stipulation of an indirect financial contribution as set out in *Lloyds Bank* v. *Rosset*.

In the case of *Ungurian* v. *Lesnoff* [1990] Ch 206, the alleged detriment was of an altogether different nature. Kamilla Lesnoff was of Polish nationality. When the couple set up home together in London, Kamilla gave up her flat in Poland, which she could have stayed in for the rest of her life, and a promising university career. She also had to enter into a marriage of convenience with a French man to enable her and her two children to get out of the country. Having severed ties with Poland, which was as the time under communist rule, both parties knew it would not be possible for her to go back. Ungurian bought a house for the couple to live in together in London, which he paid for and which they lived in together for four years, after which Ungurian left. Kamilla did not contribute financially to the property at all, but she carried out significant improvement works to the property herself, including putting in a new central heating system and various other renovations. The court held that Kamilla had a beneficial interest in the property under a constructive trust, based on the couple's agreement that Kamilla would be entitled to live in the property with her children for the rest of her life. The cumulative effect of the detriment she had suffered by leaving her position and family in communist Poland was sufficient in terms of detrimental reliance.

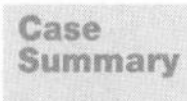

This is obviously a case of very unusual circumstances. The case of *Hammond* v. *Mitchell* [1991] 1 WLR 1127 is perhaps easier to align with everyday family break-ups, although in its way it was no less out of the ordinary. The case concerned a love affair between a second-hand car dealer named Tom Hammond and a Playboy Club Bunny, Vicky Mitchell. Tom met Vicky in a chance encounter when Vicky stopped Tom to ask for directions. The couple hit it off and within a very short time had moved in together. The couple were an item for 11 years, during which time Vicky bore Tom two children. The house in which they lived together was bought and paid for by Tom. However, Vicky ran the household and helped out with Tom's business on a day-to-day basis. When the house was purchased, Tom had told Vicky that the house was being put into his name to save complications because he was going through a divorce at the time. However, he told her not to worry because they would soon be married and half of everything would be hers anyway. The subject was never discussed again. When the couple finally split the joint assets of the house and business were worth £450,000. Tom claimed the whole of the assets belonged to him, but Vicky claimed a share. The court agreed with Vicky and held that she should have a half interest in the house under a constructive trust.

Clearly in the case of *Hammond* v. *Mitchell* there had been an express discussion between the parties as to the beneficial interest that Vicky would, albeit eventually, have in the property. The question was one of detriment. Had Vicky acted to her detriment in reliance on the agreement? The court believed that, yes, she had. Vicky had given up a highly-paid job as a croupier at the Playboy Club in Mayfair in order to set up home with Mr Hammond. In embarking with Mr Hammond on his various business ventures and in giving her support, on two occasions by waiving her occupational rights to the house with the bank so that he could take out mortgages to fund business deals, she had acted to her detriment and was therefore entitled to a half share of the house under a constructive trust.

It is clear from these cases that, provided a genuine detriment can be shown, in cases of an express **oral agreement**, financial contribution is not essential to establish a beneficial interest in the property. Following Lord Bridge's judgment in *Rosset*, whilst financial contributions are fundamental in cases of **implied common intention**, it is detriment which is key to making a claim in cases where an oral agreement between the parties can be proved.

It may be a good idea at this point to have a little recap of the law that we have learnt so far in relation to constructive trusts. Take a moment to look at Figure 7.1.

Figure 7.1 Recap of constructive trusts

Following Lord Bridge's judgment in *Lloyds Bank* v. *Rosset*, there are three requirements for the finding of a constructive trust:

1. **Common intention: there must have been some form of agreement, understanding or common intention that the person making the claim will have a beneficial interest in the property;**
2. **Reliance: the person making the claim must have acted or changed their position in reliance on that agreement; and**
3. **Detriment: it must be shown that the person will suffer a detriment if the legal owner of the property then tries to deny them an interest in it.**

Common intention can be shown in one of two ways:

1. **Express agreement: where there have been express discussions between the parties pointing to an agreement that the person making the claim is to have a beneficial interest in the property; or**
2. **Implied agreement: where such an agreement is implied from the conduct of the parties.**

Where there is an express agreement, the detrimental reliance may consist of either direct or indirect contributions to the purchase of the property as well as, it would appear, non-financial contributions – provided they are sufficient in nature that the contributing party will suffer a genuine detriment on account of having made such contributions, were they then denied an interest in the property. Where the agreement is implied by conduct, nothing less than direct contributions (including the making of mortgage payments) to the purchase of the property will be sufficient. The contributions themselves will provide evidence of the required detriment.

Now that we have reminded ourselves of how to establish a beneficial interest in the property under a constructive trust, the only thing left to do is to quantify the share. And this is what we are going to look at in this last part of the chapter.

Calculating the share

With a resulting trust, the size of the contributing party's share is directly proportionate to the amount of their contribution. So if a person pays the 10 per cent deposit on the purchase of the property, they will be entitled to a 10 per cent share of the property when it is subsequently sold. With a constructive trust, calculating the size of the share is not quite so straightforward, however. This is especially so in light of the fact that, in cases of express agreement constructive trusts, the party claiming an interest may succeed in doing so by virtue of a non-financial contribution or detriment which may be hard to quantify in terms of a cash share in the property. Unfortunately in the case of *Lloyds Bank* v. *Rosset*, there was no discussion as to how the share under a constructive trust should be calculated, because Mrs Rosset failed in her claim: such discussion was simply not necessary. So we must look to later case law for guidance on the best approach to take in such situations.

Case Summary

The Court of Appeal case of *Midland Bank plc* v. *Cooke* (1995) 27 HLR 733 is a useful starting point. The case concerned a married couple, Mr and Mrs Cooke, who were facing repossession proceedings from the Midland Bank. The house was in Mr Cooke's sole name and had been paid for out of a mixture of Mr Cooke's personal savings and a mortgage in his sole name. In addition, part of the deposit on the property had been funded out of a wedding gift which had been made to the couple by Mr Cooke's parents. When the bank sought repossession of the property following non-payment of the mortgage, Mrs Cooke resisted the application on the grounds that half the house belonged to her.

The court at first instance agreed that Mrs Cooke had a beneficial interest in the property, but limited this to a 6.47 per cent share, representing her half of the wedding present from Mr Cooke's parents. However, the Court of Appeal disagreed with the decision and gave her a half share in the house in support of her initial application.

So what was the reasoning behind this? Clearly, the Court of Appeal did not believe that the quantification of shares in a constructive trust situation should be done by reference purely to the size of financial contribution (what you might call a 'resulting trust' calculation). How, then, did the Court of Appeal reach their conclusion that Mrs Cooke was entitled to half of the property? Lord Justice Waite explained the court's reasoning:

> When the court is proceeding, in cases like the present where the partner without legal title has successfully asserted an equitable interest through direct contribution, to determine (in the absence of express evidence of intention) what proportions the parties must be assumed to have intended for their beneficial ownership, the duty of the judge is to undertake a survey of the whole course of dealing between the parties relevant to their ownership and occupation of the property and their sharing of its burdens and advantages. That scrutiny will not confine itself to the limited range of acts of direct contribution of the sort that are needed to found a beneficial interest in the first place. It will take into consideration all conduct which throws light on the question what shares were intended. Only if that search proves inconclusive does the court fall back on the **maxim** that 'equality is equity'.

So, according to *Midland Bank* v. *Cooke*, once a beneficial interest under a constructive trust has been established, albeit that the interest may have been established by virtue of direct contributions by the person making the claim, the calculation of that person's interest will not be limited to those direct contributions. Rather, the court will look at the 'whole course of dealing between the parties' and make their decision based on what appears to have been the parties' intention in light of those dealings. In *Midland Bank* v. *Cooke*, Mrs Cooke had always been treated as an equal partner in the marriage, both in terms of paying household expenses from her wages as a teacher, to signing a waiver when a first, and then second mortgage was taken out over the property, and generally in keeping house and bringing up the children. The court therefore concluded that the actions of the parties were such as to imply an intention that they intended to share everything equally, and Mrs Cooke was given a half share in the property.

> the court will look at the 'whole course of dealing between the parties'

A decade later the Court of Appeal saw fit to make comment on the finding in *Midland Bank* v. *Cooke*, in the case of *Oxley* v. *Hiscock* [2004] 3 All ER 703. The case concerned an unmarried couple, Elayne Oxley and Allan Hiscock. Elayne was living in a council house with her children when she met Allan, who owned his own house. In September 1987 Elayne exercised her **right to buy** her council house for £25,200 using funds provided by Allan from the sale of his property. In 1991 the couple bought a bigger house for £127,000, which was funded by the proceeds of sale of Elayne's house at £61,500 (of which £25,200 was attributable to Allan's original contribution and £36,300 to Elayne), by a further £35,500 from Allan's savings and by a mortgage loan of £30,000. The property was registered in the sole name of Allan.

After the purchase both Elayne and Allan contributed towards the maintenance and improvement of the property from pooled resources in the belief that each had a

beneficial interest. By 2001 the couple had paid the mortgage off. Elayne and Allan then separated and the property was then sold, each buying separate houses. Elayne applied for a declaration that the proceeds of sale of the property were held on trust for both parties in equal shares, which she was given. Allan appealed, contending that since there had been no discussion between the parties as to the extent of their respective beneficial shares at the time of purchase, the property should be held on resulting trust for both parties in beneficial shares proportionate to their contributions. Following the reasoning in *Midland Bank* v. *Cooke*, the Court of Appeal held that, where there was no evidence of any discussion between the parties as to the amount of the share each was to have, each was entitled to that share which the court considered fair having regard to the whole course of dealing between them in relation to the property, including any arrangements made to meet the various outgoings required to be met to live in the property as their home.

However, whilst the court was keen to state that:

(i) they were not required to make a finding that the property was held on trust in proportion to the couple's respective financial contributions; and that

(ii) regard should be had to the whole course of dealings between the parties;

they nevertheless found that a fair division of the proceeds of sale would be 60 per cent to the **defendant** and 40 per cent to the claimant. Taking a purely mathematical division of the parties' various contributions they therefore had, in fact, based their finding on a 'resulting trust' calculation, in proportion to the financial contributions the parties had made to the property and not taking into account any other factors. Figure 7.2 summarises the parties' financial contributions.

Figure 7.2 The parties' contributions in *Oxley* v. *Hiscock*

			% of purchase price
Elayne's equity	(£36,300)		
Half share in mortgage	(£15,000)		
Elayne's total share		£51,300	40%
Allan's sale proceeds	(£25,200)		
Allan's savings	(£35,500)		
Half share in mortgage	(£15,000)		
Allan's total share		£75,700	60%
Total (purchase price of property):		£127,000	100%

Lord Justice Chadwick justified the Court of Appeal's approach to the case by stating that it would simply be unfair to ignore the different sizes of their respective financial contributions. However, the decision rests uneasily alongside that of *Midland Bank* v. *Cooke*. Exactly how much weight is supposed to be given to financial contributions when the amount of the beneficial interest is being calculated? According to *Midland Bank* v. *Cooke*, financial contributions should be given no more than a cursory glance; but according to *Oxley* v. *Hiscock*, it would appear that financial contributions are of paramount importance in deciding how the beneficial interest in a property is to be divided. The key distinction between the two decisions would appear to be the fact that, in *Midland Bank* v. *Cooke* the couple were married, whereas in *Oxley* v. *Hiscox* they were not. In *Midland Bank* v. *Cooke* the couple had made a legal commitment to one another, in the form of their marriage vows, whereas in *Oxley* v. *Hiscox*, there was no such commitment, albeit that they had set up home together. Perhaps if Elayne Oxley and Allan Hiscock had been married their share would have been calculated on a 50/50 basis as well. Is this not a fundamentally outdated response to cohabitation, however? The Law in Action feature below may help you to form a view:

Law in action

In the recent battle between Nick Clegg, Deputy Prime Minister and David Cameron, the pair came to blows over David Cameron's proposals to give tax breaks to married couples. Whilst Nick Clegg described marriage as 'the best thing that ever happened to him', he said the Conservative government should wake up and smell the coffee as regards current social norms and recognise that there are just as many couples in stable, unmarried relationships as married ones. Figures from the Office of National Statistics published in 2011 [see the Key Stats feature below] support this. In talking about the institution of marriage, Mr Clegg, spoke out against the Conservative view, stating that: 'we should not take a particular version of the family institution, such as the 1950s model of suit-wearing, bread-winning dad and aproned, home-making mother – and try and preserve it in aspic'.

He clearly felt that the Conservatives were outdated in their approach. You can read Nick Clegg's 'open society' speech in full at: **http://www.politics.co.uk/comment-analysis/2011/12/19/nick-clegg-open-society-speechl**

Sources: http://www.telegraph.co.uk/comment/telegraph-view/8963508/Nick-Clegg-fails-to-understand-why-marriage-really-matters.html, http://www.huffingtonpost.co.uk/2011/12/18/nick-clegg-attacks-tory-plans-married-couples-tax-breaks_n_1156121.html and http://www.bbc.co.uk/news/uk-politics-16235463

Source: Janis Christie, Photodisc

The question the above feature raises is surely that, if cohabitation trends are being taken seriously enough by the government to impact on their imposition of tax regimes across the country, the judiciary should also fall in line and recognise the equality that should in the current social climate exist between married and unmarried couples in the event of a break-up of the family home. The position in the courts has until recently remained fundamentally unchanged, however.

Case Summary

In 2007 the House of Lords was, once more, given the opportunity to consider the issue when it heard the case of *Stack* v. *Dowden* [2007] UKHL 17. The facts of the case were as follows: Barry Stack and Dehra Dowden met and began a relationship in 1975. In 1983 Dehra Dowden bought a house in her sole name in which the couple lived together and brought up their four children. Dehra, who earned considerably more than Barry, made all the mortgage payments and paid the household bills. The couple made substantial improvements to the property and in 1993 sold it for three times the amount Dehra originally paid for it. Dehra and Barry then bought another property, which was purchased in their joint names. Over 65 per cent of the purchase price was paid out of funds from a building society account held in Dehra's sole name and which included the money made on the sale of the previous house. The balance of the purchase price was provided by a mortgage in the parties' joint names and two endowment policies (a type of life insurance policy which pays out at the end of a specified period or on the death of the policy holder), one in their joint names and one in Dehra's sole name. Barry paid the mortgage interest and the premiums due under the endowment policy in the couple's joint names and Dehra paid the premiums due under the endowment policy in her sole name. The parties kept separate bank accounts and made separate savings and investments. Over the course of their years in the house together the mortgage was paid off by a series of lump sum payments, of which Dehra provided just under 60 per cent. The couple separated in 2002 and Barry left the property while Dehra remained there with the children. Barry then successfully applied for an order for sale of the property and an equal division of the proceeds. However, on appeal the Court of Appeal found in Dehra's favour, ordering that the net proceeds of sale should be divided 65 per cent to 35 per cent in Dehra's favour. The House of Lords upheld this judgment in favour of Dehra.

So what was the reasoning of the Lords in upholding the decision? The facts of the case were of course different from the previous cases upon which the Court of Appeal had deliberated, in that the house in *Stack* v. *Dowden* was purchased in joint names. There was therefore no question as to whether or not Barry Stack had a beneficial interest in the property; the only question was as to the size of his share in it. The court took the view that, as the property had been purchased in joint names without any declaration as to shares, the initial presumption would be that the couple owned the house equally because of equity following the law, with the burden of proof lying with the party wishing to establish that they should have a greater beneficial interest in the property. It was therefore for Dehra Dowden to show the court that she was entitled to more than a 50 per cent share in the house. In claiming a constructive trust in her favour, Dehra would have to show a common intention between the parties that she should hold a greater interest in the property. Baroness Hale said that, in order to determine the exact amount of that share, the court would have to undertake 'a survey of the whole course of dealing between the parties . . . taking account of all conduct which throws light on the question what shares were intended'. As with previous cases, this would include whether or not the couple were married.

In divining the amount of Dehra's share in the property the Lords therefore took the following factors into account:

1. The couple were unmarried;
2. Dehra had contributed far more to the acquisition of the house than Barry;
3. The parties had never pooled their separate financial resources for the common good;
4. Everything, apart from the house and associated **endowment policy**, had been kept strictly separate.

They found that the facts of the case were highly unusual, as most couples did not put their accounts on such a separate footing. The complete segregation of the couple's finances was strongly indicative that the parties had *not* intended their shares in the property to be equal and, accordingly, Dehra should be entitled to a 65 per cent share of the beneficial interest in the house. In making their decision, the Lords stressed that each case would turn on its own facts and that many more factors than financial contributions may be relevant in divining the parties' true intentions. However, perhaps because of the unique facts in this particular case, we have been left in a slightly contradictory position. Whilst Lord Walker in *Stack* v. *Dowden* said quite clearly that the use of resulting trusts should not operate as a legal presumption in a domestic context, the facts of this case resulted in exactly that. The only question which remains is whether the calculation of share in any future case where the former couple was not married, will always be made on an arithmetical basis.

The controversy caused by this finding is not helped by the dissenting judgment given by Lord Neuberger in *Stack* v. *Dowden*. Whilst he agreed with the overall decision of the Lords, he believed that the reasoning behind their decision was made on the wrong footing. In his own words:

> where the resulting trust presumption (or indeed any other basis of apportionment) applies at the date of acquisition, I am unpersuaded that (save perhaps in a most unusual case) anything other than subsequent discussions, statements or actions, which can fairly be said to imply a positive intention to depart from that apportionment, will do to justify a change in the way in which the beneficial interest is owned. To say that factors such as a long relationship, children, a joint bank account, and sharing daily outgoings of themselves are enough, or even of potential central importance, appears to me not merely wrong in principle, but a recipe for uncertainty, subjectivity, and a long and expensive examination of facts. It could also be said to be arbitrary, as, if such factors of themselves justify a departure from the original apportionment, I find it hard to see how it could be to anything other than equality. If a departure from the original apportionment was solely based on such factors, it seems to me that the judge would almost always have to reach an 'all or nothing' decision. Thus, in this case, he would have to ask whether, viewed in the round, the personal and financial characteristics of the relationship between Mr Stack and Ms Dowden, after they acquired the house, justified a change in ownership of the beneficial interest from 35–65 to 50–50, even though nothing they did or said related to the ownership of that interest (save, perhaps, the repayments of the mortgage). In my view, that involves approaching the question in the wrong way. Subject, perhaps, to exceptional cases, whose possibility it would be unrealistic not to acknowledge, an argument for an alteration in the way in which the beneficial interest is held cannot, in my opinion, succeed, unless it can be shown that there was a discussion, statement or action which, viewed in its context, namely the parties' relationship, implied an actual agreement or understanding to effect such an alteration.

Lord Neuberger clearly favoured a more traditional resulting trust approach of initial contributions to the purchase price to be applied to such cases, feeling that, except for in a small amount of exceptional circumstances, the later actions of the parties should have no bearing on the size of the respective parties' shares.

So where do we go from here? As far as calculating the share under a constructive trust is concerned and, seemingly, in contradiction to the idea of taking into account a whole course of dealings, the outcome in *Stack* v. *Dowden* could very easily be interpreted as simply mirroring the more restrictive approach of *Oxley* v. *Hiscock*. Whatever the reasoning behind the decision, the undeniable finding of the court was that Dehra Dowden's share should be proportionate to her contributions to the purchase price of the property, which leads us straight back to square one: the 'resulting trust' arithmetical method of share calculation. This causes all manner of problems: with shares being calculated on an arithmetical basis, it makes it very difficult to tell the difference between the implied common intention constructive trust and a simple resulting trust itself. After all, why bother proving a common intention and detrimental reliance through the payment of direct contributions to the property, when the outcome of the case will still be that the contributing party is given a no greater share than that directly proportionate to their financial contribution? The argument would surely be that, taking into account the whole course of dealings between the parties, the beneficial interest could theoretically be adjudged to be considerably greater under the guise of a constructive trust. However, the reality of the decisions in *Oxley* v. *Hiscock* and now *Stack* v. *Dowden* would appear to show otherwise. The Key Stats below give us an indicator of just how serious this problem could be on a practical level.

Key stats

In the latest Office for National Statistics report entitled *Families and Households 2011*, which was released on 19 January 2012, the following figures were published:

- There were 26.3 million households in the UK in 2011. Of these 29% consisted of only one person and almost 20% consisted of four or more people.
- In 2011 there were 17.9 million families in the UK. Of these 12.0 million consisted of a married couple with or without children.
- The number of opposite-sex cohabiting-couple families increased significantly, from 2.1 million in 2001 to 2.9 million in 2011.
- The number of dependent children living in opposite-sex cohabiting-couple families increased significantly, from 1.3 million to 1.8 million over the same period.
- In 2011, 38% of cohabiting couple families had dependent children, the same percentage as married couple families.

Source: **http://www.ons.gov.uk/ons/rel/family-demography/families-and-households/2011/index.html**

With as many unmarried households with dependent children now in the UK as married households with dependents, the panic in the wake of *Stack* v. *Dowden* is perhaps understandable, with commentators crying out for a change in the law to reflect the current social norms. In Scotland an overarching law of financial claims for unmarried couples has recently been introduced, offering financial remedies, albeit lesser than those available to married couples, and calls have been made to the Coalition Government to revisit the Law Commission's proposal to introduce law reform in this area.

the panic in the wake of *Stack* v. *Dowden* is perhaps understandable

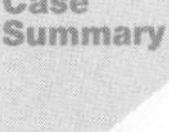

In the midst of all this panic, it was thought that the recently heard Court of Appeal decision in *Jones* v. *Kernott* [2011] 2 WLR 1121 might bring some light at the end of the tunnel. However, the decision of the Supreme Court which followed it has merely resulted in a continuation in the same vein as *Stack*. The facts in *Jones* v. *Kernott* were as follows: the parties had bought a house together in joint names with the benefit of a mortgage. They lived there together for over eight years, sharing the household expenses including the mortgage payments, until Mr Kernott moved out of the property in 1993. Ms Jones then remained in the property with their two children for a further 14 years, paying all the household expenses by herself. When the property was put up for sale, Kernott made an application to the court seeking a declaration as to his share in the property The court at first instance found in favour of Ms Jones, declaring that the beneficial interest in the property should be split between the parties, 90 per cent to Ms Jones and 10 per cent to Mr Kernott. On appeal the court reversed the decision, finding that the former couple should have a 50/50 share in the property. But the Supreme Court, overturning the decision of the Court of Appeal, held that Mr Kernott and Ms Jones would hold the shares in the house on trust in a ratio of 10 per cent to 90 per cent, to reflect their contributions to the home. Lord Kerr, disagreeing with the judgment of the Court of Appeal, held that a 90:10 split in favour of Ms Jones was 'a fair one between the parties'.

Whilst the the Court of Appeal's finding in the case for a short time provoked a hope that fears following *Stack* v. *Dowden* that unmarried couples would always be subject to an arithmetical calculation of their shares in the former family home, unfortunately the Supreme Court decision to revert to the original finding of the court has had the effect simply of underlining the difficulty and ultimately the uncertainty in the case of unmarried couples co-owning property. This is certainly an area of the law which will remain a matter for debate for some time to come.

'Surveying the whole course of dealings': does it relate to acquisition or quantification of share?

The issue of quantification of share is unfortunately not the only area in which the findings of the court in *Stack* v. *Dowden* seem to have caused controversy. The Privy Council case of *Abbott* v. *Abbott* [2007] UKPC 53 and more recently the High Court in *Hapeshi* v. *Allnatt and another* [2010] EWHC 392 have both indicated that the findings in *Stack* could be used to *award* a beneficial interest, as well as to quantify it.

In *Abbott* v. *Abbott* the case concerned the former matrimonial home of Mr and Mrs Abbott. The home had been built on land given to Mr Abbott by his mother and of which Mr Abbott was the sole legal owner. Mr Abbott's mother had contributed towards the construction costs, but subsequently the house had been paid for by Mr and Mrs Abbott with the help of a mortgage in their joint names, although Mrs Abbott had not worked for a period of nine years during their marriage. There had never been any express agreement reached between husband and wife as to what should be the wife's beneficial share in the property (if any). The Court of Appeal held that Mrs Abbott was only entitled to an 8.31 per cent share in the equity, based on her actual contributions towards the mortgage. However, the Privy Council overturned their finding. In accordance with *Stack* v. *Dowden*, they said, the parties' whole course of conduct in relation

to a property had to be taken into account in determining their shared intentions as to its ownership. The court reasoned that, if a parent gave financial assistance to a newly-married couple to acquire a home, the usual inference was that it was intended as a gift to both of them. That inference was in this case supported by the husband and wife's behaviour throughout the marriage, in the fact that they arranged their finances entirely jointly and undertook joint liability for the repayment of the mortgage. The Privy Council awarded Mrs Abbott a 50 per cent share in the house. In taking this decision, however, the court was in essence awarding the constructive trust on the basis of the 'whole course of dealings' alone. No express agreement, in the words of Lord Bridge in *Lloyds Bank* v. *Rossett*, 'however imprecise' existed (remember that *Stack* v. *Dowden* did not explore this issue as the couple were joint owners of the property in law – the only argument in *Stack* was as to share). Surely, then, what the court in *Abbott* v. *Abbott* had, in effect, done was to impute the intention of the parties as no share could be inferred from their conduct. This has always been forbidden territory and certainly not something advocated in *Stack* v. *Dowden*.

Case Summary

The 2010 case of *Hapeshi* v. *Allnatt* muddies the waters still further. Again, the case consisted of a claim by a person without any legal interest in the property. A son, Kevin Hapeshi, was claiming a beneficial interest in a property owned jointly by his mother and brother, both legal owners having died. Kevin's mother had bought the property from the local authority at a discount some years previously as part of the authority's right-to-buy scheme. The house was bought by means of a mortgage and the property was registered jointly in the name of Mrs Hapeshi and Kevin's brother. Both the brother and the mother had subsequently died, however. Kevin contended that he held the entire beneficial interest in the property pursuant to a constructive trust. He claimed that it had been the parties' intention that he should be named as a joint purchaser when his mother bought the house, but that this could not be formalised at the time because he was not eligible to purchase the house under the local authority scheme. He was therefore left off the title deeds. This could not be proved, however, leaving the court with no evidence of an express agreement to share in the property and no evidence of making direct payments to the purchase price (including the mortgage). Nevertheless the judge, interpreting Baroness Hale's judgment in *Stack*, adopted what he called a 'holistic approach' in 'undertaking a survey of the whole course of dealings between the parties and taking account of all conduct which throws light on the question of what shares were intended' to arrive at a 25 per cent share.

Again, then, we can see that here is a case in which, in the name of surveying the whole course of dealings, a statement originally applied in *Stack* v. *Dowden* specifically to the issue of quantification of share has been used to make an award of a beneficial interest. In *Hapeshi* v. *Allnatt* there was no express agreement, no contribution to the purchase price, and no contribution towards mortgage payments. However, the claimant ended up with a 25 per cent beneficial share in the family home. How did this happen? The big question that remains is whether the interpretation of Baroness Hale's judgment to allow the imputation of a beneficial interest in deserving cases is correct. Surely not, although this is how it was applied in *Hapeshi* v. *Allnatt*. It remains to be seen what will happen when the matter is brought before a higher court for discussion.

Other uses for constructive trusts

The focus of this chapter has been on constructive trusts in so far as they relate to private individuals and, in particular, the family home situation. However, although the spotlight has very much been on this area of constructive trusts in recent years, it is important to remember that this is not the only situation in which constructive trusts are used. In fact, the imposition of constructive trusts is commonplace in many situations, both individual and commercial. If we return to the beginning of the section on constructive trusts you will remember that we looked at the case of *Banner Homes Group* v. *Luff Developments Ltd*, which concerned an agreement between two developers which had gone sour. In that case, Banner Homes were awarded a beneficial interest in a piece of development land owned by Luff Developments Ltd because of the reliance they had placed on Luff Developments' representations that the companies were going to buy the property together by way of a joint venture.

Another situation in which constructive trusts are also used is where a trustee has acted in breach of their **fiduciary duties**. The most common example of this might be in the case of an unauthorised profit made by a trustee; however, a detailed discussion of the imposition of constructive trusts in this situation is more relevant in the context of a textbook on trusts and not land law. It should be noted, nevertheless, that a person guilty of receiving trust property in the knowledge that the property is the product of a breach of trust can also have a constructive trust imposed upon them, with the effect that they will hold the misappropriated trust property on trust for the **beneficiaries**. On this basis, it is easy to see how, as a matter of **public policy** alone, a constructive trust could be imposed in cases of persons seeking to profit from their crimes. It would clearly be inequitable for a person receiving stolen goods, in full knowledge that they had been acquired illegally, to be allowed to keep the product of the crime, for example. Thus, in cases of fraud, the property is held by the fraudster on constructive trust for the original owner.

One final, and rather more unusual, example of a situation in which a constructive trust will be imposed is in the case of a person who has received property as a product of murder. In *Cleaver* v. *Mutual Reserve Fund Life Association* [1892] 1 QB 147, the Court of Appeal allowed the **executors** of a man who had been murdered by his wife to claim a constructive trust in favour of the man's estate as against the wife, who was the sole beneficiary under the policy. It was held that the wife should hold the proceeds of the policy on a constructive trust on the basis that she should not be entitled to benefit from her crime. Put simply, murder will make the killer a constructive trustee of whatever property they acquire as a result.

So, as we have seen, constructive trusts can be imposed in a number of situations, not just in relation to the family home, but also in the case of businesses, and in order to protect trust property where there has been a breach of trust by a trustee. More unusually, a constructive trust may also be imposed in cases of murder, on the basis that a person should not be allowed to profit from their crime.

Summary

- Resulting and constructive trusts can be created without any formality whatever, meaning that there is no need even for writing to create them (s.53(2) LPA 1925).
- In the context of the acquisition of land, a resulting trust will be created wherever property has been bought in one person's sole name but paid for, either wholly or in part, by another.
- Only contributions to the purchase of the property will be relevant in awarding a resulting trust. This may include payments towards the mortgage, but will not include any subsequent payments to the maintenance or improvement of the property, however substantial.
- The beneficial share in a property awarded in a resulting trust situation will be calculated in proportion with the amount of the claimant's contribution to the property.
- Constructive trusts are imposed wherever it would be unconscionable for the owner of property to deny another a beneficial interest in it.
- Unconscionability in constructive trusts arises where there has been detrimental reliance by the non-owning party, based either on an express agreement made between the parties, or where a common intention that the parties should share the beneficial interest in it can be proved.
- In the absence of an express agreement, only direct contributions to the purchase of the property will traditionally be enough to suggest a common intention to share the beneficial interest – *Lloyds Bank* v. *Rosset* (but see *Abbott* v. *Abbott* and *Hapeshi* v. *Allnatt*, which suggest a more holistic approach).
- Where there has been an express agreement, the detriment need not be financial at all, however (see *Ungurian* v. *Lesnoff*).
- In calculating the share of the property to be awarded in constructive trust cases, the court will 'undertake a survey of the whole course of dealing between the parties . . . taking account of all conduct which throws light on the question what shares were intended' (*Stack* v. *Dowden*).
- There has been some recent controversy as to whether this also applies to the award of a beneficial interest, as well as the calculation of share. A step in this direction would necessarily lead to imputation of the parties' intentions by the courts, however: something which the courts have always fought to avoid (*Lloyds Bank* v. *Rosset*).

Question and answer*

Problem: Shannon and Deeroy met in 1999 and started a relationship together. In 2000 Shannon moved into Deeroy's ex-council flat in Penge, which he had previously occupied with his mother, who had recently moved into a nursing home. The flat was in his mother's name. She had bought the flat from the council under their 'Right to Buy' scheme in 1994, with the assistance of a mortgage in her sole name. The intention had been that Deeroy and his mother should both be on the title deeds, but the council's rules under the scheme would not allow this. Deeroy had never contributed towards the mortgage on the property, but had maintained the house and looked after his mother in the house before she was put into the nursing home. Since moving into the flat, Shannon has paid all of the household expenses and furnishings and has bought and installed a new fitted kitchen. Deeroy has continued to claim benefits in his mother's name to make the mortgage payments, even though she now resides in a nursing home. Twelve years later Shannon and Deeroy have now split up. Shannon wants to sell the flat and split the proceeds between them. Deeroy says the flat belongs to him and Shannon has no right to it. In the meantime Deeroy's mother dies. Deeroy's sister, Imelda, claims the flat belongs to her under the terms of her mother's will and that neither Deeroy nor Shannon have an interest. What are Shannon and Deeroy's rights respectively?

You should allow yourself no more than 40 minutes to complete this task.

Essay: The holistic approach in *Stack* v. *Dowden* has opened the floodgates to the third party acquisition of a share in properties wherever equity sees fit to award one. Discuss.

This question should be answered in 40 minutes.

* Answer guidance is provided at the end of the chapter.

Further reading

'A Failure of Trust: Resolving Property Disputes on Cohabitation Breakdown', available online at: http://www.justice.gov.uk/lawcommission/docs/Cohabitation_Cardiff_Research.pdf.
Report of a research study funded by the ESRC by Gillian Douglas, Julia Pearce and Hilary Woodward. Provides a useful insight into the practical issues surrounding the break-up of the family home in cohabitation cases.

Panesar, S., 'Quantifying beneficial interest in joint ownership disputes: is the constructive trust changing?', Cov LJ 2012, 17(1), 59–67.
This article outlines the Supreme Court judgment in *Jones* v. *Kernott* on quantifying the beneficial interests. Provides an interesting discussion and comparison on how the common intention constructive trust is used in Canada.

Pawlowski, M., 'True intention', Fam LJ, 2010, 94(Mar), 17–19.
An article discussing the recent decision in *Abbott* v. *Abbott* and considering *Abbott*'s suggestion of a more flexible way to establish a common intention constructive trust, moving from a two stage test to one composite enquiry into all the dealings of the parties in relation to the property.

Smithdale, J. 'Inference, imputation, or both? Confusion persists over beneficial interests in the family home', CSLR 2011, 7(1), 74–88.
Useful article discussing, with reference to the recent cases of *Abbott* v. *Abbott* and *Hapeshi* v. *Allnatt*, the blurring of the boundary between imputation and inference following *Stack* v. *Dowden*, and how this might be addressed by the courts.

Question and answer guidance

Please note that the following are not full answers and are intended to provide guidance in outline form only as to how to answer the questions posed.

Problem: This is a question about constructive trusts. Resulting trusts will not apply in this scenario because when his mother purchased the flat Deeroy did not contribute to the purchase price in any way. Shannon moved in a considerable time after the purchase and so there is no question of her having a resulting trust through contribution to the purchase price either.

Neither Deeroy nor Shannon have any legal interest in the property: it belonged to Deeroy's mother, who has now died, and who left the flat to her daughter, Imelda, in her will. The legal ownership of the property therefore lies with Imelda. What we need to look at is whether Deeroy or Shannon have acquired an equitable interest in the property by virtue of a constructive trust.

A constructive trust will be imposed wherever 'it would be unconscionable for the owner of property to assert their own beneficial interest in the property and deny the beneficial interests of another' (*Luff* v. *Banner Homes*). It will be unconscionable for the legal owner of the property to deny a person an equitable interest in it wherever there is a common intention between the parties that they should share the beneficial interest in that property (*Gissing* v. *Gissing*).

In the absence of an express agreement, common intention can be inferred through the conduct of the parties. However, indirect contributions to the property will only be considered sufficient by the courts where there has been an express agreement as to beneficial interest between the parties. In all other cases only direct contributions to the purchase price will suffice (*Lloyds Bank* v. *Rosset*).

Concerning Deeroy's contributions, he has made no direct contributions to the purchase price. However, we are told that the intention was that he and his mother should have joint ownership of the property, but that the council would not allow this under the right-to-buy scheme. This is suggestive of a common intention that they should beneficially own the property together. If such a common intention can be proved, Deeroy will only need to show indirect contributions in order to establish a constructive trust.

In terms of indirect contributions Deeroy has maintained the house and looked after his mother in the house before she was put into the nursing home.

He has also been claiming benefits on her behalf in order to pay the mortgage since she went into the home. However, this is not really his own contribution, but a contribution he is making in his mother's name.

With regard to Shannon's contribution, we are not told of any express agreement between the couple as to their intentions about ownership of the property. In any event, such discussions must have been with the owner of the property, Deeroy's mother, and not Deeroy. Shannon's claim to the property under a constructive trust will therefore fail. She could, however, be able to make a claim in proprietary estoppel for the fitted kitchen if Deeroy has made representations to her about her stake in the flat (see Chapter 8).

In addition to a common intention in order for Deeroy to establish an interest in the flat under a constructive trust there must also be reliance and detriment. Detrimental reliance needn't be financial in nature, although we are told he has 'maintained' the property, which is suggestive of some financial outlay. His looking after his mother could be seen to be detrimental reliance if he did so on the understanding that he was to have an interest in the house. See here *Hammond* v. *Mitchell*, where we are told that, following express discussions about the property, the woman gave up a lucrative position in order to stay at home on the understanding that she would have an interest in the property. Like Deeroy, who was prevented from going on the title deeds by the council, she was told that the only reason she was not being put on the title deeds was because of the man's personal circumstances. However, the difference here is that she gave up her position to look after the home. We are not aware of Deeroy having made such a sacrifice. See also *Grant* v. *Edwards* and *Eves* v. *Eves* in this respect.

If an equity can be established on the part of Deeroy, quantification of the interest will need to be established. In calculating the share of the property to be awarded in constructive trust cases, the court will 'undertake a survey of the whole course of dealing between the parties . . . taking account of all conduct which throws light on the question what shares were intended' (*Stack* v. *Dowden*).

Essay: This question is referring to the recent tendency of the courts to use the findings in *Stack* v. *Dowden* to award a beneficial interest under a constructive trust as well as to quantify one. In particular, the question is looking for a discussion of the two recent cases of *Abbott* v. *Abbott* and *Hapeshi* v. *Allnatt*.

You may wish to start by outlining the facts in *Stack* and explaining the judgment given by Baroness Hale, which stated that in order to quantify the share in a property under a constructive trust the court should 'undertake a survey of the whole course of dealing between the parties . . . taking account of all conduct which throws light on the question what shares were intended'.

Following this judgment, two cases, *Abbott* v. *Abbott* and *Hapeshi* v. *Allnatt*, have interpreted this as being sufficient to award a constructive trust, as well as to quantify one. You should talk through the facts of each case, explaining the findings of the court in each one.

The point to be made in *Abbott* v. *Abbott* is that the court was in essence awarding the constructive trust on the basis of the 'whole course of dealings' alone as there was no express agreement in existence between the parties at all. What the court in *Abbott* v. *Abbott* had, in effect, done, then, was to impute the intention of the parties as no share could be inferred from their conduct. This has always been forbidden territory and certainly not something advocated in *Stack* v. *Dowden*. It should be remembered that *Stack* v. *Dowden* did not explore the issue of award of share, only the quantification of it, as the couple were joint owners of the property in law in any event.

In *Hapeshi* v. *Allnatt*, again there was no express agreement, no contribution to the purchase price, and no contribution towards mortgage payments. However, the claimant ended up with a 25 per cent beneficial share in the family home. Again, then, this is a case in which, in the name of surveying the whole course of dealings, a statement originally applied in *Stack* v. *Dowden* specifically to the issue of quantification of share has been used to make an award of a beneficial interest.

There has been no judgment from a higher court to state whether or not these interpretations are correct to date. You may wish to finish by giving your own views on the matter and suggesting the way in which the problem might be remedied.

Visit **www.mylawchamber.co.uk** to access tools to help you develop and test your knowledge of land law.

Chapter 8
Informal methods of acquisition: proprietary estoppel

Key points In this chapter we will be looking at:

- ✦ What is proprietary estoppel
- ✦ Why proprietary estoppel is important
- ✦ How to establish a claim in proprietary estoppel
- ✦ Assurance, reliance and detriment in proprietary estoppel cases
- ✦ What constitutes an assurance: particular problems with estate contracts and testamentary promises
- ✦ What constitutes 'detriment'
- ✦ The issue of unconscionability
- ✦ The remedies granted in proprietary estoppel claims
- ✦ The proprietary effect of estoppel
- ✦ Similarities between proprietary estoppel and constructive trusts

Introduction

Imagine the following scenario: Anya builds a conservatory onto her house the foundations of which encroach on her neighbour's boundary by some eight inches. The neighbour, Zander, is fully aware of the conservatory being built, but says nothing during the course of the building works. Once the extension has been finished, Zander writes to Anya demanding that she pays £50,000 for the eight-inch strip of land belonging to him and on which the conservatory has been built. If she does not pay for the land, he says, he will get a court order forcing her to pull the conservatory down.

Viewed through the eyes of the law, Zander has every right to do this. He is the legal owner of the land and can enforce his rights over it. But what about the sheer inequity of the situation? Zander was clearly aware of Anya's building works and could have stopped her at any time; but he chose not to. He waited until the conservatory was finished and then threatened Anya with a view to extorting money from her. In this situation, the courts may use the equitable **doctrine** of **proprietary estoppel** to prevent Zander from enforcing his legal rights of ownership over the eight-inch strip of land. The outcome will be a transfer of the land from Zander to Anya on grounds of proprietary estoppel. Put in legal terms, Zander will be estopped by the court from asserting his **proprietary rights** in the land. The transfer is an informal one because there is no transfer of the land by **deed** (in this scenario of course the transfer would be by court order).

The doctrine of proprietary estoppel follows well after the topics of **resulting** and **constructive trusts** because:

(a) it shares many of the same features as constructive trusts (although to date the two equitable principles remain separate); and

(b) It frequently (although not always) results in the informal creation of rights in land.

Let us take some time now to look at what proprietary estoppel is and why it is important as a tool of the court of **equity**.

What is proprietary estoppel?

Proprietary estoppel is an old established equitable principle which has enjoyed a renaissance at the hands of the court of equity in the last fifty years or so. As we have seen above, the idea behind the doctrine of proprietary estoppel is that, if a landowner allows another person to act to their detriment in the mistaken belief that they either have or will gain either ownership or an interest in land belonging to the landowner, then the landowner will be 'estopped' from asserting their legal rights over the property and denying the third party an **equitable interest** in the land. In our example we saw that the landowner, Zander, allowed Anya to build a conservatory which encroached onto Zander's property, knowing that once the conservatory had been built she would be unlikely to want to pull down the conservatory and so would be forced to pay for the land she had encroached upon. In this situation it is easy to see why equity would choose to help Anya. Now take a look at the following three cases and You Be the Judge as to whether or not the landowners' claims in each case should have been estopped.

You be the judge

Q: **Take a look at the facts of the following three cases and decide whether or not the third parties' claims to the land should have been upheld.**

1. *Inwards* v. *Baker* [1965] 2 QB 29: a father, John Baker, allowed his son to build a bungalow on the father's land. On the father's death the father's mistress, Miss Inwards, and their children, sought possession of the bungalow.

2. *Pascoe* v. *Turner* [1979] 1 WLR 431: Mr Pascoe bought a house in his sole name, which he lived in with Ms Turner. Mr Pascoe told Ms Turner 'the house is yours and everything in it'. Ms Turner spent a considerable amount on repairs and improvements to the property, such as plumbing, repairs to the roof, putting in new carpets and the general redecoration of the house. When the couple later split up, Mr Pascoe sought to have Ms Turner removed from the house.

3. *Greasley* v. *Cooke* [1980] 1 WLR 1306: Doris Cooke began to work at the age of 16 as a maid in a widower's house, and to look after his four children. The widower, Mr Greasley, died in 1948 leaving the house to two of his sons, who were now grown up. Doris looked after the eldest son and his mentally ill sister without receiving any payments and on the basis of assurances by the two sons who owned the house that she could remain in the house as long as she wished. On the death of the eldest son, his share in the house passed to his three remaining siblings. Doris sought a declaration that she was entitled to remain in the house rent-free for the rest of her life.

A: In all three cases the third parties' claims for proprietary estoppel were upheld and the claimants were estopped from enforcing their legal rights as landowners.

Why is proprietary estoppel important?

it enables the courts to recognise the moral obligations of the landowner

The thread which links all of the above cases together is that, in each case, the person claiming the benefit of the doctrine of proprietary estoppel had no legal right to the ownership or occupation of the property in question. At law, each of the parties in question was helpless to defend their position. Proprietary estoppel is therefore a vital equitable tool in that it enables the courts to recognise the moral obligations of the landowner where no legal obligation exists.

Proprietary estoppel is also important because it forms one of the few methods of creating interests in or transferring **legal title** to land without the **formality** of a deed or writing. It is for this reason that you will come across lawyers using proprietary estoppel as an argument in property disputes over and over again, and why you will find an equal number of judges using the doctrine in their findings.

From the examples given above, you should now have a good idea of the nature of proprietary estoppel and in what sort of circumstances it will arise. Generally speaking, estoppel claims will arise for one of two reasons. Either:

1. to enforce a promise which has been made to a third party by the landowner; or
2. to protect the position of a buyer who has acted to their detriment in the process of negotiations to purchase a property.

We will be looking at both kinds of estoppel claim throughout the course of the chapter. However, claims made for either reason are proven in the same way. Let us now move on to consider the detail of how a claim in proprietary estoppel is established.

How to establish a claim in proprietary estoppel

In order to establish a claim in proprietary estoppel a number of requirements need to be fulfilled. Traditionally there were five separate requirements, set out by Mr Justice Fry in the case of *Willmott* v. *Barber* (1880) 15 ChD 96. The case concerned an agreement to buy a piece of land. Joseph Willmott owned a timber yard which adjoined land belonging to William Bowyer. William let part of his land to Joseph, giving him an **option to purchase** the land at any time within the following five years. Unbeknown to Joseph the land, which was itself held by William on a long **lease**, was subject to a **covenant** not to sub-let or assign (that is, to transfer) the property without the written consent of the **landlord**, and William had not obtained this consent. Joseph spent a considerable amount of money improving the land by levelling it and incorporating it into his existing business premises. He then served notice on William that he wished to exercise his option to purchase the land. However, William was unable to go through with the sale because the landlord refused to give his consent to the **assignment** of the lease. Joseph brought an **action** against both William and the landlord, claiming **specific performance** of the agreement between William and Joseph, and to compel the landlord to give his

Case Summary

agreement to the transfer. Joseph claimed that the landlord had acquiesced in Joseph's expenditure because he knew that Joseph was acting in the mistaken belief that William was able to assign the property to him.

In making his judgment in the case, Mr Justice Fry said that, in order for a claim of proprietary estoppel to be established:

1. the claimant must have made a mistake as to their legal rights;
2. the claimant must have expended some money or must have done some act (not necessarily on the land) on the faith of their mistaken belief;
3. the landowner must know that their own right is inconsistent with the right claimed by the claimant;
4. the landowner must know of the claimant's mistaken belief as to their rights;
5. the landowner must have encouraged the claimant in their expenditure of money or in the other acts which they have done, either directly or by abstaining from asserting their legal right.

As it turns out in this case, Mr Justice Fry actually found that the landowner, William, did not fulfil the knowledge requirement for estoppel and thus could not be compelled to perform his agreement. At the time of the agreement the evidence in the case showed that the landlord had been unaware of the covenant; he therefore did not know at the time of the agreement that his own rights were inconsistent with that of the claimant. As such he could not be estopped from asserting his legal rights as freeholder of the land by being forced to give his consent to the assignment.

Whilst the original requirements set out in *Willmott* v. *Barber* still stand, the courts have over the course of time relaxed the rules somewhat so that the requirements have become more of a set of guidelines or indicators, rather than a checklist for establishing a claim. In the case of *Taylor Fashions Ltd* v. *Liverpool Victoria Trustees Co. Ltd* [1982] QB 133, applications were made by the **tenants** of two adjoining shops, Taylor Fashions and Old & Campbell Ltd, for specific performance of options to renew in their leases, which the landlord was refusing to honour. Both tenants had carried out substantial improvements in reliance on the options, but the landlord said that the options were invalid because they had not been registered at the **Land Charges Registry**, which was a requirement under the Land Charges Act 1925. The problem for the court was that it was proved in the case that, at the time of the improvements being made, neither the landlord nor the tenants were aware that the options were invalid. Without this knowledge the third requirement in *Willmott* v. *Barber* (that is, knowledge of the mistake) could not be established because the landlord could not be said to have knowledge that his own rights were inconsistent with the rights claimed by the tenants. In order to get around this problem, in making his findings Mr Justice Oliver said that the courts should adopt a broad approach to the five elements set out in *Willmott* v. *Barber*, and that it was not necessarily essential for each element to be fully present in every instance. Applying this to the case, whilst the court acknowledged that the options to renew were invalid because they had not been registered, under the doctrine of proprietary estoppel the landlord would nevertheless be bound by them if it would be 'dishonest or unconscionable' for him to argue otherwise.

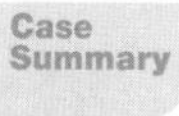

The outcome in the case is interesting because the court found differently in respect of each tenant. *Taylor Fashions* were refused specific performance on the basis that the landlord had no involvement with the work carried out to the premises. It was therefore not possible to say that the tenant would not have carried out the works if the landlord

had told them that their option to renew was invalid. However, in the case of Old & Campbell Ltd, the landlord had encouraged the tenant to carry out works, to take another lease of adjoining premises and had fixed the value of the freehold taking into account the option over it. Specific performance was granted therefore and Old & Campbell were allowed to renew their lease.

Whilst *Taylor Fashions* is only a first instance decision, Mr Justice Oliver's reasoning has been widely followed and the focus in proprietary estoppel cases is now not on the slavish fulfilment of all five criteria in *Willmott* v. *Barber*, but rather on the unconscionability of the landowner's actions in the particular case. This does not mean that the criteria in *Willmott* v. *Barber* have been removed altogether; but it is now commonplace to state them rather more simply in terms of:

1. ***assurance*** (by the landowner giving rise to the claimant mistaking their legal rights);
2. ***reliance*** (on the landowner's assurances); and
3. ***detriment*** (brought about by that reliance).

This is coupled with the fourth more general requirement set out in *Taylor Fashions*, of:

4. ***unconscionability*** (which requirement incorporates within it the prerequisites of knowledge, both of the mistake and the inconsistency of rights, and encouragement as cited in the original case).

So we can now say that, in order to establish a claim in proprietary estoppel, the claimant will need to show:

ASSURANCE + RELIANCE + DETRIMENT + UNCONSCIONABILITY

Let us now spend some time looking at these four requirements in a little more detail.

Assurance

The requirement of assurance essentially replicates Mr Justice Fry's fifth requirement in *Willmott* v. *Barber*, in that it requires the landowner to have encouraged the claimant in their belief, whether directly or indirectly. Direct assurance would be where the landowner has actively encouraged the claimant to act to their detriment; indirect assurance would be where they have simply stood by and allowed the claimant to continue in their mistaken belief as to their rights over the property, albeit knowing that this was not the correct position at law. There are many different examples of what might constitute such assurances, as we have already seen in the You Be the Judge feature, above. You will remember that these included an assurance by a man to his cohabitee that 'the house is yours and everything in it' (direct assurance); a claim by a long-standing housekeeper that she could remain in the house as long as she wished (direct assurance); and a father allowing a son to build a house on land owned by the father (indirect assurance). In particular, however, it is worth spending a little bit of time taking a look in more detail at two particular types of assurance, both of which have raised questions as to what constitutes assurance in proprietary estoppel cases in general.

Proprietary estoppel and estate contracts

The formation of **estate contracts** has recently become a key area in which claims for proprietary estoppel are prevalent, both *Willmott* v. *Barber* and *Taylor Fashions* turning on the claimants' belief that they had the benefit of options to purchase a legal estate in the land in question (you will remember from your earlier reading that an option to purchase is a type of estate contract). In both of these cases, however, the options to purchase were not valid and so the claimants asked for a remedy on the grounds of proprietary estoppel.

Writing and drafting

Here is a little piece of revision for you. Can you remember what is required for the formation of a valid estate contract in land? Take a few moments to write down the formalities required, together with details of the provision in which the rules can be found.

Source: Sozaijiten

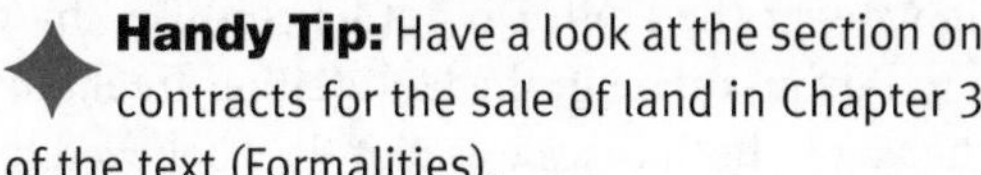

Handy Tip: Have a look at the section on contracts for the sale of land in Chapter 3 of the text (Formalities).

Reflective practice

The above Writing and Drafting exercise illustrates how interconnected the various issues arising in land law really are. Try thinking about what else you can remember about estate contracts and where this information might come in useful. You will come across estate contracts in the context of transmissibility of proprietary estoppel later in the chapter.

You will remember from your earlier reading that, under section 2 of the Law of Property (Miscellaneous Provisions) Act 1989, in order for an estate contract to be valid it must be created in writing. In cases where an agreement for the sale of land has not been put into writing, or where the purported contract falls foul of section 2 in some other way (for example, because it does not contain all the terms of the agreement), the injured party will often turn to the courts to remedy the situation on the basis of an estoppel. This was what happened in the case of *Crabb* v. *Arun District Council* [1976] Ch 179. The case concerned two neighbouring landowners, Mr Crabb and Arun District Council. Mr Crabb sold part of his land to a third party, without reserving a **right of way** over his remaining land to the **public highway**. This was because he had been led by the Council to believe that they would give him a right of way over their adjoining land, and so the **reservation** of a right of way over his own land was not necessary. However, after Mr Crabb's land had been sold, the Council then refused to give him a right of way over their land unless he paid them the sum of £3,000. The Court of Appeal held that Mr Crabb should be given the right of way under the doctrine of proprietary estoppel and that he did not have to pay the Council for it. He had sold his own land without reserving a right of way through it, based on the assurances of the Council and they were estopped from denying him a right of way as a result of this. The point to be made here is that there was no formal written contract in place for the purchase of the right of way

Case Summary

This case shows a significant step forward by the courts

from the council. All that existed was the expectation of a right of way being granted over the Council's land in the future, on which Mr Crabb acted to his detriment by selling off a part of his land which contained the only other access to the public highway. Despite there being no legally binding contract under section 2, however, the court were nevertheless willing to step in and effectively enforce an **oral agreement** on the basis of an **estoppel**, because of the Council's unconscionable actions in demanding money for the right of way. This case therefore shows a significant step forward by the courts in the area of proprietary estoppel: firstly, because it shows that the courts are willing to use proprietary estoppel as a means of enforcing contracts which have failed to be formalised under section 2 of the Law of Property (Miscellaneous Provisions) Act 1989; and, secondly, because it shows a clear extension of what will constitute the nature of the assurance on the part of the landowner to incorporate not only what are the current rights of the claimant but also as to what the claimant might expect in terms of a future interest in the land. In both *Willmott* v. *Barber* itself and in *Taylor Fashions*, the claimants' beliefs related to their current – not future – rights over the land. Do not be confused by the fact that the rights gave them the option to buy an estate in the land (either **freehold** or **leasehold**) at some point in the future. The fact in both cases was that they believed they had a *current* right in the land in the form of the option to purchase itself. The use of proprietary estoppel to enforce agreements that had not yet been reduced to writing and properly formalised is therefore a clear extension of this requirement.

Conscious that this extension of the rules of proprietary estoppel could be used as a convenient tool for the courts to allow oral contracts for the sale of land wherever they deemed it appropriate, however, there has been a more recent attempt by the House of Lords to reduce the number of instances in which proprietary estoppel can be used to enforce oral estate contracts. In the case of *Cobbe* v. *Yeoman's Row Management Ltd* [2008] 1 WLR 1752, the full facts of which are given below, Mr Cobbe claimed that he had reached an oral agreement with the owners of a block of flats that he would apply for **planning permission** for their redevelopment of a block in return for a share of the profits on the development. The owners, however, denied that any legally enforceable agreement had been entered into, saying that Mr Cobbe had incurred the expense entirely at his own risk. Rejecting the argument put forward by Mr Cobbe, Lord Walker said:

Case Summary

> . . . Mr Cobbe's case seems to me to fail on the simple but fundamental point that, as persons experienced in the property world, both parties knew that there was no legally binding contract, and that either was therefore free to discontinue the negotiations without legal liability . . . Mr Cobbe . . . stood to make a handsome profit if the deal went ahead . . . the fact is that he ran a commercial risk, with his eyes open, and the outcome has proved unfortunate for him.

Lord Walker clearly felt, then, that in a business context reliance on a verbal assurance did not hold any weight as proof in the establishment of an estoppel.

The immediate reaction from legal commentators on the outcome of the case was one of dissent. Applying the case to proprietary estoppel cases as a whole, it was felt that the case resulted in a severe curtailment of the use of proprietary estoppel as an equitable remedy in the future. However, when read in context, Lord Walker's judgment is clearly restricted to oral agreements for the sale of land made in the commercial arena. Lord Walker even went as far as to say that, in his view and clearly in the general view of the courts from judgments before him, there was a marked difference between cases in which families had relied on promises of, in the most part, security of family life in the provision of a home, and a commercial case such as *Cobbe* v. *Yeoman's Row*. In this case, despite being a very experienced businessman, Mr Cobbe had decided to take a commercial risk without putting the agreement on a formal footing. Mr Cobbe was well aware that there was no legally binding contract and that therefore the management company could pull out of the deal at any time, without legal consequence. All Lord Walker was suggesting was that it would be unrealistic to impose a remedy under proprietary estoppel based on the suggestion that an experienced man of business would be naïve enough to rely on another company's word that a £12 million business deal would go ahead without further negotiation.

The finding in *Cobbe* v. *Yeoman's Row* seems not to have dissuaded claimants from making proprietary estoppel claims in the face of failed agreements for the sale of land, however. One example of this is *Herbert* v. *Doyle* [2010] EWCA Civ 1095, in which the Court of Appeal recently followed the finding in *Cobbe*. The case concerned an agreement made between the owners of two neighbouring properties: one owned by a developer, Mr Herbert, and the other by a dental practice. Mr Herbert was redeveloping the property he owned into flats and, as part of the development, had made an oral agreement with the dentist to acquire nine of his car parking spaces, in exchange for space to park elsewhere on the development. The agreement was never formalised, however. Mr Herbert started work on the development and the dentist sought to prevent him from doing so on grounds of trespass onto the car parking spaces. Following *Cobbe*, the court found against Mr Herbert, stating that proprietary estoppel could not be invoked to save an agreement which fell foul of section 2 of the Law of Property (Miscellaneous Provisions) Act 1989. However, the judge nevertheless stated that, if all the other elements of proprietary estoppel were present, the fact that an agreement falls foul of section 2 should not by itself be enough to defeat a proprietary estoppel claim.

Case Summary

Despite the result in *Herbert* v. *Doyle*, then, the House of Lords' finding in *Cobbe* v. *Yeoman's Row* has certainly not signified the end of proprietary estoppel claims in cases of informal agreements made for the sale and purchase of land, most recently in *Whittaker* v. *Kinnear* [2011] EWHC 1479 (QB), which concerned the sale of a large house in Colchester called Marks Tey Hall. Ms Whittaker, who owned the Hall, had sold it to a developer for almost half of what it was worth on the basis that she would be allowed to continue to live in the property after the sale. However, although Ms Whittaker continued to live in the property the agreement was never properly formalised and when the developer subsequently did not keep up their mortgage payments on the property the bank sought to repossess it. Ms Whittaker claimed a right to occupy the property on grounds of proprietary estoppel. The court at first instance summarily rejected Ms Whittaker's claim (that is, without consideration of her case) on the grounds that no formal agreement had been effected under section 2 of the Law of Property (Miscellaneous Provisions) Act 1989. They stated that proprietary estoppel could not be used to revive an agreement falling foul of section 2 and so there was no case to answer. However, the High Court overturned the ruling as an incorrect interpretation of the ruling in *Cobbe* v. *Yeoman's Row* and referred the case back to the County Court for a full retrial to consider Ms Whittaker's proprietary estoppel claim. It will be interesting to see the outcome of the hearing, particularly given the practical application a positive outcome in the case will have in respect of homeowners who have fallen foul of **sale and leaseback** agreements. The following Law in Action feature explains.

Case Summary

Law in action Proprietary estoppel comes to the rescue of sale and leaseback victims

The doctrine of proprietary estoppel may help former homeowners who have sold their house in return for **tenancy** but have subsequently been given **notice to quit** the property.

In the current financial climate sale and leaseback arrangements are all too common. This is the situation in which property owners will sell their house to a company at a substantial discount, in exchange for a tenancy agreement which allows them to continue to live in their home, paying rent to the new property owners. In this way, they get their debts paid off but can still remain in the family home – or that is the theory.

Unfortunately what some unscrupulous sale and leaseback companies will do is to serve notice on their tenants only six to twelve months after buying the house, leaving the former homeowners homeless. This is not illegal, but has clear moral implications. Abuses within the sell-to-rent-back market are frequently in the news and, in the present economic climate, increasing numbers of people are likely to find themselves in this precarious position.

Former homeowners need not necessarily abandon all hope in the face of these possession claims, however. What defendants in sale and leaseback possession claims generally want to do is to continue to live in their former home as tenants and, where assurances have been made to them by the property company that they will have a secure home in the property for the foreseeable future, the equitable doctrine of proprietary estoppel may provide a mechanism to achieve this end.

Establishing detriment ought not to be problematic for the tenant of a sale and leaseback property, where the house has been sold at a discount from the full market value. Even where this has not happened (although unlikely) simply entering into a bargain which provided less security of tenure than was promised might, in any event, by itself constitute a detriment.

The general rule is that the relief granted under proprietary estoppel claims will be 'the minimum equity required to do justice'. Therefore if the promise or expectation was of something less than lifetime security, that is what the court is likely to award. Nevertheless, in these turbulent financial times the doctrine of proprietary estoppel is an equity not to be sniffed at.

Source: **http://www.lawgazette.co.uk/in-practice/practice-points/solving-sell-to-rent-back-issues-with-proprietary-estoppel**

Testamentary promises

Failed contracts for the sale of land are not the only area in which the extension of the criteria in proprietary estoppel claims has become an issue. There are many other cases in which the estoppel claim has been founded, quite successfully, on the basis of the claimant's expectation of a future right in the property. Reliance on **testamentary** promises, in other words the situation in which one person says to another 'all this will become yours one day' (i.e. when they die), have also become a common background to proprietary estoppel claims.

> the court could not be seen to be enforcing simple promises

As can be seen from the various wills cases, basing a claim of proprietary estoppel on a promise of a gift or inheritance is not an easy thing, and the acceptance of this premise initially led the courts down a confusing path. Fundamentally, the court could not be seen to be enforcing simple promises – which are not in themselves legally binding (if they were we would most likely all be in trouble!), based on the strength of that promise alone. In order to establish a proprietary estoppel claim, therefore, the courts soon established that the promise must be made somehow more substantial by the subsequent actions of the person making the promise. But where does that leave us?

Case Summary

A good starting point in defining what is required is the Court of Appeal case of *Wayling* v. *Jones* [1995] 2 FLR 1029. The background for this case was not that of a family, but rather the running of a business. Paul Wayling met Daniel Jones when he was 21 and Daniel was 56, and they entered into a relationship together. From the time they met in 1971 until Daniel's death in 1987, Daniel had bought and run various businesses, primarily hotels and guest houses. Paul acted throughout this time as Daniel's companion and chauffeur and gave substantial help in running the businesses. In return for his services Paul received pocket money, living and clothing expenses. Daniel also promised Paul on several occasions that he would leave him the business in his will, making provision first for Paul to inherit Daniel's café premises and later another hotel owned by Daniel, the Glen-y-Mor Hotel in Aberystwyth. In 1985 Daniel sold the Glen-y-Mor Hotel and bought the Hotel Royal, Barmouth which, he told Paul, was for Paul to run and to inherit after Daniel's death. Daniel told Paul that he would alter his will to substitute the Hotel Royal, Barmouth for the Glen-y-Mor Hotel, but he had not done so by the time of his death in 1987. Upon Daniel's death, Paul claimed that he was entitled to the proceeds of the sale of the Hotel Royal, Barmouth on the principles of proprietary estoppel. The Court of Appeal held in favour of the **claimant**, finding that Paul had relied on the promises made by Daniel to leave Paul property under his will, to his detriment. Daniel's **executors** were therefore required to pay the proceeds of sale of the hotel to Paul out of Daniel's estate.

Case Summary

Three years later, however, the outcome in the case of *Taylor* v. *Dickens* [1998] 1 FLR 806 came in complete contrast to *Wayling* v. *Jones*, with a finding at first instance that proprietary estoppel could *not* apply in the case of a promised **legacy**. The facts of the case were as follows: upon being told by the **defendant**, Mrs Parker, that she would leave him her bungalow in her will, Mr Taylor, Mrs Parker's part-time gardener, stated that he would work without pay from then on. Mrs Parker executed at least three wills leaving the bungalow to Mr Taylor, but then made another will leaving it to someone else, without telling Mr Taylor. When Mrs Parker died, Mr Taylor claimed to be entitled to the property on grounds of proprietary estoppel. However, the court held that Mr Taylor should not inherit. In what is now considered rather a harsh finding Judge Weeks QC said that it was not enough for Mr Taylor to believe that he was going to be left property by Mrs Parker, if he knew that the defendant had the right to change her mind. In order to effect a claim in proprietary estoppel Mr Taylor also had to establish that Mrs Parker had created or encouraged a belief that she would not revoke her will and that Mr Taylor had relied on that belief. As Mr Taylor had admitted that this was not the case, his claim for proprietary estoppel failed.

The finding in *Taylor* v. *Dickens* suggested that the cases in which a will could be relied upon would be almost negligible. After all, anyone can change their will at any time up until death. However, this state of affairs was short-lived. In the case of *Gillett* v. *Holt* [2001] Ch 210, which was heard at first instance not six months after *Taylor* v. *Dickens*, the findings in *Taylor* v. *Dickens* were disapproved. Mr Gillett had spent his working life as farm manager for a man named Ken Holt, a wealthy farmer. Mr Holt had made repeated promises and assurances over many years, usually on special family occasions, that Mr Gillett would be the **successor** to his farming business, which included the farmhouse in which Mr Gillett and his family lived. However, after living and working at the farm for some twenty-five years, the two men had a falling out and Mr Holt fired

Mr Gillett and cut him out of his will. On Mr Holt's death, Mr Gillett made a claim against his **estate** under the doctrine of proprietary estoppel. The judge at first instance, following *Taylor* v. *Dickens*, dismissed Mr Gillett's claim, stating that there had been no irrevocable promise that the claimant would inherit. However, on appeal, the Court of Appeal said that Mr Holt's assurances had been made irrevocable by Mr Gillett's reliance on them over a period of years. Mr Gillett was therefore awarded the farmhouse in which he and his family lived, together with sum of money to compensate him for his exclusion from the rest of the farming business. In commenting on Mr Gillett's reliance on the will, Lord Justice Walker said:

> . . . it is notorious that some elderly persons of means derive enjoyment from the possession of testamentary power, and from dropping hints as to their intentions, without any question of an estoppel arising. But in this case Mr Holt's assurances were repeated over a long period, usually before the assembled company on special family occasions . . . Mr Gillett, after discussing the matter with his wife and his parents, decided to rely on Mr Holt's assurances because 'Ken was a man of his word'. Plainly the assurances given . . . were intended to be relied on, and were in fact relied on.

Despite the finding in *Taylor* v. *Dickens* being disapproved, therefore, it is clear from the wording of the judgment that promises of inheritance should be substantial and repeated in order for a claim of proprietary estoppel to succeed in reliance on them. A simple, one-off statement or hints at an inheritance would not do. It should be noted that, in the case of *Gillett* v. *Holt*, particular emphasis was placed by the Court of Appeal on the fact that Mr Holt was a dour man of few words and that such statements by him, such as they were made from time to time, were therefore not to be taken lightly.

Following the Court of Appeal's finding in *Gillett* v. *Holt*, there have been two recent House of Lords cases which have really thrown the issue of expectation as a feature of proprietary estoppel into the limelight. The first is that of *Cobbe* v. *Yeoman's Row Management Ltd*, which we considered earlier in the context of failed contracts for the sale of land, and the second is *Thorner* v. *Major* [2009] 1 WLR 776. Although *Cobbe* v. *Yeoman's Row* concerned an alleged business deal and not a promise of inheritance at all, as we have seen above there was a great deal of initial concern after its outcome as to how this would affect proprietary estoppel claims in general and, in particular, claims of testamentary promise. However, in cases of testamentary promise the fears brought about by the outcome of this case appear to have now been allayed by a further House of Lords decision, that of *Thorner* v. *Major*. Following hot on the heels of *Cobbe* v. *Yeoman's Row*, this 2009 case once again concerned a promise of testamentary gift, and therefore put the discussion of expectation back into familiar territory. The facts of the case are very similar to the facts of *Gillett* v. *Holt*, in that they concern promises to inherit a farm. The claimant, David Thorner, lived at home with his parents helping his father and later his father's cousin Peter, to farm their neighbouring farmland (Peter had no children of his own to help out on the farm). In 1986, David's father gave up farming and David began to work full-time on Peter's farm, which he did until Peter's death in 2005. David was never paid for his work; however, various remarks were made by Peter that led David to expect that he would inherit the farm on Peter's death. In particular, on one occasion Peter handed David a life insurance policy bonus notice, saying 'That's for my death duties' (by this he meant the payment of inheritance tax). Peter had also made a will in which he left the farm to David, but this had been later destroyed after a falling-out between Peter and another **beneficiary**. David made a claim for the whole

Case Summary

of Peter's estate under the doctrine of proprietary estoppel. The judge at first instance found in David's favour. However, the Court of Appeal reversed the decision, stating that Peter's actions regarding the payment of inheritance tax were not sufficient to show a 'clear and unequivocal representation upon which Peter had intended David to rely'. David appealed to the House of Lords.

The decision of the Court of Appeal was duly overturned. Lord Neuberger did not agree with the Court of Appeal's suggestion that the statements made by Peter Thorner were not of a sufficiently unequivocal nature. He said that the meaning ascribed to words passing between parties would be dependent on their factual context. In Lord Neuberger's view, whilst there could be exceptional cases where it might be wrong to find estoppel on the basis of a statement relied upon, because that person had been unreasonable in their reliance, such cases would be rare. In this case, although technically 'revocable', once the statement made by Peter had been acted upon by David for a substantial period of time, it would have been inequitable for Peter to go back on that statement, at least without paying David appropriate compensation for his 14 years' unpaid work on the farm. This was unless it could be proved that the change of mind was attributable to, and could be justified by, a change of circumstances (which in this case it could not).

We can therefore see from this case that when proving the element of assurance in cases of proprietary estoppel, whilst a promise to leave a gift of property in a will can, if taken in context, be a sufficient assurance on which a party can rely:

1. The quality of the assurance made will depend on the individual facts of the case; and
2. It is the act of reliance by the claimant on the property owner's assurances that makes the assurance irrevocable, not the contractual (or otherwise) nature of the assurance itself.

You may find it helpful to read and complete the following Writing and Drafting exercise to consolidate your learning at this point.

Writing and drafting

You are a trainee solicitor at Johns Associates, solicitors. Mr Johns has asked you to get the team up to speed on the requirements for proprietary estoppel following the recent House of Lords decision in *Thorner* v. *Major*. Read Lord Neuberger's judgment in *Thorner* v. *Major* [2009] 1 WLR 776 and prepare a case report explaining his findings.

You should spend no more than 50 minutes on this task.

Handy tip: The judgment is particularly helpful in explaining what will be considered sufficient in terms of assurances in cases of proprietary estoppel. You may wish to focus on his explanation of this in your answer.

Reliance

Reliance is fairly self-explanatory and, as can be seen from the case law explored in the section on assurance, tends to overlap with the other two requirements of assurance and detriment. However, in essence, the idea is that the claimant must have relied upon the assurance or assurances made to them by the landowner, acting to their detriment in doing so. That the claimant has acted in reliance on the assurance tends to be assumed wherever assurance and detriment are proven. This was confirmed in the Court of Appeal case of *Gillett* v. *Holt*, the facts of which are given above.

Detriment

The requirement of Mr Justice Fry in *Willmott* v. *Barber*, that the claimant must have expended some money or must have done some act on the faith of the assurance made to them, is what now equates to the requirement of detriment in modern cases. The requirement that the claimant has acted to their detriment based on the assurance given to them by the landowner seems straightforward. But how can the achievement of the required level of detriment be quantified? What level of detriment will suffice?

Case Summary

If the claimant has expended money in reliance on the assurance, the court will usually find detriment. This was the finding of the Court of Appeal in *Pascoe* v. *Turner* [1979] 1 WLR 431, in which a woman had spent money on redecorations, improvements and repairs to a house in which she lived with her partner for ten years. The house had bought for the couple in the man's sole name, but he had assured her that the house and its contents would be hers and she had spent money on the house in reliance on his declaration. However, as with **detrimental reliance** in constructive trusts, detriment in proprietary estoppel can take many forms, not necessarily financial. In the case of *Re Basham* [1986] 1 WLR 1498 the claimant, Joan Bird, acted to her detriment by working in her stepfather's businesses without payment for many years and caring for him and his home. She did this on the understanding that she would inherit his estate on his death; however, the stepfather died **intestate** and his estate went to his children under the rules of intestacy, leaving Joan with nothing. Joan made a claim against the stepfather's next-of-kin and the court held that she was entitled to the estate as she had successfully established a case in proprietary estoppel in the circumstances.

Case Summary

Case Summary

The case of *Lissimore* v. *Downing* [2003] 2 FLR 308, on the other hand, provides a good illustration of what will *not* constitute detriment. The case concerned a claim by the former lover of the founder member of heavy metal band, Judas Priest, Kenneth 'K K' Downing. Sarah tried to claim half of Kenneth's 380-acre country estate in Shropshire, Astbury Hall. The couple had embarked on an eight-year relationship, with Miss Lissimore giving up her job as a pharmacist's assistant and moving in with Kenneth, but the couple did not marry. When the couple split up, Miss Lissimore made a claim for half the estate on grounds of proprietary estoppel. She said that she was entitled under the doctrine because Kenneth had promised to support her, based on his assertion, 'I'd bet you'd love to be lady of this Manor, wouldn't you?' However, the court found that there had been no representation or assurance made by Kenneth and that there had been no action by Miss Lissimore which would be construed as detrimental above and beyond actions which would have constituted the ordinary course of such a relationship. Miss Lissimore's claim therefore failed and she received no part of the estate. It would appear that Mr Downing was luckier than many in his celebrity break-up.

Case Summary

In the more recent Court of Appeal case of *Powell* v. *Benney* [2008] P&CR D31, the claimants also failed to give sufficient evidence of detriment to gain the award they requested, albeit that they were still given a sum of money in lieu of their expenditure. Mr Hobday owned several properties. He became friendly with a local pastor, Mr Powell, and his wife who, when Mr Hobday became incapable of looking after himself, took care of him and managed his affairs. Mr Hobday told the Powells several times that he was going to leave his properties to them and even signed a document purporting to leave them the properties, although this was not a valid will. He also invited them to use the properties. Powell and his wife spent time tidying and improving the properties for their own use and adapting one for the giving of music and Bible lessons, which they had previously given in their music shop premises. Mr Hobday died intestate and the properties passed to his cousins. The Powells claimed the properties on the grounds of estoppel, but their claim was rejected. Whilst the couple had decided to avail themselves of Mr Hobday's offer to use the properties and incurred some expenditure in consequence, they had done no more than this. Their expenditure did not in any way amount to a detriment in the way they described as it was expended in order to further their own enjoyment of the properties. The couple were nevertheless given a £20,000 award by the court in lieu of their expenditure on the properties 'to reflect their disappointment' at not inheriting.

A similar outcome was reached in the case of *Cobbe* v. *Yeoman's Row*, although for different reasons. You will remember that the case concerned a block of flats that the claimant, Mr Cobbe, said he had agreed with the owners to apply for planning permission to redevelop in return for a share of the profits on the development. When the owners of the block of flats reneged on the deal, Mr Cobbe took them to court, alleging that, pursuant to the agreement, he had spent considerable time and money securing the grant of planning permission and therefore claiming a lump sum payment under the doctrine of estoppel.

The judge at first instance, Mr Justice Etherton, found in favour of Mr Cobbe, awarding Mr Cobbe a one-half share in the increased value of the property as a result of the planning permission. The Court of Appeal also favoured this decision. However, the House of Lords overturned their findings. In their view, this was not a case of proprietary estoppel at all. Mr Cobbe was an experienced businessman who had carried out the work in the knowledge that the oral agreement which had been reached was not legally binding, and therefore his expenditure had been purely speculative. The property deal had never been a venture and so the outcome of the case should not be to treat it as one by giving Mr Cobbe a share of the increase in value on obtaining the planning permission. His only entitlement should therefore be the reimbursement of Mr Cobbe's outgoings and a fee for services rendered to the company. In the eyes of the House of Lords, therefore, detrimental reliance on a promise by Yeoman's had simply not been proved.

Unconscionability

Following *Taylor Fashions*, an opportunity for the unconscionability argument to be tested by the Court of Appeal came in the case of *Sledmore* v. *Dalby* (1996) 72 P&CR 196. The case concerned a house owned by the parents-in-law of Mr Dalby, a Mr and Mrs Sledmore. The Sledmores had allowed Mr Dalby, their daughter and the Dalby's children to live in the house at a time when Mr Dalby was unemployed and his wife was seriously ill. Mr Dalby had been led to believe that he and his family would have a **licence** to live there until the children left home and accordingly he carried out repairs on the property. When Mr Sledmore subsequently died Mrs Sledmore made an application to gain possession of the property, on account of the fact that she wanted to live there herself. Her own home was in a state of some disrepair and she was behind on the **mortgage**

payments. By this time Mr Dalby was employed and the children were grown up, although one still lived at home. Although the facts of the case showed that there had been detrimental reliance by Mr Dalby on a statement by the legal owner, no finding of proprietary estoppel was made and the court found in favour of Mrs Sledmore. This was because no unconscionability on her part could be established. In the court's view there had been a legitimate change in circumstances of both parties and, as the legal owner of the property, Mrs Sledmore was entitled to assert her right to possession of the house. In addition, the court found that, as Mr Dalby had already lived in the property rent-free for 20 years, it was arguable in any event that he had already received the benefit of any proprietary interest he might have been entitled to by virtue of the repairs he had carried out at the property.

So we can see that unconscionability is now a key element to proprietary estoppel. However, it is nevertheless important to remember that unconscionability alone will not suffice: assurance, reliance and detriment are also still valid prerequisites when forming an estoppel claim. This is a point Lord Walker of Gestingthorpe was keen to confirm in the recent House of Lords case of *Cobbe* v. *Yeomans' Row Management Ltd* [2008] 1 WLR 1752. The case concerned an alleged agreement between a developer and a management company. The claimant, Mr Cobbe, said that he had reached an oral agreement with the owners of the block that he would apply for planning permission for their redevelopment in return for £12 million plus 50 per cent of the gross proceeds on their subsequent sale. Mr Cobbe further claimed that, pursuant to the agreement, he spent considerable time and money securing the grant of planning permission for the development. However, the owners had subsequently refused to pay Mr Cobbe, denying that any legally enforceable agreement had been entered into and saying that Mr Cobbe had incurred the expense entirely at his own risk. In making his judgment Lord Walker said:

Case Summary

> . . . equitable estoppel is a flexible doctrine which the court can use, in appropriate circumstances, to prevent injustice caused by the vagaries and inconstancy of human nature. But it is not a sort of joker or wild card to be used whenever the court disapproves of the conduct of a litigant who seems to have the law on his side. Flexible though it is, the doctrine must be formulated and applied in a disciplined and principled way . . .
>
> The principle has been applied in quite a wide variety of factual situations, sometimes of a domestic nature, sometimes commercial. Any formulation of the principle must, if it is to be comprehensive, be expressed in such general terms as to give little idea of what it is really about – what Lord Hoffmann . . . referred to as 'the moral values which underlie the private law concept of estoppel'.
>
> The authors of *Gray & Gray* [state that]: 'The tendency in the modern case law is to synthesise the **jurisprudence** of proprietary estoppel in a more unified doctrine of "detrimental reliance".' I may have made a small personal contribution to that tendency. But . . . this appeal . . . remind[s] me that synthesis and unification, however desirable as objectives, have their dangers.

Lord Walker later went on to say that in his opinion and in the general opinion of the House of Lords 'conscious reliance on honour alone' (in other words the element of unconscionability) would not give rise to an estoppel. Lord Walker was in actual fact following the ruling in the earlier House of Lords case of *Ramsden* v. *Dyson* (1866) LR 1 HL 129, which concerned an argument over two plots of land on a large estate near Huddersfield in the north of England. The Court of Appeal had originally found in favour of the

tenants of the land in granting them long leases of the same on the grounds that they had spent money building on it on the understanding that 'they would never be disturbed'. However, the House of Lords overturned their judgment, on the basis that there had been a mistake on the part of the tenants but no encouragement of their consequent actions. It should be noted that the case was won by a slim majority, the four dissenting judges agreeing with the Court of Appeal's finding in the tenants' favour.

The effect of proprietary estoppel

So far in this chapter we have explored the nature of proprietary estoppel and we have examined in detail what will be sufficient to constitute a claim in equity under the doctrine of proprietary estoppel. What remains is for us to consider what the effect of establishing such a claim is, in practice. In order to get a feel for this let us take a further look the case of *Crabb* v. *Arun District Council*, the facts of which we considered earlier in the chapter. You will remember that the case concerned neighbouring landowners, Mr Crabb and Arun District Council. Mr Crabb had sold part of his land to a third party without reserving a right of way over his remaining land to the public highway because the Council had led him to believe that they would give him a right of way over their adjoining land. In the event, after Mr Crabb had sold his land, the Council then refused to give him a right of way over their land unless he paid them the sum of £3,000. In making his judgment in the case, Lord Justice Scarman said that estoppel cases involved three questions:

1. **Has an equity been established?**
   In other words: has there been an assurance by the legal owner on which the claimant has relied to their detriment and is the legal owner's behaviour unconscionable in all the circumstances? (in brief, the prerequisites set out in *Willmott* v. *Barber* as modified by *Taylor Fashions*).
2. **What is the extent of the equity?**
   The extent of the equity will be matter to be decided on the facts of each case, dependent on the extent to which the claimant acted to their detriment, on the basis of the assurances made to them. The court's decision as to the extent of the claimant's equity will have a direct bearing on the relief granted (below).
3. **What relief should be granted to satisfy it?**
   In other words, what remedy will the courts grant to the claimant? Again, this will be dependent on the facts of each case. In *Pascoe* v. *Turner*: Lord Justice Cumming-Bruce said that, in deciding what remedy to provide in cases of proprietary estoppel:

   > '. . . the court must decide what is the minimum equity to do justice . . . having regard to the way in which [the claimant] changed [their] position for the worse by reason of the acquiescence and encouragement of the legal owner.'

It is therefore not necessarily the case that the claimant, if successful, will be awarded the house or other property, or a share in that property, in every single case. If a claim for proprietary estoppel is established, the court has a broad equitable jurisdiction to prescribe whatever remedy they deem appropriate under the circumstances. It is particularly important to note that the remedy given cannot be punitive in nature.

the remedy given cannot be punitive in nature

The 'minimum equity to do justice' in essence means that the claimant will be given, at most, the interest in the property which they believed they would receive on account of the assurances made to them. They cannot be given an award simply based on the unconscionability of the legal owner's actions, however morally reprehensible they might be.

The remedy given by the courts will be tailored to the facts of the individual case, the court doing whatever they consider necessary to reverse the detriment which has been suffered by the claimant. Such remedies are therefore many and varied in nature, and can range from a simple transfer of the legal estate from the legal owner to the claimant outright, to something more modest, such as the grant of a licence to occupy the land for a period of time. The following are some of the different remedies that can be awarded in a proprietary estoppel case:

(a) *A transfer of the legal estate* (*Pascoe* v. *Turner* – the court held that the house belonged to Ms Turner and ordered the transfer of the property to her. Mr Pascoe was estopped from asserting his legal right over the property because he had promised Ms Turner the house and because she had believed his promise and acted to her detriment as a result of that promise)

(b) *The grant of an* ***easement*** over land (*Crabb* v. *Arun*)

(c) *The grant of a licence* to occupy land for life (*Gillett* v. *Holt*) or to occupy for as long as the claimant wishes to use the land as a home (*Inwards* v. *Baker* – he was entitled to remain in possession as a **licensee** so long as he wished to use it as his home)

(d) *The payment of cash* compensation (*Gillett* v. *Holt*)

Writing and drafting

Your client, Mrs Salée, comes to you for some advice. Last year she built a garage on the driveway between her own and her neighbour's property. The shared driveway is owned jointly by the two properties, but her neighbour never uses it as he has a separate driveway to the rear of his own house which he prefers to use. Mrs Salée asked her neighbour if he minded her building the garage on the shared driveway and he had said that no, he didn't mind. He never used it and he was happy to forgo his legal rights to use the drive so she should go ahead and build. Unfortunately Mrs Salée's neighbour has now decided to sell his property and, following some advice from his solicitor, he is claiming that he has a right to use the driveway and that the garage is obstructing it. He is demanding a payment of £10,000 to formally relinquish his right to use the driveway. If he does not receive this, he says he will force Mrs Salée to have the garage removed.

You decide that the best course of action would be to bring a claim against your client's neighbour for proprietary estoppel. Write a letter to the neighbour explaining your client's claim against them.

You should take no longer than 40 minutes on this task.

Handy tip: Remember to explain to the other side: what you are claiming; what is the basis of your claim (i.e. mistake, detriment, unconscionability) and what you want out of the claim (i.e. the remedy you are seeking).

Case Summary

A really interesting illustration of the courts' attitude towards remedies in proprietary estoppel is that of *Jennings* v. *Rice* [2002] EWCA Civ 159. The case concerned a man named Jennings and an elderly widow, Mrs Royle. Jennings had worked for Mrs Royle on a part-time basis, doing gardening, running errands and taking Mrs Royle shopping, since around 1970. In the late 1980s Mrs Royle stopped paying Jennings, telling him he need not worry about that since 'he would be all right' and that 'this will all be yours one day'. Mrs Royle subsequently became more and more dependent on Jennings, who helped her wash, dress and go to the bathroom, did her shopping, and even slept overnight at her house to provide her with security after a break-in at the house. When Mrs Royle died intestate in 1997, Jennings made a proprietary estoppel claim on the basis of Mrs Royle's assurances to him. The house was then worth £435,000. Mrs Royle's total estate was worth some £1.285 million.

The court found in favour of Mr Jennings but, rather than giving him the house or estate, instead gave him a monetary award of £200,000 which, the judge said represented the estimated cost of full-time nursing care for Mrs Royle. Jennings appealed, contending that he was entitled under the doctrine of proprietary estoppel either to the whole of Mrs Royle's estate, or alternatively to the value of the house, on the basis that that was his expectation. However, the court held, dismissing the appeal, that to have awarded Jennings the value of the house would have been excessive. In the court's view, the value of the equity will depend upon all the circumstances, including not only the expectation of the claimant but also the detriment actually suffered by them. The task of the court was to do whatever is necessary to avoid an unconscionable result, but in doing so there had to be proportionality between the expectation and the detriment. On this basis if the claimant's expectations were extravagant, or out of all proportion to the detriment which the claimant had suffered, the court felt that the claimant's equity should be satisfied in another more limited way.

The 2008 Court of Appeal case of *Powell* v. *Benney*, which we came across earlier in the chapter, also provides some useful commentary on this point. Here the Court of Appeal said that estoppel could be broken down into two different kinds: bargain and non-bargain. In the 'bargain' variety of estoppel it would have to be shown that there was some bargain or agreement between the parties. On the facts of *Powell* v. *Benney*, Mr Hobday had said he would leave the properties to Mr and Mrs Powell but he had not required them to undertake the improvements, which they had done entirely at their own discretion, albeit that Mr Hobday had known about them. This was 'non-bargain' estoppel. Whilst this form of estoppel nevertheless required the judge to satisfy the equity which had arisen on the basis of the Powells' expenditure, the value of the properties was out of all proportion to their expenditure. Therefore the judge ordered a payment of £20,000 which he considered reasonable in order to meet the Powells' expectations.

It would thus appear that, regardless of the circumstances of the estoppel, the detriment suffered must be proportionate to the award claimed in order for 'the minimum equity to do justice' to be satisfied. As with the two cases above, and even the outcome in *Cobbe* v. *Yeoman's Row*, the court will look to the extent of the expenditure made or other detriment suffered by the claimant before making the appropriate award.

The proprietary nature of estoppel

When we think of a claim in proprietary estoppel we automatically imagine a scenario such as that given at the beginning of the chapter, where a landowner such as Zander allows or encourages a third party such as Anya to act to their detriment (by expending money building a conservatory on his land) on the basis of a mistaken belief or expectation (that the land belongs to her). The example of Zander and Anya is simple: we have a simple interaction between two people with the resulting claim being against the unconscionably acting landowner. However, what would happen if Zander then sold his property to Spike? If Spike tried to force Anya to remove the conservatory from his land, would Anya be able to claim against Spike as the successor in title to Zander? Logic might tell us that Anya would be unable to bring a claim against Spike, as he has not acted unconscionably (not having been a party to Anya's mistake); but the law tells us otherwise. In actual fact, successors in title have consistently been bound under the doctrine of proprietary estoppel by the actions of their predecessors. We have even seen examples of this happening throughout the course of the chapter, particularly in cases where the land in question is the subject of a probate dispute. Obviously in these circumstances the protagonist has died and the claim is being made against the estate of that person and thus the persons who have inherited their property. Just think of *Wayling* v. *Jones* and *Jennings* v. *Rice*, to name but two examples. So how is this possible?

> successors in title have consistently been bound under the doctrine of proprietary estoppel

The answer lies in two parts:

1. firstly, the nature of the estoppel as an interest in land; and
2. secondly, the timing of the creation of the estoppel.

In the first instance it should be noted that an estoppel, once created, is an equitable interest in land. This means that, once created, it subsists in the same way as any other equitable interest in land and the benefit or burden of it can be transferred as such to third parties. In respect of cases of proprietary estoppel where the land in question is **registered**, section 116 of the Land Registration Act 2002 states that '. . . for the avoidance of doubt . . . an equity by estoppel . . . has effect from the time the equity arises as an interest capable of binding successors in title'.

The addition of the wording 'for the avoidance of doubt' is suggestive of an assumption that this is already the position in relation to **unregistered land** and there is no suggestion in case law that this should be otherwise. It should be noted that the estoppel itself is thus quite separate from any interest in land which may be granted as a remedy of that estoppel. It is this point which often causes confusion – where an interest in land is granted to satisfy a claim of another interest in land. However, it is important to keep the two as distinct and separate notions. It may help to remember the questions posed by Lord Justice Scarman in the case of *Crabb* v. *Arun*, above:

1. Has an equity been established? (that is, the equity of estoppel)
2. What is the extent of that equity?
3. What relief should be granted to satisfy it? (As we have seen, the relief may come in the form of another equitable interest, such as a constructive trust, or in the form of money, or any number of other things.)

Secondly, it is important to remember that the estoppel is created at the time when the detrimental reliance occurs: so in the case of Anya and Zander, it is created when Anya builds her conservatory, not later on when Spike buys the property and asks Anya to remove the conservatory from his land. In this way, it is possible for an estoppel to be created through the unconscionable actions of one landowner and then subsequently passed on to another.

One final point to mention in this respect relates to the transmissibility of equitable interests in land. You many remember from Chapter 4 on interests in land, that equitable interests in land will only bind a purchaser of registered land if they are either protected on the register of title at the **Land Registry** as a **registrable** or third party **interest** (not applicable here), or if they are an **overriding interest**. Due to the nature of proprietary estoppel cases, it will often be the case that the person claiming the estoppel is an occupier of the land in question and can claim an overriding interest by virtue of their occupation of the property as a 'person in actual occupation' under Schedule 3, paragraph 2 of the Land Registration Act 2002. Equitable interests in unregistered land, on the other hand, you will remember, bind everyone except a **bone fide purchaser of the land for value without notice.** Thus inheritance disputes will circumvent this because there is no purchase of the land.

Similarities to constructive trusts

You may have noticed from your reading of this chapter that the doctrine of proprietary estoppel shares a number of the features of constructive trusts. Indeed, as we have seen above, a finding of proprietary estoppel can even result in the awarding of a constructive trust. A case in point is the Court of Appeal case of *Yaxley* v. *Gotts* [2000] 1 All ER 711, the facts of which are discussed below. However, the two doctrines can also produce very different results. One only has to look at the preceding paragraphs to see how much wider the range of remedies available to a claimant of proprietary estoppel is and how much greater the court's discretion can be, than in cases of constructive trust. This does not mean that the remedies available in proprietary estoppel are superior to those available to the constructive trustee, of course. A wider discretion, as we have seen, does not necessarily equate to a more substantial reward: in fact, proprietary estoppel claims can often produce a financially lesser remedy for the claimant.

Nevertheless, due to what has been traditionally perceived as the very similar natures of the two equitable doctrines, it has been commonplace for lawyers in such claims to plead their case in the alternative, arguing the benefit of one doctrine if the other fails; and the courts have been happy to treat the two doctrines as overlapping, if not synonymous in some circumstances. Lord Scott of Foscote commented on this phenomenon in the recent case of *Thorner* v. *Major*. In his judgment Lord Scott said:

> These reflections invite some thought about the relationship between proprietary estoppel and constructive trust and their respective roles in providing remedies where representations about future property interests have been made and relied on. There are many cases in which the representations relied on relate to the acquisition by the representee of an immediate, or more or less immediate, interest in the property in question. In these cases a proprietary estoppel is the obvious remedy. The representor is estopped from denying that the representee has the proprietary interest that was promised by the representation in question. *Crabb* v. *Arun* seems to me a clear example of such a case . . . *Ramsden* v. *Dyson* (1866) LR 1 HL 129 is another . . . In cases where the owner of land stands by and allows a neighbour to build over the mutual boundary, representing either expressly or impliedly that the building owner is entitled to do so, the owner may be estopped from subsequently asserting his title to the encroached upon land. This, too, seems to me straightforward proprietary estoppel . . . Constructive trust, in my opinion, has nothing to offer to cases of this sort. But cases where the relevant representation has related to inheritance prospects seem to me difficult . . . to square with the principles of

> proprietary estoppel established by the *Ramsden* v. *Dyson* and *Crabb* v. *Arun* line of cases and, for my part, I find them made easier to understand as constructive trust cases. The possibility of a remedial constructive trust over property, created by the common intention or understanding of the parties regarding the property on the basis of which the claimant has acted to his detriment, has been recognised at least since *Gissing* v. *Gissing* . . . The 'inheritance' cases, of which *Gillett* v. *Holt*, *Re Basham* . . . and, of course, the present case are good examples, are, to my mind, more comfortably viewed as constructive trust cases.

So we can see here that, in Lord Scott's view at least, cases of testamentary promise should be viewed not as proprietary estoppel cases at all, but rather as cases of common intention constructive trust.

Case Summary

The willingness of the court to lump the two doctrines together in this way is perhaps somewhat surprising, given their very different natures. However, this train of thought is not a new one. In the earlier case of *Yaxley* v. *Gotts*, the Court of Appeal again seemed to suggest that the doctrines of resulting and constructive trusts were one and the same. The facts of the case were as follows: Mr Yaxley entered into an agreement with Mr Gotts, that Mr Gotts would buy a particular house requiring refurbishment. Mr Yaxley would then carry out repair works and convert the property into three flats, in return for which Mr Gotts agreed to transfer the ground-floor flat to Mr Yaxley. In fact, unbeknown to Mr Yaxley, the house was purchased by Mr Gott's son, Alan. Mr Yaxley carried out the renovation work and, when the flats were let, acted as agent in collecting the rents and so on. After an argument with Mr Gotts' son, Mr Yaxley was locked out of the property, the son telling Mr Yaxley that he had no interest in it. Mr Yaxley sought the grant of a long lease of the ground-floor flat, on grounds of proprietary estoppel.

Based upon the facts of the case, it was not possible to infer a common intention constructive trust, because the agreement made was not with the legal owner of the property; as it turned out, the agreement had been made with his father. For a constructive trust to be imposed, you will remember that there must be a **common intention**, whether actual or implied, between the legal owner of the property and the person making the claim. This is unlike the remedy of proprietary estoppel in which, according to the prerequisites in *Willmott* v. *Barber*, the person making the representations need not be the legal owner of the property in question. The only possible outcome in the case was therefore one of proprietary estoppel. However, Lord Justice Walker confused the issue by stating that, having established a case for proprietary estoppel, the award to be given was that of a constructive trust over the property. Thus, the remedy under the doctrine of proprietary estoppel was the imposition of a constructive trust. As we have seen above, this is quite possible; however, in practical terms the outcome in the case has only served to muddy the waters in an area already fraught with difficulty.

Case Summary

In the subsequent case of *Van Laethem* v. *Brooker* [2005] EWHC 1478 (Ch), the issue of a possible overlap between constructive trusts and proprietary estoppel was again discussed. The claimant in this case, Penelope Van Laethem, sought a declaration against the defendant, Kim Brooker, that she was entitled to an interest in a large Grade II listed mansion house called Caradoc Court. The couple had bought the property together in a dilapidated state with a view to turning the house into 20 luxury apartments and building six new houses in the grounds. The legal title to the property was split between Mr Brooker, as to the house, and a company owned by Mr Brooker, as to the grounds, which the court referred to in their judgment as 'the development land'. Mrs Van Laethem had made financial contributions to the purchase of Caradoc and assisted with

its physical restoration. Mrs Van Laethem argued that she was entitled to a half share in the house and the development land, either by virtue of a common intention constructive trust or by proprietary estoppel. Mr Brooker denied that Mrs Van Laethem had any interest in the properties and submitted that he had bought Mrs Van Laethem another property in full and final settlement of her claims.

The court held that Mrs Van Laethem had acted to her detriment by relying on Mr Brooker's assurances. In particular, Mrs Van Laethem had mortgaged her home and later invested her share of the proceeds from the sale of her home in the restoration of the house. By mortgaging her home, Mrs Van Laethem had placed herself at substantial and very real risk as there was no obvious source of funds for Mr Brooker to service the loan. Mrs Van Laethem's sale of her home in her middle age and her investment of the proceeds in the house were indicative of the fact that she thought she would ultimately have a home in which she would share her interest with Mr Brooker. Mrs Van Laethem would not otherwise have rendered herself virtually homeless by trading in her home and capital. Mrs Van Laethem had contributed a large amount of time by her physical contribution to the restoration of the grounds. Mr Brooker's unconscionable behaviour, as was required for proprietary estoppel, was his denial of her interest. In respect of the development land, the court also found that Mrs Van Laethem held an interest. Mrs Van Laethem had already received £280,000 from the sale of another property held in her sole name, and was entitled to a further £420,000 in addition in respect of her claim. As regards whether the claim was proved on grounds of proprietary estoppel or constructive trust, Mr Justice Collins had the following to say on the matter:

> . . the modern authorities . . . show that there is no substantial difference in the remedy as between constructive trust and proprietary estoppel. My primary holding is that Mrs Van Laethem is entitled to an interest by way of proprietary estoppel in relation to Caradoc Court and by way of constructive trust in relation to the Development Land. My alternative holding is that Mrs Van Laethem is entitled to an interest by way of proprietary estoppel in relation to both properties. I do not consider that it makes a difference as regards the remedy.

What remains unclear from his judgment is on what basis he differentiates between the two, if at all, and why he has chosen one possible remedy over the other. Whatever the reasons, it is clear that Mr Justice Collins views the degree of separation between the two equitable remedies as being very slim indeed. In the People in the Law feature below, litigator Greg Kilvington talks about the issues this raises:

People in the law

Name and title: Greg Kilvington, solicitor, Watson Burton LLP

What kinds of cases do you deal with on a day-to-day basis? I deal with commercial litigation, chancery and contested probate matters and trust litigation.

Are the majority of proprietary estoppel claims that you deal with commercial or non-commercial in nature? Both. The issue has arisen in the context of succession scenarios with farmer clients but I have also considered it in residential scenarios with unmarried couples (though if I can get a **ToLATA*** claim off the ground that will usually suffice). The most recent case in which it was a major part of the claim as opposed to a minor consideration or fallback provision is set out below.

Can you give an example of a recent case you have worked on in this area? Yes, I dealt with a claim in the Residential Property Tribunal, involving an application for the determination of the extent of **demised premises** in a lease. The extent of the premises affected the **premium** payable. The landlord argued that a loft area in an open ceiling set-up was owned by him and not demised, that the tenant was trespassing into the loft space and, should the tenant wish to procure a new lease including the loft space, he would have to pay a substantially higher (£50–60k higher) premium. My client (the tenant) successfully argued that 1. on a correct construction of the lease it included the loft space and 2. that the landlord, who had submitted particulars of sale to an estate agent showing the opened ceiling area (with sky lights etc.) was, by virtue of proprietary estoppel, not able claim ownership of the loft and 3. if the tenant was unsuccessful on '1' then '2' could be used to provide a remedy to rewrite the lease accordingly. The tenant was able to rely on proprietary estoppel in a positive way and it was this that made the case interesting for me.

As a litigator, is it common to claim proprietary estoppel and constructive trusts in the alternative? I haven't personally done this though the practice of claiming proprietary estoppel in the alternative is common. It is seen as a 'fall-back' claim by a lot of practitioners. Proprietary estoppel is useful if there is no obvious common intention because without it a constructive trust claim is generally a non-starter.

In your experience, is this a hindrance or a help to your work? Neither; I consider the two options to be quite different.

In the recent case of *Van Laethem* v. *Brooker* Mr Justice Collins claimed that the modern authorities show that

Source: Greg Kilvington

there is no substantial difference between constructive trusts and proprietary estoppel. Do you agree? I disagree. If a constructive trust exists it will provide an interest in the property and this will be dealt with within the terms of the constructive trust – whatever they may be. A constructive trust will only arise where there is a common intention that the claimant would have an interest in the property. I understood this not to be the case with proprietary estoppel. Where one party tricks the other a constructive trust is not often helpful whereas proprietary estoppel can be. The key difference for me, though, regardless of what test is appropriate to satisfy either proprietary estoppel or a constructive trust is that a constructive trust will only provide a party with whatever share in a property the parties are deemed to have intended. In some cases this is practically not useful or workable. Proprietary estoppel is flexible; it could result in a damages award, an interest in property or some other remedy at the court's discretion.

Do you think the law would benefit from some judicial clarification on this point? Yes – or a good chapter in a textbook at the very least.

* Trusts of Land and Appointments of Trustees Act 1996 (see Chapter 9).

Table 8.1 Differences between resulting/constructive trusts/proprietary estoppel

	Resulting (trust)	Constructive trust	Proprietary estoppel
Requirements	Direct financial contribution to purchase price	Common intention (express or implied) + Detrimental Reliance	Assurance + Reliance + Detriment + Unconscionability
Remedy	Share in property proportionate to contribution to purchase price	Share in property based on whole course of dealings between parties	Various: whatever will provide 'the minimum equity to do justice'

It remains to be seen where the courts will decide to go in light of these findings. In the meantime, Table 8.1 serves as a reminder of the differences between resulting and constructive trusts and proprietary estoppel.

Summary

- Proprietary estoppel arises where a landowner encourages or acquiesces in a third party's mistake in respect of their rights to land and they act to their detriment as a consequence of this mistake.
- Proprietary estoppel is a vital equitable tool in that it enables the courts to recognise the moral obligations of the landowner where no legal obligation exists.
- The key element in proprietary estoppel cases is the unconscionability of the landowner's actions (*Taylor Fashions*). However, the elements of assurance, reliance and detriment must also be proved.
- Assurance has over the years been enlarged to include the expectations of the claimant as to what rights in the land they will have in the future. This has caused some controversy, especially in wills cases.
- Proprietary estoppel has also been used to perfect claims where there has been an agreement for the sale of land which falls foul of section 2 of the Law of Property (Miscellaneous Provision) Act 1989. The outcome in the House of Lords case of *Cobbe* v. *Yeoman's Row* has made this more difficult to achieve in commercial cases, however.
- Detriment need not be financial, but must be real and substantial.
- The remedy granted in proprietary estoppel cases will be the 'minimum equity to do justice'. Thus, it will not necessarily be the acquisition of land, but may be a lesser interest in it, or even the payment of financial compensation.
- The similarities between proprietary estoppel and common intention constructive trusts are quite striking. This has caused some confusion in the courts and even the suggestion that the two are synonymous. The point is yet to be settled in the courts.

Question and answer*

Problem: Cindi inherits a large estate in Monmouthshire from her estranged uncle Blinko. Cindi has no interest in living on the property, having made her home elsewhere in the country. However, she sees the development potential of the property straightaway and employs architects to draw up plans and apply for planning permission to convert the house and garden into a theme park and leisure grounds. However, no sooner has the planning application been made, but a number of complaints come in from neighbouring properties, objecting to the development.

Glenys, Blinko's former gardener, says that she has been caring for Blinko and cooking meals for him for the last thirteen years without payment, because he said he would 'see her right' and that 'all this will be yours one day'. She claims the entire estate for herself.

Justin, Blinko's neighbour, says that the field to the north of the property, which is principal to the development plans, belongs by rights to him. He has been using the land as paddock for his horses, and has spent a considerable amount of money building a block of stables and indoor arena on the land. He says Blinko allowed him to do this, saying that he would leave the land to Justin in his will.

Carmen, Blinko's former girlfriend, says that the house belongs to her. During the course of their seven-year relationship, Blinko frequently said to her 'you're my lady of the manor'.

Property development company, Estates R Us, claim a half share in the development, on the grounds that they have spent two years and half-a-million pounds developing plans and liaising with the council to turn the property into a luxury flats and a new exclusive housing estate. They did this, they say, because Blinko had promised them half of the proceeds of sale of the development if they did so.

Is there any substance to their claims and, if so, on what grounds?

You should allow yourself no more than 40 minutes to complete this task.

Essay: '. . . the modern authorities . . . show that there is no substantial difference in the remedy as between constructive trust and proprietary estoppel.'

Mr Justice Collins, *Van Laethem* v. *Brooker* [2005] EWHC 1478 (Ch)

Discuss.

This question should be answered in 40 minutes.

* Answer guidance is provided at the end of the chapter.

Further reading

***Cobbe* v. *Yeoman's Row Management Ltd* [2008] 1 WLR 1752.**
This is a very useful case for students to read because the court in giving its judgment has analysed the variety of remedies that might have been available to Mr Cobbe in the circumstances. It therefore gives a very good practical overview of the law in this area.

***Thorner* v. *Major* [2009] 1 WLR 776.**
Lord Neuberger's judgment is particularly valuable and worth reading in full for a detailed explanation of what will be sufficient in terms of assurances in cases of proprietary estoppel.

McFarlane, B. and Robertson, A., 'Apocalypse averted: proprietary estoppel in the House of Lords', LQR 2009, 125 (Oct), 535–42.
This article provides an excellent discussion of the two important House of Lords decisions of *Cobbe* v. *Yeoman's Row* and *Thorner* v. *Major*, commenting on the issues raised in relation to expectation as the foundation of proprietary estoppel claims.

Waltham, A., 'Proprietary estoppel: the risks of building on land you don't own', available online at: http://www.wragge.com/analysis_3205.asp.
Gives an interesting analysis of the case of *Herbert* v. *Doyle* and the use of proprietary estoppel to perfect failed contracts under section 2 of the Law of Property (Miscellaneous Provisions) Act 1989.

Question and answer guidance

Please note that the following are not full answers and are intended to provide guidance in outline form only as to how to answer the questions posed.

Problem:

In proprietary estoppel cases the best way to approach them is by applying the four prerequisites set out in *Taylor Fashions* of assurance, reliance, detriment and unconscionability, and if all four apply there is a good chance of the courts providing an equitable remedy to the situation. You can then go on to look at what kind of equity the courts may apply in the situation given (remember it is not always an estate or interest in the land that will be granted in proprietary estoppel cases).

Glenys: Glenys, Blinko's former gardener, is claiming the entire estate for herself. *Assurance*: Glenys has received assurances from Blinko that he would 'see her right' and that 'all this will be yours one day'. *Reliance*: In reliance on these statements Glenys has acted to her *detriment* by caring for Blinko and cooking meals for him for the last thirteen years without payment. This is similar to the case of *Taylor* v. *Dickens*. *Unconscionability*: It may seem unconscionable that Blinko has made false representations to Glenys about to whom his property will go on his death, but in cases of testamentary promises the court is quite clear about what will be sufficient and what will not. The finding in *Taylor* v. *Dickens* should be contrasted with the outcome in *Gillett* v. *Holt*, although the findings in that particular case were based on the particular circumstances of the case and the fact that the assurances had been given repreatedly over a long period of time. *Equity*: It seems unlikely that Glenys will benefit from a proprietary estoppel claim in this instance. However, if she did, the likelihood is that she would be granted a sum of money to compensate her for her expenditure, rather than any stake in the property. Certainly her claim to the entire estate is disproportionate to the work she has done and therefore to the level of her detriment (see *Powell* v. *Benney*; *Jennings* v. *Rice*).

Justin: Justin, Blinko's neighbour, is claiming the field to the north of the property. *Assurance*: Blinko said he would leave the land to Justin in his will. *Reliance*: In reliance upon Blinko's statement, Justin has, to his *detriment*, spent a considerable amount of money building a block of stables and indoor arena on the land. This is similar to the facts of *Inwards* v. *Baker*, where a father allowed his son to build a house on land owned by him. *Unconscionability*: Blinko has allowed him to expend the money, whilst telling him he would leave the land to Justin in his will. Testamentary promises are difficult, the general feeling of the court being that, because a will can be revoked at any point up until death, they will not be sufficient to give rise to an equity under the rules of proprietary estoppel. Having said this, in *Inwards* v. *Baker*, a life interest in the land was granted. *Equity*: It may be that the court sees fit to grant a life interest in the land, as in *Inwards* v. *Baker*. Alternatively, the court may feel that the benefit Justin has already had from grazing his horses on the land has gone a long way to satisfying the equity in this situation. We are not told whether Justin is paying rent for the privilege of doing this. In *Sledmore* v. *Dalby*, the claimant was viewed as having already received a considerable benefit by living in the house rent-free over a number of years.

Carmen Carmen, Blinko's former girlfriend, says that the house belongs to her. *Assurance*: During the course of their seven-year relationship, Blinko frequently said to her 'you're my lady of the manor'. *Reliance*: We are not told of any action she has taken in reliance on this statement. *Detriment*: The case is similar to the facts of *Lissimore* v. *Downing*, in which there was held to be no real detriment to the girlfriend. *Unconscionability*: There has been no real assurance here, and from what we are aware no detrimental reliance either. There is therefore unlikely to be an equity granted.

Estates R Us: The property development company claim a half share in the development. *Assurance*: Blinko promised them half of the proceeds of sale of the development of the site. *Reliance*: in reliance on this, Estates R Us have, to their *detriment*, spent two years and half-a-million pounds developing plans and liaising with the council to turn the property into luxury flats and a housing estate. *Unconscionability*: On the face of it, it does seem unconscionable that Blinko should renege on their business deal. However, following *Cobbe* v. *Yeoman's Row*, the courts might take the view that Estates R Us should have taken precautions as businessmen to protect their agreement/interest. *Equity*: Following *Cobbe*, they are unlikely to get an interest in the land but may be paid agency fees for acting in the development.

Essay: This question is asking you to discuss the differences between constructive trusts and proprietary estoppel and to consider whether or not there is any real difference between the two, in line with Mr Justice Collins' comment in *Van Laethem* v. *Brooker*.

You might begin by stating briefly how the two concepts are individually proven, so as to highlight the technical differences that exist between them. Whereas a constructive trust requires that a common intention exists as between the parties as to the ownership of the property, coupled with detrimental reliance upon the parties' understanding of what that intention is, proprietary estoppel requires detrimental reliance upon an assurance given by the landowner, coupled with unconscionability on the part of the landowner. This assurance is quite different from a perceived 'common intention' or understanding between the parties.

In addition, the remedies available in constructive trusts and proprietary estoppel are quite different. With a constructive trust, the result of proving a constructive trust is always that the claimant will gain a share in the property, quantified on the basis of the perceived common intention of the parties. However, proprietary estoppel is based upon giving the claimant the 'minimum equity to do justice'. Thus, the remedies available are more wide-ranging and much more flexible in terms of the appropriateness of the claim.

You might then go on to say that, despite this, the two doctrines have traditionally been perceived as very similar in nature, and therefore that it has been commonplace for lawyers in their claims to plead their case in the alternative, arguing the benefit of one doctrine if the other fails. Equally, the courts have been happy to treat the two doctrines as overlapping, if not synonymous in some circumstances, particularly in cases involving testamentary promise (see Lord Scott of Foscote's comments in *Thorner* v. *Major* on this point).

Particular mention might be made of the case of *Yaxley* v. *Gotts*, in which the court held that the claimant should be given the remedy of a constructive trust, on grounds of proprietary estoppel. On the facts of the case a simple finding of a constructive trust was not possible because there was no agreement with the legal owner of the property. However, the outcome could be said only to have confused the issue.

Moving on from this, you may wish to focus on the case in question, from which Mr Justice Collins's quote has been taken, that of *Van Laethem* v. *Brooker*. You should spend some time outlining the facts of the case and the findings given by the court, mentioning in particular the fact that Mr Justice Collins had said that he did not consider whether a finding of constructive trust or proprietary estoppel made a difference as regards the remedy. Clearly from his comment the basis of his finding is left open. You should conclude by stating whether you think this is correct or not and perhaps whether you think there should have been a clear finding in the case. In putting forward your views you may find the comments of Greg Kilvington in the People in the Law feature useful.

mylawchamber
unrivalled support for legal education

Chapter 9 Co-ownership

Key points In this chapter we will be looking at:

- The division between legal and equitable title to the property
- Co-ownership of the legal estate – capacity and limitations
- Co-ownership in equity – joint tenants and tenants in common
- The concept of survivorship
- The four unities
- Recognising the form of co-ownership: express wording, presumptions and words of severance
- Severance of the joint tenancy in equity by notice in writing
- Methods of severance under *Williams* v. *Hensman*
- The effect of unlawful killing on the equitable joint tenancy
- Shares awarded on severance of the beneficial interest
- Bringing an end to co-ownership
- Solving disputes under sections 14 and 15 of the Trusts of Land and Appointment of Trustees Act 1996 and the Insolvency Act 1986

Introduction

During the course of your reading you will have become aware of a number of really quite complex notions relating to the ownership of land in England and Wales. In particular, in Chapter 4 we thought about the division of law and equity and the possibility that two people can own separate interests in land: one legal and one equitable. This has been considered further in our exploration of informal methods of land acquisition in the previous two chapters, particularly in our consideration of **constructive** and **resulting trusts**, in which a person is able, on account of their circumstances, to gain an **equitable interest** in the property, despite not being a legal owner of it. This is clearly a vital part of your study of land law; however, what we haven't really considered up until now is the rather more common situation in which two or more people simply decide to buy a property together, both acquiring the **legal title** to the property jointly by **deed** in the usual formal manner, as opposed to acquiring an equitable interest informally. So here we are talking about a couple, or a husband and wife, or even business partners, acquiring the legal title to a property jointly – **co-ownership** in the ordinary sense, if you like. In this chapter we are going to be exploring the mechanics of such co-ownership, how it comes about, how it operates, and how it may end.

Co-ownership as a concept

People may decide to co-own property, either because they are buying a home together, or because they need premises for their business, or a multitude of other reasons, financial or practical. Technically speaking, co-ownership may be either concurrent or successive. **Concurrent ownership** is where two or more people have the ownership of the same estate in land at the same time; **successive ownership** is where two or more people have consecutive ownership of property, such as in the case of a **life interest** (where Jill owns property for life, and then it goes to Ben). This chapter is going to concentrate on concurrent ownership, which is the most common form of co-ownership, and the one you are most likely to come across in practice. The following Key Stats feature gives you some idea of just how many residential properties alone this might affect in the UK.

Key stats Families and households in 2011

According to the Office of National Statistics there were 26.3 million households in the UK in 2011. Of these:

- 29% consisted of only one person and almost 20% consisted of four or more people.
- 17.9 million of the households were families.
- 12.0 million consisted of a married couple.
- The number of opposite sex cohabiting couple families was 2.9 million.

Source: http://www.ons.gov.uk/ons/rel/family-demography/families-and-households/2011/stb-families-households.html

Separation of legal and equitable title

The most important concept to grasp when talking about co-ownership of land is the separation or division between legal and equitable title to the property. As we mentioned in the introduction to this chapter, we have come across this division on a number of occasions during the course of the book, primarily when we have been looking at informal methods of land acquisition, either through the medium of a constructive or resulting trust. You will remember that in such cases, it is possible for a person to acquire an equitable interest in property, despite not having a claim to the property in law (because they do not appear on the title deeds as a legal owner of it). You should therefore already have an awareness that ownership of land can take one of two forms: legal or equitable. However, given the fundamental importance to the concept of co-ownership of this division of land into separate legal and the equitable rights, it would be sensible to take a moment or two to clarify the position.

> ownership of land can take one of two forms: legal or equitable

Ownership of land is divided, in English law, into two distinct parts: legal ownership and equitable (or **beneficial**) ownership. The legal owner or owners of the property are the **paper owners**: they hold the legal title to the property and have the right to dispose of it at law; the equitable or beneficial owners of the property have the right to benefit from that property in **equity**, either by living in it, receiving rents from it and so on. We have seen how the legal and equitable owners of the property can be two different people, when we explored the concept of resulting and constructive trusts in Chapter 7, but let us now take the further example of a Welsh couple, Daz and Martine, who are buying a home together. After some searching they find a little place in South Wales, 12 Port Steward Road, Port Steward, Gwenyth, which they agree to buy for the sum of £140,000. The house is put into Martine's name, because Daz is going through a sticky divorce and doesn't want his ex-wife to lay claim to the property. He does, however, pay £15,000 towards its purchase. The remainder of the purchase price is funded by a **mortgage** in Martine's name, but paid for jointly by them both. An example of how such ownership might look diagrammatically is shown in Figure 9.1.

Figure 9.1 Legal and equitable ownership in a resulting trust scenario

Law	Martine
Equity	Daz and Martine

As we can see from the diagram, Martine is the sole legal owner of the property, but the equitable ownership is shared between the couple, by virtue of Daz's contribution to the purchase of the property. Thus, whilst Martine is the paper owner, Daz and Martine both share the right to benefit from it together in equity.

Daz and Martine's situation, like all those we have seen before, is a common illustration of the situation in which only one person holds the legal title to the property. However, it is also quite possible of course for there to be more than one legal owner of land. In Daz and Martine's case, this might look as follows:

Figure 9.2 Illustration of the division between legal and equitable ownership of land

Law	Daz and Martine
Equity	Daz and Martine

As we can see from Figure 9.2, in this situation, where Daz and Martine buy the house together in their joint names, they will both be legal owners of the property at law, and also beneficial owners of the property in equity.

This division of the legal and equitable ownership of land in a co-ownership situation is achieved automatically under statute, through the imposition of a **trust of land** under section 36 of the Law of Property Act 1925. As such, Daz and Martine are viewed as holding the legal title of the property on trust for themselves in equity. This is a technical distinction, but one which will grow in significance as we learn more about co-ownership throughout the course of the chapter. The important points to remember for now, however, are that in the context of land ownership:

- the ownership of land is always divided into two: legal ownership and equitable ownership
- the two sit side-by-side, but have different qualities (legal and beneficial)
- the legal and equitable owners may be the same, or different persons

Having established that there is a division in land law between legal and equitable ownership, this leads us neatly to explore the two types of ownership in the context of a co-ownership of land. We will consider the legal ownership first.

Co-ownership of the legal estate

Let us continue to use our example above, where Daz and Martine buy a house together to live in as a couple. What can we say about their legal co-ownership of the property?

Joint tenants

At law they will become what are known as '**joint tenants**' of the legal title to that property. Do not confuse the reference to tenants with the law in relation to **leases**; the word '**tenant**' in this context refers to the way in which the couple holds the legal estate to the land: that is, their **tenure** of it. As joint tenants, Daz and Martine hold the whole of the property together as a joint, or group entity. They do not hold shares in it; they own the whole together. Think of it as buying and owning a family computer – you cannot cut it into pieces or sections, you simply own the computer as a whole, and the family shares the ownership and use of it. There is therefore no physical division of the property; the joint owners together own the whole. This proposition is given statutory authority in section 1(6) of the Law of Property Act 1925, which states that 'A legal estate in land is not capable of subsisting or being created in an undivided share in land or of being held by an infant.'

By '**undivided share**' the statute means that the legal estate can only be held by co-owners together as a whole, and thus as joint tenants. It is not divisible into shares. At law, there is no other way of co-owning property.

Legal capacity

A second point to make relates to Daz and Martine's legal **capacity** to hold the legal estate to the land. As you will remember from your earlier reading, a **minor**, that is somebody under the age of 18, cannot hold the legal title to property; and you will see that section 1(6) also provides the authority for this, stating that a legal estate in land is not capable of being held by an infant. Equally, you will remember that a person without the requisite mental capacity is also unable to be a legal owner of land, under the provisions of the Mental Capacity Act 2005. We have based Daz and Martine's legal ownership of their house upon the assumption that they both have the requisite legal and mental capacity to do so. If one of them did not, if Martine was only 17, for example, the resulting position would be that Daz would become the sole legal owner of the property, holding the legal estate on trust for the joint benefit of himself and Martine.

Number of legal owners

One other restriction on the legal ownership of land relates to the number of legal co-owners there can be of any given piece of land. In our example, we have only two co-owners: Daz and Martine. This is not a problem, but there is in fact a statutory limit put upon the number of legal co-owners of a property you can have, which is set at four. The statute says:

> Law of Property Act 1925, section 34(2)
>
> Where . . . land is expressed to be conveyed to any persons in undivided shares and those persons are of full age the conveyance shall . . . operate as if the land had been expressed to be conveyed to the grantees, or if there are more than four grantees, the first four named in the conveyance, as joint tenants in trust for the persons interested in the land.

The wording of the statute raises a couple of interesting points. Firstly, if there are more than four co-owners named on the deed of transfer of the property, then it is the first four named who will take legal ownership of the property. The fifth, and any consecutive persons named in the deed will take the property in equity only. The result, diagrammatically speaking, would be as shown in Figure 9.3.

Figure 9.3 Showing the position at law and in equity where there are more than four co-owners named on the purchase deed

Law	Sacha, Jed, Boris, Felix
Equity	Sacha, Jed, Boris, Felix and Carlos

If, on the other hand, the second of the five purported co-owners, Jed, was only 17 at the time of the transfer, the outcome would be different. Take a look at the You Be the Judge feature, below, and see if you can work out the difference.

You be the judge

Q: Sacha (18), Jed (17), Boris (18), Felix (19) and Carlos (20) decide to buy a student house together. As law students, they decide to draw up the purchase deed themselves, putting all of their names on the documentation as joint owners of the property. Assuming they state their names in the order listed above, what will be their positions in law and in equity? Draw a diagram to show this.

Source: Ingram Publishing, Alamy

A: Sacha, Boris, Felix and Carlos would hold the legal title on trust for themselves and Jed. Jed cannot hold the legal title to the property because he is a minor.

This details the position at law; now let us explore the position in equity.

Co-ownership of the equitable estate

Whereas, at law, there is only one way of holding the legal estate: as joint tenants of the whole; in equity, there are two different methods of holding the land: either as joint tenants, or as **tenants in common**. There are significant differences between the two and we shall now discuss these in turn:

Division of property

Whilst joint tenants are seen as a group entity, together owning the whole of the property, tenants in common are viewed as separate individuals, owning the whole in 'undivided shares'. This means that, unlike joint tenants, tenants in common are able to own a specified share of the property, the value of which they will recoup on its subsequent sale. So, for example, our couple, Daz and Martine, might own the property 60/40, or 70/30, as well as 50/50. If the couple decided to sell the property, they would each be entitled to their proportionate share in the proceeds of sale. Joint tenants, on the other hand, do not own shares as they are perceived as owning the whole together as a group (remember the example of the family computer, given earlier).

It should be noted that this division of the property into shares is an academic division, not a physical one. If the property were to be physically split, this would amount to the end of the co-ownership. This point will be discussed in further detail later in the chapter.

Survivorship

One of the most significant differences between joint tenants and tenants in common is the way in which the property passes on the death of one of the co-owners. In the case of tenants in common, if one of the co-owners dies, their share of the property passes to their next of kin, in the case of intestacy, or as specified under the terms of their will. This means that the surviving co-owners may find themselves sharing the beneficial interest in the property with a stranger. There is therefore no guarantee that they will be able to stay in their home, as most likely the person named in the will or other relative will want the house to be sold and the proceeds of sale divided to give them their share. In the case of unmarried couples, or in situations where, for example, there are children from a previous marriage that the co-owners wish to provide for financially in the event of their death, this can work well. However, in a family situation, especially where there are children involved, the result could be quite harrowing.

It is for this reason that couples buying property to live in as a family unit, and most commonly married couples, tend to own as joint tenants. Because of the nature of joint tenancy as this 'group ownership' of the whole, it means that if one of the co-owners dies, there are no shares to go to surviving relatives of the deceased co-owner; rather the property simply remains in the possession and ownership of the surviving member or members of the group, until the last one dies, when it will devolve to their next of kin or other person specified within their will. This is far simpler and easier for all concerned, as there is no transfer of the property necessary; and for the surviving co-owners gives them the security that they need in that no one will come along and demand the sale of the property in order to release 'their share'.

Out and about

Imagine you are buying a property together with your housemates at university. How would you choose to hold the property? Explain why.

You should spend no more than 20 minutes on this task.

The four unities

We have seen that the two methods of co-ownership are very different: from a practical perspective, one is viewed as a group ownership of the whole, the other as ownership of the property in separate but, until the point of sale of the property, undivided shares. From a legal viewpoint the two different forms of co-owning property dictate that they boast very different qualities too, however.

With a joint tenancy, there are four essential common law characteristics that the co-owners must share. These are known as the '**four unities**'. The unities, as set out in the House of Lords case of ***AG Securities* v. *Vaughan*** [1988] 3 WLR 1205, which you will remember from your reading in Chapter 5 on the lease/licence distinction, concerned a disagreement over the status of tenants of a four-bedroom flat, are:

- **possession**
- **interest**
- **title**
- **time**

Possession

All the co-owners of the property must be entitled to possession of the whole. If any single co-owner is prevented from having access to any part of the property, there is no unity of possession. Where a couple or family buys a house to live in together, this will not be an issue. In the case of house sharers, it is important that none of them claim exclusive possession of any part of the house, as this would destroy the joint interest. This can be illustrated by the case of *Wiseman* v. *Simpson* [1988] 1 WLR 35. Following the break-up of an unmarried couple, the woman had refused to allow the man access to their council flat. The woman then made an application to exclude the man from the flat, which was granted at first instance, but on appeal the court rejected her claim. There was no evidence of domestic violence and, as such, as a joint tenant of the property he had as much right to reside there as she did, regardless of their circumstances.

Interest

In the case of joint tenants, all the co-owners of the property must hold the same estate or interest in the land. This means that they buy the **freehold** or **leasehold** of the property together, rather than one of them having a freehold and one a leasehold interest, or perhaps another having a life interest in the property. They must all own the property on the same basis.

Title

This means that all of the co-owners must have obtained their interest the property by the same method. So, for example, one could not have become a freehold owner of the property through an ordinary deed of **conveyance** and the other under the terms of a will, or through their **adverse possession** of it. Usually, joint tenants will buy property through the same means, namely a single purchase deed, so this will not be an issue.

Time

In order for the unity of time to be satisfied, all the co-owners must have acquired their interest in the property at the same time. Again, where a couple is buying a property to live in together, this will usually be the case as they will do so together.

As you can see, the requirements for a joint tenancy to exist are quite stringent, although usually easy to satisfy, given the circumstances under which people usually buy a property to hold as joint tenants (that is, the desire to live in the property as a family). With the exception of the unity of possession, which must exist in all cases of co-ownership, if one of the unities is not present, the co-owners will be deemed to be holding the property in equity as tenants in common. If any of the parties are denied possession of

> the unity of possession must exist in all cases of co-ownership

any part of the property, through a physical division of the property, then there can be no co-ownership of the property at all; there will instead be separate ownership of the different parts.

Capacity

One final point worth mentioning is that of capacity. As we were reminded earlier in the chapter, the ability to own land legally requires both mental and legal capacity, in that the owner must be at least 18 years of age. This is not the case with equitable ownership. In fact, it is commonly the case that property is held on trust for the benefit of those who do not have the legal capacity to hold it themselves. This is how, in our earlier example of the five co-owners, Sacha, Jed, Boris, Felix and Carlos, Jed was unable to hold the legal title to the property due to his age (17), but the others were able to hold it on trust for themselves and him in equity.

Recognising the form of co-ownership

Now we know what co-ownership is, in legal terms, and what criteria are necessary to form any particular type of co-ownership in equity, what we need to be able to do is to recognise which form of co-ownership has been created in any particular case. As with any legal premise, the starting point is the documentation, from which much can be gleaned.

Express declaration

The first thing to look for is an express declaration by the parties as to how they intend to hold the property they are buying in equity (remember, they can only hold the legal title as joint tenants in any event). In **unregistered land**, the wording would appear in the body of the conveyance; in **registered land**, there is a simple tick-box in the transfer deed stating whether the property is to be held in equity as joint tenants or tenants in common. Where the co-owners intend to hold the property in unequal shares, this will usually be coupled with a separate deed, called a '**declaration of trust**', detailing the intentions of the co-owners more fully. An example of a declaration of trust is shown in the Documenting the Law feature, below.

Documenting the law

Example of a declaration of trust

DECLARATION OF TRUST

This Trust Deed is dated the Twelfth day of June 2012 by:

DARREN ROLAND ARCHER and MARTINE SCARBER both of 12 Port Steward Road, Port Steward, Gwenyth ('the Trustees')

WHEREAS:

(a) This Deed is supplemental to a deed of Transfer dated the twelfth day of June 2012 and made between (1) JAMES ANTHONY LOCK and JUDITH PATRICIA LOCK and (2) the Trustees WHEREBY the freehold property known as 12 Port Steward Road, Port Steward, Gwenyth ('the Property') was transferred to the Trustees in consideration of the sum of one hundred and forty thousand pounds (£140,000) as therein stated to have been paid by the Trustees to the said JAMES ANTHONY LOCK and JUDITH PATRICIA LOCK

(b) The said consideration was provided as follows:

(i) The Sandsend Building Society £125,000
(ii) DARREN ROLAND ARCHER £ 15,000

NOW THIS DEED WITNESSETH as follows:

1. The Trustees declare that they are to hold the property upon a trust of land and shall hold the net proceeds of sale (after deducting the balance of any money due to the said Sandsend Building Society) upon trust as follows:

1.1 To the sum of Fifteen Thousand Pounds for the said DARREN ROLAND ARCHER
1.2 As the remainder thereof upon trust for themselves in equal shares as tenants in common

IN WITNESS WHEREOF the parties hereto have signed this Deed the day and year first before written

SIGNED as a Deed by the said
DARREN ROLAND ARCHER D R Archer

In the presence of:

Henry Fontell
Granite Place, Port Steward

SIGNED as a Deed by the said
MARTINE SCARBER Martine Scarber

In the presence of:

Henry Fontell
Granite Place, Port Steward

If the property is to be held as tenants in common, the **Land Registry** will enter a **restriction** on the **Proprietorship Register** preventing the property from being sold by a sole proprietor of the land. This means that a purchaser of co-owned property must buy from two or more owners of the property in order to overreach any equitable interest of the co-owners and take free of their equitable rights on the purchase. For a reminder of how **overreaching** works see the section on overreaching in Chapter 4. There is no need for such a restriction where the co-owners are joint tenants, as payment will either be to the joint tenants as a whole or, if there is only one surviving co-owner, to them under the rules of **survivorship**.

Words of severance

If the deed of transfer of the property, in whatever form it may take, does not specify whether the co-owners are going to be holding their equitable interest in the property as either joint tenants or tenants in common, it may still be possible to determine their position by the existence of '**words of severance**' in the documentation. Such words, if they exist, indicate a desire to hold the property in shares and thus evidence the fact that the property is to be held as tenants in common, rather than on the basis of a joint tenancy. They might include:

- In equal shares/equally
- To be divided between
- Share and share alike
- Amongst
- One half each
- Any indication of unequal shares in the property

Failing the existence of telltale wording in the transfer documentation, we may be able to learn from the individual positions of the parties how they intend to hold the property. In this regard, equity makes certain presumptions, considered below.

Presumptions

We mentioned above the four unities, which must be present if a joint tenancy is to exist. The first assumption at **common law** and in equity is that, if all these four unities are present, then the intention is to create a joint tenancy, rather than a tenancy in common.

If a couple buy a house together, entering into possession at the same time, under the same tenure and through the same document, therefore, the assumption will be that they are holding the property in equity as joint tenants.

If co-owners provide the purchase money to buy the property in unequal shares, however, equity will presume that they intend to hold the property, not as joint tenants, but as tenants in common in proportion to their respective contributions to the purchase price. In the Court of Appeal case of *Bull* v. *Bull* [1955] 1 QB 234, a mother and son had bought a house together, with the son providing the greater part of the purchase price. He was also the legal owner of the property, the property having been purchased in his sole name. When the son later married, friction between the mother and daughter-in-law led to the son asking the mother to leave the house, but she refused. It was held that she was a tenant in common in the property, in equity, and that the son therefore had no authority to ask her to leave the property. The house should be sold and the proceeds divided between them in proportion to their initial contributions to the purchase of it.

Case Summary

A similar presumption is applied in the case of business partnerships where, again, equity will presume that the intention was not to hold the property as joint tenants, but rather as tenants in common. This is the manifestation of an old Latin **maxim**: '*jus accrescendi inter mercatores locum non habet*', which means 'there is no place in business for the right of survivorship'. The suggestion here is that people going into business together would naturally prefer to make their own plans for the disposal of their share of the assets of the business on their death. This was the finding in *Lake* v. *Craddock* (1732) 24 ER 1011, in which land on a flood plain adjacent to the Thames river at Dagenham had been purchased by a number of business partners together, with a view to draining the land for a profit. The court held that the owners held as tenants in common, the right of survivorship not being applicable in such a case.

That is not to say, in either situation, that these presumptions cannot be rebutted, however. If there is an express declaration in the **transfer deed** stating that either business partners wish to hold the property as joint tenants in equity, or that a couple who have put in differing shares wish to hold as joint tenants rather than as tenants in common, the law will uphold their written declaration above and beyond any natural presumption that may exist to the contrary. In *Pink* v. *Lawrence* (1978) 36 P&CR 98 two gentlemen had bought a house together, the purchase deed stating specifically that the two co-owners were to hold the property as joint tenants in equity. Following a dispute between the two men, Mr Pink claimed that Mr Lawrence had only been included in the paperwork to satisfy Mr Pink's mortgage lender, as Mr Pink did not, on his own, earn enough money to satisfy their lending criteria. Mr Lawrence claimed that he had contributed £500 towards the purchase of the property and so had a claim to the property under a constructive trust. The Court of Appeal found that neither argument applied: the documentation clearly stated that the two men were to hold the property as joint tenants in equity and this was the situation that applied. The co-owners could not rescind the declaration of trust that had been made between the two men just because they had subsequently fallen out.

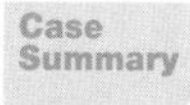

The facts of this case lead us neatly to ask the question: if the co-owners start as joint tenants in common but later wish to change their position to become tenants in common in equity, can they do this and, if so, how do they achieve it? The short answer is that, yes, it is possible for co-owners who start their equitable relationship as joint tenants to later become tenants in common. The process through which they do this is known as '**severance**'.

Severing the joint tenancy

There are many reasons for a co-owner to wish to sever their joint tenancy in equity. These reasons will usually be financial: to enable one co-owner to provide for a specific person other than their co-owner in the event of their death, or to reflect a change in the financial or personal circumstances of the co-owners.

Remember, the ability to hold land as tenants in common relates only to the equitable estate in the property; the legal estate must always be held as joint tenants. Severance, therefore, only applies to the beneficial estate: it cannot apply at law. In recognition of this, section 36(2) of the Law of Property Act 1925 specifically states that it is not possible to sever a legal joint tenancy.

In equity, the position is quite different, however, it being possible to sever the joint tenancy and become tenants in common in one of two distinct ways: either under statute by the giving written notice, or at common law, in accordance with the criteria set out in the case of *Williams* v. *Hensman* (1861) 1 John & H 546 (the facts of which are set out below). We shall consider these two methods of severance in turn.

By written notice under statute

The ability to sever the joint tenancy in equity by notice in writing is provided for in section 36(2) of the Law of Property Act 1925. The relevant wording of the statute is as follows:

> . . . where a legal estate . . . is vested in joint tenants beneficially, and any tenant desires to sever the joint tenancy in equity, he shall give to the other joint tenants a notice in writing of such desire or do such other acts or things as would, in the case of personal estate, have been effectual to sever the tenancy in equity, and thereupon the land shall be held in trust on terms which would have been requisite for giving effect to the beneficial interests if there had been an actual severance.

It should be noted from the wording of the statute that it is necessary to inform *all* of the other co-owners, if more than one, of the intention to sever, in order for that severance to take effect.

What constitutes the effective service of notice on the other tenants is set out in section 196 of the Act. This states that:

> **196. Regulations respecting notices.**
>
> (1) Any notice required or authorised to be served or given by this Act shall be in writing.
> . . .
>
> (3) Any notice required or authorised by this Act to be served shall be sufficiently served if it is left at the last-known place of abode or business in the United Kingdom of the . . . person to be served . . .
>
> (4) Any notice required or authorised by this Act to be served shall also be sufficiently served, if it is sent by post in a registered letter addressed to the . . . person to be served, by name, at the aforesaid place of abode or business . . . and if that letter is not returned by the postal operator (within the meaning of the Postal Services Act 2000) concerned undelivered; and that service shall be deemed to be made at the time at which the registered letter would in the ordinary course be delivered.

Provided that notice in writing has been served effectively on all the other joint tenants, then the joint tenancy will be severed and the co-owner will hold from the date of service their share of the tenancy as a tenant in common.

Case Summary

One interesting point here is that the notice need not have been actually received to have been deemed served, under the terms of the Act. In *Re 88 Berkeley Road, NW9* [1971] 2 WLR 307 Miss Rickwood and Miss Eldridge owned a house as joint tenants in equity. Following the marriage of Miss Eldridge and on instructions from Miss Rickwood that she wished to sever the joint tenancy, Miss Rickwood's solicitors sought to do so by sending Miss Eldridge notice of severance in the post, by recorded delivery. However, Miss Rickwood answered the door when the postman arrived and signed for the recorded delivery package (Miss Eldridge was away at the time). Miss Rickwood then put the letter to one side and forgot about it. Unfortunately Miss Eldridge never got to see the notice because she died shortly after it was delivered and the letter was never mentioned. Following the death, Miss Rickwood applied to the court for a declaration that she was beneficially entitled to Miss Eldridge's half share of the property as a joint tenant through the right of survivorship. However, her application was denied. The delivery of the notice by recorded mail was held to have been sufficient to effect severance of the equitable estate as between the two ladies under section 36(2) and, as such, Miss Eldridge's share of the property would be distributed under the terms of her will.

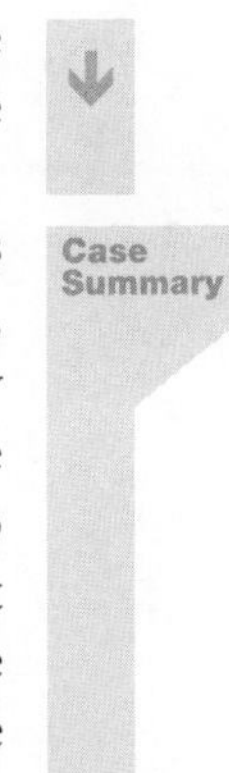

Kinch v. *Bullard* [1999] 1 WLR 423 is one other such example of the fact that it is unnecessary for the co-owner to actually have read or received notice under section 36(2), provided it is effectively served. In this case a wife, who was terminally ill, served notice by way of ordinary first class post on her husband of her wish to sever the joint tenancy on the matrimonial home. Before the husband read the notice, however, he was admitted to hospital with a heart attack. Realising that she would receive the house through the right of survivorship if the husband died without the joint tenancy having been severed, the wife destroyed the notice. The husband died a week later. However, the court held that the notice had nevertheless been effectively served because it had been delivered to his last-known place of abode. It was irrelevant that he had never had the opportunity to read it.

The form of the notice

Another point you will note from the wording of section 196 is that there is no specification as to any particular form the notice has to take. The notice does not have to be signed; nor does the notice have to be agreed by the other co-owners. As long as the notice is equivocal and immediate in its effect, therefore, this will be sufficient to sever the tenancy. In the Court of Appeal case of *Harris* v. *Goddard* [1983] 1 WLR 1203, a divorce petition served on a husband requesting 'such order in relation to the property by way of transfer or settlement as should be just' was held not to be effective notice of severance by the wife, because the wording of the petition merely asked the court to exercise its discretion as related to the property at some future date; it did not show an immediate desire to sever. This meant that, despite argument to the contrary made by the husband's relatives, when the husband was unfortunately killed in a car accident prior to the divorce petition being heard by the court, the family home went to the wife automatically under the right of survivorship.

Despite the lack of firm rules on the form of the notice itself, it should be noted that, although in itself a form of writing, it is not possible to sever a joint tenancy by will. The reason for this is that the right of survivorship operates immediately upon the death of the co-owner and therefore in advance of any provisions in the will coming into play. In the case of joint tenants there is therefore no share to dispose of under the terms of any will of a co-owner, because it continues to belong to the survivors of the group whole. This was the case in *Re Caines (deceased)* [1978] 1 WLR 540. The facts of the case were that a notice of severance had been prepared but not served on the deceased's wife. In lieu of this, the solicitors for the deceased sought to claim that the will itself was proof enough of effective severance by notice. Their claim failed, however.

Having established what is required by way of notice to sever a joint tenancy in equity, let us now go back to the wording of section 36(2) to see what else we can glean from it. If you look again at the wording of the section, you will notice that notice in writing is not the only provision made by the statute for the severance of a joint tenancy in equity: the section also says that a joint tenancy may be severed by doing 'such other acts or things as would, in the case of personal estate, have been effectual to sever the tenancy in equity . . .'.

Such a seemingly vague statement is clearly in need of judicial interpretation, and this was provided for by Vice-Chancellor Page-Wood in the authoritative case of *Williams* v. *Hensman* (1861) 1 John & H 546, mentioned above.

Williams v. *Hensman*

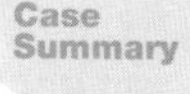

The case of *Williams* v. *Hensman* concerned an argument over a trust fund left by a woman in her will to be shared between her eight children. Following the woman's death, various of the children had purported to manage their shares of the property in different ways, one using the money for a marriage settlement, another mortgaging their share, and another requesting and receiving from the **trustees** of the fund an advance of £450 out of it. Three of the children also subsequently died. The question then arose as to whether the children owned the property as joint tenants or as tenants in common. In making his judgment in the case, the Vice-Chancellor stated that severance in accordance with the wording of section 36(2) of the Law of Property Act 1925, namely 'such other acts or things as would . . . have been effectual to sever the tenancy in equity' fell into three distinct categories:

1. severance by an act of any one of the persons interested 'operating upon their own share'
2. severance by mutual agreement
3. severance by any course of dealing sufficient to intimate that the interests of all were mutually treated as constituting a tenancy in common (also known as 'mutual conduct').

Acts operating on one's own share

In the case of the first category, you could be forgiven for questioning whether the Vice-Chancellor's interpretation gave any more clarity than the statutory description of 'such other acts of things . . .', although he did go on to illuminate the position a little by saying that any co-owner 'is at liberty to dispose of his own interest in such manner as to sever it from the joint fund . . .'.

The suggestion therefore is that an act operating upon one's own share can be recognised as any act of a co-owner that makes clear their intention to sever their interest from the interests of the other joint tenants. The category is nevertheless perhaps better understood by way of example.

Sale of the co-owner's own share

The first example of where a co-owner can be seen to be 'operating on their own share' is in the case of a sale of the co-owner's share in the property. This purported sale of the co-owner's equitable interest in the property is also known as 'total alienation', because of their attempt to transfer the whole of their interest in the property to a third party. All that is required for total alienation to take place is that the co-owner makes the transfer of their interest in the land in writing and signs it, which is the minimum **formality** required for the transfer of an equitable interest under section 53(1)(c) of the Law of Property Act 1925. No deed is therefore required for the joint tenancy to be severed in this way.

The purchase of another co-owner's share in the property is also considered sufficient to effect severance in equity, on the basis that it is acknowledging that the separate parties hold interests in the property of which they are capable of disposing. This was acknowledged in the case of ***Nielsen-Jones* v. *Fedden*** [1974] 3 WLR 583, which concerned a claim by a wife to the husband's beneficial interest in the family home through the right of survivorship. The husband had died after the couple had separated, and were in negotiations for the wife to buy the husband's share of the property. As it happened,

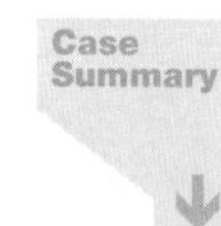

in this instance the court held that there had been no severance because the negotiations were never completed.

Interestingly, if a co-owner enters into a contract to dispose of their share in the property, this will also be considered effective severance, on the basis of the **equitable maxim** 'equity looks upon that as done which ought to be done'. In other words, if you enter into a contract to do something, in the eyes of equity you have as good as done it.

Mortgaging the co-owner's share

If one of the co-owners purports to mortgage their equitable interest in the property, this too will constitute an 'act operating on their own share', and thereby effect severance of the joint tenancy. This is known as 'partial alienation' and, again, must be in writing, signed by the severing co-owner in order to be valid.

Bankruptcy

If one of the co-owners is made bankrupt, the bankruptcy itself will effect severance on the part of the person made bankrupt. This is known as 'involuntary alienation', because on bankruptcy the assets of the bankrupt pass automatically to their **trustee in bankruptcy** to manage on their behalf.

The commencement of litigation

Apart from a purported sale or transfer of the co-owner's share of the property to a third party, the commencement of litigation against the other co-owners may often be deemed sufficient evidence of an act operating on one's own share. In the case of *Re Draper's Conveyance* [1969] 1 Ch 486, a wife commenced divorce proceedings against her husband, in which she requested that the matrimonial home be sold and the proceeds of sale divided between them. The husband died before the sale of the property took place and the wife tried to claim that the property should pass to her under the right of survivorship. However, the court held that the claim made by the wife against the husband was sufficient to show that she considered herself to have a distinct share in the property, and thus to sever the joint tenancy.

Case Summary

This outcome is, of course, quite the opposite of that in *Harris* v. *Goddard*, mentioned above. You will remember that in *Harris* v. *Goddard*, however, the divorce petition simply requested whatever order the court might think just, under the circumstances. It made no immediate or clear claim to any specific share in the property.

Mutual agreement or course of dealing

The second and third categories of severance listed in *Williams* v. *Hensman* are closely linked and consequently the line between them is often blurred, with the result that frequently severance under this heading could be categorised equally comfortably as either one or the other.

Unlike the other forms of severance, with mutual agreement or a mutual course of dealing the decision to sever is not a unilateral one; rather it comes about through a dialogue or course of action played out between the co-owners that evinces a clear intention that the co-owners no longer wish to continue on the basis of a joint tenancy in equity. It is for the person alleging that severance has occurred to prove the agreement or course of dealing that has

with mutual agreement the decision to sever is not unilateral

Case Summary

effected it. The authoritative case in this category of severance is the Court of Appeal case of ***Burgess* v. *Rawnsley*** [1975] 3 WLR 99. The case concerned an elderly couple, Mr Honick and Mrs Rawnsley, who bought a house together as joint tenants, each paying equally towards the purchase of it. Mr Honick intended to propose marriage to Mrs Rawnsley, but Mrs Rawnsley, when she became aware of this, rejected his proposal and never moved into the house. Mrs Rawnsley later agreed to sell her share of the property to Mr Honick, the pair agreeing a price for Mrs Rawnsley's interest. But she subsequently refused to go through with the sale. When Mr Honick died, Mrs Rawnsley claimed ownership of the whole of the house by right of survivorship. The Court held that severance had been effected and Mr Honick's share should be distributed in accordance with the terms of his will. This had not been severance by an act operating on one's own share, because there was nothing in writing, either contractually or in accordance with section 53(1); this had been a simple oral agreement to sever.

Case Summary

This is in contrast to the outcome in the case of *Nielson-Jones* v. *Fedden* [1974] 3 WLR 583, which was heard only a year previously. In this case a husband and wife, who owned the matrimonial home together as joint tenants, separated and the couple agreed that the house should be sold. Before this happened, however, the husband died, and the wife claimed the house under the right of survivorship. The court found that, whilst they had agreed to sell the property, there had been no agreement as to shares, or that the joint tenancy should be severed. There was therefore no severance of the joint tenancy in equity.

Case Summary

Another more recent case in which severance was declared to have been effected through mutual agreement is that of *Hunter* v. *Babbage* [1994] EGCS 8. Here a couple again owned the family home together as joint tenants, but following the breakdown of their marriage agreed that the property should be sold and the proceeds of sale divided. The couple's solicitors drafted an agreement to this effect, although exact shares were never agreed and the agreement was never finalised because the husband died before this could happen. The Court nevertheless held that the agreement, albeit in draft, was sufficient to have severed the tenancy in equity.

Case Summary

Whereas mutual agreement relies on some form of agreement between the parties, often in writing, mutual conduct or a mutual course of dealings relies on a pattern of behaviour as between the co-owners that shows they viewed themselves as being tenants in common, rather than joint tenants. This can be through a course of conduct which continues over a long period of time; however, such conduct must be clear and unambiguous. Inconclusive negotiations carried out between the co-owners will not be enough to show a mutual course of conduct. In the case of *Gore and Snell* v. *Carpenter* (1990) 60 P&CR 456, a husband and wife owned two properties together as joint tenants. During the course of divorce proceedings, an agreement was reached in principle that one property should be transferred to the wife and the other to the husband, but the agreement was never formalised and nothing further was done to effect the transfers. When the husband subsequently committed suicide, his executors made an application to the court to determine whether the properties should pass to the wife under the right of survivorship, or whether the husband's share in both should be distributed as part of his estate. The court held that there had been no express agreement to sever the joint tenancies; neither could the intention to sever be shown from any course of dealings between them. The negotiations had never been concluded and there was no evidence to show that either husband or wife had agreed to the idea of the tenancies being severed prior to the transfer of each of the properties into their sole names. The houses therefore passed to the wife under the right of survivorship.

The more recent case of *McDowell* v. *Hirschfield, Lipson & Rumney* [1992] 2 FLR 126 had a similar outcome. Here a husband had left his wife and gone to live with another woman. Divorce proceedings ensued but the husband died before the divorce had been finalised, leaving his lover as sole **executrix** and **beneficiary** under his will. The lover claimed half of the matrimonial home on the grounds that the joint tenancy had been severed when the husband petitioned for divorce. However, the court did not agree. No notice of severance had ever been served on the wife and, in fact, severance had never been mentioned in the correspondence between the husband and wife's solicitors. There was therefore nothing in the course of their dealings showing any intention to sever the tenancy.

Case Summary

There is one final way in which a mutual course of dealing can be shown to sever the joint tenancy in equity, and this is when co-owners make **mutual wills**. This may seem contradictory, given that we already know a will cannot constitute notice of severance, because the right of survivorship pre-empts the provisions of the will coming into force. However, the case of *Re Wilford's Estate* (1879) LR 11 ChD 267b explains how it works. The co-owners in this scenario were two sisters, who had each made a mutual will purporting to leave to the other their share of the property owned by the sisters as joint tenants, for life, and then to their nieces after the death of the last surviving sister. The court held that the sisters' joint tenancy in equity had been effectively severed. In making the mirror wills, the sisters showed a course of dealing which acknowledged their belief that they each had separate shares in the property that they could dispose of independently, albeit that they had been in agreement with one another as to how they would achieve this. The mutual wills, once finalised, therefore effected severance of their beneficial interest in the property.

Case Summary

Now that you know all about the different types of tenancy at law and in equity, test your knowledge with the following Writing and Drafting exercise.

Writing and drafting

Using the format shown in Figures 9.1, 9.2 and 9.3, illustrate using a diagram in each separate case the changing position in respect of the following:

1. 5 Lamp Lane is bought by five friends: Ava, Brenda, Carlos, Daffyd, Enid and Freddie. They all contribute equally to the purchase price. They tell their solicitor that they want to be able to leave their share in the property by will to other people.
2. Gregor, Harry, Ingrid, Josef and Karl buy 6 Lamp Lane as equitable joint tenants.
3. Karl writes to the others saying he wants to sever his interest in 6 Lamp Lane immediately.
4. Ingrid sells her interest in 6 Lamp Lane to Xavier.
5. Lara and Monty buy 7 Lamp Lane as beneficial joint tenants.
6. Monty dies, leaving all of his property to the Markingfield Dog Rescue Centre.

You should spend no more than 30 minutes on this task.

Handy tip: Remember you need two boxes for each scenario – one for the legal position and one for the equitable position.

So, to recap, severance of the joint tenancy in equity can take place under section 36(2) of the Law of Property Act 1925, either by notice in writing, or by such other acts or things as may be effective to sever the tenancy in equity. Such other acts or things may include an act operating on one's own share, such as an attempt by a co-owner to sell or mortgage their share of the property, a mutual agreement between the parties or a mutual course of conduct showing a clear and unequivocal intention to sever.

Unlawful killing

One last method of severance of the joint tenancy which is not mentioned in section 36(2) is that which takes place on the unlawful killing by one co-owner of the other. It is a rule of **public policy** (known as the '**forfeiture rule**') that a person who has unlawfully killed another should be prevented from acquiring any form of benefit in consequence of the killing. This, naturally, would include benefiting from the right of survivorship in the case of a joint tenancy of land or property. If one joint tenant kills the other, therefore, the forfeiture rule dictates that severance of the joint tenancy in equity will be effected, so that the killer is prevented from benefiting from their criminal act. Instead of automatically receiving the property under the right of survivorship, therefore, the deceased's share in the property will be distributed in accordance with the terms of their will or intestacy.

There are, of course, circumstances in which it could be argued that the unlawful killing should not result in the loss of property by the killer, for example, where the killer has been prompted by years of systematic abuse by the deceased. For this reason, under section 2 of the Forfeiture Act 1982 the court has the discretion to grant relief against the forfeiture rule, in cases where the justice of the case requires it. Manslaughter would be one such case. In *Re K* [1985] 3 WLR 234, a wife accidentally killed her husband with his own 12-bore shotgun, following an altercation at their home. The following excerpt from the judgment of Mr Justice Vinelott at first instance details what happened.

Case Summary

Documenting the law

Excerpt from the judgment of Mr Justice Vinelott in *Re K*:

'The widow had for many years been subjected to violent and unprovoked attacks. The doctor to whose affidavit I have referred and the probation officer who gave evidence at the trial both described her as a "battered wife". But she was fond of and loyal to the deceased. She attributed his violence to illness, a brain tumour or paranoid schizophrenia. I should add also that he was a persistent and heavy drinker and may well have suffered in his intellectual capacity and power of self-control as a result. The widow had what she considered to be a refuge in the spare room which could be locked until a violent outburst had blown over. On 30 September the deceased returned from a visit to the post office to collect his pension. The couple had a snack lunch. The widow's version of the events which followed in her evidence in this court is as follows. There was a disagreement over a trivial incident, a request that he guarantee the bank account of a friend of hers. He lost his temper and grabbed her hair, calling her a "stupid bitch". There was a lull but she feared a resumption of his attack as had happened before. She decided to escape to her bedroom. As she got to the kitchen door she decided on the spur of the moment to pick up the gun. She thought that if he saw the gun in her hands he would be deterred from following her. At that precise moment his back was towards her. He had turned towards the kitchen sink, but he could still have turned back and caught her before she reached the bedroom. That had happened before. To attract his attention and make sure that he would see that she had the gun she released the safety catch. It made an audible click. He started to turn towards her. The gun went off. She says that she has no recollection of touching, far less pulling, the trigger. She telephoned a friend in an hysterical state and then telephoned the ambulance service, but the deceased was dead when the ambulance arrived.'

Source: *In Re K, Dec'd* [1985] 3 WLR 234, 92–4

The husband and wife had been joint tenants of the matrimonial home. Mr Justice Vinelott held that, whilst the circumstances of the killing were such that the forfeiture rule must apply, he had jurisdiction under section 2(2) of the Forfeiture Act 1982 to modify the effect of the rule. He concluded that the wife should be relieved from the forfeiture rule and the joint tenancy should stand. The decision was upheld on appeal.

What share will they have in the property?

If the tenancy is severed in equity, this begs the question: what share will each party get? The answer is that, in the absence of an agreement to the contrary, the severing party will take an equitable interest in the property in equal shares, proportionate to the number of co-owners. This is regardless of the parties' initial contribution to the purchase price of the property, as we shall see shortly. In the situation where there are only two co-owners of a property, the outcome is simple: they will each receive a 50 per cent share in the property. This was the outcome in the case of *Goodman* v. *Gallant* [1986] Fam 106. Here, a husband had bought a house for him and his wife to live in. The house was in the husband's sole name, but there was an agreement between them that she should be beneficially entitled to half of the property. The couple subsequently split up and the wife began living at the house with another man. The husband later transferred the title to the property into the joint names of the wife and her lover, in exchange for payment for his half share in the property. On the subsequent break-up of the relationship between the wife and her lover, the wife served notice to sever the tenancy and made an application to the court to determine what shares they should be given. The wife contended that she should be entitled to a 75 per cent share, as she was already entitled to half and the husband's transfer of the property was for the remaining half to be shared between her and her lover. The court disagreed. The house had been transferred into the joint names of the wife and her lover beneficially as joint tenants and the wording in the transfer was conclusive of their position, regardless of what money or share had been put into the property. On a subsequent severance of the tenancy, the co-owners were each entitled to an equal share of the house.

Case Summary

Where there are more than two co-owners, however, the result looks slightly different. Let us imagine three joint tenants, let us call them Julia, Rashid and Alma, living in a house together. Alma serves notice on the other two co-owners under section 36(2), stating that she wishes her interest in the property to be severed. The notice is effective. However, rather than each of the co-owners now becoming a tenant in common of a third share of the property, what actually happens is that the severing party, in this case Alma, becomes a tenant in common with a third share of the property, the other two co-owners remain joint tenants in equity (as they have not severed as against one another) as to the remaining two thirds. Figure 9.4 shows what the split would look like.

Figure 9.4 Effect of severance on the equitable estate

Law	Julia, Rashid, Alma
Equity	Julia and Rashid are joint tenants as to two-thirds Alma is a tenant in common as to the remaining third

Bringing an end to co-ownership

Bringing the co-ownership to an end can come about in a number of different ways, dependent largely upon the circumstances of the individual co-owners.

Sale

If a jointly-owned property is sold, the proceeds of sale will be divided between the owners in accordance with their respectively owned shares and the co-ownership will come to an end. As we have seen above, however, there is not always consensus as to who owns what share of the property and, in this eventuality, the court may be asked to intervene to settle the matter.

Merger

If one co-owner buys or is given, either during their lifetime or by will, the share of another co-owner, the two shares in the property will be deemed to be merged and therefore the co-ownership will come to an end in respect of those two shares in the land.

Death of the other co-owners

Where the co-owners are joint tenants, the co-ownership will come to an end when all co-owners bar one die, leaving a sole owner of the property through the process of survivorship. At this point, the entire legal and beneficial interest in the property will **vest** in the surviving co-owner.

Physical separation

The physical partition of the land between the co-owners will result in the creation of two separately identifiable pieces of land coming into being, each part being owned absolutely by the former co-owner possessing it.

Court order

The court has power either to make an order determining the parties' respective shares or to make an order for sale under section 14 of the Trusts of Land and Appointment of Trustees Act 1996 (**ToLATA**). In exercising its power under section 14, the court must take into consideration the factors listed in section 15 of the Act. These are:

the court must take into consideration the factors listed in section 15

(a) the intentions of the person(s) who created the trust;

(b) the purposes for which the trust property is held;

(c) the welfare of any minors who occupy the trust land as their home;

(d) the interests of any secured creditor of any beneficiary. This will apply where there is a mortgage on the property;

(e) the circumstances and wishes of the beneficiaries of full age and entitled to an interest in possession in the property subject to the trust or in the case of dispute, to the wishes of the majority (according to the value of their combined interests).

Much of the case law relating to the settlement of disputes over co-owned property predates ToLATA. However, many of the issues taken into consideration remain the same and so the precedents are still of use. The following give a few good examples of how the court may frame their decisions, taking into account the requirements of section 15.

In *Jones* v. *Challenger* [1961] 1 QB 176, a married couple had bought a house together as joint tenants. When the wife subsequently left to take up residence with another man, an application was made to the court for the property to be sold. The Court of Appeal granted the application, on the basis that the purpose for which the house had been purchased, as a matrimonial home for husband and wife, had ceased to exist.

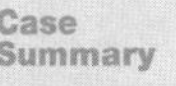

This is in contrast with the earlier decision made in *Re Buchanan-Wollaston's Conveyance* [1939] Ch 217. Here, four adjoining property owners got together to buy a plot of land adjacent to all their properties in order to preserve their collective sea views. The land was bought by the property owners together as joint tenants. Some time later, when one of the property owners sold their house, they wanted the plot of land to be sold so that they could recoup their investment in purchasing the land. The other three house owners opposed the sale and so the matter went to court. The court refused to make an order for sale because the purpose of the trust, which was to preserve the view for all four properties, still continued.

Clearly the basis upon which the decision in *Re Buchanan-Wollaston's Conveyance* was made would come within the factors for consideration of the modern-day provisions of ToLATA, because it concerned the ongoing purpose for which the trust property was held. However, the outcome may at once seem rather harsh for the selling party, who would have no further personal interest in owning the amenity land. It could be considered that perhaps a more pragmatic view was taken by the court in the case of

Case Summary

Ali v. *Hussein* (1974) 231 EG 373. Here again there were several co-owners, one of whom wished the land to be sold in order to recoup their investment. The court in this case, however, made an order postponing the sale for a number of months to allow the other co-owners to raise sufficient money to buy the co-owner out of their share in the property. The making of such an order clearly achieved a balance between the interest of the party wishing to sell and the remaining co-owners. Of course, there is considerable scope for discretion in application of the section 15 guidance and, ultimately, each case will turn upon its own facts.

Case Summary

The other main issue which often comes into consideration when the courts are making decisions under section 14 is the existence of children living in the home. A case in point is *Re Ever's Trust* [1980] 1 WLR 1327. Here an unmarried couple had bought a property together as co-owners. The husband subsequently moved out, leaving the woman and their children still living in the house. The man applied for an order for the sale of the house, but this was refused by the Court of Appeal on account of the fact that the purpose of acquiring the house, which was to house their family, could still be fulfilled. It should of course be remembered here that, in any event, one of the factors to be taken into account under section 15 is the welfare of any minors living at the property.

Case Navigator

Case Summary

It should not be a given that this will be the outcome in every case, however. In the case of ***Bank of Ireland Home Mortgages Ltd*** **v.** ***Bell*** [2001] 2 FLR 809, the Court of Appeal ordered the house be sold. Here, the Court said that following the husband's departure from the family home the purpose for which the house had been purchased had come to an end. It was perhaps significant in this case that the child of the marriage, although still living at home, was almost 18 years old at the time of the hearing.

One final point that should be raised about section 15 is that it does not apply in the case of the bankruptcy of one of the co-owners. Here, a completely separate set of statutory guidelines come into play, which are set out at section 335A of the Insolvency Act 1986. Like section 15 of ToLATA, section 335A lists a number of matters to be taken into account when a trustee in bankruptcy is selling an estate in land (or a share of it) on behalf of a bankrupt. The idea behind the section 335A requirements is that it aims to balance the needs of the creditors of the bankrupt with the needs of the other co-owners, who are likely to be innocent parties in respect of the bankruptcy. There are nevertheless clear similarities between the two sections. Section 335A states:

> (1) Any application by a trustee of a bankrupt's estate under section 14 of the Trusts of Land and Appointment of Trustees Act 1996 . . . for an order under that section for the sale of land shall be made to the court having jurisdiction in relation to the bankruptcy.
>
> (2) On such an application the court shall make such order as it thinks just and reasonable having regard to:
>
> a The interests of the bankrupt's creditors;
>
> b Where the application is made in respect of land which includes a dwelling house which is or has been the home of the bankrupt or the bankrupt's spouse or civil partner or former spouse or former civil partner:
>
> i The conduct of the spouse, civil partner, former spouse or former civil partner, so far as contributing to the bankruptcy;
>
> ii The needs and financial resources of the spouse, civil partner, former spouse or former civil partner;
>
> iii The needs of any children; and
>
> c All the circumstances of the case other than the needs of the bankrupt.

(3) where such an application is made after the end of the period of one year beginning with the first vesting . . . of the bankrupt's estate in a trustee, the court shall assume, unless the circumstances of the case are exceptional, that the interests of the bankrupt's creditors outweigh all other considerations.

Thus, generally speaking, if the application for an order for sale is made by the trustee in bankruptcy over a year after the bankruptcy has taken place, the court is more likely to order the sale of the house on the basis that, unless there are exceptional circumstances to be taken into account, at that point the needs of the creditors are deemed to outweigh those of the co-owners. If the application by the trustee in bankruptcy is made within a year of the bankruptcy, however, the court's discretion is more fluid, albeit nevertheless strictly applied.

What the courts will accept as being exceptional circumstances is usually limited to matters of extreme ill-health on the part of the co-owners. Thus, in the case of *Re Citro* (a bankrupt) [1991] Ch 142, the Court of Appeal did not consider the fact that the sale of the jointly-owned family home would result both in the eviction of the bankrupt's wife and young children, and that it would make the children's schooling very difficult, to be exceptional circumstances. On the other hand, in *Re Mott* [1987] CLY 212, a seventy-year-old woman who had lived in a house for over forty years was given precedence over the creditors of her bankrupt son, with whom she owned the house. The house was full of memories and the woman's doctor had advised that the woman's health, which was poor, would deteriorate if she was forced to move. The court held that the sale should be postponed until after the woman's death.

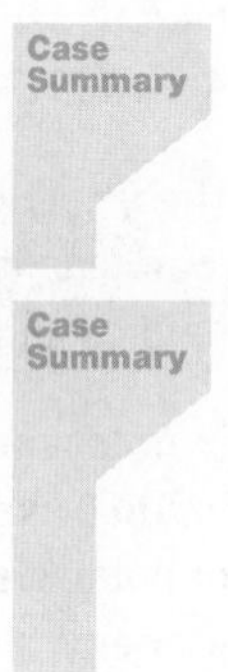

Reflective practice

Consider once again your answer to the Out and About feature above. What could you do to avoid the difficulties inherent when the co-ownership inevitably comes to an end?

It has been questioned whether there may be a separate human rights impact on innocent co-owners under the section 335A rule, although to date the courts have resisted the suggestion that there may be any conflict between the section and Article 8 of the European Convention on Human Rights, which encompasses the right to respect for the individual's home and family life. A full discussion of the issues can be found in Adam Baker's article, entitled: 'The judicial approach to "exceptional circumstances" in bankruptcy: the impact of the Human Rights Act 1998', the reference for which is given at the end of the chapter.

Summary

- Ownership of land is divided, in English law, into two distinct parts: legal ownership and equitable (or beneficial) ownership. The legal and equitable owners can be different people.
- In a co-ownership situation the division of the legal and equitable ownership is imposed by statute, through the imposition of a trust of land under section 36 of the Law of Property Act 1925.
- The legal estate in the land is always held as joint tenants; the equitable interest may be held as joint tenants or tenants in common.
- Joint tenants hold the property as a joint, or group owner; tenants in common are capable of holding separate undivided shares in the property.
- Joint tenants benefit from the right of survivorship, meaning that on the death of one of the joint tenants, the property will automatically vest in the remaining joint owners or owner. With tenants in common there is no right of survivorship, so that on the death of a co-owner, their share will pass in accordance with the terms of their will or intestacy.
- All joint tenants must share the four unities of possession, interest, title and time. Tenants in common need share only the unity of possession.
- If there is no express declaration in the documentation as to how the co-owners are to hold the beneficial interest in the property, there may be words of severance suggesting the property is to be held as tenants in common. These are words that suggest a desire to hold the property in shares.
- Failing the presence of wording in the documentation, the presumption of a tenancy in common may be made based on the circumstances of the co-owners. These include business partners and unequal contributions to the purchase price.
- Once a joint tenancy in equity has been created, it can be severed in one of two ways: by notice in writing, or by 'other acts or things' (section 36(2) LPA 1925).
- Notice in writing need not be in any particular form, as long as it unequivocal in its nature and is served on all the other joint owners at their last known place of residence. The co-owners need not have seen or read the notice, as long as it has been correctly served.
- 'Other acts or things' were defined in *Williams* v. *Hensman* as including an act operating on one's own share (through sale, mortgage or bankruptcy), mutual conduct and mutual agreement.
- Unlawful killing will also act to sever the joint tenancy in equity, although there are provisions within the Forfeiture Act 1982 to grant relief where there is no moral culpability.
- If the tenancy is severed in equity, in the absence of an agreement to the contrary, the severing party will take an equitable interest in the property in equal shares, proportionate to the number of co-owners (*Goodman* v. *Gallant*).
- Co-ownership may be brought to an end through the sale of the property, merger of the beneficial interests or the physical division of the property.
- If there is a dispute as to whether the property should be sold or as to its division into shares, the court may make an order under section 14 of ToLATA, taking into account the factors listed in section 15 of the same Act.
- If the court is making a decision in respect of a bankrupt co-owner, they will have to consider the factors listed in section 335A of the Insolvency Act 1986. Unless there are exceptional circumstances, the needs of creditors will be given preference over the needs of the remaining co-owners or occupants of the property.

Question and answer*

Problem: In 2000 Jaz, Romila and Sheila bought a flat together to live in whilst they were at university. The girls put in £5,000 each by way of deposit and the remainder of the money was supplied through a mortgage in their joint names.

In 2001 Sheila was thrown off her university course, having failed her exams in all subjects, and returned home to live with her parents. The girls have since lost touch.

In 2004 Romila wrote to Jaz, stating that she wished to sever the tenancy to the flat. She put the letter on the kitchen table, but it later got mixed up with Jaz's revision papers and was never opened.

In 2008 Romila was killed in a car accident. Jaz is now getting married and wishes to sell the flat and use her share of the proceeds to buy a new property together with her husband. Sheila opposes the sale. So does Luca, to whom Romila left all her property by will.

Advise Jaz whether Luca and Sheila can prevent the sale and, if so, on what basis.

You should allow yourself no more than 40 minutes to complete this task.

Essay: What are the difficulties inherent in the methods of severance outlined under s.36(2) of the LPA 1925 and is there a case for reform?

This question should be answered in 40 minutes.

* Answer guidance is provided at the end of the chapter.

Further reading

Thompson, M. P., 'Beneficial joint tenancies: a case for abolition?', Conv 1987, Jan–Feb, 29–35.
Whilst this article is old it makes an interesting case for the abolition of joint beneficial tenancies and gives useful insight into the pros and cons of both types of beneficial holding.

King, L., '*Quigley* v. *Masterson*: methods of severing joint tenancy', PCB 2012, 1, 20–3.
This brief case comment neatly affirms the rules relating to severance of the joint tenancy by notice under section 36(2) of the Law of Property Act 1925 in the light of the 2011 case of *Quigley* v. *Masterson* [2011] EWHC 2529.

Conway, H., 'Joint tenancies, negotiations and consensual severance', Conv 2009, 1, 67–78.
Discusses the Australian 2007 case of *Saleeba* v. *Wilke* [2007] QSC 298 and considers the difficulties of separating the two devices under *Williams* v. *Hensman* of mutual agreement and mutual course of dealings.

Baker, Adam, 'The judicial approach to "exceptional circumstances" in bankruptcy: the impact of the Human Rights Act 1998', Conv 2010, 74(5), 352–68.
Discusses the impact of section 335A of the Insolvency Act 1986 on Article 8 of the European Convention on Human Rights and the approach the courts have taken in interpreting it.

Question and answer guidance

Please note that the following is not a full answer and is intended to provide guidance in outline form only as to how to answer the questions posed.

In order to advise Jaz we need to ascertain how both the legal and equitable estates in the flat were held when it was bought in 2000 and whether the position has changed since then.

1. Whenever land is the subject of co-ownership, a trust will be imposed. A trust is essential so that there may be separate consideration of the position in law and in equity. In 2000 when the flat was purchased, a trust of land would have been imposed under s.36 LPA 1925.

2. The legal title must be held as a joint tenancy (s.1(6) LPA 1925: 'a legal estate is not capable of subsisting or being created out of an undivided share'; and s.34(2) LPA 1925: 'any attempt to create a legal tenancy in common takes effect as a joint tenancy at law and a tenancy in common in equity').

When the property is purchased the legal title to the property will therefore be held as joint tenants by Jaz, Romila and Sheila on trust for themselves in equity.

3. We then need to discover whether they bought as joint tenants or tenants in common in equity. (i) Are the four unities present? (possession, interest, title and time). It does not appear that any of the unities are missing in our scenario. (ii) Is there an express declaration in the purchase deed stating whether they are to hold as joint tenants or tenants in common? We are not told that there is any such declaration. (iii) Where the documentation is silent, the presumption is that equity follows the law and that a joint tenancy will exist in equity unless this presumption can be rebutted by evidence of words of severance (there appear to be none in our scenario), business ownership (which this was not) or unequal contributions to the purchase price (which again there are not). As there is no evidence of any of the above, it would appear that they are all joint tenants in both law and equity.

4. *Romila's letter of severance*: Romila can sever the joint tenancy in equity by giving notice in writing under s.36(2) LPA 1925. As long as the notice shows an unequivocal intention to sever, and is sent to all the other joint tenants then this will be sufficient to sever the joint tenancy. Romila has written to Jaz and left the letter on the kitchen table. The fact that she has not seen the note is irrelevant, as long as it was left at the last known address of her joint tenant, it will be valid. BUT Romila has not written to Sheila. In order to effect severance notice has to be given to all the other joint tenants. The notice to Jaz alone is therefore not effective in severing the joint tenancy.

5. *Romila dies*: when Romila died in the car accident, therefore, the two remaining co-owners, Jaz and Sheila, will remain joint owners of the property both in law and in equity, by virtue of the right of survivorship.

6. *Romila's will*: making a will leaving your jointly owned property to a third party will not effect severance of the joint tenancy, because the will takes effect after death, when the right of survivorship has already been exercised. Luca therefore has no entitlement to the property.

7. Sheila, on the other hand, is still a joint tenant of the property and can, in theory, oppose Romila's wish to sell. Under s.14 ToLATA, any person who has an interest in the property can apply for a court order. In making such an order, the court is required to have regard to

(i) the intention of the persons who created the trust;

(ii) the purpose for which the property subject to the trust is held;

(iii) the welfare of any minors;

(iv) the interest of any secured creditors.

(iii) and (iv) do not apply in our scenario. As the purpose of buying the flat was to share during their time at university, and presuming their respective university courses have now ended, it could be argued that the purpose for which the property was purchased has now ceased. In addition, of the three flat sharers, one has died and the other, Sheila, dropped out of university after the first year. It is likely therefore that the court will order sale (in support of this see *Jones* v. *Challenger*; *Ali* v. *Hussein*).

Essay: The question is in the first instance asking you to outline the different methods of severance of the equitable estate under s.36(2) LPA 1925. These are either by notice in writing or by 'any other acts or things . . .'

1. *Notice in writing*: this has no prescribed form and needn't be signed, so the notice itself is not difficult to comply with. It is also unilateral in its effect, so again, this makes it simple to impose. The main features that may be seen as causing difficulty are that:

(a) It must be unequivocal; (b) It must be served on all other co-owners (not just one). As long as the wording of the notice is clear, however, and copies of it are given to all other co-owners of the property, this should not cause a problem. If a co-owner is proving difficult to find, service at their last known address will be sufficient.

From the perspective of the person wishing to sever, as long as the notice is served in the correct way (by leaving it at the last known address or posting it to that address), whether the other joint tenants see it or not is irrelevant. This is more of a problem for the recipient, who may find themselves in a situation where their joint tenancy has been severed without their actual knowledge.

2. The concept of 'other acts or things' is more problematic. You should describe what constitutes acts or things in accordance with *Williams* v. *Hensman*, and then go on to discuss each one in turn. (a) *Act operating on one's own share*. List what will come within this category and how each can be applied. The main point to get across here is that the act must be irrevocable and therefore incomplete or inconclusive actions will not suffice (see *Harris* v. *Goddard*, for example). (b) *Mutual conduct and mutual course of dealings*. These are often difficult to prove and frequently overlap. Probably the most uncertain of the methods and subject to most judicial criticism.

One additional point worth mentioning here is the effect of severance under *Goodman* v. *Gallant*, and the fact that, in the absence of agreement to the contrary between the parties, once severed, the co-owners may be left with smaller or different shares from what they anticipated they would receive in this eventuality, and which may be unfair.

You should conclude by stating whether or not you think there is room for reform in this area of the law and where you think the focus of such reforms should be. You may wish to take up legal commentator M. P. Thompson's view ('Beneficial joint' tenancies: a case for 'abolition?', above) that all co-owners should be tenants in common in equity, to avoid the difficulties inherent in determining whether severance has occurred in the event of a disagreement between the parties. The problem with this view, of course, is that this would remove the right of survivorship in respect of the beneficial interest, which is generally thought to be the main benefit of having a joint tenancy in equity to begin with.

Visit **www.mylawchamber.co.uk** to access tools to help you develop and test your knowledge of land law.

Use Case Navigator to read in full some of the key cases referenced in this chapter with commentary and questions:

AG Securities* v. *Vaughan and others [1990] 1 AC 417
Nielson-Jones* v. *Fedden [1974] 3 All ER 38
Burgess* v. *Rawnsley [1975] 3 All ER 142
Bank of Ireland Home Mortgages Ltd* v. *Bell [2001] 2 FLR 809

Chapter 10 Interests in land: easements

Key points In this chapter we will be looking at:

- What is an easement
- Positive and negative easements and how to tell the difference between the two
- Easements compared with other rights in land
- The four essential characteristics of an easement as set out in *Re Ellenborough Park* [1955]
- The grant and reservation of easements
- How easements are created: express, implied and presumed grant
- Easements of necessity
- Easements implied through the common intention of the parties
- *Quasi*-easements and the rule in *Wheeldon* v. *Burrows*
- Easements created under section 62 of the Law of Property Act 1925
- Easements acquired by prescription and the acquisition of rights to light
- Easements and proprietary estoppel
- How to protect an easement in registered and unregistered land
- The extinguishment of easements
- Proposed reforms to the law of easements

Introduction

In Chapter 4 we examined the concept of interests in land, both legal and equitable. And we learned that whilst interests in land are lesser rights than an estate in land (which you will remember confers possession of the land on the estate holder for a defined period of time) such interests nevertheless are capable of ownership and can be transferred from person to person and used to benefit the owner and the owner's own land. Although we have already considered the various interests in land and how to protect them, in order to gain a fuller picture of land law as a whole it is necessary to get to know some of the more common forms of interest in rather more detail. This is a foundation which will become particularly important when you come to look at the sale and purchase of land in practice, because you will have to be aware of every interest that affects the land you are buying (or selling) and how to deal with those interests. Over the next three chapters, therefore, we are going to be considering three of the most important interests in land: **easements, freehold covenants** and **mortgages**.

In this first chapter we will be looking at the concept of easements.

What is an easement?

From the definition given in Chapter 4 you may remember that an easement is an interest in land which can be either legal (easements are listed under section 1(2) of the Law of Property Act 1925 as one of the five categories of interest in land which can be legal) or equitable. An easement confers the right to do something on someone else's land. This is not a right to take anything from the land; nor does it confer a right of possession. An easement is simply a **common law** right to make use of the land in some way.

There are many different kinds of easement, the most common being a **right of way**, which is the right to cross someone's land either on foot or with vehicles, depending on the nature of the easement. Some of the more usual forms of easement include:

- a **right of storage** (as in ***Wright* v. *Macadam*** [1949] 2 KB 744, which concerned the right to store coal in a coal shed);
- a **right to park a car**, which is itself also a right of storage (as in *London & Blenheim Estates Ltd* v. *Ladbroke Retail Parks Ltd* [1992] 1 WLR 1278);
- a **right of drainage** (as in *Mason* v. *Shrewsbury & Hereford Railway Co.* (1871) LR 6 QB 578);
- a **right of support** (that is, the right for a building or land to receive physical support from neighbouring land, as in *Dalton* v. *Angus* (1881) 6 App Cas 740); and
- a **right to light** (again, this is the right to receive light from neighbouring land, as in *Colls* v. *Home and Colonial Stores Ltd* [1904] AC 179).

All of these are well documented in the courts, although there are other more obscure rights, such as the right to use a lavatory (as in *Miller* v. *Emcer Products* [1956] 2 WLR 267, in which occupants of office premises on the ground floor of a building were given the right to use toilets that had been included in a lease of the first and second floor premises), and a right to put up signage on the land. Although very different in nature, each type of easement is governed by the same principle, which is that the owner of the easement is given the right to use the land in some way.

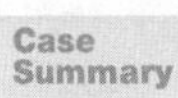

To give you some idea of just how common an interest in land easements are, take a look at the Key Stats feature below. The figures, which are taken from a Law Commission report which did a study on the subject, are a few years old now, but still give a good idea of just how widely used the concept of the easement is.

Key stats Law Commission Consultation Paper 186. Statistics on easements collated for the years 2003/4 and 2004/5.

- **Number of easements created each year in relation to registered land:**

  2003/04 – 277,668
  2004/05 – 257,881
- **Number of easements created in registrable leases:**

  2003/04 – 39,380
  2004/05 – 56,798
- **Number of new land charge registrations (Class D(iii)):**

  2003/04 – 406
  2004/05 – 375
- **Proportion of existing freehold titles that are subject to an easement:**

  Registered freehold titles – 16,643,383
  Registered freehold titles that are subject to an easement – 10,836,366
  Proportion – 65%

Source: Richard Smith

Source: http://lawcommission.justice.gov.uk/docs/cp186_Easements_Covenants_and_Profits_a_Prendre_Consultation.pdf

Positive and negative easements

Easements may, by their nature, be positive or negative. With the exception of the right to light and the right of support, all of the examples given above are positive easements, meaning they give the owner of the easement the right to use the land of someone else in some specified way. The right to light and the right of support are both negative. Do you know why this is? To find out, take a look at the You Be the Judge feature, below.

You be the judge

Source: BuildPix, constructionphotography.com

Q: Why are rights to light and rights of support negative easements:

(a) because they stop the holder of the interest from doing something on their own land;
(b) because they allow the holder of the interest to prevent someone else from doing something on their own land;
(c) because they require someone to do something on their own land or
(d) because they require someone to do something on your land?

A: (b). A negative easement has the effect of preventing a person from doing something on their own land.

In the case of a right to light, the right to receive light from someone else's land has the negative effect on the landowner who is subject to the right from doing anything on their own land that would obscure the passage of that light onto the right holder's land. This might be building above a certain height, or even building at all. The right to light is therefore negative in nature because it restricts the landowner's use of their own land. In the same way, an easement of support for a building on the benefited landowner's land would prevent the owner of the burdened land from removing that support, although the burdened landowner cannot be put under a positive obligation to maintain the means of support, for example if it is a building on the burdened owner's land, because this would necessarily mean expenditure on the part of the landowner. This was the case in *Jones* v. *Pritchard* [1908] 1 Ch 630, although in this case the court gave the benefited landowner the right to enter the burdened land to effect the necessary repairs himself. For further discussion of this point see the section on the essential characteristics of an easement, below. Because of the restrictive nature of **negative easements** the courts have now declined to allow any new types of negative easement to be created. In the Court of Appeal case of *Phipps* v. *Pears* [1964] 2 WLR 996, Lord Denning, Master of the Rolls, declined to grant an easement of protection of a side wall of a house in Warwick from the weather. The wall had previously been protected by another structure on neighbouring land, which the landowner demolished. In giving his judgment, Denning said that the courts would not readily accept the creation of new negative easements because of their tendency to restrict the burdened land and hamper property development, saying:

> . . . if such an easement were to be permitted, it would unduly restrict your neighbour in his enjoyment of his own land. It would hamper legitimate development . . . if we were to stop a man pulling down his house, we would put a brake on desirable improvement. Every man is entitled to pull down his house if he likes. If it exposes your house to the weather, that is your misfortune. It is no wrong on his part. Likewise every man is entitled to cut down his trees if he likes, even if it leaves you without shelter from the wind or shade from the sun.

A more recent case in the same vein is the House of Lords case of *Hunter* v. *Canary Wharf Ltd* [1997] 2 WLR 684. Here, Hunter and others brought an action against Canary Wharf

Ltd with regard to interference caused to their television reception as a result of the construction of the Canary Wharf Tower. The court refused to grant an easement to receive an uninterrupted television signal, however, stating that not only was the purported easement negative in nature and therefore could not be granted, but also that it would be an inconsistent finding for the courts to recognise 'such a wide and novel restriction'.

Case Summary

The ability of the courts to create new categories of **positive easement**, on the other hand, is not closed, the courts recognising that the categories of easements must be allowed to 'alter and expand with changes that take place in the circumstances of mankind', as stated in the case of *Dyce* v. *Lady James Hay* (1852) 1 Macq 305. Thus, new easements can be created so long as they are similar in nature to, or can be said to be a development of, others already established by case law. One such example is the recognition of car parking as a valid form of easement, as in the case of *London & Blenheim Estates Ltd* v. *Ladbroke Retail Parks Ltd*, which is effectively an extension of the easement of storage.

Easements compared with other forms of right

So now you know how to recognise an easement. Even with all the facts set out in front of you, however, at first glance easements can look remarkably similar to certain other forms of right or interest in land that you may have come across. In fact, they are actually quite distinct. An explanation of the differences between the most common of these rights is given below.

Licences

In the same way that a landowner may grant an easement over their land for the benefit of another, a landowner might also give a third party a **licence** to use that land in the same way. The difference between the two is in the type of benefit conferred upon the third party: with an easement, the benefiting property is given a legal or equitable interest in the land itself; with a licence, however, the third party is simply given a personal permission by the landowner, effectively giving consent to what would otherwise be a trespass on the burdened land. A licence is therefore a personal right, incapable of existing as an interest in land and benefiting from contractual remedies only, as opposed to any right in the land itself. Because a licence is simply a personal agreement between the parties, it is able to exist in a far wider context than an easement. For example, there is no need for the holder of a licence to be the owner of land themselves in order to benefit from the agreed use; neither is there any need for the use to confer any more than a personal benefit on the licence holder.

A licence is a personal right, incapable of existing as an interest in land

Restrictive covenants

Easements differ from **restrictive covenants** in that, whereas an easement is a right to do something on someone else's land, a restrictive covenant is a right to prevent someone else from doing something on their own land. We are going to be considering the nature of restrictive covenants in detail in the next chapter. A negative easement can look extremely similar to a restrictive covenant. For example, an easement of light can be almost identical in its effect to a restrictive covenant against building. In practice, the two interests in land work differently though. Covenants can be far wider in their scope and more flexible than easements. In particular, a covenant against building can effectively confer a right to maintain a view on the benefited landowner, whereas an easement cannot do this as such a right would be too vague to form the subject matter of a grant. From a technical point of view, restrictive covenants can only exist in **equity**, not being one of the interests in land mentioned in section 1(2) of the Law of Property Act 1925. As we know, easements, on the other hand, exist at law or in equity.

Profits à prendre

Whilst **profits** and easements fall within the same category of legal interest under section 1(2) of the Law of Property Act 1925, a profit is quite different in nature from an easement in two respects: firstly, it allows the benefiting party to come onto the burdened land and actually take something from it, which an easement cannot allow. So, for example, a profit might incorporate the right to graze animals on the land, or to fish in a river, or to cut wood from trees on the land or peat from the soil. An easement, being a right of user only, cannot extend beyond this to incorporate the removal of anything from the land. The second respect in which a profit is dissimilar to an easement is that it can exist 'in gross'. This means that you do not have to own land yourself in order to benefit from a profit. As we shall see, in accordance with the rules in *Re Ellenborough Park*, this same rule cannot apply to easements, which must incorporate both a burdened and a benefiting landowner.

Public rights of way

We have seen that one of the most common types of easement is a right of way over land. An easement of way should not be confused with a public right of way, however. Whereas a public right of way provides a general right of passage which can be used by any member of the general public and which does not require the user to own any land themselves, an easement of way is a private right of passage over privately owned land, not available to the general public, the use of which is specifically connected to the benefited land and the owners of it.

Quasi-easements

When a landowner makes use of land owned by them that could, if part of the land was subsequently sold, potentially form the subject of an easement, that use is known as a '**quasi-easement**'. Until the land is sold it cannot be an easement, of course, because as we know you cannot have an easement over your own land. Quasi-easements and how they can be used are explained in more detail in the context of the rule in ***Wheeldon* v. *Burrows***, later on in the chapter.

Case Navigator

Essential characteristics of an easement

Case Summary

Having established what easements are and having compared them with other forms of interest and looked at a few different examples of easements, we can already see that easements tend to share a number of similar characteristics. In fact, in order for an easement to exist either at law or in equity, the courts have specified a number of essential prerequisites. These requirements, of which there are four in number, are set out in the Court of Appeal case of *Re Ellenborough Park* [1955] 3 WLR 892. The case concerned a private park known as Ellenborough Park in Weston-super-Mare. The owners of the park sold the plots of land surrounding the park for use as building plots, specifying in the conveyances of sale that each purchaser would be granted 'the full enjoyment . . . at all times hereafter in common with the other persons to whom such easements may be granted of the pleasure ground [Ellenborough Park]'. The court at first instance held that a valid legal easement had been created for the benefit of all purchasing plot owners and on appeal the judgment of Mr Justice Danckwerts was upheld. In making his judgment, Lord Evershed, Master of the Rolls, stated that, for a right to be capable of being an easement:

1. There must be a **dominant** and a **servient tenement**;
2. The dominant and servient properties must be in separate ownership or occupation;
3. The right must accommodate the dominant tenement; and
4. The right must be capable of forming the subject matter of a grant.

The language used is fairly archaic but it can be explained quite simply.

Dominant and servient tenement

First of all, 'there must be a dominant and a servient tenement'. In plain English, this means that there must be two parcels of land, one which is benefited by the easement (the dominant tenement) and one which carries the burden of it (the servient tenement). In the case of a right of way, this would mean that the dominant land would be the land with the benefit of the right to use the access across its neighbour's land, and the servient land would be the land which had the right of way across it.

Diversity of ownership or occupation

The second requirement, that the dominant and servient properties must be in separate ownership or occupation, is self-explanatory. It is logical to say that you cannot have a right of use over your own land. Therefore the dominant and servient owners or occupiers must be different people. It follows from this that if the dominant and servient tenements are occupied by the same person, the easement is suspended, but if the **freehold** of both parcels of land are acquired by the same person, any pre-existing easement is extinguished altogether (although this is not to say that it cannot then become a 'quasi-easement', being effectively reinstated at such time as the land is again given over to separate ownership. For further explanation of this see the rule in *Wheeldon* v. *Burrows*, below).

Accommodation of the dominant tenement

The third requirement, that the right must accommodate the dominant tenement, refers to the nature of the benefit conferred on the land. It is fundamental to the nature of an easement that the right of use conveyed is not just for the benefit of the person who has the initial benefit of that easement, but that it is for the genuine use and enjoyment of the land itself. The general rule of thumb is to look at whether the right makes a genuine improvement to the benefited land, or in some way adds convenience to its use. Take the example of Leo and Sadie. If Leo gives Sadie the right to use his field to exercise her horse, we can see that Leo is giving Sadie a purely personal benefit and not a genuine benefit to the land. Future landowners may not have a horse they want to exercise and, what is more, Leo may not wish them to use his land for this purpose. In reality, what Leo is more likely to have given Sadie is a personal licence for the use of the land, and not a formal right of user. To illustrate the point with case law, we can look at two contrasting cases. The first is that of *Hill* v. *Tupper* (1863) 2 H&C 121. In this case a company leased land adjoining a canal to Mr Hill, giving him the sole and exclusive right to let out pleasure boats on it. Mr Tupper, a local inn-keeper, then rented out his own boats on the canal for his clients to use for fishing. Mr Hill tried to sue Mr Tupper on the basis that Tupper was interfering with Hill's property rights, but his claim failed. The court held that Mr Hill's rights in the land could not form an easement because they did nothing more than confer a personal advantage on him and his business. His right to let out pleasure boats on the canal provided no genuine accommodation to the land leased.

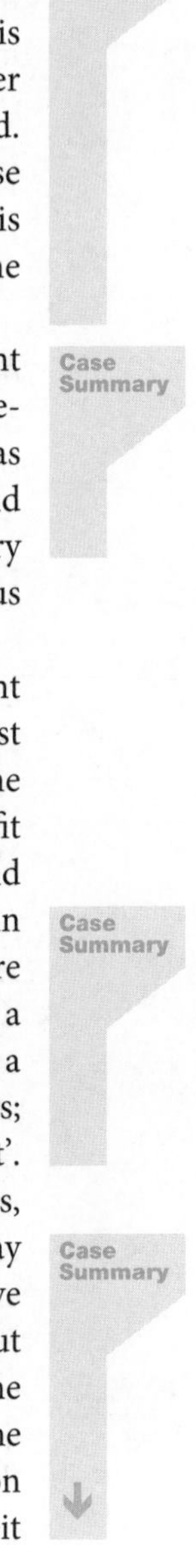

In contrast to this is the case of *Moody* v. *Steggles* (1879) 122 ChD 261. Here, a right to hang a sign on neighbouring land which pointed to a pub was held to be a valid easement. This is perhaps a surprising decision. The reasoning given for the judgment was that the business would remain on the land for a long time and therefore the land and business were inextricably linked. However, there is an argument to say that not every possible future owner of the land would consider the right to hang signage advantageous to it.

One further point to make about the need for the right to accommodate the dominant tenement is that, from a practical viewpoint, the benefited and burdened land must be sufficiently close geographically for the right to convey a genuine benefit on the dominant land. If the land benefited is too far away, the suggestion is that the benefit is personal to the landowner, and not to the land. This was dealt with famously and succinctly by Mr Justice Byles in the case of *Bailey* v. *Stephens* (1862) 12 CB (NS) 91, in which he commented about a ***profit à prendre*** affecting land, that 'there is really no more connection here, than if the owner of an estate in Northumberland were to grant a right of way to the owner of another estate in Kent'. He went on to say that a right of a personal nature could not be connected to the land merely by the design of the parties; it would have to have 'some natural connection with the estate, as being for its benefit'. That is not to say that the benefited and burdened land must be immediate neighbours, however. In the case of *Pugh* v. *Savage* [1970] 2 QB 373, a farmer's claim to a right of way over a field not immediately adjacent to the rest of his farm was held nevertheless to have created an easement, the field subject to the purported right of way being next door but one to the dominant landowner's property. This had been an unusual case in which the farmer's land was divided with another farmer's property in between. The two parts of the farm could be reached, in part, via a public highway, but to access the field in question from the road necessitated the farmer crossing the neighbouring farmer's land, albeit

not immediately adjacent to the rest of the farm. The right of way connecting the two was nevertheless held by the court to confer a genuine benefit on the farm as a whole.

The right must be capable of forming the subject matter of a grant

The final requirement of *Re Ellenborough Park* is that the right must be capable of 'forming the subject matter of a grant'. This stems from the judicial fiction that an easement can only be created by **deed** (traditionally, a 'deed of grant'), although as we will see later on in the chapter there are many cases in which easements are created without the **formality** of writing, albeit that the easement is subsequently implied into the documentation. The point to be made here is that the right must *be capable* of being created by deed, and thus must be capable of reduction into writing. The prerequisite is actually a very sensible one, therefore, in that it by its nature encompasses a number of further requirements that ensure the easement is sufficiently certain in its nature to be enforceable and transmissible as a legal interest.

Capable grantor and grantee

First of all, in order for it to be capable of being created by deed, the right must have a capable **grantor** and **grantee**. So, first and foremost, the person granting the easement must have the legal **capacity** to do so. This would mean that either an individual capable of owning land or a company would be capable of granting or benefiting from an easement, but the inhabitants of a village or locality, for example, which does not have its own separate legal personality and which is constantly changing and evolving, would not.

Use of specific land

Secondly, the right must be granted for the use and benefit of a specific piece of land. Thus, general use for a number of different pieces of land or for an undefined area of land would not be capable of being an easement.

Sufficiently definite

In addition, the right must be sufficiently definite to enable it to be reduced into writing. A purported right which is too vague in nature will therefore be incapable of forming the subject matter of an easement. A right to a view would be an example of a right which would be considered too vague as in *William Aldred's case* (1610) 9 Co Rep 57b in which an action was brought against a neighbour for erecting a piggery adjacent to the **claimant**'s house. Whilst the claimant's right to receive light to the property was recognised, his right to a prospect (a view) was not, this being considered a matter 'only of delight, not of necessity'. Similarly, in the case of *Webb* v. *Bird* (1861) 10 CBNS 268 a claim to an easement of free flowing air for a windmill was rejected, on the basis that it could not be sufficiently defined. One further example consists of a claim of a **tenant** to an easement of privacy, which was rejected in the case of *Browne* v. *Flower* [1911] 1 Ch 219. Here, the **landlord** had erected an external staircase to a block of flats which passed in between the two bedroom windows of the claimant's flat. The court was clear in stating that there could be no easement of privacy, however.

Case Summary

Case Summary

Expenditure of money

An easement must not involve a cost to the burdened property. This is illustrated in the case of *Regis Property Co. Ltd* v. *Redman* [1956] 2 QB 612, in which a tenant tried to claim the benefit of an easement by the landlord to supply hot water to the tenant's property. The court, however, held that such a claim could not be an easement, because it would impose a financial burden on the landlord. Conversely, it should be noted that where there is an easement over land, whilst the owner of the burdened land is under no obligation to do any repairs or maintenance to enable the easement to be enjoyed, the benefiting landowner has the right to enter the burdened land to effect necessary repairs. This was the case in *Jones* v. *Pritchard* [1908] 1 Ch 630, which concerned an argument over who was responsible for repairs to adjoining flues between a pair of semi-detached houses. This common law right which formerly took form in an ancillary capacity to the existence of any easement has now been given some statutory weight with the Access to Neighbouring Land Act 1992. The Act allows any person to apply to the court for an order to enter neighbouring property to carry out repairs to their own land.

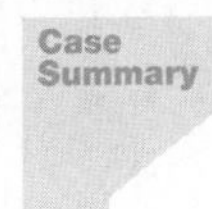

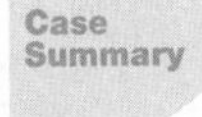

Exclusive possession

As we have already discovered above, an easement is a right of use only and thus any right which amounts to exclusive possession of the burdened property cannot be an easement. Rather, it would take effect either as a **lease** or licence (with permission) or (without permission) a trespass on the land. Rights of storage, and in particular the right to park, are consequently notoriously difficult to establish. In the case of *London & Blenheim Estates Ltd* v. *Ladbroke Retail Parks Ltd* [1992] 1 WLR 1278, it was held that the right to park a car could constitute an easement provided that the vehicles were not constantly in the same spaces and that they did not interfere with the burdened landowner's reasonable use of the land. If, however, the right had extended to a right to park a car exclusively in the same space twenty-four hours a day and seven days a week, it could not have been an easement, because this would effectively have deprived the landowner of using that part of their land on a permanent basis. It was for this reason that the claim in *Copeland* v. *Greenhalf* [1952] Ch 488 failed. Here the **defendant**, who was a wheelwright by trade, making, repairing and fitting wheels for carts and carriages, had for fifty years used a narrow strip of land by the side of the public highway, which belonged to the claimant, for the purpose of storing vehicles which were either in the process of repair or awaiting collection following such repair. He claimed the benefit of an easement over the strip of land, but his claim failed. It was held his use of the land was too extensive to constitute an easement as it, in effect, deprived the landowner of using their own land entirely. A similar verdict was reached in the more recent Court of Appeal case of *Batchelor* v. *Marlow* [2003] 1 WLR 764, in which a claim to an easement of the right to park up to six cars on a plot of land between the hours of 9.30 a.m. and 6.00 p.m., Monday to Friday, failed on the basis that the claim was too intrusive on the burdened landowner.

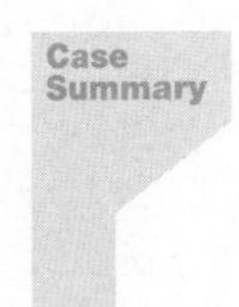

In terms of simple rights of storage, the Court of Appeal in *Grigsby* v. *Melville* [1972] 1 WLR 1355 again reached the same outcome. The case concerned a claim to the use of a cellar room underneath the floor of an adjoining property. Access to the cellar was via some stairs which led down from the benefiting owner's house. The burdened landowner had no access to the space. The benefiting landowner made a claim to an easement of storage in a cellar, but his claim was rejected, because his use of the land was

such that it amounted to an exclusive right of user over the whole of the cellar. This is in contrast to the judgment given in the earlier case of *Wright* v. *Macadam* [1949] 2 KB 744, full details of which are given later in the chapter, but which concerned a successful claim to a right to store coal on the burdened landowner's property. Mr Justice Brightman, in *Grigsby* v. *Melville*, did in fact comment on the perceived disparity between the two judgments, however, saying:

> The precise facts in *Wright* v. *Macadam* . . . in this respect are not wholly clear from the report and it is a little difficult to know whether the tenant had exclusive use of the coal shed or of any defined portion of it. To some extent a problem of this sort may be one of degree.

Similarity to existing forms of easement

Finally, in order for an easement to be capable of lying in grant it must be analogous to other forms of recognised easement. As we saw earlier in the chapter, this does not mean that no new easements can be created, only that the easement must be similar in nature to others already established by case law. You will remember that in the case of *Dyce* v. *Lady James Hay* it was stated that existing categories of easement should be allowed to 'alter and expand with changes that take place in the circumstances of mankind', thus allowing for easements of car parking to evolve more recently from the earlier established easement of storage. This is, of course, save for the exception of negative easements which, as we have seen, the courts have stated is now a closed category.

The creation of easements

Now that we have established what the essential characteristics of an easement are and how they differ from other interests in land, the next thing to do is to consider how that easement may be created. Easements can be created by way of grant or reservation either expressly or impliedly, or they may be 'presumed'.

Grants and reservations

It is important to understand the difference between the grant and the reservation of an easement because some methods of implied easement apply to grants only, and not to **reservations**. A grant is where someone gives a right over their own land to another person; a reservation is where someone sells part of their land to a third party, reserving rights over the land sold to benefit the land retained. Take the example given below in Figure 10.1.

As this figure shows, the only way to access Hazel Brow is through the garden of Hazel Dean. If Jenny sells Hazel Brow, retaining Hazel Dean, she will have to grant an easement to the purchaser to allow them to cross the garden of Hazel Dean to access Hazel Brow. However, if Jenny keeps Hazel Brow and sells Hazel Dean, she will have to retain a right to cross the garden of Hazel Dean in order for her to continue to gain access to the road after Hazel Dean has been sold.

Figure 10.1 Pictorial explanation of the grant and reservation of an easement

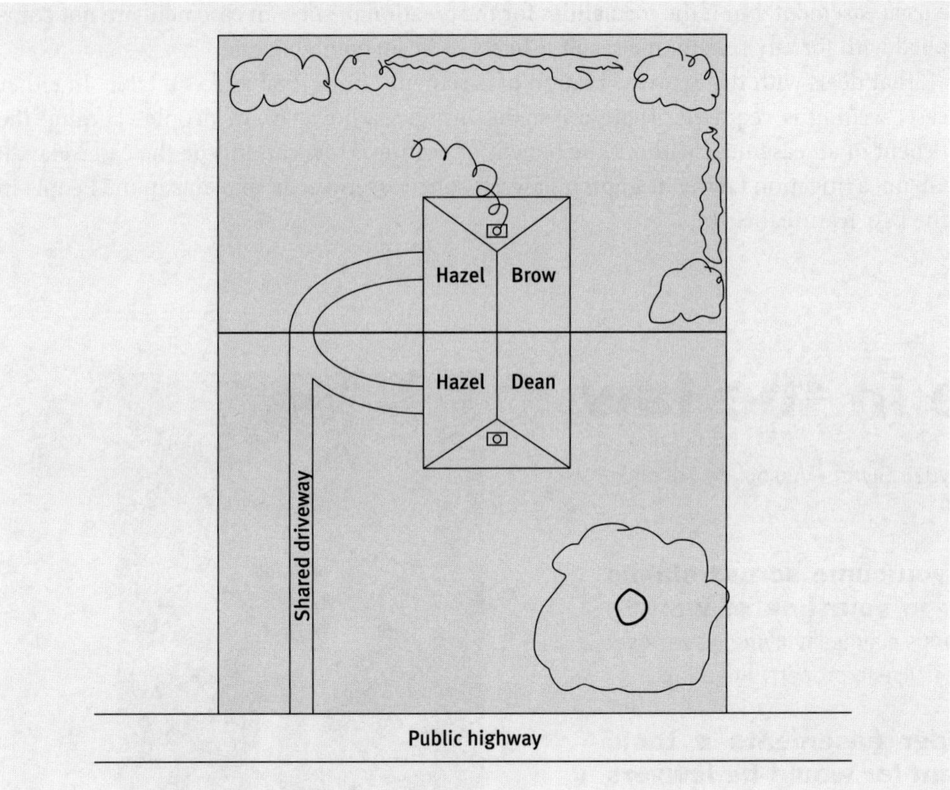

Express creation

A legal easement can be expressly created by deed. Both grants and reservations of easements can be formed in this way. This is in accordance with section 52 of the Law of Property Act 1925, which states that the creation or disposition of any estate or interest in land must be by deed.

In addition, in accordance with section 1(2) of the 1925 Act, in order for the easement to be legal, it must either be granted for a term equivalent to a freehold (that is, permanently) or for a **term of years**, meaning a specified time period, say ten years. If the easement is for any other period, for example, for life, it can exist in equity only.

Equally, if a person tries to create a legal easement by deed, but fails in some way to comply with the necessary formalities (which, you may remember from your previous reading, are that the document is clear on the face of it that it is intended to be a deed, signed, witnessed and delivered (section 1 Law of Property (Miscellaneous Provisions) Act 1989)), the easement may nevertheless take effect in equity as a contract to create an easement, in accordance with the **doctrine** of ***Walsh* v. *Lonsdale***, provided that it complies with the requirements of section 2 of the same Act which, you will remember, sets out the formalities required for the creation of a valid contract relating to land. So, in essence, a legal easement can be expressly created by deed, but if the deed fails, it may nevertheless exist in equity.

Case Navigator

Finally, in accordance with section 27(2)(d) of the Land Registration Act 2002, all new expressly granted legal easements in **registered land** must be registered at the **Land**

Registry. Until they are, they will take place in equity only and could be defeated by a purchaser of the burdened land.

So we can see that the express grant or reservation of an easement by deed will create a legal easement, but if the formalities for the creation of such an easement are not complied with for any reason, the result is likely to be an equitable one.

That deals with the express creation of easements, both legal and equitable. In either case, writing is required. There are many instances, however, of people claiming the benefit of an easement without the benefit of writing. How can this be the case? Haydn Glynn, a litigation lawyer at Lupton Fawcett solicitors in Leeds, explains in the People in the Law feature, below.

People in the law

Source: Hayden Glynn

Name and title: Hayden Glynn – Associate Solicitor, Lupton Fawcett LLB

How often do you come across claims for easements in your line of work? I come across numerous claims involving issues over easements as I specialise in property litigation.

Do you consider easements a topic that is important for would-be lawyers to learn about? I would say that it is essential that property litigators have a good understanding of the laws regarding easements.

If there is nothing in writing, on what basis is a potential claimant able to claim the benefit of a right over the land? If there is no express written grant either by way of deed, in a conveyance or transfer, then a claimant may still be able to claim the benefit of a right over land either by necessity or by prescription. If the only way of accessing a parcel of land from the public highway is over a road, track or path leading to that parcel of land then in that circumstance an easement may be created of necessity. An easement may be created by prescription if the person claiming the right has carried out an act that is capable of being an easement, openly, repeatedly and without the landowner's permission for a continuous period of 20 years.

What are the most common types of easements claimed? From my experience the most common types of easements claimed are rights of way, for example over a shared driveway, the right to lay drainage and utility cables over neighbouring land, the right to light and the right of support.

What are the difficulties encountered in proving a claimant's interest, from a practical point of view? Without an express written right, the claimant is left with the burden of having to prove the existence of the easement, the manner in which that easement has been used and over what period of time. These points are often difficult to establish, particularly when disputed.

Do these types of cases often end up in court? If not, why not and how are they resolved? The majority of cases dealing with these types of issues will settle rather than end up at court, simply because of the potential for costs to spiral disproportionately.

In your experience, how long, on average, do such matters take to be resolved and what are the expected costs? I can only say what I have found from my experience and that is that these types of cases tend to settle, but settle after a good six months plus and only generally after the appointment of an independent expert etc. I recently acted for an individual in a dispute with his neighbour over what was no more than nine inches of land and that case went on over a year and both parties spent in excess of £25k with their respective lawyers. It was a complete nonsense.

I actually hate dealing with these types of claims because I find that individuals in these circumstances lose all sense of commerciality which I suppose is why they tend to take so long to settle and are so costly.

As we can see from the interview above, then, if there is nothing in writing, one has to consider instead whether the easement may have been granted or reserved impliedly, or whether it may be presumed.

Implied grant or reservation

There are four methods through which an easement may be implied. These are:

1. necessity;
2. common intention;
3. under the rule in *Wheeldon* v. *Burrows*; and
4. under section 62 Law of Property Act 1925.

Necessity

Easements of necessity are exactly as their name suggests: the courts imply into the deed of purchase of a property an easement in favour of the land purchased on the basis that the land would be incapable of use, and therefore worthless, without it. By far the most common example of an easement of necessity being granted is where the land is completely inaccessible from the public highway without the benefit of a right of way over adjoining land. Such land is often described as being 'landlocked'. Because of the way in which an easement of necessity is engineered – by the courts implying its grant into the deed of purchase of the benefited property – implied easements of necessity will always be legal (because they are impliedly created by deed). However, the permanent burden the imposition of an easement will place upon the servient land also means that the courts are reluctant to imply an easement of necessity unless the land which has been purchased is genuinely landlocked or otherwise incapable of use without the easement. In the case of a claim to a right of way by necessity, therefore, any suggestion of another means of access to the property would defeat the claim. This was the case in *MRA Engineering Ltd* v. *Trimster Co. Ltd* (1987) 56 P&CR 1, in which the Court of Appeal held that an alternative access to the property in the form of a public footpath over neighbouring land was sufficient to prevent a claim to an easement of necessity. This was even though the public footpath did not provide the claimants with any vehicular access to the land.

implied easements of necessity will always be legal

In their strict application of this rule, the courts have been prepared to go to quite some extremes, bringing about situations in which even the most difficult or unorthodox alternative means of access to a site have prevented an easement of necessity from being granted. In the case of *Titchmarsh* v. *Royston Water Co* (1899) 64 JP 56 the court decided against a claim of necessity where the claimant had tried to make a case for an easement of necessity over a neighbour's privately owned farm track which adjoined his land. The only alternative access was a public road that did adjoin his land, but at some twenty feet below the existing level of his property. The court nevertheless said that this was an access, albeit a highly inconvenient one, and so an easement of necessity could not be implied. The claimant was left with the unenviable task of cutting his own land away so as to provide a means of access to the road twenty feet below.

Case Summary

In another exhibition of stringent adherence to the law on this point is the more recent case of *Manjang* v. *Dammeh* (1990) 61 P&CR 194. Here the Privy Council made the decision that land adjoining a river in Gambia was not landlocked and therefore ineligible for a claim to an easement of necessity because the river was a public highway and, although less convenient, was therefore a perfectly legitimate access to the property. It would appear, therefore, that even access by boat is considered a means of access for the purpose of a necessity claim.

Case Summary

All of the illustrations given above relate to claims to rights of way. It is not entirely unheard-of to have an easement of necessity of some other kind. On such example is the case of *Richard* v. *Jenkins* (1868) 18 LT 437, in which an easement of necessity in the form of a right of support was implied into the claimant's sale of the subsoil beneath his property which he had sold to a third party for the purposes of mining. However, other types of easement, even those that would be highly advantageous to the use of the land, will not be considered necessary unless not to have that right prevents the use of the property entirely. They are therefore that much more difficult to prove and therefore far more rare. In the case of *Richard* v. *Jenkins*, illustrated above, it is easy to see how the right of support was necessitated as the benefiting owner risked the collapse of his land without it. However, in the case of *Pryce* v. *McGuinness* [1966] Qd R 591 whilst Mr Justice Hanger was happy to grant an easement of necessity of a right of way over a neighbouring property as the property was landlocked, the court was quick to reject additional claims for easements for electricity and drainage over the same land because they were not 'necessary' to the use of the land.

Case Summary

Case Summary

It should also be noted that, whilst the courts will imply both grants and reservations of necessity where a property is landlocked, they are loath to imply a reservation of necessity, the judiciary taking the view that if a person sells off part of their land they should have the foresight to take any necessary steps required to secure continued access to the remaining land when they sell. The case of *Titchmarsh* v. *Royston Water Co.*, considered earlier, was a claim to an easement of necessity; and it might be said that this was one of the reasons for the harsh decision: the courts tending to disapprove reservations on principle. That is not to say that an easement of necessity will never be granted, however, and we can see this in the case of *Sweet* v. *Sommer* [2004] EWHC 1504. Here an easement of a right of way was impliedly reserved to landowners over neighbouring property that had been sold by the landowners' predecessors to a third party without reserving the necessary access. *Richard* v. *Jenkins* is another such example.

Case Summary

One final point to make about easements of necessity is that the necessity must be in existence at the time of the property is purchased, and not simply be something which arises

at a later date. *Midland Railway* v. *Miles* (1886) 33 Ch D 635 concerned a claim to an easement of necessity through underground tunnels comprising former mines which provided the only means of access across a piece of land covered in railway tracks. However, the claim to an easement of necessity was refused because, at the time of the purchase of the land, the claimant owned the mines in question. The necessity therefore only arose after the event.

Common intention

In addition to implied easements of necessity, the courts will also imply into the deed of sale the grant or reservation of an easement in situations where they think this was the intention of the genuine parties when the land was sold. An example of this is the case of *Jones* v. *Pritchard* [1908] 1 Ch 630, where shared chimneys to a pair of semi-detached houses were held to be capable of use by both parties by way of easements of common intention. Again, any such implied easement will be legal in nature and, as with easements of necessity, the law in this area is strictly applied. Whilst necessity is not a prerequisite with an easement of common intention, there is a requirement that the property was let or sold with a view to its use for a particular purpose; and it is that purpose that it must be impossible to carry out without the benefit of the easement in question. The authoritative case on the point gives a rather unusual, but nevertheless clear illustration of how this works. The case is that of *Pwllbach Colliery Co. Ltd* v. *Woodman* [1915] AC 634. The facts of the case centred around a coal mine. The neighbouring property, a slaughterhouse and sausage factory, had brought an action claiming a remedy in the tort of nuisance for coal dust polluting their property from the mine. The mining company counter-claimed the benefit of an easement to spread coal dust on the neighbouring property. As one might expect, the counter-claim was dismissed, the court stating that there could never be a case in which the courts would authorise a party to cause a nuisance. However, there is some useful dicta in the case regarding the application of the law in respect of easements of common intention, the Lord Parker of Waddington stating that such cases:

> depend . . . not upon the terms of the grant itself, but upon the circumstances under which the grant was made. The law will readily imply the grant or reservation of such easements as may be necessary to give effect to the common intention of the parties to a grant of real property, with reference to the manner or purposes in and for which the land granted or some land retained by the grantor is to be used . . . But it is essential for this purpose that the parties should intend that the subject of the grant or the land retained by the grantor should be used in some definite and particular manner. It is not enough that the subject of the grant or the land retained should be intended to be used in a manner which may or may not involve this definite and particular use.

We can see therefore that the proposed use of the property is paramount when the courts are seeking to make a decision as to whether an easement of common intention should be implied.

Because of the nature of the grant of such easements, where they are implied by the courts easements of common intention will usually be related to mutual support required between two adjoining properties or commonly shared access ways, as in *Stafford* v. *Lee* (1992) 65 P&CR 172, in which a developer, Stafford, obtained planning permission to build houses on his land, claiming right of way over his neighbour's drive for access to the road. The right of way was granted, the Court of Appeal stating that the intention of the parties when the land was sold was to be for residential purposes, and it must therefore be implied that they intended residents to have access to the road across the adjoining land.

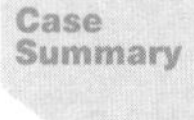

An example of a quite different situation in which an easement of common intention has been applied, however, is the case of *Wong* v. *Beaumont Property Trust Ltd* [1965] 1 QB 173. In this case a basement property was let for use as a restaurant. The tenant covenanted in the lease to eliminate cooking smells. In addition, in order to comply with public health regulations he was required to install a ventilation system to the premises. He was thus required under the terms of the lease and by law to ventilate the property in order to run it as a restaurant. The only feasible way the tenant could do this was via pre-existing ventilation ducts attached to the part of the building retained by the landlord. There was no provision for this in the lease, but the court nevertheless held that an easement of common intention could be implied into the lease. It they had not, it would not have been possible to use the premises as a restaurant, which the court said must have been the common intention of the parties when the restaurant premises were let.

Wheeldon v. *Burrows*

The third form of implied easement is that implied under the rule in *Wheeldon* v. *Burrows*. This kind of easement is implied specifically in the situation where a plot or plots of land are owned and occupied by one person and then they sell off part or parts of the land. The rule also works where the landowner sells off all of their land, parts to different people, as we shall see in our discussion of the facts of *Wheeldon* v. *Burrows* itself, later in this section. The rule works as follows:

Imagine Jacob owns a farmhouse. Access to the road is through a field in front of the farmhouse, which Jacob also owns. Figure 10.2 illustrates this.

Figure 10.2 Illustration of a quasi-easement

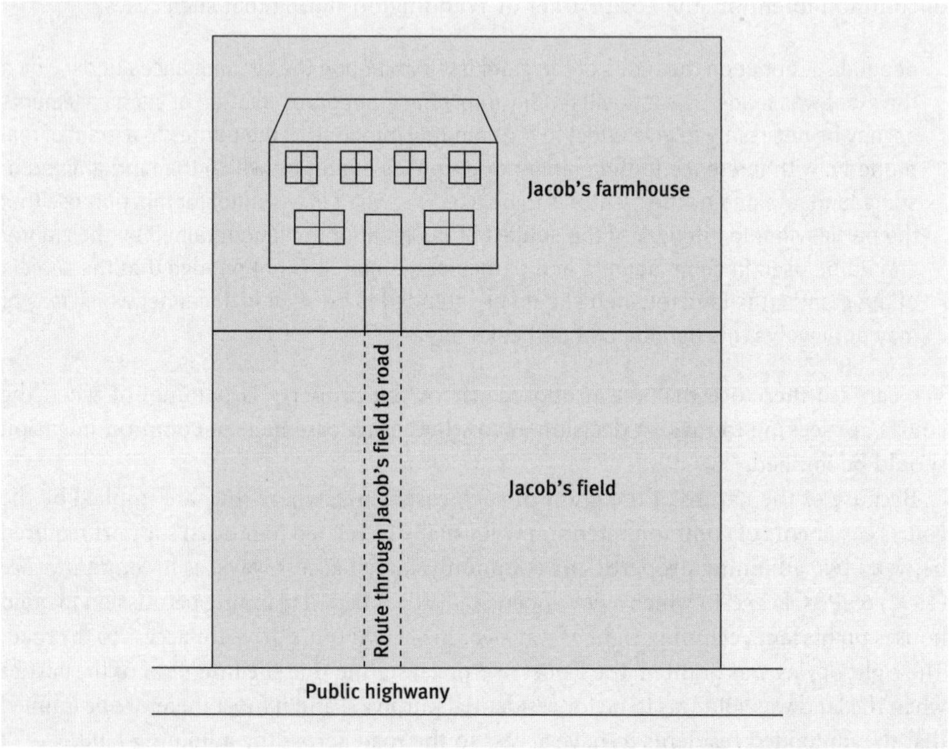

Jacob's farmhouse

Route through Jacob's field to road

Jacob's field

Public highwany

Jacob does not have an easement in the form of a right of way through the field; remember: you cannot have an easement over your own land. He is simply crossing his own property. What the access way does provide, however, is the potential to create an easement out of it at some point in the future. In legal terms, this is known as a *quasi*-easement. Some further explanation will make this clear. Imagine Jacob is now getting on a bit and is not as good on his legs as he used to be. He decides to build a bungalow in the field. Jacob then moves into the bungalow and sells the farmhouse to a younger couple. The only access to the farmhouse is through the field owned by Jacob on which he has built his bungalow. Under the rule in *Wheeldon* v. *Burrows*, Jacob is deemed to have granted a right of way through his retained field for the new owners of the farmhouse.

Case Summary

In the case of *Wheeldon* v. *Burrows* itself, the full citation for which is *Wheeldon* v. *Burrows* (1879) LR 12 Ch D 31, the landowner had sold two adjoining plots of land to separate parties. The first plot, which comprised vacant land, he sold at auction; the second plot, on which there stood a workshop, did not sell at the auction but he sold it privately shortly after the auction sale. The workshop relied upon the adjoining piece of land as a source of light to its windows, but the landowner had not thought to reserve a right to light in favour of the workshop over the vacant land when he put the two properties up for sale. As a consequence, when the new owner of the vacant land proposed to develop it in a way that would interfere with the passage of light to the workshop owner's windows, the workshop owner applied to the court for a declaration that he had an easement of a right to light from the adjoining land. The court made the following findings:

1. On a sale of part of land there will pass to the buyer all those continuous and apparent easements over the retained land that are necessary for the enjoyment of the part sold and which have been used up until the time of sale;
2. As a general rule there is no corresponding implication in favour of the seller, save where the same arises through necessity.

Unfortunately for the workshop owner the second part of the rule meant that his claim to an easement of light failed. The landowner should have reserved any rights needed for the workshop, including an easement of light, when he sold the initial plot. Because he had not, when the second plot of land comprising the workshop was sold off, the court was unwilling to imply a reservation into the first deed of sale. The buyer of the piece of land could therefore build so as to obstruct the workshop windows.

What the outcome in this case tells us is that there can be no reservation of an easement implied under the rule in *Wheeldon* v. *Burrows*. Going back to our example of Jacob, this means that if Jacob were to remain in the farmhouse and sell the bungalow, the courts would not grant him an implied reservation of a right of way over the field. This is because the courts consider that the seller of the land should have had the foresight to reserve any rights required by them at the time of the sale. In other words, the courts will not step in to save a seller from their own stupidity: they should have thought to do it at the time.

Going back now to the rules as set out in *Wheeldon* v. *Burrows*, we can see that in addition to the general requirements there are three further prerequisites that must be met before an easement under the rule will be implied. These are:

1. the right must be 'continuous and apparent';
2. the right must be necessary for the reasonable enjoyment of the land sold;
3. the right must be in use both previously and at the time of the sale for the benefit of the part of the land sold.

Continuous and apparent

That the right must be continuous indicates that it must have been uninterrupted for a number of years, rather than continuous in the literal sense. The reference to the right being apparent suggests that it must be clear upon inspection of the property that the right exists: for example in the case of a right of way by the existence of a path or road through the property. This was the case in *Hansford* v. *Jago* [1921] 1 Ch 322, which concerned a claim to a right of way to the rear of four adjoining cottages which had been sold into different ownership over a period of time.

A good illustration of the need for the right to be continuous and apparent can be seen in the case of *Suffield* v. *Brown* (1864) 46 ER 888. The case concerned the sale of a dock and adjoining land to separate parties at auction. The claimant, who had bought the dock, asserted an easement of the right for the bowsprits (which are the large sail poles that stick out from the bow of a ship) of ships coming into dock for repair to protrude over land adjoining the dock itself for the duration of the repair. If granted, this would have, in effect, prevented the purchaser who had bought the adjoining land at the auction from building on it altogether. The court rejected the claimant's case on the basis that the land adjacent from the dock would be unusable if the easement were to be granted, and that this would be a **derogation from grant** on the part of the seller. However, the court also commented that the easement claimed by the claimant could not be implied in any event, because it was neither continuous nor apparent. The court went on to say that continuous in this context meant something the use of which is constant and uninterrupted, which this was not. The right was equally not apparent, there being no sign of its existence except when a ship was actually in the dock with her bowsprit projecting over the land.

Reasonably necessary

This is a lesser test than that required for easements of necessity. In essence, an easement will be considered reasonably necessary if it enhances the enjoyment of the land. In *Wheeler* v. *JJ Saunders Ltd* [1995] 2 All ER 697 the claimants bought a farmhouse and the defendants an adjacent pig farm, both from a common seller. The claimants covenanted to erect and maintain a fence along the boundary between the farmhouse and the farm. One of the two means of access to the farmhouse was across the pig farm. This access had been used when the property was in common ownership. The defendants blocked the access. The court found that the claimants had not acquired an easement under the rule in *Wheeldon* v. *Burrows* because the access was 'not necessary' although there was evidence that the access was used before the sale. This was despite the **dissenting judgment** of Lord Justice Gibson, and the trial judge's consideration that it was the main entrance to the farm and that the use was clearly both continuous and apparent. It would thus appear that the reasonable enjoyment test is whether there could be reasonable enjoyment of the land without the quasi-easement, not whether the benefit of the easement promoted the reasonable enjoyment of it *per se*.

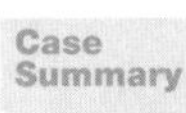

Use at the time of sale

This means that the right must have still been in use at the date of the transfer. An old abandoned track that has not been used for years would therefore not suffice under this rule. We can therefore see that in the case of *Re St Clement's, Leigh-on-Sea* [1988] 1 WLR 720 a claim to an easement of way from a former rectory across a churchyard failed under the rule in *Wheeldon* v. *Burrows* because the rectory had been vacated long before the

conveyance to the claimant's predecessor in title, and the access across the churchyard was therefore not at the time of sale being used for the benefit of the rectory.

So, just to recap, the rule in *Wheeldon* v. *Burrows* gives the courts the authority to imply into the deed of sale and purchase of part of land a grant of an easement (but not a reservation) where a quasi-easement has previously existed. This is provided that the use is continuous and apparent, reasonably necessary for the enjoyment of the land and has continued to be used up until the date of sale of the land.

One final note to make on the subject of implied easements under *Wheeldon* v. *Burrows* is that unlike easements of necessity and common intention, the court may imply either a legal or an equitable easement under this rule. If the estate transferred by the seller with the quasi-easement is the legal estate to the benefited property, then the easement implied will be legal; alternatively if the estate transferred is equitable, the easement will also be equitable, the implied easement assuming the same status as the estate transferred to which it relates. Let us now move on to the last form of implied easement, which is that implied under statute.

Section 62 Law of Property Act 1925

The final type of easement which can be implied by the courts is that implied under statute, in accordance with section 62 of the Law of Property Act 1925. You may remember in Chapter 2 when we were considering fixtures and chattels that section 62 lists all those things that will be automatically included in a sale of a legal estate in land. A reminder of the wording of the section may be helpful:

> s.62(1) A conveyance of land shall be deemed to include and shall by virtue of this Act operate to convey, with the land, all buildings, erections, fixtures, commons, hedges, ditches, fences, ways, waters, watercourses, liberties, privileges, easements, rights and advantages whatsoever, appertaining or reputed to appertain to the land or any part thereof, or, at the time of the conveyance, demised, occupied or enjoyed with, or reputed or known as part or parcel of or appurtenant to the land or any part thereof.

If we look again at section 62 we can see that it also states that privileges, easements, rights and advantages pass with the conveyance. And this is how section 62 may be used to imply the existence of an easement into the deed of sale of a property. It should be noted that, because of the method of implication, easements of this nature can only be legal in nature.

Whereas the rule in *Wheeldon* v. *Burrows* deals with the conversion of quasi-easements into easements, section 62 has the effect of upgrading a licence granted by the owner of the land to a tenant to an easement, when the land occupied by the tenant is subsequently sold to them or on the renewal of their lease.

> Section 62 has the effect of upgrading a licence to an easement

To explain further, imagine Jacob (from our earlier example) builds his bungalow but then decides he is too attached to the farmhouse to sell it quite yet. So he lets the bungalow to Mariel on an **assured shorthold tenancy** agreement for six months. The bungalow does not have any garaging, so Jacob allows Mariel to park her car in the courtyard in front of the farmhouse. The arrangement works well, so when the lease is up for renewal, Jacob agrees to let to Mariel for a longer, five-year period. He grants the lease, making no mention of the car parking arrangements. Following Mariel's recent purchase of an old rusty camper van, which she is parking in Jacob's courtyard, Jacob tells Mariel he no longer wishes Mariel to park her vehicle in front of his house, as he considers it an eyesore. Mariel, however, is able to claim an easement of parking under section 62, following the renewal of the lease. This easement will only last as long as her lease (that is, five years). However, during this time, Jacob will be powerless to stop her from exercising her right. Had Jacob sold Mariel the freehold of the bungalow, this right would have become permanent, in line with the extent of her estate in the property.

Case Summary

The facts of the case of *International Tea Stores* v. *Hobbs* [1903] 2 Ch 165 are similar to our example. Here, a landlord gave permission to a tenant of a property forming part of the landlord's premises to use an access across the yard for business purposes. The tenant subsequently bought the freehold in the property and so acquired an easement in the form of a right of way over the yard.

The seminal case in this area, however, is that of *Wright* v. *Macadam*. Again, the case involves a right of storage. A tenant was allowed to use a coal shed situated on the landlord's premises. The lease was later renewed and no mention was made of the use of the coal shed. Afterwards, the landlord tried to claim extra rent for the use of the shed. The Court of Appeal held that the renewal of the lease had been a conveyance under section 62 and that the licence had therefore become an easement of storage. The landlord could therefore neither stop the tenant from using the shed, nor charge her extra rent for the duration of the lease.

Implied easements under section 62 are therefore quite different from those implied under the rule in *Wheeldon* v. *Burrows*. Whereas *Wheeldon* v. *Burrows* requires land in the same ownership and occupation to be sold off, section 62 requires separate occupation, in the form of a lease of property, followed by a sale or lease renewal.

It should be noted that the effect of section 62 can be excluded from a sale of land by specifically excluding its provisions in writing in the contract for sale of the property. As with the rule in *Wheeldon* v. *Burrows*, you cannot have an implied reservation under section 62.

Table 10.1 provides a summary of implied easements and their application.

Table 10.1 Implied easements and their application

Type of easement	Creation	Grant or reservation	Legal or equitable
Necessity	Will only be implied where the land cannot otherwise be used (e.g. if landlocked).	Either	Legal
Common intention	Implied where the proposed use of the benefited land would not be possible without the easement. Assumes the parties must have intended the use at the time of sale.	Either	Legal
Wheeldon v. *Burrows*	Transforms quasi-easements into easements where the seller retains the burdened land.	Grant only	Either
s.62 LPA 1925	Upgrades a licence to an easement where tenanted land is sold, or the lease renewed.	Grant only	Legal

Presumed grant

If the easement has neither been created expressly, nor implied by one of the four methods detailed above, it may nevertheless be established through the benefited landowner's continued use of the easement over a long period of time. This form of acquiring an easement is known as '**presumed grant**'. It is called this because, through the benefited landowner's long user of the land, the legal assumption is made that the land has always been used in this way, in the face of evidence to the contrary. The method of acquiring land by presumed grant is commonly referred to as '**prescription**'. The formation of prescriptive rights is ancient in origin and complex in its application and could easily be the subject of a stand-alone text. It is not therefore proposed to deal with prescription in minute detail in this chapter. However, the following should give you a good basic understanding of the mechanics of presumed grant, which you can build upon through further more directed reading, should you wish to.

The three essential requirements of prescription

In order to claim the benefit of an easement by prescription, the claimant must in every case be able to satisfy three essential prerequisites. These are:

- The claimed easement must be over freehold land – prescription does not apply to rights as between landlord and tenant, or between tenants;
- There must have been at least 20 years' uninterrupted use of the burdened land by the claimant in order to claim an easement by prescription;
- The use claimed must be 'as of right'.

The freehold nature of prescriptive easements

This is significant because it means that all easements acquired by prescription, regardless of the method claimed, will be legal in nature and not equitable. This is logical when you consider the nature of prescription and the fact that it is based on the presumption that the easement was once expressly granted by a deed that has now been lost.

Uninterrupted use

The requirement for uninterrupted use means that use of the burdened land must have been continuous and regular. Sporadic use of the burdened land in a particular way would therefore not be sufficient to claim a prescriptive right over it. This is neatly illustrated by the case of *Hollins* v. *Verney* (1884) 13 QBD 304, in which a purported right of way that was used only three times over a period of 35 years was not considered sufficiently uninterrupted to acquire formal rights over the land.

Case Summary

One point that is interesting here is that, whilst the use must have been uninterrupted, there is no requirement that the use was all by the same person. If the land changed hands during the 20-year period, therefore, this will not prevent the current landowner from making a claim. If you think about it, this fits in with the premise that an easement is a right benefiting the land itself, and not the landowner.

User as of right

This prerequisite is captured in the Latin **maxim**: *nec clam, nec vi, nec precario*, which means 'without permission, without secrecy and without force'. Generally speaking, if the claimant can prove that they have been using the land for the required 20-year period without permission, secrecy or force, this will be sufficient to prove that such user has been as of right, and thus that a grant of an easement through long use can be presumed.

Secrecy

Case Summary

If the use of the land is as of right, then there will be no need for the claimant to be secretive about their use of it. A claim to an easement under the rules of prescription therefore dictates that the use of the land has not been hidden from the burdened landowner. The courts are quite strict about the application of this particular point, as can be seen in the case of *Barney* v. *BP Truckstops Ltd* [1995] CLY 1854. Here, the defendant's claim to a prescriptive easement of drainage failed because the use, whilst it had not been surreptitious, was nevertheless unknown to and unsuspected by the burdened landowner. User as of right in this context, therefore, must clearly go beyond a ban on clandestine usage of the property of others; the use of the land must be open and in full view of the burdened landowner.

Force

Again, if the use of the land is as of right then there will not be any need for the benefiting landowner to exert force or threats in order to use it; nor will it be necessary to use the land in the face of objections by the burdened landowner. Essentially, what is required of the burdened landowner, then, is acquiescence to the use claimed. This was confirmed in the case of *Dalton* v. *Angus & Co.* (1881) 6 App Cas 740, in which an easement of support for a building neighbouring the claimant's property was granted, because the building had been supported by the neighbouring property without objection of the neighbouring landowner for a period of over 20 years.

Permission

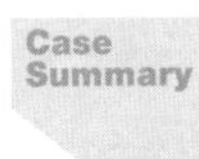

Put simply, if the use is with the burdened landowner's permission, it cannot be use 'as of right': a person using a property as of right would not need to ask the landowner's permission to do so. On this basis, a prescriptive claim of the right to park a van on burdened land failed in the case of *Green* v. *Ashco Horticultural Ltd* [1966] 1 WLR 889. Evidence given in the case showed that the claimant had always moved the van when asked to do so by the burdened landowner. The court found, therefore, that he had only been exercising his right so far as the burdened landowner permitted and therefore that the use could not be as of right (*nec precario*).

Once the necessary prerequisites have been established, the acquisition of prescriptive rights can be divided into three separate categories. These are:

1. Common law prescription;
2. The doctrine of lost modern grant; and
3. Under the provisions of the Prescription Act 1832.

Common law prescription

The common law will presume that an easement has been granted over the land if it has been enjoyed since 'time immemorial'. The commencement of time immemorial, which is seen as being the commencement of legal memory, has been set in statute, by the first statute of Westminster in 1275, at the date of Richard the Lionheart's accession to the throne of England in 1189. It is not necessary to give proof of the easement having been used for the whole of this period, of course; if it can be shown that the use has lasted for an uninterrupted period of at least twenty years it will be presumed that that use commenced in 1189.

The problem with common law prescription is that it will be defeated if it can be shown that, at any time since 1189, the right could not have existed. So, for example, an easement claimed for the benefit of a building erected after 1189 would automatically fail. Equally, a claim would fail if it could be shown that at some point in the past the benefited and burdened land was in common ownership. Because of the huge window of opportunity given to a burdened landowner in which they can prove that the claimed easement has not existed since time immemorial, it is altogether too easy to defeat a claim of common law prescription, particularly in relation to modern easements (take, for example, the right to park a car), so it is of little practical use. In order to counter this, therefore, the courts introduced the legal fiction of the 'lost modern grant'.

Lost modern grant

The doctrine of '**lost modern grant**' did much to circumvent the difficulties which can arise under common law prescription. The idea behind the doctrine is that, if the claimant can prove that there has been continuous use of the claimed easement for any single period of twenty years or more during the lifetime of the easement, there will be a judicial presumption that at one stage an easement was validly granted by deed, but that the documentation, and hence the proof of the grant, has since been lost. The doctrine of lost modern grant is thus in its own way equally as strange as common law prescription in its concept and application. As the doctrine is a fiction the court will not admit evidence from the burdened landowner that shows that there never was a grant in the first place; as long as 20 years' uninterrupted use can be proven, this will be sufficient for the easement to be presumed. This was the case in *Tehidy Minerals* v. *Norman* [1971] 2 QB 528, in which land had been requisitioned by the Ministry of Defence.

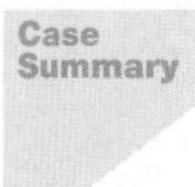

It should be noted that the rules of common law prescription must first be tested before the doctrine of lost modern grant will be applied. The report of the 1909 Court of Appeal case of *Hulbert* v. *Dale* [1909] 2 Ch 570 illustrates well how this works. In considering the case at first instance, Mr Justice Joyce said:

> There was a considerable conflict of evidence in the case, but, upon the whole, the result to my mind is that I come to the conclusion, and find as a fact, that for a period as far back as living memory extends the owners and occupiers for the time being of Fishmore Farm have openly and without interruption had an unquestioned user until quite recently, when the dispute arose, of the now disputed road . . .
>
> I should have held such user to have been as of right . . . but for the circumstance that during the period between the years 1889 and 1905 there was unity of possession (not of ownership) of the two farms, Fishmore and Crown Farms, both being in the occupation of the same tenant or tenants. This being so, the defendant could not make good any claim to a right of way along the disputed road by prescription under the second section of the Prescription Act [1832].
>
> Nor could he, I think, have succeeded upon a claim by prescription at common law, because I consider it to be tolerably plain, for various reasons, that the existence of the right of way claimed, if it does exist, originated and commenced at a date long subsequent to the reign of King Richard I – in fact very little more than one hundred years ago.

> The defendant, therefore, has to base his claim upon the existence of a grant not produced, and he contends that it is a case for presuming a grant, now lost, of the right to use the disputed road.

Prescription Act 1832

The Prescription Act 1832 was passed in order to address some of the difficulties arising under the common law rules. However, whilst it should have consolidated the law, what it in fact did was to add yet another alternative method of acquisition by prescription, this time statutory, to the already complicated system which existed. Thus there are now three different methods of prescriptive acquisition of an easement to choose from when such a matter is being argued in court, as can be seen from the case excerpt above.

To make matters worse, the Act itself is not simple to apply. Under section 2 of the Act, there is not one, but two periods of continuous user set out: one of twenty years and one of forty years. The claimant can choose which of the periods of use apply to their case and make their claim accordingly. The rules of application differ, depending upon which period of user is chosen.

If a period of twenty years' continuous user can be established, an easement will be presumed, provided that:

1. the user is of right (as detailed above);
2. the owner of the burdened land is not an infant, mental patient or tenant for life. If there are periods of user where this has been the case, these periods will be excluded, although the periods before and after such ownership may be added together; and
3. there has been no interruption for a year or more.

If a period of forty years' continuous user can be established, on the other hand, an easement will be assumed, provided that:

1. the user is as of right. This is given a different application from the user set out in cases of prescription by 20 years' use, however, as only *written* consent will defeat user as of right where the use has been continuous for forty years;
2. the burdened land is not held by a tenant for life or tenant for a term exceeding three years, in which case that term will be excluded provided the claim is resisted by the freehold owner within three years from the end of the term.
3. there has been no interruption for a year or more.

The Law Commission in its recent report entitled 'Making Land Work: Easements, Covenants and Profits à Prendre' proposes the replacement of the three existing methods of prescription with a single, statutory scheme. The key elements of use for 20 years, without force, stealth or permission would remain. The report and draft Bill, which was published in June 2011, is, at the time of writing, yet to be implemented.

Easements of light

The Prescription Act 1832 also deals with easements of light, albeit under a separate section of the Act (section 3). There is no 40-year period applicable to the acquisition of rights to light; only a 20-year period of continuous user need be proved. However, once 20-years' continuous use can be shown, the only way this can be defeated is by evidence of express written consent to the right. This is akin to the rule relating to other easements proven over a 40-year period.

It should be noted that, unlike other forms of easement, a tenant may acquire a right to light which burdens either his landlord's own property or the property of another tenant. Any right obtained, however, is deemed to be for the respective benefit and burden of the freehold estates affected by the right.

Light obstruction and the Rights of Light Act 1959

As with the other methods of statutory acquisition, if the use of the right to light is interrupted for a period of one year or more, then the continuous user will be deemed to have ceased. To disrupt the flow of light to the benefited property, therefore, and prevent such an easement from being acquired, it became common practice for burdened landowners to simply erect a wall or hoarding blocking the passage of light to the benefited land, leave it standing for a year to form the required period of interruption and then take it down again after the one year period had elapsed. To prevent this from happening, the Rights of Light Act 1959 was enacted. This allows a person with a claim to a right to light over property to register as a local land charge a '**light obstruction notice**', should the light to their property be obstructed in this way. The notice will be effective for a period of one year in preventing the continuous user from being interrupted, provided the notice is backed by a certificate from the **Lands Chamber** that notice has been given to all relevant parties.

How a right to light is quantified

Case Summary

As one might imagine, rights to light are notoriously difficult to quantify. How do you know exactly how much light the owner of the benefited land is entitled to, in order to protect that right? The general rule is that the benefited landowner is entitled to as much light as is necessary for the ordinary use and enjoyment of the premises. This is a positive and not a negative test. Therefore, in order to determine whether a right to light has been breached, the court will look, not at how much light to the premises is being obstructed, but rather at the amount of light that is still being allowed to reach it. In the House of Lords case of *Colls* v. *Home and Colonial Stores Ltd* [1904] AC 179 the claimant had sought an **injunction** against the owner of land across the street from their business premises in Shoreditch, London, on the basis that the landowner's proposed building plans would interfere with the business owner's right to light. Reversing the Court of Appeal decision to grant an injunction preventing the building works, the Lords held that to constitute an actionable obstruction of a right to light it is not enough that the light is less than before:

> There must be a substantial privation of light, enough to render the occupation of the house uncomfortable according to the ordinary notions of mankind and (in the case of business premises) to prevent the plaintiff from carrying on his business as beneficially as before.

No such obstruction was found in the case.

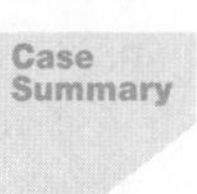

At one stage the courts adopted more specific objective tests based on arithmetical calculations in order to determine the amount of light left in such cases, but these tests have since been disapproved. In *Carr-Saunders* v. *Dick McNeil Associates Ltd* [1986] 1 WLR 922 the court said, following *Colls* v. *Home and Colonial Stores* that the landowner with the benefit of the right is entitled to such light 'as will leave his premises adequately lit for all ordinary purposes for which they may reasonably be expected to be used'. Nonetheless, when building a case where there is a dispute between the parties as to whether or not a right to light has been breached it is still customary for solicitors to employ a specialist surveyor to calculate the amount of light that has or will be lost to the premises in question. Elizabeth de Burgh Sidley from property consultancy, Carters Jonas, explains the process in the People in the Law Feature.

People in the law

Name and job description/area of expertise: Elizabeth de Burgh Sidley, property consultancy, Carters Jonas

Source: Elizabeth de Burgh Sidley

What do you see as your role in resolving right to light disputes? My role as a surveyor is to assess the technical effect of loss of light to a property and then to agree with the clients a strategy as to how they want to pursue the matter by either (a) approaching all affected parties with a view to reaching a settlement or (b) by taking out insurance or (c) taking a risk and making no contact.

Briefly, how do you calculate the amount of light left in a building after a proposed or actual development? We undertake a survey of the existing building plus all relevant adjoining buildings and then use specialist software to find how light penetrates at 850 mm above floor level at every floor in every adjoining building, first with the existing building in place and then with the proposed new development in place. The specialist software can calculate the percentage of a room lit in the existing situation and then the percentage of a room lit after the new building is built.

Was the use of arithmetical calculations not disapproved by the House of Lords in *Carr-Saunders* v. *Dick McNeil Associates Limited*? If so, why is it still customary to use these? Noted, but rights of light advisers are there to assist judges make a decision on whether or not an injunction should be given and the only way is by a technical analysis.

What the case did was highlight that any owner/occupier of an adjoining building is able to lay out the floorspace in any reasonable fashion. However, ultimately it is the penetration of light through the windows which is critical. The position will remain the same generally regardless of the layout and it is for the judge to decide whether there is adequate light taking into account all the circumstances of the case.

In your experience, what will usually happen if there is a genuine obstruction to light in a building? In the case of commercial/industrial buildings it is likely that the adjoining owners will accept the loss of light and a fair amount of compensation will be agreed. In the case of residential properties it would be normal for most adjoining owners to settle for compensation, albeit in some cases a significant sum. In fact in commercial, industrial and residential situations it is rare to find adjoining owners who demand to retain their light.

Do you think there is a move by the courts towards making demolition orders over damages for loss of light? Clearly the *Heaney** case has highlighted what the law is and the law has not changed. Basically if a loss of light is a nuisance then the first remedy is an injunction. The *Heaney* case reminded all developers of this and the likelihood that there could be a **demolition order** even after a building was completed and let.

Is there anything else you would like to add? There is real difficulty with the issue of rights of light affecting development. We have a small country with great demand for space such that developments are getting larger, and particularly so in any tight city environment. Inevitably there will be loss of light and the risk is that, if more adjoining owners do demand to keep their light, then there could be a curtailment of development with a knock-on effect on the construction industry.

* *HKRUK II (CHC) Ltd* v. *Heaney* [2010] EWHC 2245 (Ch), in which an injuction, rather than damages, was held by the court to be the appropriate remedy where the claimant had interferred with the access of light to the defendant's building by the addition of two floors to its own building.

One additional point to make about the **dicta** in *Carr-Saunders* v. *Dick McNeil Associates* is the reference to the use of the premises claiming the benefit of the right.

The amount of light required will depend upon the ordinary use of the building; a greenhouse necessarily needing more light than a warehouse, as was found in *Allen* v. *Greenwood* [1980] Ch 119. Here, after the claimants had used a greenhouse in their garden for over 20 years as an ordinary domestic greenhouse, the defendants obstructed the light to the greenhouse with the effect that it became impossible for the claimants to grow anything in it, although there remained sufficient light to work in the building. Whilst the claimants' application for an injunction was at first instance dismissed, on appeal the court held that the measure of light which could be acquired by prescription was the light required for the use of the building for its ordinary purpose; in the case of a greenhouse this could include the right to an extraordinary amount of light and the benefits of that light, including the sun's rays.

Proprietary estoppel

We have so far seen that easements can be express, implied or presumed. One final way of an equitable easement being created is by virtue of the doctrine of **estoppel**. The courts may impose such an easement where:

- The burdened landowner had allowed the injured party to believe that they would enjoy the benefit of the easement;
- The injured party had acted to their detriment in reliance on that representation or belief (for example, by buying the property); and
- The landowner then sought to take advantage unconscionably of the injured party by denying the expected benefit.

You may remember from your earlier reading a case called *Crabb* v. *Arun District Council* [1976] Ch 179, which serves as a good illustration of how this can work. The case concerned two neighbouring landowners, Mr Crabb and Arun District Council. Mr Crabb had sold part of his land which adjoined the public highway to a third party without reserving a right of way over it, on the basis that the Council had said that they would give him a right of way over their adjoining land when his own land was sold. However, the council then reneged on their promise, demanding payment of a sum of money in return for the easement. The Court of Appeal held that Mr Crabb should be given the right of way under the doctrine of **proprietary estoppel**.

For a more detailed analysis of the workings of proprietary estoppel see Chapter 8.

The protection of easements

Now that we have considered the various ways in which easements can be created, let us take some time to explore how those easements can be protected against third party purchasers of the burdened land and how we can enforce them. As with all interests in land, how to protect the easement will depend on whether the land is registered or **unregistered**, and whether the right is legal or equitable in nature.

Registered land

As stated earlier, under section 27 of the Land Registration Act 2002 express grants or reservations of legal easements are **registrable dispositions**. They therefore must be registered by putting an entry on the **Property Register** of the land that is to benefit from the easement and a **notice** on the **Charges Register** of the property that is burdened (section 38 Land Registration Act 2002).

Documenting the law

Example of an entry in the Property Register showing the benefit of an easement.

A: Property Register

containing the description of the registered land and the estate comprised in the Title.

COUNTY	DISTRICT
WEST YORKSHIRE	BRADFORD

1. (26 January 1989) The **Freehold** land shown edged with red on the plan of the above Title filed at the Registry and being The Towers, Brow Lane, Clayton, (BD14 6PT).

   NOTE: The part tinted green on the filed plan is not included in the title.

2. The land has the benefit of the following rights reserved by a Conveyance of adjoining land dated 9 February 1978 made between (1) Harold Whitehead and Frederick Vernon Whitehead (Vendors) and (2) Norman Frederick Hebron and others (Purchasers):-

   TOGETHER WITH ....as to that part of the property firstly described comprising of field numbered 8634 on the plan and the property secondly described the purchasers and their successors in title for the time being of the said field or any part or parts thereof and their tenants servants and licensees (in common with the Vendors and all persons having the like right) a right of way at all times of the day and night as a means of access to and egress from Brow Lane to the said fields numbered 8634 and 7739 and that part of the field numbered 7328 hereby conveyed but not for any other purpose whatsoever with or without vehicles of any description and with or without animals over and along the cart track and the part of field numbered 7328 retained by the Vendors coloured green on the said plan subject to the payment of a fair proportion of the expense of maintaining and keeping such cart track and land in repair

If this is not done then the easement will be equitable.

An implied grant or reservation of an easement will be **overriding** under schedule 3, paragraph 3 of the Land Registration Act 2002, provided that:

- The person buying the land knew about the easement; or
- The easement would have been obvious from a reasonably careful inspection; or
- The easement had been used in the last year before the land was sold.

The burden of proof is on the person who has used the easement to show that it is overriding.

An equitable easement should be protected by a notice on the Charges Register of the burdened land (section 32 Land Registration Act 2002). The easement will then be binding on any purchaser of the burdened land.

Out and about

Take a look at your dream property office copies. Alternatively, ask your parents or another member of your family if you can get copies of their title documentation from the Land Registry. Are there any easements benefiting or burdening the land? If so, what are they? Are they legal or equitable in nature? How can you tell?

You should take no longer than 40 minutes on this task.

Handy tip: If you cannot find any, look at the sample office copies on the accompanying website.

Unregistered land

You may remember from your reading of Chapter 4 on interests in land that legal interests in land, including legal easements, 'bind the whole world'.

Equitable easements created after 1 January 1926 are registrable as a class D(iii) land charge at the Central Land Charges Registry in Plymouth. If registered as such, they will be binding on any buyer of the burdened land. If they are not registered, they will be void against a purchaser *for money or money's worth* of a legal estate in the land. This means that, even unregistered, an equitable easement will remain binding both against someone buying an equitable, rather than a legal, interest in the land and against a person receiving the legal estate as a gift.

Equitable easements created before 1 January 1926 are bound by the doctrine of notice and as such will be binding on anyone except a ***bone fide* purchaser for value without notice** of the legal estate in the land. For a reminder of how this works, see Chapter 4.

Writing and drafting

Now that we have considered the whole of the law relating to easements, it's time to test your understanding. Imagine you are a trainee solicitor at Staithes & Partners, Solicitors. You have received a telephone message from a client from which you understand they have a dispute over a purported right to park on their neighbour's land. Before you return your client's call, make a checklist of everything you need to know in order to form an opinion as to whether their claim is valid.

You should take no more than 30 minutes on this task.

Handy tip: Go through each of the various methods of creation of an easement and think about what information you need to tell you whether the easement might have been created in each particular way. For example, is there anything in writing, first of all?

Extinguishment of easements

Up until this point in the chapter we have been concerned primarily with the creation of easements: what they are, how they are formed, and how to protect them. What remains to be considered is how they can be brought to an end. This is particularly important to those wishing to develop burdened land, whose plans to build on the affected property could be made more difficult or even prevented, should the easement continue. A right to light benefiting neighbouring property can be equally as damning as a rogue right of way across the middle of a proposed building plot.

Agreement

So if a developer wishes to remove a right of way, for example, how can this be done? The first method, as one might imagine, would be by agreement with the benefited landowner. The landowners are free to agree between them any variation or even the cessation of the easement in question, as they see fit. All that is needed to formalise the arrangement is the execution of a deed stating that the easement is to be extinguished or varied, which must be registered at the Land Registry in order to cancel the entries on the relevant registers of title. The downside to this, of course, is that the burdened landowner is entirely at the mercy of the benefited landowner, who may require payment for the variation or extinguishment of their right, or could simply refuse it. There is nothing in this circumstance that the developer can do to force the benefited landowner from continuing to exercise their right.

Unity of seisin

The second method of extinguishment of an easement is through what is known as '**unity of seisin**'. In plain terms, this simply means that both the benefited and burdened land have come into the same ownership. As we know from our earlier reading, a person cannot have an easement over their own land; therefore if the land is either occupied or owned by the same person, the easement will cease to exist, either temporarily (in the case of joint occupation by way of a lease, for example), or permanently, in the case of a purchase of the freehold. It should be noted that this method of extinguishment of an easement is not necessarily a permanent one, however. If the land at a later date falls once more into separate hands then both under the rule in *Wheeldon* v. *Burrows* and under section 62 of the Law of Property Act 1925, the easement may be revived.

if land is either occupied or owned by the same person, the easement will cease to exist

Abandonment

A third method of extinguishment of an easement is where it can be shown by the claimant that the use of the land comprising the easement has been abandoned. However, the rule is strictly construed and simple non-user of the right is insufficient for abandonment to be declared by the **Lands Chamber**; there must be deliberate abandonment.

A good illustration of this can be seen in the contrasting cases of *Swan* v. *Sinclair* [1924] 1 Ch 254 and *Benn* v. *Hardinge* (1992) 66 P&CR 246. In the earlier case of *Swan* v. *Sinclair* a right of way that had not been used for over 50 years, and which had been blocked by fences and uneven ground, was held to have been abandoned. However, in *Benn* v. *Hardinge*, a right of way that had not been not used for a staggering 175 years was not held to have been abandoned. In making their finding in *Benn* v. *Hardinge*, the court said that, just because there were alternative access routes to the property which the landowners had favoured until a flood made use of the unused accessway necessary once more, this did not mean that the alternative access had been abandoned, nor that it could not be resurrected. The difference between the two cases appears to have been the physical obstruction of the right of way in *Swan* v. *Sinclair*, which the courts deemed to signal a deliberate abandonment.

Case Summary

This is supported by the case of *Moore* v. *Rawston* (1824) 3 B&C 322, which concerned the alleged abandonment of a right to light. Here the claimant pulled down a cottage and erected in its place a stable, which did not have any windows. Nineteen years later he wished to open up a window in the stable, but it was held that the existing easement had been abandoned.

Case Summary

Once an easement has been declared abandoned by the courts it is deemed to be permanently extinguished. However, it is interesting to note the outcome of the recent case of *Jones* v. *Cleanthi* [2006] EWCA Civ 1712, which concerned the alleged abandonment of a right to use an area in the ground floor of a block of flats for rubbish disposal. The easement had become unusable after the landlord had been required to build a wall blocking the tenant's access to that area of the building, in order to comply with fire regulations. The Court of Appeal held, however, that the easement had not been abandoned and was therefore not extinguished; rather it was only suspended until such time as fire safety regulations or a different use of the building allowed the easement to be used once more.

Case Summary

Reform

In 2008, the Law Commission published their consultation paper number 186 entitled, 'Easements, Covenants and Profits à Prendre'. The results of that consultation have now been published in the Law Commission's report number 327 entitled 'Making Land Work: Easements, Covenants and Profits à Prendre'. The report contains the Commission's final recommendations to Parliament, together with a draft Bill, entitled the 'Law of Property Bill'. There are 64 proposals in total; those relating to easements are outlined below.

Exclusive use

The existing law states that, because an easement is a right of user only, any right which goes beyond this to the extent that it gives the benefiting landowner exclusive possession of the burdened land, cannot by definition be an easement. The extent of possession that will be acceptable has always been tricky to gauge, and has become a particular source of difficulty in relation to easements of storage and, more specifically, car parking easements. The report recommends clarification of the test that defines what amounts to exclusive use, but concludes for its own part that 'an easement that stops short of exclusive possession, even if it deprives the owner of much of the use of his land, or indeed of all reasonable use of it, is valid'. The consequence of this is, if the recommendations of the report are followed, that an exclusive right to park on the land of a third party will be capable of being an easement, provided the landowner can still access the land, even when that access is severely limited. If implemented the effect of the recommendation will be to put beyond question the validity of a potentially wide range of parking easements.

Creation of an easement over land in the same ownership

Another major characteristic of an easement under the current law is that you cannot have an easement over your own land. This can give rise to major difficulties for landowners and in particular developers wishing to sell off plots of land, because easements granted by them can be subject to challenge if the plots are not sold in the right order. The Commission has therefore recommended that, provided the title to the benefited and burdened land is registered, the fact that they are in common ownership or possession will not prevent the creation or existence of easements or profits. Equally, where two registered titles came into common ownership, any easement benefiting one title and burdening the other would not be extinguished unless the common owner made a specific application to the Land Registry to do so.

It is the intention of the Commission that this recommendation would apply both to easements created before the proposal was implemented, as well as after it. However, care will have to be taken in the implementation of this reform, as it could potentially result in easements which were thought to have been extinguished under the unity of seisin being subsequently revived, which may not be what the burdened landowner intended or desired.

Implied easements

The Commission recommends replacing three of the current methods of creation of implied easements, those of necessity, common intention and the rule in *Wheeldon* v. *Burrows*, with a single statutory test. The test, which will focus on what is necessary for the reasonable use of the land, will be an objective test, taking into account:

(a) the use of the dominant and servient land at the time of the grant;

(b) the presence on the servient land of any relevant physical features;

(c) any intended future use of the dominant land known, at the time of the grant, to the grantor and grantee;

(d) so far as relevant, the routes available for the easement; and

(e) the extent to which the easement would or might interfere with the servient land or inconvenience the servient owner.

The Commission has recommended that section 62 of the Law of Property Act 1925 shall no longer operate to upgrade licences to the status of easements on the subsequent sale or lease of tenanted land.

Prescription

As with implied easements, the Commission proposes the replacement of the three existing methods of prescription with a single, statutory scheme, based on 20 years' continuous qualifying use. The key elements of use without force, stealth or permission would remain. The law relating to rights to light is not included in the proposed reforms, but will be subject to a separate consultation and review, commencing in 2013.

Presumption of abandonment for easements

In order to simplify the problems surrounding the rules relating to the abandonment of easements, the Commission has suggested that, where an easement has not been used for a continuous period of 20 years, there should be a rebuttable presumption that it has been abandoned.

Powers of the Lands Chamber

The Lands Chamber of the Upper Tribunal (previously the Lands Tribunal) currently has the power to discharge or modify covenants on certain grounds. However, the Law Commission has recommended that the jurisdiction of the Lands Chamber should be extended to enable it to modify or discharge easements as well, provided it is satisfied that the modified interest 'would not be materially less convenient to the benefited owner' nor 'more burdensome to the land affected'. The practical use of this measure in the short term is questionable, however, as the Commission has recommended that the power only apply to interests created after the date of reform. This leaves a huge swathe of easements remaining untouchable by the tribunal. It is thought that the new abandonment provisions would act as a balance to this.

the Law Commission has recommended that the jurisdiction of the Lands Chamber should be extended

As with all Law Commission recommendations, the proposals will only become law if they are brought before Parliament. There is therefore no guarantee that any of the proposed reforms will be brought to fruition, and in any event it is likely to be some time before this happens.

Summary

- An easement is a right to do something on someone else's land. As it is a right of user only, any right which amounts to exclusive possession of the burdened property cannot be an easement.
- Easements may, by their nature, be positive or negative. Because of the restrictive nature of negative easements the courts have now declined to allow any new types of negative easement to be created.
- For a right to be capable of being an easement:
  - there must be a dominant and a servient tenement;
  - the dominant and servient properties must be in separate ownership or occupation;
  - the right must accommodate the dominant tenement (i.e. it must benefit the land and be sufficiently close to confer a genuine benefit);
  - and the right must be capable of forming the subject matter of a grant. (*Re Ellenborough Park*).
- An easement may be granted or reserved to the benefiting landowner. A grant is where someone gives a right over their own land to another person; a reservation is where someone sells part of their land to a third party, reserving rights over the land sold to benefit the land retained.
- An expressly created legal easement must be made by deed. In order for the easement to be legal, it must either be granted for a term equivalent to a freehold (that is, permanently) or for a term of years, meaning a specified time period, say ten years. If the easement is for any other period, for example, for life, it can exist in equity only (s.1(2) LPA 1925).
- There are four methods through which an easement may be implied. These are: necessity; common intention; under the rule in *Wheeldon* v. *Burrows*; and under section 62 Law of Property Act 1925.
- An easement of necessity is where the court implies into the deed of purchase of a property an easement in favour of the land purchased on the basis that the land would be incapable of use, and therefore worthless, without it. Implied easements of necessity will always be legal.
- The courts will also imply into the deed of sale the grant or reservation of an easement in situations where they think this was the common intention of the parties when the land was sold. In order to apply, the property must have been let or sold with a view to use for a particular purpose that it would be impossible to carry out without the benefit of the easement in question.
- The rule in *Wheeldon* v. *Burrows* transforms quasi-easements into easements on a sale of part. In order for the rule in *Wheeldon* v. *Burrows* to apply the right must be 'continuous and apparent'; necessary for the reasonable enjoyment of the land sold; and in use both previously and at the time of the sale for the benefit of the part of the land sold. There can be no reservation of an easement implied under the rule in *Wheeldon* v. *Burrows*.
- Section 62 LPA 1925 has the effect of upgrading a licence granted by the owner of the land to a tenant to an easement, when the land occupied by the tenant is subsequently sold to them or on the renewal of their lease. As with the rule in *Wheeldon* v. *Burrows*, you cannot have an implied reservation under section 62.
- If the easement has neither been created expressly nor impliedly it may still be acquired by prescription. There are three basic requirements to prescription: the right must be over freehold land; there must have been at least 20 years' uninterrupted use and the use claimed must be 'as of right' (*nec clam, nec vi, nec precario*). Acquiring

prescriptive rights is complicated and the Law Commission has proposed reform of the law in this area.

- Easements may be brought to an end through agreement, the dominant and servient land coming into common ownership (the unity of seisin), or abandonment. Abandonment is currently difficult to establish and the Law Commission has recommended that the process be simplified.

- The Law Commission has also recommended reform of the law relating to the creation of implied easements, which they suggest should be replaced with one single statutory test. It is recommended that easements acquired under s.62 LPA 1925 should be abolished.

Question and answer*

Problem: Sanjay owned two pieces of land, a barn and paddock, depicted below.

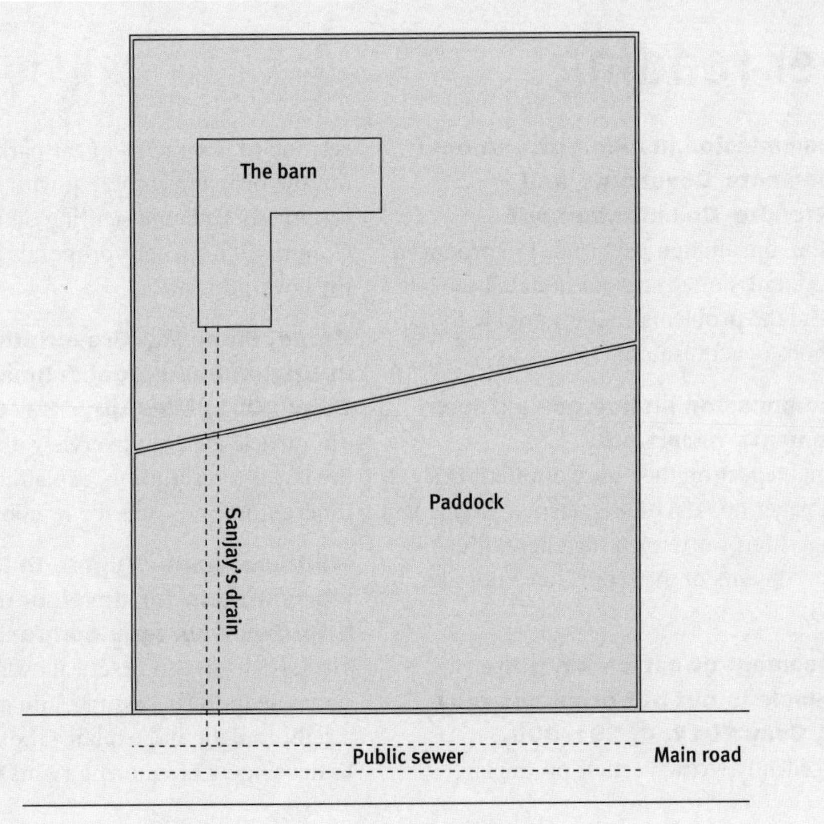

A drain runs from the barn through the paddock to the sewer in the main road.

(a) Sanjay retained the paddock but sold the barn to Petra. The conveyance to Petra made no reference to easements. Does Petra have a right to use the drain?

(b) Sanjay retained the barn but sold the paddock to Yashma. Does Sanjay retain a right to use the drain?

(c) Sanjay retained the paddock but sold the freehold to the barn to Ahmed to whom the barn has been let on a yearly tenancy for the last ten years. Sanjay now sells the paddock to Sandra. Can Ahmed enforce a right to use the drain against Sandra?

(d) Sanjay retained the barn but sold the paddock to Dean, expressly reserving the use of the drain for the benefit of the barn. Dean now sells the paddock to Yoshi. Can Sanjay enforce a right to use the drain against Yoshi?

You should allow yourself no more than 40 minutes to complete this task.

Essay: What are the difficulties with easements of car parking and how might these be resolved?

This question should be answered in 40 minutes.

* Answer guidance is provided at the end of the chapter.

Further reading

http://lawcommission.justice.gov.uk/docs/cp186_Easements_Covenants_and_Profits_a_Prendre_Consultation.pdf.
This link to the consultation paper no. 186 produced by the Law Commission seting out in detail the law as it stands and the problems encountered with the various methods of acquisition.

http://lawcommission.justice.gov.uk/docs/lc327_easements_report.pdf.
This is the final report on the Law Commission's consultation paper no. 186 on easements. The paper contains suggestions for reform together with a draft bill. The contents of the report have not yet been adopted.

Xu, Lu, 'Easement of car parking: the ouster principle is out but problems may aggravate', Conv 2012, 4, 291–306.
This is an excellently written article on the law relating to easements of car parking, setting out the problems inherent with such rights as easements and commenting on the Law Commission's recent proposals to reform the law in this area.

Burns, Fiona R., 'Prescriptive easements in England and legal "climate change"', Conv 2007, Mar/Apr, 133–47.
This article gives an overview of the development of the law of prescription, explaining the difficulties inherent in proposals for its abolition.

Waltham, Anne, 'Rights to light – a worrying tale for developers', available at: http://www.wragge.com/analysis_6183.asp.
This article gives a practical overview of the likely outcome for a successful claim against a breach of a right to light and explains the dangers and pitfalls to developers of ignoring rights to light.

Question and answer guidance

Please note that the following is not a full answer and is intended to provide guidance in outline form only as to how to answer the questions posed.

Problem: First we need to consider whether the right in question is capable of being an easement. Under *Re Ellenborough Park* (1955) there are four essential characteristics of an easement: 1. there must be a dominant and a servient tenement; 2. the tenements must be in different ownership or occupation; 3. the right must accommodate the dominant tenement; 4. the right must be capable of forming the subject matter of a grant.

The right we are discussing here is the right to use a drain which runs from the barn through the servient land and into the public sewer.

In each case: 1. the dominant tenement (benefiting) is the barn and the servient tenement (burdened) is the paddock; 2. the benefited and burdened land are in different ownership: (a) Sanjay and Petra; (b) Sanjay and Yashma; (c) Ahmed and Sandra; (d) Sanjay and Yoshi; 3. the right to use a drain can be said to provide a genuine benefit to the barn, and not just a personal benefit to the owner of it at the time; 4. the right of drainage is a recognised form of easement and capable of description.

Having established that the right is capable of being an easement, we need to look at how that easement may have been created. In each case, we must look to the documentation first to see whether an easement has been expressly created or reserved. If there has been none, we then look to see whether one can be implied.

(a) We are told in example (a) that the conveyance of the barn to Petra made no reference to easements and can therefore conclude that there has been no express grant of an easement of drainage to Petra. We therefore need to consider whether she has an implied easement. Easements can be implied in one of four ways: necessity; common intention; under the rule in *Wheeldon* v. *Burrows* and by virtue of s.62 LPA 1925. Easements of necessity only apply where the land would be useless without the right claimed, usually when the land is landlocked. Drainage, whilst useful to the barn, is not essential, and therefore an easement of necessity is unlikely to be granted. Equally, section 62 does not apply in this situation because it is a sale of part and not a lease followed by a renewal or purchase of the benefited land. This leaves common intention and the rule in *Wheeldon* v. *Burrows*. Common intention requires that it was the intention of the parties to use the property for a particular purpose when the property is sold, and without the easement the property cannot be used for that purpose. We are not told what Petra's proposed use of the property is, and whether drainage is needed for that purpose. The more likely method of implication is the rule in *Wheeldon* v. *Burrows*. This states that, if a landowner sells part of their land, over which exists a quasi-easement (in this case the right of drainage across the field), then the grant of that easement will be implied into the conveyance of the land. Petra has an implied easement under the rule in *Wheeldon* v. *Burrows*.

(b) We are not told whether there was anything express in the conveyance to Yashma, but Sanjay should have reserved a right to use the drain when he sold the paddock to her. If he did not, we need to consider methods of implication. As above, an easement of necessity is unlikely to be granted, as is an easement of common intention. This leaves *Wheeldon* v. *Burrows* and s.62. However, neither form of implied easement is available for reservations. The court will take the view that Sanjay should have reserved any rights he needed when he sold the paddock and they will not therefore be sympathetic to his claim.

(c) Again, we are not told whether there was anything express put in the conveyance to Ahmed when the barn was sold to him. Assuming not, we need to consider methods of implication. As above, easements of necessity or common intention are unlikely to be granted. This leaves *Wheeldon* v. *Burrows* and s.62. *Wheeldon* v. *Burrows* applies where the two pieces of land have been in the same ownership and occupation but one or both pieces are subsequently sold. This does not apply here as the barn and paddock have been in separate occupation (with Ahmed occupying the barn as a tenant). This leaves s.62, which has the effect of upgrading a licence granted to a tenant on a subsequent sale or lease renewal. This fits our scenario of Sanjay's sale of the barn to Ahmed, who has been letting it. We are not told whether Sanjay had given Ahmed permission to use the drain during his lease of the barn. Assuming he was, we have a likely implied easement under s.62.

Sanjay has now sold the paddock to Sandra. Whether the burden of the implied easement has passed to her will depend upon whether the land is registered or unregistered. If it is unregistered, all easements implied under s.62 are legal by nature, and legal rights bind the whole world, so Ahmed's interest will be protected. If the land is registered (and remember that registration is now compulsory on all sales of land, so it will have been subject to first registration on the sale) any implied grant of an easement will be overriding under sched.3, para.3 of the LRA 2002, provided that Sandra (as purchaser) knew about the easement; or the easement would have been obvious from a reasonably careful inspection of the paddock; or the easement had been used in the last year before the land was sold.

(d) Here we have an express reservation of the easement in favour of Sanjay. Under s.27 of the LRA 2002 express grants or reservations of legal easements are registrable dispositions. They therefore must be registered by putting an entry on the Property Register of the land that is to benefit from the easement and a notice on the Charges Register of the property that is burdened (s.38 LRA 2002). If Sanjay has not done this then the easement can take place in equity only. An equitable easement should be protected by a notice on the Charges Register of the burdened land (s.32 LRA 2002). The easement will then be binding on any purchaser of the burdened land. If Sanjay has done neither of these things Yoshi can take free of the easement and Sanjay's right to use the drain will be lost.

Essay:

The initial point to make here is that easements of car parking are an extension of the right to store, which is a well-established form of easement (*Wright* v. *Macadam* [1949]). In this respect they are nothing new and 'capable of forming the subject matter of a grant'; thus they are able to conform with the four essential characteristics of an easement as set out in *Re Ellenborough Park* (1956).

Having said this, there have always been difficulties with easements of storage because of the fact that an easement is a right of user only and not a right of possession; therefore, if the use of the land is so invasive as to prevent the landowner themselves from using their own property, the storage goes beyond that of an easement and becomes either a licence (with permission) or a trespass (without).

This is an argument which has come to the fore in particular with regard to purported rights to park. You should talk through the relevant case law on the subject, in particular the key cases of *Copeland* v. *Greenhalf* [1952], *London & Blenheim Estates* [1992] and *Batchelor* v. *Marlow* (2003), explaining why the court came to the decision they did in each case. The pivotal argument in each case seems to have been the extent of the parking right: if a car was allowed to park 24/7 in a single parking space, this effectively went beyond a right to park because it prevents the landowner from using the land. The right to park generally on a bigger plot seems to get around this problem, however.

You might mention the converse problem of permission, however, in that if a person is claiming a right to park, but then moves their car whenever asked to, they will effectively be seen to be parking with permission rather than as of right and their ability to claim the right to park by means of prescription will be lost (see *Green* v. *Ashco Horticultural Ltd* [1966]).

Having established what the difficulties with rights to park are this leaves you to discuss how these might be resolved. Guidance might be sought from the Law Commission report and draft Bill no. 327, 'Making Land Work: Easements, Covenants and Profits à Prendre'. Essentially the report is rather woolly but recommends clarification of the test that defines what amounts to exclusive use. However, it does go on to say that a right to park will still be valid even if it deprives the owner of much of the use of their land, or even all reasonable use of it 'so long as it stops short of exclusive possession'. This means that in the future an exclusive right to park on the burdened land would be capable of being an easement, provided the landowner still had access to it in some form. You should finish by drawing your own conclusions, perhaps by making comment on the Commission's findings or by making your own suggestions as to how the problem may be solved.

Visit **www.mylawchamber.co.uk** to access tools to help you develop and test your knowledge of land law.

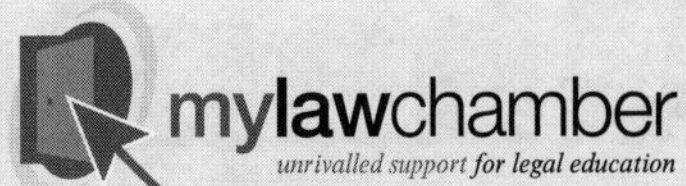

Use Case Navigator to read in full some of the key cases referenced in this chapter with commentary and questions:

Wright* v. *Macadam [1949] 2 KB 744
Wheeldon* v. *Burrows [1874–80] All ER Rep 669
Walsh* v. *Lonsdale [1881–5] All ER Rep Ext 1690

Chapter 11 Freehold covenants

Key points In this chapter we will be looking at:

- ✦ What is a covenant
- ✦ The difference between positive and negative covenants
- ✦ How covenants can be enforced as between the original parties, through privity of contract
- ✦ The inability to pass the burden of a covenant at common law and how this may be circumvented
- ✦ Indemnity covenants and the doctrine of mutual benefit and burden in *Halsall* v. *Brizell*
- ✦ The passing of the burden of a covenant in equity and the rule in *Tulk* v. *Moxhay*
- ✦ Making the benefit of the covenant pass in equity, including methods of annexation and building schemes
- ✦ How to register and protect freehold covenants
- ✦ Remedies for breach of covenant
- ✦ How covenants may be amended or discharged
- ✦ Proposals for the reform of the rules relating to covenants: 'land obligations'

Introduction

Having considered in the last chapter the topic of easements, in this chapter we are going to be thinking about another type of interest in land: the freehold covenant.

What is a covenant?

Let us start with a reminder of what a **covenant** is. A covenant is a promise made by **deed**. You may have already come across covenants in the context of **leases**: covenants by the **tenant** to pay the rent or to keep the premises in repair. The concept of **leasehold** covenants should not be confused with **freehold** covenants, however. Whereas freehold covenants are promises to do (or not to do) something on your own land, leasehold covenants are promises as to how a **landlord** and tenant will conduct themselves for the duration of a lease. The two concepts, whilst they share a common feature in that both relate to promises to do, or not to do, something in relation to an estate in land, are distinct entities with entirely different sets of rules relating to their existence and transmission, and as such they should be viewed completely separately. Accordingly, this chapter will consider freehold covenants only. Leasehold covenants are considered in Chapter 13 of the text.

Freehold covenants are also very often confused with the concept of **easements** because both involve to some extent the way in which land is used. However, in reality the two concepts are quite different in nature. As we learned in the last chapter, whereas an easement is a right to do something on someone else's land, a covenant constitutes either the right to prevent someone else from doing something on their own land, or the right to force someone to do something on their own land (for example, to maintain it). Covenants can be far wider in their scope and more flexible than easements. In particular, a covenant against building can effectively confer a right to maintain a view on the benefited landowner, whereas an easement cannot do this as such a right would be too vague to form the subject matter of a grant. In addition, from a technical point of view, freehold covenants can only exist in **equity**, not being one of the **interests** in land mentioned in section 1(2) of the Law of Property Act 1925. As we know easements, on the other hand, exist at law or in equity.

So, having established what a freehold covenant is not, the next question to ask is where you might be likely to come across them in practice. Covenants are in fact quite common in respect of freehold property, especially where land is divided and the original owner wants to ensure that the property is treated in a certain way or, if the property sold is to be developed, the seller wants to make sure that the properties built are of a certain type, number or specification. The following are a few examples of the kind of covenant you might commonly encounter in relation to freehold land:

- **not to use the property for the sale of alcoholic liquor**
- **not to keep any animal other than domestic pets on the land**
- **not to use the property for business purposes**
- **not to build without the consent of the covenantee**
- **to keep the boundary fences to the property in good repair and condition**

The possibilities are quite endless. Basically, anything the seller of the land can conceive in terms of how the property is used can be made a covenant.

Positive and negative covenants

Covenants can be positive or negative in nature. It is important to understand the difference between **positive** and **negative covenants** because, as we will see later in the chapter, whilst negative covenants will usually bind **successors in title** to the burdened land, positive covenants do not.

The essence of a negative covenant is that it is restrictive in its nature. It may forbid or limit in some way any activity on the land which has the burden of the covenant. To give a couple of examples of negative, or **restrictive covenants** as they are more commonly called, they might include a covenant not to build on the land, a covenant not to use the premises for illegal or immoral purposes or even a covenant not to park a caravan in the driveway. Positive covenants, on the other hand, require the owner of the burdened land to carry out a positive obligation in relation to the land, such as the requirement to build a wall, or to pay towards the upkeep of a shared driveway, or to paint the windows green. Positive covenants are by their nature more difficult to enforce than negative covenants, for reasons we are going to consider later in the chapter. For now, however, let us concentrate on negative covenants.

You be the judge

Q: Take another look at the list of five covenants given in the 'What is a covenant?' section, above. Which of these covenants do you think are positive and which are negative?

A: The first three are negative and the last two are positive. Whereas the first three prohibit certain actions or activities on the property, the last two both require positive action to be taken in order for the covenants to be complied with.

Do not be caught out by the wording of the covenant. Some covenants may appear to be positive but actually have a negative effect. For example, a covenant to build only a single-storey dwelling house on the land in effect is a restriction preventing any building on the land other than that of a single-storey dwelling house. It is therefore negative in nature and not positive, as it may first appear. To give another equal but opposite example, the same applies to our fourth scenario, given above: 'not to build without the consent of the covenantee'. Here, the covenant appears negative, because it says not to build; however, the second part of the covenant requires positive action in that it requires the consent of the covenantee for any development to take place on the land. The covenant not to build without consent is therefore in fact a positive covenant and not a negative covenant at all, because it requires positive action to be taken by the person with the burdened land in the form of the obtaining of consent.

It should be remembered that a negative, or restrictive, covenant may also be limited to certain permitted activities, rather than banning a particular activity altogether – so it may be only partially, not totally, negative in nature. For example, a covenant could be imposed not to build more than a certain number of houses on the land, or above a certain height, or may prohibit only certain trades, such as the running of a public house or hotel, rather than banning business use altogether. Again, the wording of such covenants may appear positive in nature, albeit that they are really negative. If you are in doubt about whether a covenant is positive or negative in nature, the following quote, taken from the Court of Appeal case of *Co-operative Retail Services Limited* v. *Tesco Stores Limited* (1998) 76 P&CR 328, is useful. In the case, which concerned an argument between two supermarket stores as to what should be included within the meaning of a covenant not to use the site 'for the purposes of food retailing', Lord Justice Millet, quoting Preston and Newsome, *Restrictive Covenants* (8th edn, 1991), paragraph 3–09, stated: 'A restrictive covenant is a burden, not on the owner's pocket, but on his land; he can comply with it completely by complete inaction.'

Case Summary

This is often referred to as the 'hand in pocket' rule, and its meaning is clear: whereas a negative covenant can be complied with simply by refraining from doing the restricted act, a positive covenant will require some form of action which, necessarily, may entail the incurring of a certain amount of expense on the part of the **covenantor** (the person whose land has the burden of the covenant).

Enforceability of freehold covenants

Having established what a freehold covenant is, we must now turn to the bulk of the law that relates to freehold covenants, which concerns not their definition but their enforceability. We will look firstly at the enforceability of covenants between the original parties to the agreement, and then to what happens when one or other of the parties sells the benefited or burdened land to another.

As between the original parties

The original parties to the covenant are bound by the ordinary rules of **privity of contract**. In essence, this means that if Jayden sells half of his land to Carla, retaining the other half for himself, and in doing so requires her to covenant not to keep poultry on that half, a contract is created between them. If Carla then subsequently breaks her covenant and starts keeping chickens on the land, Jayden can sue Carla for **damages** for **breach of contract** or seek an **injunction** to restrain the breach under the ordinary rules of contract.

Figure 11.1 Illustration of privity of contract as between the original parties

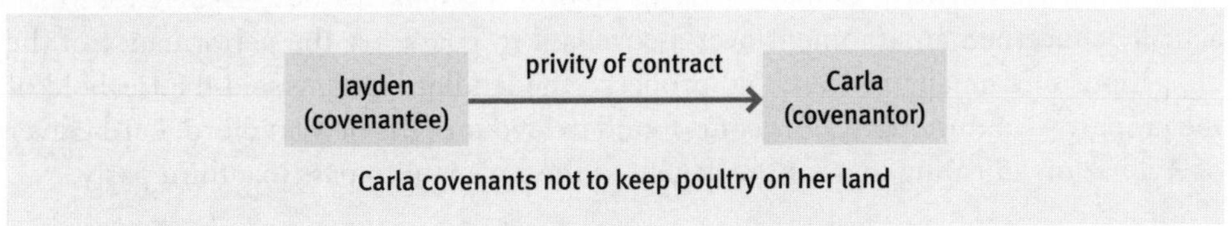

The rules of privity of contract apply regardless of whether the covenant is positive or negative in nature.

Transmission of the benefit at law

So what happens if, having sold half of his land to Carla, Jayden then sells the piece of land he had originally retained for himself to a third party, Asif? Can Asif then enforce the covenant if Carla breaches it?

Express assignment

With foresight, Jayden, as the original covenantee, could always expressly assign the benefit of the covenant to Asif by deed, in accordance with section 136 of the Law of

Property Act 1925. This says that the benefit of a covenant can be assigned provided that the assignment is in writing and express notice of the assignment is given in writing to the covenantor.

Contract (Rights of Third Parties) Act 1999

It is also possible that the benefit of the covenant might be transferred under the provisions of the Contract (Rights of Third Parties) Act 1999. The Act states at section 1 that, where a contract purports to confer a benefit on a third party, that third party may enforce the term in their own right, unless it appears that the parties did not intend this. So in our example, if the wording of the covenant between Jayden and Carla was such that it purported to enter into the covenant for the benefit of Jayden 'and his successors in title', a third party, such as Asif, could take the benefit of the covenant even though they were not a party to the original contract. The effect of the Act would at first glance appear to be an end to any potential problem regarding the transmission of the benefit of a covenant in law, provided it is properly drafted. However, it should be remembered that the Act only came into force on 11 May 2000 and so will not apply to any covenant created before this time; nor will it apply unless the covenant is specifically worded so as to include successors in title of the covenantor.

Transmission at common law

But what if neither of these things apply? Obviously there is no privity of contract, because there is no contractual relationship between Asif, the purchaser, and Carla, the original covenantor. Instead, this is the point at which the principles of the **common law** step in. At common law the benefit of any covenant over land, whether it is positive or negative in nature, is allowed to pass to a successor in title of the original covenantee, provided four conditions are met. These conditions were set out in the House of Lords case of *P&A Swift Investments* v. *Combined English Stores Group plc* [1988] 3 WLR 313, which actually concerned an argument over a covenant to guarantee the performance of the obligations of a tenant on leasehold property, the landlord having sold the freehold of the property to a third party. The court found in favour of the new landlord, Lord Oliver of Aylmerton affirming that for the benefit of the covenant to pass to a third party:

Case Summary

1. The covenant must 'touch and concern' the land of the covenantee;
2. It must have been the intention of the parties at the time of making the covenant that the benefit should pass to successors in title: that is, that the covenant should run with the land;
3. the covenantee must have held the legal estate in the land to be benefited at the time of entering into the covenant;
4. The claimant must derive their title from or under the original covenantee.

In *P&A Swift*'s case, in guaranteeing the performance of the incoming tenant each of these conditions was seen to apply. Of course we are looking at freehold covenants, but the principles remain the same. Let us take a look at the conditions in more detail:

'Touching and concerning' the land

The idea at common law of the covenant 'touching and concerning' the land of the covenantee is similar in its aim to the requirement from the previous chapter in

Re Ellenborough Park, that an easement must 'accommodate the **dominant tenement**'. Essentially, the rule seeks to ensure that the benefit of the covenant will only pass to a third party if it confers a benefit on the land itself, and that it was not purely of personal benefit to the original covenantee. The requirement that the covenant must 'touch and concern' the land, therefore, simply ensures that a covenant which is of purely personal benefit to the covenantee cannot be passed to successors in title. An example of this might be a covenant not to paint a house blue, just because the neighbour did not like the colour, for instance. Examples of covenants which have been held to touch and concern the land include:

the covenant must 'touch and concern' the land

- a covenant only to build one private dwelling house on the land (*Rogers* v. *Hosegood* [1900] 2 Ch 388);
- a covenant not to carry on any noxious trade or chemical operation on the land (*Formby* v. *Barker* [1903] 2 Ch 539);
- a covenant to maintain a river bank (*Smith and Snipes Hall Farm Ltd* v. *River Douglas Catchment Board* [1949] 2 KB 500).

In all these cases we can see that the covenant provides a clear benefit to the land itself, and not just to the covenantee in their personal capacity.

Intention to pass the benefit

The second requirement for the passing of the benefit of a covenant at common law is that it must have been the intention of the parties that the benefit of the covenant should pass to successors in title of the covenantee. Again, a purely personal covenant such as a covenant not to paint a house a particular colour, or a covenant not to allow children on the property, imposed because the covenantee did not like children, could not pass this second test because it is an agreement made with the intention of benefiting the original covenantee only. But how do you prove the intention of the original parties to the agreement in the case of non-personal covenants?

Prior to 1925, evidence of intention used to be provided by including in the wording of the original covenant specific mention of not only the original covenantee, but also their successors in title and those deriving title under them. Statute has since stepped in to help out in this regard, however. Section 78(1) of the Law of Property Act 1925 now says that the inclusion of successors in title is deemed to be included in the covenant, irrespective of the wording given in the actual deed. To quote section 78(1), it says that:

> **s.78(1)** A covenant relating to any land of the covenantee shall be deemed to be made with the covenantee and his successors in title and the persons deriving title under him or them, and shall have effect as if such successors and other persons were expressed [in the original deed].

Thus, with any covenant created after 1925 it is no longer necessary to include any specific wording in order to show evidence of an intention to pass the benefit of the covenant to third parties.

The covenantee must hold the legal estate

The third prerequisite for the transmission of the benefit of a covenant at common law is that the person with the benefit of the covenant must have held the legal estate in the land to be benefited at the time the covenant was entered into. This requirement that the covenantee owns benefited land is, in reality, simply another expression of the fact that the covenant must attach to the land itself and not merely the owner of that land or the creator of the covenant as an individual. It also means that the owner of an **equitable interest** in the land cannot benefit from covenants on the land at common law.

The claimant must derive title

The fourth and final common law rule on the passing of the benefit of a covenant at common law is somewhat historical in its nature and background. The rule says that the person claiming the benefit of the covenant must derive title from *or under* the original covenantee. It was traditionally the case that a successor claiming the benefit of a covenant at common law had to have acquired the same estate in the land as had been held by the original covenantee. This meant that, whilst a buyer of the freehold estate could enforce a covenant made between the seller and the covenantor, a tenant acquiring a lease of the benefited property, even a leasehold term of 999 years, could not.

Case Summary

The case of *Smith and Snipe Hall Farm Limited* v. *River Douglas Catchment Board* [1949] 2 KB 500, changed all this, however. The case concerned a covenant made by the water authority with a private landowner to maintain the local river banks and flood defences. The landowner subsequently sold the land to a third party, who then leased the land. The water authority failed to maintain the flood defences and the land was flooded. The court held that section 78 of the Law of Property Act 1925 (seen above) had the effect of extending the right of a successor in title of the land to enforce the benefit of a covenant to a tenant, as well as a freehold owner of the land. This is because of the wording in the section which states that a covenant shall be deemed to be made with the covenantee 'and his successors in title and the persons deriving title under him or them'.

To test your knowledge and understanding of what you have just read, have a go at the Writing and Drafting exercise, below.

Writing and drafting

You are a trainee solicitor at Hicks & Co. LLP. Your training principal has asked you to write to a client of his, explaining whether or not he can sue his neighbour for breach of covenant. Your client bought the property five years ago and understands that it came with the benefit of a covenant not to build on the land next door. The neighbours have recently built a garage right up to your client's boundary fence, which your client considers unsightly and wishes to have removed. Your client has tried to talk to the neighbours about the garage, but they say their agreement was with the previous owner of your client's house, and has nothing to do with him.

Prepare a letter of advice to the client, advising him whether or not he may be able to sue on the breach and what action he can take.

You should take no more than 30 minutes on this task.

So, going back to our earlier example, we can see that, applying the common law rules, a third party buyer of the benefit of the covenant such as Asif can enforce the covenant not to keep poultry on the land as against the original covenantee, Carla, should she be in breach of the same. It is important to remember in this context that this ability to enforce covenants by a third-party buyer of the benefited land extends to all non-personal covenants, regardless of whether they are of a positive or negative nature, and provided that the four common law provisions are met.

Transmission of the burden at law

The above establishes how the benefit of the covenant can pass at common law, so that a successor in title of the original covenantee can sue on the covenant, if breached. But what happens if the original covenantor sells their land? Will the burden of the covenant pass to their successors in title? In other words, to use our example, if Carla sells her land to a third party will that third party be bound by the covenant not to keep poultry on the land?

At common law, the short answer is no. Regardless of whether the covenant is positive or negative in nature, the common law stands firmly against restraints being placed on a person's use of their own property, and so applies the strict rules of privity in such cases. Figure 11.2 shows us how this works in practice.

Figure 11.2 Transmission of the burden of a covenant at law

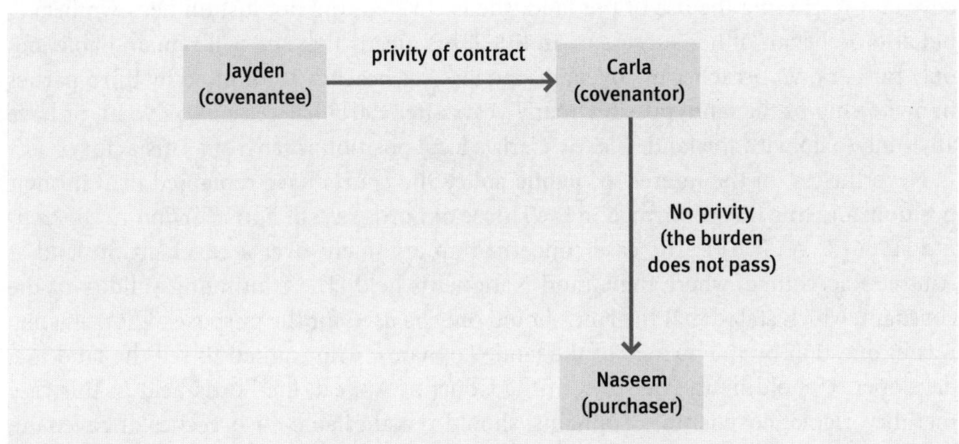

From Figure 11.2 we see that if Carla sells her land to a third party, Naseem, then Naseem will not be liable at common law for keeping chickens in breach of the covenant on the property.

The leading decision on the issue of the passing of the burden of a covenant at common law came in the case of *Austerberry* v. *Corporation of Oldham* (1885) 29 Ch D 750. In this case it was held that at common law the obligation to make up a road and keep it in good repair could not pass to the successor in title of the original covenantor. The judges in this Court of Appeal case were unanimous in agreeing that there was neither authority nor reason for the passing of the burden of a covenant to be allowed at common law. Following *Austerberry* v. *Oldham* the common law position was reaffirmed in the more recent House of Lords decision in *Rhone* v. *Stevens* [1994] 2 AC 310, which concerned a covenant by the predecessor in title of the burdened landowner to maintain a roof which overhung the benefited landowner's property. This decision still stands today.

Case Summary

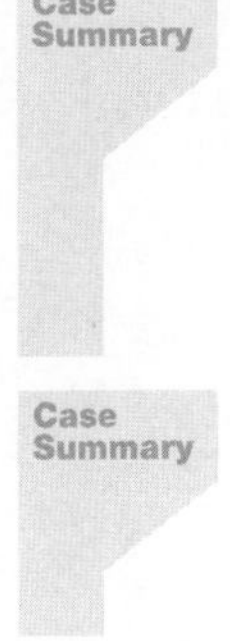

the original covenantor will remain liable having transferred their ownership

But where does this leave the original covenantor? If the burden does not pass at common law when the property is sold or transferred to a third party, what happens to it? One might assume that the covenant would simply come to an end at this point, but this is not the case. In fact, quite the opposite is true. Not only will the burden of the covenant continue to run, but the original covenantor will remain liable for it, despite having transferred their ownership of the property to someone else. This means that, taking our example of Carla and Naseem, above, whilst at common law Naseem as the buyer of the property will not be liable for breaches of covenant on the land he has purchased, Carla will continue to be liable on Naseem's behalf. The primary reason for this is because of the effects of section 79 of the Law of Property Act 1925. The section states that:

> a covenant relating to any land of a covenantor or capable of being bound by him, shall, unless a contrary intention is expressed, be deemed to be made by the covenantor on behalf of himself his successors in title and the persons deriving title under him or them . . .

The effect of the wording of the section is that when a person such as Carla enters into a covenant restricting the use of her land, she is covenanting not just on her own behalf, but also on behalf of her successors in title. This means that she will remain liable, not only for her own breaches of covenant, but also for beaches committed by third parties in ownership of the land, possibly many years after Carla has ceased to live in, or have anything to do with the land. Clearly Carla's legal position is far from satisfactory.

Case Summary

Nevertheless, in the interest of **public policy** the courts have remained firm in their position, and this was confirmed in the House of Lords case of *Earl of Sefton* v. *Tophams Ltd* [1966] 2 WLR 814. The case concerned an argument over a covenant on land at Aintree Racecourse, where the Grand National is held. The continuing validity of the covenant, which stated that the land should only be used for the purpose of horseracing, was in question by the owners of the land, Tophams, who wanted to sell the land to a developer. Upholding the decision of the Court of Appeal, the Lords held in this case that the original covenantor, Tophams, should remain liable for breaches of covenant, even after they had sold their interest in the land. Thus if Naseem, as a purchaser of Carla's land, breaches the covenant on the land not to keep poultry, whilst Naseem will be free from liability, Carla will remain statutorily liable for his breach.

Whilst this might seem harsh, it should be remembered that there are clear policy reasons for not allowing the burden of a covenant to pass at common law. It would be a singular breach of public policy to allow land to be burdened indefinitely and therefore for the uninhibited use of a person's private property to be restrained on a permanent basis. In any event, luckily for the likes of Carla, the common law did nevertheless see fit to provide a couple of ways to circumvent this problem. One way is through a chain of **indemnity covenants**; the other is through the doctrine in ***Halsall* v. *Brizell***.

Chain of indemnity

As we have seen, at common law, the original covenantor (in our case Carla) will always remain liable on the covenants they have made to the original covenantee and their successors in title. This leaves the original covenantor in a difficult position. Whilst Carla may be happy to be responsible for keeping to the terms of a covenant she herself has agreed to during her ownership of the land, she is not really going to want to remain responsible for the actions of her successors in title, long after she has sold the property and moved on. So what can she do? One answer to the problem is to try to obtain an **indemnity** from the person buying their land, indemnifying the seller should the buyer be held liable for any breach of covenant on it. This would enable the original covenantor to claim back from the buyer any damages they have had to pay the covenantee for the buyer's breaches of covenant. In our scenario, therefore, Carla would obtain an indemnity covenant from Naseem when she sells to him, and then Naseem would do the same on selling the land to a third party, and so on down the line. This would create a chain of indemnity and thus protect Carla against Naseem or his successors in title breaching the covenant at a later date. Naturally, such a chain of indemnity could be applied either to the burden of a positive or negative covenant. The wording of such a covenant would typically look as follows:

One answer to the problem is to try to obtain an indemnity

Documenting the law

Wording of a typical indemnity covenant on the sale of property

'The Transferee hereby covenants with the Transferor that the Transferee and the persons deriving title under him will at all times observe and perform the covenants and conditions contained or referred to in the charges register of the Title Number so far as they relate to the Property and will indemnify and keep the Transferor and his successors in title fully and effectively indemnified against all actions proceedings damages costs claims and expenses which may be suffered or incurred by the Transferor or his successors in title in respect of any future breach or non-observance or non-performance of those covenants and conditions.'

Of course, any of these buyers could refuse to grant an indemnity, but in practice they do not do this. The grant of an indemnity on the purchase of land is very common practice in residential **conveyancing** transactions.

In any event, if the original covenantee is concerned about this they can always place a **restriction** on the **Proprietorship Register** of registered land, preventing the land from being sold unless the purchaser enters into a direct covenant with the benefited landowner on purchase. This would mean that each new successive landowner of the burdened land would enter into a brand new covenant with the benefited landowner, thus getting around the problem of succession altogether. A benefited landowner can do this under section 40 of the Land Registration Act 2002.

The creation of a chain of indemnity covenants is nevertheless far from ideal for the original parties. In reality, it only takes one person in the chain to disappear or become **insolvent** for the chain to break down and for the original covenantor to be unable to claim reimbursement of their damages; and for the covenantee, the disappearance of the original covenantor leaves them with no recourse against any future breach.

Halsall v. *Brizell*

Case Summary

Another way to circumvent the common law rule is through the **doctrine** of mutual benefit and burden, as set out in the case of *Halsall* v. *Brizell* [1957] Ch 169. The doctrine states that a person who wishes to claim the benefit of a deed must also submit to any corresponding burden which is imposed by that deed (remember that a covenant is a promise made by deed). The facts of the case were as follows.

The case concerned the sale of a house on an estate. The deed of conveyance gave the buyer the right to use various roads, sewers and drains on the estate. The same conveyance also imposed on the buyer by way of a positive covenant the duty to contribute to the upkeep of those sewers, drains and roads. The buyer then sold the land to a third party, who refused to contribute to the upkeep of the roads, sewers and drains, arguing that the burden did not run to them as a successor in title at common law. The court held that the third-party buyer could not take the benefit of the rights of way, rights of drainage and so forth, unless they were also prepared to accept the related burden of the covenants appertaining to those rights.

In theory, liability under the doctrine of mutual benefit and burden is voluntary: if the buyer does not wish to accept the benefit of the deed, they need not be made liable for the burden. However, in the case of roadways and drainage, the choice is in most cases really a fictional one.

Case Summary

Interpretation of the doctrine by the courts tends to be narrowly construed, in that the benefit and corresponding burden imposed by the deed must be inextricably linked. So, for example, whereas the use of a roadway could carry with it the obligation to maintain that roadway, a requirement to pay towards the maintenance of landscaped and communal areas on a housing estate in which the purchaser's property stood, but which the purchaser had not been granted any right to use, would not fall within the confines of the doctrine. This was the outcome in the Court of Appeal case of *Thamesmead Town* v. *Allotey* (1998) 37 EG 161.

The doctrine of mutual benefit and burden under *Halsall* v. *Brizell* is perhaps the most effective method of passing the burden of a positive covenant at common law. The only problem with it is, of course, that there must be a corresponding benefit and burden in order for the doctrine to operate. It is therefore not possible to impose a positive covenant on the land without the burdened landowner receiving a benefit in return for their obligation.

At this point a little recap may be helpful. What we have said so far about the passing of the benefit and burden of covenants at common law is that:

- At common law the benefit of any covenant will run with the land to successors in title, provided the four requirements set out in *P&A Swift Investments* v. *Combined English Stores* are met;
- The burden of a covenant will not run directly at common law to bind successors of the original covenantor, however, other than through a chain of indemnity covenants or under the rule of mutual benefit and burden in *Halsall* v. *Brizell*.

There are a couple of points we can make about the position of the original covenantee here. One is that any remedy sought against the original covenantor will be limited to damages. As the original covenantor no longer has possession of the land, an injunction or an order of **specific performance** as against them would be worthless; the value to the covenantee of bringing an action against the original covenantor is therefore limited as it will not have the effect of restraining the breach against which the covenantee is complaining. This may seem pretty unfair to the covenantee as their covenant may effectively become unenforceable merely by virtue of the fact that the land has changed hands. From the point of view of the original covenantee in our example, Jayden, what is the value of entering into a covenant to prevent the neighbours from keeping poultry on their land, when as soon as the land is sold to a third party, the benefit of that covenant will be lost? The whole point of entering into a covenant on the sale of part of their land in the first place was to retain some control over the use of the land, and the strict application of the law frustrates this.

There are a few different ways in which Jayden could get around the issue of dealing with the passing of the burden of the covenant at common law, primarily by creating the obligation through another medium. For example, he could:

- *Grant a long lease of the land*, in which case all covenants in the lease which touch and concern the land, regardless of whether they are positive or negative in nature, would be enforceable under the doctrine of **privity of estate**, or, if the lease was granted after 1 January 1996, under the Landlord and Tenant (Covenants) Act 1995, which makes provision for the release of the landlord and the tenant from their respective covenants under the terms of the lease on **assignment** to a third party. This will be explored in more detail in Chapter 13.
- *Create a commonhold development.* In a **commonhold** development, both positive and negative covenants are enforceable by and against successors in title to the separate properties within the development. For a reminder of how commonhold works, see the section on commonhold in Chapter 1.
- *Create estate rentcharges*, supported by a right of re-entry. You will remember that a **rentcharge** is an interest in freehold land that allows the creator of the rentcharge to demand payments on another freehold property, failure to pay which entitles the owner of the rentcharge to regain possession of the property, as with a lease. By creating an **estate rentcharge** under section 2(3) of the Rentcharges Act 1977, the landowner can secure the cost of the performance of positive or negative covenants such as covenants for the provision of services and the maintenance of the property, with a right of re-entry as against the current owner of the land, should those covenants not be complied with. This will not impact upon the original covenantor, it will only be enforceable as against the current freeholder – the person who is actually in breach of the covenant.

Transmission of the burden in equity

The problem, of course, with all of the above options is that none of them achieve a clean break, where the original covenantee is wishing to sell the land. This is where the court of equity has stepped in, seeking to find its own solution to the problem by applying equitable principles. The result came in the landmark case of ***Tulk* v. *Moxhay*** (1848) 2 Ph 744.

Case Navigator

Law in action

The case of *Tulk* v. *Moxhay* concerned the very famous square in the centre of London, Leicester Square, and it is, in fact, the finding in this case that we have to thank for the fact that we can still, today, continue to enjoy this beautiful open space in the heart of London. The facts of the case were as follows. Mr Tulk owned open ground in Leicester Square. In 1808 he sold the freehold of that land to a Mr Elms. The conveyance to Mr Elms required that Mr Elms, his heirs and assigns would:

> 'keep and maintain the said piece of ground and square garden and iron railing round the same in its then form and in sufficient and proper repair as a square garden and pleasure ground, in an open state uncovered with any buildings in neat and ornamental order.'

By various conveyances the land passed to a Mr Moxhay. The conveyance to Mr Moxhay did not contain any restriction, although Mr Moxhay was aware of the terms of the 1808 conveyance. Mr Moxhay expressed the view that he had a right to build on the land in the centre of Leicester Square if he so wished. Mr Tulk, who still owned a number of houses around the square applied for an injunction against Mr Moxhay building on the land, which was granted in the first instance and upheld on appeal. The court held that Mr Tulk, as an owner of neighbouring benefited land had a right in equity to enforce the benefit of the covenant against the buyer of the burdened land, Mr Moxhay, because Mr Moxhay had known of the restriction when he acquired the land and had paid a reduced price for the land on account of this fact. The court held that it would have been unconscionable for Mr Moxhay to buy land at a reduced price on account of the covenant, but then ignore the covenant and re-sell it for a profit. Accordingly, because Mr Moxhay had been aware of the restriction on the land when he bought it, he was deemed to buy that land without the benefit of the right to build on it.

Source: Naki Kouyioumtzis, Pearson Education Ltd

The principle laid down in *Tulk* v. *Moxhay* formed the basis of an equitable doctrine that still holds good today and which, in its modern form, can now be described as follows:

1. *The covenant must be negative.* The burden of positive covenants will therefore not pass to third parties in equity. This makes sense given the likely imposition of a financial burden on the purchasing party if the covenant is positive in nature. We looked earlier in the chapter at how to establish whether a covenant is positive or negative, through the 'hand in pocket' rule.
2. *The covenant must accommodate the dominant tenement.* In order for the covenant to benefit the land of the covenantee, the person with the benefit of the covenant must have owned the land at the time the covenant was entered into. This point is illustrated by the case of *LCC* v. *Allen* [1914] 3 KB 642, in which a developer entered into a covenant with London County Council, in return for being given permission to build a new street, that he would leave the land at the end of the street undeveloped. The developer then sold the land to a Mrs Allen, who wished to build on it. The court held that the covenant could not be enforced against her as the Council did not own any land that benefited from the terms of the covenant.

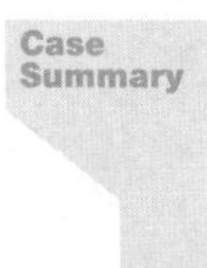

In order to accommodate the dominant tenement, the land itself must also be benefited by the covenant, rather than simply a personal benefit being conferred on the covenantee.

3. *The original parties must have intended that the burden should bind successors in title to the property.* This can either be expressly evidenced, or implied under section 79 of the Law of Property Act 1925, as we saw earlier in the chapter; and
4. *The person against whom the covenant is being enforced must have notice of the covenant.* Notice, in this context, means that, in the case of **registered land**, the restrictive covenant must be entered on the **Charges Register** of the burdened property at the **Land Registry** as a **notice**, and in the case of **unregistered land** must be registered as a class D(ii) **Land Charge** under the Land Charges Act 1972. This is unless the covenant was created before 1 January 1926, in which case the traditional **doctrine of notice** will apply. In order to refresh your memory further about the protection of equitable interests in land, you can re-read the relevant section in Chapter 4.

As we can see, then, whilst it is not possible for the burden of a covenant to pass at common law, the burden of negative covenants only can pass in equity, provided that the conditions in *Tulk* v. *Moxhay* are met. This is of course good news for the covenantee; but there is one final twist in the tale, and this is that, in order to satisfy equitable principles, in order for the burden of the covenant to pass in equity, the benefit of the covenant must also be shown to pass in equity.

Transmission of the benefit in equity

The effect of the rule that both the burden and benefit of the covenant must be shown to pass in equity is that, having established that a third party buyer has the burden of the covenant, the person wishing to enforce that covenant, if they are not the original covenantee, must also show that they are entitled to the benefit of the covenant according to equitable rules. Perhaps somewhat frustratingly, it will not be sufficient to show that they have acquired the benefit of the covenant through common law. So how can the passing of the benefit in equity be proven? The answer is that the benefit of the covenant can be made to run in equity in one of three ways:

- ✦ by express assignment of the benefit of the covenant; or
- ✦ by annexation; or
- ✦ under the rules relating to building schemes.

Express assignment of the benefit

If the benefit of the covenant has not been successfully annexed to the land, it can nevertheless be expressly assigned on the subsequent sale of that land, provided two conditions are met, which are set out in the case of *Re Union of London and Smith's Bank Ltd's Conveyance* [1933] Ch 611. These are:

1. That it must be possible to ascertain from the conveyance and all the surrounding circumstances the identity of the land it is intended to benefit; and
2. That the benefit of the covenant is assigned to the buyer of the land at the time of the conveyance or transfer to them.

So, in other words, the benefit of the covenant can be expressly assigned to a purchaser of the benefited land, provided it is done at the time of the transfer and the benefited land is identifiable in that transfer.

Case Summary

The flaw with this method of passing on the benefit of the covenant is that, as suggested in the case of *Re Pinewood Estate* [1958] Ch 280, it is necessary both to have an unbroken chain of assignments of the benefit and that the benefit has been passed to the new owner who seeks to enforce the covenant. This means that the express assignment must be repeated every time the land transfers ownership and, if the chain is broken, as with indemnity covenants, the benefit of the covenant is lost.

Annexation

Annexation means that when the covenant was made it must have been annexed, or permanently attached to, the land itself, and not just to the person with the benefit of the covenant. There are three types of annexation: express, implied or statutory.

Express annexation

Express annexation takes place when the express wording of the covenant shows that it was the intention of the original parties to the agreement that the benefit of the covenant should run with the land. There are two cases that illustrate this: *Rogers* v. *Hosegood* [1900] 2 Ch 388 and *Renals* v. *Cowlishaw* (1878) 9 Ch D 125.

Case Summary

Case Summary

In *Rogers* v. *Hosegood* a covenant that stated expressly that it was made 'for the benefit of' particular land was held to be annexed to the land because it demonstrated a clear intention that the benefit should run with the land itself. However, the case of *Renals* v. *Cowlishaw* reached a conflicting decision. Here it was found that it is not enough for the covenant to be made with the covenantee and their 'assigns'. The court found that the word 'assigns' was not enough to link any successors in title with the benefited land. It is clear, then, that if the benefit of the covenant is to be shown to run with the land through the medium of express annexation, the wording of the covenant must be both clear and precise.

Case Summary

In addition to clear wording in the covenant itself, in order for express annexation to take place the whole of the land retained by the covenantee must be capable of benefiting from the covenant. It is not sufficient that only part of the land which has the benefit of the covenant will gain from it. This of course will be a matter of fact and degree in every case. In *Re Ballard's Conveyance* [1937] Ch 473, the land in question was a large estate of some 17,000 acres in Hertfordshire, called Childwickbury. The estate sold off 16 acres of land at one edge of the estate, entering into a covenant with the buyer that the land should not be built on. When the continuing validity of the covenant was questioned, however, the court held that the whole of the estate could not benefit from the covenant: only the part of the estate nearest to the boundary with the land that had been sold could benefit. Therefore the benefit could not run on the sale of the estate.

Case Summary

So where a covenant purports to have been annexed to the land but does not affect the whole of the land, the annexation is ineffective and the covenant cannot run with the land. If you wish to annex a covenant to a large piece of land, therefore, you should draft the covenant so as to benefit the 'whole or any part of' the named land. In the case of *Marquess of Zetland* v. *Driver* [1939] Ch 1, a covenant was expressed to be for the benefit of the covenantee's retained land 'and each and every part thereof'. This was considered sufficient to ensure that the parts of the land retained that were actually affected by the breach could sue under the terms of the covenant.

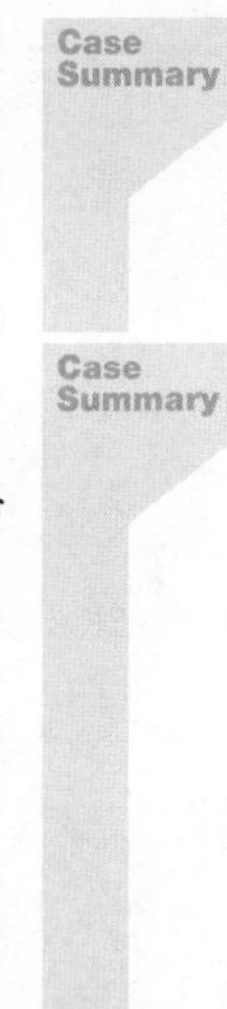

It should be noted that the rule set out in the case of *Re Ballard's Conveyance* has been relaxed in recent years, to the point where there is some question as to whether it remains good law. In particular the case of *Marten* v. *Flight Refuelling Ltd* [1962] Ch 115 made a finding that a covenant to use land sold for agricultural purposes only was annexed for the benefit of the whole of a 7,500 acre estate, after the Ministry of Defence acquired the land on a compulsory purchase basis and began to use the land as an aerodrome. The 1980 Court of Appeal case of *Federated Homes Ltd* v. *Mill Lodge Properties Ltd* [1980] 1 WLR 594, later even went so far as to say that a covenant could be presumed to be annexed to each and every part of the land without the need for any express provision to that effect being contained in the covenant at all, again on the basis of the wording of section 78(1) of the Law of Property Act 1925. The case concerned three plots of land, one of which was subject to a restrictive covenant not to develop above a certain density. When the developer of the burdened land obtained **planning permission** to develop the site with a higher density of housing than allowed by the covenant, the claimant, who owned both of the other plots of land, albeit that they had been acquired via different chains of ownership, sought an order restraining the development. The court held that the claimant was entitled to the benefit of the covenant in respect of both plots of land.

Implied annexation

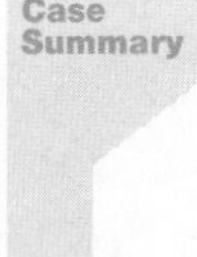

Implied annexation is in fact very rare, and something which can only be done by the courts. Stated simply, the courts will imply annexation if they find that the circumstances indicate an intention to benefit the land. This was what happened in *Marten* v. *Flight Refuelling*, and also the case of *Newton Abbott Co-operative Society Ltd* v. *Williamson & Treadgold Ltd* [1952] Ch 286. Here, the owner and occupier of business premises sold part of her premises to a company subject to a covenant that the company would not carry out the business of ironmongers at the premises, in competition with the seller's own business. When a successor in title to the burdened land later let the premises on a lease to an ironmonger, the son of the original covenantee, who had since died, sought to restrain the breach. The court held despite there being no specific assignment of the benefit of the covenant to the son, the proximity of the two businesses and the **defendant**'s knowledge at all times of the existence of the covenant were sufficient to imply that the covenant was annexed to the land in question.

Statutory annexation

In the case of *Federated Homes Ltd* v. *Mill Lodge Properties Ltd*, mentioned above, it was decided that the wording of section 78(1) of the Law of Property Act 1925 was sufficient to annex the benefit of a covenant to each and every part of the covenantee's land, provided that the covenant touches and concerns the land in question. In theory, therefore, there is no need for express words of annexation in the covenant at all: every covenant which touches and concerns the land will be statutorily annexed to the land and the benefit of it will automatically pass in equity. However, this decision has never sat comfortably with the courts.

One reason for this is the outcome of the House of Lords in *Beswick* v. *Beswick* [1968] AC 58. The case, which was about another matter entirely, stated that, since the Law of Property Act 1925 is a consolidating Act, its provisions should be accorded a construction which do not change the law. On this basis, the decision in *Federated Homes* has been viewed with scepticism by legal commentators over the years, because of its wide interpretation of section 78. It could therefore be argued that the *Federated Homes* case was wrongly decided and, as such, it is best not to work on the assumption that statutory annexation will automatically have occurred.

In 1984 the case of *Roake* v. *Chadha* [1984] 1 WLR 40 served to qualify the finding in *Federated Homes* by stating that section 78 would only annex the benefit of a covenant that is not expressed to be personal to the original parties. This is to a degree a matter of common sense, however. In order for the covenant to touch and concern the land it would by definition not be personal in any event. This decision was followed in the more recent Court of Appeal case of *Crest Nicholson* v. *McAllister* [2004] EWCA Civ 410. Here a number of plots of land bordering Claygate Common in Surrey had been sold off for individual development. Each plot was subject to a covenant not to build more than one dwelling house on the land and requiring the purchasers of the plots to submit plans to be approved prior to the commencement of building. A house builder subsequently bought three of the plots and sought to build a housing estate on them. The court found that the wording of the conveyances had been intended to be personal in nature and, as such, had not been sufficient to annex the benefit of the covenant to the land.

A further case of *Sugarman* v. *Porter* [2006] EWHC 331, in which a covenant not to build more than one private dwelling house on the burdened land was expressed to be 'for the benefit and protection of the Vendor's said adjoining property or any part thereof remaining unsold and any part of such property hereafter expressly sold with the benefit of this present covenant' also came to the same conclusion: that where the covenant was expressed to be personal it would not run with the land unless it was expressly assigned to a purchaser of that land by the seller.

The upshot of these cases is that statutory annexation should be treated with caution and that the construction of the covenant must still be considered carefully before proceeding on the assumption that it will apply.

Building schemes

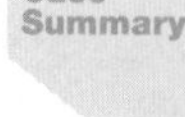

The final method of passing on the benefit of a covenant at equity is by way of a building scheme, the rules relating to which were set out in the 1908 Court of Appeal case of *Elliston* v. *Reacher* [1908] 2 Ch 382, which concerned an estate of houses in Felixstowe. The claimants wanted to prevent one of the houses from being used as a hotel. On appeal it was held that equity will allow the owners of the various plots on an estate to enforce covenants against one another, provided four conditions are satisfied. These are as follows:

1. That all the buyers acquire their property from the same seller;
2. That the seller must have divided the estate into plots prior to selling the properties;
3. That the covenants were intended by the seller to continue for the benefit of all the plots in the scheme; and
4. That every buyer must acquire the plot on the understanding that the covenants are for the benefit all the other plots in the scheme.

An injunction was therefore granted against the use of the house as a private hotel.

The following year an additional condition for the finding of a building scheme was added by the case of *Reid* v. *Bickerstaff* [1909] 2 Ch 305, which concerned a large sixty-four-acre estate on the outskirts of Liverpool. On appeal, the court reversed the decision at first instance, rejecting the claim on the basis that the claimant had not shown there was a definite building scheme in place for a particular defined area of land. Thus, the fifth condition added to the prerequisites in *Elliston* v. *Reacher* is that:

5. the area of the building scheme must be clearly identified.

You may be asking why we need special rules in relation to building schemes. The answer is that, in the ordinary scheme of things, whilst the builder may put these covenants in place to protect the estate as a whole, after the last plot has been sold the builder will no longer have any interest in enforcing the covenants. The use of a building scheme therefore, by putting the power to enforce in the hands of the individual plot owners within the scheme, avoids the problems which might otherwise occur with the enforcement of covenants meant to protect the estate after the developer has sold the last plot.

after the last plot has been sold the builder will no longer have any interest

In any event, this traditional set of five conditions has latterly been viewed more as a number of useful guidelines in deciding whether or not a building scheme exists, and the tendency of the courts is now to relax some of them, provided that it has clearly been the intention of the builder and the understanding of his buyers that the benefit of the covenants will continue for the benefit of all the plots in the scheme. This was set out in the case of *Baxter* v. *Four Oaks Properties Ltd* [1965] 2 WLR 1115, in which the land was not set out in plots before being sold off by the developer, and subsequently confirmed in the 1970 case of *Re Dolphin's Conveyance* [1970] 3 WLR 31, in which the land did not all derive from a common vendor.

Case Summary

Finally, we can make a couple of additional points of interest in relation to building schemes. Firstly, what is the effect of the sub-division of the original plots? In the case of *Brunner* v. *Greenslade* [1971] Ch 993, it was held that both the benefit and the burden of covenants in a building scheme will run to affect someone who acquires only part of the original plot. In addition, the buyer of one part may enforce the covenants against the buyer of the other part and against the other owners of plots within the scheme.

Case Summary

Secondly, what is the effect of common ownership of some of the plots? In the case of *Texaco Antilles Ltd* v. *Kernochan* [1973] AC 609, it was decided that if two plots come into common ownership and are then at a later date divided, the original covenants will revive automatically between the subsequent owners.

Case Summary

The position with positive covenants

As we have seen above, whilst it may be possible to make the burden of a restrictive covenant run in equity through the application of the principles laid down in *Tulk* v. *Moxhay*, there is actually no mechanism in equity which allows for the burden of a positive covenant to run with the land, due to the financial implications of allowing such a burden to pass. Does this mean, then, that a positive covenant simply cannot be passed to a purchaser of burdened land? The answer to this question is that the law has through necessity found various ways to circumvent this problem at common law, all of which we have in fact already been introduced to throughout the course of the chapter.

Reflective practice

Imagine you wanted to enforce the burden of a covenant to erect and maintain a boundary wall. Take a look back through the chapter and see if you can find one or more methods of doing this.

The erection and maintenance of a boundary wall is a good example of where a positive covenant may be both desirable and necessary. If a landowner sells off part of their land on the understanding that the buyer will build a wall between the two properties and subsequently maintain that wall, if the burden of the covenant is not allowed to pass to a third party, if the covenantor subsequently sells the land there will be nothing in place to ensure that the new property owner maintains the wall. In theory, they could allow the wall to fall into disrepair or even fall down, and there would be nothing the

Table 11.1 Enforceability of freehold covenants

As between the original parties	privity of contract applies	regardless of whether covenant is positive or negative in nature
Passing of the benefit at law	the original covenantee can expressly assign by deed under s.136 LPA 1925	regardless of whether covenant is positive or negative in nature
	if the covenant is created after 11 May 2000 the benefit may pass under the Contract (Rights of Third Parties) Act 1999, provided the covenant is specifically worded so as to include successors in title of the covenantor	regardless of whether covenant is positive or negative in nature
	at common law, provided the four conditions in *P&A Swift Investments* are met	regardless of whether covenant is positive or negative in nature
Passing of the burden at law	privity of contract applies and the burden will not automatically pass	regardless of whether covenant is positive or negative in nature
	the burden can be passed through a chain of indemnity covenants	regardless of whether covenant is positive or negative in nature
	through the doctrine of mutual benefit and burden under *Halsall* v. *Brizell*	applies to positive and negative covenants which are mutually interlinked (i.e. the use of a road coupled with responsibility for the maintenance of it)
Passing of the burden in equity	under the rule in *Tulk* v. *Moxhay*, provided that the benefit of the covenant can also be shown to pass in equity	applies to negative covenants only. *The burden of positive covenants cannot pass in equity*
Passing of the benefit in equity	through express assignment by deed	regardless of whether covenant is positive or negative in nature
	through annexation (express, implied or statutory)	regardless of whether covenant is positive or negative in nature
	by means of a building scheme	regardless of whether covenant is positive or negative in nature

covenantee could do about it. If it is not possible to create a positive covenant, the burden of which is transmissible to third parties, how can its longevity be ensured? The answers lie in the following mechanisms:

- granting a long lease
- commonhold developments and estate rentcharges
- indemnity covenants
- the doctrine of mutual benefit and burden under *Halsall* v. *Brizell*

The Law Commission recommended the creation of a new legal interest

As we have seen above, all the legal devices which can currently be adopted to get around the problem of the inability of the burden of a positive covenant running to successors in title suffer from drawbacks in one form or another, or are otherwise cumbersome to operate. The Law Commission has therefore recommended in its proposals the creation of a new transferable legal interest in land called the '**land obligation**', meant to replace the creation of new freehold covenants in the future. The proposals recommend that these land obligations should be capable of being either positive or negative in nature. The proposals for reform are discussed in more detail below.

Table 11.1 provides a summary of the enforceability of freehold covenants both at law and in equity.

Protection of freehold covenants

You should by now be familiar with the various methods of protecting interests in land, both at law and in equity, from your reading of Chapter 4. However, it is always helpful to have a reminder of the rules in the context of the specific interest being considered, so here is a short recap on how the benefit of a freehold covenant can be protected by the benefiting landowner.

The first thing to remember is that a freehold covenant is an equitable interest in land. You will remember that, unlike an easement or a **mortgage**, it can never be legal, because it does not appear on the list of legal interests in land set out in section 1(2) of the Law of Property Act 1925. We are therefore looking at the provisions relating to the protection of an equitable interest in land, and not a legal one.

As with all interests in land, how we protect our freehold covenant depends upon whether the land affected by the benefit and burden of the covenant is registered or unregistered. In registered land, under section 32 of the Land Registration Act 2002, a freehold covenant must be registered as a notice on the Charges Register at the Land Registry. If the landowner with the benefit of the covenant enters a notice on the register, that covenant will be capable of binding any third party purchaser of the freehold. If the benefited landowner fails to enter their notice, however, any buyer of the burdened land will take free of the covenant, in accordance with section 52 of the Land Registration Act 1925, and so will not be bound by it. So it is very important for the person with the benefit of the covenant to enter the Notice on the register.

If the title to the land is unregistered, the covenant must be registered at the central Land Charges Register in Plymouth, as a class D(ii) land charge under the Land Charges

Table 11.2 Protection of a covenant

	Method of protection	Failure will result in . . .
Registered land	By entry of a notice in the Charges Register at the Land Registry	Any purchaser of the burdened land takes free of the covenant
Unregistered land (post-1926)	By registering a Class D(ii) Land Charge at the Land Charges Registry in Plymouth	Any purchaser for value of the legal estate takes free of the covenant
Unregistered land (pre-1926)	The doctrine of notice applies.	A bone fide purchaser for value without notice takes free of the covenant

Act 1972. If the covenant is registered as a class D(ii) land charge it will bind subsequent buyers of the land; if not, in accordance with section 4(6) of the Land Charges Act 1972, a purchaser of the legal estate for value will not be bound. It should be noted that the requirement for registration of restrictive covenants in unregistered land only applies to those covenants created after 1 January 1926; in respect of those covenants created before this date the old doctrine of notice applies.

Table 11.2 provides a reminder of how a covenant should be protected.

Remedies for breach of covenant

Having established whether or not a covenant is enforceable by and against the current owners of the benefited and burdened land, and therefore whether a breach of that covenant is capable of remedy, the obvious question is what remedies are actually available to the benefited landowner. As against the original parties, of course, you can apply to the court for damages for breach of contract. However, this will in most cases not give the benefited landowner the remedy they actually want, which is to restrain the breach. The favoured course of action therefore for the majority of landowners will be to apply for an equitable remedy, either by way of an injunction or specific performance. These equitable remedies are much more flexible in that they can be applied as against any landowner who has acquired the burden of the covenant, whether through equitable or common law means.

However, it must always be remembered that the difficulty with equitable remedies is that they are discretionary and not granted to the benefited landowner as of right. This means that there is no guarantee the victim of the breach will achieve the result they want in the courts. One example is the case of *Wrotham Park Estate Co. Ltd* v. *Parkside Homes Ltd* [1974] 1 WLR 798. Here land had been sold off from the estate, subject to a covenant that plans for any building work to be carried out on the land bought should be submitted to the estate for approval prior to the work being carried out. The covenant was registered as a Class D(ii) land charge. Aware of the covenant, Parkside Homes bought the land and then built a high-density housing estate on it without seeking

approval from the covenantee. The estate asked the court to grant an injunction requiring the houses to be demolished, but, despite the clear breach of covenant, the court refused to grant their request. Instead they ordered Parkside Homes to pay damages in lieu of an injunction, based on a percentage of the purchase prices of the houses. It was the view of the court that to order the houses to be demolished would cause a detriment to the house builder disproportionate to the damage incurred by the breach of covenant. However, from the point of view of the estate owners, a permanent view of a high-density housing estate from their land would have been far from a satisfactory outcome.

Discharge of covenants

Turning once again to the point of view of a buyer of the burdened land, what can a buyer of burdened land do if the land is subject to an unwanted covenant? One answer is that they might, under certain circumstances, be able to negotiate or procure its modification or discharge. This can be achieved in several ways, as follows.

Express discharge or variation

The purchaser may be able to agree with the benefited landowner that the covenant in question be varied or discharged. This would of course be dependent upon the value of the covenant to the benefited land and the relative bargaining positions of the parties. It may be that the benefited landowner sees little need or use for the covenant and is therefore happy to discharge it, perhaps subject to a payment of money or legal costs for its discharge or variation. However, this is far from a guaranteed solution and is very much dependent upon the good will of the covenantee.

Implied agreement

On rare occasions the benefit of the covenant may be lost if the covenantee has submitted to a long usage wholly inconsistent with its continuance, for example by remaining inactive while open breaches are committed. In these circumstances, the covenantee will lose the equitable right to enforce the covenant by injunction although, if there is mere delay, without evidence of implied consent to discharge or modification, the covenantee may still be able to claim damages at common law against the original covenantor.

Declaration by the court

Application may be made to the court for a declaration as to whether any freehold land is affected by any restriction and, if so, the nature, extent and enforceability of it (s.84(2) LPA 1925). This can be used to obtain a declaration that a covenant has been impliedly waived or, for example is now **void** for want of registration as a Land Charge Class D(ii) or for failure to register a notice on the Charges Register. The advantage of a court declaration is certainty; a purchaser of the burdened land can be assured in advance that the covenant no longer affects the land.

By the Lands Chamber

The Upper Tribunal (**Lands Chamber**), formerly the Lands Tribunal, has power under section 84 of the Land Registration Act 1925 (as amended by section 28 of the Law of Property Act 1969) to modify or extinguish a restrictive covenant if an applicant can show one of four grounds, which are:

1. That the restriction ought to be deemed obsolete due to changes in the character of the property or neighbourhood. For example, where there is a restrictive covenant that the burdened property should only be used as a residential dwelling house, when all of the surrounding properties are in business use, it may be argued that the covenant is obsolete;
2. That the covenant impedes reasonable user of the land and is either of no real value to the persons entitled to the benefit of it, or is contrary to the public interest;
3. That those with the benefit of the covenant have already agreed, expressly or impliedly 'by their acts or omissions to the discharge or modification of the covenant'; and finally
4. That the proposed discharge or modification will not injure persons entitled to the benefit of the restriction. In other words, that there will be no real detriment to the covenantees if the covenant is discharged

As can be seen from the above list, the situations in which the discharge of a covenant will be genuinely appropriate are rare, unless the covenant is very old and to all intents and purposes obsolete.

Key stats Restrictive covenants statistics received from the Lands Tribunal

Number of applications to discharge and/or modify restrictive covenants received per year:

2000	2001	2002	2003	2004	2005	2006	2007
38	49	55	54	89	86	91	84

The Tribunal commented that the sustained increase in numbers of applications received is probably due to increased demand for residential development land from 2004 onwards.

Of the cases received, the statistics show that at least half are withdrawn or struck out, some after the applicant has reached agreement with objectors and no longer seeks to have a determination by the Tribunal. In other cases the application is withdrawn or struck out because the applicants give up in the face of objections or change their plans. It is half or less of received cases that proceed to a determination. The majority of determined cases are determined on the papers. An order without a hearing is made only when the parties consent to this procedure. This occurs when no objections are received after publication.

Source: http://www.official-documents.gov.uk/document/hc1012/hc10/1067/1067.pdf

It should be noted that, if the Chamber agrees to discharge the covenant, then it may require the payment of compensation to the owners of the benefited land.

Reform

The rules relating to the running of freehold covenants have been much criticised over the years due to their complexity and, in particular, because of the difficulty in enforcing positive covenants. In 1984 the Law Commission published a report in which they suggested that the rules should be abolished and should be replaced by a new class of legal interest in land, called 'land obligations'. Since then, the Law Commission has recommended a series of reforms to the law governing third-party rights over land, and in particular easements and covenants. This culminated in the publication of a consultation paper in 2008, entitled 'Easements, Covenants and Profits à Prendre', from which the Commission has now published its report, entitled 'Making Land Work: Easements, Covenants and Profits à Prendre'. The report contains the Commission's final recommendations to Parliament, together with a draft Bill. In brief, the recommendations as relate to the law on restrictive covenants are as follows:

- It will not be possible to create new freehold covenants after the date of reform, although existing freehold covenants will not be affected.
- A new type of legal interest in land will be created by statute, called 'land obligations'.
- Land obligations must be either an obligation not to do something on the burdened land, an obligation to do something on the burdened land or on its boundary or an obligation to make a payment in return for the performance of such an obligation.
- Land obligations will be capable of being positive or negative in nature. The benefit and burden of land obligations will pass to successors in title under statute.
- In order to be valid land obligations must 'touch and concern' the land. The example used by the Law Commission is that an obligation to maintain a fence between Plot A and Plot B will be a land obligation; whereas an obligation to walk a dog will not.
- Existing positive and restrictive covenants will remain unaffected by the changes. Therefore if a person owns land which either has the benefit or burden of a positive or negative covenant, their position in respect of their benefit or burden will remain unchanged. Old positive or negative covenants will not be converted into new land obligations and the old law will continue to apply to pre-existing covenants.
- Land obligations must be created by deed and must be registered at the Land Registry or (where the burdened land is unregistered) as a new class G Land Charge. If these procedures are not followed, the obligation will not be a land obligation. Land obligations will not be able to be created by implication or long user.

The Law Commission also proposes to make changes to the powers available to the Lands Chamber for the hearing of cases relating to third party interests in land. Currently, the Lands Chamber has the power to discharge or modify covenants on certain grounds. The procedure itself is not used routinely, as it can be time-consuming and costly. One particular problem with the system of application for discharge has always been that which exists in relation to establishing a ground for discharge of the covenant. Under the current system there are four grounds on which a covenant may be discharged, and the landowner seeking discharge must establish the same single ground against each and every objector to its discharge. The Commission proposes that if in future the burdened landowner can establish one ground for discharge against each objector (but not necessarily the same one), this will be sufficient to discharge the covenant. This would potentially make it much easier to discharge third party rights using this process. The Commission's proposals for reform also envisage the widening of the jurisdiction of the Lands Chamber to deal with easements and the new land obligations, as well as existing freehold covenants. This will make the system more accessible to developers as well as giving some continuity of treatment of third party interests in land.

Having said all this, the proposals will only become law if taken up by the government of the day, and allocated parliamentary time. The Commission has recommended that, in addition, as an alternative to the implementation of all its recommendations wholesale, the government may prefer for the time being to put into effect the Commission's proposals in relation to easements, without introducing land obligations. It is therefore by no means certain that the proposals in relation to land obligations will be implemented.

Summary

- A covenant is a promise made by deed. Freehold covenants are promises to do (or not to do) something on your own land.
- Covenants can be positive or negative in nature. A negative covenant forbids or limits in some way activity on the covenantor's land; a positive covenant requires the owner of the burdened land to carry out a positive obligation, such as the requirement to build or maintain a wall.
- If in doubt as to whether a covenant is positive or negative in nature, you can apply the 'hand in pocket' rule, which states that if compliance with the covenant requires expenditure, it is positive in nature.
- The original parties to the covenant are bound by the ordinary rules of privity of contract. The person with the benefit of the covenant can therefore sue the person with the burden of the covenant if the terms of the covenant are breached.
- The benefit of the covenant can be transmitted at common law either expressly (under s.136 LPA 1925), or by virtue of the common law, provided the four conditions set out in *P&A Swift Investments* are met. These are that: the covenant must 'touch and concern' the land; the parties must have intended it to run; the covenantee must have a legal estate in the benefited land; and the claimant must derive their title from or under the original covenantee.
- It is not possible to pass the burden of a covenant at common law (*Austerberry* v. *Oldham Corporation*).
- There are two ways to circumvent this rule at common law: either by the creation of a chain of indemnity covenants, or under the doctrine of mutual benefit and burden set out in *Halsall* v. *Brizell*.
- The burden of the covenant can be passed to a third party in equity, however, under the rule in *Tulk* v. *Moxhay*. This allows the burden of negative covenants only to pass, provided they accommodate the dominant tenement, were intended by the original parties to run with the land and provided that the buyer of the burdened land has notice of them.
- If the burden of the covenant is made to run in equity, then the benefit must also run in

equity. This can be done in one of three ways: through express assignment of the benefit, annexation, or by way of a building scheme.

A person with the benefit of a covenant should protect it by registering it as a notice at the Land Registry or, if the land is unregistered, as a Class D(ii) Land Charge at the Land Charges Registry in Plymouth. Failure to do so will render the covenant unenforceable as against a third-party purchaser of the land.

Once established, covenants can be varied or discharged by express agreement, implied agreement (rarely), declaration by the court or by the Lands Chamber.

There are proposals to reform the law of freehold covenants to replace them with a new type of legal interest in land called 'land obligations'. The proposal is that these should be either positive or negative in nature and transmissible by law. The proposals are yet to be implemented.

Question and answer*

Problem: In 2004 Garth, a dairy farmer, sold off 10 acres of registered freehold farmland to his neighbour, Luke. In the conveyance transferring the property, Luke entered into the following covenants: 1. to use the land for agricultural purposes only; 2. not to carry on any business on the land which competes with Garth's; and 3. to pay half the cost of maintenance of the shared access road that services both properties.

In 2008 Garth decided to retire and sold the freehold of the farm to Shane, who wished to use the farm for the manufacture and production of his own range of cheeses. Last year Luke sold the freehold of his land to Jason, who owns a neighbouring farm. Jason has obtained planning permission to build a factory unit on the site to complement his own dairy farming business. The unit will be used for the production of cream, butter and cottage cheese. The shared access road is being used by the construction lorries to gain entrance to the site and the condition of the road has deteriorated very quickly, making it difficult to drive on. Jason has refused to pay any money towards the repairs. Shane wishes to stop Jason. Advise him on his options.

You should allow yourself no more than 40 minutes to complete this task.

Essay: Statutory annexation means that there is no longer any need to show that a covenant benefits all of the land retained by the covenantee. Discuss.

This question should be answered in 40 minutes.

* Answer guidance is provided at the end of the chapter.

Further reading

Dollar, P., 'A bit of an uphill struggle', EG 2007 0715, 142–3.
This article provides a useful overview of the law relating to freehold covenants, with an emphasis on how to circumvent them. The article considers, with reference to case law, the passing of the benefit and burden of the covenant including its passage by annexation or building schemes.

Bullock, A., '*Federated Homes* revisited (2005) 155 NLJ 238.
This article gives a useful and practical discussion of the case of *Federated Homes* in the light of the more recent decision of *Crest Nicholson* v. *McAllister*. Helps to put the concept of statutory annexation into context in the light of these decisions.

Gravells, N., 'Enforcement of positive covenants affecting freehold land' [1994] 110 LQR 346.
This article discusses the enforcement of positive covenants in the light of *Rhone* v. *Stevens* and calls for a review of the law in this area.

Martin, J., 'Remedies for breach of restrictive covenants' [1996] Conv 329.
This is a really useful article setting out the various remedies available for breach of covenant and how they are applied by the courts.

Law Commission Report no. 327, 'Making Land Work: Easements, Covenants and Profits à Prendre', available online at: http://www.official-documents.gov.uk/document/hc1012/hc10/1067/1067.pdf.
Report and recommendations for reform of the law relating to restrictive covenants, including the creation of a new form of legal interest in land, the 'land obligation'. Also discusses options for the expansion of the jurisdiction of the Lands Chamber, to aid developers.

Question and answer guidance

Please note that the following is not a full answer and is intended to provide guidance in outline form only as to how to answer the questions posed.

The first question to ask is whether the covenants listed are positive or negative in nature. This will determine how they are dealt with on any subsequent transfer of the property.

1. *to use the land for agricultural purposes only* – this is worded positively 'to use the land for a certain purpose only', but is actually negative in nature, because it restricts the burdened landowner from using the land for any other purpose than for agriculture; 2. *not to carry on any business on the land which competes with Garth's* – this again restricts Luke's use of the land; and 3. *to pay half the cost of maintenance of the shared access road that services both properties* – this is a positive covenant, requiring Luke to pay for the maintenance of the access road to his property.

Since the original covenantor (Luke) and covenantee (Garth) entered into these covenants, both have sold their land to third parties – Garth has sold his benefited land to Shane and Luke has sold his burdened land to Jason. In order to discover whether Shane can stop Jason from breaching the covenants we therefore need to determine whether the benefit of the covenants has passed to Shane and whether the burden of the covenants has passed to Jason.

Passing the benefit at law: The original covenantee, Garth, could have expressly assigned the benefit of the covenants to Shane by deed under s.136 LPA 1925. Alternatively, as the covenants were created after 11 May 2000 the benefit of them may have passed under the Contract (Rights of Third Parties) Act 1999, provided that covenants were specifically worded so as to include successors in title of the covenantor. However, we are not told that either of these applies, so we need to look to the position at common law. This states that, provided the four conditions in *P&A Swift Investments* are met, the benefit of the covenants will pass to Shane. The conditions are that: (a) The covenant must 'touch and concern' the land of the covenantee – in other words the covenants must be of genuine benefit or value to the land itself and not merely personal in nature. Of the three covenants, numbers 1 and 3 seem to be genuinely for the benefit of the land; however covenant number 2, not to carry on any business which competes with Garth's, is likely to be seen as personal in nature and therefore not to fulfil the first condition in *P&A Swift*. The benefit of covenant 2 cannot therefore be said to pass to Shane at common law; (b) It must have been the intention of the parties at the time of making the covenant that the benefit should pass to successors in title. This intention is now implied under s.78(1) LPA 1925, unless stated otherwise – which in our case it is not; (c) the covenantee must have held the legal estate in the land to be benefited at the time of entering into the covenant. We are told that the original covenantee, Garth, owned the freehold of the farmland; (d) The claimant must derive their title from or under the original covenantee. We are told that Shane bought the freehold from Garth. This is therefore complied with. On the basis of the above, then, covenants 1 and 3 will pass at common law to Shane.

Passing the burden at law: at common law, the burden of the covenants will not pass to third parties (*Austerberry* v. *Oldham*; *Rhone* v. *Stevens*). The burden will therefore stay with Luke under s.79 LPA 1925, although this is of limited use to Shane because he can only sue Luke for damages. He cannot get the equitable remedies of injunction or specific performance because the breach is not Luke's. From Luke's perspective, he could have protected himself by insisting on an indemnity for future breaches when he sold the land to Jason. We are not told whether this has been done, however. We therefore have to look to see whether the burden may have passed to Jason in equity.

Passing the burden in equity: the burden of negative covenants only may pass in equity, provided that they comply with the conditions set out in *Tulk* v. *Moxhay*. We have established that covenants 1 and 2 are negative in nature; covenant 3 (to maintain the driveway) is not, and so the burden of it will not pass in equity. In addition, for the burden of covenants 1 and 2 to run with the land: 1. *the covenant must accommodate the dominant tenement*, that is, it must benefit the land in question, and not be personal to the original parties. We have established that covenant 2 is likely to be viewed as personal in nature. This leaves covenant 1, not to use for anything other than agricultural purposes – which would fit this criterion; 2. *the original parties must have intended that the burden should bind successors in title to the property* – this can either be expressly evidenced, or implied under Section 79 of the Law of Property Act 1925. There is no suggestion that it should not be implied; 3. *the person against whom the covenant is being enforced must have notice of the covenant* – in the case of registered land, the restrictive covenant must be entered on the Charges Register of the burdened property at the Land Registry as a notice. We are told that the land is registered and have been given no reason to think that the covenant would not have been registered as it should have been. Assuming it has been properly registered, the burden of covenant 1 will therefore pass with the land in equity. If the burden of the covenant has passed in equity, the benefit must also be shown to pass in equity:

Passing the benefit in equity: this can be done through express assignment (we are not told this applies here); through the medium of a building scheme (again, this doesn't apply) or through annexation, which can be express, implied or statutory. It has been suggested that s.78(1) LPA 1925 serves to automatically annex the benefit of covenants to the land (*Federated Homes*), although the construction of the covenant should be taken into account when deciding on this. With a covenant such as one not to use other than for agricultural purposes one might suggest that the intention clearly was that this should pass to successors in title.

Conclusion: Shane has obtained the benefit of covenant 1 and Jason the burden, both in equity. Shane can therefore apply to the court for an injunction to prevent Jason's non-agricultural use of the property. Covenant 2 was personal to the original parties and so the benefit would not have passed to Shane; nor the burden to Jason. There is therefore nothing Shane can do to prevent the competing business. Covenant 3 is positive in nature and therefore the burden of the covenant will not have passed in equity. However, we are told that the maintenance cost is in return for use of the shared driveway to the property. This is suggestive of a mutual benefit (the easement of access) and burden (the cost of maintenance) under the doctrine in *Halsall* v. *Brizell*. This common law doctrine will apply provided the benefit and burden are mutually linked, which would definitely appear to be the case here. Jason could refuse the benefit and thus not incur the burden, but he has not done so – we are told he is using the driveway. Shane can therefore claim the cost of maintenance of the driveway from him.

Essay: You should start by explaining what annexation is: i.e. that it is one of three methods of passing the benefit of a covenant to a third party in equity. Annexation, express assignment or a building scheme must be used to show that the benefit of the covenant has passed to the purchasing party of the benefited land wherever the burden of the covenant has also been shown to pass in equity, under the rule in *Tulk* v. *Moxhay*.

There are three types of annexation: express, implied or statutory. You should talk through briefly what each of these types of annexation is and how it applies.

Annexation means that when the covenant was made it must have been annexed, or permanently attached to, the land itself, and not just to the person with the benefit of the covenant. Express annexation takes place when the express wording of the covenant shows that it was the intention of the original parties to the agreement that the benefit of the covenant should run with the land; implied annexation is rare and can only be imposed by the courts.

Statutory annexation, according to the case of *Federated Homes* v. *Mill Lodge Properties*, is the idea that the wording of s.78(1) LPA 1925 serves automatically to annex to each and every part of the benefited land the covenant in question, provided that it touches and concerns the land benefited, and unless expressed to be personal to the original parties to the covenant (*Roake* v. *Chadha*). The decision has caused controversy, however, particularly in respect of the issue of the extent of annexation when dealing with larger pieces of land.

With express annexation, the annexation takes place when the express wording of the covenant shows that it was the intention of the original parties to the agreement that the benefit of the covenant should run with the land. In order for express annexation to take place the whole of the land retained by the covenantee must be capable of benefiting from the covenant. It is not sufficient that only part of the land which has the benefit of the covenant will gain from it. Traditionally, this will be a matter of fact and degree in every case. In *Re Ballard's Conveyance* the land in question was a large estate of some 17,000 acres and consequently a covenant not to build in a sale off of 16 acres of land at one edge of the estate was held only to benefit the land abutting the the boundary of the burdened property. The covenant could therefore not run on the sale of the estate because it did not benefit the whole of the land. This could be contrasted with the case of *Marten* v. *Flight Refuelling*, in which the opposite decision was reached, despite the estate in question extending to some 7,500 acres.

With express annexation, therefore, if you wish to annex a covenant to a large piece of land, the covenant should be drafted so as to benefit the 'whole or any part of' the named land, as in *Marquess of Zetland* v. *Driver* in which a covenant expressed to be for the benefit of the covenantee's retained land 'and each and every part thereof' was considered sufficient to ensure that the parts of the land retained that were actually affected by the breach could sue under the terms of the covenant.

The issue with *Federated Homes Ltd* v. *Mill Lodge Properties Ltd* is that the Court of Appeal here suggested that, on the basis of the wording of section 78(1), a covenant could be presumed to be annexed to each and every part of the land without the need for any express provision to that effect being contained in the covenant at all. Not only does this remove the need for express annexation of any kind, but also suggests that the extent of the annexation will extend to the full acreage of the benefited land, regardless of size. This could have impractical implications and could be unnecessarily restrictive on small sales off of land on the boundaries of large estates. There is also the issue that s.78(1) will apply only to covenants imposed since 1925, meaning that there is still the need for express or implied annexation in respect of any covenant created before this date.

You should conclude by stating whether or not you agree with the statement made and if not, why not, perhaps citing some more recent cases following *Federated Homes*, such as *Sugarman* v. *Porter* and *Crest Nicholson* v. *McAllister*.

Visit **www.mylawchamber.co.uk** to access tools to help you develop and test your knowledge of land law.

Use Case Navigator to read in full some of the key cases referenced in this chapter with commentary and questions:

Tulk **v.** ***Moxhay*** [1843–60] All ER Rep 9

Chapter 12 Interests in land: mortgages

Key points In this chapter we will be looking at:

- ✦ What a mortgage is and how they are relevant to you
- ✦ The terminology of mortgages
- ✦ The borrower's contractual right to redeem the mortgage
- ✦ The equitable rights of the borrower: the equity of redemption
- ✦ Collateral advantages and when they can be used
- ✦ The striking down of unconscionable terms in the mortgage
- ✦ Undue influence and its effects on the mortgage agreement
- ✦ The right of the lender to sue on the mortgage
- ✦ The lender's right to possession and sale and the borrower's right to postpone it
- ✦ The provisions of section 36 of the Law of Property Act 1925 and suggestions for reform
- ✦ The lender's right of foreclosure
- ✦ The lender's right to appoint a receiver
- ✦ Equitable mortgages and how they are created
- ✦ Priority and registration of mortgages

Introduction

Of all the topics featured in this text **mortgages** is the one most likely to affect the everyday lives of most of its readers. And the reason for this? Of course, it is that anyone wishing to buy their own property is likely to need a mortgage to do so. There are very few people who have enough personal funds of their own to be able to finance the purchase of a property without the help of some kind of lending, whether it is from the bank, building society, or even a substantial loan from a family member. And it is the process of securing, or mortgaging, property against such a loan of money borrowed for this purpose that we will be dealing with in this chapter.

What is the relevance of mortgages?

In the wake of the still relatively recent housing market crash and with the global recession still looming large the topic of finance and lending is rarely out of the news and the concerns of first time buyers in particular hoping to secure lending for the purchase of a home are commonly cited. The *Financial Times* article, set out in the Law in Action feature below, gives an excellent snapshot of exactly the type of coverage the press are giving to the topic on an almost daily basis.

Law in action Households feel pinch as lenders tighten mortgages

By Tanya Powley and Norma Cohen

UK households are facing a growing squeeze on their incomes as lenders hike the cost of mortgage repayments and tighten criteria for borrowers.

While the number of mortgages approved by lenders edged up slightly in March, according to Bank of England figures published on Wednesday, mortgage conditions have worsened in recent months for millions of homeowners.

New data on Wednesday, which followed a string of earnings statements from some of the UK's largest banks, illustrates why borrowers are being asked to pay more, despite the fact that official Bank of England rates are unchanged.

In short, banks' own costs of funds are rising, a reason cited by Lloyds Banking Group and Santander earlier in the week when they sought to explain why they will be more cautious in their mortgage lending activities going forwards.

Banks raise money in wholesale markets where jitters about solvency in the Eurozone are making those who normally make short term loans to banks – such as money market funds – demand higher rates in compensation.

Banks have been under pressure from regulators to raise more funds from retail depositors who are less likely to suddenly withdraw their cash. However, the costs of this more stable form of bank funding are rising, too.

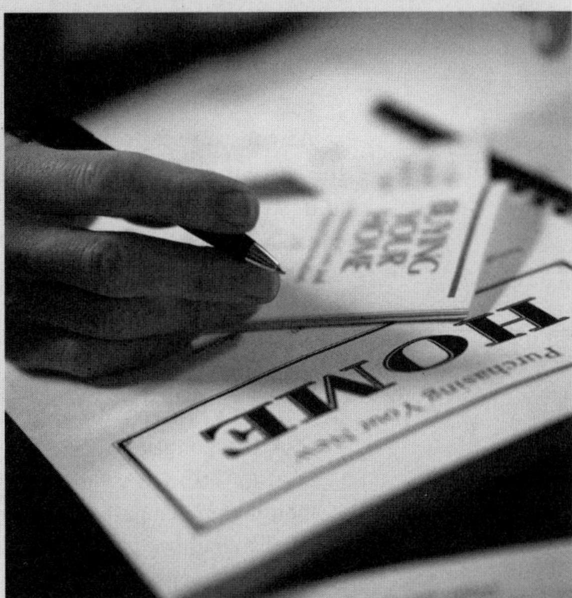

Source: Brofsky Studio Inc., Photodisc

For example, so-called time deposits – which require customers to keep their money in the bank for a minimum period to gain access to a favourable interest rate – rose to their highest level since April 2009, just after the Bank slashed rates to current lows. Rates offered to business customers to keep funds on deposit are also at their highest levels since May 2009.

Homeowners with interest-only mortgages – where the capital is only paid off at the end of the mortgage term – have been hit particularly hard following a clampdown on these type of deals by lenders and the Financial Services Authority.

Lenders have introduced stricter criteria over who can take out an interest-only loan following moves by the financial regulator to stop borrowers taking on more debt than they can afford.

On Wednesday, the Co-operative Bank became the first big high street lender to pull out of the interest-only mortgage market, further reducing the remortgage options for homeowners with interest-only loans. From 8 May, the bank will only allow customers to take out mortgages on a capital repayment basis.

Several lenders, including Santander and Nationwide, have already restricted these loans to homeowners with a deposit – or equity – of 50 per cent or more.

Meanwhile, more than a million homeowners face higher mortgage payments after several high street lenders raised rates by as much as 0.5 percentage points on Tuesday.

Halifax, the UK's biggest mortgage lender, the Co-operative Bank, Clydesdale and Yorkshire Banks all hiked the cost of their standard variable rate (SVR) mortgage deals, increasing their mortgage customers' annual repayments by an additional £300m, according to consumer group Which?

It warned that the rate rises would place further pressure on family finances. A fifth of borrowers surveyed said that a £100 increase in their monthly mortgage repayment would leave them without enough money for daily essentials like food.

Source: **http://www.ft.com/cms/s/0/f4f62e4e-947f-11e1-8e90-00144feab49a.html#axzz20OUw9Nen**

Source: Powley, T. and Cohen, C. (2012) Households feel pinch as lenders tighten mortgages, *Financial Times*, 2 May.

As you can see from the article above, mortgage lending is not an easy business in the current financial market. Do you have a mortgage? Whether you do or not, the Out and About feature below will give you some insight into your own personal borrowing capabilities and what it might mean to you.

Out and about Your 'dream' property

Look at a mortgage calculator online, such as the one at: **http://www.moneysupermarket.com/mortgages/calculator/**. How much would you need to borrow to buy your dream property? What are the features of the mortgage? Is there any tie-in? What would you have to repay?

You should take no longer than 20 minutes on this task.

Handy tip: If you already have a mortgage, you will have to look at your mortgage conditions for details of the mortgage rate and other mortgage features. If you do not have it to hand, you should find a copy of your lender's current mortgage conditions on their website.

Source: Imagemore Co. Ltd

Reflective practice

Did you find this an easy exercise and were you able to follow all of the technical language? Could you afford to take out a mortgage now? If not, how much would you have to be earning in order to afford it and what kind of deposit would you have to put in? Where would you find this deposit money? Do you think the repayment rates and borrowing are realistic in the current housing market?

Having perused the above features you should now have a reasonable understanding of the social context behind mortgage lending today and perhaps of the difficulties you may face when seeking to afford your own borrowing. Bearing this in mind, let us spend the remainder of the chapter putting mortgages into a legal context.

What is a mortgage?

As we have already alluded to above, a mortgage is a loan of money secured against property. The classic definition of a mortgage is found in the Court of Appeal case of *Santley* v. *Wilde* [1899] 2 Ch 474, which says that a mortgage is 'a **conveyance** of land as security for the payment of a debt or the discharge of some other obligation'. So it is a loan of money secured against your house. What do we mean by 'secured', exactly? Well, put simply, it means that you promise the lender that you will pay back the loan, putting up your house as **security** for the loan; if you do not repay your loan, the lender may then take your house in order to satisfy the debt.

Case Summary

The example set out in *Santley* v. *Wilde* relates specifically to land, but a mortgage does not actually have to be over land or **real property** you can actually mortgage any property, including houses, but also aeroplanes, ships, works of art, and even the assets of a company. Anything which has a commercial value can be used as security against a loan, and thus can be mortgaged. So mortgages do not apply just to land, although in the context of this text that is what we will be concentrating on.

Anything which has a commercial value can be used as security

Mortgages are quite a nice topic to be dealing with towards the end of the text, because when you start to think about mortgages, you will realise that you actually already know quite a lot about them from earlier chapters. Apart from any general knowledge of mortgages you may have picked up along the way, you also know a fair amount about the nature of mortgages from your previous reading. For example, you may remember from your reading in Chapter 4 on **interests in land**, that a mortgage is one of the five classes of legal interest in land listed in section 1(2) of the Law of Property Act 1925. So already you know that a mortgage is capable of being a legal interest in land. You also know from your study of the **formalities** for the creation of legal interests in land that, for an interest to be legal, according to section 52 of the Law of Property Act 1925 it must be made by **deed**. So it follows, then, that a legal mortgage must be created by deed. An example of the form of a standard mortgage is contained in the Documenting the Law feature, below.

Documenting the law

Example of a mortgage deed:

MORTGAGE DEED **OCTAGON BUILDING SOCIETY**

Date:

We are: The Octagon Building Society, Octagon House, Newtown NE3 0BS

You, the Borrower are:

The Mortgage Conditions are: Octagon Building Society Conditions 2012

The Property is:

Postcode: **Title number:**

1. The Mortgage Conditions form part of this mortgage. You confirm receipt of a copy of the Mortgage Conditions.
2. You charge the Property by way of legal mortgage with payment of all the money payable to us under the Mortgage Conditions. This mortgage is made with full title guarantee.
3. We are obliged to make further advances and application is made to the Registrar for a note to be entered on the Register to this effect.
4. We and you agree that this document may be destroyed at any time after it has been electronically scanned and registered by the Land Registry. An Official Copy issued by the Land Registry will then be acceptable as evidence for all purposes as if it were the original.

SIGNED AS A DEED BY:
(Signature of the borrower) ____________________

In the presence of: ____________________

(Name, address and signature of witness) ____________________

____

SIGNED AS A DEED BY:
(Signature of the borrower) ____________________

In the presence of: ____________________

(Name, address and signature of witness) ____________________

____

As you can see from the sample above, the format of a mortgage deed can be very simple indeed. The majority of detail is contained in the attached mortgage conditions, which form a part of the mortgage contract. These will contain details such as the interest rate and the date for redemption of the mortgage (for an explanation of this, see below).

Having established the nature and formalities for the creation of a legal mortgage, then, what else do we need to know about them? What other requirements are there for their creation? Prior to 1926 a legal mortgage was created by the borrower actually transferring their **legal title** in the property to the lender in exchange for the loan of money. This meant that, for the duration of the mortgage, the lender was actually the legal owner of the property, and they did not transfer the land back into the borrower's name until the loan had been repaid. This made matters very simple for the lender because, if the loan was not repaid, the lender would simply keep the property. However, it was less than satisfactory for the property owner, who would effectively lose ownership of their property for the life of the mortgage and have to deal with the stress of a reconveyance at the end of the mortgage term. The Law of Property Act 1925 therefore abolished this method of creating a legal mortgage, so that today the only way of doing so is by way of legal **charge**, or 'charge by way of legal mortgage' as is stated in section 85 of the Act. So what happens now when a mortgage is created, is that the property remains in the legal ownership of the borrower, and instead the lender is granted a charge over that property in the form of a legal interest in the land. That legal interest carries with it the right, amongst other things, to take possession of the property in repayment of the debt if the loan is not repaid. We will be considering the detail of both lenders' and borrowers' rights in the remainder of the chapter. However, before we do this, it may be prudent to learn a little bit of mortgage terminology.

if the loan was not repaid, the lender would simply keep the property

Mortgage terminology

You have already come across the term 'mortgage' itself, and have seen that, since 1925, the word is synonymous with the term 'legal charge'. This is because a mortgage by way of legal charge is the only way in which a legal mortgage can now be created; thus the terms 'mortgage' and 'legal charge' are colloquially interchangeable.

More importantly, you should become familiar with the terms '**mortgagor**' and '**mortgagee**'. Again, these terms are synonymous with two other terms that we have already come across: that of borrower and lender: the mortgagor is the person who mortgages the property: the person who borrows the money in exchange for an interest in the land; the mortgagee is the person or company who accepts the property as security for the loan, lending the money in exchange for the interest in the land. In this text we will be using the terms borrower and lender, for ease. However, you will come across the terms mortgagor and mortgagee in other texts and when reading case comments and judgments. It is therefore necessary for you to be familiar with both sets of terms and their meanings.

Rights of the borrower

Having created the mortgage, the next thing we need to know is what rights the borrower and lender have under the mortgage. Let us first consider the borrower.

The borrower's rights under the terms of the mortgage can broadly be divided into two categories:

1. firstly, their contractual, or legal right under the mortgage; and
2. secondly and much more importantly, the borrower's rights in **equity**.

The contractual right to redeem

Essentially, the borrower under a mortgage has one contractual right and that is the right to redeem, or pay off, the mortgage, thus releasing them from their obligation to the lender and the lender from their interest in the land. The mortgage deed will set out in its terms the date of the contractual right to redeem. This date, which is usually set at six months from the start of the mortgage (although it could be any time), is quite separate from the term of the mortgage, which is commonly far longer. The majority of residential mortgages are taken over 25 years.

Because the date of the contractual right to redeem is set so early on in the life of the mortgage, in reality it is of little practical use to a borrower. If someone is repaying a loan of £100,000 in instalments over a period of 25 years, the likelihood of them being able to repay the whole of the loan only six months into the mortgage term is extremely slim. Despite this, under the strict rules of contract law, if the borrower misses the date of redemption set out in the mortgage deed, they lose their contractual right to redeem. More importantly, when the redemption date in the mortgage passes the borrower also loses their property. This is because, technically speaking, once the redemption date has passed the borrower is in breach of one of the terms of the mortgage deed. By not repaying the loan before the specified date, contractually they forfeit their security under the loan, and with residential mortgages of course this means their house.

The equity of redemption

Luckily for the borrower this is the point at which the court of equity has taken steps to intervene, affording to the borrower a series of protective measures which together can be summarised as the '**equity of redemption**'. The idea behind the equity of redemption is to keep the parties focused on the true purpose of the mortgage, which is to give security to a lender in the event of the non-payment of a debt. In the eyes of equity, there should be nothing more to the mortgage than simply that; any opportunity the mortgage gives to the lender to obtain other advantages over the borrower should therefore be quashed. The equity of redemption can be broken down into four separate principles or rules. These are:

- the equitable right to redeem (which also encompasses the prevention or postponement of redemption);
- **collateral advantages**;
- **unconscionable** terms; and
- **undue influence**.

The equitable right to redeem

The first, and most important equitable right under the equity of redemption is the borrower's equitable right to redeem. Whilst we have seen that the contractual right to redeem is limited at best, equity says that, so long as the borrower pays back the loan together with interest due on the mortgage at the contractually specified rate, then they will have a continued right to redeem the mortgage right up until the end of the mortgage term. This means that, even though the contractual date for redemption under the mortgage may have passed, in equity the borrower can still redeem the mortgage even though technically they are in **breach of contract** because the legal date of redemption has passed. This is obviously a far more flexible approach: as long as the borrower pays back the money by the end of the term the courts have a discretion in equity to allow the mortgage to be redeemed. It is worth noting that a lender is unlikely to want to redeem the mortgage after six months in any event: from a commercial point of view, they are lending the money in order to earn interest on it, paid to them over the course of the mortgage term. If they bring the mortgage to an end after only six months, potentially this means they would miss out on 24-and-a-half years' worth of interest payments.

The prevention or postponement of redemption

Whilst, on one hand, the court of equity is keen to give borrowers the right to redeem their mortgages at any point throughout the term, on the other hand equity is also keen to prevent terms in mortgages which postpone or limit that borrower's right to redeem the mortgage should they wish to. In other words, the borrower should have the right to pay back the sums owed by them and be released from the mortgage whenever they choose during the lifetime of the mortgage without limitation. This is particularly the case with domestic mortgages. This does not mean that the lender cannot make administrative charges or charge a **redemption penalty** for early repayment of the loan; after all, early redemption means the lender loses their interest payments, as we have seen above. Rather, what equity seeks to prevent is a provision in the mortgage that prevents early repayment altogether.

The difference between the two extremes can be illustrated by looking at a number of commercial mortgages, which equity deals with somewhat more leniently. Because of the more equal footing between a business borrower and lender, equity is more comfortable with allowing the repayment of a mortgage to be postponed or limited, provided that:

- the mortgage is not in any other way unconscionable; and
- the right to redeem is not rendered an illusion.

So, whereas with a residential mortgage you cannot limit the right to redeem the mortgage at all, with a commercial mortgage you can have a term which limits redemption as long as the effect of that term is neither unconscionable nor inequitably harsh and so long as there is a realistic prospect of redeeming.

There are two cases which illustrate this point well. The first is the House of Lords case of *Knightsbridge Estates Trust Ltd* v. *Byrne* [1940] AC 613, which concerned a large property company, Knightsbridge Estates, who took out a mortgage over its freehold property portfolio. The mortgage deed contained a term that the mortgage, which was for the sum of £310,000, was to be repaid over a period of 40 years in six-monthly instalments. However, the borrower wanted to repay the loan early. The lender objected because they would lose out on their interest payments and the court upheld their claim. In the view of the Lords, the property that was the subject of the mortgage was **freehold** land; therefore at the end of the 40-year period, the borrower would get back no less than what they had mortgaged in the first place: the freehold. Whilst it was accepted that 40 years was a relatively long time, the transaction was a commercial one made between two parties that knew what they were doing. It was therefore not an unconscionable term: it was a valid business transaction. As it transpired the borrower later felt that they had made a bad bargain, but at the end of the day it was a business deal and the House of Lords were quite clear in stating that it is not the place of equity to intervene in such circumstances.

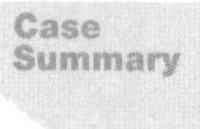

We can contrast the outcome in the *Knightsbridge Estates* case with the earlier Privy Council case of *Fairclough* v. *Swan Brewery Co. Ltd* [1912] AC 565. Here, a Mr Fairclough, who was a publican, had taken an **assignment** of the **lease** of the Federal Hotel, in Kattaning, Australia. The lease had only 20 years left to run. Two years after the assignment, Mr Fairclough took out a mortgage over the property of £500. There was a provision in the mortgage that said that Mr Fairclough could not redeem the mortgage until six weeks before the end of the term of the lease. When Mr Fairclough wanted to redeem the mortgage early, in contrast to the outcome in *Knightsbridge Estates*, the **Privy Council** said that yes, in that case, Mr Fairclough should be allowed to do so. The term in the mortgage deed had rendered the right to redeem an illusion: if the borrower was prevented from redeeming the mortgage until the term of the lease is about to come to an end, there would be nothing for the borrower to recover. No sooner would he have paid off his mortgage than he would have to return the property to the owner of the freehold reversion. This was considered an unrealistic prospect of redemption.

Collateral advantages

The third equitable right from which a borrower may benefit under the umbrella of the equity of redemption is the rule against collateral advantages. A collateral advantage can be described as getting something extra: something on the side over and above simple security for the loan. Obviously, from the point of view of equity, the idea of the lender obtaining another advantage at the same time as getting what should be just simple security for a loan is unacceptable, especially in a domestic context. However, in certain commercial **arm's length transactions**, equity will allow limited collateral advantages to exist. Typically, it will be that the borrower should buy certain products or services from the lender. One example might be in the lease of a public house where you have a **tie-in**: so the brewery lends their tenant money on the understanding that the brewery will have the sole rights to supply the tenant with alcoholic beverages to sell in the pub. This was the case in *Biggs* v. *Hoddinott* [1898] 2 Ch 307, in which a mortgage of a hotel contained provisions that the loan should not be repaid within the first five years, and that within this time the borrower should sell only the lender's beers. The court held that the tie-in did not unfairly compromise the borrower's right to redeem because it only applied during the period of the mortgage.

Generally speaking, in commercial transactions where collateral advantages are allowed, they will be subject to certain limitations:

- firstly that the collateral advantage should stop when the mortgage is redeemed; and
- secondly, that the collateral advantage should not be unconscionable.

Thus, in the case of *Noakes & Co Ltd* v. *Rice* [1902] AC 24, where a tenant of a public house had entered into a mortgage that contained a tie-in stated to last for the duration of the leasehold term, regardless of when the mortgage was repaid, it was held that the term created an unfair collateral advantage and that the collateral advantage should be brought to an end upon repayment of the loan.

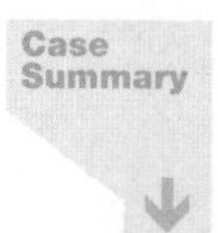

Another more recent example of where the court will strike down a term of the mortgage if they see it as unconscionable is the Court of Appeal case of *Jones* v. *Morgan* [2001] EWCA Civ 995. Here two brothers had mortgaged property subject to an agreement which gave the lender the right to have a half share in the mortgaged property transferred to them. The Court held that this was an unfair collateral advantage because it prevented the brothers from effectively redeeming the mortgage and regaining the whole of the property.

However, as with all equitable remedies their application is at the discretion of the court and how strictly the rules are applied will depend upon the circumstances of the case. The best known illustration of how a collateral advantage can work is the House of Lords case of *G&C Kreglinger* v. *New Patagonia Meat and Cold Storage Co. Ltd* [1914] AC 25. Here the Meat Company mortgaged its property to a wool broker. One of the terms of the mortgage agreement was that the Meat Company would give the wool brokers a right of first refusal on their sheepskins for a period of five years. After only two years the Meat Company redeemed the mortgage, paying back all the monies owing under it. It then argued that the agreement to sell the sheepskins to the lender should cease. But the House of Lords did not agree. In their opinion, the collateral advantage was valid as between two businesses, for the following three reasons:

1. In the grand scheme of things, the 5-year tie-in was not a particularly long time to be tied into the agreement;
2. The price to be paid for the skins as stated in the agreement was a reasonable market price; and
3. It was an arm's length business transaction. These were experienced business people who knew what they agreeing to.

So here we can see that the court was prepared to uphold a collateral advantage which continued after the redemption of the mortgage, because it was for a short period of time, the price of the agreement was reasonable and it was a business transaction. Whilst the Meat Company may have felt they had entered into a bad bargain, this was not a matter for the court. The collateral advantage obtained by the lender was not unconscionable.

Unconscionable terms

As you might imagine, equity has the power to strike down any unconscionable or oppressive terms in the mortgage agreement and not just those that relate to collateral advantages. What sort of thing is included in the wider definition of an unconscionable term is perhaps best explored by example. In the case of *Cityland & Property (Holdings) Ltd* v. *Dabrah* [1967] 3 WLR 605, a company had bought land for £3,500, with the help of a £2,900 mortgage. The terms of the mortgage were very unusual, however. There was no interest payable on the loan, but the lender instead required payment of a premium of 57 per cent of the amount of the loan, repayable over 6 years. The court held that the term was unreasonably oppressive for two reasons: firstly because of its size and secondly because of the relative strengths of the lender and the borrower. It was obvious that the borrower had been desperate for the loan and that the lender had taken advantage of this. The court struck out the term requiring payment of the premium and instead allowed for the variation of the loan to be repaid at an average interest rate of 7 per cent per annum over the course of the term.

This case can be contrasted with the result in the case of *Multiservice Bookbinding Ltd* v. *Marden* [1978] 2 WLR 535. This case concerned a mortgage over a business. The interest rate on the loan was not onerous, at only 2 per cent above the prevailing bank rate. On top of this, however, arrears were capitalised immediately after 21 days, meaning that arrears were added to the capital sum and interest would be charged on them from

that date; and there was an **'uplift' payment** calculable on the capital and interest on the loan that was index-linked to the Swiss franc. When the court calculated the effect of these clauses when applied together, in reality it meant that the interest rate payable by the borrower was actually a staggering 33 per cent. Despite this, however, the court found that the uplift clause was not an unconscionable term. In the eyes of the court, an index-linked money obligation was not contrary to **public policy** and, accordingly, the provisions of the mortgage linking repayments of capital and interest to the value of the Swiss franc were valid. The uplift clause could only be viewed as objectionable if it was imposed in a morally reprehensible manner. They said that, whilst there was no special rule applicable to mortgage contracts, the court might assume that an unfair advantage had been taken of the borrower if there were an unusual or unreasonable stipulation; however, this depended on the facts of the case, and in this instance the parties were in equal bargaining positions. Thus, while the terms of the agreement may have been unreasonable, they were not unfair, oppressive or morally reprehensible. It was not the job of the court to rewrite an 'improvident contract'. If the mortgage were unobjectionable when entered into, the hardship caused to the borrower as a result of the unforeseen fall in the value of the pound sterling since that date was not a ground for the court refusing to enforce the provisions of the mortgage.

What the court was saying, in effect, was that the lender has to have taken clear advantage of its position in order for the term to be unconscionable. This is quite a high bar that the courts impose in relation to business mortgages.

Undue influence

Whilst equity is quick to step in on behalf of domestic borrowers in the case of unconscionable terms in the mortgage, or a collateral advantage being discovered, probably the most common situation in which equity steps in on behalf of domestic borrowers is in cases of undue influence on the part of (usually) one borrower over another. The usual way in which undue influence arises is as follows: imagine the case of a husband and wife co-owning the matrimonial home. The husband wants to borrow some additional money against the house in order to help his business. The wife is unsure about the loan, but the husband tells her that if she does not agree to the borrowing, his business will go under; their lifestyle will suffer; they will no longer be able to afford the children's school fees, and so on. In fear of the wider consequences, the wife signs the agreement. This is essentially what is called undue influence. Because of the relationship of trust that exists between a husband and wife one spouse is able to unduly influence the other to enter into a transaction which is to their obvious disadvantage.

Another way in which undue influence can arise is, not where one spouse puts pressure on the other to sign the mortgage agreement, but where they lie about it. So, for example, the husband might tell the wife that it is a £5,000 loan over two years, whereas in actual fact it is a £50,000 loan over 20 years. Because the wife trusts the husband she does not bother to read the fine detail of the agreement and simply signs it. In this case, there is undue influence because one spouse has used their position of trust to deceive the other resulting in the weaker party entering into a transaction which puts them at a significant disadvantage.

Of course, undue influence does not arise solely between spouses; it can arise in any situation where one person is in a position of trust and they take advantage of that position to the detriment of the party relying on them. Thus, undue influence could arise between a mother and son, a solicitor and their client, a priest and parishioner, and any other number of circumstances. However, most of the case law on the subject relates to husband and wife situations, and this is what is most relevant to our studies.

In order to see some examples of undue influence at work, we will now take a look at some case law on the topic. But before we do, one question you may be asking is: why is the bank interested in whether or not there has been undue influence in the signing of the mortgage? And the answer to this question is that, if the bank seeks to repossess a property because the borrower has defaulted on the mortgage, but it turns out that one of the spouses signed the mortgage deed under undue influence and the lender knew it, the mortgage in respect of the innocent party will be set aside and the bank will not be able to obtain possession of the property in order to sell it and recoup their losses under the mortgage agreement.

To make things worse, under the rules of equity, where there is a relationship of trust such as that between a husband and wife the bank has **constructive notice** of any undue influence which may take place. This means that as soon as the bank is aware of the existence of a relationship in which undue influence or misrepresentation could arise, namely in the case of a married couple, they are put on notice of the possibility of that arising and, what is more, they are deemed to know about any that does arise. As we can see, then, the consequences on a mortgage lender of undue influence being established are potentially very damaging, hence the great interest of the banks and building societies in this particular issue.

Initially, in order to combat the effects of possible cases of undue influence, lenders adopted the practice of requiring any adult occupiers in the property to be mortgaged to sign a consent form which stated that they agreed to the mortgage and effectively postponing any rights they might have in the property in favour of the lender. However, it soon became clear that this was not enough to protect lenders from the far-reaching effects of an agreement entered into under undue influence. The court of equity required more. The two seminal cases in the area are the House of Lords decisions in *Barclays Bank* v. *O'Brien* [1993] 3 WLR 786 and *Royal Bank of Scotland plc* v. *Etridge (No. 2)* [2001] 3 WLR 1021.

Case Summary

In *Barclays* v. *O'Brien*, a wife had signed mortgage documentation giving the bank a second legal mortgage over the family home. When the bank sought to enforce payment of the loan, the wife said that she had signed the documentation under undue influence. She said that the husband had lied to her about the effect of the mortgage, leading her to believe that the security on the loan was limited to a £60,000 **bridging loan** for a period of only three weeks. In reality the debt had amounted some £154,000 and had not been repaid. The House of Lords, dismissing the bank's appeal, held that there had indeed been undue influence and that the bank had constructive notice of this. Unless the bank could prove, therefore, that it had taken reasonable steps to satisfy itself that the wife had entered into the agreement freely, the bank would be unable to enforce it. Whilst the bank had in fact written to Mrs O'Brien advising her to take independent legal advice, they had not followed the letter up to check that this had happened; nor had they explained to her, as a borrower, the implications of the second mortgage, either in their letter or otherwise. In the court's view this was simply not good enough. It can be seen from this case, then, that the courts were putting on lenders a positive duty to take steps to ensure that any interested party in the mortgage agreement should be fully advised of the nature of the transaction into which they were entering. The court also said **obiter** that the principles applied not only to married couples, but also to cohabitees and same-sex couples.

Case Summary

The second House of Lords case of *Etridge* gave the Lords the opportunity to review all of the previous case law in this area and to set out definitive guidance on what a lender should do in order to discharge this duty where the possibility of undue influence was apparent. The court actually heard no less than eight separate appeals in *Etridge*, all of which had arisen out of transactions in which a wife had mortgaged her interest in the family home in favour of the bank as security either for her husband's debts or for the debts of a company through which he carried on business. The Lords started their judgment by confirming that the burden of proof when claiming undue influence was on the person claiming to have been wronged. Therefore it was for the wife to prove that undue influence had occurred. That said, the Lords also confirmed that wherever a wife offered to stand **surety** for her husband's debts, the bank would be put on inquiry of the possibility of undue influence occurring, thus giving them a clear responsibility to take action to ensure proper advice has been given in any such case.

The Lords went into a huge amount of detail about the kind of advice which should be given. In brief the main requirements are as follows:

1. The advice has to be given to the wife by a solicitor. If the wife declines independent legal advice the bank should not continue with the mortgage;
2. The advice has to be given in the absence of the husband;
3. The solicitor has to explain in clear plain English both the nature of the transaction and that if the money is not repaid that they will lose their house and that the wife could be made bankrupt;
4. The wife must be advised that she has a choice whether or not to sign; and
5. If she does wish to proceed, the wife should confirm that she is happy for the solicitor to write to the bank detailing what has been explained to her.

There is a lot more detail given in the judgment of Lord Nicholls and it is worth reading through it to get a full picture of the requirements. In order to guide you through this process, why not take a look at the Writing and Drafting feature below.

Writing and drafting

Imagine you act for the Red Hills Building Society in the mortgage lending department. You have been tasked by your superior to produce a standard leaflet or memorandum to be sent to any solicitor instructed to act on your behalf in residential mortgage transactions, advising them on the steps they should take in order to satisfy the requirements of the court following *Etridge*. Read the judgment of Lord Nicholls in *Etridge* and prepare a draft of this document, setting out when the guidelines apply and what advice a solicitor needs to give to their clients under such circumstances.

You should take no more than 45 minutes on this task.

Handy tip: If you are stuck on what advice to give, try answering the following questions that are answered in the judgment: when is the bank put on inquiry? What should a solicitor be advising as a core minimum?

The most important thing to remember about *Etridge* is that it lays down guidelines to be followed by lenders that are designed to prevent them losing their security under a mortgage, on the basis that they had constructive notice of undue influence of one of the parties to the agreement. So long as the lender follows these guidelines, they will be protected from a claim of undue influence when they seek to enforce their right to possession of premises secured under the terms of the mortgage. If they do not follow the guidelines, however, they risk losing their security and having the mortgage set aside if undue influence can be proven.

Let us now turn to consider what rights the lender has under the mortgage.

Rights of the lender

There are a number of rights and remedies available to a lender under a legal mortgage: an **action** in contract for the debt; the right to possession of the property; the **power of sale**, the right to **foreclosure** and the power to appoint a **receiver**. The ones that most people are familiar with are possession and sale: where the bank repossesses the property with a view to selling it to repay the loan. Firstly, however, let us take a quick look at the right to sue on the mortgage.

The right to sue

Any legal mortgage carries with it the contractual right to sue on the debt. The mortgage deed creates a contract between borrower and lender, giving rise to an action for the debt should the borrower breach the terms of that contract and fail to repay the loan. From a practical perspective, however, the contractual right to sue is in most cases pretty useless: in 90 per cent of cases the reason the borrower has failed to pay their mortgage is because they do not have any money. Consequently, suing in contract for the debt is often pointless. For this reason the two main remedies favoured by lenders are the power of possession and the power of sale. If you think about it, the whole point of a mortgage is to give the lender the ability to realise their security: to sell the property that has been offered as security for the debt and use the money to repay what is owing to them.

There is one situation in which the right to sue in contract for the debt is a valuable remedy, however, and this is where the property is in **negative equity**. The term negative equity refers to the situation in which, usually due to a fall in house prices, the value of the property is actually less than the amount owing to the lender. In these circumstances selling the mortgaged property will not be sufficient to fully discharge the debt, and so the lender will seek to reclaim the balance of the debt by suing the borrower under the terms of the mortgage contract.

The right to possession

One of the most important rights of a lender is the right to enter into possession of the mortgaged property. If the borrower defaults on the loan, the lender needs to be able to take possession of the property in order to sell it and thereby realise their security on the debt. In short, they need to be able to get the borrower out. The question, though, is when that right to possession should arise. Consider when you think this should be, taking a look at the You Be the Judge feature below.

You be the judge

Q: When do you think the lender is entitled to take possession of the borrower's property: (a) when the borrower defaults on the mortgage; (b) once the date of redemption has passed; (c) at the end of the mortgage term or (d) as soon as the mortgage deed is completed?

A: The answer is (d) as soon as the mortgage deed is completed. For an explanation of why, see below.

It is perhaps surprising to learn that, unless the mortgage agreement provides to the contrary, in equity the lender has the right to possess the mortgaged property as soon as the mortgage agreement has been finalised. This is irrespective of whether the borrower has fallen behind in their mortgage repayments. In the words of Mr Justice Harman in the case of *Four Maids* v. *Dudley Marshall (Properties) Ltd* [1957] 2 WLR 931, 'the mortgagee may go into possession before the ink is dry on the mortgage'. So, in essence, the lender has the right to possess the mortgaged property from day one of the mortgage agreement. This is a fairly scary thought: that when you enter into the mortgage you are, in equity, giving up the right to possess your own house. However, this somewhat frightening paper reality is tempered by a number of intervening factors.

Case Summary

The first thing to remember is that, from the point of view of the mortgage lender, this is nothing more than a business transaction. They have no desire to live in the borrower's home, nor any need to. Their only interest in the property itself is as security for the debt. There is therefore no practical reason why the mortgage lender would want to go into possession of the property unless the borrower is in default.

The second little bit of reassurance that can be given to borrowers relates to the way in which the lender takes possession of the property. As with a landlord **forfeiting** a lease, a lender can take possession of mortgaged property in one of two ways: either by **peaceable re-entry** or by way of court order. However, a lender is unlikely to attempt to take possession without a court order, particularly in the case of residential property, because of the risk they run of falling foul of section 6(1) of the Criminal Law Act 1977. This provides that any person who uses or threatens violence for the purpose of securing entry to any premises will be guilty of a criminal offence and could be sentenced to up to six months in prison or a £5,000 fine. It is unlikely to envisage a situation in which a borrower would not object to the lender or their agents turning up on the doorstep and demanding possession of the borrower's home! If the lender knows the property is empty, of course, peaceable re-entry (in other words, simply going in and changing the locks) is quite possible. In the case of *Ropaigealach* v. *Barclays Bank plc* [2000] QB 263 the lender was able to take possession of the property through this method because the house was a renovation project and the owners were not living there at the time. We shall be looking at this case in more detail later in the chapter.

a lender is unlikely to attempt to take possession without a court order

Case Summary

And finally, if the borrower needs yet more reassurance, there are also some civil statutory provisions in the form of section 36 of the Administration of Justice Act 1970 and section 8 of the Administration of Justice Act 1973 which lend even further protection to homeowners. Section 36 goes right to the heart of the matter, providing a cushion for a borrower in the situation where the lender is seeking a court order for possession of the mortgaged property. This works by giving the court power to **adjourn**, **stay** or **suspend** the possession proceedings brought by a mortgage lender, or alternatively to postpone the date for delivery of possession of the property to that lender, if it believes that the borrower will be able within a reasonable period of time either to pay any sums due under the mortgage or otherwise to remedy the breach of mortgage term of which the borrower is accused. However, the provision applies only where the mortgaged property includes a dwelling house (that is, a residential property). It is therefore not a protection available to businesses.

Effectively, then, section 36 gives a residential borrower who is in arrears with their mortgage payments a second chance, if you like, to pay off any debts owed under the mortgage and get back on their feet, without the bank repossessing the property in the meantime. One immediate question that the wording of section 36 raises is, in terms of repayment of the debt, what is a 'reasonable period of time'? Traditionally, the court had set this time period at between two and four years; however, the Court of Appeal case of ***Cheltenham and Gloucester Building Society* v. *Norgan*** [1996] 1 WLR 343, determined the question rather more generously. The case, which concerned an application to suspend a warrant for possession of a farmhouse, stated that, whilst discretionary, the starting point for what should be considered by the courts to be a reasonable time period was actually no less than the outstanding term of the mortgage.

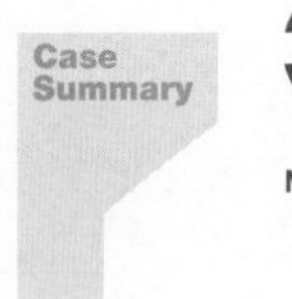

Case Navigator

It could be said, then, that this is quite a generous statutory provision: allowing the borrower to repay their arrears over the remainder of the mortgage term. However, it is important to make the point here that the borrower must have a genuine prospect of both repaying the debt and continuing to make their usual contractual mortgage payments for the court to suspend or stay the possession under section 36. Thus, some vague hope of an inheritance from a frail aunt that the borrower may receive at some point in the future will not be enough; there must be a realistic plan in place for repayment. This was confirmed in the case of *First National Bank plc* v. *Syed* [1991] 2 All ER 250. Following the redundancy of Mr Syed, an accountant, the family had fallen heavily into mortgage arrears. A first order for possession was stayed but Mr and Mrs Syed failed to keep up the arrears payments, which led to a second application by the bank. The possession order was granted, Judge James in the county court stating: 'There are always sad human facts in these cases. Considerable arrears have been outstanding for a long time. On past form I do not feel justified in assuming there is a reasonable prospect for any real change.'

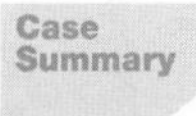

On appeal from this finding the Syeds' application under section 36 was dismissed, Lord Justice Dillon agreeing with the first instance decision.

The second statutory provision, under section 8 of the Administration of Justice Act 1973, is actually just an amendment or clarification to the interpretation of section 36 as it previously stood. You will remember that the wording of section 36 is that suspension of an order for possession may be granted provided that the borrower will be able within a reasonable period of time to repay 'any sums due' under the mortgage. The wording was causing significant difficulty with mortgages payable in instalments (which included the vast majority of residential mortgages) because in such mortgage agreements it was normal to provide that if one instalment went unpaid the whole sum borrowed fell due. Under section 36, therefore, 'any sums due' could effectively be deemed to include the whole of the mortgage advance. In the days before *Norgan*, the effect of this was that a borrower in arrears could only stay or suspend a possession order under section 36 if they could show a realistic prospect of paying off the whole of the mortgage within a 'reasonable time'. As a reasonable time was commonly considered to be two to four years, this meant a borrower struggling to make mortgage repayments would only be able to postpone possession of their home if they could prove that they could pay off the mortgage in two to four years. This effectively rendered the provisions of section 36 worthless. Section 8 was therefore passed to amend this interpretation, restoring the status quo by providing that, in the case of instalment mortgages, 'sums due' are only those payments which are in arrears and a clause requiring payment of the whole advance can be disregarded. Of course, post *Norgan*, which allows repayment of arrears over the whole of the remaining term of the mortgage, the difficulties caused by the previous interpretation of section 36 are removed, as the full sum of the mortgage would be due to be repaid by the end of the mortgage term in any event.

Case Summary

One other case which is important to consider in terms of section 36 is the case of *Ropaigealach* v. *Barclays Bank*. The case, which was mentioned earlier in the chapter, concerned a property bought by a couple as a renovation project. As you may remember, the bank had taken possession of the property by way of peaceable re-entry. They were able to do this because the owners were not living in the property at the time. The borrowers tried to make a claim under section 36 in order to reverse the repossession; however, the court rejected their claim. Making a point which had never been at issue in previous cases, the court said quite simply that they were not in a position to apply the provisions of section 36 to the Ropaigealachs' case because section 36 only operates where the lender has obtained or is seeking a court order for possession. In this case the lender had taken possession not by way of court order, but rather by physical re-entry of the property. There was therefore no court application to suspend.

A case for reform?

Case Summary

Ropaigelach v. *Barclays* caused a certain amount of concern about the possible human rights implications of what could be perceived as the 'legal loophole' left by section 36. However, matters were not brought to a head until the case of *Horsham Properties Group* v. *Clark* [2009] 1 WLR 1255 was heard almost a decade later. In this case, the ability of the borrower to invoke section 36 was again circumvented, this time because the action for possession was being brought, not by the mortgage lender, who had sold the property on, but by a third party purchaser. In finding for the purchaser, Horsham Properties, the judge in the case, Mr Justice Briggs, rejected the arguments put forward by the borrowers' legal representatives, stating that:

1. The bank's exercise of their power of sale under section 101 of the Law of Property Act 1925 (see below) was contractual and not a matter of policy. It was therefore not incompatible with the Human Rights Act 1988;
2. The wording of section 36 was clear in that section 36 could only be triggered where the claim for possession of the property was being made by the mortgage lender and not by a third party purchaser of the property.

Following *Horsham Properties*, it initially appeared that swift action was going to be taken by the government to close the loophole and proposals were made for amendments to the Administration of Justice Act 1970 in the draft Banking Bill 2008. However, the proposals were subsequently withdrawn. Another **Private Member's Bill** followed swiftly on from it in the form of the Home Repossession (Protection) Bill, which called for amendments to section 101 of the Law of Property Act 1925, to require anyone seeking to exercise their statutory right to sell first to seek the permission of the court.

Again, the Bill was withdrawn before its second reading in the House of Commons, however. More recently, there has been a Consultation Paper issued by the Ministry of Justice, again suggesting a mandatory court order in residential cases, which closed in March 2010; and most recently, a Private Member's Bill, entitled the Secured Lending Reform Bill 2010, was presented to Parliament at the end of June 2010. Amongst other things, the Bill called for:

- New provisions to be inserted into the Law of Property Act 1925 restricting the powers of a receiver appointed to act on a mortgage lender's behalf, except where an order for possession of the property has been granted by the court;
- The abolition of the right of a mortgage lender to repossess a property using peaceable re-entry;
- New regulations to be invoked which prevent the making of an order for possession by the court unless the court is satisfied that the borrower has been given sufficient opportunity to raise and have considered by the court any counter-claim, set-off or other defence that may be available to them.

Unfortunately, this latest Bill has once again failed to reach its second reading in the Commons and so, at this point in time, the suggested reforms are unlikely to be implemented. It is suggested that this may be because of the huge implications the proposed changes would have on mortgage lenders across the country.

The right to sale

Having obtained physical possession of the property, the mortgage lender will want to sell the property and repay the debt owing to them by the borrower. As we have seen above, the lender has a statutory right to do this, conferred upon them by section 101 of the Law of Property Act 1925. This Section says that the power of sale will arise in respect of every mortgage made by deed, provided that the monies owing on the mortgage have 'become due'. This is a reference to the date of redemption on the mortgage which, we established earlier in the chapter, is usually set in the mortgage deed at around six months from the date of the mortgage.

For the lender, this is not the end of the matter, however. In a slightly awkward twist of the legislation the fact that the power of sale has arisen under section 101 is not, by itself, sufficient authority to go ahead and sell the property. The lender must also have the right to *exercise* that power of sale. So the power of sale must not only have arisen, it must have become exercisable as well. The provisions that deal with the exercise of the power of sale can be found at section 103 of the Act. According to section 103, the power of sale will not become exercisable unless and until:

1. Notice requiring payment of the mortgage money has been served on the borrower and that money has remained unpaid for three months following the notice; or
2. Interest due under the mortgage is in arrears and remains unpaid for two months after becoming due; or
3. The borrower is in breach of some other provision of the mortgage (for example a provision not to let the premises).

Provided the borrower is in breach of one of these provisions, however, the lender will have the statutory right to sell the property in order to recoup the sums due under the mortgage. There is currently no requirement for the lender to procure a court order prior to exercising the right to sell the mortgaged property. To give you an idea of potentially the number of homes this might affect, take a look at the Key Stats feature, below.

Key stats Financial Services Authority mortgage lending statistics

Since the beginning of 2007, mortgage lenders have been required to submit a Mortgage Lending & Administration Return each quarter, providing data on their mortgage lending activities. The key statistics for the first quarter of 2012 are as follows:

- The total value of outstanding loans at the end of the first quarter was £1,221bn, £36bn of which comprised new loans.
- The proportion of new lending done at a loan to value* of more than 90% rose above 2% for the first time since the end of 2010.
- In the first quarter of 2012 there were 35,400 new arrears cases, an increase of 2% on last quarter but 4% lower than the first quarter of last year.
- The total number of accounts in arrears at the end of the quarter, however, fell by 3% in the first quarter of 2012 to 333,200, some 10% below the first quarter of 2011.
- The proportion of the residential loan book that is in arrears, and hence not fully performing, continued its downward trend, from 2.61% last quarter to 2.52% in the first quarter of 2012.
- The number of new possessions in the quarter increased by 7% to 9,552.
- Arrears totalling £28m on 8,120 accounts were capitalised in the first quarter of 2012.

*The term 'loan to value' indicates the amount of the loan in proportion to the value of the property to be mortgaged.
Source: http://www.fsa.gov.uk/library/other_publications/statistics

The law relating to repossession was briefly under review with a proposed Home Repossession (Protection) Bill 2009, which sought to amend section 101 of the Law of Property Act 1925 so that, in respect of residential properties, lenders can no longer exercise the power of sale granted under section 101 without first obtaining a court order to do so. The Bill came in the wake of concerns over the potential human rights implications the provisions might have on domestic borrowers, following the finding in the case of *Horsham Properties Group Ltd* v. *Clark* [2009] 1 WLR 1255, although the outcome of the case was actually that there was in that case no breach of human rights provisions in the interpretation of the statute. The case concerned a claim made against the buyer of a property sold to them by a mortgage lender under its statutory power of sale. Unusually in this case the borrower had remained in possession of the property whilst the sale had proceeded and it was the new owner, and not the mortgage lender, who was seeking possession. The borrower argued that the sale of the property without the benefit of a court order was in breach of his human rights under Protocol 1, Article 1 of the European Convention of Human Rights 1950 (peaceful enjoyment of possessions). The court held, however, that there was no infringement of the borrower's human rights. The provisions of the Law of Property Act 1925 served, not as an intervention of the State, but simply in order to help implement the personal bargain made between borrower and lender when the mortgage was entered into.

Case Summary

In any event, the bill was withdrawn before its second reading in the House of Commons. A further Private Member's Bill has still more recently been put before Parliament in the form of the Secured Lending Reform Bill, which was given its first hearing as recently as June 2010. However, the Bill again failed to get through to the second reading. It remains to be seen whether there will be further consultation on the subject.

Managing the sale

We have established that the lender does not need a court order in order to sell the property (although they may have sought a court order to gain possession of it). In exercising their power of sale, however, there are still a couple of procedural matters to be taken into account by the lender. The first relates to their conduct of the sale. It is incumbent upon the lender as the seller of the property to obtain a proper price for it. In the case of *Cuckmere Brick Co. Ltd* v. *Mutual Finance Ltd* [1971] Ch 949, the property that was subject to the mortgage was land which had the benefit of two sets of **planning permission** attached to it. The land was sold by the lender at auction but only one of the permissions was referred to in the auction guide. The result was that the property sold at a far lower price than it might otherwise have done. The lender was held liable for the difference in price.

Case Summary

Following *Cuckmere Brick*, it can reasonably be assumed that a 'proper price' equates to the lender taking reasonable steps to ensure that they achieve the best price they can for the property. This was accepted by the Privy Council in *Newport Farm Ltd* v. *Damesh Holdings Ltd* [2003] UKPC 54, in which a lender was held to be under a duty to take reasonable steps to obtain the best price for the property, looking at the steps taken in the round and in practical commercial terms. This duty does not extend to the lender having to expend time or money seeking to increase the purchase price the property will achieve, though. This is illustrated in the Court of Appeal case of *Silven Properties Ltd* v. *Royal Bank of Scotland plc* [2004] 1 WLR 997, in which the Court held that, in the exercise of their power of sale, a lender was not under a duty either to pursue applications for planning permission or to complete the grant of leases in order to increase the best price reasonably obtainable on the sale.

Case Summary

Case Summary

In contrast is the case of *Palk* v. *Mortgage Services Funding plc* [1993] Ch 330, in which an order for the sale of the property was granted to a borrower, despite the wishes of the lender to delay the sale in order to wait for a rise in property prices. The house in question was in negative equity, there being more owing on it than the house was worth. The lender had taken possession of the property and intended to let it whilst they waited for property prices to rise. However, the amount of rent they would achieve for the property was far less than the arrears payable and the action would inevitably lead to spiralling mortgage debts on the part of the borrower. The court therefore ordered that the property be sold to enable the borrower to cut their losses. This did not prevent the lender from then seeking the balance of monies owing from the borrower at **common law**.

Case Summary

Once the property has been sold, the proceeds of sale have to be applied in a particular order and the lender is considered to be in the position of **trustee** for the funds until they have been distributed. The order in which the monies are to be applied is governed by section 105 of the Law of Property Act 1925 and is as follows:

1. any prior charges (that is, any mortgages that take precedence over the mortgage of the lender exercising the power of sale. The priority of mortgages is discussed further on in the chapter);
2. costs of selling the property (that is estate agents and legal fees);

3. the lender's own mortgage;
4. any lesser charges secured over the property;
5. any remainder can go to the borrower.

The right to foreclose

This is a rarely-used remedy whereby the mortgage lender becomes the registered owner of the house in exchange for the extinguishment of the mortgage debt.

Foreclosure is problematic in that any surplus on the mortgage debt remains in the house and is therefore lost to the borrower. Conversely, in a negative equity situation the lender loses their rights to pursue the borrower in person for the balance of the debt. Unless the mortgage amounts to 100 per cent of the value of the house, therefore, foreclosure is likely to be unfair on either one or another of the parties to the mortgage. Foreclosure cannot be granted to a lender without the benefit of a court order, and the courts will more than likely commute an application to foreclose for an order for sale whenever the property is worth more than the mortgage debt. The term 'foreclosure' in English law should not be confused with the American use of the term, which equates roughly to mortgage repossession in England and Wales.

Power to appoint a receiver

The last right of the lender we need to consider is the power to appoint a receiver. Up until now we have been focusing on the lender's right to take possession of the property in order to sell it and thereby repay the mortgage debt. However, there are some situations in which it will benefit the lender to repossess the mortgaged property not to sell it, but instead to use it to provide an income. This is particularly the case with commercial properties. Consider a leased office block. If the owner of the block falls into arrears with the mortgage, the lender can appoint a receiver to collect the rent on the offices direct and use this money to pay off the **capital** and interest due under the mortgage. For a lender, this may be a more efficient way of dealing with mortgage arrears than simply requesting them from the borrower, who may have different priorities in terms of how the rent monies should be distributed. You may remember that in the case of *Palk* v. *Mortgage Services Funding plc*, the bank wished to rent out the property pending a recovery in the property market. If this had meant that the borrower's arrears and continued payments due under the terms of the mortgage were covered in the meantime, the story might have been different. However, you will remember that in this particular case it was considered by the court that this would not be in the best interests of the borrower and the lender's application was denied.

The power to appoint a receiver is implied by statute under sections 101 and 109 of the Law of Property Act 1925.

Equitable mortgages

Equitable mortgages are slightly more complicated than legal mortgages. They can be divided into two distinct categories:

1. firstly, informal mortgages of legal interests; and
2. secondly, mortgages of **equitable interests**.

Informal mortgages of legal interests

We have already been reminded at the beginning of the chapter that, in accordance with section 52 of the Law of Property Act 1925, in order for a mortgage to be legal it has to be made by deed. But what happens if there is no deed? The answer, of course, is that it cannot be a legal mortgage because the formalities required for a legal mortgage have not been complied with. However, it may nevertheless be recognised as an equitable mortgage under suitable circumstances. As with the creation of equitable leases, this is done through the doctrine in ***Walsh* v. *Lonsdale***, which you will remember states that a contract for land can create an equitable interest in that land, provided it complies with section 2 of the law of Property (Miscellaneous Provisions) Act 1989. And you will remember that under section 2 a valid contract in land will be created if it is in writing, contains all the terms as agreed between the parties and is signed by both parties to the agreement. So essentially you can create an equitable mortgage: a contract for a mortgage, if it complies with section 2 of the 1989 Act.

Case Navigator

Let us have a look at a couple of examples of this in practice. In the Court of Appeal case of *United Bank of Kuwait plc* v. *Sahib* [1996] 3 WLR 372 some creditors of the **defendants** tried to claim that they had the benefit of an equitable mortgage over the defendants' property on the basis of the deposit of the defendants' **title deeds** with the bank. However, the court on appeal dismissed their claim. The deposit of title deeds was no longer a method of creating a contract for land. As section 2 of the 1989 Act had not been complied with, there could therefore have been no equitable mortgage created.

Case Summary

A similar outcome was reached in the case of *De Serville* v. *Argee Ltd* [2001] NPC 82. Here an exchange of letters between a debtor and creditor was held not to have created an agreement to create a mortgage (and thus an equitable mortgage), because the correspondence between the parties did not satisfy the requirements of section 2. You will remember that since the 1989 Act you can no longer create a contract by correspondence.

Case Summary

As you can see, the level of formality that is required in order to create an equitable mortgage is therefore really quite high. This means that in reality an equitable mortgage will only come into existence where there has been some mistake made with the production of the mortgage documentation, for example, if the deed is not properly witnessed and so the formalities for the creation of a deed have not been complied with. This type of equitable mortgage is therefore relatively rare.

Mortgages of equitable interests

Mortgages of equitable interests, on the other hand, are very commonly seen in commercial property practice. Take, for instance, the following example of how a mortgage of an equitable interest may be of use to a property developer: imagine a property developer is in the process of building a new estate of 50 houses on a 10-acre site. The developer will not want to purchase the building land until they have planning permission for the development; they will therefore either have entered into an **option to purchase** the land with the seller, or **exchanged contracts** for the sale of the land, conditional upon planning permission being granted. Either way, as we know from our earlier reading, the developer will have acquired an equitable interest in the land, through their entering into an **estate contract** with the seller, although they will not have a legal interest in it yet. The problem is that the developer still needs to raise money on the land in order to pay for their architects' fees and costs of obtaining the planning permission, which are considerable. The developer will therefore seek to mortgage their equitable interest in the land.

As it is not possible to create a legal mortgage of an equitable interest (you cannot give what you do not have), any mortgage deal entered into by the developer of their equitable interest in the land can only be equitable in character. The creation of such a mortgage is, as one might expect, less formal than the requirements for the creation of a legal mortgage. Technically speaking, the creation of an equitable mortgage is treated as a disposal of an equitable interest in the land and, as such, must comply with section 53(1)(c) of the Law of Property Act 1925. As you may again remember from your earlier reading when we looked at formalities for the creation of interests in land in Chapter 4, section 53(1)(c) simply requires that the disposal (or mortgage in this case) must be made in writing. So, to put it simply, the only formality required for the creation of a mortgage of an equitable interest is that it must be made in writing.

Rights of lenders and borrowers under equitable mortgages

As the lender under an equitable mortgage only has an equitable, and not a legal, interest in the land, the only remedies that are available to it are equitable and therefore discretionary in nature. Equally, the borrower's rights will also be governed by equity. For the borrower, the equity of redemption will therefore apply, subject to the usual **equitable maxims**. However, for the lender, the position is more difficult.

> the lender does not have any right to possession

The primary difficulty is with the lender taking possession of the property. As the holder of an equitable interest in the land only, the lender does not have any right to the possession of the legal estate. How, then, under these circumstances, can the lender take possession of the land and release their security in it? The power of sale prompts similar difficulties. Under statute, the power of sale under section 101 of the Law of Property Act 1925 only applies when the mortgage is made by deed. There is therefore no power of sale implied into the mortgage agreement under an equitable mortgage. In a leading case on the subject, *Re White Rose Cottage* [1965] Ch 940, Lord Denning suggested that there must be an equivalent right in equity allowing a property to be sold. He said:

Case Summary

> The subject of the mortgage here was the property itself, both the legal and equitable estate in it: and I see no reason why an equitable mortgagee, exercising his power of sale, should not be able to convey the legal estate.

This does not change the basic legal position in terms of possession, however, the result being that a lender will not be able to physically **re-enter** mortgaged property in order to sell it. They will need first to obtain an order of the court for possession.

Protection of the mortgage interest

So far in the chapter we have concentrated on what mortgages are, how they are created, and what rights they afford both to lender and borrower. An equally important issue to consider, however, is how the lender can protect their mortgage against third party purchasers of it. In other words, if the borrower is loaned a sum of money by the lender, giving their house as security for the debt, what is to stop them from then selling their property and absconding with the money? Equally, what can the lender do to ensure that this does not happen or, if it does, that the new owner of the property will be bound by the terms of the mortgage? As we know from our reading in Chapter 4, under section 1(2) of the Law of Property Act 1925, a mortgage takes the form of a legal or equitable interest in the land. How the rights of the mortgage lender are protected therefore depends, as with other forms of interest in land, on whether the title to the land which is the subject of the mortgage is legal or equitable, and whether it is **registered** or **unregistered**.

Registered land

According to section 27(2)(f) of the Land Registration Act 2002, legal mortgages are **registrable dispositions**, meaning that it is compulsory to register them. The effect of this is significant because it means not only that non-registration of a legal mortgage will render it unprotected as against a third party purchaser of the land (so that a buyer of the land gets the legal and **beneficial interests** in the property without being responsible to pay the charge on it), but also that the mortgage cannot actually take place at law until **registration** has been completed; in other words, the mortgage can only exist in equity until this time. We have seen above how significant the disadvantage to the holder of an equitable mortgage can be, in comparison with the holder of a legal mortgage. It is therefore vital that whenever a lender takes a mortgage over property that they register it at the **Land Registry**.

Once registered, details of the lender's mortgage will appear on the **Charges Register** as a registered charge. The entry on the register is shown in two parts: the first states brief details along with the date of the mortgage and the second gives the name and address of the lender, who is the registered proprietor, or owner of the legal interest in the land (the mortgage). See the Documenting the Law section for an example of what this looks like.

Documenting the law

Example of the Charges Register showing a registered charge

C: Charges register

This register contains any charges and other matters that affect the registered estate.

1. (01.08.2002) REGISTERED CHARGE dated 15 July 2002 to secure the moneys including the further advances therein mentioned.
2. (01.08.2002) Proprietor: OCTAGON BUILDING SOCIETY of Octagon House, Newtown NE3 0BS

End of register

It is also common practice for the lender to enter a **restriction** on the **Proprietorship Register** for the property, preventing a change of ownership in the land from being registered without their prior consent. Naturally, consent will not be given by the lender unless their mortgage debt has been repaid.

An equitable mortgage is not a registrable disposition, but a lender may still protect it by entering **notice** of their equitable interest on the Charges Register. If the lender does this, the equitable mortgage will then bind any purchaser of the land. Failure to register an equitable mortgage will, in the first instance, render it unenforceable against third party purchasers. However, if the borrower is living at the mortgaged property, they may still be able to claim the benefit of an **overriding interest** in the land on the basis of an interest in actual occupation under Schedule 3, paragraph 2 of the Land Registration Act 2002. This is subject to the usual provisos of which you may wish to remind yourselves by taking a look back at interests in actual occupation in Chapter 4.

Unregistered land

If the land to be mortgaged is unregistered, you will remember that the title to the property is proven by reference to a bundle of title deeds showing the unbroken line of ownership of the property over a specified period of years. If the owner wishes to sell the property, they will have to show the title deeds to their buyer's representative to check through. For a lender taking a mortgage over an unregistered property, therefore, the position is straightforward in that the lender will simply take custody of the title deeds as security and prevent the owner from selling to anyone else without their knowledge or consent. Add to this the common law mantra that 'legal rights bind the whole world' and the lender finds themselves in a nice, secure position. From a legal point of view, the deposit of the title deeds with the lender is sufficient notice to a buyer of a prior interest in the land (the assumption arising when the selling borrower is unable to produce them for inspection). Unfortunately this is a position that can obviously only apply to the first mortgage the owner takes out over their property, however. If the owner then wishes to take out a second, or subsequent, mortgage on the property, they will not be able to offer their title deeds as security, because these are already with the holder of the initial mortgage. These must therefore be protected in a different way. Mortgages not protected by the deposit of title deeds then, whether legal or equitable, may be registered as **land charges** under the Land Charges Act 1972, either as a Class C(i) (legal) or C(iii) (equitable) land charge respectively. You may remember that a legal mortgage not protected by the deposit of title deeds is referred to in the context of land charges as a **puisne mortgage**. If a mortgage not protected by deposit of title deeds is not registered it will be **void** as against any purchaser of the land. This is in accordance with section 4(5) of the Land Charges Act 1972.

Priorities of mortgages

When we talk about mortgages it is easy to assume that a borrower will only have one single mortgage over their property: in a residential context in particular, we assume that it is that which they took out in order to purchase their house. This is often not the case, however, with borrowers taking out multiple mortgages over their homes or business premises. Consider the case of Alexander. He buys a house for him and his growing family to live in. The house, which is called Apple Tree Grove, is rather smaller than he wanted but it is all he can afford at the time and it has a large garden for his young son to play in, so he buys it with the help of a mortgage from the Moon Alliance Bank. Five years later, Alexander has two small children, with another on the way, and Apple Tree Grove is growing pretty crowded. He has been given a management position at work, however, money is not so tight, and the value of their house has increased quite significantly, following some home improvements. After some discussion with his wife, therefore, Alexander decides to borrow some further money from another lender, the Orange Bank, to carry out a loft conversion at Apple Tree Grove and create two additional bedrooms. Another twelve months on, the new baby has arrived and Alexander realises that the family car is not big enough to accommodate them all. Reluctantly the family takes the decision to borrow a further £10,000 from a different lender, Pit Stop Lending Solutions, which is again secured against the house. Then the worst happens. There is a global recession, house prices fall dramatically and Alexander is made redundant, following cuts in the workplace. He falls behind with his mortgage payments and it becomes clear that the next step will be for the lenders to repossess the property. The house is now worth less than the total amount Alexander has borrowed, though. The question that remains is how the three lenders are to be paid.

The answer lies in the order of priority of the mortgages. In such a situation, there is no reduction of the individual debts *pro rata*, so that each lender gets, for example, 80 per cent of their debt repaid. Instead, the mortgages will take priority in order of the date on which they were registered so that, whereas the first lender may succeed in having the whole of its debt repaid, the second lender may only receive part payment of their debt, and the third lender may end up with nothing. An illustration of how this might work is given in Figure 12.1.

Figure 12.1 Receipt of proceeds of sale of a repossessed property in order of mortgage priority

Current value of house:	£200,000	
	Amount owing	Amount received
Mortgage with Moon Alliance Bank	£180,000	£180,000
Mortgage with Orange Bank	£25,000	£20,000
Mortgage with Pit Stop Lending Solutions	£10,000	£0
Total	£215,000	£200,000

In these circumstances, both the Orange Bank and Pit Stop Lending will be left with a deficit that they will have to seek to recover in another way, perhaps by suing the borrower personally for the debt. A fuller explanation of the position is given below.

Registered land

In accordance with section 48 of the Land Registration Act 2002, legal mortgages in registered land are prioritised in accordance with the date on which they are registered whichever mortgage is registered first takes priority

at the Land Registry. This is regardless of the order of their creation: whichever mortgage is registered first takes priority over subsequently registered mortgages, even if those subsequent mortgages were created on an earlier date.

Equitable mortgages in registered land are also protected in date order, under sections 34 to 36 of the 2002 Act. An equitable mortgage protected by notice in the Charges Register may therefore take priority over a later legal mortgage, although its remedies will nevertheless remain limited to its status as an equitable interest in land. Interestingly, however, an equitable mortgage protected as an interest in actual occupation will also override subsequent legal mortgages, despite not appearing as an entry on the Register. Such mortgages rank in order of their creation, as against other unregistered mortgages. We can thus see that a mortgage lender lending money against property is in the same position as a potential purchaser of the land, taking subject to prior charges and overriding interests on it.

You be the judge

Q: **Put the following mortgages in order of priority: (a) legal mortgage dated 1 October 2008. Registered 15 October 2008; (b) equitable mortgage dated 1 August 2008. Registered 1 October 2008; (c) legal mortgage dated 1 September 2008. Registered 15 September 2008; (d) equitable mortgage dated 1 July 2008. Protected as an overriding interest under Sched.3 para.2 LRA 2002.**

A: (d), (c), (b), (a).

Unregistered land

In unregistered land, as we have seen above, legal mortgages protected by deposit of title deeds take precedence over all other mortgages, on the basis that 'legal rights bind the whole world'. This priority can be lost under three sets of circumstances:

1. Where there is fraud on the part of the lender (so, for example, where a subsequent lender is led to believe that there is no earlier mortgage on the property). In this situation, the subsequent lender's mortgage will take precedence over that of the deed-holding lender.
2. Where there is an **estoppel**. If the lender with possession of the title deeds either expressly or by implication makes a misrepresentation which deceives a subsequent lender, the deed-holding lender will be estopped from asserting the priority of their mortgage. An example of this would be a first mortgage which incorrectly shows a receipt indicating that it has been repaid, or where the lender hands the deeds over to the borrower knowing that the deeds will be used to raise further money on the property.
3. Where the lender has been negligent in relation to the title deeds to the property. For example, this may happen where a lender who is entitled to hold the title deeds to the property negligently fails to obtain them from the borrower.

The position in relation to mortgages not protected by deposit of title deeds is more straightforward, being comparable to the position in registered land. In accordance with section 97 of the Law of Property Act 1925:

> Every mortgage affecting a legal estate in land made after the commencement of this Act, whether legal or equitable (not being a mortgage protected by the deposit of documents relating to the legal estate affected) shall rank according to its date of registration as a land charge pursuant to the Land Charges Act 1925.

Thus, whereas a first legal mortgage protected by the deposit of title deeds will take precedence over all others (subject to the above provisos), second and subsequent mortgages are ordered by the date on which they are registered. As can be seen from the wording of Section 97, this is the case regardless of whether those mortgages are legal or equitable in nature.

There is one small problem with the registration of mortgages under section 97, which arises out of a conflict in the existing legislation. The problem arises where a mortgage of unregistered land is created but has not been registered by the time a further subsequent mortgage is created. This creates a situation in which the later of the mortgages has been registered after the earlier mortgage, but created before that earlier mortgage has itself been registered, thus creating an overlap.

Figure 12.2 Overlap between creation and registration of mortgages in unregistered land

1 January 2012
Mortgage A is created
8 January 2012
Mortgage B is created
15 January 2012
Mortgage A is registered
23 January 2012
Mortgage B is registered

In this situation, section 4(5) of the Land Charges Act 1972 states that the earlier mortgage is void for failure to register it before the creation of a further legal charge. There is an argument that the earlier mortgage should prevail, however, as the first in time to be registered, regardless of the respective dates of creation of the mortgages. This theory has not been tested by the courts.

Summary

- A mortgage is a loan of money secured against property. Anything which has a commercial value can be used as security against a loan, and thus can be mortgaged.
- A mortgage is one of the five classes of legal interest in land listed in section 1(2) of the Law of Property Act 1925.
- In order for a mortgage to be legal it must be created by deed (section 52 of the Law of Property Act 1925).
- Today the only way of creating a mortgage is by way of a legal charge, as stated in section 85 of the Law of Property Act 1925.
- A borrower has only one contractual right under the mortgage and this is the contractual right to redeem, or pay off, the mortgage. The mortgage deed will set out in its terms the date of the contractual right to redeem and this is usually set at six months from the start of the mortgage. In reality it is therefore of little practical use to a borrower.
- The equitable right to redeem is far more flexible, however, allowing the borrower a continued right to redeem the mortgage right up until the end of the mortgage term, provided they continue to pay back the loan together with interest due on the mortgage at the contractually specified rate throughout this period.
- Equity is also keen to prevent terms in mortgages which postpone or limit that borrower's right to redeem the mortgage should they wish to (see the contrasting cases of *Knightsbridge Estates* v. *Byrne* and *Fairclough* v. *Swan Brewery Co.*).
- Equity also disallows collateral advantages as a general rule, although these are allowed in commercial lending cases, as long as the advantage is not unconscionable and does not extend beyond the life of the mortgage (see *Kreglinger* v. *New Patagonia Meat Co.*).
- Equity in addition has the power to strike down any unconscionable or oppressive terms in the mortgage agreement (see *Cityland* v. *Dabrah; Multiservice Bookbinding* v. *Marden*).
- Equity will step in, in cases of undue influence, so that the person so influenced is not bound by the terms of the mortgage. In order to protect lenders in this situation, the House of Lords case of *Etridge* has set out extensive guidelines which should be followed wherever one spouse acts as surety for the debts of the other.
- From the lender's point of view, they have a contractual right to sue on the mortgage debt, although this is often of little assistance to the lender, as the borrower will have no money to recoup against the debt.
- More important is the lender's right to possession of the property, which the lender has 'before the ink is dry on the mortgage' (*Four Maids* v. *Dudley Marshall Properties*).
- The lender can exercise their right to possession of the property either by peaceable re-entry or by obtaining a court order. In most cases, especially residential ones, the lender will seek a court order, however, unless the property is empty (*Ropaigealach* v. *Barclays*).
- Under Section 36 of the Administration of Justice Act 1970 (as amended), if the lender applies for a court order for possession, the borrower can apply to the court for this to be stayed or suspended, where there is a realistic prospect of repayment of the mortgage debt within a reasonable time. A 'reasonable time' is taken to mean the remaining life of the mortgage (*Cheltenham and Gloucester Building Society* v. *Norgan*).
- The provisions of section 36 do not apply in cases of peaceable re-entry (*Ropaigealach* v. *Barclays*).

- The lender is given the power of sale over the property under section 101 of the LPA 1925. The power of sale will arise wherever the mortgage monies have become due (in other words from the date of redemption under the mortgage).
- The power of sale must not only arise, but must become exercisable under statute. This occurs wherever there are either three months' mortgage arrears and notice has been served under the mortgage; there are two months' interest payments outstanding; or another of the terms of the mortgage has been breached (s.103 LPA 1925).
- When selling the mortgaged property, the lender has a duty to obtain a 'proper price' for it (*Cuckmere Brick Co.* v. *Mutual Finance*).
- The proceeds of sale must be applied in order, paying off any prior charges first, then the costs of sale of the property, then the selling lender's own mortgage, then lesser charges. The remainder can go to the borrower (s.105 LPA 1925).
- Equitable mortgages fall into two categories: attempts to create legal mortgages which have failed and therefore become equitable under the rule in *Walsh* v. *Lonsdale*, and mortgages of equitable interests in land. Protection of equitable mortgages is more difficult, particularly because there is an argument that an equitable lender has no automatic right to possession of the property. They can nevertheless be granted a court order for possession and sale, however.
- A legal mortgage is a registrable disposition (s.27(2)(f) LRA 2002) and can only take effect in equity until registered. An equitable mortgage can be protected by way of notice on the Land Register. Alternatively, it may form an overriding interest by virtue of actual occupation under Sched.3 para.2 LRA 2002.
- In unregistered land, first legal mortgages are protected by the deposit of title deeds, and 'bind the whole world'. Second and subsequent mortgages, both legal and equitable, must be protected by registration at the Land Charges Registry in Plymouth, either as a class C(i) or C(iii) land charge.
- As a general rule, mortgages will be given priority in order of the date of their registration (and not their creation), either at the Land Registry (s.48 LRA 1925) or as land charges in unregistered land (this is subject to the priority given to mortgages protected by deposit of title deeds).

Question and answer*

Problem:

In 2007 Dave and Joachim bought their dream house, Ten Bells, for £200,000. The house was registered with freehold title at the Land Registry. They bought Ten Bells with the aid of a registered mortgage of £175,000 from the First and Last Bank and a £25,000 interest-free loan from Dave's Nan. Dave and Joachim were registered as joint legal owners of the property. Dave's Nan also moved in to live with them shortly after the purchase.

Joachim is a freelance fitness instructor, running personal training sessions at a local gym. Dave does not work, but stays at home and runs the house. Unfortunately with the recession there has been less call for personal trainers over the last few years and Joachim's business has dropped off significantly. To make matters worse, in 2010 Joachim suffered an ankle injury whilst playing five-a-side football for his local team and was unable to work for six months.

As a result he decided to borrow a further £25,000 from LendSafe, a small mortgage provider, to help him get through this bad period, secured against Ten Bells. Joachim told Dave, who has no interest in the financial running of the house, that this was just a temporary measure and Dave signed the loan papers without really thinking about it.

Unfortunately by the time Joachim had recovered, many of his clients had gone elsewhere and Joachim's business was in real trouble. The couple has been unable to pay interest or capital payments on either mortgage since November. Last week they received a letter from LendSafe telling them that if they do not pay off the full arrears by the end of the month the lender will seek to seek to repossess Ten Bells and sell it to recover the debt.

The couple have no savings with which to pay off the debt, although Joachim says that the gym may be able to give him some extra shifts to help with his finances, covering sickness and holidays for the other fitness instructors.

Dave says he knows nothing about the loan from LendSafe and that he is therefore not bound by their loan. Dave's Nan says she has nothing to do with the debts and has every right to stay in the property, having put money into its purchase. Advise Joachim and Dave, and Dave's Nan as to their positions.

This question should be answered in 40 minutes.

Essay: 'Section 36 of the Administration of Justice Act 1970 does not go far enough to balance the rights of borrowers against the lender's right to possession.' Discuss.

This question should be answered in 40 minutes.

✱ Answer guidance is provided at the end of the chapter.

Further reading

McMurtry, L., 'The Section 36 discretion: policy and practicality', Conv 2002, Nov/Dec, 594–601.
This article gives a clear and useful discussion of the law relating to section 36 of the Administration of Justice Act 1970, as amended, through discussion of the case of *Barclays Bank Plc* v. *Alcorn* [2002] EWHC 498 (Ch).

***Royal Bank of Scotland plc* v. *Etridge (No.2)* [2001) 3 WLR 1021.**
It is well worth reading the full judgment in this case for full details of the guidelines given to lenders when dealing with possible cases of undue influence in residential mortgages.

Mujih, E. C., 'From manifest disadvantage to transactions that call for explanation: have the difficulties been eliminated ten years after *Royal Bank of Scotland Plc* v. *Etridge (No.2)*?' JIBLR 2012, 27(10), 395–405.
This article gives a good insight into the practical application of *Etridge*, in particular highlighting the shift in the burden of proof between pre- and post-*Etridge* cases.

McAuslan, P. 'Whose mortgage is it anyway? Producers, consumers and the law in the UK mortgage market', available online at: http://www.gla.ac.uk/media/media_129711_en.pdf.
This University of Glasgow conference paper makes a clear and thorough survey of the law of mortgages as it stands and makes suggestions for change, taking into account economic and financial factors as well as legal ones. For a really good overview of the law on this subject this is a must-read.

The Law after *Horsham Properties*, available online at: http://www.legalmortgage.co.uk/#/orders-for-sale-after-horsham/4538803765.
This is a nice, concise article giving in brief the circumstances which led to the Secured Lending Reform Bill and what it proposed to achieve. It should be remembered that, at present, there is no plan to take this Bill further forward although, given the flurry of activity in Parliament there has been in this area of the law over the last couple of years, we are likely to see more movement in this area in the future.

Question and answer guidance

Please note that the following is not a full answer and is intended to provide guidance in outline form only as to how to answer the questions posed.

Problem:

Here we have a first registered mortgage for £175,000 in favour of the First and Last Bank plc, a second registered mortgage of £25,000 with LendSafe and an unsecured loan from Dave's Nan for £25,000. The second mortgagee, LendSafe, is seeking to repossess the property and recoup what is owing to them.

They can obtain possession without a court order but as the property is occupied they would be advised not to, as if they use or threaten violence to do so this will be a criminal offence under the Criminal Law Act 1977 s.6(1). The safer course of action would be for them to apply for a court order for possession.

Once LendSafe have obtained possession of the property, they will wish to sell the property in order to recoup the debt. We need to look at, firstly, whether the power of sale has arisen under s.101 LPA 1925, and secondly whether that power of sale has become exercisable under s.103.

In order for the power of sale to arise under s.101 the mortgage has to be created by deed (we assume it has been as the mortgage is registered) and the mortgage money has to have become due i.e. the legal date for redemption must have passed. This is usually six months after the mortgage has been created. As the mortgage was taken out over six months ago, we can assume that the power of sale has arisen.

In order for the power of sale to become exerciseable under s.103 there are several options, but the easiest to apply in this instance is that there are more than two months' interest in arrears on the loan. We are told that Joachim and Dave have not been able to pay capital or interest on the loan since November, so this would qualify.

If LendSafe obtain possession of the property and seek to sell it they will have to hold the proceeds of sale of the property on trust and pay out the monies in the order prescribed by s.105 LPA 1925, which states that the First and Last Bank plc, as the holder of the first legal mortgage, must be paid off first, followed by the costs relating to the sale, before LendSafe can get any money. Whether they will get back the whole of the monies owing to them will therefore depend on the current value of the property and whether there is enough money after the sale to cover all the debts.

What can Joachim and Dave do to prevent the repossession? They could apply under s.36 AJA 1970 for an order postponing possession of the property but they will have to provide a financial plan to the court showing how they can pay both the outstanding monies owed within a reasonable time and to continue to make ongoing payments on the loan. Due to s.8 AJA 1973 they would not have to pay back the full amount of the loan, only any arrears. They would also not have to pay back arrears due under the first legal mortgage, although it is likely that the First and Last Bank will start chasing them for this eventually, and the court is likely to take their ability to pay their other debts into account when assessing their ability to repay the loan to LendSafe. A reasonable period means the remaining term of the mortgage (*C&G* v. *Norgan*). Joachim has said that the gym may be able to supplement his wage with relief work, but this is no guarantee of additional income, so they are unlikely to get this.

What can Dave do? Dave could argue undue influence, as he signed the second loan to LendSafe 'without really thinking about it' having been told by Joachim this was just a temporary measure. We are told that Joachim dealt with the household finances. If Dave can prove undue influence, that is that he has been induced to enter into the second mortgage through the abuse of Joachim's position of confidence or trust with Dave, then the lender, LendSafe, may have their loan set aside. Whether this will happen depends on whether the bank lender has followed the guidelines set out in *Etridge*. LendSafe should have ensured that Dave received independent legal advice from a solicitor and should not have proceeded with the mortgage until they had received written confirmation that such advice had been given. If LendSafe had not followed the guidelines the courts could set aside the mortgage contract and the loan would become unsecured. As a consequence they would simply become an unsecured creditor and simply have to fall into line with the couple's other creditors for payment.

What can Dave's Nan do? Dave's Nan has an unsecured loan against the property. She does not have an overriding interest as although she is living at the property (and thus in actual occupation) she does not have any equitable interest in the property. Although she has contributed towards the purchase price by making the loan to Dave, there can be no resulting trust due to this being a loan and not a permanent contribution towards the purchase of the property. The presumption of a resulting trust in this case will therefore be rebutted. Even if she had an interest in the property, her right to remain would have been overreached by the payment of the mortgage monies to two trustees of the property (Joachim and Dave).

Essay: This question is asking you to set out what the lender's right to possession is in respect of mortgaged property and what protection the statute has afforded in respect of this.

To begin with, you should set out the premise that a lender has the right to enter into possession of the mortgaged premises 'as soon as the ink is dry on the mortgage', unless the agreement provides to the contrary (*Four Maids* v. *Dudley Marshall*). This is the case irrespective of whether the borrower has fallen behind in their mortgage payments. The lender can take possession of the premises either by way of peaceable re-entry or by obtaining a court order for possession.

At first glance this seems very onerous. However, it should be remembered that, unless the premises are empty, a lender will rarely do this without first seeking a court order because of the risk of falling foul of the Criminal Law Act 1977, s.6(1). This provides that if there is any violence towards the borrower, whether threatened or actual, during the course of possession of the premises being obtained the lender will be guilty of a criminal offence. In most cases this will rule out the lender taking possession by way of peaceable re-entry in the case of a residential property, therefore.

If the lender does apply to the court for an order for possession, s.36 AJA 1970 gives protection to the borrower where the property includes a dwelling house (in other words if it is residential). Under s.36 the court may do a number of things, including adjourning the proceedings, staying or suspending judgment or even postponing the date for delivery of possession to the lender, if it appears that the borrower is likely within a reasonable period to be able to pay any sums due under the mortgage.

The court will only exercise this power, however, where the borrower can both continue to pay their current instalments and be seen to be able to clear the debt within a 'reasonable time' (*First National Bank* v. *Syed*). Thus, the borrower must be able to demonstrate a realistic prospect of paying the arrears, not simply a hope or possibility. A 'reasonable time' is now considered to be the remainder of the life of the mortgage (*C&G Building Society* v. *Norgan*).

It would be worth mentioning at this point the amendment to the statute made by s.8 AJA 1973, preventing 'any sums due' from including the whole mortgage advance in the case of instalment mortgages.

The crux of the question, however, is the fact that s.36 does not come into play if you use either peaceable re-entry (because there is no application for a court order by the lender which can be stayed, as in *Ropaigealach* v. *Barclays*), or where a third party purchaser of the property, and not the lender, is seeking possession (as in *Horsham Properties* v. *Clark*).

The purported ability of the lender to circumvent the effects of s.36 by repossessing in either of these circumstances has led to considerable controversy and calls for reform. You may wish to set out the facts of both these cases and to discuss the outcomes and the courts' reasoning for their judgments.

In particular, it should be mentioned that the outcome in *Horsham Properties* led to a Private Member's Bill, entitled the Secured Lending Reform Bill 2010, being presented to Parliament at the end of June 2010 which suggested, amongst other things, that the LPA 1925 should be amended so that a court order is always compulsory in respect of residential properties prior to possession being sought. However, at this point the Bill is being taken no further forward and therefore the suggested reforms are unlikely to be implemented. You should finish by commenting on the position, possibly mentioning the human rights aspect, bearing in mind the ruling on this in *Horsham Properties*.

Chapter 13 Covenants in leases

Key points In this chapter we will be looking at:

- The basic structure and format of a lease
- What are leasehold covenants
- Implied tenant covenants, including the covenant not to commit waste
- Implied landlord covenants, including the covenant for quiet enjoyment and not to derogate from grant
- The limited repairing liability of the landlord
- The most commonly used express covenants, including assignment and use
- Absolute, qualified and fully qualified covenants
- Repairing covenants and the issue of inherent defects
- Remedies for breach of covenant on behalf of landlord and tenant
- The landlord's right of forfeiture or re-entry onto the premises
- Transmission of leasehold covenants pre-1996
- Transmission of leasehold covenants under the Landlord and Tenant (Covenants) Act 1995

Introduction

Throughout the last three chapters we have been considering various interests in land, predominantly relating to **freehold** estates, although of course it is possible to have a **mortgage** over **leasehold** property (lenders commonly assist in purchases of residential flats on long **leases,** for example) and, as we have seen in Chapter 10 on **easements,** to acquire an easement over leasehold land under section 62 of the Law of Property Act 1925. In this penultimate chapter of the text we are going to return to the concept of leasehold property as a method of landholding, and the rights and obligations commonly found within the structure of a lease. We will be looking at the more usual types of rights and obligation which are both implied into the lease by **common law** and statute and at those rights and obligations which are commonly specified within a lease by the parties to it. We will also be considering the transmission and preservation of such rights and obligations to third parties when the leasehold interest is sold or otherwise transferred or alternatively when the landlord disposes of the property which is subject to the lease.

The structure of a lease

In Chapter 5 we spent some time considering how leases are created and their essential characteristics, and in doing this, we briefly touched in passing upon some of the common features of leasehold agreements. At the beginning of this chapter, in which we are considering the rights and obligations contained within leases in some detail, however, it would make sense first to take a look at the structure of a typical lease. Although there are bound to be variations in the detail of the agreement, the vast majority of leases will share broadly the same format.

Writing and drafting

Imagine you are a landlord renting out your dream property. What terms would you expect to see in the lease? Which of those terms would you consider essential? Why not have a go at drafting your own lease of the property and then compare it with the sample lease below. Try to do it without looking at the example for inspiration though! Remember, it is the basic form we are interested in at this stage, not a perfect piece of legal drafting.

You should spend no more than 30 minutes on this task.

Source: Nick Pope © Dorling Kindersley

Handy tip: If you are stuck, consider the following to get you started – who are you renting to and what are you renting? How long for and for how much?

The Writing and Drafting feature should have got you thinking about the essential ingredients of any lease. We will now spend some time going through the basic elements of a lease in more detail, following the format of the example lease shown in the Documenting the Law feature, below.

Documenting the law

Form of a basic lease

THIS LEASE dated 27th January 2009 is made between HARRISON RIDLEY ('the Landlord') and JAMES GILBERT COCKBURN ('the Tenant').

1. The Landlord lets to the tenant all those premises known as FLAT 4, THE GRANGE, WETHERKNOLL in the county of BARKINGHAMSHIRE for a term of 5 years commencing 1st September 2009 for the sum of £5,000 per annum payable in advance by monthly instalments on the first of each month.

2. The Tenant covenants with the landlord as follows:
   (a) To pay the rent at the time and manner it falls due;
   (b) Not to use the premises for any purpose other than as a private dwelling house;
   (c) To keep the premises (excluding the structural parts) in repair;
   (d) Not to assign, sub-let or part with possession of any part of the premises without the prior written consent of the landlord.
3. The Landlord hereby reserves the right to re-enter the premises and thereby determine the lease if at any time the rent is 14 days in arrears (whether formally demanded or not) or if the Tenant has failed to observe any of the covenants contained within the lease. This shall not prejudice any other claim by the Landlord in respect of any breach of any covenants within the lease.

Signed as a deed by
THE LANDLORD
and witnessed:

Signed as a deed by
THE TENANT
and witnessed:

1. ***The date***: The first thing you will note from the above lease is the date of the lease. Be aware, however, that this is the date that the parties entered into the lease and not necessarily the date on which the term of the lease commenced (although these are often the same day). Remember that leases can take effect **in reversion**, which means that they can start at some point in the future. They do not have to commence immediately as a freehold does. In the sample lease above the commencement date is actually 1 September 2009.
2. ***The parties***: In order for the lease to be enforceable in a court of law (as well as from a practical viewpoint), there needs to be certainty as to who the parties to the lease are: in other words who is the landlord and who is the tenant. In our example the **landlord** is Harrison Ridley and the **tenant** is James Cockburn.
3. ***The term***: You will remember from Chapter 5 on the leasehold estate that one of the requirements of the creation of a leasehold interest in land is a **determinate term**, which means that the lease has to have a definite start date and definite or calculable end date. The term is therefore an essential ingredient of any lease. In our example lease, the term is five years from 1 September 2009. The end date can therefore be calculated as 31 August 2014.
4. ***The rent***: Whilst rent is not an essential part of a lease, as we have seen from the Law of Property Act 1925 section 205 definition of the **term of years absolute**, as confirmed in *Ashburn, Anstalt* v. *Arnold* [1988] 23 EG 128, the payment of rent is a usual part of any lease. In our lease the tenant is agreeing to pay to the landlord £5,000 a year in monthly instalments.
5. ***Covenants in the lease***: A **covenant** is simply a legal term meaning a promise that is contained in a deed. In the example lease above, the tenant has entered into a number of covenants with the landlord whereby he promises to do certain things during the **tenancy**. The first is to pay the rent on time and in the method stated in the lease (that is, to pay the rent on a monthly basis in advance); the second is a covenant not to use

the property for anything other than as a private dwelling house: in other words, the tenant cannot use the premises for business purposes; the third covenant is to keep the premises in repair, apart from the structure (by implication this is the responsibility of the landlord); and the fourth covenant is that the tenant will not assign or sublet the premises without the landlord's consent. There are no landlord covenants in our example, although some will commonly be included. Landlord and tenant covenants will form the basis of the greater part of the remainder of the chapter.

6. ***Forfeiture clause***: The **forfeiture**, or **re-entry**, clause is almost always present in any lease. You may remember that you came across rights of re-entry in Chapter 4: it is one of the five legal **interests** in land capable of subsisting under section 1(2) of the Law of Property Act 1925. A right of re-entry or the right to forfeit in a lease is the right of the landlord to enter onto the leased premises if the tenant is in breach of certain specified terms within the lease, thereby reclaiming the property and bringing an end to the **letting**. The right is not automatic however, and so if a landlord wishes to take advantage of the legal right of re-entry they must ensure that there are forfeiture, or re-entry, provisions specifically contained within the lease. In our example lease the forfeiture clause allows the landlord to re-enter the premises either if the rent remains unpaid for 14 days after it becomes due, or if the tenant is in breach of any of their other covenants under the terms of the lease. Thus, for example, if the tenant let the property fall into disrepair the landlord could forfeit under the terms of this clause.
7. ***Execution clauses***: To '**execute**' a lease means to sign it in the presence of a witness, in accordance with the requirements for a valid **deed** under section 1 of the Law of Property (Miscellaneous Provisions) Act 1989. The **execution clause** is therefore the term given to the part of the lease which contains the signatures of the parties to the lease and their witnesses. You will remember from Chapter 5 that in order to create a valid legal lease under section 52 of the Law of Property Act 1925 any lease for more than three years' duration must be created by deed. In the example above, the lease is for a term of five years, and therefore must be created by deed in order to comply with the **formalities** of section 52.

You be the judge

Q: Take another look at the example lease in the Documenting the Law feature above. Imagine the term is three years, rather than five. Would it still need to be created by deed?

A: Yes. Remember that one of the provisos under the exception to the requirement for a deed contained in section 54(2) LPA 1925 is that the lease takes effect in possession: in other words, that it starts immediately. Our example lease is in reversion – the commencement date is almost nine months after the date of the lease.

So we can see from our brief tour of the basic example lease in our Documenting the Law feature that there are certain elements that will be essential to the creation of any valid lease: the identities of the landlord and tenant; the commencement and term of the lease; the rent payable (if appropriate) and the property to be let. We have also been reminded that the lease must also be created in the correct form (in this case a deed) in order to comply with the necessary statutory formalities for its creation. In addition, however, we can see that there are a number of other clauses that may be included in a lease which are not compulsory, but which either the landlord or the tenant may require in order to reach agreement over what is acceptable for them, both practically and commercially, in the terms of the letting. The most obvious of these is the forfeiture clause; any landlord will want to ensure this is included in the lease so that they have the legal right to comply with it and bring an end to the tenancy if the tenant does not comply with their obligations under the lease. The remainder is the covenants made on the part of both landlord and tenant, detailing their rights and obligations under the lease. It is these covenants, these leasehold rights and obligations, on which we will be focusing for the remainder of the chapter.

Reflective practice

Compare the example lease in the Documenting the Law feature with your own draft lease. You should be able to see some similarities. Consider the differences. Did you miss anything out that you now consider essential, or is there anything missing from the example that you would ordinarily expect to see in a lease?

What is a covenant?

As we saw earlier in the chapter, a covenant is simply a promise made in a deed: so it might be a promise on the part of the tenant to pay the rent, or a promise on the part of the landlord to keep the structure or exterior of the premises in repair, for example. Whereas the rest of the lease tends to deal with the operative provisions of the tenancy, such as when it starts and ends, what the property consists of, how much the rent will be, and so on, the covenants form the basis of the bargain between the parties: setting guidelines or rules about how the parties will behave towards the property and each other for the duration of the lease. It is for this reason that you will tend to see the most variation in terms of leasehold covenants as components of a lease, because these are the things which are specific to the original parties when the lease is created. It should be mentioned here that the concept of leasehold covenants should not be confused with **freehold covenants**. Whereas freehold covenants are promises to do (or not to do) something on your own land, leasehold covenants are promises as to how a landlord and tenant will conduct themselves for the duration of a lease. The two concepts, whilst they share a common feature in that both relate to promises to do, or not to do, something in relation to an estate in land, are distinct entities with entirely different sets of rules relating to their existence and transmission, and as such they should be viewed completely separately.

Implied covenants

Whilst the majority of leasehold covenants are expressly recorded within the lease, there are a number of landlord and tenant covenants which common law and statute have seen fit to imply into all leases of property, and it would make sense to deal with these first.

On the part of the tenant

To pay the rent

The common law implies a covenant on the part of the tenant to pay all rates and taxes (such as council tax, water rates or business rates) which are payable on the property. Perhaps unusually, there is no implied covenant to pay the rent, rent not being a compulsory element of a lease; however, it is usual for the landlord to want to deal with the payment expressly in the lease in any event because they will want to specify when the rent has to be paid and by what method.

To use the property in a tenant-like manner

This common law obligation imposes on the tenant a very basic obligation to look after the property – to treat it with respect, if you like. The authority for this proposition is the 1815 case of *Horsefall* v. *Mather* (1815) 171 ER 141, in which a tenant successfully defended an action against him for repairs to a property in which he had been living. The court in this case said that the obligation to keep the property in a 'husbandlike manner' put a certain obligation on the tenant, but that this did not extend to general repairs. This begs the question, however, what does it include, exactly? Lord Justice Denning most famously attempted to answer this question in the 1954 case *Warren* v. *Keen* [1954] 1 QB 15, in which he described it as the duty to do 'all those little jobs about the place which a reasonable tenant would do'. He then went on to give examples, which included turning off the water if he (the tenant) is going away for the winter, cleaning the chimneys and the windows, mending the electric light when it fuses and unblocking the sink when it is blocked by his waste.

Case Summary

Case Summary

Not to commit waste

If the tenant has 'committed **waste**', it means that they have carried out an unauthorised act or an omission which physically alters the state of the land. So in other words they have done something that changes the land in some way. Usually this will mean that the property has been damaged in some way, but the term does actually include '**ameliorating waste**', which means that an unauthorised improvement has been made to the premises. Waste can be divided into two categories:

- **voluntary waste**, which is where the tenant does some positive act that changes the property; and
- **permissive waste**, which is where the tenant fails to do some act which ought to be done, and as a result damage is caused.

The most common example to be given of voluntary and permissive waste is that of a wall on the tenant's premises. If the tenant knocks the wall down without the landlord's consent, this is voluntary waste; if they do not keep the wall in repair and as a result the wall falls down, this is permissive waste. However, to give a different example in which a tenant was found to have committed waste, we might also look at the case of *Mancetter Ltd* v. *Garmanson Ltd* [1986] QB 1212, in which the tenant removed an extractor fan from the wall of the premises without repairing the resulting hole. It is easy to see from an example such as this how tenants can be found liable for waste in situations where they have made unauthorised alterations to rented property.

Case Summary

If there is nothing in the lease to the contrary, all tenants are liable for voluntary waste. This was the case in *Yellowly* v. *Gower* (1855) 11 ExD 274, which concerned an argument over a clause in a lease exempting the tenant from responsibility for waste. However, the extent of liability for permissive waste depends on the type of lease. A tenant of a fixed-term lease will always be responsible for permissive waste, unless the lease states otherwise; but the liability of a **periodic tenant** will depend on the length of the periodic term. A tenant on an annual periodic tenancy has been held to be liable for permissive waste that results only from the tenant's failure to keep the premises wind and watertight. However, tenants on shorter periodic tenancies have been held only to be liable for voluntary waste (so they can knock the wall down, but they cannot let it fall down).

To allow the landlord to enter and view

Case Summary

We have seen that the grant of **exclusive possession** to the tenant means that the tenant can exclude everyone from the premises, including the landlord. However, where the landlord has either an implied or express obligation to repair, either under the terms of the lease or under statute, this carries with it an implied obligation on the tenant to allow the landlord access to the premises to inspect them and carry out necessary repairs. This was confirmed in the Court of Appeal case of *Mint* v. *Good* [1951] 1 KB 517, which concerned an argument between the landlord and tenant regarding responsibility for injury caused by the falling down of a wall in a tenanted property.

On the part of the landlord

Quiet enjoyment

Case Summary

A covenant is implied into every lease at common law that the landlord will not breach the **quiet enjoyment** of the tenant in respect of the premises. This means that the landlord will allow the tenant to occupy the premises without disturbance. The implied covenant of quiet enjoyment is not usually about the landlord making noise, although continuous and excessive noise could amount to a breach of quiet enjoyment, if it was sufficient to prevent the tenant from enjoying their use of the property. This was confirmed by Lord Hoffman in the House of Lords case of *Southwark LBC* v. *Mills* [1999] 4 All ER 449, which concerned complaints by two council tenants about excessive noise coming from neighbouring properties. Other more typical examples of a landlord's breach of quiet enjoyment include:

Case Summary

- ✦ Removing the doors and windows to the premises (*Lavender* v. *Betts* [1942] 2 All ER 72;
- ✦ The erection of scaffolding around the property which hinders the tenant's access to it (*Owen* v. *Gadd* [1956] 2 QB 99);
- ✦ Disconnection of the gas and electricity (*Perera* v. *Vandiyar* [1953] 1 WLR 672);
- ✦ Where the landlord persistently intimidates the tenant in an attempt to force them to leave the premises (*Kenny* v. *Preen* [1963] 1 QB 499).

It should be noted that actions by the landlord that merely cause inconvenience to the tenant will not amount to a breach of the implied covenant of quiet enjoyment. Usually the breach will have to constitute an actual physical interference with the tenant's enjoyment of their property in order for a breach of quiet enjoyment to occur. This can be illustrated by the case of *Browne* v. *Flower* [1911] 1 Ch 219, where the landlord built an external staircase outside the tenant's premises which allowed people using the staircase to look through the windows of the tenant's premises. Whilst the court acknowledged that the erection of the staircase caused an inconvenience to the tenant in that it reduced her privacy to the bedrooms in her flat, the landlord's actions were held not to be a breach the tenant's quiet enjoyment of the premises, because the landlord had done nothing to prevent or hinder the tenant in her ordinary use of the property.

Breach of quiet enjoyment must relate to interference by the landlord which has taken place since the tenant has entered into their tenancy. Pre-existing issues will not constitute a breach of quiet enjoyment, because the tenant will have known about the issue before they entered into the lease. For this reason, the House of Lords rejected the claim in *Southwark Borough Council* v. *Mills*, mentioned above, because the noise issues were on account of a lack of sufficient soundproofing to the flats which had existed for many years before they entered into their tenancies with the Council.

The landlord will also not be in breach of this implied covenant if they were acting lawfully, as in the case of *Brent LBC* v. *Botu* (2001) 33 HLR 14, where the tenant had failed to pay the rent and the landlord obtained an order for possession of the premises and forfeited the lease. The tenant then applied to the court for **relief** from forfeiture, which was granted, and the order for possession was reversed. The tenant claimed breach of quiet enjoyment, but the court held that the landlord was entitled to take possession whilst he was acting under the authority of the court order. Therefore the landlord had not breached the tenant's quiet enjoyment of the property. The concepts of forfeiture and relief from forfeiture will be dealt with in the section on landlord remedies later in the chapter.

One final point to make about breaches of quiet enjoyment is that section 1 of the Protection from Eviction Act 1977 makes harassment and unlawful eviction of tenants criminal offences carrying a sentence of up to two years' imprisonment or a fine; so whilst the covenant itself is implied at common law, the breach of that covenant has been given a statutory remedy. In addition, the aggrieved tenant can also make a statutory claim for substantial **damages** under section 27 of the Housing Act 1988. It is therefore important that the landlord does not breach this provision under any circumstances, even where it is not dealt with expressly in the lease.

Not to derogate from grant

The implied covenant not to **derogate from grant** means that the landlord, having let the premises for a particular purpose, cannot then do anything which would prevent them from being used for that purpose. The phrase commonly used to describe this is that the landlord 'cannot give with one hand and then take away with the other' (Lord Millet, *Southwark Borough Council* v. *Mills*). An example of the landlord derogating from grant might be where a landlord let a field to a tenant on which to keep his horses, but then let the adjoining field out to a firework company to practise their firework displays, thereby making it impossible to keep the horses next door. As you can see there may be some overlap between this and the implied covenant for quiet enjoyment. A further example of derogation from grant is given in the Court of Appeal case of *Harmer* v. *Jumbil (Nigeria) Tin Areas Ltd* [1921] 1 Ch 200, where a landlord let a warehouse to a tenant for the storage of explosives. One of the requirements of the tenant in keeping the explosives was that

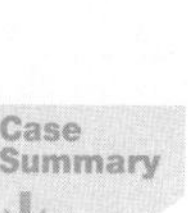

they obtained a licence for this use of the premises. The licence was granted on the proviso that there were to be no other buildings within a certain radius of the storage unit. This in turn meant that the landlord could not build within this area without derogating from his grant to the tenant.

In order to breach the implied covenant of non-derogation from grant, the landlord must have been aware of the tenant's intended use of the property at the time of the letting. Thus, in the Court of Appeal case of *Robinson* v. *Kilvert* (1889) 41 Ch 88, a landlord let the ground floor of a building to a tenant for use as a paper warehouse, retaining the cellar immediately below. The landlord then used the cellar for the manufacture of paper boxes, which required the air to be hot and dry. The manufacturing process raised the temperature of the floor in the tenant's room to a level that dried out the brown paper being stored by him and made it less valuable, even though the temperature was not such a heat as would damage paper generally. The landlord was not aware at the time of the letting that the tenant was going to store a kind of paper which had particular sensitivities and therefore the court held that the landlord was not liable for the breach.

What will not amount to derogation from grant are circumstances in which the landlord lets premises adjacent to the tenant to a competing business, however. This was the case in *Port* v. *Griffith* [1938] 1 All ER 295, in which the landlord let premises adjoining the tenant's shop, which was used for the sale of wool and general trimmings, for use as a tailor's and for the sale of dressmaking trimmings.

Repair

At common law there is no implied covenant on the landlord to keep the premises in repair; therefore the responsibility of the landlord and tenant for the repair of the premises should always be dealt with specifically in the lease. Having said this, there are a number of limited circumstances where certain covenants relating to repair will be implied on the landlord, either at common law or by statute. These can be summarised as follows:

Fitness for human habitation

In respect of furnished lettings of residential property, there is an implied covenant at common law that the premises will be fit for human habitation when they are let: in other words, that they will be in a condition suitable for a person to live in. Thus, in the case of *Smith* v. *Marrable* (1843) 11 M&W 5, a landlord had let a property to a tenant which turned out to be infested with bugs. The property was found not to be fit for human habitation and the tenant was held by the court to be entitled to quit the premises immediately without giving notice under the lease.

Case Summary

This covenant is generally only implied in respect of the condition of the premises at the start of the lease term. This was confirmed by the Court of Appeal in *Sarson* v. *Roberts* [1895] 2 QB 395, in which the tenants tried to claim that the infection of their child with scarlet fever, and its subsequent spreading to other tenants in the building, made them uninhabitable. This suggestion was rejected by the Court. The only exception to this is the statutory provision made by section 8 of the Landlord and Tenant Act 1985, which imposes a duty on the landlord to keep the property fit for human habitation throughout the continuation of tenancy; however, this relates only to premises where a very low rent is paid under the Rent Acts (£80 a year in London and £52 elsewhere), and so applies to an extremely small proportion of properties.

Liability under the Defective Premises Act 1972

Under section 4 of the Defective Premises Act 1972, wherever a landlord is responsible for the repair of a building either expressly or impliedly, or if they have a right to enter leased premises to carry out repairs or maintenance, then they will have imposed upon them a statutory duty to ensure that 'all persons who might reasonably be expected to be affected by defects in the premises' are kept reasonably safe from injury or damage to the property that might result from the defect. The duty to ensure the safety of 'all persons who might reasonably be affected' means that this duty extends not only to the tenants within the landlord's building, but also their visiting family and friends. The fact that the provision applies wherever the landlord has a right to enter premises to carry out repairs is also significant, because it effectively extends the landlords' liability to repair, converting a simple right to enter into a duty to carry out repairs where they are found necessary.

The duty is owed by the landlord wherever they either know about the defect or ought to have known about it. There is therefore no positive obligation upon the tenant to notify the landlord of defects to the property. However, it is up to the landlord to ensure that they monitor the building and keep up to their repairing obligations under the terms of the lease. In the case of *Clarke* v. *Taff Ely Borough Council* (1980) 10 HLR 44, the court found a landlord liable under the statutory provision because the age and construction of the house was such that it had been reasonably foreseeable that the floors in the building might rot due to dampness. However, the landlord had failed to carry out inspections on the property and ascertain the condition of the floors or carry out a structured maintenance programme. The facts of the case were that a woman had been visiting the council-owned house where her sister and brother-in-law lived, to help out with some redecorating. She stood on a table in order to wash down the ceiling in the living room, but the leg of the table went through the floorboards, which were rotten, causing her to fall and injure her leg and shoulder, resulting in the need for surgery.

There will be no liability if the damage or lack of repair was outside the scope of the landlord's duties, however. This was the case in *McNerny* v. *Lambeth LBC* [1989] 1 EGLR 81, in which the court confirmed that liability to repair an unfurnished property under the Act was relevant only as far as the landlord had any obligation to repair the premises under the repairing covenant in the lease. As there was none, condensation in the house causing discolouration and mould growth was held not to be the liability of the landlord.

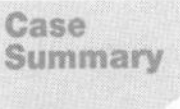

Liability for repairs under the Landlord and Tenant Act 1985

Perhaps the most significant repairing obligation imposed upon the landlord by statute is in relation to short residential leases under the Landlord and Tenant Act 1985. Section 11 of the Act provides that, in respect of a letting of any dwelling house for a period of less than seven years there shall be implied into the lease a covenant by the landlord:

(1) to keep in repair the structure and exterior (including drains, gutters and external pipes); and

(2) to keep in repair and proper working order the installations in the house –

- (i) for the supply of water, gas and electricity and for sanitation (including basins, sinks, baths and sanitary conveniences but not other fixtures, fittings and appliances for making use of water, gas and electricity); and
- (ii) for space heating or heating water.

Under section 11(3), the standard of repair is determined by having regard to the age, character and prospective life of the dwelling house and the locality in which it is situated. This is similar to the common law test for repair set out in *Proudfoot* v. *Hart* (1890) 25 QBD 42, except that it takes into account the prospective life of the house in addition to the other common law elements (for more detail on the common law test for repair see the section on repairing covenants, below).

According to the case of *Irvine's Estate* v. *Moran* [1990] 24 HLR 1, the structure of the dwelling house 'consists of those elements of the overall dwelling-house which give it its essential appearance'. It is therefore not confined to the load-bearing elements of the building and can include the windows of the property. However, in respect of matters such as the decoration of the exterior, this would only be relevant in so far as this was necessary to keep the building wind- and water-tight. A rather more extreme example of the meaning of repair under the Act can be seen in *Quick* v. *Taff-Ely BC* [1986] QB 809. Here, inadequate ventilation and heating to the building which was part of the design of the original house meant that the house suffered badly from condensation, so much so that in the winter the house was almost uninhabitable through damp. The Court of Appeal nevertheless found, however, that the council was not liable under the Landlord and Tenant Act 1985, because there was no actual disrepair that they should have remedied. Rather, it was a simple design defect in the house that was causing the damage.

As for the term 'proper working order', in the case of *Wycombe Health Authority* v. *Barnett* (1982) 47 P&CR 394 this was held to mean that the water and other installations in the house are in good mechanical order; in other words that they are in proper working condition. On this basis, on the facts of *Wycombe HA* v. *Barnett*, a failure on the part of the landlord to lag the water pipes was not considered by the court to be a breach of their statutory duty to repair under the Act. The court commented that if the water pipe had burst due to being rusted away, this would fall within the remit of the landlord's repairing obligations, but for it to burst through freezing, this was no different from the electrics blowing a fuse, which could not in all reasonableness be said to constitute a lack of repair.

The installation of a sub-standard system, on the other hand, was in *O'Connor* v. *Old Etonian Housing Association Ltd* (2002) held to be quite another matter. The case concerned a complaint by a tenant about a defect in the water pressure to the property. The landlord had refurbished the property, installing water pipes of a smaller bore than previously and this had disrupted the water flow. The Court of Appeal said that the wording of the Act meant that the landlord had an obligation at the start of the tenancy to check the installation was working and capable of performing its function. A defect in the design or construction of the installation did not relieve the landlord of their liablility under the Act. Presumably, then, if the landlord were to install an electrical system which was overloaded and caused the fuse box to blow on a recurring basis, this would come within the statute.

Unlike the liability of the landlord under the Defective Premises Act 1972, the obligation under the Landlord and Tenant Act 1985 does not arise until the landlord is notified of the disrepair. There is therefore no obligation on the landlord to carry out a regular inspection or maintenance programme in the property in order to discover potential defects. After receiving notice of the disrepair under the 1985 Act, the landlord then has a reasonable time within which to carry out any necessary repairs. This was confirmed in the House of Lords case of *O'Brien* v. *Robinson* [1973] 2 WLR 393 in which a husband and wife were injured when the bedroom ceiling fell in on them. The couple had complained to the landlord some three years before about the tenant in the flat

Table 13.1 Summary of implied covenants

Landlord	Tenant
• quiet enjoyment (*Owen* v. *Gadd*) • not to derogate from grant (*Harmer* v. *Jumbil*) • premises should be fit for human habitation when let (*Smith* v. *Marrable*) • limited statutory repair obligations, s.4 Defective Premises Act 1972 • repairing obligations in respect of short leases under s.11 Landlord & Tenant Act 1985	• to pay rates and taxes • to use the property in a tenant-like manner (*Warren* v. *Keen*) • not to commit waste (*Mancetter* v. *Garmanson*; *Yellowly* v. *Gower*) • to permit the landlord entry to view and repair

above them persistently dancing and banging on the floor and had commented that if they carried on the ceiling was likely to collapse. However, no defects in the ceiling had become visible either at that time or since then, and the landlord was unaware of any structural defect that needed to be remedied (the noise issue was duly dealt with by the landlord at the time of the complaint).

Table 13.1 gives a brief summary of the covenants implied into a lease on behalf of both landlord and tenant.

Express covenants

As we have seen, those covenants which are implied into a lease are extremely limited in scope. It is therefore common for leases to contain express covenants relating to matters such as the use of the property, provisions for its **assignment** and subletting, alterations and responsibility for repairs. The following are the more common covenants that you are likely to come across in a standard form of lease.

To pay the rent

As we have seen, there is no implied covenant to pay the rent owing under the terms of a lease, and therefore it is vital for the landlord to include such a covenant in the lease documentation. From a practical viewpoint, the landlord will also want to specify certain things about the payment of the rent, such as how often the rent is to be paid and on which days (for example the first of each month, or the usual **quarter days**); the method of payment (for example cash, cheque or standing order); and whether the rent is to be paid in advance or arrears. This last point is particularly important, as if the landlord does not specify it will be assumed that the rent is to be paid in arrears. If it is a longer lease, the landlord may also want to state provisions for the rent to be reviewed during its term. Again, this is important because there is no implied right for the landlord to increase the rent during the term if such a covenant is not included.

Not to assign or sublet

You will remember from Chapter 5 that assignment is the sale or transfer by the tenant of the remainder of the term of the lease to a third party; it is a disposition of the tenant's leasehold interest. After an assignment, subject to certain restrictions which we will be considering further on in the chapter, the tenant has no further business with the landlord or the property. Subletting, or underletting, on the other hand, is where the tenant creates a new lease out of their own leasehold interest. In this situation, the tenant remains in the position of a tenant, but also becomes the landlord of their **sub-tenant**, who takes possession of all or part of the premises, depending on what area of the property the sub-lease consists of. A reminder of the figure from Chapter 5 may help to refresh your memory of how the two concepts differ.

Figure 13.1 Assignment and subletting

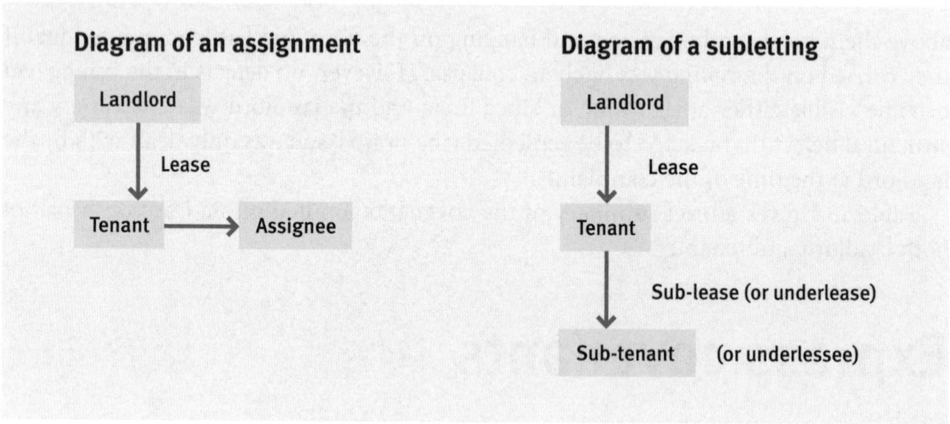

In respect of assignment or subletting, the common law position is that, if the lease is silent (in other words, there is nothing mentioned in the wording of the lease), no restrictions on assignment or subletting are implied. This means that the tenant can assign or sublet the leased property to anyone they wish without the landlord's consent, or even knowledge. Furthermore, the law acts in the tenant's favour in respect of any wording in the lease which does serve to restrict assignment or subletting: thus a restriction against assignment will not prevent subletting (this was settled in the case of *Church* v. *Brown* (1808) 15 Ves Jr 258, which concerned a lease of premises on Croydon High Street by a grocer), and a subletting of the whole of the property will not prevent a subletting of part (as stated in *Wilson* v. *Rosenthal* (1906) 22 TLR 233). It is therefore vital that if the landlord wants to retain some control over who is entering their property during the term of the lease, that they should insert some provisions into the lease restricting, or even prohibiting, these actions on the part of the tenant. Whether the landlord wants to prevent an assignment or subletting altogether, or just to restrict it so that the tenant needs to obtain the landlord's permission to do so, will be dependent on the length of the lease and the bargaining position of the parties, and will therefore vary significantly from lease to lease. However, there are certain things the landlord should bear in mind when making their decisions as to what provisions to include:

Case Summary

Absolute, qualified and fully qualified covenants

The landlord may make the tenant's covenant against assignment or subletting '**absolute**', '**qualified**', or '**fully qualified**':

- 'Absolute' means that there is an absolute bar on assignment or subletting; so the tenant is not allowed to assign or sublet at all. To do so would be a breach of covenant and the only way an assignment or subletting of the premises could be achieved during the term of the lease would be if the landlord and tenant agreed a variation to the provisions of the lease.
- 'Qualified' means that the tenant must obtain the landlord's consent to any proposed assignment or subletting. The landlord's grant of consent is entirely at their discretion, however, and the landlord may therefore refuse to allow the proposed disposition.
- 'Fully qualified' means that the tenant must obtain the landlord's consent to the proposed assignment or subletting, but that the landlord cannot unreasonably withhold their consent. It is important to note that a qualified covenant against assignment or subletting in the lease will be automatically converted into a fully qualified covenant under the provisions of section 19(1) of the Landlord and Tenant Act 1927. Therefore a covenant against assignment or subletting can, in reality, be either absolute (so that the tenant cannot assign or sublet at all) or fully qualified, so that the landlord cannot refuse their consent without good reason.

Alternatively, if the lease is a long lease, say, a 99-year lease of a flat, the landlord may simply want to be notified of changes in ownership of the property. In this case the covenant would not be against assignment; rather it would simply state that the tenant must give notice to the landlord on an assignment of the lease.

Matters the landlord should consider on receiving a request to assign or sublet

the landlord must respond within a 'reasonable time'

According to section 1(3) of the Landlord and Tenant Act 1988, the landlord must respond in writing to any request to assign or sublet within a 'reasonable time', giving reasons for their refusal if applicable. If a landlord exceeds this reasonable time period when making their decision, they will be viewed as having unreasonably withheld their consent to the assignment or subletting, regardless of the reasons for their refusal. Unfortunately, the act does not state what a reasonable time is considered to be, but in the case of *Midland Bank plc* v. *Chart Enterprises* (1990) 44 EG 68 a period of two-and-a-half months from the date of the initial request was considered an unreasonable delay. The tenants had sent various reminders to the landlord during this time, but the landlords had failed to respond. The delay was held to have effectively amounted to an unreasonable refusal on the part of the landlord. The more recent Court of Appeal case of *Go West Ltd* v. *Spigarolo* [2003] 2 WLR 986 which concerned a request to assign a twelve-year lease of shop premises on Camden High Street, has subsequently confirmed that a reasonable time period would be measured in weeks rather than months. Here a request for consent to assign had been put in to the landlord in March and the landlord had not given its refusal until May, with further correspondence between them continuing until July.

Case Summary

The year 2003 was quite a busy one for the courts for dealing with this particular topic, with two further first instance decisions being made, both of which had their own comments

Case Summary

to make on the issue of how quickly a landlord should be expected to make a decision on a proposed assignment. In *Mount Eden Land Ltd* v. *Folia Ltd* [2003] EWHC 1815, the court made the quite sensible observation that the urgency of the application should be taken into account when making a decision, the landlord dealing with more urgent cases more quickly. The landlord in this case was criticised because evidence showed that they had made their decision not to give their consent to the assignment within 24 hours of receiving the tenant's request, but then had taken 24 days to communicate this to the tenant. In a falling market this had a significant impact on the tenant's ability to find another suitable applicant. Then in *Blockbuster Entertainment Ltd* v. *Barnsdale Properties Ltd* [2003] EWHC 2912 damages were awarded to the tenant on the grounds that the landlord should have given their consent to an application to sublet the premises within a week of receiving all of the required information. In actual fact the landlord had taken around a month to make their decision.

Case Summary

The decision in *Blockbuster* v. *Barnsdale Properties* obviously placed a great deal of pressure on landlords to make their decisions on assignment quickly. However, this position proved to be short-lived and the requirements placed upon a landlord when faced with a request for consent to assign or sublet are now governed by the case of *NCR Ltd* v. *Riverland Portfolio No. 1 Ltd (No. 2)* [2005] 2 EGLR 42. The case concerned a request for consent to sublet office premises on Finchley High Road in London. The premises, which were substantial, were let on a 25-year lease at a rent then standing at £710,000 per annum. The judge at first instance held that the landlords were in breach of their statutory duty to respond within a reasonable time and that they should have made their decision within two weeks of the request being made. However, the Court of Appeal did not agree, stating that, under the circumstances, a period of less than three weeks could not be categorised as an inherently unreasonable timescale within which a landlord could make their decision on subletting. The position following *NCR* v. *Riverland*, then, is a common-sense approach: the landlord should act as quickly as is reasonable for them to do so under the circumstances.

Case Summary

It is not just the timescale within which the landlord must respond that has to be reasonable, however. The actual reasons for refusal to a proposed assignment or subletting must be reasonable too. When deciding what is and is not reasonable in terms of refusal, it is the courts that will have the final say in the event of a dispute. The traditional view has always been that refusal of consent will be reasonable only if it relates specifically either to the character of the proposed **assignee** or to the unsuitability of the proposed use of the premises by the assignee. This was confirmed in the Court of Appeal case of *Houlder Bros & Co Ltd* v. *Gibbs* [1925] Ch 575. The case concerned a request to assign a property at 10 Market Street in Sheffield, known as The White Building. The tenants held the property on a lease which contained a covenant against assignment without the landlord's consent, 'such consent not to be withheld unreasonably in the case of a respectable and responsible person or corporation'. The tenant applied for consent to assign the premises to the tenants of the neighbouring property at 12 Market Street. However, the landlord also owned number 12 and refused consent to the assignment because it knew that this would mean losing their tenant at the neighbouring premises, which would then be hard to re-let. The court at first instance held that this was an unreasonable refusal of consent, and the Court of Appeal confirmed this, stating that it could not be reasonable as the reason given for the refusal was one which had no reference either to the personality of the proposed assignee or to the subject matter of the lease. The tenant was therefore free to assign to the neighbouring tenant.

This remained the position for many years, until the Court of Appeal case of *Bickel* v. *Duke of Westminster* [1977] QB 517 was heard. The case, which concerned an application for consent to assign residential property in Belgravia, London, was unusual in its facts because new legislation which had come in since the granting of the lease effectively meant that an assignment of the property would give the assignee the right to buy the freehold. The landlord did not want this because it would mean they would be forced to sell off part of their substantial estate at far less than its market value, and they preferred to keep the estate intact. They therefore refused consent to the proposed assignment. At first instance the court held that the landlord's refusal to consent to the assignment was unreasonable because it related neither to the personality of the proposed assignee or the use of the premises. However, the Court of Appeal disagreed. In a landmark judgment Lord Denning, who was Master of the Rolls at that time, said that:

Case Summary

> I do not think the court can, or should, determine by strict rules the grounds on which a landlord may, or may not, reasonably refuse his consent. He is not limited by the contract to any particular grounds. Nor should the courts limit him . . . The landlord has to exercise his judgment in all sorts of circumstances. It is impossible for him, or for the courts, to envisage them all. When this lease was granted in 1947 no one could have foreseen that 20 years later Parliament would give a tenant a right to buy up the freehold. Seeing that the circumstances are infinitely various, it is impossible to formulate strict rules as to how a landlord should exercise his power of refusal. The utmost that the courts can do is to give guidance to those who have to consider the problem. As one decision follows another, people will get to know the likely result in any given set of circumstances. But no one decision will be a binding precedent as a strict rule of law. The reasons given by the judges are to be treated as propositions of good sense – in relation to the particular case – rather than propositions of law applicable to all cases. It is rather like the cases where a statute gives the court a discretion. It has always been held that this discretion is not to be fettered by strict rules and that all that can be properly done is to indicate the chief considerations which help to arrive at a just conclusion.

In other words, reasonable refusal should not be limited to a set of particular circumstances, but should be judged on the facts of each individual case.

One further case to mention on the subject of the reasonableness of a landlord's refusal to consent to an assignment or subletting is that of *International Drilling Fluids Ltd* v. *Louisville Investment Ltd* [1986] 2 WLR 581. The case concerned an application for consent to assign office premises on an industrial estate. The lease contained a restriction on the use of the premises, stating that they could be used as offices only. The tenant applied for consent to assign the lease to a company that wished to use the premises as serviced office accommodation for multiple users of the office space on a short-term let basis. The landlord refused consent on the basis that this would diminish the value of the freehold; however, the court disagreed. There was no evidence to show that this would be the case. The tenant had already moved out of the premises and taken up a new lease elsewhere. The Court of Appeal dismissed the landlord's appeal against the decision. In their view, the detriment to the landlord existed only on paper and the reality was that there was little or no danger of the new assignee not paying their rent or the premises becoming less valuable as a result of their occupation of it. In this case, the detriment of the landlord's refusal to the outgoing tenant was far greater than any alleged detriment to the landlord in granting their consent to the assignment. The tenant was therefore allowed to assign by the court.

Case Summary

It should be noted that a licence will automatically be deemed to have been unreasonably withheld if the landlord withholds their consent on grounds of colour, race, ethnic or national origins or sex. This is in accordance with section 24 of the Race Relations Act 1976 and section 31 Sex Discrimination Act 1975 respectively. There is, however, an exception made in both acts for situations in which the premises are shared with the landlord or a near relative of the landlord and the premises are classed as 'small'. The topic of discrimination has recently hit the news, not in relation to an assignment or subletting, but in respect of a very similar situation in which a small bed and breakfast establishment operated from the owners' home was sued for refusing guests based on their sexual orientation. Take a look at the Law in Action feature below for details.

Law in action Is an Englishman's home still his castle? Not if he invites guests, it would appear

In 2011 the Court of Appeal upheld a ruling that two Christian guest house owners had acted unlawfully when they refused to allow a gay couple to stay in a double room in their establishment. Peter and Hazelmary Bull had refused to allow civil partners Steven Preddy and Martyn Hall, from Bristol, the room at their guest house in Cornwall in 2008. The couple were ordered in January 2011 to pay £3,600 in damages for breaches of equality legislation on the ground of sexual orientation under the Equality Act (Sexual Orientation) Regulations 2007.

At a hearing last month, the Bulls denied the claim, saying they have a longstanding policy of banning all unmarried couples both heterosexual and gay from sharing a bed at their Private Hotel in Marazion near Penzance. Mr Bull, 70, and his wife, 66, said their policy, operated since they bought the hotel in 1986, is based on their beliefs about marriage and not hostility to sexual orientation.

Sources: http://www.bbc.co.uk/news/uk-england-15811223 and http://www.telegraph.co.uk/news/uknews/law-and-order/8266097/Gay-couple-awarded-damages-after-Christian-hotel-owners-refused-to-let-them-share-double-room.html

This recent ruling does beg the question whether there is an inconsistency in the law in this area. Given that the same rules would not apply to a refusal of consent to assign or sublet in the case of a tenant of small premises, it is suggested at least that this raises the issue of where to draw the line in such cases. However, given that the provisions of the recently enacted Equality Act 2010 have replaced both of the earlier statutory provisions without amendment, it looks unlikely that a further change will be made in the near future.

One further point to make is that the landlord is not entitled to demand payment in return for giving their consent to the requested assignment or subletting. This is a statutory restriction, set out under section 144 of the Law of Property Act 1925. The landlord can, however, under section 19(1)(a) of the Landlord and Tenant Act 1927, claim reasonable legal and other expenses incurred in connection with the giving of consent.

The above examples in case law should give you a good idea of the sorts of cases that would warrant refusal to consent to assign or sublet on the part of the landlord and those which would not. Why not take a moment to test your judgment in the following You Be the Judge feature, below.

You be the judge

Q: In which of the following scenarios do you think the landlord would be reasonable in refusing their consent to an assignment: (a) where the proposed tenant has provided unsatisfactory references; (b) where the proposed assignee intends to use the premises to run a rival business next door to the landlord; (c) where the proposed tenant is a well-known campaigner for gay and lesbian rights; (d) where the existing tenant is already in breach of covenant or the proposed assignee intends to put the premises to a use which will be in breach of covenant?

A: They are all examples of where a refusal will be deemed reasonable. In the case of the tenant' breach of covenant, the landlord can insist upon the breach being remedied before giving consent unless it is clear that the incoming tenant can remedy the breach on assignment (this was the case in *Orlando Investments Ltd* v. *Grosvenor Estate Belgravia* [1989] 2 EGLR 74).

The following are examples of unreasonable refusal:

- Where the proposed assignee was a diplomat who would be protected by diplomatic immunity (*Parker* v. *Boggon* [1947] KB 346);
- Where the landlord's intention was to bring the tenancy to an end and they did not therefore propose to give consent to any assignee, not just to the particular assignee in question (*Bickel* v. *Duke of Westminster*);
- Where the proposed assignee was already a tenant of the landlord in another property which would have been difficult to re-let (*Houlder Bros* v. *Gibbs*).

Despite the relaxing of the acceptable criteria for refusal that has taken place since *Houlder Bros* v. *Gibbs*, the landlord still remains on their guard whenever taking a decision not to consent to an assignment or underletting. One statutory provision that has helped soften the blow, however, is section 22 of the Landlord and Tenant (Covenants) Act 1995. The provision, which relates to business leases only and so has no impact on residential tenancies, states that in leases commencing on or after 1 January 1996, the landlord is able to include in the lease circumstances in which their consent to assignment will be withheld and also conditions subject to which any consent may be given. As long as the landlord refuses consent to assignment for a reason specified in the lease, whatever this may be, their refusal to consent to an assignment will therefore not be deemed unreasonable. It should be noted that the provisions of section 22 relate only to assignments and not sublettings.

What can the tenant do if the landlord unreasonably withholds consent?

In this situation, the tenant has three basic options:

1. They could assign or sublet regardless. This is not a wise course of action as if the court later finds that the landlord was reasonable in withholding their consent, the tenant will be in breach of the covenant not to assign and liable to forfeiture by

Case Summary

the landlord. It should be noted that if the tenant assigns the lease without asking the landlord for their consent at all they will be in breach of covenant, even if the landlord could not have reasonably withheld their consent if they had been asked. This was the outcome in *Eastern Telegraph Co Ltd* v. *Dent* [1899] 1 QB 835.

2. They could apply to the court for a declaration that the landlord is acting unreasonably. However, this takes time and money, so may not be an option for the tenant;
3. They could sue for damages under the Landlord and Tenant Act 1988 on the grounds that the landlord has breached their statutory duty not to unreasonably withhold their consent.

Alterations

Landlords will usually seek to restrict or prevent the tenant from making structural alterations to the property. If the landlord allows a qualified covenant against alterations, section 19(2) of the Landlord and Tenant Act 1927 will automatically convert this into a fully qualified covenant in the case of improvements to the premises.

Use

If the lease is silent on the subject of user, the tenant will be free to use the premises for any lawful purpose. The landlord will usually wish to restrict the use of the premises, however, at least to limit its use to what is appropriate for the nature of the building. An example of this would be to use a house as a residential dwelling only, or to use a warehouse for storage or distribution. If there is a qualified covenant against change of use, there is no provision under section 19 of the LTA 1927 that the covenant shall become fully qualified. The landlord is therefore free to withhold consent without having to justify the reasonableness of their decision.

Repair

> the longer the lease, the more repairing obligations will rest on the tenant

We have already seen that a landlord is, generally speaking, not under any implied duty to repair premises, except in the case of short leases of residential premises, and certain other rare circumstances. It is therefore customary to include in any lease of property an express repairing covenant, detailing what is the responsibility of the landlord in respect of repairs and what is the responsibility of the tenant. As a general rule of thumb, the longer the lease, the more repairing obligations will rest on the tenant. The interpretation of repairing clauses is fraught with difficulty, however, mainly because even well-worded repairing covenants are often the subject of unintentional ambiguity. One problem to consider is what constitutes a lack of repair in the first place. In the case of *Post Office* v. *Aquarius Properties Ltd* (1987) 54 P&CR 61, the basement of a building flooded due to a structural defect. The landlord required the tenant to remedy the defect, but the flooding had caused no actual damage to the building. The court therefore held that there was no responsibility on the tenant to resolve the problem.

Case Summary

Standard of repair

Another issue is the standard of repair required. The general standard of repair required was set out in the case of *Proudfoot* v. *Hart* (1890) 25 QBD 42, in which Lord Justice Hopes said that premises should be repaired in such a way as 'having regard to the age, character and locality would make it reasonably fit for the occupation of a reasonably minded tenant of the class likely to take it'; this was taking into account the age, character and condition of the premises at the time the lease was granted. Perhaps the more significant (and, on the part of the tenant, worrying) part of the decision in this case, however, was the statement that a covenant to keep premises in repair imposed upon the tenant a requirement to put the premises into repair. Therefore, if the premises were leased to the tenant in a state of disrepair, they would be required to repair them first and then to keep them in a suitable state of repair. A tenant should thus be mindful of the condition of the premises at the time of letting and make sure their responsibility for repair is modified if necessary to reflect this.

The main difficulty seems to be where to draw the line between the repair of premises and their renewal: when does a repair become a renewal and should the tenant be responsible for this? In the case of *Lurcott* v. *Wakely* [1911] 1 KB 905, the front wall of a house had become unsound due to old age and had to be taken down in its entirety and rebuilt. Despite this being an obvious renewal of the wall, the tenant was nevertheless held to be liable for the work under the terms of his repairing covenant in the lease. In making the distinction between renewal and repair in the case, the judge said that: 'Repair is restoration by renewal or replacement of subsidiary parts. Renewal, as distinguished from repair, is reconstruction of the entirety, meaning by the entirety not necessarily the whole but substantially the whole . . .'

What he was saying therefore was that a tenant can be required to replace defective parts of the premises but not to rebuild the whole. This can be illustrated by looking at the Court of Appeal case of *Lister* v. *Lane* (1983) 2 QB 212, in which the tenant was held not to be liable for the cost of rebuilding a house that had become unsafe because of poor foundations. The house had been built some 100 years previously on a timber platform which rested on boggy soil. The timber had rotted, causing the house to sink into the soil and the walls to bulge. In making their judgment in the case, Lord Esher, Master of the Rolls, held that a covenant to repair was '. . . not a covenant to give back a different thing from that which the tenant took when he entered into the covenant'.

In the same way that a repair does not constitute a renewal, a covenant to repair also does not constitute a requirement to improve the premises. In the case of *Morcom* v. *Campbell-Johnson* [1955] 3 WLR 497 Lord Denning stated that 'if the work which is done is the provision of something new for the benefit of the occupier, that is, properly speaking, an improvement; but if it is only the replacement of something already there, which has become dilapidated or worn out, then, albeit that it is a replacement by its modern equivalent, it comes within the category of repairs and not improvements'. The case in question actually concerned a claim by the landlords of the property that they had carried out a series of improvements and were therefore entitled to elevate the rent. However, the Court of Appeal disagreed. The works, which had constituted the replacement of water pipes and installation of water tanks and works to prevent rising damp to the ground floor flats were simply to renew that which had reached the end of its life and to repair defects to the building. None of them could constitute improvements.

The judgment was more recently followed in the case of *New England Properties plc* v. *Portsmouth New Shops Ltd* [1993] 23 EG 130, where substantial works carried out to the

roof of a building following damage caused by gale force winds did not alter the roof structure sufficiently to be called improvements to, rather than repair or replacement of, the original roof.

Inherent defects

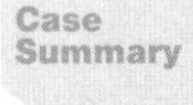

It used to be considered that damage caused to a property by '**inherent defects**', that is, defects in the design or construction of the building, did not come within the ambit of a tenant's repairing covenant. In the case of *Brew Brothers Ltd* v. *Snax (Ross) Ltd* [1970] 1 All ER 587, a lease of a fish and chip shop contained a full repairing covenant on the part of the tenant. This meant that the tenant was responsible for repairs to the whole of the premises, including the structure. A dispute arose over who should be responsible for underpinning works which became necessary due to a bowing wall caused by defective drains to the property. The court held that the damage was caused by an inherent defect to the building and that therefore the work did not fall within the scope of the tenant's repairing covenant. It is significant that the cost of the repairs was estimated at £8,000 and the value of the building as a whole was estimated at between £7,500 and £9,500.

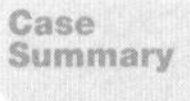

However, in the contrasting case of *Ravenseft Properties Ltd* v. *Davstone (Holdings) Ltd* [1980] 1 QB 12 the court made the opposite finding. The case concerned concrete cladding on a new building that had fallen off, necessitating the insertion of expansion joints into the structure of the building which had been omitted from the original design. The court held that, as the cost of the joints formed only a small percentage of the value of the building as a whole, the tenant was liable for the repair, even though the defect was inherent in its design. In the light of this case it would now appear, therefore, that whether the defect is inherent is wholly irrelevant and, like all other repairs, whether the tenant will be responsible for the repair of such defects will be a matter of fact and degree in every case.

Now test your knowledge about the rules relating to repairs by taking a look at the Writing and Drafting exercise, below.

Writing and drafting

In 2010 Amani granted Roger a five-year legal lease of a two-bedroom house in Agincourt Street, Gainstown. The lease contained a clause stating that the tenant should keep the premises in a good state of decoration and repair throughout the term. Roger has told you that during the winter storms a number of roof tiles were blown off the roof, and it now leaks. The guttering is also full of leaves and debris, which is causing them to overflow and cause dampness to the outer wall, which is in turn causing the wallpaper to peel off the wall in the sitting room; and a window frame is also broken, causing cold and drafts in the main bedroom. Roger has told you that he cannot afford to do the necessary repair work and is concerned about his responsibility for the repairs. He has not spoken to the landlord about this. Draft a letter of advice to Roger.

You should take no more than 40 minutes on this task.

Reflective practice

Would your advice to Roger differ if it was a 10-year lease?

Having now considered the various express covenants which you are likely to find in a lease of residential or business premises alike, it may be worth reminding ourselves what the effect of a qualified covenant in each case will have (Table 13.2).

Table 13.2 Effect of s.19 LTA 1927 on qualified tenant covenants within a lease

Type of covenant	Effect
Assignment or Underletting	A qualified covenant is automatically turned into a fully qualified covenant, meaning that the landlord cannot unreasonably refuse consent to assign or underlet.
Alterations	Section 19(2) of the Landlord and Tenant Act 1927 will automatically convert this into a fully qualified covenant in the case of improvements to the premises.
Use	There is no provision in respect of user covenants under s.19. A qualified covenant therefore remains so and a landlord can refuse consent to change of use without the necessity of reasonableness.
Repair	Section 19 of the Landlord and Tenant Act 1927 only applies to qualified covenants (that is, covenants where consent is required to do the act specified in the covenant), and thus does not apply to repairing covenants.

Remedies for breach of covenant

We have so far in the chapter considered what the various covenants on the part of landlord and tenant are, both express and implied. What we need to consider now is what to do if there is a breach of those covenants, either by the landlord or tenant respectively. We shall deal firstly with the remedies available to the tenant if the landlord is in breach of one of their covenants within the lease; then we shall look at breaches of tenant covenant and what the landlord can do in respect of those.

Breach by the landlord

If the landlord is in breach of one of their covenants within the lease, whether express or implied, the tenant has the following remedies available to them:

- damages
- specific performance
- injunction
- appointment of a receiver

Damages

If the landlord is in breach of one of their covenants in the lease, the most obvious action available to the tenant is to bring an action for damages against them. If the tenant sues for damages under the lease, the normal contractual rules will apply, which means that the court will aim to restore the tenant to the position they would have been in had there been no breach. In a case of breach of covenant, therefore, this means that damages will be measured as the difference between the value of the tenant's interest in the property if the covenant was complied with, and the value with the covenant breached. Take the example of a breach of repairing covenant on the part of the landlord: the tenant will be able to sue for damages equal to the difference between what the property would have been worth in good repair, and what the diminished value of the property is with the landlord's repairs outstanding. The tenant will also be able to claim damages for consequential loss, meaning they can make a claim for any of their property which is damaged as a result of the disrepair – so if the roof has leaked and caused water damage to furnishings owned by the tenant, the tenant can make a claim for their replacement. A claim for consequential loss will also cover the cost of temporary accommodation, should the damage be so bad as to force the tenant out of the premises whilst the repairs are being carried out.

Case Summary

The landlord will not become liable to carry out repairs to the property until they are notified of the existence of disrepair by the tenant. However, once the landlord is notified of the disrepair, they should act within a reasonable time to carry out the repairs for which they are responsible under the lease. If they do not, the tenant is within their rights, having given the landlord reasonable opportunity to do so themselves, to carry out the repairs and deduct the cost of doing so from the rent. This was confirmed in the case of *Lee-Parker* v. *Izzet* [1971] 1 WLR 1688.

Specific performance or injunction

In certain circumstances, the tenant may feel that damages are not an appropriate remedy, and in these cases may seek an equitable remedy, such as **specific performance** or an **injunction**. Specific performance may be an appropriate course of action where the landlord is in breach of their repairing covenant under the lease and the tenant wants the landlord to carry out the works. However, it should be noted that this will only be granted if damages are not a suitable remedy. One example of where this was deemed an appropriate remedy is the case of *Jeune* v. *Queen's Cross Properties* [1973] 3 WLR 378. The landlord was under a duty to repair the premises under the terms of the lease, including the exterior and structure. The landlord had failed to repair a balcony which had collapsed at first floor level. The court granted the tenants an order for specific performance to reinstate the balcony in its original form. Injunction may be a suitable remedy for restraining a breach of implied covenant on the part of the landlord, such as a breach of quiet enjoyment or derogation from grant. Thus, the tenant could obtain an order preventing the landlord from continuing to carry out an act that prevented the tenant from using their property for its purpose. Injunctions are usually prohibitory by nature (that is, that they prevent an action being carried out), but exceptionally they can be used to compel the performance of a covenant. This was the case in *Parker* v. *Camden LBC* [1986] Ch 162, in which the Court of Appeal ordered a landlord to supply the tenants with heat and hot water from which they had been deprived due to strike action.

Case Summary

Case Summary

As specific performance and injunction are both equitable remedies, they will usually be subject to the standard equitable restrictions, in particular in that the remedies are both entirely at the discretion of the court. However, in the case of landlord's repairing covenants, there is an exception under section 17 of the Landlord and Tenant Act 1985. This states that the court can order specific performance of a landlord's repairing covenant regardless of the usual equitable rules relating to delay, the requirement for '**clean hands**' and so on (for a further explanation of the **maxims of equity** see Chapter 1 of Warner-Reed on *Equity and Trusts*, in Pearson's Living Law series). Section 17 is also useful because it allows a tenant to require specific performance of the landlord's repairing covenant, even where the repair does not relate to the tenant's own premises – so the tenant can require repairs to a neighbouring property owned by the landlord in order to prevent consequential damage to their own.

Appointment of a receiver

One final remedy available to the tenant where the landlord is in breach of their covenants under the lease is the appointment of a **receiver**. If the landlord is in breach of their covenants under the lease, most commonly where they have abandoned the property, but also where the landlord fails to carry out urgent repairs, the tenant can apply to the court for a receiver to be appointed to manage the property in accordance with the terms of the lease, collecting the rent and performing the landlord's covenants. In accordance with section 37 of the Senior Courts Act 1981, the High Court has the power to appoint a receiver wherever it is just and convenient to do so. This happened in *Daiches* v. *Bluelake Investments Ltd* [1985] 2 EGLR 67, in which the tenants of a block of 110 flats known as Elm Park Mansions requested a receiver to be appointed where the landlord had repeatedly ignored the tenants' requests for urgent repair works to be carried out to the building. The repairs, which were substantial, were estimated to cost in the region of, at the lowest estimate, £300,000, and at the highest, as much as £1 million. Although it was doubtful that the landlord could afford to do the repairs, a receiver was nevertheless appointed because the tenants had said that they were prepared to pay for the cost of the works in this eventuality.

Unlawful eviction and harassment

You will remember from your earlier reading that there is also a statutory remedy available to tenants who have been the victim of harassment or unlawful eviction under section 1 of the Protection from Eviction Act 1977. The statute makes harassment and unlawful eviction of tenants criminal offences carrying a sentence of up to two years' imprisonment or a fine; the aggrieved tenant can also make a statutory claim for damages under section 27 of the Housing Act 1988.

Breach by the tenant

A landlord's remedies for breaches of covenant by the tenant are best divided into two categories: remedies for non-payment of rent, and remedies for other breaches of covenant.

Non-payment of rent

If the tenant has not paid their rent, the landlord has the following remedies available to them:

- ✦ action for the debt
- ✦ distress
- ✦ forfeiture

Action for the debt

The landlord can sue the tenant at common law for breach of their covenant to pay rent. In accordance with the ordinary rules of limitation, the landlord can only recover a maximum of six years' rent arrears (Limitation Act 1980, section 19). Under certain circumstances, the landlord may also be in a position to sue former tenants of the property for rent owing by the current tenant. We will be considering when such circumstances apply later on in the chapter. If this is the case, section 17 of the Landlord and Tenant (Covenants) Act 1995 requires that the landlord gives the former tenant notice that they intend to sue for non-payment of rent within six months of the rent becoming due. This ensures that the most the landlord can collect from a former tenant is six months' arrears of rent. This is rather fairer than the previous situation, in which a former tenant could be required to pay up to six years' worth of rent arrears if the landlord had not been quick to deal with the issue.

Distress

Distress, or '**distraint**', is an ancient common law remedy which entitles the landlord to enter the premises of the tenant and confiscate goods belonging to the tenant to the value of any rent payments which are outstanding. Once the landlord is in possession of these goods, they must keep them for a period of five days, after which if the rent has not been paid the landlord can sell the goods in lieu of their rental payment. The rules relating to the seizure of goods are strict: the landlord must not carry out the distress themselves but must use the services of a **certificated bailiff**. There are also restrictions on what the bailiff can take. Clothes, bedding, tools of the tenant's trade up to £150 in value, and also things the tenant is using at the time of distraint, must not be taken.

tools of the tenant's trade must not be taken

The ancient remedy of distress is a much criticised remedy, particularly as it relates to residential tenancies. Of particular concern is that the use of the remedy may result in a violation of human rights under Article 8 of European Convention on Human Rights, the respect for private life. As a result of this, in May 2001 the Ministry of Justice issued a consultation paper, called 'Enforcement Review Consultation Paper No. 5: Distress for Rent', which contained proposals to abolish distraint in respect of residential leases, retaining it only in respect of commercial premises, subject to certain safeguards to ensure compliance with the Human Rights Act 1988. Following this, the Tribunals, Courts and Enforcement Act 2007 has been enacted, which contains provisions under section 71 to abolish the landlord's right of distress against their tenant and instead introduces a new regime for rent arrears recovery available only to landlords of commercial premises. However, whilst the Act was passed on 19 July 2007, the relevant section will not come into force until further legislation has been introduced. There has been concern, amid a series of delays, that the subsequent enactment of the legislation was going to be shelved, but in February 2012 the Government launched a public consultation confirming its intention to abolish distress for rent and replace it with a more modern regime. Managing Director of Able Investigations & Enforcements, Steve Wood, talks about the problems surrounding the remedy of distress as it exists in its current form in the People in the Law feature, below.

People in the law

Name and title: Mr Steve Wood. Managing Director of Able Investigations & Enforcements, Bristol.

What does your company do? Our company works as private investigators and certificated bailiffs, carrying out a variety of work from tracing missing persons to personal injury surveillance, status enquiries and asset recovery from motor vehicles to complete commercial kitchens. We also carry out commercial rent management for a number of high-profile shopping centres in the United Kingdom.

Is there still a lot of call by landlords to use the remedy of distress? Does it form a large percentage of your company's work? Yes, it is a large percentage of clients that still use distress for commercial rent matters. Along with forfeiture of commercial properties, clients find it a cheap and quick alternative method of collecting outstanding rent and service charges.

How useful is distress as a remedy? Why might it be considered better than other remedies which might be available to the landlord, e.g. suing for damages on the debt? Distress is very useful. Rather than going down the court route or using a solicitor to chase rent arrears, it gives the landlord the opportunity of a speedy recovery of the rent. The debtor pays the cost of the enforcement, unless there is a *nil bona* (meaning the debtor has nothing to levy against), in which case the landlord will have to pay a small visit fee. In most cases we rarely remove goods: it is the threat of removal that ensures that the client/landlord gets their rent speedily. If, however, the client takes action in the court, it may take at least eight weeks to get a judgment, and the county court bailiffs are not that effective, along with which the cut backs that are currently in the court system mean that the court bailiffs are usually about eight weeks behind. Instructing a certificated bailiff the client could have their money within 48 hours or, if we do have to remove the goods, then you are still only looking at ten days.

Source: Steve Wood

Do you believe that the recent suggestions for change to the law of distress are either useful or necessary? In my opinion some of CRAR gives the debtor more rights than the landlord. The current suggestions are not going to assist the landlord in collecting his rent. The recent suggestion that bailiffs have to give 14 days' notice to the tenant before any action takes place is only going to ensure that the tenant either removes his goods from the property or applies to court to stop the bailiff action. This in turn is going to increase fees for the landlord who will have to use a solicitor to issue proceedings, or do so themselves. Nor do I believe that bailiffs should have the power to force entry into a property without a court action unless it is for peaceful possession such as in forfeiture.

Having said this, I do believe that the law of rent and distress needs updating to bring it in line with the twenty-first century, especially the way that the fees are worked out and bringing the fees in line with each other. Many bailiffs use a number of variations rather than sticking to local authority guidelines, so one bailiff may charge one fee and another may charge a completely different fee for collecting on the same level of debt.

How is Commercial Rent Arrears Recovery a better system (if you think it is)? I do not believe that CRAR is going to be a useful tool for landlords; I also have my doubts if it will come into force. CRAR is going to make the life of a bailiff more difficult with tenants. The best tool for a landlord who employs the services of a bailiff is the act of surprise; if this is to be taken away from us then the tenant is going to move goods, place them in hiding or may just close up shop and move on.

Any other comments you would like to make? The role of a bailiff is one of the most ancient legal roles in the country, the first bailiff having been mentioned in the year 998. I believe that there is still a role for the bailiff in the twenty-first century, but to do so the government must not tie our hands, giving the debtor more powers than the creditor. Bailiffs always appear to have a bad reputation, some of which they have brought on themselves. To ensure that bailiffs are not seen as 'thugs in leather jackets' I feel that we have to have a recognised training programme.

Forfeiture

As you will remember from your previous reading, forfeiture, or the right of re-entry, is where the landlord can enter the premises in the event of tenant default and retake possession, thereby terminating the tenant's lease. You may also remember that the right of forfeiture is not automatic: the landlord has to reserve the right to forfeit or re-enter the premises in the terms of the lease in order to be able to take advantage of it. Provided there is a forfeiture clause in the lease, the landlord has two methods of forfeiture available to him:

- court order; or
- peaceable re-entry.

The usual method of forfeiture chosen by a landlord is to obtain a court order for possession of the premises. Landlords are often reluctant to use the **peaceable re-entry** method, which is essentially simply re-entering the premises and retaking physical possession of them, usually by changing the locks. The reason for this is that if the landlord uses threats of violence or commits an act of violence whilst in the course of re-entering the premises, or even if the landlord is aware that there is someone on the premises who opposes the re-entry, they can be guilty of a criminal offence under section 6 of the Criminal Law Act 1977. In addition, there are further restrictions placed on the right of peaceable re-entry where the premises are residential. This is under the Protection from Eviction Act 1977.

In order to exercise the right to forfeit (by whichever method the landlord chooses) they must first make a formal demand for the rent; that is, unless the wording of the lease exempts them from doing so. Most leases will include wording in the forfeiture clause to ensure that the landlord does not have to jump through this additional administrative hoop. So, for example, the lease will state that the landlord will have a right of re-entry if the tenant is 14 days or more in arrears of rent 'whether the rent is formally demanded or not'. If you look back at the example lease given in the Documenting the Law feature earlier in the chapter, you will see such wording written in brackets in the relevant clause.

Unfortunately, the landlord either making a simple application to the court or effecting a peaceable re-entry of the premises is not always the end of the matter. The tenant can apply for relief from forfeiture, meaning that the forfeiture does not take effect and the tenant continues under the terms of the existing lease. However the landlord chooses to forfeit, the tenant's request for relief must be by application to the court. In order to obtain relief before the landlord is granted a court order for forfeiture of the premises, the tenant must pay all the rent arrears plus the landlord's costs in advance of the hearing. However, in the case of both an order for re-entry being granted and the landlord taking peaceable re-entry of the premises, the tenant may also apply at any time up to six months from the forfeiture taking place in order to request relief. Again, the tenant must pay all arrears due in order to be granted relief. In addition, it must be possible for relief to be granted. If the landlord has already let the premises to a new tenant it may not be possible to allow the defaulting tenant back into possession. There are exceptional circumstances in which the court has used its inherent jurisdiction to give relief outside of the six-month time period; however, this is rare. One such case is that of *Thatcher* v. *Pearce* [1968] 1 WLR 748. Here, the landlord had re-entered a scrap yard by peaceable re-entry whilst his tenant was in prison. Due to his circumstances, the tenant was unable to apply for relief from forfeiture within the six-month time period. However, the court nevertheless granted his application. The grant of relief is entirely at the discretion of the court and they will look at the particular circumstances of each case when making their decision.

Other breaches of covenant

If the tenant has committed breaches of covenant other than the non-payment of rent due under the lease, the landlord can choose from the following remedies:

- damages
- injunction
- specific performance
- forfeiture

Damages

If a tenant is in breach of any of their covenants in the lease the landlord can bring an action for damages at any time during the term of the lease or even after it expires. Generally speaking, the ordinary contractual rules as to the measure of damages will apply. To give an example, if the tenant is in breach of their covenant to insure and have not insured the premises, and the premises are damaged, the landlord's measure of damages will be the cost of rebuilding the property. This was the case in *Burt* v. *British Transport Commission* (1955) 166 EG 4. Where the tenant is in breach of a repairing covenant, however, there is a statutory limit placed upon the amount of damages recoverable by the landlord. Under section 18 of the Landlord and Tenant Act 1927, the landlord cannot recover damages for breach of repair exceeding the amount by which the lack of repair has diminished the value of the freehold. This means that if the cost of repairs exceeds the diminution in the value of the property caused by the breach, the landlord will not be able to recover those losses. In addition, if the term of the lease is for seven years or more and there are at least three years left to run on the lease, the landlord must serve notice under the Leasehold Property (Repairs) Act 1938 notifying the tenant of the breach and requiring them to carry out the repairs before they can sue. The notice, which actually takes the form of a **section 146 notice** (to see an example of such a notice take a look at the Documenting the Law feature, below), must notify the tenant that they have the right to serve a counter-notice within 28 days claiming the benefit of the 1938 Act. If the tenant does serve counter notice, the landlord cannot then take any further action without the leave of the court. The court will give leave to the landlord to proceed with an action for damages only if:

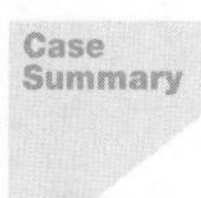

- the value of the property has been substantially reduced on account of the disrepair; or
- immediate repair is required either to prevent a substantial decrease in the property's value, or to comply with statute, or in order to protect the interests of other occupiers

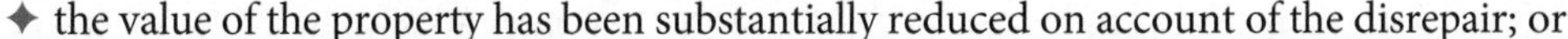

of the building if it is in multiple occupation, or in order to avoid much more substantial future cost; or

- ✦ there are special circumstances in existence which make the giving of leave by the court both just and equitable.

The decision of the court to grant leave to sue for damages is entirely discretionary.

Injunction

Case Summary

Dependent upon the nature of the breach, the landlord may feel that their needs will be better served by the grant of an injunction by the court, rather than a claim for damages. Such circumstances might include where the landlord wishes to prevent the tenant from assigning the lease in breach of their covenant for assignment, such as in the case of *Hemingway Securities Ltd* v. *Dunraven Ltd* (1995) EG 322, in which the landlord was granted an injunction to prevent an unauthorised sublease of a 25-year lease of premises in Islington, London. Alternatively the landlord may seek an injunction to prevent the tenant from carrying out unauthorised alterations to the premises, or from using the premises in a way which is not authorised by the lease. It should be remembered that injunction is an equitable remedy and therefore its grant is entirely at the discretion of the court.

Specific performance

Case Summary

The equitable remedy of specific performance is very rarely ordered in respect of a tenant's repairing covenant as damages will usually be adequate. However, it may be considered a suitable remedy under certain circumstances. One such instance is that of *Rainbow Properties Ltd* v. *Tokenhold* [1998] 3 WLR 980. The case concerned a property known as Gaynes Park Mansion, a Grade II listed property in Epping. The property, the repair of which was the responsibility of the tenants under the terms of the lease, had fallen into a considerable state of disrepair. However, there was no clause contained within the lease either to allow the landlord to enter to carry out repairs or to forfeit in the event of the tenant's non-compliance with the repair covenant. This left the landlord in a difficult position. They therefore sought an order for specific performance requiring the tenants to carry out the necessary works to the property. The court stated that, whilst they would usually be cautious in granting an order of specific performance to a landlord for the purpose of carrying out repairs (primarily because an order for specific performance is not subject to the limitations of the Leasehold Property (Repairs) Act 1938 and therefore the cost of repairs which could be required would remain unfettered), because of the particular circumstances of the case this was the only sensible remedy available. They were keen to stress, however, that the court in giving such an order 'should be astute to ensure that the order was not being sought by the landlord simply to harass or otherwise put pressure on the tenant' and, in doing so, could take into account considerations similar to those in the 1938 Act. They also stated that, where the court granted an order for specific performance, the order must be sufficiently clear in its description of the works to be done so as to enable the defendant to comply with the order.

Forfeiture

Assuming the landlord has reserved the right to forfeit for any breach of covenant within the lease, if the tenant is in breach of covenant the landlord may re-enter the premises either peaceably or by court order in the same way that they are able to do when there has been a failure to pay rent on the part of the tenant. The only difference is that, whereas with forfeiture for non-payment of rent the landlord can take action immediately (assuming the forfeiture clause excludes the requirement for a formal rent demand), before re-entering the premises of a tenant in breach of any other covenant within the lease the landlord must serve a notice on the tenant under section 146 of the Law of Property Act 1925. The notice, colloquially referred to as a 'Section 146 Notice', must contain certain specified information in order to be valid. It must:

1. specify the breach complained of by the landlord;
2. require the breach to be remedied within a reasonable time, if it is a breach which is capable of remedy; and
3. require the tenant to pay compensation for the breach, if the landlord requires this.

An example of a section 146 notice is given in the Documenting the Law feature below.

Documenting the law

Example of a Section 146 Notice

NOTICE UNDER SECTION 146 OF THE LAW OF PROPERTY ACT 1925

To: [name of tenant] of [address of tenant] ('the **Tenant**').
From: [name of landlord] of [address of landlord] ('the **Landlord**').
Re: [address of leased property] ('the **Premises**') as demised by the lease dated [date] made between [the landlord] and [the tenant] ('the **Lease**').

We, the Landlord, **GIVE YOU NOTICE THAT**:
The Lease contains the following covenants:

3.1 To pay the rents as hereinbefore provided and without deduction or set off.

3.5.1 To keep the demised property in good repair and condition.

3.5.2 To decorate the interior of the demised property in a good and workmanlike manner and with appropriate materials of good quality as often as in the opinion of the Landlord is reasonably necessary.

3.6.1 Not without the consent in writing of the Landlord (the same not to be unreasonably withheld) to make any alteration or addition to the demised property.

You are in breach of the above covenants. The breaches complained of are:

1. Non-payment of rents, outgoings and charges in the sum of £7,380 as at the date of this notice.
2. Breach of the Tenant's Repair and Decoration, and Alterations covenants as set out in the attached Interim Schedule of Dilapidations dated 2 April 2012.

You are required to remedy the breaches within a reasonable time so far as they are capable of remedy.
You are required to pay compensation in money for the breaches. You are required to also pay all costs, fees, charges, disbursements and expenses incurred by the Landlord and any VAT payable by them in relation or incidental to the preparation and service of this notice pursuant to clause 3.15 of the Lease.
If you fail to comply with this notice within a reasonable time the Landlord intends to re-enter the premises pursuant to clause 5 of the Lease and claim damages for the above breaches of covenant.

DATED: ....
SIGNED: ....

for and on behalf of the Landlord.

Having served the section 146 notice on the tenant, if the tenant does not remedy the breach within a reasonable time the landlord can then proceed to re-enter the premises, either by peaceable re-entry or with a court order.

How long is a reasonable time?

Case Summary

What is considered a reasonable time will differ according to the circumstances of the breach. This was confirmed in the case of *Albany Holdings Ltd* v. *Crown Estate Commissioners* [2003] EWHC 1480 (Ch), in which a tenant had argued that a reasonable time to remedy the breach should be a period of two months, because this was the notice period he had to give his licensee under the terms of the licence of part he had given to occupy the premises for the provision of computer study courses. The court held that the reasonableness of the time frame given by the landlord under a section 146 notice to remedy a breach was a matter between the landlord and tenant, and should not be decided with reference to the needs of any third party. A section 146 notice does not need to specify the exact time frame within which the breach complained of must be remedied: it is for the landlord to decide what is reasonable before they exercise their right to forfeiture. In any event, it should be a matter of fact and degree in each instance.

Case Summary

If the breach is not capable of remedy, on the other hand, the landlord simply has to give the tenant enough time to consider their position. In this case, 14 days is considered sufficient. This was decided in the Court of Appeal case of *Scala House and District Property Co. Ltd* v. *Forbes* [1974] QB 575). Here, a landlord had served a section 146 notice for breach of a covenant not to assign without the landord's consent. The landlord served a notice on the tenant requiring them to remedy the breach. Then 14 days later they commenced possession proceedings. The tenant complained this was not a reasonable time frame within which the breach could be remedied. The court held, however, that as the breach was one which was incapable of remedy, 14 days was not an inadequate period after which to commence possession proceedings.

Is the breach capable of remedy?

Case Summary

One of the main pitfalls of the section 146 notice is deciding when the breach is a remediable one. There is no exhaustive list detailing which breaches of covenant are considered remediable, and which are not; however, precedent gives us sufficient guidance to make an educated judgment in most cases. As a general rule of thumb, breaches by the tenant of **positive covenants** within the lease, that is covenants to do something, such as to repair the premises, are remediable. So if the tenant is required to do something under the terms of the lease, but has failed to do it, the landlord can under the section 146 notice require the tenant to comply with their covenant by carrying out the act which they have omitted within a reasonable time. This was the case in *Expert Clothing Service & Sales Ltd* v. *Hillgate House Ltd* [1986] Ch 340, which concerned a breach of covenant to do work on the premises. However, the issue of covenants within the lease not to do a certain act is less clear-cut. It was traditionally thought that, once an act prohibited under the terms of the lease had been committed, then that breach of covenant by the tenant could never be taken back – it was not remediable. This would clearly be the case where a tenant had assigned the lease to a third party without the landlord's consent, for example, as was the case in *Scala House & District Property Co. Ltd* v. *Forbes*, the facts of which are given above. Another such example would be a covenant against using the property for an immoral purpose. This can be shown in the Court of Appeal case of

Rugby School (Governors) v. *Tannahill* [1935] 1 KB 87, in which a breach of a covenant of this kind was held to be irremediable because of the stigma that would attach to the premises following the immoral use. The case concerned a house in Great Ormond Street owned by the school which had been let to a Marian Tannahill. Miss Tannahill had habitually used the house for the purposes of prostitution (she had run a brothel from the premises) over a period of time and it was the view of the Court that, even if the use complained of ceased the value of the house was irrevocably damaged due to the stigma which attached to it.

With breaches of other kinds of **negative covenant**, however, it can easily be seen that to remedy the breach would be simple and logical. One such example would be where a tenant was in a breach of a covenant not to erect signage on the premises. Although the covenant is negative in nature, it would be simple to remedy, by the tenant taking the signage down. There have even been **dicta** to suggest that unauthorised alterations to property being carried out by a tenant may be considered remediable. This was the case in the House of Lords finding in ***Billson* v. *Residential Apartments Ltd*** [1992] AC 494), which concerned an application for relief from forfeiture where the tenant had made substantial alterations to premises without the landlord's consent. Despite the Vice Chancellor, Lord Browne-Wilkinson, stating that the Lords did not intend to make a finding on whether or not the breach was remediable, in his judgment he nevertheless sought to question the judge at first instance's finding that the breach was not capable of remedy.

If the breach cannot be remedied, and the landlord does not want compensation, all that it is necessary for the notice to contain is a description of the breach alleged. This was confirmed in the case of *Rugby School (Governors)* v. *Tannahill*, previously mentioned.

Service of counter-notices

It should be noted that the provisions of the Leasehold Property (Repairs) Act 1938 that we came across when considering claims for damages for breaches of repair in the case of leases of over seven years' duration also apply to a landlord's application to forfeit a lease. As with claims for damages under the Act, the provisions have the effect of severely limiting the ability of a landlord to forfeit for breach of a repairing covenant until the last three years of a longer lease.

Relief from forfeiture for other breaches of covenant

As well as the act of forfeiture itself carrying with it additional requirements for breaches of covenant other than the requirement to pay rent, relief from forfeiture for breach of a covenant other than the non-payment of rent is also slightly more complicated. There is no standard right to apply for relief with forfeiture for other breaches – whether or not the tenant can apply for it will depend upon the circumstances of the case:

- ✦ If the landlord obtains a court order to forfeit the lease, the tenant can only seek relief before the landlord re-enters the premises: after this point, their right to ask for relief from forfeiture will be lost.
- ✦ If the landlord re-enters the premises peaceably, however, the tenant can still seek relief after the landlord has re-entered the premises, albeit that the court will be under a duty to consider the circumstances of the case, including any delay on the part of the tenant, when deciding whether or not to grant relief. An example of when relief

was granted under these circumstances is that of *Billson* v. *Residential Apartments*, mentioned earlier.

✦ If the landlord's application under the section 146 notice relates to internal decorative repairs, the tenant may in addition apply to the court under section 147 of the Law of Property Act 1925 to be relieved, either wholly or in part, from liability to carry out the works if they believe the notice is unreasonable. Section 147 does not apply, however, where:

1. the notice relates to breach by the tenant of an express covenant to put the property into a state of decorative repair at the start of the lease; or
2. the repairs are required to keep the property in a sanitary condition, or in order to maintain or preserve its structure; or
3. there is a statutory liability to keep the house fit for human habitation; or
4. the tenant is in breach of a covenant to return the property to the landlord in a specified state of repair at the end of the term.

As with the application for relief from forfeiture in cases of non-payment of rent, the decision as to whether to grant relief is entirely at the discretion of the court. Generally, it will depend upon the nature of the breach, how much damage has been caused to the premises as a result and whether the breach can be put right; however, the landlord's motives for wanting to forfeit the lease will also be taken into account. In the case of *St Marylebone Property Co.* v. *Tesco Stores Ltd* [1988] 2 EGLR 40, a sub-tenant had breached a number of covenants under the lease, including breaches of the user covenant, which restricted the use of the premises as a general store. The sub-tenant had been using the premises, amongst other things, as a video hire outlet. After the tenant promised to remedy the breach, but then failed to do so, the landlord sought to forfeit the lease. The court granted the landlord possession of the premises, rejecting the tenant's application for relief on the basis that the breaches had continued to be committed by the tenant over the period of a year or more despite the landlord's requests for the breaches to cease, and that the future commission of similar breaches would be very difficult for the landlord to police.

Case Summary

A contrasting decision was reached in the case of *Ropemaker Properties Ltd* v. *Noonhaven Ltd* [1989] 34 EG 40. In this case the tenant was in breach of a user covenant not to use the premises for illegal or immoral purposes. The property, which was supposed to be run as a high-class restaurant and night club establishment, was being used for the provision of prostitutes. The court, it might be said rather surprisingly, granted the tenant relief from forfeiture on a number of grounds, including:

Case Summary

✦ the substantial value of the lease;

✦ the substantial loss forfeiture would cause to the tenant company, which the court considered disproportionate to the breach;

✦ the fact that the immoral use had been brought to an end and was unlikely to be renewed;

✦ the fact that any stigma attaching to the premises was likely to be short-lived and, in any event, would not be removed by getting rid of the tenant company; and

✦ the poor health of the tenant company's sole director, and his intention to dispose of the lease.

The court also specified that the user covenant in the lease should be varied so that all that was sufficient for a future breach of covenant to be proved would be the tenant's knowledge that girls were 'acting as hostesses' in the tenant's establishment: that is to say that they were providing their services, however innocently, for reward.

Effect of forfeiture on a sub-tenant

If a landlord forfeits their tenant's lease, then any sub-lease granted by that tenant is also forfeit. The effect of this is that a sub-tenant who has not breached any of the covenants in their lease may have their lease brought to an abrupt end through no fault of their own. Luckily, statute has thought to intervene to relieve the harsh effect of this fact of the common law, by providing under section 146(4) of the Law of Property Act 1925 that a sub-tenant may apply for relief against forfeiture where it is the **head lease** that has been forfeited. If relief is granted by the court, the sub-tenant will then become the immediate tenant of the landlord, rather than a sub-tenant. The terms of relief will often include that the sub-tenant complies with all of the covenants that were contained in the original head lease, but it is entirely at the discretion of the court (at the request of the landlord) as to what terms will apply. If a sub-tenant is going to apply for relief they must do so before the landlord has repossessed the premises.

Waiver of the right to forfeit

It is possible for the landlord, either expressly or impliedly, to waive their right to forfeit under the lease, which means they lose their right to re-enter the property and bring the lease to an end. **Waiver** will be implied where the landlord, aware that a breach has occurred, carries out an act or series of acts that recognise the continuance of the lease. Usually this means that the landlord has received payments of rent after the event of a breach, but can also include the landlord distraining after the breach has occurred. Either way, whether the landlord intended by their actions to waive the breach is irrelevant: a simple clerical error on the part of the landlord's agent in accepting rent will be just as effective in constituting a waiver as an intentional act of distraint on the part of the landlord. This is illustrated in the case of *Central Estates (Belgravia) Ltd* v. *Woolgar (No. 2)* [1972] 1 WLR 1048 in which Mr Woolgar rented a house from Central Estates under a long lease. The lease contained a covenant against nuisance by the tenant, with a proviso for re-entry on breach. When Mr Woolgar was convicted of keeping a brothel on the premises, Central Estates served a section 146 notice notifying Mr Woolgar that they intended to forfeit the lease on the ground that he had breached the covenant against nuisance. However, due to a clerical error the next quarter's rent was subsequently demanded by Central Estates' agents, which Mr Woolgar paid. Central Estates then sought possession but their application was denied. The court held that the demand for and acceptance of rent had constituted a waiver of the breach.

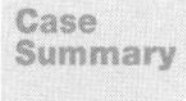

Continuing and 'once and for all' breaches

Once waiver has occurred, the landlord can no longer forfeit the lease on the grounds of the breach that has been waived. This is very serious in the case of a 'once and for all' breach. However, if the breach is one which is 'continuing', whilst waiver may cause annoyance or delay, it will not necessarily prevent the landlord from forfeiting at a later date. The consequences of the waiver will differ depending on the type of breach that has been waived. With a **'once and for all' breach**: that is, for example, a breach of covenant not to assign or sublet, in which the tenant has assigned the lease to a third party without the landlord's consent, then waiver of that breach will prevent the landlord from forfeiting the lease for that assignment once and for all. This means that it would take another assignment without consent by the new tenant to a third party before the landlord could forfeit for this reason again. However, if the breach is what is known as an '**ongoing**' or '**continuing' breach**: that is, a breach that continues over a period of time, like breach of a repairing covenant, for example, then the landlord only waives their right to forfeit for the rental period for which the rent has been received. If the property continues to be in disrepair after the end of the rental period in question and the landlord refuses to accept rent for the following rental period, the landlord will be able to re-enter the premises at this point. This was the case in the Court of Appeal case of *Greenwich LBC* v. *Discreet Selling Estates Ltd* [1990] 48 EG 113, which concerned a breach of a repairing covenant by the tenants. The landlords had served a section 146 notice but had continued to receive rent whilst waiting for leave from the court to re-enter the premises. The tenants contended that this constituted a waiver of the landlord's right to forfeit the lease. However, the court denied their claim. No repairs had been carried out to the premises since the original notice had been served and therefore there was no need for the landlord to serve a fresh forfeiture notice. The breach was ongoing.

Case Summary

We have now considered the various remedies available to a landlord and tenant for breaches of covenant within the lease. Consolidate your knowledge by undertaking the Writing and Drafting feature, below.

Writing and drafting

There are a number of different remedies available to both landlord and tenant for breach of covenant and, in the case of the landlord, these differ according to the type of breach. In order to make sure you have a firm grasp of the array of remedies on offer, why not spend some time now creating a table setting out what the remedies available to both landlord and tenant are and when they are applicable. It should provide you with a good revision aid when you come to this point in your studies.

You should spend no more than 40 minutes on this task.

Law reform

Amid particular concerns about possible breaches in human rights legislation in relation to forfeiture in residential tenancies, in January 2004 the Law Commission published a consultation paper which proposed the abolition of the law of forfeiture and set out proposals for a new statutory scheme for the termination of tenancies in the event of tenant default. This consultation paper was followed by a final report of the Law Commission, which was published in October 2006 and entitled, 'Termination of Tenancies for Tenant Default' (Law Com. No. 303). The paper recommended the abolition of the law of forfeiture and its replacement by a new statutory scheme, which was set out in a draft 'Landlord and Tenant (Termination of Tenancies) Bill' attached to the report. The report can be summarised as follows:

- Forfeiture will be abolished. Instead, if a tenant is in breach of covenant the landlord will instead be able serve a 'tenant default notice', setting out the terms of the breach, any remedial action required and the date by which it should be completed. This date should be no less than seven days from the date of the notice.

- ✦ If the tenant does not remedy the breach before the expiry of the notice the landlord may make a 'termination claim'. The court may then grant one of a number of orders, including a 'termination order', which brings an end to the tenancy, and a 'remedial order', which requires the tenant to remedy the breach. The latter **stays** (that is, it puts a stop on) the landlord's termination claim for a period of three months from the day by which the tenant is required to have carried out the work. During that period the landlord can apply for the stay to be lifted and proceed with the termination claim.
- ✦ There will be no requirement for a forfeiture or 'tenant default' clause in the lease. However, the parties will be able to exclude or limit the right to terminate by agreeing that particular breaches will not comprise tenant default.
- ✦ Peaceable re-entry will be abolished. However, in its place there will be a '*summary termination procedure*', under which the landlord can bring a tenancy to an end without applying to the court. The procedure will apply where the tenant has no realistic prospect of contesting a termination claim. The landlord will have to serve a '*summary termination notice*' that will bring the tenancy to an end one month after service of the notice. During that one-month period, the tenant will be able to apply to the court to have the notice discharged. The burden will be on the landlord to show that the tenancy should be terminated.
- ✦ For six months after summary termination the tenant will be able to apply for a '*post termination order*' which will be similar to relief from forfeiture, except that the order will allow the court to grant a new tenancy or the payment of compensation but will not allow the reinstatement of the original tenancy. This will apply in cases of summary termination (i.e. without court order) only.
- ✦ The concept of waiver will also be abolished, meaning the landlord will be able to continue to accept rent after the tenant defaults.

At the time of writing, there have been no further moves to enact the draft bill. Whether the legislature will choose to do so in the future remains to be seen.

The transmission of leasehold covenants

Having established the nature of leasehold covenants, which are the most commonly found in leases of property and which are implied by common law and statute, and having discussed the remedies available to landlord and tenant for breach of those covenants, the only question which remains to be asked is whether those covenants can be transferred to a third party, either on the assignment of the lease to a new tenant, or on the sale of the landlord's reversionary interest in the land, whether this is freehold or leasehold.

Perhaps before asking this question, however, it may be sensible to look at the position as between the original parties. We assume that the original landlord and tenant have the right to sue or to seek other equitable remedies under the terms of the lease, if these are breached, but on what grounds? The answer is found in the law of contract. The relationship between the original landlord and tenant is a contractual one, creating

The relationship between the original landlord and tenant is a contractual one

what is known as '**privity of contract**' between them. All this term actually means is that there is a legal relationship based upon the law of contract which exists between the landlord and tenant. And it is by virtue of this contractual relationship, this privity of contract, that the landlord and tenant as the original parties to the agreement are able to enforce all of the promises, conditions or covenants contained in the lease against one another. A lease is, at the end of the day, only a special type of contract which carries with it additional **proprietary rights** (for a more detailed reminder of the concept of a lease you may wish to refer to Chapter 5 on the leasehold estate).

So what happens after this, when one of the parties transfers their rights under the lease to a new landlord or tenant? There will be no privity of contract between them because they are not the original parties to the agreement, so how can the terms of the lease be enforced against them? The answer to this question is twofold, the reason being that the traditional common law position was significantly altered by the Landlord and Tenant (Covenants) Act 1995. Unfortunately, however, the provisions of the Act were not retrospective, and therefore students of law must learn the two separate sets of rules appertaining to the running of leasehold covenants and apply them dependent on when the lease was created. Let us begin with the position before the imposition of the Act on 1 January 1996.

Pre-1 January 1996

We have seen above that, under the rules of contract, the original landlord and tenant can enforce their obligations under the lease as against one another because there is privity of contract between them. Before the coming into force of the Landlord and Tenant (Covenants) Act 1996, this position continued for the whole term of the lease (that being the duration of the contractual agreement made between them), even after one or both of the original parties to the lease had assigned their rights under it to a third party. This meant that, for example, an original tenant under a lease would continue to remain liable for the payment of rent to the landlord even after they had assigned their interest under the lease to a third party and ceased to have possession of the premises. As you could imagine, the consequences of this could be extremely far-reaching and potentially very unfair.

The only way to escape the consequences of being subject to privity of contract was to expressly exclude the continuation of the liability by the parties to the original agreement in the terms of the lease. Originally an established common law exception, the rule was enshrined in statue under section 79 of the Law of Property Act 1925, which states that:

> a covenant relating to any land of a covenantor shall, *unless a contrary intention is expressed*, be deemed to be made by the covenantor on behalf of himself, his successors in title and the persons deriving title under him or them. (emphasis added).

Having said this, the fact of the matter was that it was simply not common practice to include such an exclusion. Landlords obviously wanted to protect their position as well as they could, and so were unlikely to agree to an exclusion of liability from their original tenant. The position with the original parties, then, most commonly was that they remained liable for the full duration of the lease. But what about the position of the incoming landlord or tenant on an assignment of the lease? The answer lies with the doctrine of **privity of estate**.

Privity of estate

We now know that a lease forms a contractual relationship between the original parties to it. However, we also know from our reading in Chapter 5 that the creation of a lease forms far more than just a contract: as we learned previously, a lease also creates proprietary rights – it creates a legal estate in land. And it is this sharing of the land, this division of the land into two **tenures**, one freehold, one leasehold, at common law which creates an additional bond between the landlord and tenant; one which is completely unique to land law: that of privity of estate.

Privity of estate will exist as between the current landlord and current tenant of a lease, whoever they may be and however many times the property changes hands. So it will exist regardless of whether the parties are original to the lease or not. This means that whilst the original landlord and tenant have privity of contract between them, they will at the same time also have privity of estate. But once the property changes hands, bringing in either a new landlord or new tenant, or both, the new parties to the lease will share only the bond of privity of estate between them, privity of contract being reserved for the original parties to the agreement. To make sure you have understood this, why not work through the examples given in the You Be the Judge feature, below.

You be the judge

Q: What is the relationship between the following parties in respect of 5 Harold Road: privity of contract or privity of estate? (a) A landlord, Lenny, grants a lease of 5 Harold Road, Heatherwell to a tenant, Tobia. What is the relationship between Lenny and Tobia? (b) Tobia assigns the lease to Alfred. What is the relationship between Alfred and Lenny? (c) Following the assignment, what is the relationship between Tobia and Lenny? (d) Alfred assigns his lease to Bernice. What is the relationship between Bernice and Lenny? (e) Following the assignment to Bernice, what is the relationship between Alfred and Lenny? (f) Bernice sublets to Saima. What is the relationship between Bernice and Saima? (g) Following the subletting, what is the relationship between Lenny and Saima? (h) Lenny sells the freehold reversion to Raoul. What is the relationship between Raoul and Bernice? (i) Following the sale of the reversion, what is the relationship between Lenny and Tobia?

A: (a) There is both privity of contract (as the original parties to the lease) and privity of estate between Lenny and Tobia. (b) There is privity of estate between Alfred and Lenny. (c) There is still privity of contract between Tobia and Lenny as they were the original contracting parties to the lease. There is no longer privity of estate between them, however. (d) There is privity of estate between Bernice and Lenny. (e) There is no longer any relationship between Alfred and Lenny. There used to be privity of estate but this ended when Alfred assigned the lease. (f) There is privity of contract and privity of estate between Saima and Bernice. In subletting the premises, a new lease has been created. As the original parties to this lease Saima and Bernice share privity of contract between them. (g) There is no relationship between Lenny and Saima. Lenny is not Saima's landlord: Bernice is. (h) There is privity of estate between Raoul and Bernice. (i) There is privity of contract between Lenny and Tobia as the original parties to the lease.

Handy tip: If you are struggling, a pictorial image of the relationships between the parties may help:

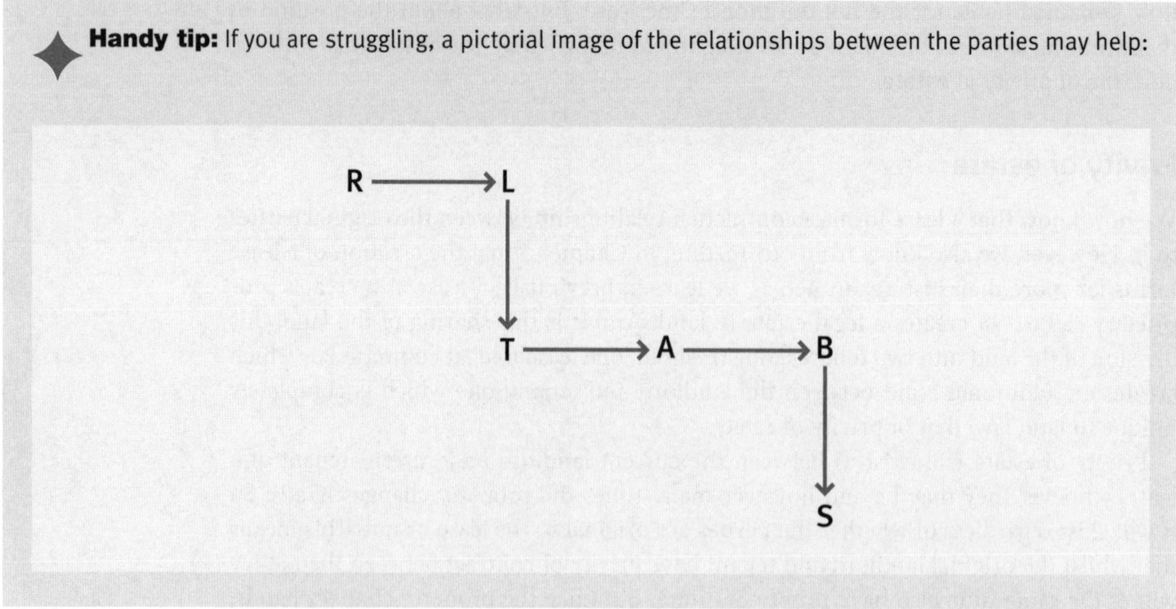

This is all very interesting, but what is the actual effect of privity of estate, where it exists? We have seen that, prior to 1 January 1996, the original landlord and tenant remain liable for breaches of covenant under the lease, regardless of any change of ownership, because of privity of contract. But when is an assignee liable under the terms of the lease and for how long? The answer is that they will be liable to the landlord for breaches of covenant for as long as privity of estate exists between them: in other words, until they assign the lease to a third party. So, taking some of our examples in the You Be the Judge feature above, the assignee, Arthur, remains liable for breaches of covenant against Lenny until he assigns the lease to Bernice. This is because at this point privity of estate between Arthur and Lenny ceases and privity of estate between Lenny and Bernice starts. Once the lease has been assigned to Bernice, however, it is Bernice as the new tenant who becomes liable for breaches of covenant under its terms. The authority for this is *Spencer's Case* (1583) 5 Co Rep 16a, which concerned a covenant entered into by the original tenant to the lease, on behalf of himself and his assignees, to build a wall. The court held that the assignees were required to comply with the covenant.

Case Summary

We have established, then, that privity of estate means that, as a general rule, the current landlord and current tenant of the property will be the responsible parties in respect of complying with the covenants contained within a lease. However, as with all rules, there are a number of provisos that apply to its operation. These are:

1. Firstly, that the assignee must have taken a legal assignment of the lease in order for privity of estate to be created;
2. Secondly, that the outgoing tenant on assignment will remain liable for breaches of covenant committed whilst they were a tenant of the property. These will not be passed on to the assignee, who will only be liable for breaches committed during their ownership of the lease; and
3. Thirdly, that an assignee will only be liable under privity of estate for covenants that 'touch and concern the land'.

We shall consider these in turn.

Legal assignment

In order for privity of estate to be formed as between the landlord and the assignee of the lease, the assignment of the lease must be legal. As we know from section 52 of the Law of Property Act 1925, which states that any disposition of land must be made by deed in order to take effect in law, this means that the assignment must be made by deed. It is important not to forget, however, that under the exception in section 54(2) of the Act, it is possible to create a legal lease for three years or less informally without a deed, or even writing; and it follows that such formality is not required for their transfer. This is confirmed at section 52(2)(d) of the Act. The application of this exception can be seen in the case of *Bower* v. *Warby* [1953] 1 QB 234, which concerned a lease of a flat for three years which had been created in writing, but not by deed. The lease contained a covenant on the part of the tenant to contribute £40 towards the redecoration of the flat at the end of the term. However, before the lease expired the tenant assigned his interest to a third party, who subsequently refused to make the contribution. The assignee's argument was that the covenant did not run with the land because there had not been a legal assignment. However, the court found against him.

Breaches committed before or after the assignee's ownership of the lease

As privity of estate lasts only for as long as the lease is in the ownership of the current tenant it follows that, once that tenant has assigned their lease they will not be liable for breaches committed after their ownership of the property has ceased. In the same way, they are not responsible for breaches of covenant that were committed by their **assignor**, prior to them acquiring the lease. What a tenant does remain liable for on assignment, however, are any breaches they committed during their ownership of the lease. They may also remain liable if they enter into direct covenants with the landlord on assignment to guarantee the performance of the assignee under the terms of the lease. What this means is that the outgoing tenant will promise, in the deed of assignment, to remain responsible for breaches of covenant made by their assignee. In this way, if an assignee is in breach of covenant, the landlord will be able not only to seek damages from the original tenant, but also from any subsequent tenant who has entered into direct covenants with them on assignment. Taking our example in the You Be the Judge feature, above, this would mean that if Bernice was to breach her covenants under the lease, Lenny could look not only to Bernice to rectify the breach, but also to Tobia, as the original tenant and Arthur if he entered into direct covenants with Lenny to guarantee Bernice's performance as an incoming tenant.

Which covenants 'touch and concern the land'?

The final proviso relating to the running of covenants on an assignment is that the covenants in the lease will only pass to an assignee of the lease if they 'touch and concern the land'; but what exactly does this mean? According to the Court of Appeal case of *Breams Property Investment Co. Ltd* v. *Stroulger* [1948] 2 KB 1, which concerned a disagreement over the interpretation of a provision that prevented the tenant from serving notice to quit on the landlord for the first three years of the tenancy, a covenant touches and concerns the land if it affects the landlord '*qua* landlord' and the tenant '*qua* tenant': in other words that it affects the landlord as landlord and the tenant as tenant. This may not seem particularly helpful, but what it means to say is that the covenant has to affect the landlord and tenant in their relationship as landlord and tenant and be connected directly to the lease, as opposed to any personal relationship they might share. The Court

of Appeal in this case held that the covenant restricting the tenant's right to bring an end to the tenancy did touch and concern the land. As for which other covenants touch and concern the land: essentially, all of the usual covenants contained within a lease which are discussed in this chapter will come under this heading. This would necessarily include a covenant to pay rent; to keep the premises in repair; and a covenant not to assign or sublet. A covenant by the tenant to wash the landlord's car once a week, on the other hand, clearly has no connection with the use and enjoyment of the land forming the subject matter of the lease and therefore cannot touch and concern the land or in any way be connected with the subject matter of the lease, even if the tenant is using the premises to run a car wash business. It is a personal agreement made between the original parties to the agreement and nothing more.

Indemnity covenants

Under the pre-1996 rules, we have seen that, even after assignment of the lease, the original tenant would remain liable for the duration of the term. Obviously this was not an ideal situation for the tenant to be in, so in order to limit their liability it became standard practice for the outgoing tenant to require their assignee to enter into express **indemnity covenants** with them in the deed of assignment, the assignee promising the tenant that if they ever defaulted and the tenant was sued, the assignee would make good the loss. Whilst the insertion of express indemnity covenants into the lease had become standard practice, however, there are also implied covenants that the tenant could rely upon. These are contained in section 77 of the Law of Property Act 1925. The section states that an indemnity covenant will be implied into the assignment, wherever it is made for **value** (so as long as the assignee pays for the lease to be assigned to them, an indemnity will be implied). In the case of **registered land**, these provisions have been further modified so that, under Schedule 12 paragraph 20 of the Land Registration Act 2002, an indemnity covenant will be implied regardless of whether or not the land is sold for value. The upshot of this is that statute will imply into any assignment of a pre-1996 lease an indemnity covenant on the part of the assignee, except in the case of a gift of a lease of **unregistered land**. This is rarely an issue, however, because the entering into of indemnity covenants on assignment is standard practice in any event.

And if this did not provide enough protection for an outgoing tenant on assignment, there is also the common law **rule in *Moule* v. *Garrett***. This says that where a person is compelled to pay damages because of somebody else's legal default, then they are entitled to recover from that person the sum that has been paid on the defaulting party's behalf. The rule is based on quasi-contractual principles, the idea being that if the assignee has defaulted on their legal responsibilities and, as a result, the tenant is required to compensate the landlord, provided that it is not the tenant's fault, then under the rule in *Moule* v. *Garrett*, the tenant should be entitled to compensation.

The problem, of course, with all of these safeguards, both the express and implied statutory indemnity covenants and the rule in *Moule* v. *Garrett*, is that usually the reason why the landlord has decided to sue the tenant in the first place is because the assignee has no money. The most common circumstance in which the landlord will sue their original tenant for default by an assignee is because either the assignee is bankrupt or has vanished. These safeguards, which provide seemingly so much protection to an original tenant, in reality are a slim comfort. The moral of this story is, perhaps, to make sure as a tenant that you assign to someone who you know will be able to pay the rent!

Assignment of the reversion

Let us move on, then, to consider the position in relation to assignees of the **reversion** (which you will remember is the landlord's interest in the lease). As with assignees of the tenant, when the landlord assigns the reversion to a third party the covenants under the lease do pass on to them. However, it is not the common law which assists in this case: the provisions in respect of assignment of the reversion are statutory. Under sections 141 and 142 of the Law of Property Act 1925, the benefit and burden of covenants in the lease pass from the landlord to their assignee; the benefit passes under section 141 and the burden under section 142. So if the landlord sells the freehold of the property the purchaser will obtain the benefit and burden of the covenants in the lease under statute, and the landlord will at the same time be released from them. This is illustrated in the Court of Appeal case of *Re King* [1963] 2 WLR 629, which concerned an argument over liability for fire damage to leased premises. The Court held that the landlords purchasing the reversion in doing so had acquired the right to sue for breach of the covenant to insure the premises within the lease, by virtue of section 141 of the Law of Property Act 1925. A further example is the case of *Arlesford Trading Company Ltd* v. *Servansingh* [1971] 3 All ER 113, in which it was held that the purchaser of the reversionary interest of a lease was entitled to sue for arrears of rent that had accrued before their purchase of the property. It should be noted that the effect of this relates to the benefit of the lease covenants as well as the burden of them: this means that not only is the landlord released from their obligations under the lease, but they will also be unable to sue on the tenant covenants contained within the lease after they have assigned their interest.

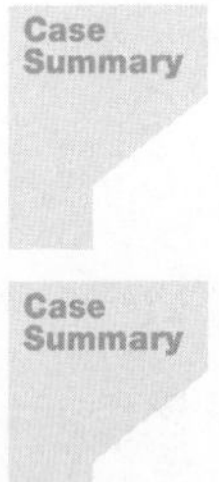

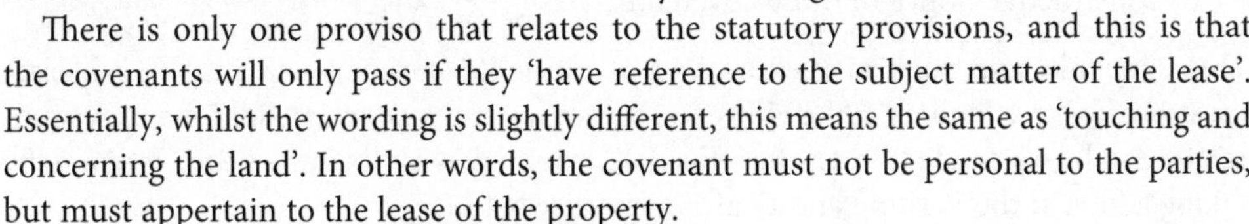

There is only one proviso that relates to the statutory provisions, and this is that the covenants will only pass if they 'have reference to the subject matter of the lease'. Essentially, whilst the wording is slightly different, this means the same as 'touching and concerning the land'. In other words, the covenant must not be personal to the parties, but must appertain to the lease of the property.

Head landlords and sub-tenants

As we saw in the You Be the Judge exercise above, there is no relationship, either contractual or proprietary, between a **head landlord** and a sub-tenant, so there exists neither privity of contract nor privity of estate between them. What happens, then, if the sub-tenant breaches one of the covenants in their lease? Obviously the tenant, who is the direct landlord of the sub-tenant, can sue, but is there anything the landlord can do about it? The answer is 'yes': there are a couple of options available to the landlord, one method of enforcement which is indirect, and one which is direct against the sub-tenant.

Taking the indirect method of enforcement first, whilst the landlord cannot sue a sub-tenant for breaches of covenant within the **sub-lease**, they can sue their direct tenant for breaches of covenant in the lease. This is by virtue of section 79 of the Law of Property Act 1925, which we came across earlier in the chapter, which you will remember states that a tenant covenants on behalf of themselves, their assignees and their sub-tenants. And of course what this means is that the tenant can be sued for any breach of covenants. So the tenant is liable to be sued if their sub-tenant breaches a covenant. In this way, the landlord can enforce the sub-tenant's covenants indirectly, by putting pressure on their direct tenant to sue on the breach.

But as well as indirect enforcement, there is also a method of direct enforcement available, and this is something we came across in the context of freehold covenants: the

rule in ***Tulk* v. *Moxhay***. So **equity** will, in certain circumstances, permit direct enforcement by the head landlord against a sub-tenant under the rule in *Tulk* v. *Moxhay*. You may remember that there are four requirements under the rule in *Tulk* v. *Moxhay*, and these are as follows:

1. The covenant must be restrictive or negative. Remember that equity will only enforce restrictive or negative covenants; equity will not enforce positive obligations.
2. The covenant in question must touch and concern the land or, to put it in a different way, the covenant must confer a benefit on the landlord's reversion. So it has to confer a benefit on the landlord's estate.
3. The original parties to the lease must have intended that the burden of the covenants within the lease would bind successors in title to the lease. This is an easy requirement to fulfil, of course, because section 79 of the Law of Property Act 1925 implies this intention in any event.
4. Notice. You will remember that the fourth requirement of *Tulk* v. *Moxhay* is that of notice. So, applied to the leasehold covenants scenario, the sub-tenant has to have notice of the covenants in the head lease. But how is this achieved? Well, according to the case of *Hall* v. *Ewin* (1888) 37 ChD 74, the sub-tenant is not only entitled to inspect the head lease but they are deemed to have done so, giving them constructive, if not actual, notice of the covenants contained in it. In essence, the sub-tenant is deemed to know about anything the head lease contains. Equity will therefore enforce the covenants in the head lease against the sub-tenant because they have either actual or constructive notice of those covenants.

This concludes our look at the running of leasehold covenants in respect of leases created prior to 1 January 1996. However, before we move on to consider the provisions relating to leases created on or after this date, you may wish to embed your learning by taking a look at the Writing and Drafting exercise below.

Writing and drafting

In order to help you to understand how landlord and tenant covenants will pass on the assignment of a lease, try creating a flowchart showing whether or not a covenant will run to the assignees.

You should spend no more than 40 minutes on this task.

Handy tip: Remember to ask 'yes/no' questions at each stage of the exercise. You may prefer to create two flowcharts – one for landlord covenants and one for tenant covenants.

Post-1 January 1996

You may be relieved to learn that the Landlord and Tenant (Covenants) Act 1995 made things a whole lot simpler. The Act abolishes the effects of privity of contract for all leases created on or after 1 January 1996, the date on which the Act came into force.

This means that, as stated in section 5 of the Act, the tenant remains liable for the covenants in the lease only for so long as they remain a tenant. As soon as the tenant assigns their interest in the property to a third party, they are automatically released from their responsibilities under the terms of the lease and their liability to the landlord ceases. The one exception to this is if the tenant has made what is termed in section 11 of the Act an '**excluded assignment**', in which case the original tenant's liability will continue, but only until their direct assignee's interest is assigned to a third party. After this it will automatically cease. An assignment of the lease will be excluded if it has been made in breach of covenant (that is, without the consent of the landlord).

Landlords under the new provisions are not quite so lucky because there is no automatic release of responsibility for them; instead, they have to apply to the tenant to be released under section 6 of the Act after they have completed their assignment of the reversion. The tenant may, of course, refuse to give their consent to release the landlord from their obligations under the lease, but if the landlord disagrees with the tenant's decision, they do have the option under section 8 of the Act to apply to the county court for a release and the court has jurisdiction to make a declaration that release would be reasonable in all the circumstances, provided that the covenants are not personal to the parties. Nevertheless, this provision may be said to give some small measure of protection to the tenant in that, if the landlord assigns to a landlord who is completely disreputable, the tenant may legitimately object to the outgoing landlord being released from the covenants under the lease.

So that deals with the original parties under the lease, but what about assignees? What is their responsibility? The answer to this question can be found in section 3(1) of the Act, which reads as follows:

> **3 Transmission of benefit and burden of covenants**
>
> (1) The benefit and burden of all landlord and tenant covenants of a tenancy—
>
> (a) shall be annexed and incident to the whole, and to each and every part, of the premises demised by the tenancy and of the reversion in them, and
>
> (b) shall in accordance with this section pass on an assignment of the whole or any part of those premises or of the reversion in them.

As you can see, the section states very clearly that both the landlord and the tenant covenants are annexed both to the lease itself (to the '**demised premises**'), and to the freehold reversion, and will pass on assignment. So section 3 effectively, in respect of leases created on or after 1 January 1996, abolishes *Spencer's Case* and repeals section 141 and 142 and now, very simply, the benefit and burden of the covenants in the lease pass on assignment by either party. There is no longer any reference to covenants having to 'touch and concern the land' or to have 'reference to the subject matter of the lease'; however, section 3(5) clearly states that covenants that are expressed to be personal between the parties will not pass on assignment.

At first glance these new provisions may appear to have swung the balance the other way, in terms of fairness to the parties. Whereas the ability of the landlord to sue the original tenant for the full duration of the lease, regardless of how many times the lease had been assigned, could have been considered unfair on the tenant, the automatic release of the tenant from their obligations on assignment could be considered unfair on the landlord. In order to give the landlord back a little control, however, section 16 of the Act allows the landlord to require an outgoing tenant to guarantee the performance of any new tenant coming in by signing a form of agreement known as an '**authorised guarantee agreement**', guaranteeing the performance of their assignee's obligations under the terms of the lease. The burden this imposes on the tenant is far less onerous than under the previous law, however, because, where one is provided, the authorised guarantee agreement will last only for as long as the outgoing tenant's direct assignee remains a tenant under the lease. Once the assignee in turn assigns their interest to a third party, the tenant is released. It should be noted that the right of the landlord to require the tenant to enter into an authorised guarantee agreement is not automatic: the landlord must reserve the right to do so under the terms of the lease when it is drafted.

Head landlords and sub-tenants

But what about the position of sub-tenants? Having seen the difficulties inherent in the pre-1996 system of law, the Landlord and Tenant (Covenants) Act 1995 seeks to provide for this under section 3(5), which states that any landlord or tenant covenant 'which is restrictive of the user of the land' is also capable of being enforced by any other person who is the owner or occupier of the demised premises. Effectively, then, a head landlord will be able to enforce all restrictive covenants in the head lease against the sub-tenant, regardless of notice. This removes the need for the application of the rule in *Tulk* v. *Moxhay* and the need for indirect enforcement through the direct tenant of the landlord, enabling the landlord to go straight to the source of the breach (the sub-tenant).

Retrospective provisions

Having said that the provisions of the 1995 Act are not retrospective, whilst this is true as regards the changes to the rules relating to the running of leasehold covenants, there are a couple of provisions which do relate to all leases, regardless of the date of their creation. These are sections 17 and 19 of the act, respectively.

Section 17 default notices

Section 17 provides that if the landlord wants to sue a former tenant for arrears of rent accrued by a current tenant, then the landlord can only do so if they serve a notice on the tenant within six months of the arrears being accrued, notifying the tenant of the arrears and of their intention to claim them from the former tenant. In the case of a post-1996 lease we of course now know that this will only apply either where the tenant has assigned the lease in breach of covenant, in which case it will be an excepted tenancy and they will still be on the hook for breaches of covenant committed by their assignee, or where the outgoing tenant has entered into an authorised guarantee agreement with the landlord. In the case of pre-1996 leases, the tenant remains liable for the duration of the lease due to privity of contract, so the landlord will be able to sue them at any time during the currency of the lease.

The idea behind this section is that it prevents the landlord from allowing substantial rent arrears to build up before chasing their former tenant for payment. In the case of pre-1996 leases, this is especially important, as the landlord could theoretically leave arrears to build up for years before taking action.

The service of default notices applies to any 'fixed charge' due under the lease, so it can include any payments owed to the landlord, including rent, rates and service charges.

Figure 13.2 Effect of an overriding lease

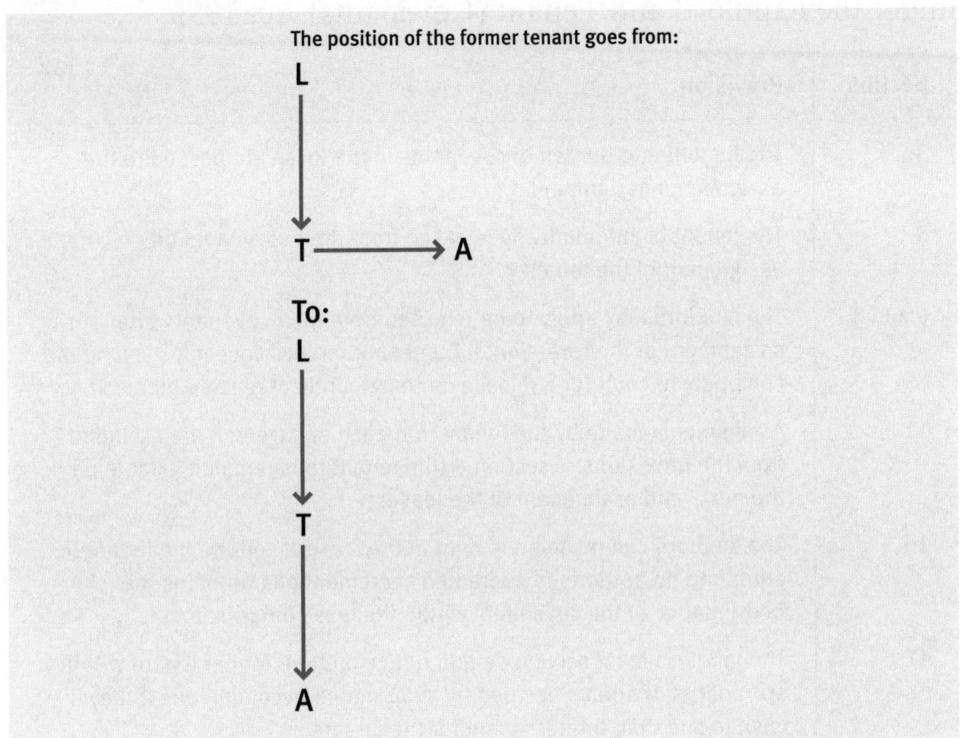

Overriding leases

Section 19 is also relevant to both pre- and post-1996 leases and relates to the situation where a former tenant is required to pay rent owing by their assignee. The provisions of section 19 allow a former tenant who has, under section 17 of the Act, been given notice of monies owing under the lease, to regain control of the premises by calling for the landlord to grant them an '**overriding lease**'. An overriding lease has the effect of putting the former tenant in the position of tenant and the assignee in the position of sub-tenant. In diagrammatic form, the position would look like Figure 13.2.

An overriding lease has the effect of putting the former tenant in the position of tenant

So the effect of an overriding lease is to make the former tenant the immediate landlord of the assignee. The question is, why would a former tenant want to do this? The answer is that it gives the former tenant control. The former tenant will have an interest in the land again. As the assignee's landlord they could forfeit their lease, sue them for arrears of rent, and so on. It puts the tenant back in control of the premises.

This concludes our look at the running of covenants in leases from 1 January 1996 as governed by the Landlord and Tenant (Covenants) Act 1995, the relevant provisions of which can be summarised as shown in Table 13.3.

Table 13.3 Summary of the running of leasehold covenants under the Landlord and Tenant (Covenants) Act 1995

Section	Provision
3	The benefit and burden of covenants in the lease are passed to the assignee on assignment
5	The tenant is automatically released from their covenants on assignment of the tenancy
6 and 8	The landlord may apply to be released from their covenants after assignment of the reversion. If the tenant refuses consent, the landlord can apply to court for a release on the grounds of reasonableness
11	Assignments made by the tenant in breach of covenant are excluded from the provisions of section 5 (the tenant thus remaining liable until the next valid assignment of the lease)
16	The landlord can reserve the right in the lease to require the tenant to enter into an authorised guarantee agreement guaranteeing the performance of the covenants within the lease on assignment
17	The landlord must serve a default notice on their former tenant within six months of arrears accrued by an assignee becoming due if they wish to sue their former tenant for the arrears
19	If served notice under section 17, a former tenant can require the landlord to grant them an overriding lease of the premises, making them the immediate landlord of the assignee

Summary

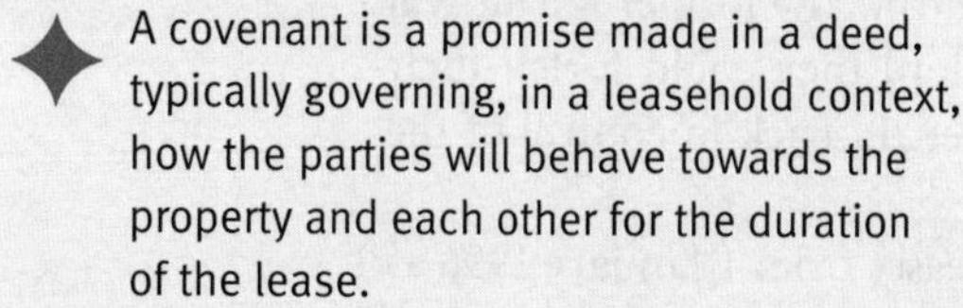

- A covenant is a promise made in a deed, typically governing, in a leasehold context, how the parties will behave towards the property and each other for the duration of the lease.
- Leasehold covenants can be express or implied. Implied covenants on the part of the tenant are: to pay rent, to use the property in a tenant-like manner, not to commit waste and to allow the landlord to enter and view. On the part of the landlord, the implied covenants are quiet enjoyment, not to derogate from grant and limited statutory obligations of repair.
- There is typically an express covenant in the lease governing the assignment or subletting of the premises. Such covenants can be absolute, qualified or fully qualified. Section 19(1) LTA 1927 automatically converts a qualified covenant against subletting into a fully qualified one.

- On receiving a request to assign or sublet, under s.1(3) LTA 1988, the landlord must respond in writing within a 'reasonable time', giving reasons for their refusal if applicable. What is considered a reasonable time will depend upon the circumstances of the case (*NCR* v. *Riverland*).

- The reason for refusal must also be reasonable. Traditionally this has meant that refusal of consent will be reasonable only if it relates specifically either to the character of the proposed assignee or to the unsuitability of the proposed use of the premises (*Houlder Bros* v. *Gibbs*). However, since *Bickel* v. *Duke of Westminster*, the position has been modified so that reasonable refusal should not be limited to a set of particular circumstances, but should be judged on the facts of each individual case.

- Generally speaking, a landlord is not under any implied duty to repair premises. It is therefore customary to include in any lease of property an express repairing covenant, detailing what is the responsibility of the landlord and tenant respectively.

- The general standard of repair required is that premises should be repaired in such a way as 'having regard to the age, character and locality would make it reasonably fit for the occupation of a reasonably minded tenant of the class likely to take it', taking into account the age, character and condition of the premises at the time the lease was granted *Proudfoot* v. *Hart*).

- Where a tenant is responsible for repair, this will include repair only, not renewal or improvement of the premises (*Lurcott* v. *Wakely*; *Morcom* v. *Campbell-Johnson*). Whether the defect is inherent or not is irrelevant; whether the tenant is responsible for the repair will be a matter of fact and degree in each case (*Ravenseft Properties* v. *Davstone*).

- If a tenant is in breach of their covenants under the lease, the most valuable remedy available to a landlord is that of forfeiture, which allows the landlord to re-enter the premises and bring an end to the tenancy.

- If the breach is for a breach of covenant other than the non-payment of rent, the landlord will have to first serve a section 146 notice on the tenant, specifying the breach, requiring it to be remedied within a reasonable time, if possible, and requesting compensation if the landlord requires it. Again, what is a reasonable time will be a matter of fact and degree in each case (*Albany Holdings Ltd* v. *Crown Estate Commissioners*).

- As a general rule of thumb, breaches by the tenant of positive covenants within the lease are remediable, negative covenants are not (but see *Billson* v. *Residential Apartments*).

- A tenant whose lease is forfeit may apply to the court for relief from forfeiture. Whether this is granted is entirely at the discretion of the court.

- A landlord can expressly or impliedly waive their right to forfeit by doing some unequivocal act that acknowledges the continuation of the tenancy (such as collecting the rent).

- Prior to 1 January 1996 the doctrine of privity of contract meant that the original landlord and tenant remained liable for the obligations in the lease for the full duration of the term, regardless of any assignment to third parties.

- This has been abolished in leases granted on or after 1 January 1996. Under the LTCA 1995 tenants are now automatically released from their obligations on assignment and landlords can apply to be released. Consent to release the landlord should be given unless it would be reasonable in all the circumstances not to do so.

Question and answer*

Problem: In June 1993 Clarice granted a 25-year lease of 44 Sinder Street to Ahmed, under which Ahmed, as tenant, promised to keep the property in good repair. In 1998 Ahmed assigned the lease to Gerard, with Clarice's consent. In 2000 Clarice sold the freehold of the property to Josh. Gerard has failed to carry out repairs to the property and it is now in a considerable state of disrepair.

1. Who is liable for the disrepair and what remedies are available to Josh? 2. How would your answer differ (if at all) if the lease had been granted to Ahmed in June 1996?

You should allow yourself no more than 40 minutes to complete this task.

Essay: What were the difficulties inherent in the provisions relating to the running of leasehold covenants prior to 1 January 1996 and how, and to what extent, have these been resolved?

This question should be answered in 40 minutes.

* Answer guidance is provided at the end of the chapter.

Further reading

Kidd, Daniel, 'Licences and consents: where are we now?', L&T Review 2006, 10(5), 140–42.
This is a useful article considering the meaning of what is a 'reasonable time' for the giving of refusal to consent to an assignment under the Landlord and Tenant Act 1988. The article considers the approach adopted by the courts to the issue of reasonableness and the remedies available to landlords and tenants.

Kodilinye, Gilbert, 'Refusal of consent to assign: the unreasonable landlord', Conv 1988, Jan–Feb, 45–56.
This article gives a clear and comprehensive explanation of the law relating to reasonableness in cases of landlord refusal of consent to assign a nd gives reasons for the Law Commission's reluctance to impose statutory guidelines.

Holland, David, 'Landlord's consent to assign or sublet: is the pendulum swinging back?', L&T Review 2005, 9(4), 88–92.
This second article on the issue of reasonableness in respect of refusals of consent to assign discusses changes in the law in the light of *NCR* v. *Riverland* and discusses whether this has tipped the balance back in favour of landlords.

'Enforcement Review Consultation Paper No.5: Distress for Rent'.
The consultation paper gives a detailed insight into the difficulties inherent with the ancient remedy of distress and why changes in the law were felt necessary.

Law Commission report, 'Termination of tenancies for tenant default' (Law Com. No. 303), available online at: http://www.official-documents.gov.uk/document/cm69/6946/6946.pdf.
The Law Commission report sets out suggestions for the reform of the law of forfeiture, including a draft 'Landlord and Tenant (Termination of Tenancies) Bill' which details the statutory provisions intended to take its place. The report also contains a very useful summary of the proposed new law.

Question and answer guidance

Please note that the following are not full answers and are intended to provide guidance in outline form only as to how to answer the questions posed.

Problem:

Question 1: Here we have a long lease of 25 years with an express tenant covenant to repair. The lease was granted in 1993 and so is an 'old lease' under the terms of the Landlord and Tenant (Covenants) Act 1995. Therefore the old common law rules in respect of the running of leasehold covenants apply to it. These are as follows.

Under the rules of privity of contract, Ahmed remains liable under the terms of the original lease for the whole of the lease term. This is despite the authorised assignment of the lease to Gerard in 1998 (s.79 LPA 1925 – the original tenant is automatically deemed to covenant on behalf of their assignees).

Gerard too will be liable for the repairs under the doctrine of privity of estate, provided that there was a legal assignment of the lease to him from Ahmed (s.52 LPA 1925) and provided the covenant in question 'touches and concerns the land'. A repairing covenant clearly would touch and concern the land and is not merely personal as between the parties. Neither is there any suggestion here that there has not been a legal assignment. Josh can therefore choose whether to sue Ahmed or Gerard for the breaches of the repairing covenant within the lease.

In order to protect himself when the assignment of the lease to Gerard took place, Ahmed should have asked Gerard to enter into an indemnity covenant requiring Gerard to indemnify Ahmed against any breaches committed in respect of the lease after assignment. If he did not, such an indemnity will have been implied into the assignment in any event, unless the assignment was of unregistered land for nil value (s.77 LPA 1925 and Sched.12 para.20 LRA 2002). We are not told whether or not the land is registered. In addition to this, Ahmed could make a claim from Gerard for reimbursement of any monies incurred by him due to Gerard's default, under the common law rule in *Moule* v. *Garrett*.

Having established who is liable for the breach of repairing covenant under the terms of the lease we also have to establish whether the new landlord, Josh, has the benefit of the covenants under the lease, following his purchase of the freehold reversion from Clarice. Under s.141 LPA 1925 the benefit of covenants under the lease passes from a landlord to their assignee on assignment, provided that the covenants 'have reference to the subject matter of the lease'. A repairing covenant clearly does this. Josh will therefore be able to benefit from the covenant to repair and can sue on the terms of the lease.

The remedies available to Josh for breach of the repairing covenant are damages, injunction or specific performance and forfeiture of the lease.

Where the tenant is in breach of a repairing covenant there is a statutory limit placed upon the amount of damages recoverable by the landlord, which is the amount by which the lack of repair has diminished the value of the freehold (s.18 Landlord and Tenant Act 1927). This means that if the cost of repairs exceeds the diminution in the value of the property caused by the breach, Josh will not be able to recover those losses. In addition, if the term of the lease is for seven years or more and there are at least three years left to run on the lease, which is the case in our scenario, the landlord must serve a s.146 notice notifying the tenant of the breach and requiring them to carry out the repairs before he can sue. The notice gives the tenant the right to serve a counter-notice within 28 days and, if counter-notice is served, Josh will be prevented from taking any further action without the leave of the court. The court will give leave to the landlord to proceed with an action for damages only if the value of the property has been substantially reduced on account of the disrepair or immediate repair is required either to prevent a substantial decrease in the property's value, or to comply with statute, or in order to protect the interests of other occupiers of the building if it is in multiple occupation, or in order to avoid much more substantial future cost or there are special circumstances in existence which make the giving of leave by the court both just and equitable.

The decision of the court to grant leave to sue for damages is entirely discretionary.

The better claim from Josh's point of view is therefore one for specific performance – a court order forcing Gerard to carry out the repairs under the terms of the lease (although see *Rainbow Properties* v. *Tokenhold*, which suggests that specific performance will only be granted for breach of a repairing covenant in exceptional circumstances), or forfeiture.

Josh can only forfeit if there is a right of re-entry contained within the lease. Assuming there is one, in order to forfeit the lease for the breach of a covenant other than one to pay the rent, Josh will need to serve a s.146 notice on Gerard. The notice must specify the nature of the breach, require Gerard to remedy it within a reasonable time and, if required, ask for compensation. If Gerard does not then carry out the repairs within a reasonable time Josh can forfeit the lease either by peaceably re-entering the premises or by court order. What is a reasonable time will depend upon the urgency of the repairs and how long it will take to carry them out. The downside of forfeiture is that Josh will then have to find another tenant for his property, although the majority of the lease has now run so he may be content with this.

Question 2: If the lease had been entered into in 1996, the provisions of the Landlord and Tenant (Covenants) Act 1995 would apply. This abolishes privity of contract in respect of all leases created after 1 January 1996, meaning that, following his assignment of the lease to Gerard, Ahmed would be released from his responsibility for the repairing covenant (s.5) unless the assignment was excluded i.e. without consent, which it is not in this case – we are told the assignment is with consent (s.11).

The only way in which Ahmed would remain liable is if he had been required under the terms of the lease to enter into an 'authorised guarantee agreement' (s.16), requiring him to guarantee the performance of the covenants in the lease by his assignee. Again there is no mention of him having done this in this scenario.

As for Gerard, he will automatically take up responsibility for the covenants under the lease under s.3 of the Act, provided the covenants are not expressed to be personal within the lease. Again, that is not the case here. The benefit of the repairing covenant will also pass to Josh under the same section.

Essay: As we have seen above, the biggest difficulty with the running of leasehold covenants prior to 1 January 1996 was the issue of privity of contract and the fact that the original tenant under the terms of the lease remained liable for the full extent of the lease term, even after the lease had been assigned to a third party. With a longer lease, in particular, this meant that where the lease had been assigned several times during the course of the tenancy, the original tenant could find themselves liable for breaches of covenant carried out by a third party they had no connection with whatever. Never 'being off the hook' was a considerable burden on a tenant, as the landlord could decide to come after them for breaches of covenant of their assignees at any time, simply because they were a better person to sue than the current tenant.

Whilst a tenant could require their assignees to enter into an indemnity covenant on assignment, in reality this was of little use if the current tenant had no money, which was likely to be the case if the landlord was choosing to sue the original tenant in the first place. Equally, a chain of indemnity could easily break down if one of the former assignees had become insolvent or disappeared.

For leases created after 1 January 1996 the issue has largely been resolved because s.5 of the Landlord and Tenant (Covenants) Act 1995 abolishes privity of contract and specifies that a tenant shall only be responsible under the terms of the lease for as long as they are the tenant of it. On an assignment to a third party, therefore, they are released from their responsibilities under the lease and can no longer be chased for breaches carried out by the new tenant. This is assuming that the assignment is not an excluded one under s.11 of the Act, which essentially means that it must have been done with the landlord's consent.

The only way in which an outgoing tenant can now remain liable is if they are required by the landlord to enter into an authorised guarantee agreement under the terms of the lease, which means that they must guarantee the performance of their immediate assignee on an assignment (s.16). However, even this is limited to the period during which their immediate assignee remains a tenant under the lease, so that if the assignee then transfers the lease to a third party the original tenant will be released from the agreement. Obviously this is considerably better than the original position, pre-1996.

The provisions of the LT(C)A 1995 are unfortunately for the most part not retrospective, so although they solve the problem in respect of leases granted after the Act came into force (1 January 1996), they do not help in respect of 'old' leases granted before this date. Obviously there will be fewer and fewer of these as time goes on, but there are still a considerable number which are affected.

There are two provisions within the Act which do provide some assistance in respect of 'old' leases, as they are retrospective in nature. These are under sections 17 and 19 of the Act, and are as follows.

Section 17 provides that if the landlord wants to sue a former tenant for arrears of rent accrued by a current tenant, then the landlord can only do so if they serve a notice on the tenant within six months of the arrears being accrued, notifying the tenant of the arrears and of their intention to claim them from the former tenant. This prevents the landlord from allowing substantial rent arrears to build up before chasing their former tenant for payment. In the case of pre-1996 leases, this is especially important, as the landlord could, prior to the provision being put into place, theoretically leave arrears to build up for years before taking action.

The provisions of section 19 allow a former tenant who has been given notice under section 17 of monies owing under the lease, to regain control of the premises by calling for the landlord to grant them an 'overriding lease'. An overriding lease has the effect of putting the former tenant in the position of tenant and the assignee in the position of sub-tenant. This at least allows the original tenant to regain control of the premises and threaten the assignee with forfeiture or otherwise if they do not comply with the lease terms.

Visit **www.mylawchamber.co.uk** to access tools to help you develop and test your knowledge of land law.

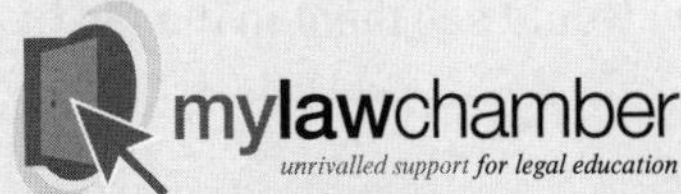

Use Case Navigator to read in full some of the key cases referenced in this chapter with commentary and questions:

Billson and others* v. *Residential Apartments [1992] 1 All ER 141

Tulk* v. *Moxhay [1843–60] All ER Rep 9

Chapter 14
Lawyer's brief

Introduction

So you have reached the end of Chapter 13 and the substantive part of the text has finished – now for something a little different! This final chapter of the text gives you the opportunity to put into practice many of the skills and much of the knowledge that you have learned throughout the rest of the text. Aptly named the 'Lawyer's Brief', what you will see in the following chapter is a series of documents presented in much the same way as you would see them in the file of a working solicitor.

In addition to these documents are a number of questions and tasks, which have been designed both to test your understanding of land law and to give you a real flavour of how the law is applied in practice. We hope that you will find this a valuable and worthwhile learning tool as well as a fun exercise. You will play the part of a trainee solicitor working in the conveyancing department of law firm, Wardell James – good luck in your task!

The brief

You are Angela Bennett, a trainee solicitor at the firm of Wardell James, in Wakebury, West Deanshire. On your arrival at the office on Monday morning you find a memorandum on your desk from your principal, managing partner at Wardell James, Jonathan James, giving you instructions. The contents of the memo are as follows:

Document 1

INTERNAL MEMORANDUM

To:	Angela Bennett
From:	Jonathan James
File Reference:	FISCHER/FIS02936
Date:	25 March 2013

Dear Angela,

My niece, Carly Fischer, is buying a house together with her boyfriend, Ted Landings. The house is called Tall Trees and is in Ossell, which is just outside Wakebury. It is a large house with several acres of grounds and a number of outbuildings, including a gatehouse and stable block, which the couple intends to let to produce an income. The stable block is already let to a charity on a 20-year lease and Carly and Ted intend to keep them on as tenants, letting out the gatehouse to a family for an additional rent. They also intend to convert the west wing of the main house into flats.

The property will be in Carly's sole name as Ted is currently going through the process of a divorce and doesn't want any complications with his ex-wife in terms of the property in case it is construed as forming part of his assets for the divorce settlement. The purchase price of £750,000 is being funded by a gift of £100,000 to Carly from me and the remainder through a mortgage with the Crisis Bank plc, which will also be in Carly's sole name, albeit that it is the couple's intention that the majority of the monthly mortgage payment will be raised through income from the lettings. Carly intends to provide any shortfall through her job as a nursery assistant at the Little Flowers nursery whilst Ted, who is currently unemployed, will manage the property business and maintain the house and grounds.

Please would you act on behalf of Carly in relation to the transfer of the estate into her name and any related matters that arise in relation to the property. The official copies and title plan relating to the house and grounds are attached at [**Documents 2** and **3**]. This is a large property with a number of outbuildings and additional land, so it may not be straightforward. You may need to speak to me about the various aspects of the purchase as you go through the documentation. Feel free to discuss with me any questions you may have.

I am naturally protective of Carly, with her being my niece, and am a little concerned about the mortgage situation. I should therefore be grateful if you would give this matter your best attentions and keep me informed of any problems you foresee with the legal aspects of the purchase.

Regards,

Jonathan

Clearly Mr Wardell has a personal, as well as a professional, interest in the matter, so you had better be seen to do a good job! Eager to get started, you turn your attentions to the attached document:

Document 2

This is a copy of the register of the title number set out immediately below, showing the entries in the register on 22 March 2013. This copy does not take account of any application made after that time even if still pending in the Land Registry when this copy was issued.

A: PROPERTY REGISTER

This register describes the land and estate comprised in the title.

Title number: WK384983

DEANSHIRE: WAKEBURY

1. The Freehold land shown edged with black on the plan of the above Title filed at the Registry and being Tall Trees, Edge Hill, Ossell, Wakebury, West Deanshire (DN14 3BQ).

END OF PROPERTY REGISTER

B: PROPRIETORSHIP REGISTER

This register specifies the class of title and identifies the owner. It contains any entries that affect the right of disposal.

Title Absolute

1. PROPRIETOR: TREVOR HARRISON AINSWORTH of Tall Trees, Edge Hill, Ossell, Wakebury, West Deanshire (DN14 3BQ).
2. (18 October 2004) The price stated to have been paid on 20 August 2004 was £500,000.
3. (18 October 2004) The Transfer to the proprietor contains a covenant to observe and perform the covenants in the Deed dated 26 November 1984 referred to in the Charges Register and of indemnity in respect thereof.

END OF PROPRIETORSHIP REGISTER

C: CHARGES REGISTER

This register contains any charges and other matters that affect the land.

1. (18 October 2004) An agreement affecting the land tinted green on the title plan dated 26 November 1997 made between (1) Trevor Harrison Ainsworth ('the Purchaser') and (2) King's Mead Developments Limited ('the Vendor') contains the following covenants:

   'No trees or hedges existing on the site at the date of this agreement shall be removed other than with the prior written consent of the Vendor.

   No poultry or other domestic or wildfowl shall be kept or reared at the property.

   The property shall not be used for anything other than as a single residential dwelling house and garden.'
2. (12 March 2009) The parts of the land affected thereby are subject to the leases contained in the schedule of leases hereto.
3. (27 March 2011) UNILATERAL NOTICE in respect of an Agreement for Sale dated 26 March 2011 made between (1) Trevor Harrison Ainsworth and (2) Geoffrey Lindley Scott.
4. (27 March 2011) BENEFICIARY: Geoff Lindley Scott of 12 King's Mead, Ossell, Wakebury DN14 3BS.

Schedule of notices of leases

1. (12 March 2009)	Stable Block at Edge Hill Edged green	6 years from 21.02.09

END OF REGISTER

Document 3

Land Registry
Current title plan

Title Number **WK384983**
Ordinance Survey Map Reference **SE3072SE**
Scale **1:1250 enlarged from 1:2500**
Administrative Area **West Deanshire: Ossell**

N

*: Small Trees

KINGS MEAD

*

11
12
13
14
15
16

KINGS MEAD

8616

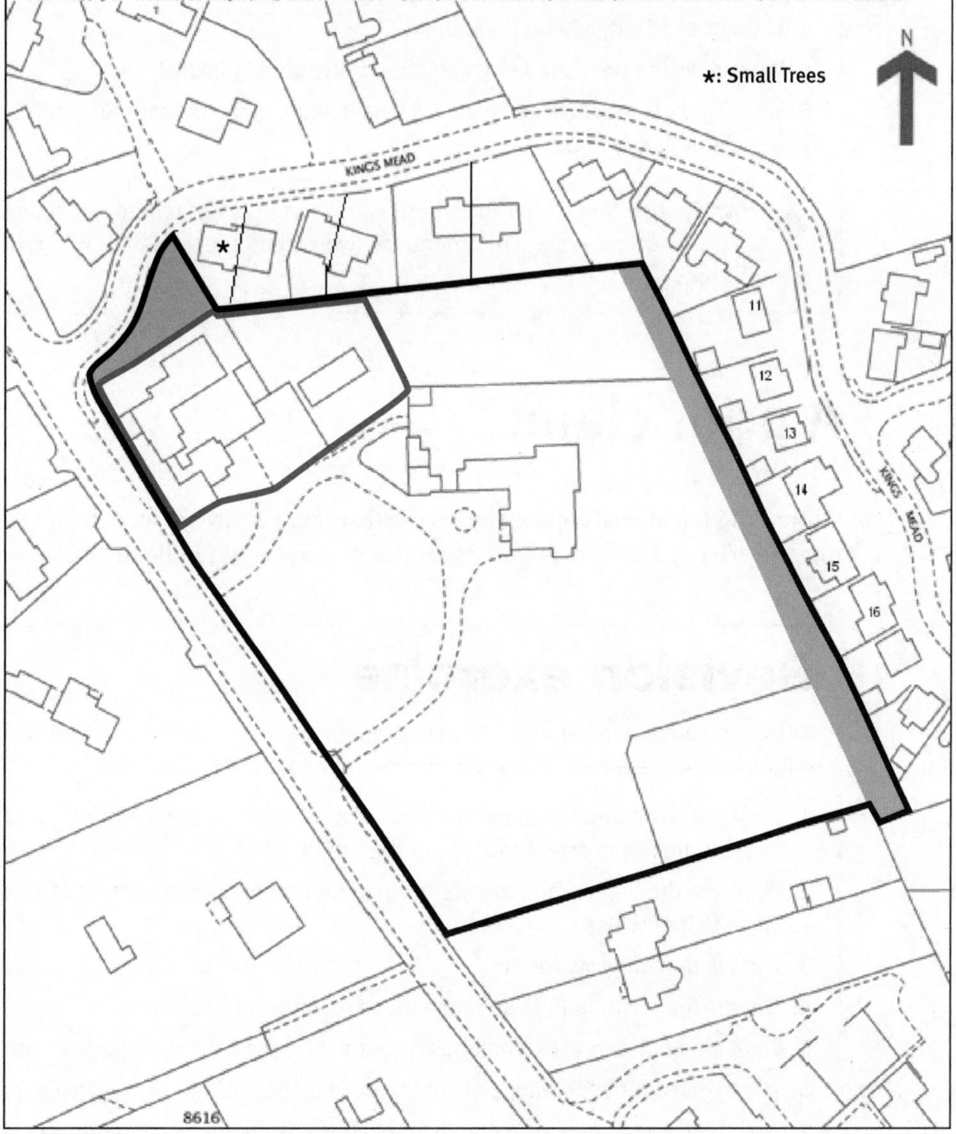

Consider this

Take a look at the official copies and title plan for the property and answer the following questions:

1. What is the legal tenure and estate of the property being purchased?*
2. What is the address of the property?
3. Who is the current owner?
4. Is there any mortgage on the property?
5. What does the area shaded green on the title plan indicate?
6. What kind of interest is listed at numbers 3 and 4 in the Charges Register? Who has the benefit of this interest?

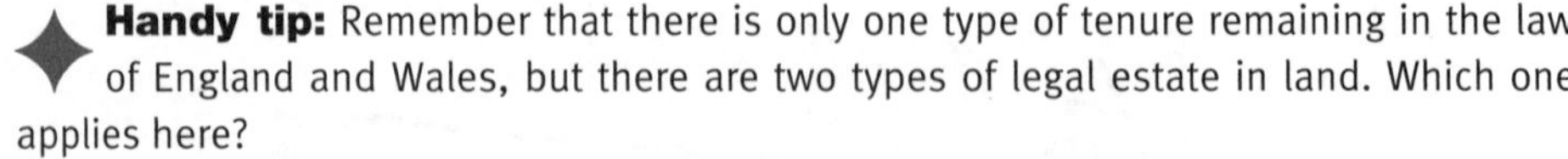

Handy tip: Remember that there is only one type of tenure remaining in the law of England and Wales, but there are two types of legal estate in land. Which one applies here?

A prior claim?

On reading the official copies, you realise that there is already a contract for the sale of the property registered in favour of another buyer: Geoff Lindley Scott.

Revision exercise

What can you remember about the conveyancing process in England and Wales? Here is a little revision exercise. You should answer the following questions:

1. What is the position as between a buyer and seller of land *before* they have entered into a formal contract for the sale of the property?
2. What are the legal requirements for the creation of a contract for the sale of land in England and Wales?
3. What is the authority for this?
4. What is the position if these formalities are not complied with?
5. What kind of interest in land does a contract for the sale of property create?
6. What is meant by 'exchange of contracts' in respect of the conveyancing process?
7. What is the position at law and in equity once exchange of contracts has taken place?
8. Once a contract for the sale of land has been created, what can the buyer do to protect their interest?

Handy tip: You will not find all the answers you need in statute. If you need a reminder, take a look at the outline of the conveyancing process contained in Chapter 3 of the text.

You quickly put a telephone call in to the seller's solicitors, and are told that this was a conditional contract which has now lapsed. They undertake to have the entries on the Register of Title removed before your client contracts to purchase the property.

No sooner have you done this, than you receive a telephone call from reception to tell you that Miss Fischer has called into the office and wishes to see you immediately. You rush downstairs. Miss Fischer is in a noticeably distressed state. You usher her into the interview room and ask her what the matter is. She tells you that the seller says he no longer wishes to go through with the sale, but that they have an agreement and that he cannot renege on the deal.

You set out the legal position to Miss Fischer as gently as you can, explaining to her that until an exchange of contracts has been finalised between her and the seller the seller is perfectly within his rights to pull out of the sale. 'But we *have* exchanged contracts', exclaims Carly. 'Look'. Carly produces from her bag an envelope, which contains three letters. The letters read as follows:

Document 4

Tall Trees,
Edge Hill,
Ossell,
Wakebury,
West Deanshire
DN14 3BQ

6 January 2013

Miss Carly Fischer
3 Sand Dunes
Seahouses
Halifeld

Dear Miss Fischer,

Further to our recent conversation please accept this letter as confirmation that I am willing to sell Tall Trees to you for the price of £750,000. As discussed, the sale will include all fixtures and fittings at the property.

Please confirm your agreement to the terms of the sale by return.

Yours sincerely,

T H Ainsworth

Trevor Ainsworth

Document 5

3 Sand Dunes
Seahouses
Halifeld
West Deanshire
DN12 6DS
9 January 2013

Mr T Ainsworth
Tall Trees,
Edge Hill,
Ossell,
Wakebury,
DN14 3BQ

Dear Trevor,

Tall Trees, Ossell

Thank you for your letter of 20th February. I confirm that I am happy to accept your offer to sell Tall Trees, Ossell to me for the price of £750,000, subject to the grant of planning permission for the conversion of the West Wing of Tall Trees into flats, as mentioned during our meeting.

As discussed, we will try to move things along as swiftly as possible but, following advice from Deanshire County Council, we anticipate that grant of planning permission will take in the region of 6–8 weeks.

Kind regards.

Yours sincerely

Carly Fischer

Document 6

Email correspondence

From: trevorharrisonainsworth@ptinternet.com
To: **carlywarly@jive.co.uk**
Date: **21 February 2013**
Time sent: **21.33**

Dear Carly,

Further to our telephone conversation I understand that things are progressing well with the planning permission, albeit a little more slowly than we had anticipated. As I explained previously, due to a previous sale falling through following a formal exchange of contracts I am understandably a little nervous of conditional sales. Do let me know as soon as you have any news from the planning office.

As I said on the 'phone, I am happy to let you have the ride-on lawnmower as part of the sale. It is fairly old now, although perfectly serviceable, and will be of little use to me after my move to Puerta Ventura in the spring.

Kind regards,

Trevor

Carly explains tearfully that they have spent a fortune on architects' fees and the services of a planning consultant in order to obtain planning permission for the flats. Without the flats they would be unable to afford the repayments on the mortgage for the house, so it is vital to their purchase that they obtain this. As the correspondence states, Mr Ainsworth knew all about this and had said he was happy with it, but he now appears to have cold feet. Carly is insistent that he should not be able to walk away from the deal.

Consider this

Now that you have read through the letters, take some time to think about whether in your view:

1. a valid contract has been created; and
2. whether this can be enforced against the seller.

Handy tip: You need to consider the requirements for a valid contract for the sale of land. If you need to remind yourself, take a look at the provisions of section 2 of the Law of Property (Miscellaneous Provisions) Act 1989.

Outside the box

If the contract cannot be enforced against the seller, what other equitable route might you consider taking, bearing in mind that your client has, arguably, acted to her detriment in reliance on the assurances of the seller regarding the sale of the property?

Writing and drafting

You think that a threat in the right direction might just do the trick and decide to run it by Mr James. Draft an internal memo to Mr James confirming the position as you understand it and explaining how you think the situation might be resolved.

You should take no more than 30 minutes on this task.

Fortunately, you never have any need to send the letter to the seller, as you receive word from Mr James that the situation has now resolved itself. It would appear that the seller was becoming impatient waiting for planning permission to be obtained, but that this was granted last Friday and Mr James himself was able to organise a swift, but formal, exchange of contracts shortly thereafter.

A situation arises

All is quiet on the file until the following morning, when you receive a telephone call from Carly's boyfriend, Ted. Ted is extremely aggravated, to say the least. Apparently there is some problem with the terms of the contract and he is furious. Carly did not want to make a fuss as it was her uncle who drafted the contracts, but Ted has no such concerns and is demanding a call back within the hour to resolve the problem. You reassure him that you will deal with the matter without delay and ask for details. The information you are given is as follows:

Document 7

TELEPHONE ATTENDANCE

Name:	Ted Landings
File Reference:	FISCHER/FIS02936
Date:	26 March 2013
Time:	11.35 am
Length of Call:	40 minutes

Ted is very upset because on moving into the property he and Carly have noticed that a number of things are missing from the property that they had expected to be left for them as part of the sale.

His main concern centres around the following:

- Firstly, although the house is in need of considerable renovation, it nevertheless boasted a fully equipped billiard room, barely touched since the time of its creation by the original owners of the house at around the turn of the century. The room came complete with wooden scoreboards inset into the wall panelling and a full size billiard table with a period glass light fitting above.
- Secondly, there was a large wood burning stove in the sitting room which, although modern, made a pleasing focal point within the room and upon which Ted and Carly were relying to provide heat in the house whilst the new central heating system was being installed.

The seller had told the couple that the house would be 'sold as seen' and they had taken this to mean that the contents of the house, including the stove and billiard table, would be left in the house following the sale. They were therefore surprised to see that both items had been removed, in particular the billiard table, which was extremely large and heavy and which they believed to be original to the house. In addition, the light fitting above the table had been ripped down, leaving only exposed wires where it had been, and the scoreboards had been removed from the walls using some force and leaving splinters in the wooden panelling.

Ted tried to phone the seller but he is in Puerta Ventura and his phone is not working, He has not responded to any of their emails and Ted wants to know if the seller can keep the items that he has removed or whether he can be forced to return them.

Consider this

You have promised that you will respond before 1 o'clock. You realise that it is already 12.20 p.m. so you have only forty minutes to answer Mr Landings' call. Take a look at the telephone attendance note and consider how you are going to respond.

Handy tip: You need to consider whether the items in question are fixtures or fittings and whether they will have formed part of the sale. Do you need any more information and where would you look for it? If there is no such information available, what rules must you apply to find your answer?

Writing and drafting

You should now draft a fax to the seller's solicitors requesting the return of items, as appropriate, stating your reasons for doing so. You should support your assertions with case law, wherever possible.

You should take no more than 30 minutes on this task.

You phone Ted and update him as to the position and what you have done about it. You tell him you will let him know as soon as you receive a response from Mr Ainsworth's solicitors. Ted thanks you for acting so promptly on their behalf, but in the meantime says that they have come across another, more major problem in one of the other buildings on the property. Ted tells you that he was surprised to hear what appeared to be chanting coming from the gatehouse and, when he went to investigate, has found that there is actually someone living in there. The occupant, who goes by the name of Muhatma Walla, says he has a lease of the gatehouse and has shown Ted a copy of a document which he purports to be a lease, signed by Trevor Ainsworth. Ted has photocopied it and now gives this to you to look at:

Document 8

1. I, TREVOR HARRISON AINSWORTH hereby let to you, MUHATMA WALLA the property known as THE GATEHOUSE, EDGE HILL, OSSELL.
2. In return I, MUHATMA WALLA, will:
   (a) Pay all bills and outgoings on the property as and when they become due; and
   (b) Keep the house and garden in a clean and tidy condition.

Signed: T H Ainsworth

M Walla

Dated: 4 April 2012

Consider this

Does the document create a valid lease of the gatehouse? If so, what kind of lease does Muhatma have? If not, why not?

Outside the box

You have checked the official copies of the Register of Title for Tall Trees and can find no note of the lease there. Is there any other way in which Muhatma's interest could be protected? What additional questions might you want to consider asking in order to help you answer this question?

Document 9

OVERRIDING INTERESTS QUESTIONNAIRE

Tall Trees, Edge Hill, Ossell, West Deanshire

The Land Registration Act took effect on 13th October 2003. It places a strict obligation on your Buyer to notify the Registry after completion of all "Overriding Interests" which affect the property. Overriding Interests are rights or liabilities in favour of third parties which burden (as opposed to benefit) the property and you as owners but which are not spelt out on the face of your property title documentation.

Accordingly it is necessary to disclose to your Buyer all overriding interests of which you are aware or suspect may exist. Failure to disclose such an interest can result in an action for damages against you.

Please consider the list below and tick the box opposite any right or liability that may affect your property. Most (if not all) will not apply. If any do apply please give details below in the box provided.

1. Private Rights of Way	☐	12. Any other rights or liabilities affecting the Property of which you are aware	☐
2. Rights of fishing or shooting.	☐	13. Rights to coal or other minerals	☐
3. Drainage rights.	☐	14. Rights of persons in occupation	☐
4. Liability to pay Crown Rents.	☐	15. Rights to timber or crops	☐
5. Public rights (e.g. public paths crossing your property)	☐	16. Leases or Tenancy Agreements	☐
6. Special rights of support (e.g. retaining wall on your land supporting adjoining land)	☐	17. Squatters rights affecting the Property	☐
7. Water courses (Streams / ditches etc running through your land)	☐	18. Liability to repair the chancel of any Church	☐
8. Liability in respect of embankments, sea and river walls	☐	19. Manorial Rights (e.g. the Lords rights of sporting, mines and minerals, holding fairs and markets, etc)	☐
9. Rights of common	☐	20. Rights of water (e.g. right of someone else to take water from a well or stream on your land)	☐
10. Liability to pay corn rent	☐	21. Franchises	☐
11. Customary rights (e.g. rights to pasture and graze animals on your land)	☐	**If none of the above are applicable please tick this box**	✓

Details in respect of any Interests ticked

Signed by: T H Ainsworth

On probing for a little further detail, Ted tells you that when he questioned Mr Walla about the absence of any sign of either him or his possessions in the property when they looked around it in January, Mr Walla said that he had been on a Buddhist retreat for two months and that, as a strictly religious man who did not believe in the burden on the soul of worldly possessions, he had few personal belongings and had taken everything he owned with him to the retreat.

Concerned, you check the file for anything else which might help you. You find Document 9.

Consider this

What is the significance of this form and how it has been completed? How can it be used to prevent the tenant from pursuing his rights under the agreement?

Letter from residents of King's Mead

A new day brings a new letter relating to the Fischer file. It is from the chairman of the residents' association for King's Mead, the cul-de-sac which winds around the north and east sides of Tall Trees. The land used to belong to Tall Trees, but was sold off to a developer some 15 years ago and a small housing estate of bungalows has now been built there. The letter appears to relate to a strip of land to the east of Tall Trees, abutting a number of the bungalows. The letter reads as follows:

Document 10

Mr R Hartbury
11 King's Mead
Ossell
West Deanshire

Miss C Fischer
Tall Trees
Edge Hill
Ossell
West Deanshire
DN14 3BQ

27 March 2013

Dear Miss Fischer,

It is with much dismay that I and my fellow residents have observed you erecting fencing to the east of Tall Trees, immediately abutting the existing boundaries of number 11 to 16 King's Mead, and thereby blocking access to the residents from the strip of woodland that divides our properties. This is without notice or discussion with the residents of King's Mead.

The woodland is a strip of 'no man's land' which the residents of King's Mead have for many years been using for the purposes of storage, as a play area for their children, for rear access on foot between the bungalows (of which the children of the various residents have made particular use), and for the walking of residents' dogs. As such, you have no right to fence it off and claim it as yours.

In any event, we believe it is our right to continue to use this woodland as amenity land for King's Mead and in particular for the houses abutting it. Your fencing serves to prevent access to the woodland from King's Mead, and we must insist that it be removed immediately. If you fail to do so we will have no choice but to instruct solicitors in the matter.

Yours sincerely,

Roger Hartbury

On behalf of the King's Mead residents' association

Reading the letter obviously gives you considerable cause for concern. You take a look at the title plan to the property (Document 3) and see that the land to which Mr Hartbury is referring is the land shaded grey on the plan. The land clearly falls within the boundary of your client's property and is not 'no man's land', as Mr Hartbury suggests. However, you cannot help but wonder whether there is any substance to their claims.

Consider this

What kind of rights or interests over the woodland might the residents of King's Mead have, or have acquired?

Handy tip: Look at the facts and consider whether the residents have rights of possession of the property or simply rights of user. Once you have your answer, consider how these rights might have been acquired.

Bearing in mind what you have discovered, above, you should now prepare the following:

Writing and drafting

Write a response to Mr Hartbury, stating your client's position and setting out the law as you understand it in relation to their claim.

You should take no more than 30 minutes on this task.

Handy tip: Do not forget to use plain English – you are writing to a lay person, not a lawyer!

Reflective practice

Think about the answer you have given above. Would it have made any difference if the residents had been using the woodland for a longer period of time, say 20 years?

An adversarial email

It is Thursday afternoon and you receive an email from Levine & Co., a local firm of solicitors. As if the relationship with the residents of King's Mead are not already strained enough, it would appear that your clients have upset another one of their residents, a Ms Sandy Meyer at 'Small Trees':

Document 11

Email correspondence

From: **shirley.levisson@levines.co.uk**

To: **a.bennett@wardelljames.com**

Date: **28 March 2013**

Time sent: **15.41**

Dear Ms Bennett,

Re: Tall Trees, Edge Hill, Ossell

I act for Sandy Meyer of Small Trees, King's Mead, Ossell and I understand you act for her neighbour, Miss C Fischer, at Tall Trees, Edge Hill, Ossell.

Ms Meyer informs me that your client is in breach of certain covenants of which my client has the benefit. These are namely that:

- Your client has removed the boundary hedge which borders onto King's Mead and abuts the public highway;
- Your client has been for the last year keeping chickens on the property. These are not only a nuisance in that the cockerel crows at 3am each morning but they also cause an offensive smell which pervades the Mead and is unpleasant for the residents, including Ms Meyer.
- Your client has been selling eggs from these hens at the garden gate, which is in breach of your client's covenant not to use the property for business purposes.

Please confirm that your client has will replace the hedge and forthwith remove the chickens from the property and cease to sell their eggs (or any other produce) from the property.

Your client has seven days within which to carry out our client's wishes, after which time I am instructed by my client to commence proceedings against your client. I should be grateful if you would confirm once our instructions have been complied with.

Yours sincerely

Shirley Levisson

Solicitor, Levine & Co.

It would appear that if you do not comply with her requests, Ms Meyer intends to commence proceedings against your client. You decide that you had better find out whether there is any basis to her claim.

Consider this

Take some time to think about the situation as described by Ms Meyer's solicitor, and answer the following questions:

1. What are the covenants that your client has allegedly breached and where on the file can you find evidence of these covenants?
2. Has the burden of the covenants passed to your client?
3. On what basis could the benefit of the covenant have passed to Ms Meyer?
4. What are the rules relating to building plots and how are they applied?
5. What additional questions do you need to ask of Ms Meyer's solicitor in order to apply them?
6. If Ms Meyer succeeds in her claim, what kind of order could the court make in her favour?
7. Are your client's tenants responsible for breaches of the covenants mentioned by the solicitor? If so, how?
8. What can you do to make the tenants cease their breaches of the freehold covenant of which Ms Meyer is complaining?

Handy tip: Take another look at Documents 2 and 3 on the file (the Official Copies of the Register of Title and Title Plan). You should find something that helps you in the Charges Register.

You decide you had better touch base with your client and discuss the matter with her to see what she wishes to do about it. You are relieved to find Carly quite relaxed about the whole thing. Apparently she has had a chat with both her tenants at the Stable Block and Ms Meyer, with whom she made an instant connection. They have reached an informal agreement that the tenants will supply Ms Meyer with a dozen eggs free of charge once a week, and that the tenants will re-home the cockerel. They have promised to do this within the next week. On this basis, she is not bothered about the hedge. Therefore the problem should be resolved. You make a note for the file.

A repairing issue

You receive an email from Carly attaching a copy of a letter she has received from the tenants of the stable block. The tenants are the Ossell Community Project, a registered charity who provides temporary residential care at the stable block for children with physical and learning disabilities. The letter reads as Document 12.

Document 12

Ossell Community Project
The Stable Block
Tall Trees
Edge Hill
Ossell
West Deansuire

Miss C Fischer
Tall Trees
Edge Hill
Ossell
West Deanshire
DN14 3BQ

27 March 2013

Dear Miss Fischer,

The Stable Block, Tall Trees, Ossell

We write to notify you of a number of repairing issues we have with the stable block and should be grateful if you would resolve these:

1. A hole in the roof due to storm damage, which has caused damage to the ceilings in bedrooms 5 and 6;
2. Rising damp in the kitchen and utility area;
3. A persistent blockage in the downstairs toilet, making it impossible to use.

As you can imagine, the condition of the premises is extremely important to the fragile health of some of our residents and we should therefore be grateful if you would give this matter your immediate attention.

We look forward to hearing from you.

Yours sincerely,

Jean Ledbury
Ossell Community Project

Carly tells you that the lease is a 'fully repairing and insuring lease' and that she had understood this to mean that the responsibility for repairs rested solely with the tenants.

Writing and drafting

Is your client liable for the repairs? Write a response to Carly advising her on her position in relation to the stable block. In doing so, you should consider:

1. The nature of the tenants in occupation
2. The nature and length of the lease
3. Any common law or statutory measures that may exist to protect tenants and whether these might apply to the Stable Block.

You should take no more than 35 minutes on this task.

Handy tip: What kind of premises are these? Could they be described as a residential dwelling? Is it likely that any of the implied covenants prescribed by statute would apply here?

A private matter

It is 5 to 5 on Friday afternoon and you are just heading out of the office to join your fellow trainees at the Pen and Wig public house for a well-deserved end of week pint, when Mr James comes into you office and says he needs a 'quick word'. Apparently he has just been on the telephone to his niece. It appears that the strain of the house purchase and all the difficulties they have had with the house have proved just too big a strain on their relationship and she and Ted have split up, following a massive row.

Mr James goes on to explain that Ted is now claiming an interest in the house and demanding sale of the property at once in order to realise his share. In the meantime, Ted has moved into one of the newly-converted flats in the west wing of the house. Carly wants him to leave the property but he says he is refusing to go. Consequently, Mr James needs answers to the following:

1. Is Ted entitled to a share in the property, either by way of a resulting or constructive trust;

Consider this

Take some time to think about whether or not Ted may be entitled to a share in the property by way of resulting or constructive trust. Consider what share he might be entitled to and if so, why. Don't forget to back up your findings with case law.

Handy tip: If you look back through the Lawyer's Brief (**Document 1**) you should find all the information you need to get an initial feel of whether you think Ted's claim has any merit.

2. If Ted is entitled to a share of the house:
   (a) what can he claim in accordance with the provisions of ToLATA; and
   (b) does this give him any right to occupy the property?

Research point

Go online and find a copy of the Trusts of Land and Appointment of Trustees Act 1996. Now answer the following questions:

1. Which provisions under the Act might relate to the occupation of property by Ted?
2. If Ted does have an interest, does Carly have the right to exclude or restrict Ted's occupation in any way?
3. Which are the relevant provisions of the act with reference to claims made under a resulting or constructive trust?
4. Who is able to make a claim under the terms of the Act?
5. What kind of order could the court make under these provisions?
6. What matters should the court take into account when making an order under the terms of the Act?
7. Would it make a difference if Ted was declared bankrupt?

Handy tip: If you are struggling to find a copy of the Act, try going onto the National Archives UK litigation website at **http://legislation.gov.uk** and carrying out a search for the Act there either by title or reference to the year. If you need a reminder of the specific provisions that are relevant take a look back at Chapter 9 of the text.

Mr James has arranged a meeting with Mike Askey, who is head of the litigation department on Monday morning, and would like you to present your findings at the meeting. With your vision of a quiet, work-free weekend in tatters you sit back down at your desk and pick up the file . . .

Present your findings

You should prepare a PowerPoint presentation explaining your findings, both in relation to Ted's purported share in the property (including your opinion on what share might be awarded and on what grounds) and what claim Ted might have both in relation to his occupation of the property and the sale of the house.

You should take no more than 60 minutes on this task.

The last straw

Following a further row with Carly, Ted has now barricaded himself into his flat in the west wing and is refusing to come out or to continue to manage the other properties. He has told Carly that if she wants to have it all to herself she can manage it by herself too.

As a consequence, Carly has been struggling to manage the properties and hold down her full time job at the nursery as well. On account of the stress, Carly has started drinking heavily and, following complaints from several parents who had noticed alcohol on her breath, Little Flowers nursery has had to let Carly go.

In addition, the Ossell Community Project has given its notice on the stable block, on account of the repairs to the roof and the rising damp still not having been taken care of. Whilst they sympathise with Carly's plight they say they simply cannot continue to risk the health of their staff and residents with the property in its current condition.

Without her job at the nursery and the sizeable income from the rental of the stable block, Carly cannot afford to keep up mortgage payments on her own and has now fallen two months behind with the mortgage payments. Yesterday she received a letter from the Crisis Bank plc, Document 13.

Document 13

Crisis Bank plc
Crisis House
Watersedge
North Deanshire

Dear Miss Fischer,

Property: Tall Trees, Edge Hill, Ossell, West Deanshire

Mortgage account number: 4239408540985

As at 31 March 2013 you will be three months in arrears with your mortgage interest and capital payments. On this basis, we write to inform you that if you do not clear the full amount of your mortgage debt by 7 April 2013 we will commence possession proceedings against you with a view to recouping the debt.

Payments should be made to the Crisis Bank plc. If you have any queries, you should contact our customer service centre, which is open from 8am until 6pm Monday to Friday.

Yours faithfully,

Crisis Bank plc

Carly tells you that she has tried to contact the bank on several occasions, but has only managed to get through to an automated system. She is petrified that she has been asked to come up with £650,000 within the next seven days and is completely unable to do this. Currently, she does not even have enough money to pay the balance of the arrears.

Consider this

What are the bank's rights and can it call in the whole of the debt like this? If not, why not? Advise what Carly can do, if anything, to prevent or delay any prospective repossession from going ahead.

Handy tip: Consider what the bank will need to do in order to repossess the property. Is there any statutory defence or assistance Carly can claim when such repossession action is taken?

Following a long chat with her uncle, Carly decides that the best course of action may actually be to allow the bank to repossess the property and sell it to pay off the mortgage debt. There is plenty of equity in the property due to the renovation works that the couple undertook, and because of the creation of the flats making it a more commercially viable enterprise for a buyer. In all likelihood, therefore, the whole of the mortgage debt will be covered by the sale and she may even get her deposit money back. Unfortunately, however, Ted disagrees with her view and is now saying that his interest in the property is sufficient to prevent the mortgage company from selling it. The mortgage is in Carly's sole name.

Consider this

Is there any truth in Ted's claim and, if so, on what grounds can he make it? What should the mortgage company have done in order to prevent any such claim being made?

Handy tip: Can Ted make a claim of undue influence? What would he have to show in order to make such a claim? What are the recommendations in *Etridge* for lenders in such a situation?

Unfortunately the bank's threat to seek the repossession of the property and the impending court action against your client has taken the matter beyond the scope of your department. You have no choice but to pass the file over to the litigation team.

File round-up

Before you pass your file over to the litigation department it might be helpful to have a look back through the chapter and reflect upon the various areas of law which you have considered. The key academic areas from the text which you have covered in this chapter follow.

Firstly you considered the doctrines of tenure and estates which we covered in Chapter 1 of the text; and then you took a look at some official copies of a registered title and a title plan, focusing in particular on the various interests in land as they appeared on the register. Interests in land were dealt with in Chapter 4 of the text.

You then moved on to look at contract for the sale of land and some of the difficulties which can be encountered with formalities for the sale of land which were dealt with in Chapter 3. There was also a little bit of thinking outside the box with the consideration of a possible claim in proprietary estoppel (covered in Chapter 8 of the text). You then took a brief look at the outline of the conveyancing process, also detailed in Chapter 3 of the text, and considered the issue of fixtures and chattels, were considered in Chapter 2.

Then you moved on to consider leases (Chapter 5) and you made some practical decisions on whether an overriding interest under Schedule 3 paragraph 2 of the Land Registration Act 2002 might have been created, which you will remember was again covered in Chapter 4 of the text. You were also given the opportunity to consider easements by prescription and freehold covenants and their operation under building schemes, which were covered at Chapters 10 and 11. There was a Writing and Drafting exercise on covenants to repair, recapping on what you learned in Chapter 13, and then you were asked to consider resulting and constructive trusts (Chapter 7), as well as carrying out a little bit of a recap and research on the Trusts of Land and Appointment of Trustees Act 1996, which was covered in Chapter 9 of the text (on co-ownership). And finally, you were asked to consider the topic of mortgages, which we read about in Chapter 12 of the text, and the borrower's right to postpone under the Administration of Justice Act 1970.

The various writing and drafting exercises were designed to get you thinking practically as a lawyer would and to give you practice in some of the skills you will need to use as a solicitor or barrister. The little bit of academic research into trustee rights of occupation which took you outside the scope of the text at the end of this chapter was hopefully both a useful and interesting tool which should help to form the foundation of your practical legal research skills.

If you have been struggling with any of the areas covered in this chapter, the above summary should point you in the right direction in terms of the chapters you perhaps need to look back at or revise a little more. In addition, you will find guidance on the accompanying website to this text at **www.mylawchamber.co.uk**.

Visit **www.mylawchamber.co.uk** to access tools to help you develop and test your knowledge of land law.

Glossary

absolute covenant A covenant that puts an absolute bar on the action restricted by the covenant.

absolute title/absolute freehold This denotes that the right is not ended upon the happening of any certain event i.e. it is not conditional.

action The legal term for a case or law suit brought in the civil courts.

actual notice When a person has direct knowledge of a fact or situation or is assumed to do so on account of their actions.

adjourn/adjournment (of proceedings) To suspend or postpone court action until a later date.

adverse possession The process of acquiring an estate in land informally through possession over an uninterrupted period of time.

alienation (total or partial) Refers to the transfer of property to a third party.

ameliorating waste An unauthorised improvement made to leased premises.

annexation The process through which fixtures merge with the land at law.

'arm's length' transaction A transaction between two unrelated people or businesses that are not connected to each other in any way: that is, that they are not related or married.

assignee The person receiving the benefit of a lease on the assignment of leasehold property (also called the incoming tenant).

assignment The transfer of the tenant's interest in leasehold property in the form of the remaining term of a lease to a third party.

assignor The person transferring the benefit of their lease to a third party in an assignment (also called the outgoing tenant).

assured shorthold tenancy A short form of tenancy created under the Housing Act 1988 which confers on the tenant no rights of renewal or rent-capping.

authorised guarantee agreement An agreement guaranteeing the performance of the tenant's assignee's obligations under the terms of the lease.

bare legal title Where the legal owner of property holds the legal title to the property but does not retain any beneficial interest in it, such as in the case of trustees of a trust.

beneficial right/interest Refers to the person with the right to benefit from the land or interest in question, regardless of whether they also have legal ownership of it. Also termed the equitable right or interest.

beneficiary A person who has the right to benefit from the land, either by occupying it, or by receiving income from it.

bona fide Good faith/in good faith.

***bona fide* purchaser for value without notice** A person who buys property in good faith, or innocently, without knowledge of any claim a third party might have to that property.

bona vacantia The common law doctrine under which property for which no owner can be found is claimed by the Crown.

breach of contract The simple failure of a party to a contract to adhere to its terms and conditions.

break clause A clause in a lease that gives either the landlord or tenant (or both) the option to bring an end to the lease at prescribed times or intervals, upon the service of a notice on the other party.

bridging loan A short term loan, usually at high interest, taken by the lender until permanent or longer term finance can be put into place.

Building Control The government department that ensures that all buildings comply with building regulations, which are national standards for health and safety, energy conservation and access to and about buildings. Building Control also makes sure that existing buildings are not a danger to the public.

building survey An inspection carried out on property by a building surveyor to establish the physical condition of property.

building regulations The regulations in place requiring building or renovation works are carried out to a particular standard of health and safety.

capacity In the context of land law, the ability of a person to create an interest in land or to transfer an estate in land, encompassing both mental capability and being of the required age.

capital A lump sum of money or assets upon which interest or income can be earned.

caveat emptor Latin maxim underpinning all sales and purchases of land and meaning 'let the buyer beware'.

certificated bailiff A bailiff is someone authorised to collect a debt on behalf of a creditor. A certificated bailiff is where the firm employing the bailiff has provided references to the county court and the bailiffs they employ are considered to be 'fit and proper' persons.

chain of ownership The method of showing how the property has passed from owner to owner in unregistered land.

charge (registered charge/legal charge) The process whereby a third party imposes an obligation or claim against property in respect of money owing to them by the owner. The charge entitles the person in possession of it to claim that property as against the loan, should the property owner fail to repay them. A mortgage is a type of legal charge.

Charges Register The section of the Land Register recording any charges affecting the property and showing the burden of any interests affecting the land.

chattel Another word for personal, moveable property (as opposed to real property, or land), for example a car or pocket watch.

chattels real Personal property which can be protected through a real action. A term which applies only to leasehold property.

claimant The person who brings an action in a civil court of law. Formerly called the plaintiff.

'clean hands' The requirement of the court of equity that anyone asking for a remedy in equity must be blameless in the action and not in any way responsible for the fate which has befallen them.

coal mining search A search made to establish whether there are any mine shafts on or near the property which might be a danger or cause subsidence.

collateral advantage In the context of mortgages a payment or other advantage given to the lender which does not have reference to the payment of the loan.

collateral contract A secondary contract which induces a person to enter into the main contract or which depends upon the main contract for its existence.

common areas/common parts The parts of a building or estate which are shared or common to more than one person or property such as roads, paths or corridors in a shared building.

common intention constructive trust A constructive trust imposed in the situation where there is no evidence of an actual agreement between the parties, but where it can be shown that it was the intention of both parties that they would share the beneficial ownership of the property.

common land/the right of common Privately owned land which is subject to a right of user either by the general public or by a specific group of people, such as the residents of a particular locality.

common law The system of legal principles developed through the courts and by the decisions of judges to form legal precedent. The system of law which runs parallel to the law of equity.

common socage The only form of tenure still in existence in England and Wales today.

commonhold An alternative method of holding freehold land devised primarily to overcome difficulties faced by owners of leasehold property in enforcing covenants contained in a lease as against neighbouring property. It enables neighbouring property to maintain control of common areas on the commonhold estate.

commonhold association A company limited by guarantee which is responsible for the management and maintenance of the common parts in a commonhold development.

commonhold community statement The document which sets out the rules and regulations of the commonhold.

commonhold unit The name given to each separate property within a commonhold development.

commons search A search made to check the status of any open land near the property which may carry grazing or other public rights.

completion The legal term for the point of legal transfer of the property to a third party in a sale or gift of land.

compulsory purchase The right of the government or local authority to require a private landowner to sell their land to the State in any situation where they can show that the development in question will promote or improve the economic, environmental or social well-being of the area, or where the land is needed for public use.

concurrent ownership Where two or more people have the ownership of the same estate in land at the same time.

conservation area An area of land designated by the local authority as having protected status by virtue of its architectural appearance or character.

consideration A legal term for payment, either monetary or in the form of goods or reciprocal services.

constructive notice Notice of any information which a person should have learned by undertaking 'usual' searches and enquiries.

constructive trust An informal trust imposed by operation of law in any situation where the conduct of one party is so unconscionable that to allow any other outcome would be unjust.

continuing breach See **'ongoing/continuing' breach**.

conveyance (deed of) The document transferring the legal ownership of property to a third party purchaser in unregistered conveyancing.

conveyancing The legal term used to describe the legal process of buying and selling land.

co-ownership (of land) The situation in which the ownership of land is shared by more than one person.

copyhold A former tenure of land abolished by the Law of Property Act 1925.

corporeal hereditament An inheritable right of a physical nature, such as the land itself, any buildings on it and anything affixed to the land.

covenant A promise made by deed. In the context of land law, a promise to do or not to do something in relation to the land. Covenants can relate to freehold or leasehold property.

covenantee The person with the benefit of a covenant.

covenantor The person who makes the covenant and who has the burden of it.

Crown Estate The portfolio of property in the United Kingdom owned by the Crown.

damages The common law remedy under which a sum of money is paid by the defaulting party in respect of loss or injury, in an action for a breach of contract or tort.

declaration of trust A deed or document which has the effect of creating a trust.

deed A legal document which is signed and witnessed. Unlike a contract, a deed does not require consideration in order to be valid. A deed is usually used for the transfer of property or the grant of a right.

deed of gift A deed used to transfer property from one person to another by way of gift.

defendant The person against whom the claim is made in a legal action.

degree of annexation Denotes the extent of the physical attachment of an item to property.

demise/demised premises The property transferred to the tenant under the terms of a lease.

demolition order An order made by the local authority requiring the owner of privately owned land to demolish buildings on that land, either because they are in a dangerous condition or because they have been built in breach of planning control.

derogate/derogation from grant Where the landlord, having let the premises for a particular purpose, then does something which prevents the premises from being used for that purpose.

determinate term With reference to a lease, a term which starts on a specified date and ends on a date which is either known or calculable at the commencement of the term.

detrimental reliance In the context of land law, where a person has relied on the statement or actions of the landowner and as a consequence has suffered a loss, usually financial, but can be a loss of another kind, for example the loss of employment or prospects.

dictum/dicta A judge's expression of opinion in a case.

dissent/dissenting judgment A judgment given by one or more of the judges in a case which conflicts or disagrees with the decision of the majority.

distress/distraint An ancient common law remedy which entitles the landlord to enter the premises of the tenant and confiscate goods belonging to the tenant to the value of any rent payments which are outstanding.

doctrine A legal rule or principle.

doctrine of notice The equitable principle which says that when a person takes an estate in land with notice that someone else had a claim on it at the time of the transfer, that claim may still be asserted against the new owner even if it might otherwise have been disregarded at law.

dominant tenement Property which has the benefit of an interest in land, such as the benefit of an easement or covenant.

drainage search A search made to establish the position and maintenance of drains and sewers to the property.

easement A right of user over someone else's land, such as a right of way or a right of storage.

encumbrance (also spelled incumbrance) A burden on property. A right or interest over the property of another that affects its value or marketability. An example of an encumbrance might be an easement or mortgage.

endowment policy A life insurance policy designed to pay a lump sum after a specified term or on the earlier death of the insured.

Energy Performance Certificate (or **EPC**) A certificate rating the energy efficiency of the building and giving recommendations for improvements.

enforcement notice A notice issued by the council to the owners of private property requiring the rectification of an unlawful development of the land.

environmental report A report confirming whether there is any contaminated land near the property making it dangerous to use or live there.

equitable interest/right An interest in the equitable, or beneficial, rights in property. The person with the equitable interest in property has the right to benefit from it, or enjoy it. A beneficiary under a trust is the holder of the beneficial interest in the trust property.

equitable maxim See **maxims of equity**.

equity The system of law in England and Wales designed to provide remedies for wrongs which were traditionally not legally recognised under the common law.

equity of redemption The right of a person who has mortgaged property to redeem the charge and reclaim their property by payment of the sum due within a reasonable amount of time after the due date.

estate A right to use the land for a certain period of time. The word 'estate' is also used to describe the whole of the property comprised in a parcel of land in one person's ownership or, in the context of wills and inheritance, all the deceased's assets, including land and personal property.

estate contract The formal legal term for a contract for the sale of land.

estate rentcharge A rentcharge created to secure the performance of covenants for the provision of services and maintenance on an estate.

estoppel Where a person is prevented from making a claim against a third party that contradicts what they have previously warranted as true.

exception A right that has been held back or excepted by the seller on the transfer of an estate in land.

exchange/exchange of contracts The point at which the buyer and seller enter into a formal binding contract for the sale of land and become legally and contractually bound to complete the transfer of the property.

excluded assignment An assignment of a lease made in breach of covenant, thereby preventing the assignor, as outgoing tenant, from being released from their obligations under the terms of the lease.

exclusive possession In the context of leasehold property, this is the right to exclude all others from the property, including the landlord.

execute/execution (of a deed) Means to sign it in the presence of a witness, in accordance with the requirements for a valid deed.

execution clause The term given to the part of a deed which contains the signatures of the parties to the deed and their witnesses.

executor/executrix The person who is appointed to administer the estate of someone who has died leaving a valid will.

fee simple This means that the right is inheritable by anyone, including women.

fee simple absolute in possession The formal legal name for a freehold estate in land. A current (rather than a future) estate in land which can be sold, gifted or handed down by will, and which will continue for an unlimited period of time.

fee tail An estate in land which was an estate passed down through the family line, usually from father to son. The fee tail is no longer a legal estate in land and can only exist behind a trust.

fiduciary duty The legal duty of any person in a position of trust to act in the best interests of the person for whom they are responsible, for example the duty of a solicitor to their client or a company director to their company or employees.

fine or **premium** A lump sum payment made by a tenant at the beginning of the lease term or on an assignment in exchange for the grant or transfer of the lease.

fittings A non-legal term used to describe items within a house which will be removed on sale. Generally refers to items which are not freestanding or not attached to the building, such as a fridge, curtains or freestanding furniture.

fixed term tenancy A lease granted for a fixed period of time, ceasing at the end of the term granted.

fixture An object with physical form, which is regarded as being part of the land and is thus transferred with it on a sale of that land, for example a fitted wardrobe or the units in a fitted kitchen.

foreclosure A rarely-used remedy whereby the mortgage lender becomes the registered owner of the house in exchange for the extinguishment of the mortgage debt.

foreshore The land between the high and low tide marks.

forfeiture The right for a landlord to enter tenanted property in order to repossess it, where the tenant has breached one or more of the terms of the letting. Also known as the right of re-entry.

forfeiture rule The rule of public policy that a person who has unlawfully killed another should be prevented from acquiring any form of benefit in consequence of the killing.

formality(ies) The formal steps which need to be taken to complete the creation or transfer of a legal estate or interest, or of a trust.

four unities The common law prerequisites for the existence of a joint tenancy of possession, interest, title and time.

free and common socage More commonly known as the 'freehold', formerly the most common form of freeholding (now the only kind), requiring the tenant to plough the fields or graze the land for a certain portion of the year.

'free' tenures Otherwise known as 'freeholds', these were the highest form of land tenure, held by the nobles. Free tenures required the party holding the land to provide the king with any number services in exchange for their landholding, although they did not necessarily require the tenant to actually farm the land.

freehold The right to possess the land for an unlimited period of time. As one of the two remaining legal estates in land, it is the closest to absolute ownership it is possible to achieve in England and Wales (ultimate ownership remaining with the Crown).

freehold covenant A covenant over freehold land (as opposed to leasehold land).

fully qualified covenant A covenant by which the covenantor can carry out the restrited action with the consent of the covenantee, such consent not to be unreasonably witheld.

General Boundaries Rule The rule which states that a boundary shown on the Register of Title of a registered property is a general boundary only and therefore does not determine the exact line of the boundary.

grand sergeanty A form of land tenure which required the landholder to act as the king's chamberlain, or to carry his banner.

grantee A person who is granted an estate or interest (in land) by the grantor.

grantor A person who grants an estate or interest (in land).

***Halsall* v. *Brizell* (rule in)** Also known as the doctrine of mutual benefit and burden. This states that a person who wishes to claim the benefit of a deed must also submit to any corresponding burden which is imposed by that deed.

head landlord Where there is a sub-lease, the landlord of the freehold.

head lease A lease between the freehold owner of land and a tenant, where the tenant has subsequently granted an underlease.

Hedge and Ditch rule The rule which says that, where two pieces of land are separated by a hedge or bank and an artificial ditch, it is presumed that the boundary runs along the side of the ditch furthest from the hedge or bank.

hereditament An inheritable right.

Home Information Packs (or **HIPs)** These were the product of a government initiative aimed to simplify the conveyancing process in England and Wales, by providing the majority of information required by the buyer 'up front' in a standard format. The initiative was unpopular and has now been suspended indefinitely by the current government.

implied common intention In the context of constructive trusts, where the intention of the parties to share the beneficial ownership of the property is implied because there is no evidence of an express agreement between them.

implied trust A trust created informally through implication, rather than by deed. A generic term encompassing resulting and constructive trusts of land.

imputed notice Where an agent of the person in question has either actual or constructive notice of an interest.

indirect contributions In the context of resulting and constructive trusts, contributions which do not relate directly to the purchase price of the property, such as payment for improvements to the property or household expenses.

in personam A claim made against an individual, as opposed to against a piece of property.

in possession This denotes that a right is immediate, and does not take place in the future. One does not have to be in actual physical possession of the property in order to be in possession; if the freeholder is in receipt of rents or profits made from the land, this will be sufficient to denote 'possession' for legal purposes.

in rem A proprietary claim directed at a specific piece of property, rather than a claim being made against a person.

in reversion Denotes an interest which will take effect at some time in the future. Often referred to in the context of leases.

incorporeal hereditaments Intangible rights, such as rights of way over the land or a right to take something from the land, such as firewood or grass for hay.

incumbrance (also spelled encumbrance) Legal term for a burden or other third party right over the property.

indemnity Where a person or persons are given protection or immunity against damage or loss.

indemnity covenant In the context of covenants this enables the original covenantor to claim back from the buyer of the burdened property any damages they have had to pay the covenantee for the buyer's breaches of covenant.

independent person A person who is in no way related to or connected with another. Not a family member of anyone who may benefit from the transaction in question.

inherent defect A defect in the design or construction of a building.

injunction An order of the court requiring the person in question to do something, or refrain from doing something. An injunction is an equitable remedy.

insolvent The legal term for a person or more commonly a company that has insufficient funds to cover its debts. Bankrupt.

instrument An official legal document, such as a will, conveyance or deed.

intangible property Property which can be owned but which has no physical presence, such as a right of user over land.

interest (in land) A right to use (or restrict the use of), enjoy or possess land belonging to a third party, such as a right of way or the benefit of a restrictive covenant.

intestate Refers to a person who dies without having made a will.

investigation of title The process of looking at the title to a property being bought to make sure it is suitable for purchase.

joint tenancy/joint tenants A method of co-ownership of property whereby the co-owners together own the whole as a single group, rather than having divisible quantified shares.

jurisprudence The study of law; the science or principles which underpin legal rules.

knight service A form of land tenure which required the landholder to provide the king with a certain number of horsemen equipped with arms, for a certain number of days in the year.

Land Charge An interest in unregistered land recorded at the central Land Charges Registry in Plymouth.

Land Charges Register A central register of equitable interests in unregistered land recorded against the name of the owner of the property affected by that interest.

land obligation A new kind of interest in land proposed by the Law Commission to supersede freehold covenants.

Land Register The central register on which a record of all registered land in England and Wales is kept.

Land Registry The central registry at which the records of all registered land in England and Wales is kept.

Land Tax A long-standing annual tax on land first introduced in 1692 but abolished in 1963.

landlord A person who grants a leasehold estate of freehold or leasehold property to a third party (tenant).

Lands Chamber (of the Upper Tribunal) The name given to the former Lands Tribunal. A specialist tribunal with High Court status, deciding disputes concerning land.

lease The document or agreement by which a leasehold estate in property is granted.

leasehold One of the remaining legal estates in land. Denotes an estate in land which exists only for a finite period of time, the estate expiring when that period comes to an end, the land returning to the freeholder.

legacy A gift made in a will.

legal title The legal basis on which a person is able to assert their ownership of property.

lessee Legal term denoting the tenant of leasehold property.

lessor Legal term denoting the landlord of leasehold property.

letting Colloquial term providing an alternative to the word 'tenancy', often used in the context of shorter leases.

licence A contractual agreement between two parties whereby one gives the other a personal right of user or occupation of property.

licensee The person who is granted the benefit of a licence by the licensor.

licensor The landowner who grants a licence over their property.

life estate/interest An estate or interest in land which lasts only for the lifetime of the beneficiary of that interest. Now exists only in equity.

life tenant The holder of a life interest.

light obstruction notice Where light is being obstructed by neighbouring property, a notice served on the owners of neigbouring land preventing continuous user from being interrupted in a claim for right to light.

listed building A building listed on a central government register as being of particular architectural or historic importance.

local authority search A search of the local land charges register via the local authority providing information about any planning restrictions affecting the property.

lost modern grant (doctrine of) In the context of easements, the judicial presumption that, if land has been used by the claimant for 20 years or more, a valid easement must have been granted by deed, albeit that the deed in question has subsequently been lost.

majority (age of) Refers to a person who has reached the legal age of adulthood (currently 18 years in England and Wales).

management or service charge A charge made to leaseholders or commonhold property owners for maintaining or managing the common parts.

maxim An established legal principle.

maxims of equity/equitable maxims A set of guidelines or standards devised by the court of equity as an aid to deciding cases which come before them.

merger Where the tenant of a lease buys the freehold, thereby causing the leasehold and freehold titles to merge.

Mines Royal The portfolio of mines owned by the Crown, including all gold and silver mines in the United Kingdom.

minor A child; someone under the age of 18.

minor interest A third party right which needs to be protected by an entry on the Register of Title at the Land Registry.

mortgage An interest in land given in exchange for a loan of money, in order to provide security for the debt. A mortgage or legal charge entitles the person with the benefit of the charge to take possession of the property in settlement of the debt if it is not repaid in accordance with the terms of the mortgage agreement.

mortgagee The person or company who accepts the property as security for the loan, lending the money in exchange for the interest in the land. Otherwise known as the lender.

mortgagor The person who mortgages the property: the person who borrows the money in exchange for an interest in the land. Otherwise known as the borrower.

***Moule* v. *Garrett* (rule in)** This says that where a person is compelled to pay damages because of somebody else's legal default, then they are entitled to recover from that person the sum that has been paid on the defaulting party's behalf.

mutual wills Where two people agree to execute separate wills disposing of their property in a particular way. The terms of each will are usually identical or very similar and give reciprocal benefits – for instance, spouses may leave property to each other with the same provision if the other should die before them.

negative covenant A covenant which prevents the landowner from using their own land in some way. Also known as a restrictive covenant.

negative easement An easement which prevents the burdened landowner from using their land in a particular way.

negative equity The situation in which, usually due to a fall in house prices, the value of the property is actually less than the amount owing to the lender.

notice A written statement appearing on the Charges Register of a registered property giving notice of an interest claimed by a third party over the property in question.

notice to quit The service of a notice by either party to a lease stating that they wish to bring the lease to an end.

nuisance A legal action in tort arising from a use of the defendant's own property which causes offence, annoyance, trouble or injury to a third party.

obiter A remark or comment made by the judge in giving judgment, which is not relevant or necessary to deciding the case in question.

objective Where a person is judged on the basis of the ordinary standards of reasonable and honest people, irrespective of their own views of their actions. So, for example, a person would be judged dishonest objectively if a reasonable and honest person considered their behaviour to be dishonest, even if the person themselves had believed themselves to be acting honestly at the time.

'once and for all' breach (of covenant) A one-off breach of covenant such as a breach of a covenant against assignment in a lease.

'ongoing/continuing' breach A breach of covenant that continues over a period of time, like breach of a repairing covenant.

oral agreement A purely verbal agreement made without the need for writing.

option to purchase A contract giving a person the right to purchase an asset (usually land) within a set period of time at an agreed price, upon service of a notice to the seller.

overreaching The process by which the beneficial interest in property attaches to the purchase price of that property on its sale, so that the beneficiaries retain a beneficial interest in the purchase moneys and the buyer is able to take the property free of the beneficiaries' interest.

overriding interest An interest in land which will bind a third party purchaser despite the fact that it cannot be registered on the Register of Title at the Land Registry.

overriding lease A lease claimed by a former tenant under their guarantee in the event of default in the terms of the lease by the current tenant. An overriding lease has the effect of putting the former tenant in the position of tenant and the assignee in the position of sub-tenant.

'paper' owner (of property) A colloquial term meaning the legal owner of the property.

peaceable re-entry The re-entering of leased premises by the landlord and retaking physical possession of them, usually by changing the locks.

periodic tenancy A short-term tenancy automatically renewable at the end of each rental period until notice to end the lease is served by either party to the agreement.

permissive waste Where the tenant fails to do some act which ought to be done in respect of leased premises, and as a result damage is caused; for example failure to maintain a wall which subsequently falls down.

personal property, or 'personalty' The term used to describe all property that can be owned by a person other than land, such as cars, books and so on.

personal remedy/claim A claim made against an individual for a sum of money, as opposed to a claim against a piece of property.

'personam' (action in) An action taken against the person who has misappropriated property, as opposed to an action to recover the property itself (a real action).

petty sergeanty A form of land tenure which required the landholder to provide hay for the kings horses or feed the king's dogs.

plaintiff The term which used to be used for the person who brings an action in a civil court of law. Now called the claimant.

Planning Control Generic term used for the statutory control of building and demolition works relating to both public and privately owned property by the council and local government.

planning permission Permission granted by the local authority under planning regulations to carry out development, building or demolition works on land or to existing property.

positive covenant A covenant which requires the landowner to carry out a particular act in relation to their own land, such as the requirement to maintain a boundary wall or fence.

positive easement An easement which allows someone to use the land of another in some way.

possessory title The class of title given by the Land Registry to property which is being claimed by virtue of the doctrine of adverse possession.

power of sale The right of a lender to sell the mortgaged property.

precedent A legal authority created by the decision of the court which can be followed in later cases.

pre-emption right A right of first refusal to purchase property.

premium See **fine**.

prescription An informal method of acquiring an easement, based upon continued uninterrupted use over a period of years. Also known as 'presumed grant'.

preservation order An order requiring the owner of privately owned land to repair buildings on that land, usually because they are in a dangerous condition.

presumed grant An informal method of acquiring an easement, based upon continued uninterrupted use over a period of years. More commonly known as 'prescription'.

priority period In the case of registered land, the Land Registry's prescribed period of 30 working days within which registration of the transfer of property must be applied for.

Private Member's Bill Proposed laws introduced by MPs and Lords who are not government ministers.

privilege An old-fashioned legal term for a profit à prendre.

privity of contract The legal relationship based upon the law of contract which exists between the original parties to an agreement.

privity of estate The relationship that exists as between the current landlord and current tenant of a lease.

Privy Council The court of final appeal for the UK overseas territories and Crown dependencies, and for those Commonwealth countries that have retained the appeal to the Crown, such as Australia.

profit à prendre The right to take something from the land of another, such as the right to fish in a lake or stream or to collect wood from a forest.

profits See **profit à prendre** (above).

Property Register The section of the Land Register recording the description and extent of the property included in any particular title number, including any interests benefiting that property.

proprietary estoppel The equitable doctrine which prevents the legal owner of property from asserting their legal rights in the property to the detriment of a third party (thereby preventing them from having an interest or benefit in the property), on account of the legal owner's unconscionable behaviour.

proprietary remedy A proprietary remedy asserts that some property in the defendant's possession belongs to the claimant, either at common law or in equity. This is as opposed to a personal remedy, whereby the claimant asserts that the defendant must pay them a sum of money.

proprietary right or **interest** An interest in the ownership of property which can be transferred or sold by the owner of the right or interest, in the same way as an estate in land can. The holder of a proprietary right can also protect that right against third party purchasers of the land over which the right is held.

Proprietorship Register The section of the Land Register recording the names of the person holding an estate in the land and showing any restrictions affecting the transfer of the property.

public highway A road or thoroughfare which is publicly owned and maintained at the public expense.

public policy The rule of law which states that the courts will not make a decision which acts against the public interest.

puisne mortgage A legal mortgage not protected by the deposit of the title deeds with the lender.

purchaser The buyer in a sale and purchase of property.

purpose of annexation In respect of fixtures, denotes the reason for placing or attaching an item on any particular property.

qualified covenant A covenant under which the covenantor can do the action restricted by the covenant with the prior permission of the covenantee.

quarter days The usual days on which the rent is paid in a commercial lease. These days are four times yearly and fall on 25 March, 24 June, 29 September and 25 December.

quasi-easement A use of property by its current owner which could become an easement if the land benefited by the easement was at a later date sold to a third party.

quiet enjoyment The ability of the tenant to occupy leased premises without interference or disturbance from the landlord.

quit rents A fixed payment made by freehold landowners in lieu of services due under the terms of their tenure.

'real' action A court action in which one is able to recover possession of the property itself (as opposed to simply claiming damages for the loss of it).

'real' property/'realty' The term given to all estates and interests in land, on account of the 'real' rights which attach to them. Property that includes land or buildings, and anything affixed to the land.

receiver A person appointed by the court to take charge of the property or business of a business which has run into financial difficulty and is unable to pay its debts.

rectification An order correcting a document which has, because of a mistake by the person drafting the agreement, recorded the agreement made between the parties incorrectly.

redemption penalty A charge made for the early repayment of a loan.

re-entry/right of re-entry The right for a landlord to enter tenanted property in order to repossess it, where the tenant has breached one or more of the terms of the letting. Also known as forfeiture.

registered land/land registration The system of land ownership whereby ownership of land is proven by registration at the Land Registry, as opposed to by the production of title deeds (as with unregistered land).

registrable interests or **dispositions** Legal interests in land which have to be registered at the Land Registry in order to take legal effect.

registration The process of registration of legal title of land at the Land Registry.

relief (from forfeiture) The situation in which the court exempts a defendant, either in whole or in part, from liability for a breach of contract or trust.

remainderman The person who is entitled to inherit property upon the death of another. The beneficiary under the terms of a trust on the death of a person with a life interest.

rentcharge The right to receive a periodic payment from the owner of freehold land.

repossession This is where the lender takes possession of the property following non-payment of a mortgage debt or other secured loan.

rescission An equitable remedy which has the effect of restoring the parties to the position they would have been in before the infringement of the interest occurred.

reservation A right which is either held back or created for the benefit of the original landowner on the sale or transfer of property.

restriction A condition appearing in the Proprietorship Register of a registered property which prevents the property from being sold unless the conditions set out within the restriction are complied with.

restrictive covenant A covenant that restricts the landowner's use of their property in some way, for example a covenant not to use the property for business purposes.

resulting trust An informal trust usually created, in the context of land law, where someone has paid towards the purchase price of property but does not appear on the title deeds to the property.

reversionary estate/reversion A freehold (or leasehold) estate that is subject to a lease.

right of support The right for a building or land to receive physical support from neighbouring land. The right to support is an established form of easement.

right of way The most common form of easement over land, giving the person with the benefit of the easement the right to cross the landowner's property, with or without vehicles.

right *'in rem'* Something which has attached to it the right to a real action, that is: the right to recover the thing itself. The owner of an estate in land has the benefit of a right *in rem*.

Right to Buy This is a government scheme which enables those living in council housing to buy their council house at a discounted rate.

right to light The right to receive light from neighbouring property. The right to light is an established form of easement.

***Rylands* v. *Fletcher* (rule in)** The common law rule that a person is responsible for injuries caused to third parties by the acts carried out by them in respect of their own land.

sale and leaseback agreement An agreement in which property owners sell their property to a company at a substantial discount, in exchange for a tenancy agreement which allows them to continue to live in their home, paying rent to the new property owners.

section 146 notice A statutory notice notifying the tenant of breaches of covenant under the terms of a lease.

security (for a loan) Collateral given to a lender (usually land or property) in return for the loan of monies, in order to secure the provision of the loan. The lender will then be entitled to keep the security if the loan is not repaid.

security of tenure The right of a tenant to continue in their occupation of property, in the absence of certain prescribed actions carried out by the landlord, usually through the courts.

service occupancy Where property is occupied as a term of the occupier's employment.

service or management charge A charge made to leaseholders or commonhold property owners for maintaining or managing the common parts.

servient tenement In the context of easements, the land which has the burden of the easement; that is, the land over which the right of user is granted.

set aside The process whereby the court orders a transaction to be cancelled, revoked or annulled.

severance (of the joint tenancy) Refers to the situation in which the equitable ownership of property is divided into shares by the co-owners to create a tenancy in common in equity.

severance (words of) Words in a conveyance or transfer that indicate a desire to hold co-owned property in shares showing that the property is to be held as tenants in common.

specific performance An equitable remedy which forces the defaulting party to meet their obligations under the terms of a contract or agreement.

squatter/squatting A person in occupation of property who has no legal claim to it. Someone in adverse possession of property.

Standard Conditions of Sale A set of terms and conditions in agreed form covering a number of matters such as who should be liable for insuring the property between exchange and completion, what will happen in the event of default, and so on.

statute-barred Where no legal action is available to the claimant because of the operation of an Act of Parliament, usually because a statutory time limit has elapsed.

statutory charge A charge imposed by statute, as opposed to by the usual method of formal creation by deed.

statutory instrument An order or set of regulations put into place by the government to enable statutory measures to be enforced.

stay (of proceedings) A ruling by the court halting any further progress from being made in a court case. The court can subsequently lift the stay and resume proceedings; however, a stay is often used as a device to postpone proceedings indefinitely.

stop notice A notice issued by the council to the owners of private property requiring the cessation of unlawful use of the land.

subjective Where a person is judged taking into account their own standards. So, for example, a person would only be judged dishonest subjectively if they considered their own behaviour to be dishonest at the time.

sub-lease A lease which is granted out of leasehold property. Also referred to as an underlease.

sub-tenant The tenant of the sub- or underlease.

successive ownership Where two or more people have consecutive ownership of property, such as in the case of a life interest.

successors in title Persons who take over the interest or estate of another when property is sold or gifted to them, or inherited.

Supreme Court The highest court of authority in England and Wales (superseding the House of Lords).

surety A person who guarantees the performance of another under the terms of a loan or other contractual agreement.

surrender Where a tenant enters into a formal agreement with the landlord to bring their lease to an end.

survivorship The automatic right of the surviving party to receive the whole of co-owned property.

suspend/suspension (of proceedings) A ruling by the court halting any further progress from being made in a court case. The court can subsequently lift the suspension and resume the court action. Also known as a stay of proceedings.

ToLATA The Trusts of Land and Appointment of Trustees Act 1996.

tenancy Alternative term for a lease of property. Often used to denote a shorter lease term.

tenancy at will A purely personal agreement created where the landlord allows the tenant to occupy the premises on an informal basis, on the understanding that either party may end the agreement at any time.

tenant The holder of a leasehold interest in land. Someone who occupies leasehold property under the terms of a lease.

tenants/tenancy in common A form of joint ownership of property in which the owners are able to hold individually quantifiable shares in a property.

tenure The right to hold, or use land, granted by the Crown.

term of years A specified period of time: for example, ten years.

term of years absolute The formal name for the leasehold estate. An estate in land limited to a defined period of time, contained within the lease.

testamentary Something which is made by will.

testator/testatrix The legal term for a person making a will.

tie-in An agreement whereby one party gives the other access to a product only if the buyer agrees to purchase other products as well. In the context of mortgages, the lender would agree to let the borrower have the loan on the condition that they bought other products or services from them as well.

tithe rentcharge A type of statutory rentcharge imposed in lieu of the ancient right of the church to receive one tenth of the produce of the land. Tithe rentcharges were abolished in 1977.

title (to property) The legal basis of the ownership of land or property.

title deeds A series of linked documents showing how property has passed down from owner to owner over a period of time. The deeds and documents which form the basis of legal title to property in unregistered land.

Title Number The unique reference number given to each individual piece of registered and at the Land Registry.

Title Plan The plan attached to any particular title number, indicating the extent of the property included within that title.

town and country planning/planning control The generic term used for the control of building and demolition works relating to both public and privately owned property by the council and local government.

transfer/transfer deed The document transferring the legal ownership of property to a third party purchaser in registered land.

treasure trove An ancient common law doctrine determining the ownership of ancient artefacts found on or beneath the surface of the land. Now superseded by the provisions of the Treasure Act 1996.

tree preservation order An order preventing the cutting down of certain protected trees on land.

trust A creation of the court of equity whereby a person gives property to another to hold for the benefit of a third person.

trust corporation A company paid to act professionally in the place of trustees to a trust.

trust instrument Any deed or document (including a will) which has the effect of creating a trust.

trust of land The equitable process whereby the owner of a legal estate in land holds the land on trust for the benefit of a third party.

trustee The person who administers a trust on behalf of the beneficiaries and who has legal ownership of the trust property.

trustee in bankruptcy A person appointed by the court to administer the affairs of a person who has been declared bankrupt.

unconscionable/unconscionability To act in a way which is morally reprehensible, or which would prick the conscience of the ordinary reasonable man.

underlease A lease which is granted out of leasehold property. Also referred to as a sub-lease.

underlessee The tenant of the sub- or underlease.

undivided shares In the context of co-owned property, the situation in which tenants in common have separate and distinct shares in the property, but which have yet to be realised through the sale of the property and the division of the proceeds of sale.

undue influence Where one person is able to unduly influence the other, on account of the relationship of trust that exists between them, to enter into a transaction which is to the other's obvious disadvantage.

'unfree' or **copyhold tenure** A lower form of tenure requiring a more onerous level of servitude to the person granting the tenure. Copyhold tenure effectively amounted to nothing more than a right to occupy the land, in exchange for various menial services of the grantor's choosing.

unity of seisin In the context of easements, where an easement is extinguished because both the benefited and burdened land have come into the same ownership.

unregistered interest The correct legal term for an overriding interest under the Land Registration Act 2002.

unregistered land Land which has not been registered at HM Land Registry and which is therefore still subject to the unregistered system of conveyancing.

unregistered (title) The system of legal ownership of land in England and Wales which pre-dates Land Registration. Ownership proved by the production of title deeds, as opposed to registration on a central government register.

unsecured loan A loan which does not have the backing of any collateral security. Such debts are only as good as the personal worth and reputation of the debtor.

'uplift' payment Where the purchaser of land is required to make an additional payment upon the happening of certain events, for example, on the grant of planning permission.

value (for value) Refers to the payment of money or money's worth; so an exchange of property for goods or services instead of money is included in the definition.

vendor The seller in a sale and purchase of property.

vesting The process by which a right is transferred to another person unconditionally. In the case of land this might refer to an interest in land vesting in the grantee, for example.

void Legal term meaning 'invalid'.

voluntary waste Where a tenant does something that changes the property that has been let to them, such as the knocking down of a wall in the leased property.

volunteer Someone who receives a benefit without consideration. The term would include the recipient of a gift of property.

waiver To relinquish a right to action by engaging in conduct which suggests the surrender of that right. Waiver can be intentional or unintentional on the part of the claimant.

***Walsh* v. *Lonsdale* (doctrine in)** States that a contract for land can create an equitable interest in that land.

waste (to commit waste) Where a tenant of leased property carries out an unauthorised act or an omission which physically alters the state of the land leased.

words of severance See **severance (words of)**.

Index